THE MASTER

CATHOLIC HIGH SCHOOL ENTRANCE EXAMS

EVE P. STEINBERG
CONTRIBUTING EDITOR, JULIE REYNOLDS

2003

THOMSON
ARCO

Australia • Canada • Mexico • Singapore • Spain • United Kingdom • United States

THOMSON
ARCO

An ARCO Book
ARCO is a registered trademark of Thomson Learning, Inc., and is used herein under license by Peterson's.

About The Thomson Corporation and Peterson's
With revenues of U.S. $7.2 billion, The Thomson Corporation (www.thomson.com) is a leading global provider of integrated information solutions for business, education, and professional customers. Its Learning businesses and brands (www.thomsonlearning.com) serve the needs of individuals, learning institutions, and corporations with products and services for both traditional and distributed learning.

Peterson's, part of The Thomson Corporation, is one of the nation's most respected providers of lifelong learning online resources, software, reference guides, and books. The Education Supersite℠ at www.petersons.com—the Internet's most heavily traveled education resource—has searchable databases and interactive tools for contacting U.S.-accredited institutions and programs. In addition, Peterson's serves more than 105 million education consumers annually.

For more information, contact Peterson's, 2000 Lenox Drive, Lawrenceville, NJ 08648; 800-338-3282; or find us on the World Wide Web at www.petersons.com/about.

ISBN : 0-7689-0886-8

Printed in the United States of America

10 9 8 7 6 5 4 3 2 1 03 02 01

CONTENTS

INTRODUCTION

WHY YOU SHOULD USE THIS BOOK

If you're in the eighth grade and are preparing to continue your education at a Catholic high school, then this book is just what you need. An essential part of getting into the school of your choice is taking and passing an entrance exam. That's where this book will help you. This book has been specially designed to assist you with preparing for and taking the two most commonly used Catholic high school entrance exams, the COOP and the HSPT. It will also introduce you to the SSAT and the ISEE, two other widely used tests. You'll find help with answering questions in every test subject and plenty of practice to get you ready for the exam.

If you have selected one or several parish, private, or diocesan high schools you'd like to attend, you're probably already aware of the importance of doing well on an entrance exam. Competition to get into the school of your choice will be fierce. Many other students have chosen the same schools as you, and openings for entering the freshman class are often limited. The school must therefore choose its students from among the many applicants. That's where an entrance exam comes into play.

How selective a school is depends on the ratio of applicants to places in the class. The basis of selection might vary somewhat, but most schools consider your elementary or middle school record, your standing in relation to other eighth-graders in your school, the recommendations of your teachers and principal, and your score on one of several widely used Catholic high school entrance examinations.

If you live within the Archdiocese of New York, or the Diocese of Brooklyn and Rockland County, or the Archdiocese of Newark, NJ, you will probably have to take the Cooperative Entrance Examination, familiarly known as the COOP. Many other cities with Archdiocese- or Diocese-wide testing—among them Baltimore, Boston, Detroit, Miami, Houston, Kansas City, Louisville, Trenton, Fall River and Worcester, MA, Metuchen, NJ, and San Antonio—will ask you to take the Scholastic Testing Service High School Placement Test (known as the HSPT exam). In many other cities—Buffalo, Chicago, Cleveland, Indianapolis, Philadelphia, San Francisco, and Seattle, to name a few—each high school may determine which test to use. A good many of these choose the HSPT. In fact, more than 50 percent of the Catholic high schools in the country require the HSPT exam for admission.

Competitive schools that require neither the COOP nor the HSPT might ask you to take the Secondary School Admission Test (SSAT) or the Independent School Entrance Exam (ISEE), as is the case in Atlanta. These schools may construct their own exams. If you find that you must take the SSAT or ISEE exam, you should purchase ARCO's *Master the SSAT and ISEE, High School Entrance Exams,* which is designed to prepare you for those exams. If your required entrance exam turns out to be other than the four exams mentioned here, you can still get excellent preparation by working your way through either or both of these books. You can quickly find out which exam you will have to take by making a phone call to the school of your choice.

This book will not only help you develop your test-taking skills, but it also includes descriptions and examples of each type of entrance exam and four full-length model exams—two COOPs and two HSPTs. The model exams simulate the type of questions you can expect to find on the actual exams. In addition, the book provides skills reviews and practice questions in each of the subject areas covered by typical entrance exams. Use these sections to help you strengthen your weak areas.

By the time you have finished this book, you should feel quite comfortable with the type of exam questions you can expect to encounter. You'll be able to pace yourself to do your best on all kinds of test topics, and you should be ready to take whichever Catholic high school entrance exam your school requires without the usual test-day panic. Are you ready? Don't worry—you soon will be!

HOW TO USE THIS BOOK

The mere mention of the word "test" is enough to send a wave of anxiety through most students. This is especially true when the test is an important exam like a high school entrance exam. Before you give in to panic, however, stop and let out a deep sigh of relief—you hold in your hands a book that can help you prepare and take the typical entrance exam needed for entry to any Catholic high school. Although the idea of taking a test makes many students nervous, entrance exams are simply tools for measuring how much you've learned. In most instances, you probably know more than you think you do! Put your nervousness aside and prepare to study—just remember, this isn't the first test you've ever taken and it certainly won't be the last.

PREPARING TO STUDY

In order to use this book wisely, there are a few ways you must approach your preparation for an entrance exam: follow instructions, observe time limits, and do not cheat. Don't rush your preparation, rather, take time to read every section of this book and answer every question that applies to your exam. Here are a few things you can do before you get started:

- Find a quiet spot with good lighting and a clear work space.
- Eliminate as many distractions as possible. (It's not very likely that your favorite CD will be playing at the actual test site!)
- Set aside specific periods of at least one hour for your test preparation. In addition, reserve one exam-length time stretch for the model exam. It is best to work straight through the model exams under "battle" conditions so that you can fully appreciate the time pressures and the need for pacing yourself.

HOW THE BOOK IS ORGANIZED

There are three main parts of this book that can help you with your preparation:

- Use Part 1 of this book to learn more about each exam type and how it's scored. You'll find examples of typical questions from each exam.
- Use Part 2 to review the verbal skill sections of the exams, such as analogies, verbal logic, reading, and composition.
- Use Part 3 to review quantitative and nonverbal skills, such as mathematics.
- The last part, Part 4, includes model exams for the COOP and HSPT (two of each) for you to practice taking. We recommend you take one model exam after completing Part 1, then take the second model exam after completing Parts 2 and 3.

Start at Part 1 of the book. Carefully read through the introductory sections so that you fully understand each exam type and how it's scored. The sections in Parts 2 and 3 are keyed to the exams to which they apply. Study those sections that teach you how to answer questions on your exam. Give extra time to those sections dealing with the subjects in which you need to improve your skills. Answer the practice questions and study the explanations.

If you discover that there are subjects you feel you never covered and need additional help with, seek out a teacher who is knowledgeable in that area and ask for recommendations for further study. Don't be shy; your high school career is at stake. If you find that you have forgotten much of what you learned in a subject, go back to your notes, borrow a textbook, or approach a teacher for extra help. A review session with a friend might prove helpful, too.

TAKING THE MODEL EXAMS

When you're ready to try a model exam, have your pencils sharpened beforehand so that you won't have to stop in the middle of your test to hunt for a pencil sharpener. It's important to time yourself, so if you have a portable kitchen timer, bring it to your work area. If you don't have a timer, put a clock or watch in a clearly visible spot. Tear out the answer sheet for the appropriate exam, then set your timer or write down the time you begin. General instructions are given by the test administrators before the clock is started, but directions for answering questions within each timed portion must be read within the time limit. When you finish a section of the model exam, allow yourself a very short, untimed break to stand up and stretch between timed sections.

If you finish an exam portion before the time limit is up, check your work. If the time runs out before you have completed an exam portion, stop working and mark the place where time ran out. When you calculate your score, you must consider only those questions you answered within the time limit. (Later on, however, just for further practice, you should return to the exams and answer the remaining questions.)

After you have completed the entire model exam, check your answers against the Answer Key that follows each exam. Calculate and enter your scores on the Score Sheet provided. Read the explanations that follow the Answer Key. Concentrate first on the explanations for those questions you answered incorrectly, then check those you weren't too sure about, and finally check those you answered correctly with a lucky guess. But be sure to read *all* of the explanations! By studying the explanations you might gain new insights into methods of reasoning out the answers.

It's a good idea to have a dictionary nearby while taking the model exam or reading the sections of this book. If you run across a word you don't know, circle the word and look it up later. Look up words you find in the reading passages, new words from among answer choices, words you find in the explanations, and words you find in the study sections. You are far more likely to remember a word you have looked up for yourself than a word you memorized from a long list. Look up every unfamiliar word in this book. If you can understand every word used in this book, you should have no trouble with the vocabulary used on your exam.

Keep in mind that all exams are subject to change. The exam writers like to experiment with different types of questions. Students occasionally report to us that they find exam questions that we have not described. The examiners might be trying to decide if a new question type provides a useful measure, or they might already have decided to make it a permanent part of the test. Give some attention to all of the questions in this book, familiarity with all styles of questions can do you no harm and might give you a real advantage. Also, if you have the time, you might find it instructive to take the model exam for the other test. For example, if you're required to take the COOP exam, you might also test yourself with the HSPT exam.

After you have completed all of the study sections, take your second model exam. You should find the second model exam much easier now and after your study and practice, should be able to answer more questions than you could on the first model. After you finish the second exam, score yourself and compare your scores for both models—if you've prepared as directed, you're sure to see some improvement.

If you have followed all the preparation instructions listed above, then you're well on your way to doing your very best on the actual exam. Be sure to read the test-taking techniques at the end of Part 1 for additional tips to help you on the day of the exam.

PART 1

Get to Know the Exams

PREVIEW

Chapter 1

Facts About the Cooperative Entrance Exam (COOP)

ROAD MAP

- *About the COOP Exam Format*
- *Timetable and Analysis of the COOP*
- *How the COOP Is Scored*
- *About the COOP Questions*

The two most widely used entrance exams for Catholic high schools are the COOP and the HSPT. Trailing these in popularity and acceptance are the SSAT and ISEE exams. In the first portion of Part 1, you'll be introduced to each of these four exam types, their formats, and how they are scored.

What exactly is the COOP exam? The Cooperative Entrance Examination (called COOP, for short) is a multiple-choice-style exam designed to determine the academic aptitude and skills achievement of eighth-graders seeking admission to selective high schools. The COOP tests your understanding of language, reading, and mathematics, among other things.

The COOP is administered only to students planning to enter ninth grade. It is given once each year, during either October or November. If you plan on taking the COOP, you must first preregister for this exam, either through your parochial elementary school, or, if currently enrolled in public school, as directed on the application form obtained from a parochial school.

Once registered, you'll receive a handbook of instructions that includes some sample questions to familiarize you with the exam. Upon registration you will also receive an admission ticket that you must bring with you to the assigned testing location on the assigned testing date.

ABOUT THE COOP EXAM FORMAT

The multiple-choice answer format is used throughout the COOP exam. Most answer choices are given in sets of four and, the sets are grouped as either (A), (B), (C), (D) or as (F), (G), (H), (J). For example, the first question might use (A), (B), (C), (D) as the answer choices, and the next question might use (F), (G), (H), (J). The test is designed this way to make it easy for you to keep your place as you flip back and forth between the test booklet and the answer sheet.

In the past, various sections of the test have offered five answer choices, so (E) and (K) are added to the answer group range. Note that there is no choice (I). (I) has been omitted to avoid any possible confusion with the number

NOTE

Because the number of questions varies in each section of the exam, scaled scores allow the test administrators to compare your performance on other parts of the exam. Using scaled scores ensures that the value of each section is equivalent to the other sections.

"1."Each year, the publisher of the COOP (CTB/McGraw-Hill) changes 30 percent of the content of the exam. Most of the changes consist of substituting new questions for old ones. Changes also include new question styles, changing numbers of questions or time limits of test sections, or eliminating or combining test sections. The following Timetable and Analysis chart was accurate at the time this book was written. Your own exam might not adhere precisely to these section titles, the number of questions, or the exact timing, but it is similar enough for you to use as your guide.

TIMETABLE AND ANALYSIS OF THE COOP

Test begins with presentation of 20 definitions for memorization.

Test Number and Topic	Time Allotted	Number of Questions
1 Sequences	15 minutes	20
2 Analogies	7 minutes	20
3 Memory	5 minutes	20
4 Verbal Reasoning	15 minutes	20
15-minute break		
5 Reading Comprehension	40 minutes	40
6 Mathematics Concepts and Applications	35 minutes	40
7 Language Expression	30 minutes	40

TIP

On the COOP exam, all questions count the same. You won't get more points for answering a really difficult math question than you get for answering a very simple analogy. Remember that when you're moving through the test. The more time you spend wrestling with the answer to one "stumper," the less time you have to whip through several easier questions.

HOW THE COOP IS SCORED

Raw scores for each test section of the COOP are determined by crediting one point for each question answered correctly. There is no deduction or penalty for any question answered incorrectly. Because each part of the exam contains a different number of questions, your raw score is converted to a scaled score according to a formula devised by the test administrators. The use of scaled scores enables schools to compare your performance on one part of the exam with your performance on other parts of the exam. Your scores are compared to the scores of other students taking the exam and are reported as percentiles. Your percentile rank shows where you stand compared to others who took the test. A percentile rank is reported for each part of the test.

There is no passing grade on the COOP, nor is there a failing grade. All of the high schools to which you have applied receive your scaled scores and your percentile rankings. Each has its own standards, and each makes its own admissions decisions based on test scores, school grades, recommendations, and other factors.

ABOUT THE COOP QUESTIONS

The following questions are examples of what you can expect on the COOP. Each question is preceded by directions like those on the actual exam and is followed by an explanatory answer. Later in this book, you will find two full-scale COOP model exams you can take to prepare for the actual exam.

NOTE

The directions ask you to choose the best answer. That's why you should always read all the choices before you make your final decision.

TEST 1. SEQUENCES

Directions: There are three forms of questions designed to measure sequential reasoning ability. In each case, you must choose the answer that would best continue the pattern or sequence.

1. 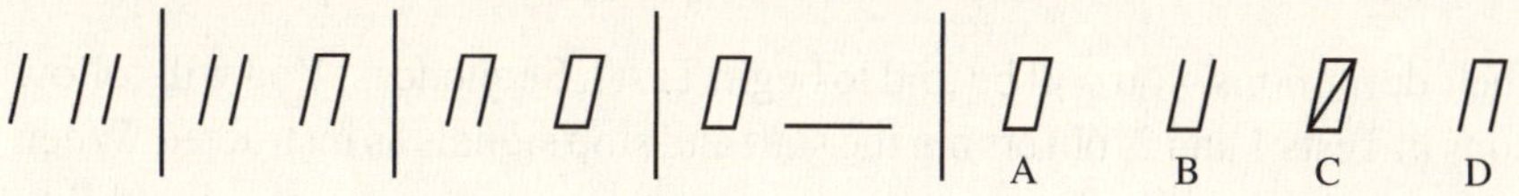

Choice (C) is correct. Each frame contains two figures. The second figure within each frame has one more line than the first figure. In the final frame, the first figure has four lines; the second must have five, as in (C).

2. 2 4 6 | 3 5 7 | 15 17 __

18	16	19	15
(F)	(G)	(H)	(J)

Choice (H) is correct. Within each frame, the pattern is simply the number plus 2, plus 2. 17 plus 2 equals 19.

3. Abcde aBcde abCde ____ abcdE

AbcdE	abCDe	aBcDe	abcDe
(A)	(B)	(C)	(D)

Choice (D) is correct. In each group of letters, the single capitalized letter moves progressively one space to the right.

TEST 2. ANALOGIES

Directions: Analogy questions test your ability to recognize and understand relationships. In these questions you must choose the picture that would go in the empty box so that the bottom two pictures are related in the same way that the top two are related.

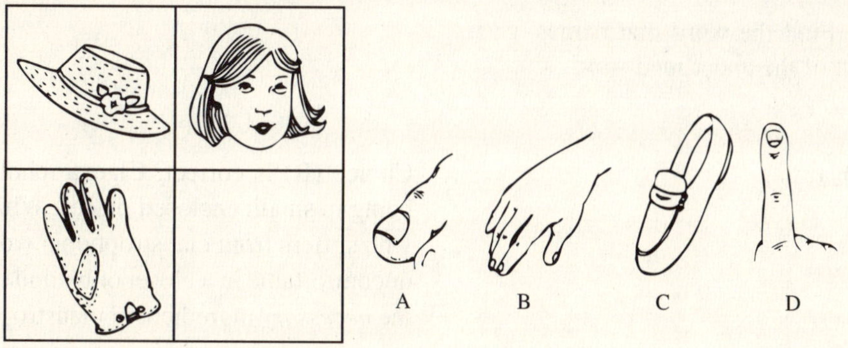

Choice (B) is correct. The relationship of hat to head is that a hat is a head covering; therefore, the best answer is hand, because a glove is a hand covering.

TEST 3. MEMORY

At the very beginning of the testing session, after you fill out forms and receive general directions, but before Test 1, question 1, you will learn 20 nonsense words and their definitions. The administrator will read the words aloud slowly while you read them. You will then have 10 additional minutes to commit the words and their definitions to memory.

Here are some typical nonsense words and their definitions.

1. A *polat* is a kind of reptile.
2. *Adrole* means to fall.
3. *Charop* is a poisonous gas.
4. *Rhumpf* means very high.
5. An *injing* is a fruit.

After you learn the words and their definitions, you will be told to begin Test 1, Sequences. You will follow directions for answering questions in Tests 1 and 2, observing the start and stop signals as instructed. When you turn to Test 3, you will have to answer questions that measure your memory—not your reasoning ability or your reading comprehension, just your power of memorization.

Directions: Choose the word that means the same as the underlined phrase.

1. Which word means <u>very high</u>?
   (A) charop
   (B) rhumpf
   (C) polat
   (D) injing
   (E) adrole

2. Which word means <u>to fall</u>?
   (F) injing
   (G) polat
   (H) rhumpf
   (J) adrole
   (K) charop

TEST 4. VERBAL REASONING

Four different question styles are used to measure how well you reason with words. Each question style has its own directions.

Directions: Find the word that names a **necessary** part of the underlined word.

1. <u>claustrophobia</u>
   (A) closet
   (B) fear
   (C) door
   (D) space

Choice (B) is correct. Claustrophobia is fear of being in small, enclosed places. While the person who suffers from claustrophobia would surely be uncomfortable in a closet or behind a closed door, the *necessary* ingredient of claustrophobia is *fear*.

Directions: The words in the top row are related in some way. The words in the bottom row are related in the same way. Find the word that completes the bottom row of words.

2. best better good

   worst worse _____

   (F) bad

   (G) worser

   (H) okay

   (J) good

Choice (F) is correct. The words in the top row are in a comparative series, with the superlative on the left. Likewise, the words in the bottom row must be a similar comparative series. The comparison descends from *worst* to *worse* to *bad.*

Directions: Find the statement that must be true according to the given information.

3. Julie is in second grade. Laura is in third grade. Julie's sister Anne rides a tricycle.

   (A) Laura is smarter than Julie.

   (B) Anne is physically handicapped.

   (C) Julie is behind Laura in school.

   (D) Julie and Laura are sisters.

Choice (C) is correct. The only certainty is that Julie is behind Laura in school. The fact that Laura is ahead in school does not necessarily mean that she is smarter, possibly only older. Anne might be a normal, healthy two-year-old. Julie and Anne are sisters, but Laura's relationship to them is not given.

Directions: Here are some words translated from an artificial, imaginary language. Read the words and answer the question.

4. ababawayla means somewhere

   parimoodu means nobody

   pariwayla means somebody

   Which word means nowhere?

   (F) waylapari

   (G) pariababa

   (H) mooduababa

   (J) ababamoodu

Choice (J) is correct. You will notice that elements of words are repeated among the English words as well as among the artificial words. By noticing the pattern of repetition, you can define and isolate word elements. In this sample wayla means some; pari means body; ababa means where; moodu means no. The order of the elements of words in this artificial language is the reverse of the order in English but is consistent within the language. Your answer choice must reflect that order, which is the reason that choice (H) is not correct.

NOTE

It's an open-book test. In COOP reading comprehension questions, the answers will be directly stated or implied in the passage.

TEST 5. READING COMPREHENSION

Directions: Read the passage and the questions following it. Answer each question based upon what you have read.

As he threw his head back in the chair, his glance happened to rest upon a bell, a disused bell, that hung in the room and communicated, for some purpose now forgotten, with a chamber in the highest story of the building. It was with great astonishment, and with a strange inexplicable dread, that, as he looked, he saw this bell begin to swing. Soon it rang out loudly, and so did every bell in the house.

This was succeeded by a clanking noise, deep down below as if some person were dragging a heavy chain over the casks in the wine merchant's cellar. Then he heard the noise much louder on the floors below; then coming up the stairs; then coming straight toward his door.

It came in through the heavy door, and a specter passed into the room before his eyes. And upon its coming in, the dying flame leaped up, as though it cried, "I know him! Marley's ghost!"

—from *A Christmas Carol*
by Charles Dickens

1. The bell that began ringing
   (A) was large and heavy.
   (B) did so by itself.
   (C) was attached to every bell in the house.
   (D) rested first on his glance.

Choice (B) is correct. The bell began to ring by itself. The bell might have been large and heavy, but we have no way of knowing this from the passage. The ringing of every bell in the house would likely be due to the same supernatural factors that caused the first bell to ring.

2. The man who was listening to the bell
   (F) dragged a chain across the wine casks.
   (G) sat perfectly still.
   (H) was apparently very frightened.
   (J) is Marley's ghost.

Choice (H) is correct. Obviously, this was a frightening experience. Also, *inexplicable dread* indicates fear.

3. The man in the story
   (A) first heard noises in his room.
   (B) is probably a wine merchant.
   (C) recognized Marley's ghost.
   (D) set the room on fire.

Choice (C) is correct. If the man imagined the flame crying out the identity of the specter, he must have recognized it himself.

4. How would you describe the mood being created by the author?
   (F) festive
   (G) depressing
   (H) exciting
   (J) spooky

Choice (J) is correct. Unexplained bells, creaking, clanking, and ghosts all create a spooky mood. The man in the story might have found the scene depressing, and you, the reader, might find the story exciting, but the overall mood is best described as *spooky*.

TEST 6. MATHEMATICS CONCEPTS AND APPLICATIONS

The computations in this test are not complicated, but you must have a firm grasp of the meaning of mathematics and a little bit of common sense in order to answer the questions.

1. 350 students are taking this examination in this school today; $\frac{4}{7}$ of these students are girls. How many boys are taking the exam in this school?
   (A) 150
   (B) 200
   (C) 500
   (D) 550

Choice (A) is correct. If $\frac{4}{7}$ are girls, $\frac{3}{7}$ are boys.

$$\frac{3}{7} \text{ of } 350 = \frac{3}{7} \times \frac{350}{1} = 150$$

2. Which number sentence is true?
   (F) $-12 > 9$
   (G) $-5 > -8$
   (H) $-3 = 3$
   (J) $2 < -6$

Choice (G) is correct. Draw a number line to prove this to yourself, if necessary.

3. Mrs. Breen came home from the store and put two half-gallon containers of milk into the refrigerator. Jim came home from school with a few friends, and they all had milk and cookies. When they had finished, only $\frac{1}{2}$ of one container of milk remained. How much milk did the boys drink?
   (A) $1\frac{1}{2}$ pints
   (B) $1\frac{1}{2}$ quarts
   (C) 3 quarts
   (D) $1\frac{1}{2}$ gallons

Choice (C) is correct. There are four quarts in a gallon; so there are two quarts in each half-gallon container.

4. Look at the figure below. Then choose the statement that is true.

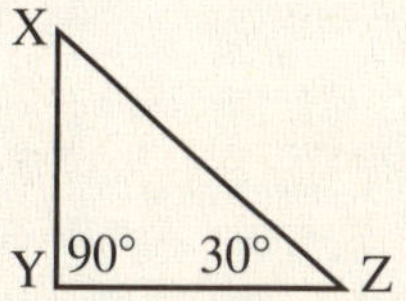

   (F) $m\angle X < m\angle Y < m\angle Z$
   (G) $m\angle X > m\angle Y > m\angle Z$
   (H) $m\angle X = m\angle Z + m\angle Y$
   (J) $m\angle X > m\angle Z < m\angle Y$

Choice (J) is correct. Because the sum of the angles of a triangle is 180°, angle x must be 60°. 60 is greater than 30, which is smaller than 90.

5. Look at the graph below. Then read the question and choose the correct answer.

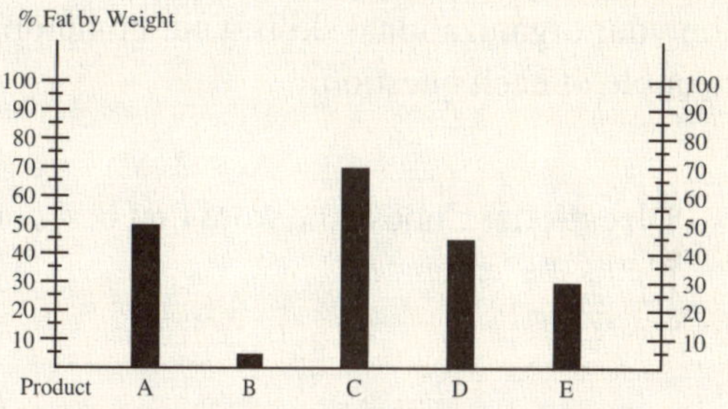

According to FDA regulations, in order to print the designation "light" on its labels, a product must contain no more than 45% fat by weight. Which of these products may be labeled "light"?
   (A) D only
   (B) B and E only
   (C) B, D, and E only
   (D) A and C only

Choice (C) is correct. The regulations state that a "light" product contains *no more than 45% fat.* Product D, which contains exactly 45% fat, may be labeled "light" along with (B) and (E).

6. The piece of property shown below is to be divided into uniform building lots of 100 × 100 sq. ft. Twenty percent of the property must be left undeveloped. How many houses may be built on this property?

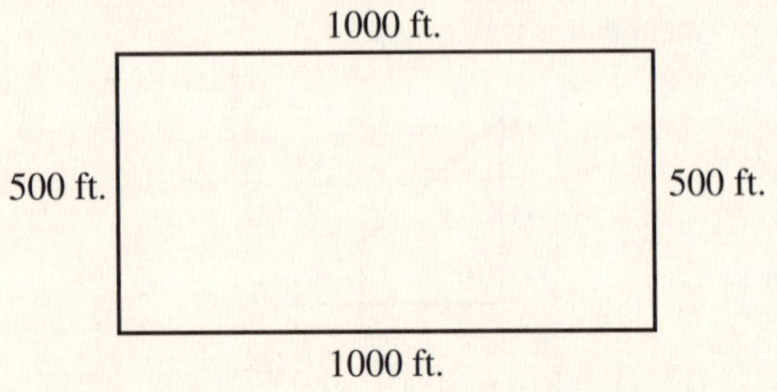

(F) 20

(G) 40

(H) 50

(J) 100

Choice (G) is correct. The entire property is 1000 ft. × 500 ft., which cquals 50,000 sq. ft. Twenly percent must be left undeveloped. 500,000 × 20% = 100,000. 500,000 – 100,000 = 400,000 sq. ft. to be developed. Each building lot is 100 × 100 = 10,000 sq. ft. 400,000 divided by 10,000 = 40 houses.

TEST 7. LANGUAGE EXPRESSION

The COOP uses ten different question styles to test your knowledge of English usage and structure. In this portion of the exam, you will have to answer only a few questions of each style, but you will have to draw on your organizational skills, your common sense, and your knowledge of grammar. We will give you a sample of each question.

Directions: Choose the word that best completes the sentence.

1. I would bring grandma to visit you, ____ I have no car.

(A) while

(B) because

(C) but

(D) moreover

(E) therefore

Choice (C) is correct. The conjunction *but* is the only choice that makes any sense in the context of the sentence.

Directions: Choose the sentence that is complete and correctly written.

2. (F) Cold-blooded reptiles with no mechanism for controlling body temperature.
   (G) Reptiles, which have no mechanism for controlling body temperature, are described as cold-blooded animals.
   (H) Reptiles are described as cold-blooded animals, this means that they have no mechanism for controlling body temperature.
   (J) Reptiles are described as cold-blooded animals and they have no mechanism for controlling body temperature.
   (K) Cold-blooded animals with no mechanism for controlling temperature, a description of reptiles.

Choice (G) is correct. Choice (F) is a sentence fragment; (H) is a comma splice of two independent clauses; (J) is a run-on sentence; (K) has no verb, so it is nothing more than a sentence fragment.

Directions: Choose the sentence that uses verbs correctly.

3. (A) While we were waiting for the local, the express roared past.
   (B) The sky darkens ominously and rain began to fall.
   (C) The woman will apply for a new job because she wanted to earn more money.
   (D) I wish I knew who will be backing into my car.
   (E) The wind blows, the thunder clapped, lightning will fill the sky, and it rains.

Choice (A) is correct. All other choices mix tenses in illogical order.

Directions: Choose the underlined word that is the simple subject of the sentence.

4. The first <u>step</u> (F) in <u>improving</u> (G) your <u>writing</u> (H) is to know <u>what</u> (J) makes a good <u>sentence.</u> (K)

Choice (F) is correct.

Directions: Choose the underlined word or group of words that is the simple predicate (verb) of the sentence.

5. A <u>decrease</u> (A) in the <u>incidence</u> (B) of contagious diseases <u>proves</u> (C) that sanitation <u>is</u> (D) <u>worthwhile.</u> (E)

Choice (C) is correct. The subject of the sentence is *decrease*, and the decrease *proves* the value of sanitation.

Directions: Choose the sentence that best combines the two underlined sentences into one.

6. <u>Fish in tropical waters are colorful. They swim among coral reefs.</u>
   (F) In tropical waters there are coral reefs swimming with colorful fish.
   (G) Fish swim among coral reefs in tropical waters, and they are colorful.
   (H) When fish swim among coral reefs, they are colorful in tropical waters.
   (J) Colorful fish swim among coral reefs in tropical waters.
   (K) Colorful tropical waters are home to swimming fish and coral reefs.

Choice (J) is correct.

Directions: Choose the topic sentence that best fits the paragraph.

7. ______________________ However, in reality, they are adaptable, intelligent, and often beautiful. A squid's body appears to be all head and feet. These feet, commonly referred to as arms, have little suction cups on them.

   (A) Because the squid is shy, it is often misunderstood.

   (B) Scientists consider squid the most intelligent mollusks.

   (C) Squid are considered a tasty treat by the other inhabitants of the sea.

   (D) The body of the squid is uniquely adapted for locomotion and for grabbing in its liquid environment.

   (E) Squid are considered by many to be ugly, unpleasant creatures.

Choice (E) is correct. The second sentence contradicts the topic statement about the squid's appearance.

Directions: Choose the pair of sentences that best develops the topic sentence.

8. Children's tastes in literature tend to change with age.

   (F) Picture books should be lavishly illustrated. Artists should depend heavily on primary colors.

   (G) Young girls often enjoy adventure stories. Teenage girls prefer romantic novels.

   (H) Some boys like to read science fiction. Other boys read only animal stories.

   (J) Historical fiction is an excellent teaching medium. It holds one's interest while introducing historical facts.

   (K) Fairy tales and science fiction represent two manifestations of the same interest. We never outgrow our delight with fantasy.

Choice (G) is correct. This is the choice that carries through with an illustration of how girls' reading tastes tend to change with age. Choice (K) is almost a contradiction of the topic sentence in that it suggests that tastes do not really change; they only mature.

Directions: Choose the sentence that does not belong in the paragraph.

9. 1) Modern computers are no longer the size of a large room. 2) These contain no wires. 3) Some are so small that they can be held in one hand. 4) The large vacuum tubes of the early computers were replaced by tiny transistors. 5) These, in turn, have given way to infinitesimal microchips.

    (A) Sentence 1

    (B) Sentence 2

    (C) Sentence 3

    (D) Sentence 4

    (E) Sentence 5

Choice (B) is correct. The paragraph is about the size of computers, not about computer wiring.

Directions: Read the paragraph and choose the sentence that best fills the blank.

10. A glass case in the British Museum houses the mummified remains of two Egyptian kings who lived beside the Nile. The exhibit includes a broken plow, a rusted sickle, and two sticks tied together with a leather strap. _______________. They are not unlike the tools used by 18th-century American farmers, and, in fact, similar sickles can be viewed at Mount Vernon, George Washington's Virginia home.

    (F) The two kings were the most important kings of ancient Egypt.

    (G) The farm implements were preserved by the same methods as were the remains of the kings.

    (H) English farmers have spent hours at the British Museum studying these tools in hopes of improving the yields of their farms.

    (J) It is interesting to note that no farm animals were found buried in the kings' tombs.

    (K) These were the "bread tools" of Egyptians who lived 4,000 years ago during the reigns of the two kings.

Choice (K) is correct. This sentence explains the use of the tools described in the previous sentence and is followed by a sentence explaining the continued usefulness of tools of this type.

NOTE

You can review the basic principles of grammar in Part 2 of this book.

Summary: What You Need to Know About the COOP

- When you register, you will receive an admission ticket. Be sure to bring it with you to the exam.
- The COOP uses a multiple-choice answer format.
- There is no deduction or penalty for wrong answers on the COOP. Therefore, if you don't know the answer, guess.

Chapter 2

The Scholastic Testing Service High School Placement Test (HSPT)

ROAD MAP

- *The HSPT Exam Format*
- *How the HSPT Is Scored*
- *About the HSPT Questions*
- *The HSPT Optional Tests*

The Scholastic Testing Service High School Placement Test, called HSPT for short, is a five-part, multiple-choice test of verbal, quantitative, reading, mathematics, and language skills. The basic exam takes nearly 2 hours. It contains 298 questions that are designed to indicate how well a student performs tasks that can be expected of an eighth-grader.

Scholastic Testing Service also provides, along with the High School Placement Test, a choice of one optional test, in Mechanical Aptitude, Science, or Catholic Religion. Because many schools do not choose any of these tests, and because the results on the optional test are not included as part of the HSPT composite score, this book doesn't cover the optional tests. However, to give you some idea of what you can expect on an optional test, an outline of the Science test is provided at the end of this section. This outline shows you the typical structure and scope of the optional tests. If you are required to take one of the optional tests, be sure to seek study advice from the school to which you are applying.

THE HSPT EXAM FORMAT

Like the COOP exam, the HSPT exam uses a multiple-choice format. Each question offers three or four answer choices, lettered (A), (B), (C), and (D). Take a look at the Timetable and Analysis chart on page 16 to see the timing, number of questions, and question types of the basic HSPT exam. Questions on the HSPT exam are numbered consecutively from 1 to 298. This numbering system helps you avoid the pitfall of answering questions in the wrong section of the answer sheet. For example, because there is only one question 25, you aren't able to mark your answer to question 25 in the wrong part of the sheet.

NOTE
You may be required to take one of the three optional tests: Mechanical Aptitude, Science, or Catholic Religion. There is an outline of the science test at the end of this section. The school to which you are applying can assist you with study advice for the optional tests.

TIMETABLE AND ANALYSIS OF THE HSPT

Test Section	Number of Questions	Time Allotted
VERBAL SKILLS	**60**	**16 minutes**
Verbal Analogies	10	
Synonyms	15	
Logic	10	
Verbal Classifications	16	
Antonyms	9	
QUANTITATIVE SKILLS	**52**	**30 minutes**
Number Series	18	
Geometric Comparison	9	
Nongeometric Comparison	8	
Number Manipulation	17	
READING	**62**	**25 minutes**
Comprehension	40	
Vocabulary	22	
MATHEMATICS	**64**	**45 minutes**
Concepts	24	
Problem-Solving	40	
LANGUAGE SKILLS	**60**	**25 minutes**
Punctuation and Capitalization	12	
Usage	28	
Spelling	10	
Composition	10	

TIP
On the HSPT exam, your score is based on the number of questions you answer correctly. You won't lose points for incorrect answers, so answer as many questions as possible.

HOW THE HSPT IS SCORED

Your score on the HSPT is based on the number of questions you answer correctly. No points are subtracted for incorrect answers, so it pays to answer as many questions as possible—even if you have to guess.

Scholastic Testing Service converts your raw scores to standard scores that are reported on a scale of 200 to 800. Your HSPT score report includes your standard scores, your national and local percentile rank, your grade equivalent, and your Cognitive Skills Quotient.

Scholastic Testing Service will compare your performance with that of the other 120,000 students taking the exam in some 1,000 schools throughout the United States, many of these among the 1,570 Catholic secondary schools in the country. Scholastic Testing Service will also compare your performance with that of other students in your own area. All of this information is sent to the high schools you have indicated on your answer sheet. It is up to each school to decide what is an acceptable score for admission to the freshman class.

NOTE
Don't worry that you don't see directions or instructions about how to answer these question types. In Part 2 of this book, you'll find in-depth reviews of each question type contained in the entrance exams discussed here.

ABOUT THE HSPT QUESTIONS

The following questions are typical of what you can expect on the HSPT exam. Each question is followed by an explanatory answer. At the end of Part 1, you will find two full-length HSPT model exams you can take to prepare for the actual exam.

PART 1. VERBAL SKILLS

Verbal Analogies

Throw is to ball as shoot is to

(A) policeman

(B) kill

(C) arrow

(D) hunting

Choice (C) is correct. This is an action to object relationship. You *throw* a ball, and you *shoot* an arrow.

Synonyms

Meager most nearly means

(A) well received

(B) long overdue

(C) valuable

(D) scanty

Choice (D) is correct. *Meager* means "lacking in quality or quantity." *Sparse* or *scanty* are synonyms for *meager*.

Logic

Bill runs faster than Mike. Jeff runs faster than Bill. Jeff is not as fast as Mike. If the first two statements are true, the third statement is

(A) true

(B) false

(C) uncertain

Choice (B) is correct. If the first two statements are true, Jeff runs faster than both Bill and Mike.

Verbal Classification

Which word does *not* belong with the others?

(A) car

(B) plane

(C) van

(D) truck

Choice (B) is correct. A plane is the only vehicle that flies; all others are modes of ground transportation.

Antonyms

Loyal means the opposite of

(A) lovely

(B) unfaithful

(C) unlucky

(D) usual

Choice (B) is correct. *Loyal* means "faithful." The best antonym is *unfaithful*.

PART 2. QUANTITATIVE SKILLS

Number Series

Look at this series: 10, 14, 18, 22, 26, . . . What number should come next?

(A) 28

(B) 29

(C) 30

(D) 32

Choice (C) is correct. The pattern in this series is to add 4 to each number. 26 + 4 = 30.

Geometric Comparisons

Examine hourglasses A, B, and C and find the best answer.

A B C

(A) B shows the most time passed.

(B) A shows the most time passed.

(C) C shows the most time passed.

(D) A, B, and C show the same time passed.

Choice (B) is correct. Be especially careful to avoid response errors when answering these questions. The correct answer is hourglass A, but you must mark the letter of the correct statement, which, of course, is choice (B).

Nongeometric Comparisons

Examine (I), (II), and (III) and find the best answer.

(I) $(4 \times 2) - 3$

(II) $(4 \times 3) - 2$

(III) $(4 + 3) - 2$

(A) (A) is greater than (C)

(B) (A), (B), and (C) are equal

(C) (C) is greater than (B)

(D) (A) and (C) are equal

Choice (D) is correct. Determine the numerical value of (A), (B), and (C). Then test each answer choice to see which one is true.

(A) $(4 \times 2) - 3 = 8 - 3 = 5$

(B) $(4 \times 3) - 2 = 12 - 2 = 10$

(C) $(4 + 3) - 2 = 7 - 2 = 5$

Number Manipulation

What number is 5 more than $\frac{2}{3}$ of 27?

(A) 14

(B) 32

(C) 9

(D) 23

Choice (D) is correct: First find $\frac{2}{3}$ of 27. $\frac{2}{3} \times 27 = 18$. Then add: 18 + 5 = 23.

PART 3. READING

Comprehension

The impressions that an individual gets from his environment are greatly influenced by his emotional state. When he is happy, objects and people present themselves to him in a favorable aspect; when he is depressed, he views the same things in an entirely different light. It has been said that a person's moods are the lenses that color life with many different hues. Not only does mood affect impression, but impression also affects mood. The beauty of a spring morning might dissipate the gloom of a great sorrow, the good-natured chuckle of a fat man might turn anger into a smile, or a telegram might transform a house of mirth into a house of mourning.

According to the passage, an individual's perception of his environment

(A) depends on the amount of light available.

(B) is greatly influenced by his emotional state.

(C) is affected by color.

(D) is usually favorable.

Choice (B) is correct. The first sentence of the passage makes the point that one's perceptions are influenced by one's emotional state.

Vocabulary

As used in the passage above, the word dissipate probably means

(A) condense

(B) draw out

(C) melt away

(D) inflate

Choice (C) is correct. Other synonyms for dissipate are "scatter," "dissolve," and "evaporate."

PART 4. MATHEMATICS

Concepts

To the nearest tenth, 52.693 is written

(A) 52.7

(B) 53

(C) 52.69

(D) 52.6

The correct choice is (A). To "round off" to the nearest tenth means to "round off" to one digit to the right of the decimal point. The digit to the right of the decimal point is 6. However, the next digit is 9, which means you must round up to 52.7.

Problem-Solving

On a map, 1 inch represents 500 miles. How many miles apart are two cities that are $1\frac{1}{2}$ inches apart on the map?

(A) 750

(B) 1,000

(C) 1,250

(D) 1,500

Choice (A) is correct. If 1 inch = 500 miles, then $\frac{1}{2}$ inch = 250 miles. Therefore, $1\frac{1}{2}$ inches = 500 + 250 = 750 miles.

PART 5. LANGUAGE SKILLS

Punctuation and Capitalization

Find the sentence that has an error in capitalization or punctuation. If you find no mistake, mark (D) as your answer.

(A) Sally asked, "What time will you be home?"

(B) Doug hopes to enter John F. Kennedy High School next Fall.

(C) The letter arrived on Saturday, January 15.

(D) No mistakes.

Choice (B) has an error in capitalization. The word *fall* should not be capitalized.

Usage

Find the sentence that has an error in usage. If you find no mistake, mark (D) as your answer.

(A) Many children adopt the beliefs of their parents.

(B) "Is he always so amusing?" she asked.

(C) All the officers declined except she.

(D) No mistakes.

Choice (C) has an error in usage. The word *she* should be *her* since it acts as the object of the preposition "except."

Spelling

Find the sentence that has an error in spelling. If you find no mistake, mark (D) as your answer.

(A) We recieved a letter from the principal.

(B) The library closes at 5 o'clock tomorrow.

(C) I have an appointment with the doctor on Wednesday.

(D) No mistakes.

There is an error in choice (A). The word *received* is incorrectly spelled.

Composition

Choose the best word or words to join the thoughts together.

I left my key at school; ________ I had to ring the bell to get in the house.

(A) however

(B) nevertheless

(C) therefore

(D) None of these

Choice (C) is correct. *Nevertheless* and *however* are used to express a contrast. *Therefore* is used to express a result. The second half of this sentence is clearly a result of the first half.

TIP
Answer as many questions as possible because points are not subtracted if you choose the wrong answer.

THE HSPT OPTIONAL TESTS

Some schools might require that you take one of the three optional tests described at the beginning of this section: Mechanical Aptitude, Science, or Catholic Religion. Not every school to which you apply will require this extra test. However, if you do have to take an optional test, the test is chosen by the school, and like the basic HSPT exam, the test will involve multiple-choice questions and answers.

Your score on the optional test will not be included with your score on the basic HSPT exam. Rather, the school will receive a report on your overall performance on the optional exam and a topic-by-topic evaluation of your performance. The school will use this information to place you in appropriate classes. It might also use the information about the background of the student body as a whole in preparing the curriculum for the following year.

The optional science test consists of 40 questions covering a wide variety of topics. The questions are not neatly categorized. For example, a biology question might be followed by a physics question, and then a laboratory methods question might be followed by a chemistry question. The outline below gives you an idea of how many topics are covered and of how many questions touch on each topic.

DISTRIBUTION OF TOPICS ON HSPT OPTIONAL TESTS

Topic/Content	Number of Items
Concepts and Application of General Science	
Biological Sciences:	
Plants	2
Animals	2
Life Processes	2
Health and Safety	1
Ecology	2
Earth Sciences:	
Astronomy	2
Geology	2
Weather	1
Air	2
Water	2
Physical Sciences:	
Matter and Energy	2
Machines and Work	2
Magnetism and Electricity	2
Sound	1
Heat and Light	1
Chemistry	2
Implications of Scientific Technology:	
Societal Benefits	3
Technical Applications	3
Principles of Scientific Research and Experimentation:	
Laboratory Methods	3
Research Practices	3

Summary: What You Should Know About the HSPT

- The HSPT is a five-part multiple-choice test of verbal, quantitative, reading, mathematics, and language skills.
- The test takes nearly 2 hours and contains 298 questions.
- No points are subtracted for incorrect answers, so it pays to answer as many questions as possible, even if you have to guess.

Chapter 3

About the Secondary School Admission Test (SSAT)

ROAD MAP

- *The SSAT Exam Format*
- *How the SSAT Is Scored*
- *About the SSAT Questions*

The SSAT (which stands for Secondary School Admissions Test) is an established independent high school entrance exam that's been around for quite some time. The exam is administered by the Educational Testing Service of Princeton, NJ. You can take the exam on any one of seven Saturday morning test dates scheduled every year at numerous locations throughout the country. Special arrangements can be made for Sabbath observers, applicants with handicaps, and students who live far from an established test center.

SSAT scores are accepted by more than 600 schools, either exclusively or as an alternative to another exam (most often the Independent School Entrance Examination—ISEE). The schools that accept SSAT scores include independent unaffiliated private schools, non-diocesan Catholic schools or Catholic schools operated by religious orders, and non-Catholic religion-affiliated schools. Many boarding schools also require the SSAT.

The SSAT is offered at two levels. The lower level of the exam is taken by students who are currently in grades 5, 6, and 7; the upper level is taken by students in grade 8 and above. Because each level includes a range of ages and grade levels, scoring takes these factors in mind, and percentile comparisons are made separately within each grade group. Because the emphasis of this book is on Catholic high school entrance exams, it focuses on the upper level exam. The lower level exam is similar in structure, but it is geared toward younger students.

THE SSAT EXAM FORMAT

The SSAT is a multiple-choice exam testing quantitative and verbal abilities and reading comprehension. The exam is administered in five separately timed sections. Two sections always contain mathematics questions; one includes synonyms and analogies; and one tests reading comprehension. The fifth section is similar to any one of the four, and is experimental.

NOTE
The experimental section of the SSAT exam will not be identifiable, because it resembles the other four sections of the exam. That's why you must do your best on all five sections.

This "experimental section" does not count toward your score. It is included for purposes of testing and validating new questions for use in future exams. Because the experimental section closely resembles a section that counts, you will be unable to identify it. Because you will not know which is the experimental section, you must do your best on all five sections.

Each question on the SSAT offers five answer choices. The odd-numbered questions have choices lettered (A), (B), (C), (D), and (E). The even-numbered questions have choices lettered (F), (G), (H), (J), and (K). There is no choice (I) because it might easily be confused with the number "1." The lettering of the answer choices is staggered to help you keep your place on the answer sheet.

The five test sections of the SSAT may be given in any order. Because each section has a 25-minute time limit, not every person in a test room will be taking the same section at the same time. Each test booklet is bound separately, and the person next to you might be answering verbal questions while you are doing math in the same 25-minute time block. The chart below shows a typical SSAT timetable.

TIMETABLE AND ANALYSIS OF THE SSAT

Section	Time allotted	Number of Questions
I. Mathematics	25 minutes	25
II. Verbal Ability	25 minutes	60
Synonyms questions		30
Analogies questions		30
III. Mathematics	25 minutes	25
IV. Reading Comprehension (questions based on approximately 7 reading passages)	25 minutes	40
V. Any one of the above	25 minutes	

CAUTION
On the SSAT exam, you earn one point for each correct answer. One-fourth of a point is deducted for every incorrect answer, so random guessing is not a good idea on this exam.

HOW THE SSAT IS SCORED

The SSAT awards you one point for each question you answer correctly. One fourth of a point is deducted for every question that you answer incorrectly. This means that random guessing is not a good idea on this exam. If you have absolutely no idea of the answer to a question, you should leave it blank. On the other hand, if you can eliminate some obviously wrong answer choices, then guessing is a wise move. The more answer choices you can eliminate, the more advisable it is to guess.

ABOUT THE SSAT QUESTIONS

The following questions are typical of what you can expect on the SSAT. Each question is followed by an explanatory answer.

TIP
Educated guessing will boost your score. You should use common sense and the process of elimination to assist you in choosing the best possible answer. If you cannot make an educated guess, leave the answer blank.

VERBAL ABILITY

Directions: Choose the word or phrase whose meaning is most similar to the meaning of the word in CAPITAL letters.

1. NOVICE
   (A) competitive
   (B) clumsy
   (C) aged
   (D) beginning
   (E) impulsive

Choice (D) is correct. A NOVICE is a *beginner.* A novice might, of course, be competitive, clumsy, aged, or impulsive, but it is his being a beginner that makes him a novice. You might recognize the root of *novel*, meaning *new*, as a clue to the definition.

2. CONVOY
   (F) hearse
   (G) thunderstorm
   (H) group
   (J) jeep
   (K) journey

Choice (H) is correct. A CONVOY is a *group* travelling together for protection or convenience. You have probably seen convoys of military vehicles traveling single file up the highway toward summer reserve camp. A jeep might be part of a convoy.

Directions: Find the relationship between the words. Read each question and then choose the answer that best completes the meaning of the sentence.

3. Lid is to box as cork is to
   (A) float
   (B) bottle
   (C) wine
   (D) blacken
   (E) stopper

Choice (B) is correct. The relationship is one of purpose. The purpose of a *lid* is to close a *box;* the purpose of a *cork* is to close a *bottle*. Cork is easily associated with all the choices, so you must recognize the purposeful relationship of the initial pair to choose the correct answer.

CAUTION

Don't spin your wheels. Make sure not to spend too much time on any one question. Give it some thought, take your best shot, and move along.

4. Poison is to death as
   (F) book is to pages
   (G) music is to violin
   (H) kindness is to cooperation
   (J) life is to famine
   (K) nothing is to something

Choice (H) is correct. This is a cause-and-effect relationship. *Poison* might cause *death; kindness* might lead to *cooperation*. Neither outcome is a foregone conclusion, but both are equally likely, so the parallel is maintained. Choice (G) offers a reversed relationship.

MATHEMATICS

Directions: Calculate each problem in your head or in the margin of the test booklet and choose the best answer.

5. $\frac{1}{4}$% of 1,500 =
   (A) 7.50
   (B) 1.50
   (C) 15.00
   (D) 3.75
   (E) 60.00

Choice (D) is correct. $\frac{1}{4}$% written as a decimal is .0025. (1,500)(.0025) = 3.75. You could have done this problem in your head by thinking: 1% of 1,500 is 15; $\frac{1}{4}$ of 1%= 15 ÷ 4 = 3.75

6. If psychological studies of juvenile delinquents show *K* percent to be emotionally unstable, the number of juvenile delinquents not emotionally unstable per one hundred juvenile delinquents is
   (F) 100 minus *K*
   (G) I minus *K*
   (H) *K* minus 100
   (J) 100 ÷ *K*
   (K) *K* ÷ 100

Choice (F) is correct. "Percent" means out of 100. If *K* percent are emotionally unstable, then *K* out of 100 are emotionally unstable. The remainder, 100 – *K*, are stable.

7. A piece of wood 35 feet, 6 inches long was used to make four shelves of equal length. The length of each shelf was
   (A) 9 feet, $1\frac{1}{2}$ inches
   (B) 8 feet, $10\frac{1}{2}$ inches
   (C) 7 feet, $10\frac{1}{2}$ inches
   (D) 7 feet, $1\frac{1}{2}$ inches
   (E) 8 feet, $1\frac{1}{2}$ inches

Choice (B) is correct. First convert the feet to inches. 35 feet, 6 inches = 420 inches, add the 6 inches to get 426 inches. 426 ÷ 4 = 106.5 inches per shelf, which makes the answer 8 feet, $10\frac{1}{2}$ inches per shelf.

8. ∢ ABD is

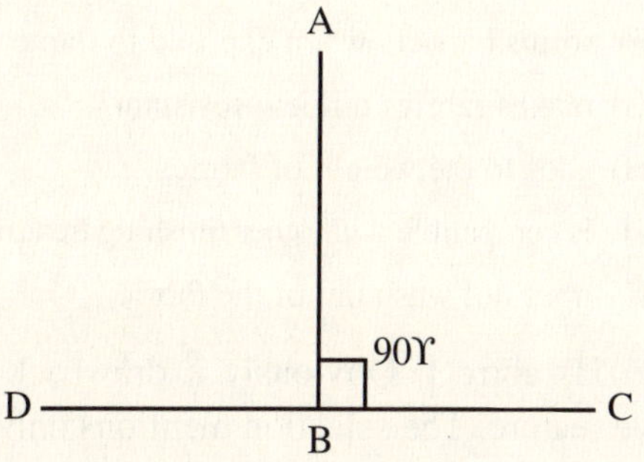

(F) a straight angle and contains 180°

(G) an acute angle and contains 35°

(H) an obtuse angle and contains 360°

(J) a right angle and contains 45°

(K) a right angle and contains 90°

Choice (K) is correct. ∢ ABC and ∢ ABD are supplementary angles. Because ∢ ABC = 90°, ∢ ABD must also equal 90° (180°–90° = 90°). A right angle contains 90°.

READING COMPREHENSION

Directions: Carefully read each passage and the questions that follow it. Choose the best answer to each question.

Cotton fabrics treated with the XYZ Process have features that make them far superior to any previously known flame-retardant-treated cotton fabrics. XYZ Process-treated fabrics are durable to repeated laundering and dry cleaning and are glow resistant as well as flame resistant; when exposed to flames or intense heat they form tough, pliable, and protective barriers; are inert physiologically to persons handling or exposed to the fabric; are only slightly heavier than untreated fabrics; and are susceptible to further wet and dry finishing treatments. In addition, the treated fabrics exhibit little or no adverse change in feel, texture, and appearance, and are shrink-, rot-, and mildew-resistant. The treatment reduces strength only slightly. Finished fabrics have "easy care" properties in that they are wrinkle-resistant and dry rapidly.

9. It is most accurate to state that the author in the preceding selection presents

(A) facts but reaches no conclusion concerning the value of the process

(B) a conclusion concerning the value of the process and facts to support that conclusion

(C) a conclusion concerning the value of the process, unsupported by facts

(D) neither facts nor conclusions, but merely describes the process

(E) the case for making all fabrics flame-retardant

Choice (B) is correct. This is a combination main idea and interpretation question. If you cannot answer this question readily, reread the selection. The author clearly thinks that the XYZ Process is terrific and says so in the first sentence. The rest of the selection presents a wealth of facts to support the initial claim.

10. The one of the following articles for which the XYZ Process would be most suitable is

(F) nylon stockings

(G) woolen shirt

(H) silk tie

(J) cotton bedsheet

(K) polyester slacks

Choice (J) is correct. At first glance you might think that this is an inference question requiring you to make a judgment based upon the few drawbacks of the process. Closer reading, however, shows you that there is no contest for the correct answer here. This is a simple question of fact. The XYZ Process is a treatment for *cotton* fabrics.

11. The main reason for treating a fabric with the XYZ Process is to
   (A) prepare the fabric for other wet and dry finishing treatments
   (B) render it shrink-, rot- and mildew-resistant
   (C) increase its weight and strength
   (D) reduce the chance that it will catch fire
   (E) justify a price increase

Choice (D) is correct. This is a main idea question. You must distinguish between the main idea and the supporting and incidental facts.

12. The one of the following that would be considered a minor drawback of the XYZ Process is that it
   (F) forms barriers when exposed to flame
   (G) makes fabrics mildew-resistant
   (H) adds to the weight of fabrics
   (J) is compatible with other finishing treatments
   (K) does not wash out of the fabric

Choice (H) correct. Obviously a drawback is a negative feature. The selection mentions only two negative features. The treatment reduces strength slightly, and it makes fabrics slightly heavier than untreated fabrics. Only one of these negative features is offered among the answer choices.

If you will be taking the SSAT for any of the Catholic high schools to which you are applying, we strongly suggest that you purchase ARCO's *Master the SSAT and ISEE.* This book contains two full-length model SSAT exams with instruction and practice specific to the question types on the SSAT.

Summary: All About the SSAT

- The SSAT is a multiple-choice exam testing quantitative and verbal abilities, and reading comprehension.
- It is important to understand the scoring proceedures. On this exam, $\frac{1}{4}$ of a point is subtracted for an incorrect answer, so try to eliminate one or more answer choices before guessing.
- There are five separately timed sections: two cover mathematics, one contains synonym and analogies, one tests reading comprehension, and the last is experimental and does not count toward your score.
- The five sections have identical time limits and may be given in any order. Not every person in a test room will be taking the same section at the same time.

Chapter 4

The Independent School Entrance Examination (ISEE)

ROAD MAP

- *The ISSE Exam Format*
- *How the ISEE Is Scored*
- *Sample ISEE Questions*

The Independent School Entrance Examination (ISEE) is a newer independent high school admission test that is gaining rapid acceptance around the country. The exam is administered by the Educational Records Bureau. Scheduled exam dates vary from region to region and are centered around major cities, but small group and even individual testing can be arranged for students who don't live near a major city. You can write to the following address for specific information on registering for the exam in your area or call 800-446-0320.

ISEE Operations Office
423 Morris Street
Durham, NC 27701

You may also request additional information and an ISEE Student Guide from:

Educational Records Bureau
345 East 47th Street
New York, NY 10017
800-989-3721

ISEE is accepted by more than 1,000 independent schools around the country, most often by day schools. Many boarding schools now accept ISEE scores as an alternative to SSAT, though few mandate the ISEE. ISEE is accepted by all member schools of the Independent Schools Association of New York City and is the exam of choice at most of the independent schools in Philadelphia, San Diego, and Nashville. ISEE has especially good acceptance at non-Catholic religiously affiliated day schools and is gaining acceptance at independent Catholic high schools.

ISEE is offered at two levels. The middle level of the exam is given to candidates for grades 6, 7, and 8, and the upper level is given to candidates for grades 9 through 12. Because each level includes a range of ages and grade levels, scoring and percentile ranking are done separately for members of each grade group. The upper and middle levels of the exam differ chiefly in the difficulty of the questions and in the mathematical subjects covered.

The information here provides you with a good foundation for ISEE preparation. If you learn that you will be taking the ISEE as part of the application process for any of your Catholic high schools, and you want further study for this exam specifically, you might also want to pick up a copy of ARCO's *Master the SSAT and ISSE, High School Entrance Exams.* That book covers the ISEE in more detail. It provides instructions for answering questions unique to the ISEE, and it gives special advice and assistance for the ISEE essay section. It also includes two full-length model ISEE exams.

THE ISEE EXAM FORMAT

The ISEE is a multiple-choice exam testing verbal ability, quantitative ability, reading comprehension, and mathematics achievement. ISEE also requires each applicant to write an essay. Of the four exam types described in this book, only the ISEE includes an essay section. The ISEE is administered in five separately timed test sections. The time limit for each section is different, so all applicants take the tests in the same order. The ISEE does not include an experimental section; so every test section and question count.

Each question on the ISEE offers four answer choices, lettered (A), (B), (C), and (D). The Timetable and Analysis chart below gives you an example of the order of subjects and time limits you can expect.

NOTE

On the ISEE exam, your score is based on the number of questions you answer correctly. You won't lose points for incorrect answers, so answer as many questions as possible.

TIMETABLE AND ANALYSIS OF THE ISEE

Test Number and Content	Time Allotted	Number of Questions
1: Verbal Ability	20 minutes	40
Synonyms		
Sentence Completions		
2: Quantitative Ability	35 minutes	40
Concepts and Understanding and Application measured by Problem Solving and Quantitative Comparisons		
3: Reading Comprehension based on approximately 9 reading passages	35 minutes	40
Science Passages		
Social Studies Passages		
4: Mathematics Achievement	40 minutes	50
Upper level: Arithmetic concepts		
Algebraic concepts		
Geometric concepts		
Essay	30 minutes	

HOW THE ISEE IS SCORED

Scoring of the ISEE is very straightforward. You receive one point for every question that you answer correctly. There is no penalty for a wrong answer. This means that even a wild guess cannot hurt you. Obviously, you want to mark correct answers to as many questions as possible, but when you're in a pinch, a guess will do.

TIP

If you guessed on any answers, mark EG (educated guess) or WG (wild guess) next to the number on your answer sheet. If you have time left after you finish the section, go back and see if you can make a better choice. Remember, you don't lose points for incorrect answers.

SOME TEST-TAKING TIPS FOR THE ISEE

Because you don't lose points for wrong answers on the ISEE, you have nothing to lose by guessing. If you can eliminate one or more answers, you can make an educated guess. If you've made an educated guess, write "EG" (for educated guess) next to it on the answer sheet. If you don't have a clue which answer choice is correct, just mark one choice, then write "WG" (for wild guess) next to it on the answer sheet. If you have time left after you finish the remaining exam questions, go back to these "guesses" to see if you can make a better choice. One big benefit of choosing an answer for every question on the exam is that you don't run the risk of losing your place on the answer sheet, as you do if you just skip a question. Be sure to go back and erase all of the "EGs" and "WGs" that you wrote. If they are not erased, the computer might mark the question wrong.

Because you have a 25 percent chance of making a correct "wild guess," we have one more recommendation: Don't leave any answers blank at the end of a test. A couple of minutes before the test time ends, mark an answer for each of the remaining questions. The odds are that you'll pick up extra points.

SAMPLE ISEE QUESTIONS

VERBAL ABILITY

Directions: Choose the word that is most nearly the same in meaning as the word in CAPITAL letters.

1. TENANT
   (A) occupant
   (B) landlord
   (C) owner
   (D) farmer

Choice (A) is correct. The most common sense of the word TENANT is *occupant.* As such, the tenant is never the landlord. The owner might be an occupant, but unless he occupies on a very temporary basis he is not considered a tenant. A tenant farmer lives on and cultivates the land of another.

2. CALCULATED
   (A) multiplied
   (B) added
   (C) answered
   (D) figured out

Choice (D) is correct. CALCULATING might include multiplying or adding to arrive at the answer, but not all calculations need be mathematical. It is the *figuring out* that is the *calculating.*

Directions: The blanks in the following sentences indicate that words are missing. Choose the one word or pair of words that will best complete the meaning of the sentence as a whole.

3. Utility is not _______, for the usefulness of an object changes with time and place.
   (A) planned
   (B) practical
   (C) permanent
   (D) understandable

Choice (C) is correct. If the usefulness of an object changes, then that usefulness is by definition *not permanent.*

4. A string of lies had landed her in such a hopeless ______ that she didn't know how to ______ herself.
   (A) status .. clear
   (B) pinnacle .. explain
   (C) confusion .. help
   (D) predicament .. extricate

Choice (D) is correct. "Hopeless predicament" is an idiomatic expression meaning "impossible situation." This is a reasonable position for one to be in after a string of lies. The second blank is correctly filled with a term which implies that she couldn't get out of the mess she had created.

QUANTITATIVE ABILITY

Directions: Work out each problem in your head or on the space available on the pages of the test booklet and choose the correct answer.

5. If $a^2 + b^2 = a^2 + x^2$, then b equals
   (A) $\pm x$
   (B) $x^2 - 2a^2$
   (C) $\pm a$
   (D) $a^2 + x^2$

Choice (A) is correct. Subtract a^2 from both sides of the equation: $b^2 = x^2$, therefore $b = \pm x$.

6. How much time is there between 8:30 a.m. today and 3:15 a.m. tomorrow?
   (A) $17\frac{3}{4}$ hrs.
   (B) $18\frac{2}{3}$ hrs.
   (C) $18\frac{1}{2}$ hrs.
   (D) $18\frac{3}{4}$ hrs.

Choice (D) is correct.

From 8:30 a.m. until noon today:	12:00 =	11:60
	–8.30 =	8.30
		3 hrs. 30 min.
From noon until midnight:	+	12 hrs.
From midnight until 3:15 a.m		3 hrs. 15 min.
		18 hrs. 45 min.
	=	$18\frac{3}{4}$ hours

Directions: For each of the following questions, two quantities are given—one in Column A, and the other in Column B. Compare the two quantities and choose:

(A) if the quantity in Column A is greater

(B) if the quantity in Column B is greater

(C) if the quantities are equal

(D) if the relationship cannot be determined from the information given

7. Column A Column B

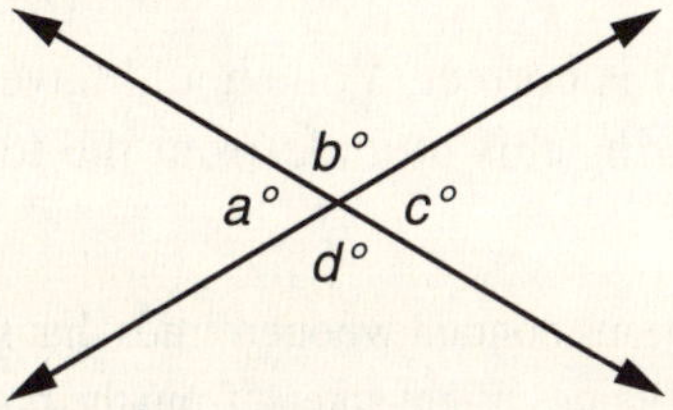

Note: Figure not drawn to scale

Column A	Column B
$180 - a$	$d + c - b$

Choice (D) is correct.

$180 - a$ versus $d + c - b$

$180 - b$

Because we do not know if $a \gtreqless b$, we cannot determine which column is greater.

8.

Column A	Column B
$\dfrac{2}{\frac{3}{4}}$	$\dfrac{\frac{2}{3}}{4}$

Choice (A) is correct.

$$\frac{2}{\frac{3}{4}} = \frac{2}{1} \bullet \frac{4}{3} = \frac{8}{3} \text{ versus } \frac{\frac{2}{3}}{4} = \frac{2}{3} \bullet \frac{1}{4} = \frac{2}{12}$$

Column A > Column B

NOTE
In some questions, information concerning one or both of the quantities to be compared is centered above the entries in the two columns.

READING COMPREHENSION

Directions: Each passage is followed by questions based on its content. Answer the questions following each passage on the basis of what is stated or implied in the passage.

Passage I

"A large proportion of the people who are behind bars are not convicted criminals, but people who have been arrested and are being held until their trial in court. Experts have often pointed out that this detention system does not operate fairly. For instance, a person who can afford to pay bail usually will not get locked up. The theory of the bail system is that the person will make sure to show up in court when he is supposed to since he knows that otherwise he will forfeit his bail—he will lose the money he put up. Sometimes a person who can show that he is a stable citizen with a job and a family will be released on "personal recognizance" (without bail). The result is that the well-to-do, the employed, and the family men can often avoid the detention system. The people who do wind up in detention tend to be the poor, the unemployed, the single, and the young."

9. According to the preceding passage, people who are put behind bars
   (A) are almost always dangerous criminals
   (B) include many innocent people who have been arrested by mistake
   (C) are often people who have been arrested but have not yet come to trial
   (D) are all poor people who tend to be young and single

Choice (C) is correct. The answer to this question is directly stated in the first sentence. (B) might be possible, but it is neither stated nor implied by the passage. The word *all* in choice (D) makes (D) an incorrect statement.

10. Suppose that two men were booked on the same charge at the same time and that the same bail was set for both of them. One man was able to put up bail, and he was released. The second man was not able to put up bail, and he was held in detention. The writer of the passage would most likely feel that this result is
   (A) unfair, because it does not have any relation to guilt or innocence
   (B) unfair, because the first man deserves severe punishment
   (C) fair, because the first man is obviously innocent
   (D) fair, because the law should be tougher on poor people than on the rich

Choice (A) is correct. You should have no difficulty inferring this attitude from the tone of the passage.

Passage II

Fire often travels inside the partitions of a burning building. Many partitions contain wooden studs that support the partitions, and the studs leave a space through which the fire can travel. Flames might spread from the bottom to the upper floors through the partitions. Sparks from a fire in the upper part of a partition might fall and start a fire at the bottom. Some signs that a fire is spreading inside a partition are: (1) blistering paint, (2) discolored paint or wallpaper, or (3) partitions that feel hot to the touch. If any of these signs is present, the partition must be opened up to look for the fire. Finding cobwebs inside the partition is one sign that fire has not spread through the partition.

11. Fires can spread inside partitions because
   (A) there are spaces between studs inside of partitions
   (B) fires can burn anywhere
   (C) partitions are made out of materials that burn easily
   (D) partitions are usually painted or wallpapered

Choice (A) is correct. This statement of fact is made in the second sentence.

12. If a firefighter sees the paint on a partition beginning to blister, he should first
   (A) wet down the partition
   (B) check the partitions in other rooms
   (C) chop a hole in the partition
   (D) close windows and doors and leave the room

Choice (C) is correct. Blistering paint (line 4) is a sign that fire is spreading inside a partition. If this sign is present, the firefighter must open the partition to look for the fire (line 5). The way to open the partition is to chop a hole in it.

MATHEMATICS ACHIEVEMENT

Directions: Choose the correct answer to each question based on either calculations made in your head or those made in the margins of the test booklet.

13. If $\frac{3}{4}$ of a class is absent and $\frac{2}{3}$ of those present leave the room, what fraction of the original class remains in the room?

(A) $\frac{1}{24}$

(B) $\frac{1}{4}$

(C) $\frac{1}{12}$

(D) $\frac{1}{8}$

Choice (C) is correct. If $\frac{3}{4}$ are absent, $\frac{1}{4}$ are present. If $\frac{2}{3}$ of the $\frac{1}{4}$ present leave, $\frac{1}{3}$ of the $\frac{1}{4}$ remain.

$\frac{1}{3} \times \frac{1}{4} = \frac{1}{12}$ remain in the room.

14. A cog wheel having 8 cogs plays into another cog wheel having 24 cogs. When the small wheel has made 42 revolutions, how many has the larger wheel made?

(A) 14

(B) 16

(C) 20

(D) 10

Choice (A) is correct. The larger wheel is 3 times the size of the smaller wheel, so it makes $\frac{1}{3}$ the revolutions.

$42 \div 3 = 14$

15. 75% of 4 is the same as what percent of 9?

(A) 36

(B) 25

(C) 40

(D) $33\frac{1}{3}$

Choice (D) is correct.

75% of 4 = 3

$3 = 33\frac{1}{3}\%$ of 9

16. If $\frac{1}{2}$ cup of spinach contains 80 calories and the same amount of peas contains 300 calories, how many cups of spinach have the same caloric content as $\frac{2}{3}$ cup of peas?

(A) $\frac{2}{5}$

(B) $1\frac{1}{3}$

(C) 2

(D) $2\frac{1}{2}$

Choice (D) is correct.

$\frac{1}{2}$c spinach = 80 calories

$\frac{1}{2}$c peas = 300 calories

1c peas = 600 calories

$\frac{2}{3}$c peas = 400 calories

$400 \div 80 = 5$ half-cups of spinach

$= 2\frac{1}{2}$ cups of spinach

TIP
Create an outline for your essay that contains 2 to 4 main points. If you try to work with too many main ideas, your essay will be long and difficult to effectively organize in 30 minutes.

ESSAY

Below is a typical essay topic. You are allowed 30 minutes to organize your thoughts; prepare an outline; and write, proofread, and edit a legible essay. Only the final copy will be scored.

Topic: *City life is criticized as being dangerous, expensive, and noisy, while suburban and country life is described by some as dull, culturally empty, and narrow. Explain some of the advantages and disadvantages of living where you do now: Be specific.*

If you learn that you will be taking the ISEE as part of the application process for any of your Catholic high schools, purchase and study ARCO's *Master the SSAT and ISEE, High School Entrance Exams.* This book includes instructions for answering questions unique to the ISEE and gives special advice and assistance with writing the ISEE essay. It also contains two full-length model ISEE exams.

Summary: About the ISEE

- The ISEE is a multiple-choice exam testing verbal ability, quantitative ability, reading comprehension, and mathematics achievement.
- There is no penalty for a wrong answer; you should guess if you are not sure.
- The ISEE is offered at two levels; a middle level is given to candidates in grades 6–8, and an upper-level exam is given to students in grades 9–12.

Chapter

5

Test-Taking Techniques

No test preparation book would be complete without a rundown of surefire test-taking techniques. Some of the techniques and tips listed here are common sense, but it never hurts to be reminded. For example, you should always assemble your materials the night before the exam, get a good night's sleep, get up early enough so that you don't need to rush, and eat breakfast. Here are some more tips:

- The only materials you need to bring to your exam are a few sharpened #2 pencils with clean erasers, positive identification, and your admission ticket (if you were issued one).
- Unless you were expressly instructed to bring a calculator, do not bring one to your exam. Calculators are not permitted at most high school entrance exams.
- It is important to wear a watch even though the room will most likely have a clock. The clock might not be conveniently located to keep track of time. If calculators are not allowed, be sure that your watch is not a calculator watch, because all calculator watches will be confiscated for the duration of the exam. If your watch has an alarm, be sure to turn it off.
- Enter the room early enough to choose a comfortable seat. After you're settled, relax. You'll concentrate more and perform better on the test if you're relaxed and comfortable. Besides, you studied hard for the exam, so what have you got to worry about, right?

ROAD MAP

- *What to Expect When You Take the Exam*
- *Question-Answering Tips*

WHAT TO EXPECT WHEN YOU TAKE THE EXAM

The first thing you will do in the exam room is fill out forms. You will be given detailed instructions for this procedure. Listen, read, and follow the directions; filling out forms is not timed, so don't rush. The exam will not begin until everyone has finished.

Next, the administrator will give you general instructions for taking the exam. You will be told how to recognize the stop and start signals. You will also find out what to do if you have a problem, such as all your pencils breaking or you find a page missing from your test booklet. Pay attention to the instructions. If you have any questions, ask them before the test begins.

TIP
You should lay out all the materials you need the night before the exam.

When the signal is given, open your test booklet and **read:**

- **Read** all directions carefully. The directions will probably be very similar to those in this book, but don't take anything for granted. Test makers do periodically change the exams.
- **Read** every word of every question. Be alert for little words that might have a big effect on your answer—words such as *not, most, all, every,* and *except.*
- **Read** all of the choices before you select an answer. It is statistically true that the most errors are made when the correct answer is the last choice given. Too many people mark the first answer that seems correct without reading through all of the choices to find out which answer is best.

QUESTION-ANSWERING TIPS

One of the best test tips we can offer is this: Try to answer every question on the exam, especially if you're running out of time. If you answer every question—even if you guess wildly—you are more likely to earn a high score. (The SSAT is an exception to this rule. Remember that there's a penalty for wrong answers on that test, so an educated guess can help, a wild guess might not.) There is no penalty for wrong answers on the COOP, HSPT, or ISSE examinations, so even a wild guess gives you a 20 or 25 percent chance for credit! Here are some basic tips for making an educated guess.

- If you're uncertain as to the answer to a question, guess—you can always mark the question and return to it for another try later if you have the time.
- An educated guess is worth more than a random guess. To make an educated guess, look carefully at the question and eliminate any answers that you are sure are wrong. Chances are that you can spot some obviously wrong answers among the choices to vocabulary, reading, and language questions. You will probably find some of the choices to math questions to be so way off as to make you chuckle. When it boils right down to it, you have a better chance of guessing correctly when you have three options instead of four or five. Your odds improve even more if you can guess between two choices.
- Keep alert for the moment during the exam when time is about to run out. In those last few seconds, pick one response—preferably not the first, because the first answer tends to be the correct one less often than the others—and mark all remaining blanks on your answer sheet with that same answer. By the law of averages, you should pick up a free point or two.

Another way to make sure you do as well as you can on the exam is to make sure that you don't lose any points through carelessness. Here's a list of suggestions that apply to any entrance exam, including the model exams you'll take later in Part 4.

TIP
The machine that scores your test can only "read" the bubbles. Be sure to shade in the entire bubble and erase all stray marks.

1. Mark your answers by completely blackening the answer space of your choice. Be sure not to make any marks outside the lines.
2. Mark only **one** answer for each question, even if you think that more than one answer is correct. If you mark more than one answer, you lose all credit for that question.
3. If you change your mind, erase the answer completely. Leave no doubt as to which answer you mean.
4. Answer every question in the right place on the answer sheet. Make sure that the number of the answer blank matches the number of the question you are answering. You could lose a lot of time if you have to go back and change a lot of answers.
5. Don't spend too much time on any question, even if it poses an interesting challenge. Pick an answer and move on. You can always mark the question in your test booklet and go back to it later if time permits.
6. You are not required to answer every question; however, if you do skip one, **be sure to skip its answer space,** otherwise, you might throw off your entire answer sheet. For that reason, it's safer to guess than to skip. Just mark the guesses in your test booklet so that you can go back and deliberate some more if you have time.
7. If you use scratch paper (you may on the HSPT but not on the COOP), be sure to mark the answer on the answer sheet. Only the answer sheet is scored, the test booklet and the scratch paper are not.
8. Stay alert. Getting a good night's sleep the night before and eating breakfast on the morning of the test will help you to be alert.
9. If you don't finish a section before the time is up, don't worry. Few people can actually answer every question. If you are accurate, you might earn a high score even without finishing every test section.
10. Don't let your performance on any one section affect your performance on any other part of the exam. For example, if you don't think you did very well on mathematics, forget about that section after you are finished and start on the next section. Worrying about a section that is finished will cause you a lot of stress.
11. Check and recheck. If you finish any part before the time is up, don't waste time. Go back and check to be sure that each question is answered in the right space and that there is only one answer for each question. Return to the difficult questions and rethink them.

GOOD LUCK!

Summary: Test-Taking Techniques

- Always assemble everything you will need the night before the exam. You will need a few #2 pencils and a watch. Don't bring a calculator unless you have been instructed to do so.
- Get a good night's sleep and get up early enough so that you don't have to rush, you can eat breakfast, and you will be sure to arrive at the testing center early. Enter the room early enough to find a comfortable seat and relax.
- READ. Read all of the directions carefully, read every word of every question, read all of the choices before selecting an answer.
- PRACTICE. Practice all of the question-answering tips in this chapter when you study and when you take the practice exams. This way, they will come as second nature when you take the exam.

Verbal Skills

PART 2

PREVIEW

Chapter 6

Synonyms

Synonym questions test your understanding of words. You are asked to choose another word that has the same, or nearly the same, meaning as the given word. On the HSPT, synonyms are tested in the Verbal Skills section of the exam, under the categories of Reading and Vocabulary. Each exam may indicate the synonym in a different fashion. For example, some exams will identify the word they want you to match by italicizing or capitalizing the word, then ask you to choose a synonym from the answer choices. Other exams will use the word in a sentence, usually identifying the synonym in question by underlining, italicizing, or capitalizing the word, then you must select a matching synonym from the answer choices. For example:

The surface of the placid lake was smooth as glass.

(A) cold
(B) muddy
(C) deep
(D) calm

In this example, the word "calm" is the correct choice. As you can see, the nice thing about a sentence example is that it might give you contextual clues that make it easier to figure out the synonym's meaning. In the example, when you read that the lake was "smooth as glass," you could infer that, although the lake might have been muddy, deep, or cold, it definitely must have been calm. That made choice (D) the **best** choice for this question.

TIPS FOR ANSWERING SYNONYM QUESTIONS

Here's a tip to use when choosing the answer for a synonym question: If the given word is in a sentence, you should always try substituting the choices in the place of the indicated word. This process can help you find and check your answer.

Sometimes the underlined or italicized word has multiple meanings, which can make the contextual clues of the sentence even more important. Consider the following question:

ROAD MAP

- *Tips for Answering Synonym Questions*
- *Synonym Exercises*
- *Answers and Explanations*

The camel is sometimes called the ship of the desert.

(A) abandon

(B) ice cream

(C) sandy wasteland

(D) leave

Here, the sentence is absolutely necessary to the definition of the word. Without the sentence, you would not know whether the word *desert* is to be pronounced *de-sert'*, which means to leave or to abandon, or *des'-ert*, which means a sandy wasteland. If you are not sure of your spelling, the sentence can also spare you the confusion of *desert* with *dessert*, which is the last course of a meal.

On the other hand, the phrase or sentence might be of little or no use at all in helping you to choose the synonym. The sentence might help you to determine the part of speech of the indicated word, but not its meaning, as in:

The robbery suspect had a sallow complexion.

(A) ruddy

(B) pale

(C) pock-marked

(D) freckled

The sentence shows you the proper use of the word *sallow*. It is an adjective used to describe a complexion, but the sentence gives no clue that *sallow* means *pale*. You either know the meaning of the word or you must guess. When the given word isn't part of a sentence, or if the sentence doesn't help define the word, you might have to guess. But before you guess blindly, you need to make sure there are no other clues that could lead you to the correct answer.

Perhaps you have seen the word used but were never sure what it meant. Look carefully. Do you know the meaning of any part of the word? If you can associate the word with something else you've read or you know, you might be able to find the answer. An example:

Remedial most nearly means

(A) reading

(B) slow

(C) corrective

(D) special

Your association is probably "remedial reading." That association can help you, but be careful! *Remedial* does not mean *reading*. *Remedial* is an adjective, and *reading* is the noun it modifies. Slow readers might receive remedial reading instruction in special classes that are intended to correct bad reading skills. Do you see the word *remedy* in *remedial?* You know that a *remedy* is a *cure* or a *correction* for an ailment. If you combine all the information you now have, you can choose *corrective* as the word that most nearly means *remedial.*

Sometimes you can find the correct answer to a synonym question by eliminating the answers that you know are wrong. If you can eliminate even one of the answers, you have a 33% chance of choosing the correct answer. Eliminate two incorrect answers, and you have a 50/50 chance of choosing the right answer from the two remaining choices. For example:

<u>Infamous</u> most nearly means

(A) well-known
(B) poor
(C) disgraceful
(D) young

The first word you see when you look at *infamous* is *famous. Famous*, of course, means well known. Because *in,* meaning *not,* is a negative prefix, you should be looking for a negative word as the meaning of *infamous.* With that in mind, you can eliminate choice (A). There is no choice meaning *not famous,* so you must look for negative fame. A person who is not well known might or might not be poor. You should carefully consider the other choices before choosing poor. Choice (D), *young,* probably can be eliminated for the same reasons. Though many young people are not famous, the terms aren't necessarily synonymous. *Disgrace* is a negative kind of *fame.* A person who behaves *disgracefully* is well known for his bad behavior; he is *infamous.* Therefore, choice (C) becomes the best answer for this question.

All of the above suggestions can help you use clues to determine the meaning of words and find their synonyms. But many synonym questions might give you no clues at all. The best way to minimize the number of synonym questions that you simply cannot answer is to learn as many vocabulary words as you can. One way to increase your vocabulary is to work with a dictionary when preparing for your exam. Try to read as much as you can during the time before your exam. When you run into a word that's totally unfamiliar to you, look it up. If you run across a word you don't know while doing the model exams, circle the word and look it up later. Look up words you find in the reading passages, new words from among answer choices, words you find in the explanations, and words you meet in the study chapters. Looking up words for yourself is the best way to learn them.

If you understand every word in this book, you are well on your way toward a broad-based vocabulary and should be able to handle not only the synonym questions, but the other verbal questions as well.

Now try the following exercises. Answers and explanations are at the end of the chapter.

SYNONYM EXERCISES

EXERCISE 1

Directions: In the following questions, choose the word that means the same as or about the same as the underlined word. Circle the letter of your answer.

1. a display of affluence
   (A) power
   (B) wealth
   (C) glibness
   (D) junction

2. the gloss of her lips
   (A) goblet
   (B) shadow
   (C) brightness
   (D) blush

3. a devout monk
   (A) reverent
   (B) lacking
   (C) growing
   (D) lonely

4. a thrilling encounter
   (A) meeting
   (B) bar
   (C) ledge
   (D) spaceship

5. to concede one's guilt
   (A) hide
   (B) invent
   (C) admit
   (D) contradict

6. to emerge from hiding
   (A) bury
   (B) come out
   (C) join
   (D) show anger

7. to teem with humanity
   (A) abound
   (B) play
   (C) group
   (D) adolescent

8. to permit to attend
   (A) discourage
   (B) allow
   (C) drive
   (D) card

9. to abate the fury
   (A) minnow
   (B) grow
   (C) formula
   (D) ebb

10. a recurrent theme
    (A) refined
    (B) resultant
    (C) electrifying
    (D) returning

11. on the verge of disaster
(A) boat
(B) force
(C) brink
(D) violence

12. to ponder deeply
(A) peruse
(B) think
(C) delay
(D) reveal

13. to aspire for success
(A) hope
(B) breathe
(C) exhaust
(D) plot

14. an era of apathy
(A) mistake
(B) war
(C) place
(D) age

15. temerity to speak out
(A) fear
(B) nerve
(C) flutter
(D) cowardice

16. a feat of skill
(A) body part
(B) celebration
(C) big meal
(D) achievement

17. zest for adventure
(A) relish
(B) fluency
(C) garment
(D) haste

18. a plaintive sound
(A) musical
(B) famous
(C) mournful
(D) patient

19. to view with consternation
(A) dismay
(B) telescope
(C) relief
(D) pretense

20. flagrant disobedience
(A) disguised
(B) glaring
(C) repeated
(D) perfumed

EXERCISE 2

Directions: Choose the word or phrase that has the same or nearly the same meaning as the underlined word or group of words.

1. The veracity of her story is without doubt.
   (A) persistence
   (B) truthfulness
   (C) poetry
   (D) horror

2. The drawings were completely identical.
   (A) twin
   (B) unclear
   (C) breathtaking
   (D) same

3. In our cellar, we accumulate old clothes.
   (A) affirm
   (B) donate
   (C) refurbish
   (D) collect

4. This legislation will transform the railroad system.
   (A) improve
   (B) electrify
   (C) change
   (D) sell

5. Candy will gratify the baby.
   (A) satisfy
   (B) fatten
   (C) excite
   (D) teach

6. The arena was girded with ribbons.
   (A) gay
   (B) established
   (C) decorated
   (D) encircled

7. How shall we quell the rebellion?
   (A) begin
   (B) cushion
   (C) crush
   (D) fire

8. His face looked pale and sickly.
   (A) wan
   (B) gabled
   (C) paltry
   (D) ponderous

9. The father was stern and impersonal with his children.
   (A) morose
   (B) gruff
   (C) opinionated
   (D) endeared

10. He was regarded as an outcast by his community.
    (A) paragon
    (B) parasite
    (C) pariah
    (D) pagan

11. Let us hoist the banner now.
    (A) raise
    (B) lower
    (C) wave
    (D) fold

12. The town took drastic measures to ensure its security.
    (A) well-informed
    (B) ill-advised
    (C) haphazard
    (D) extreme

13. The newscaster alluded to the weather forecast.
(A) changed
(B) complained about
(C) praised
(D) referred to

14. The strength of the cord exceeds government standards.
(A) surpasses
(B) equals
(C) challenges
(D) falls short of

15. The confused old gentleman was an affable soul.
(A) appetizing
(B) unappetizing
(C) foolish
(D) amiable

16. I wish that you would stop beating around the bush.
(A) running in circles
(B) avoiding the subject
(C) sweeping the driveway
(D) repeating the same thing over and over

17. I generally accept Jim's pronouncements with a grain of salt.
(A) some question
(B) criticism
(C) pleasure
(D) relief

18. That explanation is little more than an old wives' tale.
(A) a deliberate falsehood
(B) a half-truth
(C) feminist propaganda
(D) folklore

19. The medicine man shared his tried and true remedy with me.
(A) new and unusual
(B) tested and proven
(C) experimental
(D) unorthodox but effective

20. You should not look a gift horse in the mouth.
(A) question authority
(B) quibble over details
(C) expose yourself to danger
(D) be suspicious of good fortune

ANSWERS AND EXPLANATIONS

EXERCISE 1

1. **(B)** Affluence is wealth. Influence is power; confluence is junction.
2. **(C)** Gloss is brightness, polish, or shine.
3. **(A)** Devout means reverent, religious, or pious.
4. **(A)** An encounter is a face-to-face meeting.
5. **(C)** To concede is to admit or to acknowledge.
6. **(B)** To emerge is to come out. The word *emerge* is almost opposite to the word *merge,* which means join.
7. **(A)** To teem is to abound or to overflow.
8. **(B)** The word *permit,* pronounced *permit',* means allow. If the word were pronounced *per'mit*, it would mean license (which is not offered as a choice), but in no event would it mean drive or card.
9. **(D)** Abate means to subside, diminish, or ebb.
10. **(D)** That which is recurrent returns from time to time.
11. **(C)** Verge means brink or threshold.
12. **(B)** To ponder is to think or to consider. Peruse means read.
13. **(A)** To aspire is to hope or to desire. To breathe is to respire.
14. **(D)** An era is an age or period. Read carefully to avoid careless mistakes such as reading *err* or *area.*
15. **(B)** Temerity is audacity or nerve. Timorousness is timidity, fear, or cowardice.
16. **(D)** A feat is an achievement. Beware of homonyms when choosing synonyms.
17. **(A)** Zest means relish or gusto.
18. **(C)** Plaintive means mournful or melancholy.
19. **(A)** Consternation is amazement or dismay that throws one into confusion.
20. **(B)** Flagrant means glaring or conspicuously objectionable. The word meaning perfumed is fragrant.

EXERCISE 2

1. **(B)** Veracity is truthfulness or accuracy.
2. **(D)** Identical means same. Identical twins are genetically the same.
3. **(D)** To accumulate is to collect or to amass.
4. **(C)** To transform means to change. A transformer converts variations of current in a primary circuit into variations of voltage and current in a secondary circuit. The word *transform* in itself has nothing to do with electricity. One might hope that when the railroad system is transformed, it will be improved, but the change in itself is no guarantee.
5. **(A)** To gratify is to indulge, to please, or to satisfy.
6. **(D)** Girded means encircled.

7. **(C)** To quell is to put down, to suppress, or to crush.
8. **(A)** Wan means pale, sickly, or feeble.
9. **(B)** Gruff means rough or stern.
10. **(C)** A pariah is an outcast. A paragon is a model of perfection. A parasite lives off others and might well become an outcast, but the words are not synonymous. A pagan is a heathen. The pagan might be cast out by the religious community, but again, the words are not synonyms.
11. **(A)** To hoist is to raise or to lift.
12. **(D)** Drastic means extreme or severe.
13. **(D)** To allude is to make indirect reference or to refer.
14. **(A)** To exceed is to surpass.
15. **(D)** Affable means pleasant, gracious, and sociable.
16. **(B)** Beating around the bush is talking about irrelevant topics and raising side issues to avoid talking about or committing oneself on a particular subject.
17. **(A)** When one takes something with a grain of salt, one does not accept it at face value but questions details, motives, or conclusions.
18. **(D)** An old wives' tale is a story or explanation that has been handed "from woman to woman" as an oral tradition until it becomes folklore.
19. **(B)** Tried and true means tested and proven.
20. **(D)** Quite literally, the expression means that because one does not know the disposition of a gift horse, one should not risk sticking one's head in its mouth; furthermore, accept a gift as a gift without questioning its value (checking the quality of its teeth). In other words, be happy with what you get and don't be suspicious of good fortune.

Summary: Answering Synonym Questions

- If the given word is in a sentence, you should try substituting the answer choices in the place of the indicated word.
- When the given word is in a sentence, there are several ways to select the best answer. Look for contextual clues to determine which meaning of the word is being used. Determine which part of speech the word is and look for an answer choice of the same part of speech.
- When you don't know the meaning, try to take apart the word. Look for prefixes, suffixes, and the root word.
- Eliminate answers that you know are wrong and concentrate on the others.

Chapter 7

Antonyms

ROAD MAP

- *Tips for Answering Antonym Questions*
- *Antonym Exercises*
- *Answers and Explanations*

Antonym questions are similar to synonym questions in that they test your understanding of words. However, antonym questions are a bit trickier because they challenge you to demonstrate your mental flexibility as well as your verbal skills. On the HSPT, antonym questions appear on the Verbal Skills portion of the exam.

The task in an antonym question is to define the indicated word and pick its opposite. That sounds simple enough, right? Here's why it gets tricky. Where there is no true opposite, you must choose the word or phrase that is most nearly opposite. Where there appear to be two or more opposites, you must choose the best opposite. You must guard against choosing an associated word or phrase that is different in meaning but is not a true opposite. After struggling to define a word, you must then take care to choose its antonym, not its *synonym* (the word or phrase that is most similar in meaning).

Let's try an example. Suppose the test question looks like this:

INAUDIBLE means the opposite of

(A) invisible

(B) bright

(C) loud

(D) clear

You do not know the meaning of the word inaudible, but you might recognize some of the word's parts. You might know that the prefix *in* typically means *not.* You also might recognize a part of audio in the word, and you know that the audio of your TV is the sound. You might also see *able* in *ible* and thereby reconstruct not soundable or not heard.

BEWARE! This is the point at which your reasoning can easily lead you astray. If you associate the word with your TV, you might think, "The opposite of not heard is not seen or invisible, choice (A)." Wrong. These are not true opposites. Or you might associate not heard with not seen and choose answer (B), *bright*, as the opposite of not seen. Wrong again. Or you might think of inaudible as hard to hear and choose (D), *clear.* Clear would

CAUTION
Antonym questions require you to choose the **opposite** of the indicated word. Keep this in mind while you are reading the possible answers.

not be a bad answer, but (C), *loud,* is better and is indeed the best answer. The best opposite of inaudible is loud. You can now see how tricky finding the answer can be! To find the right answer to an antonym question, you need to be certain that you remember exactly what you're looking for as you reject or choose an answer choice.

TIPS FOR ANSWERING ANTONYM QUESTIONS

Thankfully, there is a sound approach to handling antonym questions if you're not sure of the correct answer. After reading the word and its four possible answers very carefully, run through the following possibilities.

Possibility #1: You know the meaning of the word, but no answer choice seems correct.

- Perhaps you misread the word. Are there other words that look similar to the word in the question? For example, did you read *revelation* for *revaluation* or *compliment* for *complement*?
- Perhaps you read the word correctly but accented the wrong syllable. Some words have alternative pronunciations with vastly different meanings. Remember *de-sert'* and *des'-ert*?
- Perhaps you are dealing with a single word that can be used as two different parts of speech and in those two roles has two entirely unrelated meanings. A *moor* (noun) is a boggy wasteland. To *moor* (verb) is to secure a ship or a boat in place. The proper noun *Moor* refers to the Moslem conquerors of Spain.
- Perhaps the word can appear as a number of parts of speech with numerous meanings and shades of meaning within each of these. *Fancy* (noun) can mean inclination, love, notion, whim, taste, judgment, imagination. *Fancy* (verb) can mean to like, to imagine, to think. *Fancy* (adjective) can mean whimsical, ornamental, extravagant. Your task is to choose from among the four choices one word or phrase that is opposite to *one* of these meanings of the word *fancy.*

Possibility #2: You do not know the meaning of the word, but it appears to contain prefix, suffix, or root clues. Examine those clues. For example, the word inaudible uses the prefix *in,* which means *not,* so look for the best opposite of "not audible."

Possibility #3: You do not know the meaning of the word, can see no clues, but have a feeling that the word has some specific connotation, be it sinister, gloomy, or positive. Play your hunch. Choose a word with the opposite connotation.

Possibility #4: You are stumped. There is no penalty for guessing on the COOP or HSPT exam, so when all else fails, guess. If you can eliminate one or more of the choices, you improve the odds of guessing correctly. Eliminate choices as you can, choose from the remaining options, and move on. There's no need to waste time on a question for which you cannot figure out the answer.

Now try the following exercises using the tactics outlined. Answers and explanations begin right after the exercises.

TIP
Examine the prefix, suffix, or root of the word to provide clues for determining the meaning of a word.

ANTONYM EXERCISES

EXERCISE 1

Directions: Choose the best answer.

1. Accelerate means the *opposite* of
   (A) stop
   (B) slow
   (C) quicken
   (D) hasten

2. Docile means the *opposite* of
   (A) active
   (B) health
   (C) probable
   (D) teachable

3. Candor means the *opposite* of
   (A) frankness
   (B) doubt
   (C) deception
   (D) enthusiasm

4. Nomadic means the *opposite* of
   (A) secret
   (B) anonymous
   (C) stationary
   (D) famous

5. Humble means the *opposite* of
   (A) simple
   (B) just
   (C) hurt
   (D) proud

6. Defy means the *opposite* of
   (A) desire
   (B) embrace
   (C) fight
   (D) abscond

7. Gorge means the *opposite* of
   (A) duck
   (B) diet
   (C) stuff
   (D) valley

8. Curtail means the *opposite* of
   (A) curry
   (B) open
   (C) shorten
   (D) extend

9. Initiate means the *opposite* of
   (A) instruct
   (B) begin
   (C) terminate
   (D) invade

10. Grant means the *opposite* of
    (A) confiscate
    (B) money
    (C) land
    (D) swamp

11. Clamor means the *opposite* of
    (A) ugliness
    (B) beauty
    (C) silence
    (D) dishonor

12. Rouse means the *opposite* of
    (A) lull
    (B) alarm
    (C) complain
    (D) weep

13. Credible means the *opposite* of
    (A) believable
    (B) unbelievable
    (C) honorable
    (D) dishonorable

14. Thorough means the *opposite* of
    (A) around
    (B) circumvented
    (C) sloppy
    (D) slovenly

15. Wooden means the *opposite* of
    (A) iron
    (B) slippery
    (C) rubbery
    (D) green

EXERCISE 2

1. Succumb means the *opposite* of
   (A) arrive
   (B) yield
   (C) eat
   (D) conquer

2. Divert means the *opposite* of
   (A) instruct
   (B) include
   (C) bore
   (D) amuse

3. Assent means the *opposite* of
   (A) agree
   (B) disagree
   (C) climb
   (D) fall

4. Diminish means the *opposite* of
   (A) lessen
   (B) begin
   (C) complete
   (D) expand

5. Brazen means the *opposite* of
   (A) frozen
   (B) humble
   (C) rustproof
   (D) leaky

6. Intent means the *opposite* of
   (A) alfresco
   (B) busy
   (C) uninterested
   (D) shy

7. Smother means the *opposite* of
   (A) cuddle
   (B) expel
   (C) aerate
   (D) rescue

8. Lavish means the *opposite* of
   (A) filthy
   (B) elegant
   (C) squander
   (D) conserve

9. Aloof means the *opposite* of
   (A) sociable
   (B) humble
   (C) public
   (D) ignorant

10. Elated means the *opposite* of
   (A) on time
   (B) tardy
   (C) ideal
   (D) depressed

11. Furnish means the *opposite* of
   (A) dress
   (B) decorate
   (C) remove
   (D) polish

12. Ostracize means the *opposite* of
   (A) include
   (B) shun
   (C) hide
   (D) delight

13. Exorbitant means the *opposite* of
   (A) priceless
   (B) worthless
   (C) reasonable
   (D) straight

14. Chastise means the *opposite* of
   (A) dirty
   (B) cleanse
   (C) praise
   (D) straighten

15. Profit means the *opposite* of
   (A) gain
   (B) money
   (C) suffer
   (D) disgust

ANSWERS AND EXPLANATIONS

EXERCISE 1

1. **(B)** To accelerate is to quicken or to hasten. Its best opposite is to slow. *Accelerate* implies that the object was already in motion. Stop would be the opposite if the original word had meant *to put into motion*.
2. **(A)** *Docile* means calm and easily led. Of the choices offered, its best opposite is active.
3. **(C)** *Candor* is frankness; its opposite is deception.
4. **(C)** *Nomadic* means wandering; its opposite is stationary, staying in one place. The word *nomadic* has nothing to do with names.
5. **(D)** *Humble* means meek and modest. Its best opposite is proud.
6. **(B)** To *defy* is to challenge; its opposite is embrace.
7. **(B)** To *gorge* oneself is to overeat; the opposite is to diet.
8. **(D)** To *curtail* is to shorten; the opposite is to extend.
9. **(C)** To *initiate* is to begin; its opposite is to terminate or to end.
10. **(A)** To *grant* is to give; its opposite is to confiscate.
11. **(C)** *Clamor* is noise; its opposite is silence. You must read carefully. Clamor is *not* glamour.
12. **(A)** To *rouse* is to awaken; to lull is to soothe and to cause to sleep.
13. **(B)** *Credible* means believable; its opposite is unbelievable.
14. **(C)** *Thorough* means careful and complete; its opposite is sloppy, which means careless and inattentive to detail. Slovenly also means careless, but it also implies dirty, so sloppy is the better opposite.
15. **(C)** *Wooden* means stiff and unbending; its opposite, rubbery, means flexible.

EXERCISE 2

1. **(D)** To *succumb* is to yield or to give in; its opposite is to conquer.
2. **(C)** To *divert* is to amuse (think of *diversion*); its opposite is to bore. To divert also means *to change the direction of,* but no opposite to this meaning is offered.
3. **(B)** To *assent* is to agree; its opposite is to disagree. *Assent* is in no way related to *ascend* or *ascent*.
4. **(D)** To *diminish* is to lessen. Therefore, its opposite is expand.
5. **(B)** *Brazen* means bold or impudent; its opposite is humble.
6. **(C)** To be *intent* is to be engrossed or determined; the opposite is to be uninterested.
7. **(C)** To *smother* is to shut out all air; to aerate is to supply with air. Although the act of smothering might be reversed by rescuing, aerate is the more direct antonym.
8. **(D)** To *lavish* is to spend profusely or to squander; its opposite is to conserve.
9. **(A)** One who is *aloof* is distant or reserved; an opposite type of person is sociable.

10. **(D)** One who is *elated* is bursting with pride; his opposite is depressed.
11. **(C)** To *furnish* is to provide; its opposite is to remove.
12. **(A)** To *ostracize* is to shut out or to exclude; its opposite is to include.
13. **(C)** *Exorbitant* means excessive; its opposite is reasonable.
14. **(C)** To *chastise* is to scold; its opposite is to praise.
15. **(C)** To *profit* is to benefit; its opposite is to suffer.

Summary: Answering Antonym Questions

- When you think you know the meaning of the given word but can't find the answer, go back and check; did you misread the word, did you accent the wrong syllable, can the word be used as two different parts of speech, does the word have multiple meanings?
- If you don't know the meaning of the word, look for prefixes, suffixes, and root words. Be sure you are clear on the context and look for the opposite meaning.
- When you have to guess, try to eliminate some answer choices. Consider connotation and the part of speech.

Chapter 8

Analogies

Verbal analogy questions test your ability to see a relationship between words and to apply that relationship to other words. It is a test of your ability to think things out clearly and logically. Analogies are tested on the Verbal Reasoning sections of the COOP; on the HSPT, analogies are tested in the Verbal Skills sections.

Depending on the exam, verbal analogy questions might be presented in a number of different forms. In the HSPT exam, you are given two example words that are related to each other in a certain way. Then you are given a third word and four answer choices. The correct answer choice will have the same relationship to the third word as that shared by the example words. For example:

MAN is to BOY as WOMAN is to:

(A) child
(B) sister
(C) girl
(D) offspring

The correct answer in this example is choice (C). Thus, the completed analogy reads "MAN is to BOY as WOMAN is to GIRL." A woman is an adult girl, just as a man is an adult boy.

The Analogies Test on the COOP exam takes a different form, using pictures instead of words. After you have named the object in each picture, you must proceed as with a verbal analogy question, defining and completing the relationships. The Related Words section of the COOP exam's Verbal Reasoning Test uses yet another form for analogy questions. You must define the relationship among three words and then complete a second group of three words, this time choosing the third word for the second group. Regardless of which form an analogy question might take, the task is always the same: Define relationships and then apply the relationships to different words.

ROAD MAP

- *Tips for Answering Analogy Questions*
- *Analogy Exercises*
- *Answers and Explanations*

TIPS FOR ANSWERING ANALOGY QUESTIONS

CAUTION

Don't be fooled by similar words. In analogy questions, you're looking for similar relationships, not similar words.

The first step in tackling an analogy question is to define the first set of words and determine their relationship. Most often you will know the meanings of both words (if you're not sure, make a guess and move on to the next step). Your next step will be to determine how those words are related. Define a specific relationship between the words. Here's an example: Suppose you are confronted with an analogy question that begins BRIM is to HAT. BRIM and HAT are immediately associated in your mind; a BRIM is a part of a HAT, so the relationship between the two is that of a part to the whole.

Now take a look at the third word in the analogy question and the four choices available. By process of elimination, you must find among the choices a word that bears the same relationship to the third word that the second word bears to the first. The analogy question would look like this:

BRIM is to HAT as HAND is to

(A) glove
(B) finger
(C) foot
(D) arm

To figure out the answer, consider each answer choice in turn. *Hand* is certainly associated with (A), *glove*, but in no way is a hand part of a glove. *Hand* and (B) *finger*, are certainly associated and, indeed, a *finger* is part of a *hand*. But BEWARE! Re-examine the relationship of the first two words: *Brim* is a part of *hat,* or in other words, *hat* is the whole of which *brim* is a part. The relationship in choice (B) is the reverse of the relationship of the first two words. *Hand* is the whole and *finger* is the part. Your answer must maintain the same relationship in the same sequence as the original pair.

The relationship of *hand* and answer (C), *foot,* is only one of association, not of part to whole. This answer is no more likely to be correct than (A). In fact, because you have found two answers that have equal chances of being correct, you now know that neither of them is the answer you are looking for. There must be a best answer.

TIP

What if none of the answer pairs seems exactly right? Just remember: the directions tell you to choose the *best* answer. The correct answer won't necessarily be a perfect fit, but it will work better than the other choices.

A *hand* is part of an *arm* in the same way that a *brim* is part of a *hat,* or the *arm* is the whole of which a *hand* is a part in the same way that *hat* is the whole of which a *brim* is the part. When you've determined this, you know that answer (D) is the *best* answer.

And so the process is:

1. Define the initial terms.
2. Describe the initial relationship.
3. Eliminate incorrect answers.
4. Refine the initial relationship, if necessary.
5. Choose the best of the remaining answer choices.

Usually your biggest problem in solving an analogy question will be that of narrowing your choices down to the *best* answer. Sometimes, however, your difficulty will be in finding even one correct answer. If this happens, you might have to shift gears and completely redefine your initial relationship. Let's look at another analogy example.

Consider an analogy that begins LETTER is to WORD. Initially, you will probably think, "A letter is part of a word; therefore, the relationship is that of part to whole." If the relationship of the third word to any of the choices is also part to whole, then all is well. However, suppose the question looks like this:

LETTER is to WORD as SONG is to

(A) story
(B) music
(C) note
(D) orchestra

Three of the choices offer an association relationship, so, clearly, you must go along with a more refined definition of the relationship. None of the choices offers a whole of which a song might be a part (such as an opera). Therefore, you must return to the original pair of words and consider other relationships between letter and word. If letter is not "letter of the alphabet," but rather "written communication," then a word is part of a letter and the relationship of the first to the second is whole to part. Then the answer becomes clear: A song is the whole of which *note,* answer (C), is the part. The relationship of *song* and *note* is the same as that of *letter* and *word*.

Analogy questions are a real challenge and can even be fun. Here's a list of a few of the most common, very general relationships:

Part to whole, e.g., BRANCH to TREE

Whole to part, e.g., OCEAN to WATER

Cause and effect, e.g., GERM to DISEASE

Effect and cause, e.g., HONORS to STUDY

Association, e.g., BAT to BALL

Degree, e.g., HUT to MANSION

Sequence, e.g., ELEMENTARY to SECONDARY

Function, e.g., TEACHER to STUDENT

Characteristic, e.g., WISE to OWL

Antonym, e.g., BAD to GOOD

Synonym, e.g., SPRING to JUMP

Purpose, e.g., MASK to PROTECTION

TIP
Know the six most common analogy connections:

1. Characteristic
2. Purpose
3. Antonym
4. Part to whole
5. Whole to part
6. Degree

Analogy questions also offer many opportunities for errors if every answer is not given careful consideration. A few of the most common pitfalls to avoid are listed on the next page.

TIP

Make the sentence connection. Turn the analogy pairs into sentences to help you see the connection. Then fit the answer pairs into the same sentence until you find the one that works best.

- Reversal of sequence of the relationship:

  Part to whole is *not* the same as whole to part.

  Cause to effect is *not* the same as effect to its cause.

  Smaller to larger is *not* the same as larger to smaller.

  Action to object is *not* the same as object to action.

- Confusion of relationship:

  Part to part (geometry to calculus) with part to whole (algebra to mathematics)

  Cause and effect (fire to smoke) with association (man to woman)

  Degree (drizzle to downpour) with antonyms (dry to wet)

  Association (walk to limp) with synonyms (eat to consume)

- Grammatical inconsistency: The grammatical relationship of the first two words must be retained throughout the analogy. A wrong analogy would be IMPRISONED is to CONVICT as CAGE is to PARROT. While the meaningful relationship exists, the analogy is not parallel in construction. A correct analogy of this sort would have to read PRISON is to CONVICT as CAGE is to PARROT, or IMPRISONED is to CONVICT as CAGED is to PARROT. In analogy questions, you have to create a pair that is grammatically consistent with the first pair, as well as meaningfully correct.
- Concentration on the meanings of words instead of on their relationships. In this type of error, you see FEATHERS to BEAK, and you think *bird* instead of part-to-part relationship. Then, you choose as your answer WING to BIRD instead of WING to FOOT.

Remember: The key to answering verbal analogy questions lies in the relationship between the first two words!

If you are having trouble determining the relationship between the words of the initial pair, you might find it useful to mentally reverse their order. If this works, just remember to mentally reverse the order of the third and fourth terms as well, to maintain parallelism in your answer.

Now try the following verbal analogies exercises and study the answers and explanations that follow the exercises.

ANALOGY EXERCISES

EXERCISE 1

Directions: In the following questions, the first two words are related to each other in a certain way. The third and fourth words must be related to each other in the same way. Choose from among the four choices the word that is related to the third word in the same way that the second word is related to the first.

1. Gasoline is to petroleum as sugar is to
   (A) sweet
   (B) oil
   (C) plant
   (D) cane

2. Fly is to spider as mouse is to
   (A) cat
   (B) rat
   (C) rodent
   (D) trap

3. Volcano is to crater as chimney is to
   (A) smoke
   (B) fire
   (C) flue
   (D) stack

4. Petal is to flower as fur is to
   (A) coat
   (B) rabbit
   (C) warm
   (D) woman

5. Retreat is to advance as timid is to
   (A) bold
   (B) cowardly
   (C) fearful
   (D) shy

6. Attorney is to trial as surgeon is to
   (A) doctor
   (B) operation
   (C) patient
   (D) ether

7. Picture is to see as speech is to
   (A) view
   (B) enunciate
   (C) hear
   (D) soliloquize

8. Soprano is to high as bass is to
   (A) guitar
   (B) bad
   (C) low
   (D) fish

9. Addition is to addend as subtraction is to
   (A) difference
   (B) sum
   (C) subtrahend
   (D) minus

10. Obese is to eat as elected is to
    (A) advertise
    (B) run
    (C) count
    (D) fraud

11. Acute is to chronic as temporary is to
    (A) persistent
    (B) sick
    (C) pretty
    (D) narrow

12. Prostrate is to flat as vertical is to
    (A) circular
    (B) horizontal
    (C) geometric
    (D) erect

13. Chariot is to charioteer as automobile is to
    (A) passenger
    (B) engine
    (C) motor
    (D) driver

14. Team is to league as player is to
    (A) piano
    (B) team
    (C) tournament
    (D) football

15. Honor is to citation as speeding is to
    (A) citation
    (B) hurry
    (C) race
    (D) stop

EXERCISE 2

Directions: In the following questions, the first two words are related to each other in a certain way. The third and fourth words must be related to each other in the same way. Choose from among the four choices the word that is related to the third word in the same way that the second word is related to the first.

1. Net is to fisherman as gun is to
    (A) bullet
    (B) policeman
    (C) deer
    (D) hunter

2. Educated is to know as rich is to
    (A) poor
    (B) wise
    (C) own
    (D) money

3. Distracting is to noise as soothing is to
    (A) medicine
    (B) music
    (C) volume
    (D) bleeding

4. Year is to calendar as hour is to
    (A) decade
    (B) minute
    (C) clock
    (D) month

5. Father is to brother as mother is to
    (A) daughter
    (B) sister
    (C) aunt
    (D) niece

6. Words are to books as notes are to
    (A) songs
    (B) letters
    (C) pianos
    (D) fragrances

7. Pungent is to odor as shrill is to
    (A) whisper
    (B) sound
    (C) piercing
    (D) shriek

8. Present is to birthday as reward is to
   (A) accomplishment
   (B) medal
   (C) punishment
   (D) money

9. Mouse is to rodent as whale is to
   (A) animal
   (B) gigantic
   (C) aquatic
   (D) mammal

10. Sky is to ground as ceiling is to
   (A) floor
   (B) roof
   (C) top
   (D) plaster

11. Food is to nutrition as light is to
   (A) watt
   (B) bulb
   (C) electricity
   (D) vision

12. France is to America as meter is to
   (A) gallon
   (B) degree
   (C) yard
   (D) pound

13. Square is to triangle as cube is to
   (A) circle
   (B) tetrahedron
   (C) ball
   (D) pyramid

14. Abacus is to calculator as propeller is to
   (A) jet
   (B) airplane
   (C) mathematics
   (D) flight

15. Dizziness is to vertigo as fate is to
   (A) adversity
   (B) order
   (C) destiny
   (D) pride

ANSWERS AND EXPLANATIONS

EXERCISE 1

1. **(D)** The relationship is that of the product to its source. Gasoline comes from petroleum; sugar comes from cane.
2. **(A)** The relationship is that of the eaten to the eater. The fly is eaten by the spider; the mouse is eaten by the cat. You have to refine this analogy to eating in order to solve it. If you were to consider only catching, then you would not be able to distinguish between the *cat* and the *trap*.
3. **(C)** The relationship is functional. The crater is the vent for a volcano; the flue is the vent for a chimney.
4. **(B)** The relationship is that of part to whole. A petal is part of a flower; fur is part of a rabbit. Fur might be part of a coat, but it is not a necessary part, so *rabbit* makes a better analogy.
5. **(A)** The relationship is that of antonyms. *Retreat* is the opposite of *advance; timid* is the opposite of *bold*.
6. **(B)** This is an object-to-action relationship. An attorney performs a trial; the surgeon performs at an operation.
7. **(C)** This is another variety of object-to-action relationship. You see a picture; you hear a speech.
8. **(C)** The relationship is that of synonyms or definition. A soprano voice is high; a bass voice is low. Bass has a number of possible meanings. You must define the word in light of the relationship of the first two words.
9. **(C)** The relationship is that of the whole to a part. The addend is one term of an addition problem; the subtrahend is one term of a subtraction problem.
10. **(B)** This is an essential cause-and-effect relationship. You cannot become obese if you do not eat; you cannot be elected if you do not run.
11. **(A)** The relationship is that of antonyms. *Acute* means sudden and short; *chronic* means always present. Temporary is the opposite of persistent.
12. **(D)** The relationship is that of synonyms. *Prostrate* means flat; *vertical* means erect.
13. **(D)** The relationship is that of object and actor. The charioteer drives the chariot; the driver drives the automobile. You must consider the action in this analogy in order to differentiate between *driver* and *passenger*.
14. **(B)** The relationship is that of the part to the whole. The team is part of the league; the player is part of the team.
15. **(A)** This analogy is probably more difficult than any you will get. The trick lies in the fact that citation has two distinct meanings. The relationship is that of cause to effect. When you are to be honored, you receive a citation, which is a formal document describing your achievements. When you are stopped for speeding, you receive a citation, which is an official summons to appear in court.

EXERCISE 2

1. **(D)** The relationship does not fall into a category with a precise name. The fisherman uses a net for his sport; the hunter uses a gun for his sport. The policeman also uses a gun, but not for sport. You must refine your relationship so as to eliminate all but one choice.
2. **(C)** The relationship is that of cause and effect. When you are educated, you know; when you are rich, you own. When you are rich, you also have money. An analogy must maintain parallelism in parts of speech. For *money* to have been the correct answer, the second term would have had to have been a noun such as *knowledge*.
3. **(B)** The relationship is that of effect to its cause. Noise is distracting; music is soothing.
4. **(C)** This is a functional relationship. Years are measured on a calendar; hours are measured on a clock.
5. **(B)** The relationship of *father* to his same-sex sibling, *brother,* is analogous to the relationship of *mother* to her same-sex sibling, *sister*.
6. **(A)** The relationship is of parts to wholes. Words are parts of books; notes are parts of songs.
7. **(B)** The relationship is that of adjective to the noun it modifies. An odor may be described as pungent, though there are many other adjectives that may be also used. A sound may be described as shrill, though certainly not all sounds are shrill. *Shriek* is not the best answer because a shriek is always shrill.
8. **(A)** This is a purpose relationship. The purpose of a present is to celebrate a birthday; the purpose of a reward is to celebrate an accomplishment.
9. **(D)** The relationship is one of definition. A mouse is a rodent; a whale is a mammal.
10. **(A)** The relationship is one of antonyms. Sky is the opposite of ground; ceiling is the opposite of floor.
11. **(D)** The relationship is that of cause and effect. Food promotes nutrition; light promotes vision.
12. **(C)** The relationship cannot be defined by looking at the first two words alone. After you look at the third word and see that it is a European measure of length (metric), you might then look for another measure of length. Because the only choice offered is *yard,* you might state the relationship as *European* is to *American* as it applies to countries and measures of length.
13. **(D)** You might loosely state the relationship as *four* is to *three*. A square is a four-sided plane figure in relation to a triangle, which is a three-sided plane figure. A cube is a solid figure based on a square; a pyramid is a solid figure based on a triangle.
14. **(A)** The relationship is sequential. An abacus is an earlier, more primitive calculator; a propeller is an earlier, less sophisticated means of propulsion than is a jet.
15. **(C)** The relationship is that of synonyms. Vertigo is dizziness; destiny is fate. One's fate may well be to suffer adversity, but fate is not necessarily negative.

Summary: Analogy Tips

- Analogies are tested on the Verbal Reasoning sections of the COOP; on the HSPT analogy questions are in the Verbal Skills Section.
- Analogy questions on the COOP use pictures instead of words. Once you have named the object in each picture, proceed the same way you would with a verbal analogy.
- Follow the steps: define the initial terms, describe the initial relationship, eliminate incorrect answers, refine the initial relationship, and choose the best answer.
- Study and learn the 12 types of analogy questions; part to whole, whole to part, cause and effect, effect and cause, association, degree, sequence, function, characteristic, antonym, synonym, and purpose.

Chapter

Verbal Logic

You'll definitely be tested on your logical thinking in both the COOP and HSPT exams. A test of your reasoning skills will show how you think through a problem or scenario. The HSPT exam tests several types of verbal logic, one under the Logic test section and the other under the Verbal Classifications section. In the COOP exam, the verbal logic test is titled Test of Verbal Reasoning.

One measure of verbal logic requires you to extract indisputable information from a series of short sentences. Another asks you to consider a single word and to decide which of four choices is an absolutely necessary component of that word. The third measure of logical thinking is an exercise in translating an artificial language. Let's look at how each exam handles a typical test question for each of these areas of measurement.

HSPT LOGIC

HSPT logic questions take a slightly different form than other questions on the exam. In these questions, you're given a series of sentences. You are asked to determine if, based on the truth of the other sentences, the final sentence is (A) true, (B) false, or (C) uncertain. If it is not possible to determine if the final sentence is true or false, then the correct answer is (C).

> **Note:** On the HSPT exam, you only have three answer choices for logic questions. (A) True, (B) False, and (C) Uncertain. Never mistakenly choose (D).

Let's look at an example of an HSPT logic question:

The black horse jumped over more hurdles than the spotted horse. The white horse jumped over more hurdles than the spotted horse. The white horse jumped over more hurdles than the black horse. If the first two statements are true, the third statement is

(A) true

(B) false

(C) uncertain

ROAD MAP

- *HSPT Logic*
- *HSPT Verbal Classification*
- *COOP Extraction of Information*
- *COOP Logic*
- *COOP Artificial Language*
- *Sample Exercises*
- *Answers and Explanations*

From the first two statements we know that both the black horse and the white horse jumped over more hurdles than the spotted horse. This is all that we know. The first two statements do not give us any information about the comparative achievements of the black horse and the white horse. The answer, therefore, is (C). The third statement can be neither affirmed nor denied on the basis of the first two statements.

HSPT VERBAL CLASSIFICATION

Here's another type of verbal logic question you'll find on the HSPT. In verbal classification questions, you are presented with four words and you're asked to determine which of the words doesn't fit with the other three. Here's an example:

Which word does not belong with the others?

(A) crack
(B) cleave
(C) split
(D) pare

The first three words are synonyms. All refer to dividing something by opening it into two or more pieces. Choice (D), on the other hand, refers to opening by peeling off the outer layer (to pare is to peel). The key to answering this kind of question lies in figuring the relationship among three of the words. The relationships might be of synonyms, degrees, parts of speech, functions, or along any of a myriad of dimensions.

COOP EXTRACTION OF INFORMATION

The COOP extraction of information questions present you with a series of related statements and four answer choices. You must choose the answer statement that is supported by the series of statements that precede the choices. That process probably sounds a lot more complicated than it really is, so let's look at an example:

The little red house on our block is very old. It was once used as a church, and Abraham Lincoln might have worshipped there. It also served as a schoolhouse.

(A) At one time schools were used for worship.
(B) Abraham Lincoln prayed in school.
(C) The house has an interesting history.
(D) Red is a popular color for schools.

Take one statement at a time. Choice (A) cannot be supported by the paragraph. The paragraph states that the house was once used as a church, not that it was used as a church and a school at the same time. Choice (B) also cannot be supported by the paragraph. If Abraham Lincoln worshipped in the house, he did so when it was a church. Although Abraham Lincoln might have prayed in school as a child, such information is extraneous to the paragraph. Choice (C) is clearly correct. The house does have a long and interesting history dating back to or before the Civil War and having been at various times a church, a school, and a house. Chances are that (C) is the correct answer, but check out choice (D) before choosing your answer. Choice (D) makes a statement of fact that is true in its own right, but one that is not supported by the information in the passage. You must therefore choose (C).

COOP LOGIC

The COOP logic questions ask that you choose a word that names a necessary part or component of an italicized or underlined word. Here's an example:

Which word names a *necessary* part of the underlined word?

colander

(A) water

(B) holes

(C) food

(D) dirt

A colander is a perforated dish or bowl for draining off liquids as in rinsing pasta, fruit, or vegetables. The holes (B) are absolutely necessary; all other choices are related, but none is necessary to the existence of the colander.

COOP ARTIFICIAL LANGUAGE

The COOP artificial language questions test your ability to transfer information that you have about one word to help define another, related word. The trick here is that all the words you deal with in these questions are nonsense-words, so you have to carefully read the definitions you're given and use those clues to help find the right answer choice. Here's an example:

Here are some words translated from an artificial language.

lobobatoba means insult

lomonatoba means inspect

lobobatabo means result

Which word means respect?

(A) tabolomona

(B) tobatabo

(C) lomonatabo

(D) lobobalomona

Look first at the English words. Notice that each word consists of a prefix and a stem and that among the four words there are only two prefixes and two stems. Now look at the three artificial-language words. Notice that each appears to have two parts, one beginning with *l* and ending with *a* and the other beginning with *t*. Now return to the first pair of words and separate each into its two halves.

loboba toba = in sult

lomona toba = in spect

You now have gathered useful information. In the artificial language, the stem comes first and is followed by the prefix. Furthermore, you now know that

toba means *in*

loboba means *sult*

lomona means *spect*

Confirm this information by looking at the third pair of words:

loboba tabo = re sult

You already knew that *loboba* means *sult;* now you also know that *tabo* means *re*.

At this point, you can figure the answer. Look at the four choices. Immediately eliminate choices (A) and (B) because you know that the stem must be followed by the prefix, and in these two choices the order of the parts of the words is reversed. If you look quickly ahead, you will see that in choice (D) you are offered joined stems with no prefix. You can confidently pick choice (C) as the answer to this question. Confirm: *tabo* means *re; lomona* means *spect*.

At first glance, the artificial-language type of verbal logic question seems rather weird, even intimidating. Actually, with concentration and practice the procedure can become mechanical and not at all difficult.

Try your hand at using the reasoning processes we have just taught you as you tackle the following exercises. Answers and explanations follow exercise 3.

SAMPLE EXERCISES

EXERCISE 1

Directions: Choose the correct answer.

1. George is older than Bob. Fred is younger than George. Bob is older than Fred. If the first two statements are true, the third statement is
   (A) true.
   (B) false.
   (C) uncertain.

2. Group A sings higher than Group C. Group B sings lower than Group C. Group A sings higher than Group B. If the first two statements are true, the third statement is
   (A) true.
   (B) false.
   (C) uncertain.

3. Percolator coffee is weaker than electric-drip coffee. Extractor coffee is stronger than electric-drip coffee. Electric-drip coffee is stronger than extractor coffee. If the first two statements are true, the third statement is
   (A) true.
   (B) false.
   (C) uncertain.

4. Red kites fly higher than yellow kites. Yellow balloons fly higher than red kites. Yellow kites fly higher than yellow balloons. If the first two statements are true, the third statement is
   (A) true.
   (B) false.
   (C) uncertain.

5. The New York team lost f
   Boston team. The Boston t
   than the Baltimore team but not as many
   the New York team. The Baltimore team lost the fewest games. If the first two statements are true, the third statement is
   (A) true.
   (B) false.
   (C) uncertain.

6. The history book has more pages than the poetry book but fewer pages than the math book. The math book has more pages than the science book but fewer pages than the English book. The poetry book has the fewest pages. If the first two statements are true, the third statement is
   (A) true.
   (B) false.
   (C) uncertain.

7. Which word does *not* belong with the others?
   (A) ceiling
   (B) window
   (C) floor
   (D) wall

8. Which word does *not* belong with the others?
   (A) orange
   (B) apple
   (C) tomato
   (D) carrot

9. Which word does *not* belong with the others?
   (A) emotion
   (B) love
   (C) anger
   (D) disappointment

10. Which word does *not* belong with the others?
    (A) hurricane
    (B) tornado
    (C) typhoon
    (D) earthquake

11. Which word does *not* belong with the others?
    (A) medicine
    (B) healing
    (C) therapy
    (D) surgery

12. Which word does *not* belong with the others?
    (A) orange
    (B) brown
    (C) red
    (D) purple

EXERCISE 2

Directions: Choose the statement that is true according to the given information.

1. Mr. Stonehill worked in the corporate headquarters of a large corporation. Another company acquired Mr. Stonehill's company and sold off the operating divisions one by one. There can be no corporate headquarters without any operating divisions. Mr. Stonehill is
    (A) unemployed.
    (B) working for one of the operating divisions.
    (C) no longer working in corporate headquarters.
    (D) working for the new company.

2. Mr. Moffitt is a high school chemistry teacher. As a young man, Mr. Moffitt worked in the textile dyes division of a chemical company. Besides teaching chemistry, Mr. Moffitt operates a business cleaning Oriental carpets.
    (A) Mr. Moffitt changes jobs often.
    (B) Mr. Moffitt teaches students how to clean carpets.
    (C) Mr. Moffitt is a wealthy man.
    (D) Mr. Moffitt is well-qualified for the work he does.

3. Sally and Susie are twins. Sally lives near her parents in a Chicago suburb with her husband and children. Susie lives in a remote area of Alaska and raises dogs.
    (A) Susie does not get along with her parents.
    (B) Twins may have different interests and tastes.
    (C) Sally does not like dogs.
    (D) There are special bonds between twins.

4. The baby woke and cried in the middle of the night. Molly Davis changed the baby's diaper, gave him a warm bottle, and put him back to bed.
    (A) The baby woke because it was time for his bottle.
    (B) The baby's mother's name is Molly Davis.
    (C) The baby woke with a wet diaper.
    (D) After his bottle, the baby went back to sleep.

5. Eight children went trick-or-treating together on Halloween. Each child carried a lighted flashlight and a big bag. Jill and Mary did not wear masks.
    (A) The children went trick-or-treating at night.
    (B) Six children wore masks.
    (C) The bags were heavy.
    (D) The youngest children were Jill and Mary.

Directions: For questions 6–10, find the correct answer.

6. Here are some words translated from an artificial language.

    pritibondo means construct

    kwalaropipiwi means diverge

    kwalarobondo means converge

    Which word means <u>destruct</u>?
    (A) pritipepewe
    (B) kwalaropepewe
    (C) bondopriti
    (D) pipiwipriti

7. Here are some words translated from an artificial language.

hohoysiri means larger

hohosiriyi means smaller

hohohoysiri means largest

Which word means smallest?

(A) ysirisiriyi

(B) siriyihoho

(C) ysirihoho

(D) hohohosiriyi

8. Here are some words translated from an artificial language.

biblithrop means import

thropganum means portable

libibnadgrul means express

Which word means impress?

(A) bibliganum

(B) biblinadgrul

(C) nadgulthrop

(D) thropganum

9. Here are some words translated from an artificial language.

eselklup means black dog

eselrifoulof means white puppy

finiklupulof means gray cat

Which word means gray kitten?

(A) finikluprifo

(B) finirifoklupulof

(C) finiulofklup

(D) klupulofrifofini

10. Here are some words translated from an artificial language.

nipilazokople means base hit

frixzokople means home run

nipilazokoptaha means first down

Which word means touchdown?

(A) nipilazokoptaha

(B) zokopfrixtaha

(C) frixlezokop

(D) frixzokoptaha

EXERCISE 3

Directions: Choose the word that names a necessary part of the underlined word.

1. mother

(A) nurturing

(B) home

(C) responsibility

(D) child

2. essay

(A) words

(B) organization

(C) paper

(D) outline

3. fantasy

(A) entertainment

(B) dream

(C) imagination

(D) music

4. carpenter

(A) house

(B) wood

(C) saw

(D) repair

5. history
   (A) past
   (B) social studies
   (C) documents
   (D) culture

6. editorial
   (A) newspaper
   (B) rebuttal
   (C) publisher
   (D) opinion

7. skeleton
   (A) anatomy
   (B) death
   (C) bones
   (D) skull

8. geometry
   (A) lines
   (B) forms
   (C) numbers
   (D) mathematics

9. disappointment
   (A) loss
   (B) discouragement
   (C) failure
   (D) expectation

10. heirloom
    (A) antique
    (B) nostalgia
    (C) ancestor
    (D) jewelry

ANSWERS AND EXPLANATIONS

EXERCISE 1

1. **(C)** We know only that George is the oldest. There is no way to tell whether Bob is older than Fred, or Fred is older than Bob.
2. **(A)** Group A sings the highest of the three.
3. **(B)** Extractor coffee is the strongest, electric-drip comes next, and percolator coffee is the weakest.
4. **(B)** Balloons appear to fly higher than kites.
5. **(C)** We know for certain that Baltimore *won* the fewest games, but without information about how many games were played, we have no knowledge of how many games Baltimore *lost*.
6. **(C)** The English book has the most pages, followed by the math book. The history book has more pages than the poetry book. However, we do not have enough information to rank the science book; it might have more or fewer pages than the poetry book.
7. **(B)** The window is transparent or, at the very least, translucent and probably is movable as well. All of the other choices are solid, opaque, and fixed.
8. **(D)** The carrot is a root vegetable. All of the other choices are seed-bearing fruits.
9. **(A)** The other three choices are all actual emotions.
10. **(D)** All other choices are wind-based natural disasters.
11. **(B)** Medicine, therapy, and surgery are all procedures leading to healing.
12. **(C)** Red is a primary color; all of the others are red-based mixtures.

EXERCISE 2

1. **(C)** There is no information as to whether or not Mr. Stonehill is now working, nor for whom. However, if the operating divisions have been sold, there is no corporate headquarters. If there is no corporate headquarters, most certainly Mr. Stonehill does not work there.
2. **(D)** With the credentials required of all schoolteachers and with his specialized experience in a chemical company, Mr. Moffitt is clearly qualified to teach high school chemistry. The training that Mr. Moffitt received working in the textile dyes division applies beautifully to his sideline occupation, cleaning Oriental carpets. The other choices, while all possible, are in no way supported by the paragraph.
3. **(B)** The only statement definitely supported by the paragraph is that twins may have different interests and tastes.
4. **(C)** Nobody changes a dry diaper in the middle of the night. The other choices are possibilities but not certainties. The baby might have waked for any number of reasons; Molly Davis might be a baby-sitter; the baby might have played happily in his crib after he was dry and fed.
5. **(A)** If all eight children carried *lighted* flashlights, we might be pretty sure that it was dark. The information that Jill and Mary did not wear masks implies that the other children did, but does not prove it. Some of the others might also have not worn masks or might have worn sheets over their heads. Sometimes the youngest children wear masks while older youngsters apply complicated makeup. Jill and Mary were not necessarily the youngest.
6. **(A)** In this language, prefix and stem appear in reverse order. Among these words, the stems are *priti* meaning *struct* and *kwalaro* meaning *verge*. Within the three given words, *bondo* means *con,* and *pipiwi* means *di*. Because the word you must translate includes the stem *struct,* it must begin with *priti.* Only one choice begins with *priti,* so you need look no further. With no further information, you might conclude that because *pipiwi* means *di, pepewe* could reasonably stand for *de*.
7. **(D)** In this language, stem and suffix appear in reverse order. *Hoho* is the comparative suffix (*er*) and *hohoho* the superlative suffix (*est*). *Ysiri* means *large* and *siriyi* means *small*. The choice of answer is easy because only one choice begins with *hohoho*.
8. **(B)** In this language, the words are formed in the same order as words in the English language. You learn this fact by studying the first two words. Because *port* appears at the end of *import* but at the beginning of *portable,* and *throp* appears at the end of the first word and at the beginning of the second, you know that *throp* means *port*. If *throp* means *port*, then *bibli* must mean *im*. You can already narrow to answers (A) and (B). Looking back at the original words, if *throp* means *port,* then *ganum* means *able*. You can thus eliminate choice (A). With time pressure, choose (B) and go on to the next question. If you have time to confirm, note that *nadgrul* is the second half of *express,* so *nadgrul* undoubtedly means *press*.
9. **(B)** Because *esel* is the only word segment appearing in both the first and second words, *esel* must mean *dog*. The noun appears before its modifier. *Klup* means *black*. For the moment, we cannot tell within the second word which

segment means *white* and which signifies that the dog is young. Moving on to the third word, we find *klup* in the middle. Because the noun comes first, we know that *fini* means *cat.* Black cat *ulof?* But we want *gray* cat. *Ulof* also appears in the second word that defines a white puppy. *Ulof* must mean *white,* and the juxtaposition of *blackwhite* (*klupulof*), means gray. The remaining segment of the second word, *rifo,* must indicate that the dog is young. Now put together the answer. It must begin with *cat, fini*. The second segment, *rifo,* makes it young, hence a kitten. Finally, *klupulof* (blackwhite) makes it *gray.*

10. **(D)** This one takes even more logical thinking than most. Because the English words do not have common elements, you must first figure out the basis on which the artificial-language words are formed. The first two words are both related to baseball and both end in *le,* which does not appear in the word related to football. The first and third words begin with *nipila,* and both refer to an initial advance toward scoring in a sport, though not the same sport. Appearing in all three words is *zokop*. Evidently, *zokop* has something to do with either sports or balls. The meaning of *zokop* is unimportant, but because the word you must translate relates to football, *zokop* must appear in the word. If *nipila* refers to the initial advance toward a score and *frix* appears only in the word meaning home run, chances are that *frix* is a scoring word portion. Now, remembering that *taha* appeared only in the word relating to football and was not otherwise accounted for, you can construct the word for *touchdown*. The degree of scoring comes first. A touchdown is a scoring play, so our word must begin with *frix.* *Zokop* must come into the middle of all words having to do with scoring activities in football or baseball. A touchdown is a scoring play in football, so our word ends in *taha*.

EXERCISE 3

1. **(D)** One cannot be a mother without having or having had a child. All the other choices are usual and desirable adjuncts of motherhood, but they are not necessary to its existence.
2. **(A)** An essay is created of words. The most commonly seen essays are well organized and appear on paper, but a poor essay might be disorganized and any essay might appear on electronic media rather than paper.
3. **(C)** Fantasy is based on imagination. Fantasy might be dreamlike, might entertain, might be musical or embellished by music, but imagination is what is crucial to fantasy.
4. **(B)** A carpenter works with wood. What the carpenter does with wood or how the carpenter accomplishes a goal is immaterial to the existence of the carpenter.
5. **(A)** History is that which is past.
6. **(D)** An editorial is an expression of opinion. We tend to first think of editorials as being essays that are published in newspapers; but editorials, that is, statements of opinion, may also be broadcast on radio or television. Although an editorial might lead to a rebuttal or might be a rebuttal of a previously expressed opinion, the rebuttal is not necessary to the editorial.

7. **(C)** The skeleton is the bony structure of the body. After death and decomposition, the skeleton might become visible, but death is not necessary to the existence of the skeleton. The skull is a part of the skeleton, necessary in a living person, but not necessary to the existence of any skeleton. The bones themselves, however, are the necessary component.
8. **(A)** There is no geometry without lines. The lines might be straight or curved and might be shaped into forms. Numbers might be assigned and mathematics computed, but there must be lines in geometry.
9. **(D)** Disappointment is what occurs when expectations are not fulfilled. This is the necessary connection.
10. **(C)** An heirloom is an object handed down from an ancestor. Without an ancestor to hand down the object, the object might be an antique, but it is not an heirloom.

Summary: Verbal Logic Skills

- The HSPT exam tests several measures of verbal logic, one under the Logic test section and the other under the Verbal Classifications section.
- In the COOP, the verbal logic test is titled Test of Verbal Reasoning.
- On the HSPT Logic questions, you only have three answer choices. NEVER mistakenly choose (D).
- On the COOP, verbal logic questions sometimes take the form of artificial language questions. All of the words you deal with are nonsense words. Each word consists of a prefix and a stem and among the four words, there are only two prefixes and two stems. At this point you can choose the correct answer.

Chapter 10

How Reading Is Tested on the Exams

ROAD MAP

- *How to Improve Your Reading Skills*
- *Tips for Answering Reading Comprehension Questions*
- *Reading Exercises*
- *Answers and Explanations*

Both the COOP and the HSPT include sections on reading comprehension. They are called "Reading Comprehension" on both the COOP and the HSPT. The format for reading questions on both exams differs from the other question types you've learned about so far. The exams present reading passages followed by a series of questions based on the passages. The questions test not only how well you understand what you read, but also how well you can interpret the meaning of the passage and the author's intent. These questions also test how well you draw conclusions based on what you have read.

To do well on the reading comprehension sections of an exam, reading quickly is crucial. You won't be able to answer questions based on a passage if you have not had time to read it. Even if you are able to read the passage through once, you must have enough time left over to reread the selection for detail questions.

HOW TO IMPROVE YOUR READING SKILLS

One of the best techniques for increasing your reading speed and comprehension is also one of the techniques that will help you improve your vocabulary—and that is **reading.** The best way to increase your reading speed between now and the actual exam is to read as much as possible. Read everything in sight—newspapers, magazines, novels, billboards, and so on. Newspaper reading is an especially good way to improve your reading skills. Don't stop with just the opening paragraph of each article. Push yourself to read the whole story and give it your full attention as you read. If your mind wanders, you will not comprehend what you read.

To read with understanding, your eyes must occasionally stop on the page. Most people stop on each word because that is the way reading is taught in the early grades. But once you know how to read well, this method wastes a great deal of time. The key to increasing your reading speed is to take in more words each time your eyes stop. If a line had ten words in it and you were able to read the line by stopping only twice instead of ten times, you would be reading five times as fast as you do now. Try to train yourself.

TIP

The reading comprehension section of the HPST and COOP exams requires that you can read quickly **and** comprehend what you are reading. The best way to increase your reading speed is to read as much as possible between now and the time of the exam.

If you have a habit of softly speaking words as you read, *break that habit now!* This habit is called *subvocalizing*, and no matter how fast you can talk, you can read faster if you stop subvocalizing. Some people chew gum to stop subvocalizing. For others, just being aware of the habit is enough to help them correct it. Not only will it slow you down, but if you're reading aloud during your exam, the administrator will ask you to stop, so you don't disturb other test-takers.

In building your reading speed, try moving your index finger or pencil underneath the line you are reading. Because your eyes tend to move as quickly as your pencil, you will not stop on every word. You will not regress (look back), and you probably will not subvocalize. However, what you might do is concentrate on your pencil and not on the reading passage. This is why you must practice this technique before using it on your test. Start your finger or your pencil at the second or third word in the line and stop it before the last word in the line. Your peripheral vision (what you see at the edges) will pick up the first and last words in the lines, and you will save time by not having to focus on them.

Become more aware of words. Earlier in this part, you were advised to use a dictionary while you read, to help increase your vocabulary. That exercise can help you with reading comprehension questions, as well. Vocabulary and reading comprehension are very closely interrelated. You cannot have a large vocabulary without reading. You cannot understand what you read without an understanding of the words. When you look up words, study the roots, prefixes, and suffixes so that you can apply all that you know whenever you meet unfamiliar words.

TIPS FOR ANSWERING READING COMPREHENSION QUESTIONS

1. Begin by reading over the questions—not the answer choices, just the questions themselves. With an idea of what the questions will be asking, you will be able to focus your reading.
2. Skim the passage to get a general idea of the subject matter and of the point that is being made. Pay special attention to the first and last sentences in each paragraph. Those sentences often state the main idea of the passage.
3. Reread the passage, giving attention to details and the point of view. Be alert for the author's hints as to what he or she thinks is important. Phrases such as *Note that. . .*, *Of importance is. . .*, and *Do not overlook. . .* give clues to what the writer is stressing.
4. If the author has quoted material from another source, be sure that you understand the purpose of the quote. Does the author agree or disagree?
5. Carefully read each question or incomplete statement. Determine exactly what is being asked. Watch for negatives or all-inclusive words such as *always, never, all, only, every, absolutely, completely, none, entirely,* and *no.* These words can affect your choice of answer.

6. Read all four answer choices. Do not rush to choose the first answer that might be correct. Eliminate those choices that are obviously incorrect. Reread the remaining choices and refer to the passage, if necessary, to determine the *best* answer.
7. Don't confuse a *true* answer with the *correct* answer. You can do this best if you avoid inserting your own judgments into your answers. Even if you disagree with the author, or even if you spot a factual error in the passage, you must answer on the basis of what is stated or implied in the passage.
8. Don't spend too much time on any one question. If looking back at the passage does not help you to find or figure out the answer, choose from among the answers remaining after you eliminate the obviously wrong answers, and go on to the next question or passage.

NOTE
Many people find it helps them to focus their reading if they read the questions before reading the passage.

Now try these exercises. Correct answers follow the exercises.

READING EXERCISES

EXERCISE 1

Directions: The following questions are based on a number of reading passages. Each passage is followed by a series of questions. Read each passage carefully, then answer the questions based on it. You may reread the passage as often as you wish. When you have finished answering the questions based on one passage, go right on to the next passage.

Passage for questions 1–4

Like the United States today, Athens had courts where a wrong might be righted. Since any citizen might accuse another of a crime, the Athenian courts of law were very busy. In fact, unless a citizen was unusually peaceful or very unimportant, he would be sure to find himself in the courts at least once every few years.

At a trial, both the accuser and the person accused were allowed a certain time to speak. The length of time was marked by a water clock. Free men testified under oath as they do today, but the oath of a slave was counted as worthless.

To judge a trial, a jury was chosen from the members of the assembly who had reached 30 years of age. The Athenian juries were very large, often consisting of 201, 401, 501, 1,001 or more men, depending upon the importance of the case being tried. The juryman swore by the gods to listen carefully to both sides of the question and to give his honest opinion of the case. Each juryman gave his decision by depositing a white or black stone in a box. To keep citizens from being too careless in accusing each other, there was a rule that if the person accused did not receive a certain number of negative votes, the accuser was condemned instead.

1. The title that best expresses the main idea of this selection is
   (A) Athens and the United States.
   (B) Justice in Ancient Athens.
   (C) Testifying Under Oath.
   (D) The Duties of Juries.

2. People in Athens were frequently on trial in a law court because
   (A) they liked to serve on juries.
   (B) a juryman agreed to listen to both sides.
   (C) any person might accuse another of a crime.
   (D) the slaves were troublesome.

3. An Athenian was likely to avoid accusing another without a good reason because
   (A) the jury might condemn the accuser instead of the accused.
   (B) the jury might be very large.
   (C) cases were judged by men over 30 years old.
   (D) there was a limit on the time a trial could take.

4. Which statement is *true* according to the selection?
   (A) An accused person was denied the privilege of telling his side of the case.
   (B) The importance of the case determined the number of jurors.
   (C) A jury's decision was handed down in writing.
   (D) A citizen had to appear in court every few years.

Passage for questions 5–13

When a luxury liner or a cargo ship nudges into her slip after an ocean crossing, her first physical contact with land is a heaving line. These streamers with a weight at the end called a "monkey fist" arch gracefully from deck to pier. On board the ship the heaving lines are tied to heavy, golden yellow manila mooring lines. Longshoremen quickly pull in the heaving lines until they can fasten the mooring lines to iron bollards (posts). Soon the ship is strung to her pier by four, eight, or as many as twenty-one nine-inch or ten-inch manila lines with perhaps a few wire ropes to stay motion fore and aft. The ship is secure against even the wrath of the storm or hurricane. A ship could dock without the aid of tugboats—and might have in New York in maritime strikes—but not without the lines to moor her to her berth.

The maritime and the related fishing industry find perhaps 250 applications for rope and cordage. There are hundreds of different sizes, constructions, tensile strengths, and weights in rope and twine. Rope is sold by the pound but ordered by length and is measured by circumference rather than by diameter. The maritime variety is made chiefly from fiber of the abaca, or manila plant, which is imported from the Philippines and Central America. Henequen from Mexico and Cuba and sisal from Africa, the Netherlands East Indies, and other areas are also used, but chiefly for twine. Nylon is coming into increasing use, particularly by towing companies. But it is six times more expensive than manila. However, nylon is much stronger, lighter in weight, and longer-wearing than manila. It is also more elastic and particularly adaptable for ocean towing.

5. In docking a ship, rope is
   (A) only a little less important than a tugboat.
   (B) essential.
   (C) helpful but not necessary.
   (D) seldom used.

6. A monkey fist is a
   (A) device for weaving a rope.
   (B) slang term for a longshoreman.
   (C) rope streamer.
   (D) weight at the end of a rope.

7. Heaving lines are
   (A) tied around iron posts.
   (B) ocean currents.
   (C) used as a means of getting mooring lines to shore.
   (D) used to prevent motion in the bow.

8. A ship is held to her berth by
   (A) wire ropes only.
   (B) wire and fiber ropes.
   (C) heaving ropes.
   (D) hundreds of ropes.

9. Mooring ropes are
   (A) 10 inches in diameter.
   (B) 21 inches in circumference.
   (C) six times thicker than heaving ropes.
   (D) 9 inches in circumference.

10. There are
   (A) more than 200 uses for rope in fishing and shipping.
   (B) few differences in rope construction.
   (C) equal tensile strengths in all ropes.
   (D) no differences in the materials preferred for the making of ropes and twines.

11. Rope is
   (A) ordered by length.
   (B) ordered by the pound.
   (C) paid for by length.
   (D) paid for by tensile.

12. Which of the following are *not* correctly paired?
   (A) sisal from the Philippines
   (B) henequen from Cuba
   (C) abaca from Central America.
   (D) sisal from the Netherlands East Indies

13. As compared with manila rope; nylon rope is
   (A) stronger and cheaper.
   (B) more elastic and more expensive.
   (C) more elastic and heavier.
   (D) longer wearing and six times cheaper.

Passage for questions 14–20

A phase of my life which has lost something through refinement is the game of croquet. We used to have an old croquet set whose wooden balls, having been chewed by dogs, were no rounder than eggs. Paint had faded; wickets were askew. The course had been laid out haphazardly and eagerly by a child, and we all used to go out there on summer nights and play good-naturedly, with the dogs romping on the lawn in the beautiful light, and the mosquitoes sniping at us, and everyone in good spirits, racing after balls and making split shots for the sheer love of battle. Last spring we decided the croquet set was beyond use, and invested in a rather fancy new one with hoops set in small wooden sockets, and mallets with rubber faces. The course is now exactly seventy-two feet long and we lined the wickets up with a string, but the little boy is less fond of it now, for we make him keep still while we are shooting. A dog isn't even allowed to cast his shadow across the line of play. There are frequent quarrels of a minor nature, and it seems to me we return from the field of honor tense and out of sorts.

14. The word *refinement* in this context means
   (A) politeness.
   (B) distinction.
   (C) improvement.
   (D) his own dignity.

15. The author of the paragraph is
   (A) very angry.
   (B) deeply grieved.
   (C) indifferent.
   (D) mildly regretful.

16. The mood of the paragraph is
   (A) dogmatic.
   (B) very earnest.
   (C) wistful.
   (D) belligerent.

17. In comparing the earlier and later ways in which they played croquet, the author considers the new way
   (A) more exact and less attractive.
   (B) more beneficial for children.
   (C) more conducive to family life.
   (D) more fun for the dogs.

18. The "quarrels of a minor nature" occur because
   (A) the dog chases the croquet balls.
   (B) the balls do not roll well.
   (C) efficiency has become more important than sociability.
   (D) the little boy interrupts the game with his shouts.

19. The author
    - (A) is opposed to all progress.
    - (B) is very exact in everything he does.
    - (C) dislikes games.
    - (D) feels that undue attention to detail can lessen enjoyment.

20. The author thinks that
    - (A) children should be seen and not heard.
    - (B) dogs are pleasant companions.
    - (C) dogs are a nuisance.
    - (D) children should not be trusted to arrange croquet wickets.

Passage for questions 21–25

On entering the amphitheater, new objects of wonder presented themselves. On a level spot in the center was a company of odd-looking personages playing at nine-pins. They were dressed in a quaint, outlandish fashion, some wore short doublets, others jerkins, with long knives in their belts, and most of them had enormous breeches, of a type similar to that of the guide's. Their visages, too, were peculiar, one had a large beard, broad face, and small piggish eyes. The face of another seemed to consist entirely of nose and was surmounted by a white sugar-loaf hat set off with a little red cock's tail. They all had beards of various shapes and colors. There was one who seemed to be the commander. He was a stout old gentleman, with a weather-beaten countenance; he wore a lace doublet, broad belt and hangar, high crowned hat and feather, red stockings, and high-heeled shoes with roses in them. The whole group reminded Rip of the figures in an old Flemish painting, in the parlor of the village parson, which had been brought over from Holland at the time of the settlement.

What seemed particularly odd to Rip was that though these folks were evidently amusing themselves, yet they maintained the gravest faces, the most mysterious silence, and were the most melancholy party of pleasure he had ever witnessed. Nothing interrupted the stillness of the scene but the noise of the balls, which, whenever they were rolled, echoed along the mountains like rumbling peals of thunder.

—from *Rip Van Winkle*
by Washington Irving

21. Looking at this scene, the observer is apparently
    - (A) fascinated.
    - (B) frightened.
    - (C) repulsed.
    - (D) bored.

22. The word *Flemish* probably refers to
    - (A) something from the area near Holland.
    - (B) the village parson.
    - (C) a certain painter.
    - (D) an old-fashioned parlor.

23. The characters were probably playing
    - (A) a game like bowling.
    - (B) soccer.
    - (C) a type of baseball.
    - (D) golf.

24. The person observing all of this is
    - (A) Flemish.
    - (B) a parson.
    - (C) melancholy.
    - (D) named Rip.

25. The observer was surprised that
    - (A) the men's beards were of so many shapes and colors.
    - (B) the men appeared to be so serious while they were playing a game.
    - (C) the leader was so stout.
    - (D) the rolling balls sounded like thunder.

Passage for questions 26–31

Powdered zirconium is more fiery and violent than the magnesium powder that went into wartime incendiary bombs. Under some conditions, it can be ignited with a kitchen match, and it cannot be extinguished with water. Munitions makers once tried to incorporate it into explosives, but turned it down as too dangerous for even them to handle.

But when this strange metal is transformed into a solid bar or sheet or tube as lustrous as burnished silver, its temper changes. It is so docile that it can be used by surgeons as a safe covering plate for sensitive brain tissues. It is almost as strong as steel, and it can be exposed to hydrochloric acid or nitric acid without corroding.

Zirconium is also safe and stable when it is bound up with other elements to form mineral compounds, which occur in abundant deposits in North and South America, India, and Australia. Although it is classified as a rare metal, it is more abundant in the earth's crust than nickel, copper, tungsten, tin, or lead. Until a few years ago, scarcely a dozen men had ever seen zirconium in pure form, but today it is the wonder metal of a fantastic new industry, a vital component of television, radar, and radio sets, an exciting structural material for chemical equipment and for superrockets and jet engines, and a key metal for atomic piles.

26. The title that best expresses the main idea of this selection is
    (A) A Vital Substance.
    (B) A Safe, Stable Substance.
    (C) Zirconium's Uses in Surgery.
    (D) Characteristics of Zirconium.

27. The word *docile* in the second paragraph means
    (A) calm.
    (B) pliable.
    (C) strong.
    (D) profuse.

28. The selection emphasizes that
    (A) zirconium rusts easily.
    (B) chemists are finding uses for zirconium.
    (C) keys are often made of zirconium nowadays.
    (D) zirconium is less abundant in the earth's crust than lead.

29. Zirconium is *not* safe to handle when it is
    (A) lustrous.
    (B) powdered.
    (C) in tubes.
    (D) in bar form.

30. The selection tells us that zirconium
    (A) is a metal.
    (B) is fireproof.
    (C) dissolves in water.
    (D) is stronger than steel.

31. Zirconium is likely to be useful in all of these fields *except*
    (A) surgery.
    (B) television.
    (C) atomic research.
    (D) the manufacture of fireworks.

Passage for questions 32–36

In August of 1814, when news came that the British were advancing on Washington, three State Department clerks stuffed all records and valuable papers—including the Articles of Confederation, the Declaration of Independence, and the Constitution—into coarse linen sacks and smuggled them in carts to an unoccupied gristmill on the Virginia side of the Potomac. Later, fearing that a cannon factory nearby might attract a raiding party of the enemy, the clerks procured wagons from neighboring farmers, took the papers thirty-five miles away to Leesburg, and locked them in an empty house. It was not until the British fleet had left the waters of the Chesapeake that it was considered safe to return the papers to Washington.

On December 26, 1941, the five pages of the Constitution together with the single leaf of the Declaration of Independence were taken from the Library of Congress, where they had been kept for many years, and were stored in the vaults of the United States Bullion Depository at Fort Knox, Kentucky. Here they "rode out the war" safely.

Since 1952, visitors to Washington may view these historic documents at the Exhibition Hall of the National Archives. Sealed in bronze and glass cases filled with helium, the documents are protected from touch, light, heat, dust, and moisture. At a moment's notice, they can be lowered into a large safe that is bombproof, shockproof, and fireproof.

32. The title that best expresses the main idea of this selection is
    - (A) Three Courageous Clerks.
    - (B) The Constitution and Other Documents.
    - (C) How to Exhibit Valuables.
    - (D) Preserving America's Documents of Freedom.

33. Before the War of 1812, the Constitution and the Declaration of Independence were apparently kept in
    - (A) Independence Hall.
    - (B) Fort Knox, Kentucky.
    - (C) the office of the State Department.
    - (D) a gristmill in Virginia.

34. Nowadays, these documents are on view in the
    - (A) National Archives Exhibition Hall.
    - (B) Library of Congress.
    - (C) United States Bullion Depository.
    - (D) United States Treasury Building.

35. An important reason for the installation of apparatus for quick removal of the documents is the
    - (A) possibility of a sudden disaster.
    - (B) increasing number of tourists.
    - (C) need for more storage space.
    - (D) lack of respect for the documents.

36. The documents have been removed from Washington at least twice in order to preserve them from
    - (A) dust, heat, and moisture.
    - (B) careless handling.
    - (C) possible war damage.
    - (D) sale to foreign governments.

Passage for questions 37–41

Few animals are as descriptively named as the varying hare (*Lepus americanus*), also commonly known as the snowshoe hare, white rabbit, or snowshoe rabbit. The species derives its various names from its interesting adaptations to the seasonal changes affecting its habitat.

The color changes are affected by means of a molt, and are timed (although the hares have no voluntary control over them) to coincide with the changing appearances of the background. The periods of transition—from white to brown in the spring, and from brown to white in the fall—require more than two months from start to completion, during which time the hares are a mottled brown and white. In addition to the changes in color, in the fall the soles of the feet develop a very heavy growth of hair that functions as snowshoes.

In New York State, hares are most abundant in and around the Adirondack and Catskill Mountains. Thriving populations with less extensive ranges, are found in Allegany, Cattaraugus, Rensselaer, and Chenango counties. Smaller colonies of limited range are found in scattered islands.

37. The title that best expresses the main idea of this selection is
    - (A) Seasonal Changes in Birds.
    - (B) The Varying Hare.
    - (C) An American Animal.
    - (D) The Abundance of Hares.

38. Terms used to name these rabbits are related to their
    - (A) abundance in many parts of New York State.
    - (B) sensitivity to weather conditions throughout the state.
    - (C) ability to adapt to the change of seasons.
    - (D) thick white coats.

39. These rabbits have both brown and white markings in
    - (A) summer and winter.
    - (B) spring and fall.
    - (C) spring and summer.
    - (D) fall and winter.

40. The parts of New York State where rabbit populations are most plentiful are
    (A) Allegany, Cattaraugus, Rensselaer, and Chenango counties.
    (B) Adirondack and Catskill Mountain regions.
    (C) islands within the state.
    (D) snowy areas in the hills.

41. Which statement about these rabbits is *true* according to the selection?
    (A) They are becoming fewer in number.
    (B) They are capable of leaping great distances.
    (C) They are more plentiful in winter.
    (D) They have no control over their color changes.

Passage for questions 42–45

Between 1780 and 1790, in piecemeal fashion, a trail was established between Catskill on the Hudson and the frontier outpost, Ithaca, in the Finger Lakes country. This path, by grace of following the valleys, managed to thread its way through the mountains by what are on the whole surprisingly easy grades. Ultimately, this route became the Susquehanna Turnpike, but in popular speech it was just the Ithaca Road. It was, along with the Mohawk Turnpike and the Great Western Turnpike, one of the three great east-west highways of the state. Eventually it was the route taken by thousands of Yankee farmers, more especially Connecticut Yankees, seeking new fortunes in southwestern New York. Along it, the tide of pioneer immigration flowed at flood crest for a full generation.

As the road left Catskill, there was no stream that might not be either forded or crossed on a crude bridge until the traveler reached the Susquehanna, which was a considerable river and a real obstacle to his progress. The road came down out of the Catskills via the valley of the Ouleout Creek and struck the Susquehanna just above the present village of Unadilla. Hither about the year 1784 came a Connecticut man, Nathaniel Wattles. He provided both a skiff and a large flat-bottomed scow so that the homeseeker, his family, team, and household baggage, and oftentimes a little caravan of livestock, might be set across the river dry-shod and in safety. Wattles here established an inn where one might find lodging and entertainment, and a general store where might be purchased such staples as were essential for the journey. So it was that Wattles' Ferry became the best known landmark on the Ithaca Road.

42. The author indicates that the Susquehanna Turnpike
    (A) began as a narrow trail.
    (B) was the most important north-south highway in the state.
    (C) furnished travelers with surprising obstacles.
    (D) went out of use after a generation.

43. The western end of the Susquehanna Turnpike was located at
    (A) the Hudson River.
    (B) the Connecticut border.
    (C) Ithaca.
    (D) Catskill.

44. The Susquehanna Turnpike was also known as
    (A) the Ithaca Road.
    (B) Wattles' Ferry.
    (C) the Catskill Trail.
    (D) the Mohawk Turnpike.

45. According to this selection, Nathaniel Wattles was prepared to offer travelers all of the following *except*
    (A) guides.
    (B) a place to sleep.
    (C) entertainment.
    (D) groceries.

Passage for questions 46–50

About the year 1812, two steam ferryboats were built under the direction of Robert Fulton for crossing the Hudson River, and one of the same description was built for service on the East River. These boats were what are known as twin boats, each of them having two complete hulls united by a deck or bridge. Because these boats were pointed at both ends and moved equally well with either end foremost, they crossed and recrossed the river without losing any time in turning about. Fulton also contrived, with great ingenuity, floating docks for the reception of the ferryboats and a means by which they were brought to the docks without a shock. These boats were the first of a fleet that has since carried hundreds of millions of passengers to and from New York.

46. The title that best expresses the main idea of this selection is
    (A) Crossing the Hudson River by Boat.
    (B) Transportation of Passengers.
    (C) The Invention of Floating Docks.
    (D) The Beginning of Steam Ferryboat Service

47. The steam ferryboats were known as twin boats because
    (A) they had two complete hulls united by a bridge.
    (B) they could move as easily forward as backward.
    (C) each ferryboat had two captains.
    (D) two boats were put into service at the same time.

48. Which statement is *true* according to the selection?
    (A) Boats built under Fulton's direction are still in use.
    (B) Fulton planned a reception to celebrate the first ferryboat.
    (C) Fulton piloted the first steam ferryboats across the Hudson.
    (D) Fulton developed a satisfactory way of docking the ferryboats.

49. Robert Fulton worked in the
    (A) seventeenth century.
    (B) eighteenth century.
    (C) nineteenth century.
    (D) twentieth century.

50. In this paragraph, the word *shock* is used to mean
    (A) an unpleasant surprise.
    (B) an impact.
    (C) an illness following an accident.
    (D) an electrical impulse.

EXERCISE 2

Directions: Read each selection, then answer the questions that follow it. Indicate your answer by circling its letter.

Passage for questions 1–5

If you are asked the color of the sky on a fair day in summer, your answer will most probably be, "Blue." This answer is only partially correct. Blue sky near the horizon is not the same kind of blue as it is straight overhead. Look at the sky some fine day and you will find that the blue sky near the horizon is slightly greenish. As your eye moves upward toward the zenith, you will find that the blue changes into pure blue, and finally shades into a violet-blue overhead.

Have you heard the story of a farmer who objected to the color of the distant hills in the artist's picture? He said to the artist, "Why do you make those hills blue? They are green; I've been over there and I know!"

The artist asked him to do a little experiment. "Bend over and look at the hills between your legs." As the farmer did this, the artist asked, "Now what color are the hills?"

The farmer looked again, then he stood up and looked. "By gosh, they turned blue!" he said.

It is quite possible that you have looked at many colors which you did not really recognize. Sky is not just blue; it is many kinds of blue. Grass is not plain green; it might be one of several varieties of green. A red brick wall frequently is not pure red. It might vary from yellow-orange to violet-red in color, but to the unseeing eye it is just red brick.

1. The title that best expresses the ideas of this passage is
   (A) The Summer Sky.
   (B) Artists vs. Farmers.
   (C) Recognizing Colors.
   (D) Blue Hills.

2. At the zenith, the sky is usually
   (A) violet-blue.
   (B) violet-red.
   (C) greenish-blue.
   (D) yellow-orange.

3. The author suggests that
   (A) farmers are color-blind.
   (B) ability to see color varies.
   (C) brick walls should be painted pure red.
   (D) some artists use poor color combinations.

4. The farmer might be best described as being
   (A) opinionated.
   (B) stubborn.
   (C) uninterested.
   (D) open-minded.

5. The author would probably be pleased if
   (A) more days were sunny.
   (B) more people became farmers.
   (C) more people became artists.
   (D) people looked more carefully at the world around them.

Passage for questions 6–11

The Alaska Highway, which runs 1,523 miles from Dawson Creek, British Columbia, to Fairbanks, Alaska, was built by U.S. Army Engineers to counter a threatened Japanese invasion of Alaska. It was rushed through in an incredibly short period of nine months and was therefore never properly surveyed. Some of the territory it passes through has not even been explored. Although the story that the builders followed the trail of a wandering moose is probably not true, the effect is much the same. The leading bulldozer simply crashed through the brush wherever the going was easiest, avoiding the big trees, swampy hollows, and rocks. The project was made more complicated by the necessity of following not the shortest or easiest route, but one that would serve the string of United States-Canadian airfields that stretch from Montana to Alaska. Even on flat land, the road twists into hairpin curves. In rough terrain it goes up and down like a roller coaster. In the mountains, sometimes clinging to the sides of cliffs 400 feet high, it turns sharply, without warning, and gives rear seat passengers the stomach-gripping sensation of taking off into space. There is not a guardrail in its entire 1,500-mile length. Dust kicks up in giant plumes behind every car and on windless days hovers in the air like a thick fog.

Both the Canadian Army and the Alaskan Road Commission, which took over from the Army Engineers in 1946, do a commendable but nearly impossible job of maintaining the road. Where it was built on eternally frozen ground, it buckles and heaves; on the jellylike muskeg it is continually sinking, and must be graveled afresh every month. Bridges thrown across rivers are swept away in flash floods. Torrential thaws wash out miles of highway every spring. On mountainsides, you can tell the age of the road by counting the remains of earlier roads that have slipped down the slope.

6. The title that best expresses the main idea of this selection is
   (A) The Alaskan Road Commission.
   (B) Building and Maintaining the Alaska Highway.
   (C) Exploring Alaska.
   (D) Driving Conditions in the Far North.

7. The Alaska Highway was built to
   (A) make the route between Alaska and the United States shorter.
   (B) promote trade with Canada.
   (C) meet a wartime emergency.
   (D) aid exploration and surveying efforts.

8. The job of maintaining the road is complicated by the
   (A) threat of invasion.
   (B) forces of nature.
   (C) lack of surveying.
   (D) age of the road.

9. The route followed by the Alaska Highway
   (A) was determined by a moose.
   (B) follows the shortest route from Dawson Creek, British Columbia, to Fairbanks, Alaska.
   (C) connects a number of airfields.
   (D) connects a number of oil fields.

10. The road twists into many hairpin curves because
   (A) bulldozers are hard to steer.
   (B) the road goes around trees, swamps, and rocks.
   (C) the ground is eternally frozen.
   (D) flash floods wash it down the mountainside.

11. A trip on the Alaska Highway is dangerous because
   (A) some of the territory was never explored.
   (B) there are no guardrails.
   (C) snow cuts down on visibility.
   (D) wild animals abound in the area.

Passage for questions 12–18

The seasonal comings and goings of birds have excited the attention and wonder of all sorts of people in all ages and places. The oracles of Greece and the augurs of Rome wove them into ancient mythology. They are spoken of in the Books of Job and Jeremiah.

Nevertheless, it has been difficult for many to believe that small birds, especially, are capable of migratory journeys. Aristotle was convinced that the birds that wintered in Greece were not new arrivals, but merely Greece's summer birds in winter dress. According to a belief persisting in some parts of the world to this day, swallows and swifts do not migrate, but spend the winter in hibernation. (Swifts and swallows *do* migrate, just as most other northern hemisphere birds do.) Another old and charming, but untrue, legend enlists the aid of the stork in getting small birds to and from winter quarters: Small birds are said to hitch rides on the European stork's back.

It is clear why northern hemisphere birds fly south in the fall; they go to assure themselves of food and a more favorable climate for the winter months. It is also clear where most of the migrants come from and where they go. Years of bird-banding have disclosed the routes of the main migratory species.

But there are other aspects of migration that remain, for all our powers of scientific investigation, as puzzling and mysterious to modern man as to the ancients. Why do migrant birds come north each spring? Why don't they simply stay in the warm tropics the whole twelve months of the year? What determines the moment of departure for north or south? Above all, how do birds—especially species like the remarkable golden plover, which flies huge distances directly across trackless ocean wastes—find their way?

12. The best title for this selection would be
   (A) The Solution of an Ancient Problem.
   (B) Mysterious Migrations.
   (C) The Secret of the Plover.
   (D) Aristotle's Theory.

13. Bird banding has revealed
   (A) the kind of food birds eat.
   (B) why the birds prefer the tropics in the summer.
   (C) why birds leave at a certain time.
   (D) the route taken by different types of birds.

14. Swallows and swifts
   (A) remain in Greece all year.
   (B) change their plumage in winter.
   (C) hibernate during the winter.
   (D) fly south for the winter.

15. The article proves that
   (A) nature still has secrets that man has not fathomed.
   (B) the solutions of Aristotle are accepted by modern science.
   (C) we live in an age that has lost all interest in bird lore.
   (D) man has no means of solving the problem of bird migration.

16. Aristotle, the famous Greek philosopher,
   (A) explained the function of storks during migration.
   (B) deciphered the explanations of the oracles.
   (C) traveled south to watch the birds.
   (D) was wrong in his disbelief in migration.

17. Birds fly south in the winter
   (A) for breeding purposes.
   (B) to avoid bad weather.
   (C) for travel and adventure.
   (D) out of habit.

18. The mysteries about birds include
   (A) the routes they follow, the dates they leave, and the food they eat.
   (B) where they hibernate, how they find their way, and who put on their bands.
   (C) why they return north, how they find their way, and what triggers migration dates.
   (D) where storks winter, why birds fly over oceans, and why there are so many birds in Greece.

Passage for questions 19–23

The proud, noble American eagle appears on one side of the Great Seal of the United States, which is printed on every dollar bill. The same majestic bird can be seen on state seals, half dollars, and even in some commercial advertising. In fact, though we often encounter artistic representations of our national symbol, it is rarely seen alive in its native habitat. It is now all but extinct.

In the days of the founding fathers, the American eagle resided in nearly every corner of the territory now known as the continental United States. Today the eagle survives in what ornithologists call significant numbers only in two regions. An estimated 350 pairs inhabit Florida, and perhaps another 150 live in the Chesapeake Bay area of Delaware, Maryland, and Virginia. A few stragglers remain in other states, but in most, eagles have not been sighted for some time.

A federal law passed in 1940 protects these birds and their nesting areas, but it came too late to save more than a pitiful remnant of the species' original population.

19. An ornithologist is a person who studies
   (A) geographic regions.
   (B) the history of extinct species.
   (C) the populations of certain areas.
   (D) the habits and habitats of birds.

20. Today eagles are found in the greatest numbers in
   (A) Florida.
   (B) Delaware.
   (C) the Chesapeake Bay region.
   (D) Virginia.

21. The selection implies that
   (A) the number of eagles is likely to increase.
   (B) the eagle population decreased because of a lack of protective game laws.
   (C) there were only two localities where eagles could survive.
   (D) the government knows very little about eagles.

22. A 1940 federal law
   (A) established wildlife sanctuaries for eagles.
   (B) declared the American eagle to be our national bird.
   (C) banned the use of the eagle in commercial advertising.
   (D) protects American eagles and their nesting areas.

23. The American eagle is able to live
    (A) only east of the Mississippi.
    (B) only in bird sanctuaries.
    (C) almost anywhere in the United States.
    (D) only in warm climates.

Passage for questions 24–28

The Rhodora

In May, when sea-winds pierced our solitudes,
I found the fresh Rhodora in the woods,
Spreading its leafless blooms in a damp nook,
To please the desert and the sluggish brook.
The purple petals, fallen in the pool,
Made the black water with their beauty gay;
Here might the red-bird come his plumes to cool,
And court the flower that cheapens his array.
Rhodora! if the sages ask thee why
This charm is wasted on the earth and sky,
Tell them, dear, that if eyes were made for seeing,
Then Beauty is its own excuse for being:
Why thou wert there, O rival of the rose!
I never thought to ask, I never knew:
But, in my simple ignorance suppose
The self-same Power that brought me there brought you.

Ralph Waldo Emerson

24. The poet is impressed with the beauty of
    (A) the sea.
    (B) the woods.
    (C) a bird.
    (D) a flower.

25. When the poet says that the flower cheapens the array of the red-bird, he means that
    (A) the bird gets nothing from the flower.
    (B) the flower gets nothing from the bird.
    (C) the color of the flower is brighter than that of the bird.
    (D) the bird ruins the flower.

26. In saying "This charm is wasted on the earth and sky," the poet means that
    (A) the earth and sky do not appreciate beauty.
    (B) no one sees a flower that blooms deep in the woods.
    (C) wise men sometimes ask foolish questions.
    (D) the bird does not even notice the beauty of the flower.

27. The poet believes that
    (A) flower petals pollute the water.
    (B) red birds are garish.
    (C) beauty exists for its own sake.
    (D) sea-wind is refreshing.

28. The poet probably
    (A) is an insensitive person.
    (B) dislikes solitude.
    (C) is a religious person.
    (D) is ignorant.

ANSWERS AND EXPLANATIONS

EXERCISE 1

1. **(B)** The entire selection is about court practices in ancient Athens.
2. **(C)** The answer is in the second sentence.
3. **(A)** See the last sentence.
4. **(B)** You will find the correct answer in the third paragraph.
5. **(B)** The last sentence of the first paragraph states unequivocally that a ship cannot dock without rope.
6. **(D)** See the second sentence.
7. **(C)** The heaving lines are tied to mooring lines. The mooring lines are the heavy ropes that secure the boat to the pier.
8. **(B)** The ship is held to her pier by up to 21 manila-fiber mooring lines and a few wire lines.
9. **(D)** You need to incorporate information from both paragraphs to answer this question. The second paragraph tells us that rope is measured by circumference. The first paragraph tells us that mooring lines are nine- or ten-inch manila lines.
10. **(A)** The first sentence of the second paragraph answers this question. All the other choices are contradicted by the selection.
11. **(A)** "Rope is sold by the pound but ordered by length."
12. **(A)** Sisal comes from Africa and the Netherlands East Indies, not from the Philippines. Abaca, also known as the manila plant, comes from the Philippines, as well as from Central America.
13. **(B)** Reread the last three sentences for the answer.
14. **(C)** Find this answer by substituting the choices for the word *refinement*. Then continue reading the passage following the substituted word, and the correct contextual meaning should be clear.
15. **(D)** The author is not terribly upset but does seem to regret the changes that have been made.
16. **(C)** This answer ties in with the answer to question 15.
17. **(A)** The author's description of the new set and new croquet course as compared to the old makes clear that the new arrangement is far more exact. On the other hand, all concerned seem to have less fun.
18. **(C)** You should be able to infer this answer from the selection.
19. **(D)** This answer is also to be inferred from the selection.
20. **(B)** The author appears to be a genial sort who enjoys children, animals, sunsets, and sport for sport's sake. All of the other choices imply negativism on the part of the author.
21. **(A)** If necessary, reread the selection. Clearly, the observer is fascinated by the scene before him. He gives no indication of being frightened or repulsed and is far too interested to be bored.
22. **(A)** The Flemish painting was brought over from Holland.

23. **(A)** At the beginning of the selection, the game is being played on a level spot with nine pins. At the end of the passage, balls are rolled, presumably at the pins. This is a variety of bowling.
24. **(D)** The second paragraph begins "What seemed particularly odd to Rip. . . ." Rip must be the observer. All of the other choices *could* be true, but we have no confirming evidence in the selection, whereas the selection does tell us that the man's name is Rip.
25. **(B)** In the first sentence of the last paragraph, Rip found it "particularly odd" that the men maintained such grave faces while evidently amusing themselves.
26. **(D)** The selection describes the properties of zirconium in its various forms.
27. **(A)** Consider the use of the word *docile* as applied to solid zirconium, in contrast to the use of the world *violent* as applied to powdered zirconium.
28. **(B)** An emphasis of the selection is that increasing uses are being found for zirconium.
29. **(B)** The first paragraph makes this point.
30. **(A)** In both the second and third paragraphs, zirconium is described as a metal.
31. **(D)** If zirconium is too dangerous to be used in ammunition, it is most certainly too dangerous to be used in fireworks.
32. **(D)** The selection traces the history of protection of our documents of freedom during times of war.
33. **(C)** If State Department clerks in Washington scooped up the documents and stuffed them into linen sacks, the documents must have been lying around the office.
34. **(A)** See the last paragraph.
35. **(A)** Bombs, shock, and fire are sudden disasters.
36. **(C)** The British advanced on and burned Washington in 1814 during the War of 1812; December 26, 1941, occurred during the opening days of World War II. The Japanese attacked Pearl Harbor on December 7, 1941.
37. **(B)** The selection describes the varying hare.
38. **(C)** As the names imply, the rabbits vary with the seasons.
39. **(B)** The rabbits are mottled brown and white while in the middle of the molting process in spring and fall.
40. **(B)** So stated in the first sentence of the last paragraph.
41. **(D)** The second paragraph states that the hares have no voluntary control over the changes in their appearance.
42. **(A)** The first paragraph describes the original trail as a path. The road is also described as an east-west route. It presented travelers with surprisingly few obstacles.
43. **(C)** The frontier outpost, Ithaca, was at the western end of the highway.
44. **(A)** Reread the first paragraph.
45. **(A)** Guides are not mentioned.
46. **(D)** The selection describes the construction and use of ferryboats.
47. **(A)** See the second sentence.
48. **(D)** The next-to-last sentence describes Fulton's ingenious docking method.

49. **(C)** 1812 was in the nineteenth century.
50. **(B)** In the context of the paragraph, *shock* must refer to the *impact* of the boat running into the dock.

EXERCISE 2

1. **(C)** The subject of the passage is variations in the composition and appearance of color. The story of the farmer and the artist is included only by way of illustration; it is not the subject of the selection.
2. **(A)** The zenith is straight overhead. The last sentence of the first paragraph answers this question.
3. **(B)** The author makes this point in the last paragraph.
4. **(D)** The farmer was willing to do the artist's bidding and look at the hills through his legs. A highly opinionated or stubborn person would not have submitted to the experiment. An uninterested person would not have noticed the difference between the artist's colors and his own observations.
5. **(D)** The author finds variations of color fascinating; he certainly would be pleased if others could have their lives enriched by appreciating this variety.
6. **(B)** The article is all about the building and maintaining of the Alaska Highway.
7. **(C)** The Alaska Highway does provide an overland route from Alaska to the 48 contiguous states, and it might promote some trade with Canada, but the reason for its original construction is stated in the first sentence.
8. **(B)** The last paragraph describes in detail the interference of nature with maintenance of the road. The poor layout of the road itself might be blamed on the threat of invasion and the lack of proper surveying. While a poorly built road is more difficult to maintain, the chief culprit in the maintenance situation is nature.
9. **(C)** The answer to this question is buried in the middle of the second paragraph. If you missed it, reread.
10. **(B)** This question is answered near the beginning of the second paragraph.
11. **(B)** The second paragraph is full of details. The answer to this question is near the end of the paragraph.
12. **(B)** The selection is about the migration of birds and raises a number of questions about migration which are not yet understood.
13. **(D)** See the last sentence of the third paragraph.
14. **(D)** A parenthetical remark in the second paragraph specifically makes this statement.
15. **(A)** The last paragraph poses a number of questions about migration which still puzzle scientists. Although we might not understand much about bird migration, it does not pose any problem that must be solved, so (D) is not the correct answer.
16. **(D)** Aristotle was a very clever man, but he erred in thinking that all birds change their plumage and remain in the same region despite the change of seasons.

17. **(B)** Birds fly south so that they might enjoy warmer weather and avoid problems of finding food in snow-covered or frozen areas.
18. **(C)** The last paragraph details the major puzzles regarding bird migration.
19. **(D)** An ornithologist studies birds.
20. **(A)** Approximately 350 pairs live in Florida, 150 pairs in the Chesapeake region, and only a few elsewhere.
21. **(B)** In stating that the 1940 protective law came too late to save the eagles, the last sentence implies that the eagle population decreased because of the lack of such a law. (You might be aware that the eagle population has indeed rebounded, but you must answer this question, and all questions, on the basis of what is stated or implied by the passage.)
22. **(D)** The 1940 law protects American eagles and their nesting areas everywhere in the United States, not just in bird sanctuaries.
23. **(C)** If in the 1700s the American eagle resided in nearly every corner of the territory that became the 48 states, its habitat is not limited to any particular climatic or geographic region.
24. **(D)** The poem really is an ode to the flower.
25. **(C)** The poet is saying that while the bird is splendid, the flower is even more beautiful.
26. **(B)** The flower blooms deep in the woods where, except for the occasional wanderer like himself, no one sees it.
27. **(C)** "Then beauty is its own excuse for being."
28. **(C)** In saying "The self-same Power that brought me there brought you," the poet is expressing his faith in a Supreme Being that created man and nature.

Summary: Reading Comprehension Review

- This section is called Reading Comprehension on both the COOP and the HSPT. Each test presents reading passages followed by a series of questions.
- To do well on this section, you will need to be able to read quickly. If you do not read quickly, study the section How to Improve Your Reading Skills, in this chapter.
- Study and remember all of the steps for answering reading comprehension questions: read over the question, skim the passage for the main idea, reread the passage with attention to details and point of view, carefully read each question or incomplete statement, read all four answer choices, and don't spend too much time on any one question.

Chapter 11

Spelling

The HSPT exam is the only entrance exam to include several test questions that check spelling skills. In these questions, you are presented with a series of four answer choices. Three of the choices contain sentences; choice (D) is "No Mistake." You are asked to read the sentences and check for errors in capitalization, punctuation, usage or spelling. If you believe that none of the sentences contains an error, you choose (D).

Spelling is a weakness for many students. The ability to spell well does not seem to be directly related to any measurable factor. A few fortunate individuals are just natural spellers—they can hear a word and instinctively spell it correctly. Most people, however, must memorize rules, memorize spellings, and rely on a dictionary.

To help you excel on the spelling questions found in the HSPT exam, this section includes tips for improving your spelling and a list of spelling rules.

TIPS FOR IMPROVING YOUR SPELLING SKILLS

You can improve your spelling by keeping a list of words that you spell incorrectly or that you must often look up. Add to your list whenever you find a word you cannot spell. When you have a few minutes to study spelling, write each word correctly ten times. If you know how to type, type each word ten times, too. Let your hand get used to the feel of the correct spelling, and let your eye become accustomed to seeing the word spelled correctly. Periodically, ask someone to read your list aloud to you, and try writing them correctly. Frequent self-testing of problem spelling words should help you learn the correct spellings. On the day before the test, read over your list carefully.

Another way to improve your spelling is by developing *mnemonic devices*. A mnemonic device is a private clue that you develop to help you remember something. For example, if you have trouble spelling the word *friend*, you might find it helpful to remember the sentence, "A *friend* is true to the *end*." This little sentence will help you remember to place the "i" before the "e." If you have trouble distinguishing between *here* and *hear* try a sentence like "To listen is to hear with an ear." If you confuse the spellings *principle* and *principal*, remember (whether you believe it or not) "The princiPAL is your

ROAD MAP

- *Tips for Improving Your Spelling Skills*
- *Spelling Rules*
- *Spelling Exercise*
- *Answers and Explanaions*

NOTE
If spelling is difficult for you, don't be discouraged. Many intelligent people have problems spelling, but you can improve your spelling skills by frequently testing yourself on words that you spell incorrectly.

PAL." When you have trouble spelling a word, try to invent your own mnemonic device, and you will have a built in "prompter" when you encounter spelling questions on the exam. Much of spelling must simply be learned. However, there are some rules that apply to the spelling of root words and more rules that apply to the adding of suffixes. The following list presents some of the most useful spelling rules and some of the most common exceptions to those rules. Try to learn them all! The explanations that accompany the spelling exercises, as well as the exam questions that test spelling, refer to these rules by number when they apply.

SPELLING RULES

- **RULE 1:** *i* before *e*
  Except after *c*
  Or when sounded like *ay*
  As in *neighbor* or *weigh*.
  Exceptions: Neither, leisure, foreigner, seized, weird, heights.
- **RULE 2:** If a word ends in *y* preceded by a vowel, keep the *y* when adding a suffix.
  Examples: day, days; attorney, attorneys
- **RULE 3:** If a word ends in *y* preceded by a consonant, change the *y* to *i* before adding a suffix.
  Examples: try, tries, tried; lady, ladies
  Exceptions: To avoid double *i*, retain the *y* before *-ing* and *-ish*.
  Examples: fly, flying; baby, babyish
- **RULE 4:** Silent *e* at the end of a word is usually dropped before a suffix beginning with a vowel.
  Examples: dine + ing = dining
  locate + ion = location
  use + able = usable
  offense + ive = offensive
  Exceptions: Words ending in *ce* and *ge* retain *e* before *-able* and *-ous* in order to retain the soft sounds of *c* and *g*.
  Examples: peace + able = peaceable
  courage + ous = courageous
- **RULE 5:** Silent *e* is usually kept before a suffix beginning with a consonant.
  Examples: care + less = careless
  late + ly = lately
  one + ness = oneness
  game + ster = gamester
- **RULE 6:** Some exceptions must simply be memorized. Some exceptions to the last two rules are: *truly, duly, awful, argument, wholly, ninth, mileage, dyeing, acreage, canoeing*.

- **RULE 7:** A word of one syllable that ends in a single consonant preceded by a single vowel doubles the final consonant before a suffix beginning with a vowel or before the suffix *-y*.
  Examples: hit, hitting; drop, dropped; big, biggest; mud, muddy; **but:** *help, helping* because *help* ends in two consonants; *need, needing, needy* because the final consonant is preceded by two vowels.
- **RULE 8:** A word of more than one syllable that accents the last syllable and that ends in a single consonant preceded by a single vowel doubles the final consonant when adding a suffix beginning with a vowel.
  Example: begin, beginner; admit, admitted; **but:** *enter, entered* because the accent is not on the last syllable.
- **RULE 9:** A word ending in *er* or *ur* doubles the *r* in the past tense if the word is accented on the last syllable.
  Examples: occur, occurred; prefer, preferred; transfer, transferred
- **RULE 10:** A word ending in *er* does not double the *r* in the past tense if the accent falls before the last syllable.
  Examples: answer, answered; offer, offered; differ, differed
- **RULE 11:** When *-full* is added to the end of a noun, the final *l* is dropped.
  Examples: cheerful, cupful, hopeful
- **RULE 12:** All words beginning with *over* are one word.
  Examples: overcast, overcharge, overhear
- **RULE 13:** All words with the prefix *self* are hyphenated.
  Examples: self-control, self-defense, self-evident
- **RULE 14:** The letter *q* is always followed by *u*.
  Examples: quiz, bouquet, acquire
- **RULE 15:** Numbers from twenty-one to ninety-nine are hyphenated.
- **RULE 16:** *Per cent* is *never* hyphenated. It may be written as one word (*percent*) or as two words (*per cent*).
- **RULE 17:** *Welcome* is one word with one *l*.
- **RULE 18:** *All right* is always two words. There is no such word as *alright*.
- **RULE 19:** *Already* means *prior to some specified time. All ready* means *completely ready.*
  Example: By the time I was *all ready* to go to the play, the tickets were *already* sold out.
- **RULE 20:** *Altogether* means *entirely. All together* means *in sum* or *collectively.*
  Example: There are *altogether* too many people to seat in this room when we are *all together*.

- **RULE 21:** *Their* is the possessive of *they*.
  They're is the contraction for *they are*
  There means *at that place*.
  Example: *They're* going to put *their* books over *there*.
- **RULE 22:** *Your* is the possessive of *you*.
  You're is the contraction for *you are*.
  Example: *You're* certainly planning to leave *your* muddy boots outside.
- **RULE 23:** *Whose* is the possessive of *who*.
  Who's is the contraction for *who is*.
  Example: Do you know *who's* ringing the doorbell or *whose* car is in the street?
- **RULE 24:** *Its* is the possessive of *it*.
  It's is the contraction for *it is*.
  Example: *It's* I who lost the letter and *its* envelope.

SPELLING EXERCISE

Directions: Look for errors in spelling. Choose the letter of the sentence that contains the error. No question contains more than one sentence with a spelling error. If you find no error, choose (D) as your answer.

1. (A) In the teacher's absence, the pupils had an eraser fight.
   (B) The laws of apartheid prohibited marriage between blacks and whites.
   (C) We may be haveing a fire drill this afternoon.
   (D) No mistakes.

2. (A) The Indian squaw carried her papoose strapped to a board on her back.
   (B) Christopher Columbus is credited with discovary of America.
   (C) Innocent victims should not have to stand trial.
   (D) No mistakes.

3. (A) The sailor shouted, "All ashore that are going ashore."
   (B) The turtle crawled accross the street.
   (C) For lunch I ate a turkey sandwich.
   (D) No mistakes.

4. (A) Meet me at the bus depot promptly at four.
   (B) On Saturday, we will have dinner at a restaurant.
   (C) The whipping post was in use as punishment in Delaware until recent times.
   (D) No mistakes.

5. (A) The shepherd would be lonely without his dog.
   (B) The experiment served to confirm the hypothesis.
   (C) The divinity fudge was truly deliscious.
   (D) No mistakes.

6. (A) The golfer took a break after the nineth hole.
   (B) Let me acquaint you with the new rules.
   (C) The slugger wields a heavy bat.
   (D) No mistakes.

7. (A) Biology is always a laboratory science.
   (B) The short story is really a memoir.
   (C) My neice will enter college in the fall.
   (D) No mistakes.

8. (A) The currency of Mexico is the peso.
   (B) The detective traveled incognito.
   (C) Is there anything one can buy for a nickel?
   (D) No mistakes.

9. (A) Our senator is a staunch supporter of the President.
   (B) I hear a rumer that our principal is about to retire.
   (C) A surgeon must have steady hands.
   (D) No mistakes.

10. (A) To grow crops in the desert, we must irrigate daily.
    (B) Most convenience stores have very long hours.
    (C) There was a lovly centerpiece on the table.
    (D) No mistakes.

ANSWERS AND EXPLANATIONS

1. **(C)** having (rule 4)
2. **(B)** discovery (The base word is *discover.* There is no reason to change the *e* to *a.*)
3. **(B)** across (No special rule applies. Learn to spell *across.*)
4. **(D)** No mistakes.
5. **(C)** delicious (There is no s in the middle of this word.)
6. **(A)** ninth (rule 6)
7. **(C)** niece (rule 1)
8. **(D)** No mistakes.
9. **(B)** rumor (No rule; just learn the spelling.)
10. **(C)** lovely (rule 5)

Summary: Understand Spelling Questions

- The HSPT exam has several questions specifically testing spelling.
- You are given three choices containing sentences and choice (D) which is "no mistake." You must find the spelling error and choose that sentence, or choose (D) if you can find no mistake.
- Keep a list of words that you spell incorrectly or that you have to look up. Periodically write the words and have someone test you on them.
- Read the section on Spelling Rules, and write some examples for yourself.

Chapter 12

Punctuation and Capitalization

ROAD MAP

- *Punctuation Rules*
- *Capitalization Rules*
- *Punctuation and Capitalization Exercise*
- *Answers and Explanations*

Along with spelling, the HSPT exam also tests your knowledge of punctuation and capitalization. You'll find these questions under the test section titled "Language Skills." To help you review, check out the following list of punctuation and capitalization rules. Because rules can be boring and very difficult to study, we've broken the rules into categories, to help you study them in "chunks." Most will be familiar to you, but if you find anything surprising, or if you have trouble understanding any of the rules, be sure to talk to your teacher.

PUNCTUATION RULES

THE PERIOD

1. Use a period at the end of a sentence that makes a statement, gives a command or makes a "polite request" in the form of a question that does not require an answer.

   Examples: I am brushing up on my verbal skills.
   Study the chapter on verbs for tomorrow.
   Would you please read this list of words so that I may practice my spelling lesson.

2. Use a period after an abbreviation and after an initial in a person's name.

   Examples: Gen. Robert E. Lee led the Confederate forces.
   Minneapolis and St. Paul are known as the "twin cities."

   Exception: Do not use a period after postal service state name abbreviations.

   Example: St. Louis, MO

3. Use a period as a decimal point in numbers.

   Examples: A sales tax of 5.5% amounts to $7.47 on a $135.80 purchase.

THE QUESTION MARK

1. Use a question mark at the end of a direct and genuine question.

   Example: Why do you want to borrow that book?

2. Do not use a question mark after an indirect question; use a period.
   Example: He asked if they wanted to accompany him.
3. A direct and genuine question must end with a question mark even if the question is only part of the sentence.
   Example: "Daddy, are we there yet?" the child asked.
4. Use a question mark (within parentheses) to indicate uncertainty as to the correctness of a piece of information.
   Example: John Carver, (first governor of Plymouth colony) was born in 1575 and died in 1621.

THE EXCLAMATION MARK

1. The only reason to use an exclamation mark is to express strong feeling, emotion, or extreme importance.
   Examples: Congratulations! You broke the record.
   Rush! Perishable contents.

THE COMMA

TIP
Commas are often used to separate introductory phrases, clauses, names, or appositives from the rest of the sentence.

1. The salutation of a personal letter is followed by a comma.
   Example: Dear Mary,
2. The complimentary close of a letter is ordinarily followed by a comma, though this use is optional.
   Example: Cordially yours,
3. An appositive must be set off by commas.
   Example: Jim Rodgers, my next-door neighbor, is an excellent baby-sitter.
4. A noun of address is set apart by commas.
   Example: When you finish your homework, Jeff, please take out the garbage.
5. Use commas to set off parenthetical words.
   Example: I think, however, that a move might not be wise at this time.
6. When two or more adjectives all modify a noun equally, all but the last must be followed by commas. If you can add the word *and* between the adjectives without changing the sense of the sentence, then use commas.
   Example: The jolly, fat, ruddy man stood at the top of the stairs.
7. An introductory phrase of five or more words must be separated by a comma.
   Example: Because the prisoner had a history of attempted jailbreaks, he was put under heavy guard.
8. After a short introductory phrase, the comma is optional. The comma should be used where needed for clarity.
   Examples: As a child she was a tomboy. (comma unnecessary)
   To Dan, Phil was friend as well as brother. (comma clarifies)
   In 1978, 300 people lost their lives in one air disaster. (comma clarifies)
9. A comma is not generally used before a subordinate clause that ends a sentence, though in long, unwieldy sentences like this one, use of such a comma is optional.

10. A comma precedes the coordinating conjunction unless the two clauses are very short.
    Examples: Kevin wanted to borrow a book from the library, but the librarian would not allow him to take it until he had paid his fines.
    Roy washed the dishes and Helen dried.
11. Words, phrases, or clauses in a series are separated by commas. The use of a comma before *and* is optional. If the series ends in *etc.,* use a comma before *etc.* Do not use a comma after *etc.* in a series, even if the sentence continues.
    Examples: Coats, umbrellas and boots should be placed in the closet at the end of the hall.
    Pencils, scissors, paper clips, etc. belong in your top desk drawer.
12. A comma separates a short direct quotation from the speaker.
    Examples: She said, "I must be home by six."
    "Tomorrow I begin my new job," he told us.
13. Use a comma to indicate that you have omitted a word or words, such as *of* or *of the*
    Example: President, XYZ Corporation
14. Use a comma to separate a name from a title or personal-name suffix.
    Examples: Paul Feiner, Chairman
    Carl Andrew Pforzheimer, Jr.
15. Use a comma when first and last names are reversed.
    Example: Bernbach, Linda
16. Use a comma to separate parts of dates or addresses.
    Example: Please come to a party on Sunday, May 9, at "The Old Mill" on Drake Road, Cheswold, Delaware.
    Exception: Do not use a comma between the postal service state abbreviation and the zip code.
    Example: Scarsdale, NY 10583
17. A comma ordinarily separates thousands, millions, and trillions.
    Example: 75,281,646
18. A nonrestrictive adjective phrase or clause must be set off by commas. A nonrestrictive phrase or clause is one that can be omitted without essentially changing the meaning of the sentence.
    Example: Our new sailboat, which has bright orange sails, is very seaworthy.
    A restrictive phrase or clause is vital to the meaning of a sentence and cannot be omitted. Do not set if off with commas.
    Example: A sailboat without sails is useless.
19. A comma must be used if the sentence might be subject to different interpretation without it.
    Example: He saw the woman who had rejected him, and blushed.
20. If a pause would make the sentence clearer and easier to read, insert a comma.
    Examples: Inside the people were dancing. (confusing)
    Inside, the people were dancing. (clearer)
    After all crime must be punished. (confusing)
    After all, crime must be punished. (clearer)
    The pause rule is not infallible, but it is your best resort when all other rules governing use of the comma fail you.

THE HYPHEN

1. Use a hyphen to divide a word at the end of a line.
2. Hyphenate numbers from twenty-one through ninety-nine, except for multiples of ten; twenty, thirty, forty, etc.
3. Use a hyphen to join two words serving together as a single adjective before a noun.

   Examples: We left the highway and proceeded on a well-paved road.

   That baby-faced man is considerably older than he appears to be.
4. Use a hyphen with the prefixes *ex-*, *self-*, *all-*, and the suffix *elect.*

   Examples: ex-Senator, self-appointed, all-State, Governor-elect.
5. Use a hyphen to avoid ambiguity.

   Example: After the custodian recovered the use of his right arm, he re-covered the office chairs.
6. Use a hyphen to avoid an awkward union of letters.

   Examples: semi-independent; shell-like.
7. Refer to a dictionary whenever you are uncertain as to whether you should write two words, a hyphenated word, or one word.

THE DASH

1. You may use a dash—or parentheses () for emphasis or to set off an explanatory group of words.

   Example: The tools of his trade—probe, mirror, cotton swabs—were neatly arranged on the dentist's tray.

   Unless the set-off expression ends a sentence, dashes must be used in pairs.
2. Use a dash to mark a sudden break in thought that leaves a sentence unfinished.

   Example: He opened the door a crack and saw—

THE COLON

1. Use a colon after the salutation in a business letter.

   Example: Dear Board Member:
2. Use a colon to separate hours from minutes.

   Example: The eclipse occurred at 10:36 A.M.
3. A colon may, but need not always, be used to introduce a list, introduce a long quotation, or introduce a question.

   Example: My question is this: Are you willing to punch a time clock?

THE SEMICOLON

1. A semicolon may be used to join two short, related independent clauses.

   Example: Anne is working at the front desk on Monday; Ernie will take over on Tuesday.

Two main clauses must be separated by a conjunction or by a semicolon or must be written as two sentences. A semicolon never precedes a coordinating conjunction. The same two clauses may be written as follows:

Autumn had come and the trees were almost bare.
Autumn had come; the trees were almost bare.
Autumn had come. The trees were almost bare.

2. A semicolon may be used to separate two independent clauses that are joined by an adverb such as *however, therefore, otherwise,* or *nevertheless.* The adverb must be followed by a comma.

   Example: You may use a semicolon to separate this clause from the next; however, you will not be incorrect if you choose to write two separate sentences.

   If you are uncertain how to use the semicolon to connect independent clauses, write two sentences instead.

3. A semicolon should be used to separate a series of phrases or clauses when each of them contains commas.

   Example: The old gentleman's heirs were Margaret Whitlock, his half-sister; James Bagley, the butler; William Frame, companion to his late cousin, Robert Bone; and his favorite charity, the Salvation Army.

THE APOSTROPHE

1. In a contraction, insert an apostrophe in place of the omitted letter or letters.

   Example: have + not = haven't
   we + are = we're
   let + us = let's
   of the clock = o'clock
   class of 1985 = class of '85

   Note: Never begin a paragraph with a contraction.

2. The apostrophe, when used to indicate possession, means *belonging to everything to the left of the apostrophe.*

   Example: lady's = belonging to the lady
   ladies' = belonging to the ladies
   children's = belonging to the children

   To test for correct placement of the apostrophe, read *of the.*

   Example: childrens' = of the childrens (therefore incorrect)girls' = of the girls (correct if it is the meaning intended)

QUOTATION MARKS

1. All directly quoted material must be enclosed by quotation marks. Words not quoted must remain outside the quotation marks.

   Example: "If it is hot on Sunday," she said, "we will go to the beach."

2. An indirect quote must not be enclosed by quotation marks.

   Example: She said that we might go to the beach on Sunday.

3. When a multiple-paragraph passage is quoted, each paragraph of the quotation must begin with quotation marks, but ending quotation marks are used only at the end of the last quoted paragraph.
4. A period always goes inside the quotation marks, whether the quotation marks are used to denote quoted material, to set off titles—such as chapters in a book or titles of short stories—or to isolate words used in a special sense.

   Examples: Jane explained: "The house is just around the corner."
   The first chapter of *The Andromeda Strain* is entitled "The Country of Lost Borders."
   Pornography is sold under the euphemism "adult books."
5. A comma always goes inside the quotation marks.

   Examples: "We really must go home," said the dinner guests.
   If your skills have become "rusty," you must study before you take the test.
   Three stories in Kurt Vonnegut's *Welcome to the Monkey House* are "Harrison Bergeron," "Next Door," and "EPICAC."
6. A question mark goes inside the quotation marks if it is part of the quotation. If the whole sentence containing the quotation is a question, the question mark goes outside the quotation marks.

   Examples: He asked, "Was the airplane on time?"
   What did you really mean when you said "I do"?
7. An exclamation mark goes inside the quotation marks if the quoted words are an exclamation, outside if the entire sentence including the quotation is an exclamation.

   Examples: The sentry shouted, "Drop your gun!"
   Save us from our "friends"!
8. A colon and a semicolon always go outside the quotation marks.

   Example: He said, "War is destructive"; she added, "Peace is constructive."
9. Words used in an unusual way may be placed inside quotation marks.

   Example: A surfer who "hangs ten" is performing a tricky maneuver on a surfboard, not staging a mass execution.
10. A quotation within a quotation may be set apart by single quotes.

    Example: George said, "The philosophy 'I think, therefore I am' may be attributed to Descartes."

CAPITALIZATION RULES

- **RULE 1:** Capitalize the first word of a complete sentence.

  Example: Your desk top should appear neat and orderly.
- **RULE 2:** Capitalize the first word of a quoted sentence.

  Example: The teacher said, "Please write your name at the top of the paper."

Do *not* capitalize the first word within quotation marks if it does not begin a complete sentence.

Examples: "I was late," she explained, "because of the snow."

Some groups would like to restrict certain liberties in the interest of "patriotism."

- **RULE 3:** Capitalize the letter *I* when it stands alone.
- **RULE 4:** Capitalize the first letter of the first, last, and each important word in the title of a book, play, article, etc.

  Examples: "The Mystery of the Green Ghost"
  A Night at the Opera
- **RULE 5:** Capitalize a title when it applies to a specific person, group, or document.

  Examples: The President will give a press conference this afternoon.

  Senators Goldwater and Tower are leading figures in the Conservative Party.

  Our Constitution should be strictly interpreted.

  Do *not* capitalize the same type of title when it does not make a specific reference.

  Examples: Some congressmen are liberal; others are more conservative.

  It would be useful for our club to write a constitution.
- **RULE 6:** Capitalize days of the week, months of the year, and holidays, but do *not* capitalize the seasons.

  Examples: Labor Day, the last holiday of the summer, falls on the first Monday in September.
- **RULE 7:** Capitalize all proper names, including but not limited to: names of people, *John F. Smith;* buildings, *World Trade Center;* events, *Armistice Day;* places, *Panama,* and words formed using those places, *Panamanian;* organizations, *The United Fund;* and words referring to a sole God. *Allah.*
- **RULE 8:** Capitalize the points of the compass only when referring to a specific place or area.

  Example: Many retired persons spend the winter in the South.

  Do *not* capitalize the points of the compass when they refer to a direction.

  Example: Many birds fly south in the winter.
- **RULE 9:** The only school subjects that are regularly capitalized are languages and specific place names used as modifiers.

  Examples: Next year I will study French, biology, English literature, mathematics, European history, and ancient philosophy.

- **RULE 10:** A noun not regularly capitalized should be capitalized when it is used as part of a proper name.

  Example: Yesterday I visited Uncle Charles, my favorite uncle.

- **RULE 11:** In a letter:

  a. Capitalize all titles in the address and closing.

  Examples: Mr. John Jones, President Mary Smith, Chairman of the Board

  b. Capitalize the first and last words, titles, and proper names in the salutation.

  Examples: Dear Dr. Williams,
  My dear Sir:

  c. Capitalize only the first word in a complimentary closing.

  Example: Very truly yours,

PUNCTUATION AND CAPITALIZATION EXERCISE

Directions: Among the following sentences, look for errors in capitalization or punctuation. If you find no mistake, mark (D).

1. (A) He was not informed, that he would have to work overtime.
   (B) The wind blew several papers off his desk.
   (C) This is the man whom you interviewed last week.
   (D) No mistakes.

2. (A) If an employee wishes to attend the conference, she should fill out the necessary forms.
   (B) Mr. Wright's request cannot be granted under any conditions.
   (C) Charles Dole, who is a member of the committee, was asked to confer with commissioner Wilson.
   (D) No mistakes.

3. (A) He is the kind of person who is always willing to undertake difficult assignments.
   (B) The teacher entered the room and said, "the work must be completed today."
   (C) The special project was assigned to Mary Green and me.
   (D) No mistakes.

4. (A) Mr. Barnes, the bus dispatcher, has many important duties.
   (B) We checked the addresses once more and sent the letters to the mailroom.
   (C) Do you agree that this year's class is the best yet?
   (D) No mistakes.

5. (A) The new teacher aides were given their assignments and, they were asked to begin work immediately.
   (B) Jim's sister, Carol, will begin college in the fall.
   (C) My favorite subjects are English, science and American history.
   (D) No mistakes.

6. (A) Although I am willing to work on most holidays, I refuse to work on Labor Day.
   (B) Every Tuesday afternoon Joan volunteers at Children's Hospital.
   (C) If you wish to be considered for the scholarship, you must file your application promptly.
   (D) No mistakes.

7. (A) The new student asked the gym teacher if he could join the baseball team?
   (B) Girl Scout Troop 71 will march in the parade.
   (C) Mrs. Garcia asked Louisa and Henry to help bake cookies for the party.
   (D) No mistakes.

8. (A) I find his study of the birds of North America to be fascinating.
   (B) The doctor suggested that my grandfather go South for the winter to avoid frequent colds.
   (C) Under the new rules, when do we revert to Eastern Standard Time?
   (D) No mistakes.

9. (A) If you would like to spend the night, you may sleep in Tom's room.
   (B) The attack on Pearl Harbor, on December 7, 1941, came as a complete surprise.
   (C) "May I use the computer this afternoon," the boy asked?
   (D) No mistakes.

10. (A) "If it rains on Friday," the boy mused, "the game may be played on Saturday instead."
    (B) The child's new bicycle lay on its side near the curb.
    (C) Whenever I drive on a New York street, I watch for potholes.
    (D) No mistakes.

ANSWERS AND EXPLANATIONS

1. **(A)** There is no reason for a comma between the verb and its object.
2. **(C)** Commissioner Wilson is a specific commissioner, and so the *C* must be capitalized.
3. **(B)** The direct quote must begin with a capital *T*.
4. **(D)** No mistakes.
5. **(A)** The comma is misplaced. The comma must be placed before the conjunction (in this case *and*) that joins two independent clauses.
6. **(D)** No mistakes.
7. **(A)** This is a declaratory statement, not a direct question; it must end with a period.
8. **(B)** Do not capitalize directions, only place names.
9. **(C)** The boy's question is: "May I use the computer this afternoon?" The question must end with a question mark. The entire sentence is a simple statement that should end with a period.
10. **(D)** No mistakes.

Summary: The Rules of Punctuation and Capitalization

- The HSPT exam tests your writing skills regarding punctuation and capitalization in the Language Skills section.
- To prepare for this section you must PRACTICE. Read the rules listed in this chapter and practice them.

Chapter 13

English Usage

Both the HSPT and the COOP exam will quiz you on your expertise in language usage. The COOP exam does this in the test section "Language Expression." The HSPT lumps this subject with spelling, punctuation and capitalization, and composition in the test section "Language Skills."

Language usage includes a student's grasp of correct English and how it's used. Your expertise in this area is based on years of reading and hundreds of hours of classroom instruction on grammar. In answering language usage questions, you may have to consider problems of agreement, double negatives, and dangling modifiers. Word choice, punctuation, tense, and case may also enter into your decision on which answer is best.

The "Twenty Principles of Grammar" that follow may prove useful to you as you prepare for English usage questions. Just remember, a simple, direct statement is more effective than a wordy one.

ROAD MAP

- *Twenty Principles of Grammar*
- *Troublesome Words*
- *English Usage and Expression Exercises*
- *Answers and Explanations*

TWENTY PRINCIPLES OF GRAMMAR

SUBJECT-VERB AGREEMENT

1. A verb must agree with its subject in number.
   Single subjects require singular verbs.
   Example: *She walks* to school every day. Plural subjects need plural verbs.
   Example: *They walk* home together.
2. The number of the subject is not affected by a prepositional phrase that follows it.
   Examples: The *girl together with* her friends *walks* to school every day.
   One of the apples *is* rotten.
3. In sentences beginning with *there* or *here*, the verb must agree with the noun that follows it.
   Examples: There *are* six *boys* in the class.
   Here *is* the *book* you wanted.

> **TIP**
> One way to decide between who and whom in a sentence is to remember two things: 1. who is followed by a verb 2. whom is followed by a noun (which can also be a subject or a pronoun).

4. *Each, every, everyone, everybody, someone, somebody, anyone, anybody, no one, nobody, either,* and *neither* are singular and require singular verbs and pronouns.
   Example: *Everyone* on the team *thinks he can* win the prize.
5. Singular subjects joined by *and* take a plural verb.
   Example: *John and Ted are* good friends.
6. Two singular subjects joined by *or* or *nor* take a singular verb.
   Example: Meg or Mary is always first to answer.
7. A singular and a plural subject joined by *or* or *nor* take a singular or plural verb depending on which subject is nearer the verb.
   Examples: Neither Kim nor her *sisters are* ready yet.
   Neither her sisters nor *Kim is* ready yet.
8. *Don't* is a contraction for *do not*. It is correct for first and second person singular and plural *(I don't, you don't, we don't)* and for third person plural *(they don't)*. Use *doesn't* with third person singular pronouns or nouns.
   Examples: *It doesn't* matter to me.
   Bill doesn't know that song.

PRONOUN AGREEMENT

9. A pronoun agrees with the words to which it refers in person (first, second, or third), number (singular or plural), and gender (masculine, feminine, or neuter).
   Examples: When the *boys* left, *they* took *their* books with *them*.
   Each *girl* must have *her* ticket.
10. A pronoun following a linking verb must be in the subject form *(I, you, he, she, it, we, they)*.
    Example: The woman in the photo *was she*.
11. If a pronoun is the object of a preposition or an action verb, the pronoun must be in the object form (*me, you, him, her, it, us, them*).
    Examples: Would you like to go to the movies *with* John and *me*?
    The teacher *selected* Joan and *me* to lead the class.
12. When a pronoun is used as an appositive, it must be in the same form as the word to which it refers. An appositive is a noun or pronoun that follows another noun or pronoun to identify or explain it: e.g., Ms. Ross, *my adviser,* suggested that I apply to this school.
    If the appositive refers to a subject, use the subject form.
    Example: The two pilots, Captain Miller and *he,* sat in the cockpit. (*Captain Miller* and *he* are appositives referring to the subject. Therefore, the subject form, *he,* is required.)
    If the appositive refers to an object, use the object form.
    Example: The class chose two representatives—Jeff and *him*—to attend the meeting.
    (*Jeff* and *him* are appositives referring to *representatives*, the object of the verb *chose*. Therefore, the object form, *him,* is required.)

13. A noun ending in *-ing* (a gerund) takes a possessive pronoun.
Example: My mother objected to *my getting* home so late.

14. Use the pronouns *who* and *whom* the same way you would use *he/she* and *him/her*. Use *who* wherever you could substitute *he,* and *whom* where you could substitute *him.*
Examples: The prize was won by a man *who* everyone agreed was deserving of it.
(Think: Everyone agreed *he* was deserving of it.)
The woman *whom* they elected to be chairperson accepted with pleasure.
(Think: They elected *her* to be chairperson.)

15. *This* and *that* are singular and refer to singular words: *this kind* of book, *that sort* of book.
These and *those* are plural and refer to plural words: *these kinds* of books, *those sorts* of books.

ADJECTIVE AND ADVERB USAGE

16. Use adverbs to modify action verbs.
Example: The car drove *slowly* and *carefully* (not *slow* and *careful*) on the icy road.

17. Use an adjective after a linking verb.
Example: The flower smelled *sweet* (not *sweetly*).

18. Use the comparative form of an adjective or adverb (the form that ends in *-er* or uses the word *more*) when comparing two things.
Examples: Jim runs *faster* than Joe.
Beth is *taller* than Amy.

19. Use the superlative form of an adjective or adverb (the form that ends in *-est* or uses the word *most*) when comparing more than two things.
Examples: Of all the boys on the team, Jim runs fastest.
Beth is the *tallest* girl in the class.

20. Avoid double negatives.
Examples: The rain was so heavy we *could hardly* see.
(*not:* The rain was so heavy we couldn't hardly see.)
They *don't have any* homework tonight.
(*not:* They don't have no homework tonight.)

TROUBLESOME WORDS

There are a few groups of words that span the realms of spelling, punctuation, and usage. You probably have many of these under control. Others might consistently give you trouble. Your choice of the best version of a sentence might hinge upon your understanding the correct uses of the words in these troublesome groups.

- **their, they're, there**
  Their is the possessive of *they.*

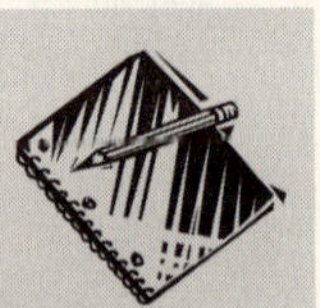

NOTE

The English language has many irregularities; therefore, items like the troublesome words must be memorized in order to use them correctly in a sentence.

Example: The Martins claimed their dog from the pound because it belonged to them.

They're is the contraction for *they are*.

Example: Tom and Marie said that they're going skiing in February.

There means at that place.

Example: You may park your car over there.

This last form is also used in sentences or clauses where the subject comes after the verb.

Example: There is no one here by that name.

- **your, you're**

  Your is the possessive of *you*.

  Example: Didn't we just drive past *your* house?

  You're is the contraction for *you are*.

  Example: When we finish caroling, *you're* all coming inside for hot chocolate.

- **whose, who's**

  Whose is the possessive of *who*.

  Example: The handwriting is very distinctive, but I cannot remember *whose* it is.

  Who's is the contraction for *who is*.

  Example: Who's calling at this hour of night?

- **its, it's**

  Its is the possessive of *it*.

  Example: The injured cat is licking *its* wounds.

  It's is the contraction for *it is*.

  Example: *It's* much too early to leave for the airport.

- **which, who, that**

  Which as a relative pronoun refers only to objects.

  Example: This is the vase *which* the cat knocked over.

  Who and *whom* refer only to people.

  Example: The boy *who* won the prize is over there.

  That may refer to either objects or people. *That* is used only in restrictive clauses.

  Example: This is the vase *that* the cat knocked over. The boy *that* won the prize is over there.

- **learn, teach**

  To *learn* is to *acquire* knowledge.To *teach* is to *impart* knowledge.

  Example: My mother *taught* me all that I have *learned*.

- **between, among**

  Between commonly applies to only two people or things.

  Example: Let us keep this secret *between you and me*.

  Among always implies that there are more than two.

  Example: The knowledge is secure *among the members* of our club.

  Exception: *Between* may be used with more than two objects to show the relationship of each object to each of the others, as in "The teacher explained the difference *between* adjective, adverb, and noun clauses."

- **beside, besides**
  Beside is a preposition meaning *by the side of.*
  Example: He sat *beside* his sick father.
  Besides, an adverb, means *in addition to.*
  Example: *Besides* his father, his mother also was ill.

- **lay, lie**
  The verb *to lay,* except when referring to hens, may be used only if you could replace it with the verb *to put.* At all other times use a form of the verb to *lie.*
  Examples: You may *lay* the books upon the table. Let sleeping dogs *lie.*

- **many/much, fewer/less, number/amount**
  The use of *many/much, fewer/less, number/amount* is governed by a simple rule of thumb.
  If the object can be counted, use *many, fewer, number.* If the object is thought of as a single mass or unit, use *much, less, amount.*
  Examples: *Many* raindrops make *much* water.
  If you have *fewer* dollars, you have *less* money.
  The *amount* of property you own depends upon the *number* of acres in your lot.

- **I, me**
  The choice of *I* or *me* when the first person pronoun is used with one or more proper names may be tested by eliminating the proper names and reading the sentence with the pronoun alone.
  Examples: John, George, Marylou, and (me *or* I) went to the movies last night. (By eliminating the names you can readily choose *I went to the movies.*)
  It would be very difficult for Mae and (I *or* me) to attend the wedding.
  (Without *Mae* it is clear that *difficult for me* is correct.)

- **as, like**
  As is a conjunction introducing a subordinate clause, while *like,* in cases where the two words are confused, is a preposition. The object of a preposition is a noun or phrase.
  Examples: Winston tastes good *as* a cigarette should. (*Cigarette* is the subject of the clause; *should* is its verb.)
  He behaves *like* a fool.
  The gambler accepts only hard currency *like* gold coins.

- **already, all ready**
  Already means *prior to some specified time.*
  Example: It is *already* too late to submit your application.
  All ready means *completely ready.*
  Example: The cornfield is *all ready* for the seed to be sown.

- **altogether, all together**
  Altogether means *entirely.*
  Example: It is *altogether* too foggy to drive safely.
  All together means *in sum* or *collectively.*
  Example: The family will be *all together* at the Thanksgiving dinner table.

- **two, to, too**
  Two is the numeral 2.
  Example: There are *two* sides to every story.
  To means *in the direction of.*
  Example: We shall go *to* school.
  Too means *more than* or *also.*
  Examples: It's *too* cold to go swimming today.
  We shall go, *too.*

ENGLISH USAGE AND EXPRESSION EXERCISES

EXERCISE 1

Directions: In the following questions, choose which of the four sentences is constructed best.

1. (A) It is the opinion of the commissioners that programs which include the construction of cut-rate municipal garages in the central business district is inadvisable.
   (B) Having reviewed the material submitted, the program for putting up cut-rate garages in the central business district seemed likely to cause traffic congestion.
   (C) The commissioners believe that putting up cut-rate municipal garages in the central business district is inadvisable.
   (D) Making an effort to facilitate the cleaning of streets in the central business district, the building of cut-rate municipal garages presents the problem that it would encourage more motorists to come into the central city.

2. (A) Since the report lacked the needed information. it was of no use to him.
   (B) This report was useless to him because there were no needed information in it.
   (C) Since the report did not contain the needed information, it was not real useful to him.
   (D) Being that the report lacked the needed information, he could not use it.

3. (A) In reviewing the typists' work reports, the job analyst found records of unusual typing speeds.
   (B) It says in the job analyst's report that some employees type with great speed.
   (C) The job analyst found that, in reviewing the typists' work reports, that some unusual typing speeds had been made.
   (D) In the reports of typists' speeds, the job analyst found some records that are kind of usual.

4. (A) They do not ordinarily present these kind of reports in detail like this.
   (B) A report of this kind is not hardly ever given in such detail as this one.
   (C) This report is more detailed than what such reports ordinarily are.
   (D) A report of this kind is not ordinarily presented in as much detail as this one is.

5. (A) Nobody but you and your brother know the reason for my coming.
   (B) The reason for my coming is only known to you and your brother.
   (C) My reason for coming is known by nobody except you and your brother.
   (D) My reason for coming is known only by you and your brother.

6. (A) If properly addressed, the letter will reach my mother and I.
   (B) The letter had been addressed to myself and my mother.
   (C) I believe the letter was addressed to either my mother or I.
   (D) My mother's name, as well as mine, was on the letter.

7. (A) The paper we use for this purpose must be light, glossy, and stand hard usage as well.
   (B) Only a light and a glossy, but durable, paper must be used for this purpose.
   (C) For this purpose, we want a paper that is light, glossy, but that will stand hard wear.
   (D) For this purpose, paper that is light, glossy, and durable is essential.

8. (A) This kind of worker achieves success through patience.
   (B) Success does not often come to men of this type except they who are patient.
   (C) Because they are patient, these sort of workers usually achieve success.
   (D) This worker has more patience than any man in his office.

9. (A) You have got to get rid of some of these people if you expect to have the quality of the work improve.
   (B) The quality of the work would improve if they would leave fewer people do it.
   (C) I believe it would be desirable to have fewer persons doing this work.
   (D) If you had planned on employing fewer people than this to do the work, this situation would not have arose.

10. (A) It is quite possible that we shall reemploy anyone whose training fits them to do the work.
    (B) It is probable that we shall reemploy those who have been trained to do the work.
    (C) Such of our personnel that have been trained to do the work will be again employed.
    (D) We expect to reemploy the ones who have had training enough that they can do the work.

EXERCISE 2

Directions: Choose the word or group of words that should go into the blank to make a correct sentence.

1. All of the boys and Joyce took ________ baseball gloves to the ball game.
   (A) her
   (B) their
   (C) his
   (D) our

2. Dana was the ________ person who dared go into the haunted house.
   (A) most only
   (B) onliest
   (C) sole only
   (D) only

3. My father will drive Althea and ________ to the airport.
   (A) me
   (B) I
   (C) myself
   (D) we

4. If Duncan had joined the soccer team, he _______ been the star.
(A) should have
(B) could of
(C) would of
(D) might have

5. Even before the wind had stopped, the rain _______ down.
(A) was slowed
(B) has been slowing
(C) had been slowing
(D) had been slowed

6. Last week I had lunch with the girl _______ won the English prize.
(A) who
(B) whom
(C) which
(D) what

7. In choosing between chocolate and vanilla ice cream, I like chocolate ice cream _______.
(A) most
(B) best
(C) better
(D) more better

8. The jury is depending _______ the witness' statements.
(A) about
(B) of
(C) upon
(D) from

9. I would bring grandma to visit you _______ I have no car.
(A) except
(B) while
(C) because
(D) moreover

10. The little girl next door _______ on her swings all day.
(A) swinged
(B) swang
(C) swung
(D) has swinged

11. Neither Kenneth nor Larry _______ book report.
(A) has completed their
(B) have completed their
(C) have completed his
(D) has completed his

12. We had just finished shoveling the driveway _______ the plow came through again.
(A) if
(B) until
(C) when
(D) than

13. You must wait for the election results until we _______ the ballots.
(A) had counted
(B) have counted
(C) are counting
(D) have had counted

Directions: Make a complete sentence by choosing the words that should go into the blank.

14. After completing the lifesaving course _______.
(A) and taking both the written and practical exams
(B) gaining months of practical experience as an apprentice
(C) you will be eligible to take the examination
(D) at the YMCA under the auspices of the Red Cross

15. _______, when the telephone rang.

(A) Returning from a frustrating day at the office

(B) No sooner said than done

(C) In the middle of dinner

(D) We had just turned off the lights

Directions: Select the sentence that means the same or most nearly the same as the underlined sentences.

16. The hiker was lost. A St. Bernard rescued him. It happened in the Alps.

(A) The hiker was rescued by a St. Bernard lost in the Alps.

(B) The lost Alpine hiker was rescued by a St. Bernard.

(C) The hiker in the lost Alps was rescued by a St. Bernard.

(D) In the Alps the hiker was rescued by a lost St. Bernard.

17. Taxes are deducted from all wages. Workers who must work at night are paid overtime. The rate of tax to be withheld is fixed by law.

(A) The law requires that people who are paid overtime must pay taxes.

(B) According to the law, people who work at night must be paid overtime and deduct taxes.

(C) The tax rate on overtime pay is deducted from wages by law and is paid at night.

(D) By law a fixed rate of taxes is deducted from all wages, including those paid as overtime for night work.

Directions: Choose the word or group of words that makes the second sentence have the same meaning as the underlined sentence.

18. The accident victim was not only frightened but also in pain.

The accident victim was _______.

(A) neither frightened nor in pain

(B) both frightened and in pain

(C) either frightened or in pain

(D) only frightened, not in pain

19. I may go to the movies tomorrow if I baby-sit today.

_______ baby-sitting today I may go to the movies tomorrow.

(A) By

(B) While

(C) Until

(D) Once

20. The criminal received consecutive sentences for his three crimes.

The criminal has to serve his sentences _______.

(A) all at once

(B) after a period of delay

(C) one at a time

(D) with no opportunity for parole

21. We bought the house; moreover, we bought the adjacent lot.

We bought _______

(A) the house because we bought the lot next door

(B) the lot because we bought the house next door

(C) the house but not the lot next door

(D) the house and the lot next door

EXERCISE 3

Directions: Among the following sentences, look for errors in grammar, usage, or composition. If you find no mistakes, mark (D).

1. (A) He got off of the horse.
   (B) Your umbrella is better than mine.
   (C) How could I be other than glad.
   (D) No mistakes.

2. (A) No one was there except Charles.
   (B) Your sample is the most satisfactory of all that I have seen.
   (C) I couldn't hardly do it.
   (D) No mistakes.

3. (A) There should be no secrets between you and me
   (B) I knew him to be the ringleader.
   (C) Everyone has studied his lesson.
   (D) No mistakes.

4. (A) There are a piano and a phonograph in the room.
   (B) This is the man whom you interviewed last week.
   (C) He is reported to be killed.
   (D) No mistakes.

5. (A) I have met but one person.
   (B) She is the tallest of the two girls.
   (C) The child is able to shape the clay easily.
   (D) No mistakes.

6. (A) I wish I were going to Mexico with you.
   (B) Please loan me five dollars until payday.
   (C) The audience was enthusiastic.
   (D) No mistakes.

7. (A) Because of the downpour, the carnival was postponed.
   (B) He walks up and said "Hello."
   (C) I already anticipate the good time I shall have at camp.
   (D) No mistakes.

8. (A) The student gave the most unique excuse for being late.
   (B) We watched the kite soar high in the sky.
   (C) Whom did you ask to go to the dance?
   (D) No mistakes.

Directions: Choose the answer that best describes the group of words.

9. The worst feature of my summer camp was the food next was the latrine.
   (A) run-on sentence
   (B) complete sentence
   (C) *not* a complete sentence

10. The man with the wart on the end of his nose gave his seat to the old woman.
    (A) run-on sentence
    (B) complete sentence
    (C) *not* a complete sentence

11. Tom, Jerry, Brad, and Genevieve, all wearing jeans and riding bicycles.
    (A) run-on sentence
    (B) complete sentence
    (C) *not* a complete sentence

12. Once upon a time in a corner of the kitchen lived a small black cricket and the cricket made a lot of noise which annoyed the woman who lived in the house and so the woman swept the cricket out the door.
    (A) run-on sentence
    (B) complete sentence
    (C) *not* a complete sentence

13. Bob and his brother Ted, who is a Civil War buff, went to Gettysburg during summer vacation and studied the battlefield together.
    (A) run-on sentence
    (B) complete sentence
    (C) *not* a complete sentence

14. The strong wind suddenly increased to gale force and the sailboat to capsize.
    (A) run-on sentence
    (B) complete sentence
    (C) *not* a complete sentence

Directions: Choose the sentence that is correctly written.

15. (A) She had done much the people began to realize.
    (B) When the people began to realize how much she had done.
    (C) Soon the people began to realize how much she had done.
    (D) The people began to realize and how much she had done.

16. (A) Mounting the curb, the empty car crossed the sidewalk and came to rest against a building.
    (B) The empty car mounts the curb, crossed the sidewalk, and will come to rest against a building.
    (C) Mounting the curb when the empty car crosses the sidewalk and comes to rest against a building.
    (D) The curb was mounted by the empty car and crossed the sidewalk and came to rest against a building.

17. (A) I had forgotten my gloves realizing and returning to the theater.
    (B) Because I will realize that I forgot my gloves, I returned to the theater.
    (C) My gloves forgotten, realized, and returned to the theater.
    (D) Realizing I had forgotten my gloves, I returned to the theater.

18. (A) She learned that further practice will have had a good effect on her swimming ability.
    (B) She learned that further practice had had a good effect on her swimming ability.
    (C) Having learned and practiced had a good effect on her swimming ability.
    (D) Learning and practicing to have a good effect on her swimming ability.

19. (A) Assisting him his friend who lives in the next house.
    (B) Assisting him and living in the next house his friend.
    (C) His friend who lives in the next house assisting.
    (D) He was assisted by his friend who lives in the next house.

20. (A) The driver does all that it will be possible to do.
    (B) The driver, having done all that was possible.
    (C) The driver did all that it was possible to do.
    (D) Doing all that is possible to do and driving.

ANSWERS AND EXPLANATIONS

EXERCISE 1

1. **(C)** (A) has an agreement error (*programs. . . are*); (B) is incorrect because the program did not review the material; (D) is totally garbled.
2. **(A)** In (B), the subject of the second clause is *information,* which is singular. In (C), the adverb should be *really*. *Being that,* in (D), is not acceptable form.
3. **(A)** The indefinite pronoun *it,* in (B), refers to nothing at all, so it means nothing. In (C), the *that* after *found* should be omitted. (D) uses colloquial language, which is unacceptable in standard written English.
4. **(D)** (A) contains an error of agreement (*these kind*); (B) contains a double negative, *not hardly; what* is an extra word in (C).
5. **(D)** In (A), the subject is *nobody,* which is singular and requires the singular verb *knows*. (B) and (C) are awkward and poorly written.
6. **(D)** Sentences (A) and (C) use the subject-form pronoun, *I,* where the object-form, *me,* is required. In (B), the object of the preposition *to* should be *me,* not *myself.*
7. **(D)** The first three sentences are not parallel in construction. All the words that modify *paper* should be in the same form.
8. **(A)** In (B), *men* is the implied subject of the verb *are.* Inserting the subject into the phrase, you can see that it must read . . . *except to those (men) who are patient.* (C) contains an error of number; to be correct, the phrase must read either *this sort of worker* or *these sorts of workers.* In (D) the comparison is incomplete. It must read "than any other man."
9. **(C)** (A) is wordy. In (B), the correct verb should be *have* in place of *leave.* In (D), *arose* is incorrect; the correct form is *arisen.*
10. **(B)** In (A), *them* should be *him* because it refers to *anyone,* which is singular. (C) and (D) are wordy and awkward.

EXERCISE 2

1. **(B)** The subject is plural and the object is plural; therefore, the possessive pronoun must be plural. The subject is in the third person, not the first.
2. **(D)** *Only* is an exclusive term. It cannot be modified in any way.
3. **(A)** The objects of the verb *drive* are *Althea* and *me*.
4. **(D)** *Of* is not an auxiliary verb, so (B) and (C) are automatically incorrect. (D) is more in tune with the nature of the sentence than is (A).
5. **(C)** To show that one past activity (the *slowing*) occurred before another past activity (the *stopping*) requires the *had been* construction (past perfect). *Had been slowed* implies that an external force was working on the rain. *Had been slowing* more accurately describes the end of a storm.
6. **(A)** *Who* is the subject of the verb *won. Which* may only be used to apply to things. *What* is not a pronoun. *That* would also be correct, but it is not offered as a choice.

7. **(C)** The comparison between two objects requires *more* or *better. More better* is redundant and incorrect. *Most* and *best* refer to comparison among three or more objects.
8. **(C)** The proper idiomatic use is *depend on* or *depend upon.*
9. **(A)** In this sentence *except* serves as a conjunction. *But* would fit into the blank in the same way. All of the other choices make no sense in the context of the sentence.
10. **(C)** The past tense of *swing* is *swung*.
11. **(D)** The construction *neither/nor* creates a singular subject (or object). Because the subject is singular, both the verb and the possessive pronoun must be singular as well.
12. **(C)** The sentence describes two activities in terms of their relationship in time. Only (C) makes sense.
13. **(B)** A present activity that is dependent on a future activity requires that the future activity be stated in the present perfect, *have counted.*
14. **(C)** The sentence fragment is nothing more than an introductory prepositional phrase. The completion must supply both subject and verb.
15. **(D)** The fragment is a subordinate clause. The sentence needs an independent clause.
16. **(B)** The correct answer must give correct information as to who was lost, where he was lost, and how he was rescued.
17. **(D)** The tax rate and the fact of withholding are established by law. Overtime pay is not established by law, but it does constitute wages subject to withholding.
18. **(B)** The term *not only/but also* is inclusive.
19. **(A)** The sentence is conditional and in reverse sequence: "I may do something tomorrow *if* I do something today." Reverse the sentence: "By doing something today, *then* I may do something else tomorrow."
20. **(C)** *Consecutive* means *one after the other*. The word that means *all at the same time* is concurrent.
21. **(D)** The word *moreover* simply means *in addition to* or *also.* It does not imply any causality.

EXERCISE 3

1. **(A)** *Off of* is an unacceptable construction: He got off the horse.
2. **(C)** *Hardly* is a negative word, and so *couldn't hardly* is an unacceptable double negative: I could hardly do it.
3. **(D)** No mistakes.
4. **(C)** The activity began in the past (he *was* killed), and is completed in the present (is reported *now*).Therefore, the present perfect tense should be used. The sentence should read: "He is reported to *have been killed.*"
5. **(B)** The comparison is between two girls, therefore *taller* is correct.
6. **(B)** *Loan* is a noun. The sentence requires the verb *lend.*
7. **(B)** The two verbs should be in the same tense. He *walked* up and *said* "Hello."

8. **(A)** *Unique* means that there is only one like it. Because there is only one, there can be no comparison. The construction *most unique* is meaningless and impossible.
9. **(A)** The two complete, independent clauses must either be separated into two sentences or be joined by a semicolon.
10. **(B)** This sentence is complete.
11. **(C)** This sentence fragment consists of subject and modifying clause. *Wearing* and *riding* are *verbals* (gerunds), not verbs. They cannot make a statement, ask a question, nor give a command, so they cannot act alone as verbs.
12. **(A)** There are actually three independent clauses here. The best correction would be to eliminate the first *and* and to begin a second sentence with "The cricket." The second *and* should be eliminated and be replaced by a comma.
13. **(B)** This sentence is complete.
14. **(C)** The sentence fragment, as organized, calls for a compound verb: *increased* to gale force and . . . . Try inserting *caused.*
15. **(C)** Choice (A) is a run-on sentence; (B) is a sentence fragment; in (D) the "and" is superfluous.
16. **(A)** Choice (B) mixes tenses illogically; (C) is a sentence fragment; in (D), the curb crosses the street and comes to rest against the building.
17. **(D)** No other choice makes sense.
18. **(B)** Choice (A) confuses tenses; (C) and (D) are sentence fragments.
19. **(D)** No other choice is a complete sentence.
20. **(C)** Choice (A) confuses tenses; (B) and (D) are sentence fragments.

Summary: Conquering English Usage Questions

- The COOP exam tests English usage in the Language Expression section. The HSPT includes it in the Language Skills section with spelling, punctuation, and capitalization.
- Study, learn, and practice the Twenty Principles of Grammar given in this chapter. They will help you not only on the test, but throughout school and life.

Chapter 14

How Composition Is Tested

Your studies of spelling, punctuation, capitalization, and grammar all contribute to your skills in language expression, another crucial part of any entrance exam. Language expression, also called language composition, is a skill that you'll use in all kinds of high school course work, exams, and in your college applications, as well.

The Catholic high school entrance examinations multiple-choice format does not lend itself to testing your ability to write a well-organized paragraph. Essay-writing is the best measure of your skills in composition, but of the exams covered in this book, only the ISEE includes an essay question.

But never fear! The COOP and HSPT exams have found a few ways to test your language expression skills. These exams have tucked questions into test sections of English usage and language expression that are designed to tap your potential for composition. Among these are questions that ask you to move a sentence to another location in the paragraph or to remove a sentence that does not belong. Other composition questions require you to identify topic sentences or to choose the best development of topic sentences that are given.

The area of language expression is one in which all test makers are experimenting at this time. New measures might crop up on the next edition of many of the high school exams administered over the next few years.

ROAD MAP

- *Tips for Answering Language Composition Questions*
- *Composition Exercise*
- *Answers and Explanations*

TIPS FOR ANSWERING LANGUAGE COMPOSITION QUESTIONS

Composition questions make up only a small portion of the exam, but those few questions might be among the most difficult and time-consuming on the test. Though you can't become an expert essayist in just a few weeks, you can familiarize yourself with some of the basic guidelines of composition, and you can learn how to focus your concentration to address these questions on your exam. Language expression questions typically test topic development and appropriateness. The following sections give

TIP
You can prepare for composition questions by reviewing essays that you have written and examine the way you developed the topic of the essay. If you have trouble developing ideas in a paragraph, review the comments your teacher has made on your compositions and learn from your mistakes.

you some common-sense tips and guidelines to use when you encounter questions dealing with these areas of language expression.

TACKLING TOPIC DEVELOPMENT QUESTIONS

What do we mean by "topic development?" The concept is relatively simple, though the task can be a bit more difficult. Topic development requires that you be able to clearly understand the main point or idea of information, and then recognize additional information that logically expands upon or further clarifies that main point or idea. Topic development is much like finishing a story that someone else has started.

Topic development questions come in a number of forms. Here are a few tips that will help you tackle these questions on the exams:

- If the question gives you a topic sentence and asks you to develop that sentence, your task is to choose a second and third sentence that best develop the idea presented in the first sentence. You aren't just choosing some sentences that refer to the same subject presented in the topic sentence. You have to choose the sentences that best expand upon or clarify the topic.
- The question might give you an essay title and then ask that you choose a topic sentence that would best express the idea of that essay. You have to choose a sentence that relates well to the subject presented by the title and that is broad enough to allow for further development of a paragraph.
- If the question gives you a title and asks you simply to choose a sentence that belongs under that title, you must weed out the sentences that are related to but not entirely relevant to the topic.
- The occasional answer choice "None of these" complicates your task and makes the question much more difficult. On the other questions, you know that one of the answers is the best solution to topic development, and you can use the process of elimination to improve your odds of landing on the correct response. When you're faced with a "None of these" response, you might not be able to use your guessing skills to find the right answer. If you can't find the answer to one of these questions, just move on. Don't let it hold you up too long.

BEATING APPROPRIATENESS QUESTIONS

Questions that ask whether a particular sentence is appropriate to a specific paragraph are, in a way, asking you to perform the same skills you use in topic development, but in reverse! With these questions, rather than choose the best way to add to the information about a topic, you're asked to choose which information definitely does or does not belong, or to determine where the best placement of that information might be.

If you can write a well-organized composition, you'll know how to allocate ideas into paragraphs. Unfortunately, these are not skills that you can develop right this minute. Take time to go over your returned written class work and learn from your teachers' comments. If you do not understand some comments or the reasons for some low grades, ask your teachers for explanations and help.

COMPOSITION EXERCISE

Directions: Choose the pair of sentences that best develops the topic sentence.

1. Salting highways in winter is undoubtedly helpful to the motorist, yet this practice may actually cause a great deal of harm.
   (A) Salt works more quickly than chemical ice melters because it does not require heat to go into action. Salt mixed with sand offers especially good traction.
   (B) While melting the ice and eliminating slippery conditions, the same salt eats into the road surface itself, creating dangerous potholes. Further, the salty runoff leaches into the soil and kills surrounding vegetation.
   (C) A small amount of salt is a dietary necessity, especially in hot, dry climates. Large amounts of dietary salt, however, lead to water retention and high blood pressure.
   (D) Salt is inexpensive because it occurs abundantly in nature. Highways in the Rocky Mountains should have good safety records because they are so close to Utah, a great source of salt.

2. Mesa Verde is a great flat-topped mountain which rises dramatically above the surrounding Colorado desert.
   (A) In contrast to this desert, Mesa Verde is fertile and well-watered, a green oasis to which men have been drawn since ancient times. Within the sheer cliff walls of these canyons, nature has carved out vast caverns in soft sandstone rock.
   (B) In 1275, a severe 24-year drought hit the Mesa Verde area. The Cliff Dwellers, hounded by their relentless enemies and forces they could not comprehend, abandoned their cities and fields and fled from Mesa Verde.
   (C) At Mesa Verde the *Anasazi* found favorable growing conditions. The legends call them the *Anasazi,* the Ancient Ones.
   (D) Villages, towns, and ultimately great cities appeared on the mesa tops. Tools and implements became more diverse and elaborate.

Directions: Choose the topic sentence that best fits the paragraph.

3. ______________________

   They set fires for many different reasons. Sometimes a shopkeeper sees no way out of losing his business and sets fire to it to collect the insurance. Another type of arsonist wants revenge and sets fire to the home or shop of someone he feels has treated him unfairly.
   (A) They don't look like criminals, but they cost the nation millions of dollars in property loss and sometimes loss of life.
   (B) Arsonists of this type have even been known to help fight the fire.
   (C) Arsonists are persons who set fires deliberately.
   (D) Some arsonists just like the excitement of seeing the fire burn and watching the firefighters at work.

4. ______________________________

But you ought not to despise it, for it can help you and your family obtain many of the good things of life. It can buy an adequate diet, one of the basics of good health. It can make it easier for your children to secure an education. When necessary, it can provide medicine and medical care.

(A) Money can offer a great opportunity for you to help others.

(B) Money can be the means for a comfortable house, for travel, for good books, and for hobbies and recreation.

(C) Mainly people consider that amassing great wealth is a goal in itself.

(D) Certainly money should not be your chief aim in life.

Directions: Choose the sentence that does not belong in the paragraph.

5. (1) The geologist studies the earth as it is today and as it has been throughout its long history. (2) He is interested in every aspect of the history of the earth, its changing geography, its life, its climate, the way the frost breaks away the tops of the highest mountains, and the way mud accumulates in the deepest parts of the sea. (3) Being mere man, the geologist can only study the surface of this planet. (4) Of course, geology is not necessarily a man's science; it is open to women as well. (5) By using the methods of modem physics, the geologist can make some inspired guesses as to what lies below, but his first concern is with rocks at the surface and with the natural processes which affect them.

(A) sentence 2

(B) sentence 3

(C) sentence 4

(D) sentence 5

6. (1) If something becomes suddenly popular, it is called a fad. (2) Parents are often dismayed by teenage fads. (3) If something's popularity endures, it is called a trend. (4) If something's popularity affects other things, it is called a style.

(A) sentence 1

(B) sentence 2

(C) sentence 3

(D) sentence 4

Directions: Choose the best answer.

7. Where should the sentence, "Prior to the Civil War, the steamboat was the center of life in the thriving Mississippi towns," be placed in the paragraph below?

(1) With the war came the railroads. (2) River traffic dwindled, and the white-painted vessels rotted at the wharves. (3) During World War I, the government decided to relieve rail congestion by reviving the long-forgotten waterways. (4) Today steamers, diesels, and barges ply the Mississippi.

(A) before sentence 1

(B) between sentences 2 and 3

(C) between sentences 3 and 4

(D) The sentence does not fit in this paragraph.

8. Where should the sentence, "Drivers who use alcohol tend to disregard their usual safety practices," be placed in the paragraph below?

(1) Many experiments on the effects of alcohol consumption show that alcohol decreases alertness and efficiency. (2) It decreases self-consciousness and at the same time increases confidence and feelings of ease and relaxation. (3) It impairs attention and judgment. (4) It destroys fear of consequences. (5) Usual cautions are thrown to the winds. (6) Their reaction time slows down; normally quick reactions are not possible for them.

(A) between sentences 1 and 2

(B) between sentences 2 and 3

(C) between sentences 4 and 5

(D) between sentences 5 and 6

9. Which of the following sentences best fits under the topic, "The Symbolic Use of Bears"?
   (A) Dancing bears provide a comical form of entertainment at street fairs.
   (B) Small children love to hug teddy bears because they are soft and warm.
   (C) The bear has long been the symbol of Russia.
   (D) None of these.

10. Which topic is best for a one-paragraph theme?
    (A) Development and Decline of the Whaling Industry
    (B) The Effects of Automation upon the Farming Industry
    (C) The Advantage of Using a Heavier Baseball Bat
    (D) None of these

ANSWERS AND EXPLANATIONS

1. **(B)** Choice (B) picks up where the topic sentence leaves off. It explains how the salt is helpful and then gives examples of the harm caused by salt. Choice (A) is also not a bad one. This choice amplifies the action of salt on ice and tells of its beneficial effects. Choices (C) and (D) do not develop the topic sentence at all. If you were not offered choice (B), you could choose (A) over (C) and (D) and have an acceptable answer. However, because you must choose the *best* from among all of the choices, (B) is the answer.
2. **(A)** The topic sentence introduces both Mesa Verde and the Colorado desert, and choice (A) flows naturally by contrasting Mesa Verde to the desert and then further describing Mesa Verde. A clear second best choice is (C). However, a transitional sentence would be desirable to introduce the *Anasazi*. Choices (B) and (D) do nothing to develop the topic sentence.
3. **(C)** Most often a definition makes a good topic sentence. This definition sets a good reference point for the pronoun, "they," which begins the next sentence. Choices (A) and (B) cannot be first sentences since they refer to antecedents that aren't there. Choice (D) might serve as a topic sentence, but not as the topic sentence for this particular paragraph. (D) would lead to a very different paragraph development.
4. **(D)** Choice (D) as topic sentence sets up a nice contrast with the "but" that follows it. (A) and (B) set up meaningless contrasts. (C) makes a weak topic sentence creating confusion of person (people. . . you) and leaving an unclear reference for the "it" that is not to be despised.
5. **(C)** Use of "man" and "he" may be politically incorrect, but clarification of the possibility of the term's being gender-inclusive has no place in the middle of the paragraph.
6. **(B)** This paragraph serves to define the terms fad, trend, and style. While the reaction of parents to teenage fads is certainly a related topic, it belongs in another paragraph.
7. **(A)** The organization of this paragraph is chronological. Because the third sentence discusses relief of rail congestion during World War I, it is clear that the war of the first sentence is the Civil War. Events prior to the Civil War should be mentioned before events that happened during the Civil War.
8. **(D)** The topic sentence introduces the subject of the deleterious effects of alcohol. The second, third, and fourth sentences clearly follow with their use of "it" to refer to alcohol. The sentence being placed might logically follow the fourth sentence, but that would leave the "their" of the sixth sentence without a reference noun. Sentence six obviously refers to "drivers" so the sentence about the drivers must appear between sentences (5) and (6).
9. **(C)** Choices (A) and (B) tell of actual uses of bears.
10. **(C)** This is a limited topic that could be dealt with in one paragraph. The topic also lends itself to being one paragraph in a longer, more comprehensive essay.

Summary: Composition Questions

- Only the ISEE includes an essay question.
- The COOP and HSPT use multiple-choice questions that ask you to move a sentence to another location in the paragraph, to remove a sentence that does not belong, to identify topic sentences, or to choose the best development of topic sentences.
- Topic development requires that you be able to clearly understand the main point or idea of information, and then recognize additional information that logically expands upon or further clarifies that main point or idea.
- Appropriateness questions ask you to choose which information definitely does or does not belong, or to determine where the best placement of that information might be.

Chapter 15

Memory

The COOP is the only exam out of the four described in this book that specifically includes questions that test your memory. Unlike all other verbal test components, the memory test does not test knowledge, reading ability, or reasoning ability. The memory test measures your ingenuity in fashioning ways to help you memorize unfamiliar material.

Here's how the test works. After filling out forms for the COOP exam, you'll be presented with a list of memory items. This happens before you even start the actual exam. The test administrator will distribute and then read aloud a list of 20 nonsense words and their definitions. That's right, I said nonsense! The words are completely made up. You will have 10 minutes to work at memorizing the words with their definitions. If you are not issued scratch paper, write words, definitions, and associations right on the page of definitions the proctor distributed. No one will judge the jottings you make for yourself. Then the administrator will collect the lists and will give instructions for Test 1, Sequences. After Test 1, you will read directions and answer questions on Test 2, Analogies.

Finally, after about 25 minutes, you'll move on to Test 3, Memory. Here's where the nonsense words come back to haunt you! The memory test section consists of 20 questions. In each question, the definition is given, and you must choose the correct nonsense word from among five possible answers. You'll have 5 minutes to complete the test. The pressure is on! But you won't need to feel so much pressure on this portion of the exam, if you can remember and follow a few basic tips and guidelines for tackling this portion of the exam.

ROAD MAP

- *Tips for Preparing for the Memory Test*
- *Memory Exercise*
- *Answers and Suggested Associations*

TIPS FOR PREPARING FOR THE MEMORY TEST

The process of memorizing is a very individualized one. Some lucky people are endowed with photographic memories. These people can commit a page of material to memory by staring hard at it and later conjuring up a mental "photograph," an exact image of the printed page. If you are one of the lucky few, the memory test will be a snap for you. You'll just need to read the list, look at the page, and take your "mental photograph."

TIP

You can prepare for memory questions in one or more of the following ways. Remember, one of these ways will work better for you than other techniques.

1. Memorize the list you are given
2. Read the list to yourself
3. Create a written list of the words
4. Associate the words with meaningful things or ideas

Another very small group of people have what are called *phonographic* memories. These people can repeat exactly that which they have heard. Because presentation of the memory material for the COOP memory test is made both visually and orally, those with phonographic memories can listen carefully and then draw upon the information they heard to answer the questions. During the 10 minutes that you are given to memorize the list, you can read to yourself (softly, of course) from the list. For the rest of us, some other techniques might be necessary to ace the memory portion of the exam.

WRITE IT DOWN

Write down the information you want to remember. Somehow, many people seem to learn and to remember through their fingers. The act of writing a word or phrase or idea can really cement that element in our mind. If you have ever written out a shopping list and then left it at home, you probably were able to remember most of the items on the list. Writing a list during the memorization portion of the exam might be the best way for you to "record" in your mind the information that you later will be asked to recall. If you aren't issued scrap paper, just write on the "memorization" list the proctor distributes. The paper will be taken away at the end of the memorization time, but just like your grocery list, you might remember your writing even after the paper is gone.

USE THE PROCESS OF ASSOCIATION

Although writing works very well with meaningful material—spelling words, vocabulary words, and such—when the material to be memorized is totally meaningless, writing alone might not be sufficient. Everyone has his or her own technique, but here's how the association technique might work for you. Suppose you are presented with the memory item: "A *bluflop* is a silly person." You might see "buffoon," a fool or a clown, in *bluflop* and so associate *bluflop* with *silly* person. Or you might visualize a picture of a person flopping over in a silly fashion. You would then write out your association—bluflop = silly person = buffoon or clown or fool.

Here is another example: "Kawash means to waddle." You might think, "A duck waddles; quack, kawash, duck, waddle; or splish, splash, kawash, duck, waddle." Imagine the sound; imagine the picture; write down the association. Chances are, if you can make some sort of association, you'll probably choose the correct nonsense word 25 minutes from now.

Associating nonsense words with their definitions presents an exercise in imagination. And you will have to be very imaginative. Don't worry, no one will ever see your associations, so you may be as outlandish and outrageous as you wish without fear of embarrassment.

To see how well association can work, try the following Memory exercise.

Use a piece of scrap paper to write out the words in the list and your associations. Read the nonsense words and their definitions aloud. Allow yourself 12 minutes to memorize. Then cover the list and put your paper of associations well out of sight. Distract yourself for about 25 minutes. Have a snack, read a newspaper article, or work in another part of this book. After 25 minutes, do your best with the questions. Along with the correct answers, you will find suggested associations. These are only suggestions, not "correct" associations. Only your own clues will work for you.

MEMORY EXERCISE

DEFINITIONS

1. A *pnupyts* is a wedding.
2. A *plub* is a lilac bush.
3. *Glidge* means to "bounce."
4. A *tocup* is a skyscraper.
5. A *lafavo* is a green vegetable.
6. *Sowso* is wastewater.
7. A *himph* is a long tail.
8. *Bonka* means "to study."
9. A *ridan* is a mosquito.
10. *Kaboz* means "charming."
11. A *nollon* is a chain.
12. A *dister* is a parrot.
13. An *alapt* is an evergreen tree.
14. *Wanok* means "dryclean only."
15. *Mosal* means "to daydream."
16. An *ictopan* is a monster.
17. *Elgofta* means "happiness."
18. An *olg* is a stork.
19. An *ijubean* is a prisoner.
20. *Yacklis* is licorice.

Directions: Choose the word that means the same as the italicized word or phrase.

1. Which word means *to bounce*?
   (A) wanok
   (B) ijubean
   (C) glidge
   (D) tocup
   (E) kaboz

2. Which word means *a green vegetable*?
   (A) elgofta
   (B) lafavo
   (C) pnupyts
   (D) mosal
   (E) ictopan

3. Which word means *wastewater*?
   (A) yacklis
   (B) dister
   (C) wanok
   (D) mosal
   (E) sowso

4. Which word means *charming*?
   (A) olg
   (B) nollon
   (C) alapt
   (D) kaboz
   (E) lafavo

5. Which word means *a parrot*?
(A) dister
(B) bonka
(C) yacklis
(D) ictopan
(E) wanok

6. Which word means *to daydream?*
(A) ridan
(B) himph
(C) mosal
(D) elgofta
(E) alapt

7. Which word means *a monster?*
(A) ictopan
(B) ijubean
(C) pnupyts
(D) plub
(E) himph

8. Which word means *happiness?*
(A) ridan
(B) glidge
(C) yacklis
(D) elgofta
(E) lafavo

9. Which word means *a wedding*?
(A) alapt
(B) wanok
(C) mosal
(D) ijubean
(E) pnupyts

10. Which word means *a long tail*?
(A) olg
(B) himph
(C) plub
(D) kaboz
(E) nollon

11. Which word means *a lilac bush*?
(A) glidge
(B) lafavo
(C) plub
(D) tocup
(E) mosal

12. Which word means *a skyscraper*?
(A) bonka
(B) ictopan
(C) yacklis
(D) elgofta
(E) tocup

13. Which word means *to study*?
(A) ijubean
(B) bonka
(C) dister
(D) glidge
(E) pnupyts

14. Which word means *an evergreen tree*?
(A) glidge
(B) elgofta
(C) alapt
(D) himph
(E) lafavo

15. Which word means *dry-clean only*?
(A) tocup
(B) kaboz
(C) ictopan
(D) olg
(E) wanok

16. Which word means *a mosquito*?
(A) sowso
(B) yacklis
(C) ridan
(D) himph
(E) kaboz

17. Which word means *licorice*?
   (A) nollon
   (B) yacklis
   (C) tocup
   (D) glidge
   (E) pnupyts

18. Which word means *a stork*?
   (A) plub
   (B) ridan
   (C) mosal
   (D) wanok
   (E) olg

19. Which word means *a chain*?
   (A) dister
   (B) nollon
   (C) elgofta
   (D) sowso
   (E) lafavo

20. Which word means *a prisoner*?
   (A) ijubean
   (B) dister
   (C) himph
   (D) bonka
   (E) pnupyts

ANSWERS AND SUGGESTED ASSOCIATIONS

1. **(C)** bounce over the edge; bounce the opposite of glide = glidge
2. **(B)** a green leafy vegetable full of vitamins = lafavo
3. **(E)** wastewater in the sewer = sowso
4. **(D)** charming—the snake charmer is charming the boa from the basket in the casbah (crowded middle-eastern marketplace) = kaboz; or charm = deceive or trick = bamboozle = kaboz
5. **(A)** parrot is a disrespectful disturber = dister
6. **(C)** daydream = mosey through your thoughts = mosal
7. **(A)** monster—panic at the thought of a monster = ictopan; or, if you happen to be into prehistoric animals, you might think ichthyosaur = ictopan
8. **(D)** happiness = elation = elgofta; also, lofted by happiness = elgofta
9. **(E)** wedding = nuptials = pnupyts
10. **(B)** long tail or prehensile tail on a chimp = himph
11. **(C)** The lilac bush has a plum color = plub
12. **(E)** The skyscraper is too up or touches up = tocup
13. **(B)** When you study you bang your head with the book = bonka
14. **(C)** An evergreen tree is always leafed = alapt
15. **(E)** If the label says "dry clean only," washing is not OK = wanok
16. **(C)** A mosquito will drain your blood = ridan (an anagram)
17. **(B)** Licorice rhymes with lis = yacklis; if you don't care for licorice, it is yucky = yacklis
18. **(E)** A stork stands on one leg = olg
19. **(B)** chain = nollon; there is no meaningful association, but the configuration of the nonsense word gives the feeling of interlocking connection—nollonnollon, etc.
20. **(A)** prisoner in jail, in the bag, in the bean bag = ijubean

Summary: Mastering Memory Questions

- COOP is the only exam that specifically includes questions that test your memory.
- After filling out the forms for the COOP, the administrator will distribute and then read aloud a list of 20 nonsense words and their definitions. You will have 10 minutes to memorize the words. Take notes directly on the page the administrator gives you. After about 25 minutes, you will come to Part 3 of the test and be asked to remember the terms.
- Write down all of the nonsense words. Many people remember things better if they write them down.
- Use the process of association. Break the word into pieces and make a sentence, rhyme the word with a similar English word, find similar words with some of the same parts.

PART 3

Quantitative and Nonverbal Skills

PREVIEW

Chapter 16

Mathematics

Whether you love math or hate it, it's always a part of your life. Mathematics questions are found on all scholastic aptitude and achievement tests, including Catholic high school entrance exams. On the COOP exam, these questions are called Mathematics Concepts and Applications. On the HSPT, Math questions include the categories of Concepts, Problem-solving, and Quantitative Skills.

In the pages that follow, we have tried to condense eight years of mathematics instruction into a comprehensive review that touches on most of the topics covered on the exams. This is only a review, not a course. If you find that you're having special difficulties with any mathematic topic, talk with a teacher or refer back to any of your mathematics textbooks. This chapter really helps you most by letting you know what you **don't** know, so you can focus some of your test-prep time on brushing up your skills in problem areas. The explanations that accompany the mathematics exercises and the mathematical questions in the practice exams are very complete. These explanations will be a big help to you, because they help you understand the processes involved in finding the right answers to mathematics questions. For extra practice with math questions, do the math sections of all the model exams.

The following sections in this part outline some of the basic mathematic rules, procedures, and formulas that you've learned over the past eight years in school. You also have an opportunity to practice your skills with some exercises, and you can judge your progress by checking your work against the answer explanations that follow the exercises. Work through these sections and the exercises carefully, and be honest with yourself about the accuracy and speed with which you solve these problems. Note which problems are difficult for you as well as those that are easy. After you've completed this section, you'll know exactly which areas you need to strengthen.

ROAD MAP

- *The Number Line*
- *Decimals*
- *Fractions*
- *Percentages*
- *Algebra*
- *Geometry*
- *Coordinate Geometry*
- *Word Problems*
- *Answers and Solutions*
- *Mathematics Exercises*
- *Answers and Solutions to Mathematics Exercises*

THE NUMBER LINE

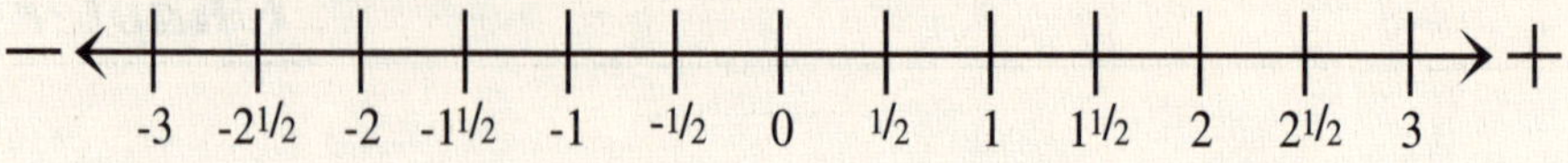

A number line is a convenient concept to keep as a mental picture. The number line above shows whole numbers and fractions greater than zero and less than zero. Numbers increase in size as you move to the right and decrease in size as you move to the left. The number line above has an arrow at each end, meaning that the number line goes on infinitely in both positive and negative directions.

Number lines can be drawn up to aid in basic mathematical calculations. Either fractions, whole numbers, or decimals can be used to name the intervals on the line. We suggest that you use number lines when dealing with signed (+, –) numbers and inequalities.

Here is a list of a few basic rules that must be mastered for speed and accuracy in mathematical computation. You should memorize these rules:

Any number multiplied by 0 = 0.

$5 \times 0 = 0$

If 0 is divided by any number, the answer is 0.

$0 \div 2 = 0$

If 0 is added to any number, that number does not change.

$7 + 0 = 7$

If 0 is subtracted from any number, that number does not change.

$4 - 0 = 4$

If a number is multiplied by 1, that number does not change.

$3 \times 1 = 3$

If a number is divided by 1, that number does not change.

$6 \div 1 = 6$

A number added to itself is doubled.

$4 + 4 = 8$

If a number is subtracted from itself, the answer is 0.

$9 - 9 = 0$

If a number is divided by itself, the answer is 1.

$8 \div 8 = 1$

If you have memorized these rules, you should be able to write the answers to the questions in the following exercise as fast as you can read the questions.

Exercise 1

Answers appear on page 187.

1. $1 - 1 =$
2. $3 \div 1 =$
3. $6 \times 0 =$
4. $6 - 0 =$
5. $0 \div 8 =$
6. $9 \times 1 =$
7. $5 + 0 =$
8. $4 - 0 =$
9. $2 \div 1 =$
10. $7 - 7 =$
11. $8 \times 0 =$
12. $0 \div 4 =$
13. $1 + 0 =$
14. $3 - 0 =$
15. $5 \times 1 =$
16. $9 \div 1 =$
17. $6 + 6 =$
18. $4 - 4 =$
19. $5 \div 5 =$
20. $6 \times 1 =$

The more rules, procedures, and formulas you are able to memorize, the easier it will be to solve mathematical problems on your exam and throughout life. Become thoroughly familiar with the rules in this section and try to commit to memory as many as possible.

When multiplying a number by 10, 100, 1000, etc., move the decimal point to the right a number of spaces equal to the number of zeros in the multiplier. If the number being multiplied is a whole number, push the decimal point to the right by inserting the appropriate number of zeros.

$.36 \times 100 = 36.$

$1.2 \times 10 = 12.$

$5. \times 10 = 50.$

$60.423 \times 100 = 6042.3$

When dividing a number by 10, 100, 1000, etc., again count the zeros, but this time move the decimal point to the left.

$123. \div 100 = 1.23$

$352.8 \div 10 = 35.28$

$16. \div 100 = .16$

$7. \div 1000 = .007$

Exercise 2

Answers appear on page 187.

1. $18 \times 10 =$
2. $5 \div 100 =$
3. $1.3 \times 1000 =$
4. $3.62 \times 10 =$
5. $9.86 \div 10 =$
6. $.12 \div 100 =$
7. $4.5 \times 10 =$
8. $83.28 \div 1000 =$
9. $761 \times 100 =$
10. $68.86 \div 10 =$

TIP
Remember decimals are a way of writing fractions using tenths, hundredths, thousandths, etc.

DECIMALS

Decimals are a way of writing fractions using tenths, hundredths, thousandths, and so forth. If you can count money, make change, or understand a batting average, decimals should present no problem.

When writing decimals, the most important step is placing the decimal point. The whole system is based on its location. Remember the decimal places?

1,	MILLIONS
2	HUNDRED THOUSANDS
3	TEN THOUSANDS
6,	THOUSANDS
5	HUNDREDS
4	TENS
0	ONES
.	DECIMAL POINT
1	TENTHS
3	HUNDREDTHS
2	THOUSANDTHS
4	TEN THOUSANDTHS
5	HUNDRED THOUSANDTHS
6	MILLIONTHS

When adding or subtracting decimals, it is most important to keep the decimal points in line. After the decimal points are aligned, proceed with the problem in exactly the same way as with whole numbers, simply maintaining the location of the decimal point.

Q Add 36.08 + 745 + 4.362 + 58.6 + .0061.

Solution:

```
  36.08       If you find it easier, you     036.0800
 745.         may fill in the spaces         745.0000
   4.362      with zeros. The answer         004.3620
  58.6        will be unchanged.             058.6000
 + .0061                                   + 000.0061
 844.0481                                    844.0481
```

Q Subtract 7.928 from 82.1.

Solution:

$$\begin{array}{r} 82.1 \\ -\underline{7.928} \\ 74.172 \end{array} \qquad \begin{array}{r} 82.100 \\ -\underline{7.928} \\ 74.172 \end{array}$$

Exercise 3

Try these problems. Answers appear on page 187.

1. 1.52 + .389 + 42.9 =
2. .6831 + .01 + 4.26 + 98 =
3. 84 – 1.9 =
4. 3.25 + 5.66 + 9.1 =
5. 17 – 12.81 =
6. 46.33 – 12.1 =
7. 51 + 7.86 + 42.003 =
8. 35.4 – 18.21 =
9. .85 – .16 =
10. 7.6 + .32 + 830 =

When multiplying decimals, you can ignore the decimal points until you reach the product. Then the placement of the decimal point is dependent on the sum of the places to the right of the decimal point in both the multiplier and number being multiplied.

$$\begin{array}{rl} 1.482 & \text{(3 places to the right of decimal point)} \\ \times\underline{.16} & \text{(2 places to the right of decimal point)} \\ 8892 & \\ \underline{14820} & \\ .23712 & \text{(5 places to the right of decimal point)} \end{array}$$

You cannot divide by a decimal. If the divisor is a decimal, you must move the decimal point to the right until the divisor becomes a whole number, an integer. Count the number of spaces by which you moved the decimal point to the right and move the decimal point in the dividend (the number being divided) the same number of spaces to the right. The decimal point in the answer should be directly above the decimal point in the dividend.

$$.06\overline{)4.212}\ \text{ (quotient } 70.2\text{)}$$ Decimal point moves two spaces to the right.

Exercise 4

Solve the following problems. Answers are on page 187.

1. $3.62 \times 5.6 =$
2. $92 \times .11 =$
3. $18 \div .3 =$
4. $1.5 \times .9 =$
5. $7.55 \div 5 =$
6. $6.42 \div 2.14 =$
7. $12.01 \times 3 =$
8. $24.82 \div 7.3 =$
9. $.486 \div .2 =$
10. $.21 \times 12 =$

FRACTIONS

Fractions are used when we wish to indicate parts of things. A fraction consists of a numerator and a denominator.

$$\frac{3}{4} \begin{matrix} \leftarrow \text{numerator} \rightarrow \\ \leftarrow \text{denominator} \rightarrow \end{matrix} \frac{7}{8}$$

The denominator tells you how many equal parts the object or number has been divided into, and the numerator tells how many of those parts we are concerned with.

Q Divide a baseball game, a football game, and a hockey game into ` convenient numbers of parts. Write a fraction to answer each equation.

1. If a pitcher played two innings, how much of the whole baseball game did he play?
2. If a quarterback played three parts of a football game, how much of the whole game did he play?
3. If a goalie played two parts of a hockey game, how much of the whole game did he play?

Solution 1: A baseball game is conveniently divided into nine parts (each an inning). The pitcher pitched two innings. Therefore, he played $\frac{2}{9}$ of the game. The denominator represents the nine parts the game is divided into; the numerator, the two parts we are concerned with.

Solution 2: Similarly, there are four quarters in a football game, and a quarterback playing three of those quarters plays in $\frac{3}{4}$ of the game.

Solution 3: There are three periods in hockey, and the goalie played in two of them. Therefore, he played in $\frac{2}{3}$ of the game.

EQUIVALENT FRACTIONS

Fractions having different denominators and numerators might actually represent the same amount. Such fractions are equivalent fractions.

For example, the following circle is divided into two equal parts. Write a fraction to indicate how much of the circle is shaded.

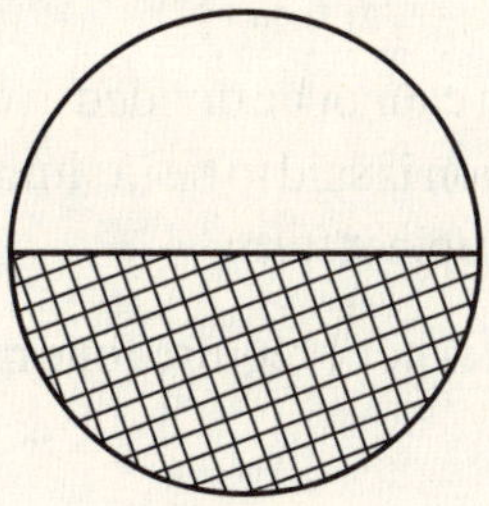

$\frac{\text{1 shaded}}{\text{2 parts}} = \frac{1}{2}$ of the circle is shaded.

The circle below is divided into four equal parts. Write a fraction to indicate how much of the circle is shaded.

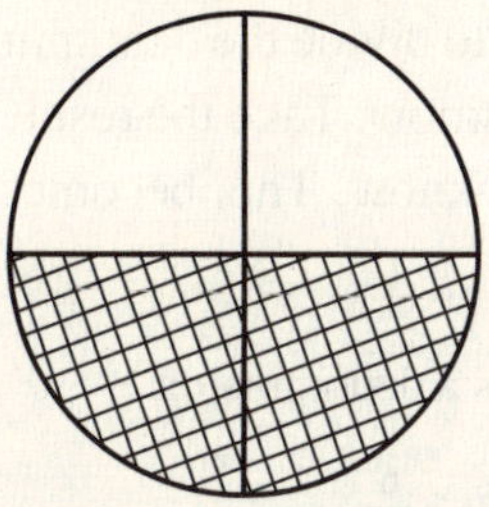

$\frac{\text{2 shaded}}{\text{4 parts}} = \frac{2}{4}$ of the circle is shaded

This circle is divided into eight equal parts. Write a fraction to indicate how much of the circle is shaded.

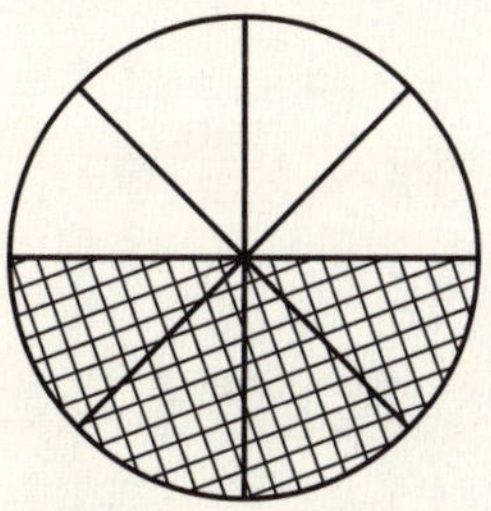

$\frac{\text{4 shaded}}{\text{8 parts}} = \frac{4}{8}$ of the circle is shaded

In each circle the same amount was shaded. This should show you that there is more than one way to indicate one half of something.

The fractions $\frac{1}{2}$, $\frac{2}{4}$, and $\frac{4}{8}$ that you wrote are *equivalent fractions* because they all represent the same amount. Notice that the denominator is twice as large as the numerator in every case. Any fraction you write that has a denominator that is exactly twice as large as the numerator will be equivalent to $\frac{1}{2}$.

Example 1: Write other fractions equivalent to $\frac{1}{2}$.

Example 2: Write other fractions equivalent to $\frac{1}{4}$.

Example 3: Write other fractions equivalent to $\frac{2}{3}$.

Solution 1: Any fraction that has a denominator that is twice as large as the numerator: $\frac{3}{6}$, $\frac{5}{10}$, $\frac{6}{12}$, $\frac{32}{64}$, etc.

Solution 2: Any fraction that has a denominator that is four times as large as the numerator: $\frac{2}{8}$, $\frac{4}{16}$, $\frac{5}{20}$, $\frac{15}{60}$, etc.

Solution 3: Any fraction that has a denominator that is one and one-half times as large as the numerator: $\frac{4}{6}$, $\frac{10}{15}$, $\frac{14}{21}$, $\frac{16}{24}$, etc.

When the numerator and denominator of a fraction cannot be divided evenly by the same whole number (other than 1), the fraction is said to be in simplest forms. In the examples above, $\frac{1}{2}$, $\frac{1}{4}$, $\frac{2}{3}$ are in simplest form.

To write equivalent fractions where the numerator is not 1 requires one more step.

Q What is the equivalent fraction for $\frac{4}{5}$ using 10 as a denominator?

Solution: Each $\frac{1}{5}$ is equivalent to $\frac{2}{10}$; therefore, $\frac{4}{5}$ is equivalent to $\frac{8}{10}$.

The quickest way to find an equivalent fraction is to divide the denominator of the fraction you want by the denominator you know. Take the result and multiply it by the numerator of the fraction you know. This becomes the numerator of the equivalent fraction.

Q Rename $\frac{3}{8}$ as an equivalent fraction having 16 as a denominator.

Solution: $16 \div 8 = 2$ $\quad 2 \times 3 = 6$ $\quad$ *Answer:* $\frac{6}{16}$

Q Rename $\frac{3}{4}$ as equivalent fractions having 8, 12, 24, and 32 as denominators.

Solution:

$$\frac{3}{4} = \frac{6}{8} \ (8 \div 4 = 2; 2 \times 3 = 6)$$

$$\frac{3}{4} = \frac{9}{12} \ (12 \div 4 = 3; 3 \times 3 = 9)$$

$$\frac{3}{4} = \frac{18}{24} \ (24 \div 4 = 6; 6 \times 3 = 18)$$

$$\frac{3}{4} = \frac{24}{32} \ (32 \div 4 = 8; 8 \times 3 = 24)$$

A fraction that has a numerator greater than the denominator is called an *improper fraction*. A number expressed as an integer together with a proper fraction is called a *mixed number*.

Examples of improper fractions include $\frac{3}{2}$, $\frac{12}{7}$, and $\frac{9}{5}$. Note that each is in simplest form because the numerator and denominator cannot be divided evenly by a number other than 1.

Examples of mixed numbers include $1\frac{1}{2}$, $1\frac{5}{7}$, and $1\frac{4}{5}$. These are called mixed numbers because they have a whole number part and a fractional part. These mixed numbers are equivalent to the improper fractions given above.

To rename a mixed number as an improper fraction is easy.

Q Rename $2\frac{1}{4}$ as an improper fraction.

Solution: The whole number 2 contains 8 fourths. Add to it the $\frac{1}{4}$ to write the equivalent fraction $\frac{9}{4}$.

An alternative way of figuring this is to multiply the denominator of the fraction by the whole number and add the numerator.

Q Rename $2\frac{1}{4}$ as an improper fraction.

Solution: $4 \times 2 = \frac{8}{4} + \frac{1}{4} = \frac{9}{4}$

To rename an improper fraction as a mixed number, just proceed backwards.

Q Rename $\frac{9}{4}$ as a mixed number.

Solution: Divide the numerator by the denominator and use the remainder (R) as the fraction:

$9 \div 4 = 2\text{ R}1$ or $9 \div 4 = 2\frac{1}{4}$

ADDING AND SUBTRACTING FRACTIONS

To add fractions having the same denominators, simply add the numerators and keep the common denominator.

Q Add $\frac{1}{4} + \frac{3}{4} + \frac{3}{4}$.

The denominators are the same, so just add the numerators to arrive at the answer, $\frac{7}{4}$ or $1\frac{3}{4}$.

To find the difference between two fractions having the same denominators, simply subtract the numerators, leaving the denominators alone.

Q Find the difference between $\frac{7}{8}$ and $\frac{3}{8}$.

Solution: $\frac{7}{8} - \frac{3}{8} = \frac{4}{8}$ Simplified to simplest form $\frac{4}{8} = \frac{1}{2}$

To add or subtract fractions having different denominators, you will have to find a *common denominator*. A common denominator is a number which can be divided by the denominators of all the fractions in the problem without a remainder.

TIP

To add or subtract two fractions quickly, remember that a sum can be found by adding the two cross products and putting this answer over the denominator product.

Q Find a common denominator for $\frac{1}{4}$ and $\frac{1}{3}$.

Solution: 12 can be divided by both 4 and 3:

$$\frac{1}{4} \text{ is equivalent to } \frac{3}{12}$$

$$\frac{1}{3} \text{ is equivalent to } \frac{4}{12}$$

We can now add the fractions because we have written equivalent fractions with a common denominator.

$$\frac{3}{12} + \frac{4}{12} = \frac{7}{12}$$

Therefore,

$$\frac{1}{4} + \frac{1}{3} = \frac{7}{12}$$

Seven-twelfths is in simplest form because 7 and 12 do not have a whole number (other than 1) by which they are both divisible.

Q Add $\frac{3}{8}$, $\frac{5}{6}$, $\frac{1}{4}$, and $\frac{2}{3}$.

Solution: Find a number into which all denominators will divide evenly. For 8, 6, 4, and 3, the best choice is 24. Now convert each fraction to an equivalent fraction having a denominator of 24:

$$\frac{3}{8} = \frac{9}{24} \ (24 \div 8 = 3; 3 \times 3 = 9)$$

$$\frac{5}{6} = \frac{20}{24} \ (24 \div 6 = 4; 4 \times 5 = 20)$$

$$\frac{1}{4} = \frac{6}{24} \ (24 \div 4 = 6; 6 \times 1 = 6)$$

$$\frac{2}{3} = \frac{16}{24} \ (24 \div 3 = 8; 8 \times 2 = 16)$$

Now add the fractions:

$$\frac{9}{24} + \frac{20}{24} + \frac{6}{24} + \frac{16}{24} = \frac{51}{24}$$

The answer, $\frac{51}{24}$, is an improper fraction; that is, the numerator is greater than the denominator. To rename the answer to a mixed number, divide the numerator by the denominator and express the remainder as a fraction.

$$\frac{51}{24} = 51 \div 24 = 2\frac{3}{24} = 2\frac{1}{8}$$

Exercise 5

Express your answers as simple mixed numbers. Answers are on page 187.

1. $\frac{2}{4} + \frac{3}{5} + \frac{1}{2} =$
2. $\frac{6}{8} - \frac{2}{4} =$
3. $\frac{1}{3} + \frac{1}{2} =$
4. $\frac{4}{5} - \frac{3}{5} =$
5. $\frac{7}{8} + \frac{3}{4} + \frac{1}{3} =$
6. $\frac{1}{2} + \frac{1}{4} + \frac{2}{3} =$
7. $\frac{5}{6} - \frac{1}{2} =$
8. $\frac{5}{8} - \frac{1}{3} =$
9. $\frac{5}{12} + \frac{3}{4} =$
10. $\frac{8}{9} - \frac{2}{3} =$

MULTIPLYING AND DIVIDING FRACTIONS

When multiplying fractions, multiply numerators by numerators and denominators by denominators.

$$\frac{3}{5} \times \frac{4}{7} \times \frac{1}{5} = \frac{3 \times 4 \times 1}{5 \times 7 \times 5} = \frac{12}{175}$$

In multiplying fractions, try to work with numbers that are as small as possible. You can make numbers smaller by dividing out common factors. Do this by dividing the numerator of any one fraction and the denominator of any one fraction by the same number.

$$\frac{{}^{1}\cancel{3}}{\cancel{4}_{2}} \times \frac{{}^{1}\cancel{2}}{\cancel{9}_{3}} = \frac{1 \times 1}{2 \times 3} = \frac{1}{6}$$

In this case the numerator of the first fraction and the denominator of the other fraction were divided by 3, while the denominator of the first fraction and the numerator of the other fraction were divided by 2.

To divide by a fraction, multiply by the reciprocal of the divisor.

$$\frac{3}{16} \div \frac{1}{8} = \frac{3}{\cancel{16}_{2}} \times \frac{\cancel{8}^{1}}{1} = \frac{3}{2} = 1\frac{1}{2}$$

Exercise 6

Divide out common factor wherever possible and express your answers in simplest form. Answers are on page 187.

1. $\frac{4}{5} \times \frac{3}{6} =$
2. $\frac{2}{4} \times \frac{8}{12} \times \frac{7}{1} =$
3. $\frac{3}{4} \div \frac{3}{8} =$
4. $\frac{5}{2} \div \frac{3}{6} =$
5. $\frac{8}{9} \times \frac{3}{4} \times \frac{1}{2} =$
6. $\frac{7}{8} \div \frac{2}{3} =$
7. $\frac{4}{6} \times \frac{8}{12} \times \frac{10}{3} =$
8. $\frac{1}{6} \times \frac{7}{6} \times \frac{12}{3} =$
9. $\frac{3}{7} \div \frac{9}{4} =$
10. $\frac{2}{3} \div \frac{2}{3} =$

The fraction bar in a fraction means "divided by." To rename a fraction as a decimal, follow through on the division.

$$\frac{4}{5} = 4 \div 5 = .8$$

To rename a decimal as a percent, (multiply by 100, move the decimal point two places to the right) and attach a percent sign.

$$.8 = 80\%$$

Exercise 7

Rename each fraction, first as a decimal to three places, and then as a percent. Answers are on page 188.

1. $\frac{2}{4}$
2. $\frac{7}{8}$
3. $\frac{5}{6}$
4. $\frac{6}{8}$
5. $\frac{3}{4}$
6. $\frac{2}{3}$
7. $\frac{3}{5}$
8. $\frac{4}{10}$
9. $\frac{1}{4}$
10. $\frac{2}{5}$

PERCENTAGES

One percent is one one-hundredth of something. The last syllable of the word *percent, -cent,* is the name we give to one one-hundredth of a dollar.

One percent of $1.00, then, is one cent. Using decimal notation, we can write one cent as $.01, five cents as $.05, twenty-five cents as $.25, and so forth.

Twenty-five cents represents twenty-five one-hundredths of a dollar. Rather than say that something is so many one-hundredths of something else, we use the word *percent*. Twenty-five cents, then, is twenty-five *percent* of a dollar. We use the symbol % to stand for *percent*.

Percentage ("hundredths of") is a convenient and widely used way of measuring all sorts of things. By measuring in hundredths, we can be very precise and notice very small changes.

Percentage is not limited to comparing other numbers to 100. You can divide any number into hundredths and talk about percentage.

Q Find 1% of 200.

Solution: 1% of 200 is one one-hundredth of 200.

$200 \div 100 = 2$

Using decimal notation, we can calculate one percent of 200 by:

$200 \times .01 = 2$

Similarly, we can find a percentage of any number we choose by multiplying it by the correct decimal notation. For example:

Five percent of fifty:	$.05 \times 50 = 2.5$
Three percent of 150:	$.03 \times 150 = 4.5$
Ten percent of 60:	$.10 \times 60 = 6.0$

All percentage measurements are not between one percent and 100 percent. We may wish to consider less than one percent of something, especially if it is very large.

For example, if you were handed a book 1,000 pages long and were told to read one percent of it in five minutes, how much would you have to read?

$1000 \times .01 = 10$ pages

Quite an assignment! You might bargain to read one-half of one percent, or one-tenth of one percent. in the five minutes allotted to you.

Using decimal notation, we write one-tenth of one percent as .001, the decimal number for one one-thousandth. If you remember that a percent is one one-hundredth of something, you can see that one-tenth of that percent is equivalent to one one-thousandth of the whole.

NOTE

There is a relationship between decimals, fractions, and percents. The following notes will help you to convert numbers from one of these forms to another:

1. To change a % to a decimal, remove the % sign and divide by 100. This has the effect of moving the decimal point two places to the LEFT.
2. To change a decimal to a %, add the % sign and multiply by 100. This has the effect of moving the decimal point two places to the RIGHT.
3. To change a % to a fraction, remove the % sign and divide by 100. This has the effect of putting the % over 100 and reducing the resulting fraction.
4. To change a fraction to %, add the % sign and multiply by 100.

In percent notation, one-tenth of one percent is written as .1%. On high school entrance exams, students often mistakenly think that .1% is equal to .1. As you know, .1% is really equal to .001.

Sometimes we are concerned with more than 100% of something. But, you may ask, since 100% constitutes all of something, how can we speak of *more* than all of it?

Where things are growing, or increasing in size or amount, we may want to compare their new size to the size they once were. For example, suppose we measured the heights of three plants to be 6 inches, 9 inches, and 12 inches one week, and discover a week later that first plant is still 6 inches tall but the second and third ones are now 18 inches tall.

The 6-inch plant grew *zero percent* because it didn't grow at all.

The second plant *added 100%* to its size. It doubled in height.

The third plant *added 50%* to its height.

We can also say:

The first plant is 100% of its original height.

The second plant grew to 200% of its original height.

The third plant grew to 150% of its original height.

Here are some common percentage and fractional equivalents you should remember:

Ten percent (10%) is one tenth $\left(\frac{1}{10}\right)$, or .10.
Twelve and one-half percent (12.5%) is one eighth $\left(\frac{1}{8}\right)$, or .125.
Twenty percent (20%) is one fifth $\left(\frac{1}{5}\right)$, or .20.
Twenty-five percent (25%) is one quarter $\left(\frac{1}{4}\right)$, or .25.
Thirty-three and one-third percent ($33\frac{1}{3}\%$) is one third $\left(\frac{1}{3}\right)$ or .333.
Fifty percent (50%) is one half $\left(\frac{1}{2}\right)$, or .50.
Sixty-six and two-thirds percent ($66\frac{2}{3}\%$) is two thirds $\left(\frac{2}{3}\right)$, or .666.
Seventy-five percent (75%) is three quarters $\left(\frac{3}{4}\right)$, or .75.

Warning: When solving problems involving percentages, be careful of common errors:

- **Read the notation carefully.** .50% is *not* fifty percent, but one-half of one percent.
- When solving problems for percentage increases or decreases in size, **read the problem carefully.**
- **Use common sense.** If you wish to find less than 100% of a number, your result will be smaller than the number you started with. For example, 43% of 50 is less than 50.
- Using common sense works in the other direction as well. For example, 70 is 40% of what number?

The number you are looking for must be larger than 70, since 70 is only $\frac{40}{100}$ of it. Moreover, you can estimate that the number you are looking for will be a little more than twice as large as 70, since 70 is almost half (50%) of that number.

To find a percent of a number, rename the percent as a decimal and multiply the number by it.

Q What is 5% of 80?

Solution: 5% of 80 = $80 \times .05 = 4$

To find out what a number is when a percent of it is given, rename the percent as a decimal and divide the given number by it.

Q 5 is 10% of what number?

Solution: $5 \div .10 = 50$

To find what percent one number is of another number, create a fraction by placing the part over the whole. Simplify the fraction if possible, then rename it as a decimal (remember: the fraction bar means divided by, so divide the numerator by the denominator) and rename the answer as a percent by multiplying by 100, moving the decimal point two places to the right.

Q 4 is what percent of 80?

Solution: $\frac{4}{80} = \frac{1}{20} = .05 = 5\%$

Exercise 8

Solve each of the following. Answers are on page 188.

1. 10% of 32 =
2. 8 is 25% of what number?
3. 12 is what percent of 24?
4. 20% of 360 is
5. 5 is what percent of 60?
6. 12 is 8% of what number?
7. 6% of 36 =
8. 25 is 5% of what number?
9. 70 is what percent of 140?
10. What percent of 100 is 19?

ALGEBRA

If you are finishing the eighth grade this year, you might not yet have had a formal algebra class. Nevertheless, you have probably used algebraic terms and expressions, and you have probably solved simple equations. This section will review the skills you have acquired so far and will show you the kinds of questions you can expect to find on a high school entrance examination.

SIGNED NUMBERS

The number line exists to both sides of zero. Each positive number on the right of zero has a negative counterpart to the left of zero. The number line below shows the location of some pairs of numbers (+4, –4; +2, –2; +1, –1).

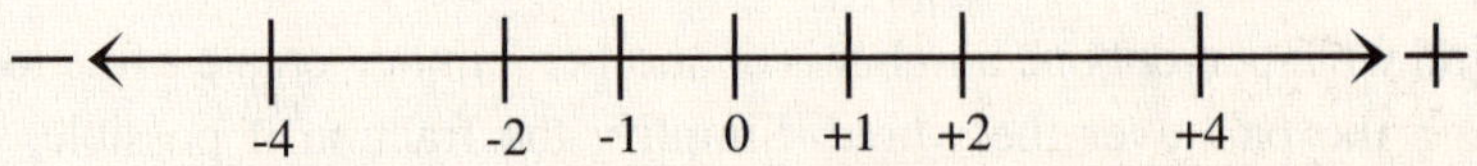

Because each number of a pair is located the same distance from zero (though in different directions), each has the same absolute value. Two vertical bars symbolize absolute value:

$|+4| = |-4| = 4$

The absolute value of + 4 equals the absolute value of –4. Both are equivalent to 4. If you think of absolute value as the distance from zero, regardless of direction, you will understand it easily. The absolute value of any number, positive or negative, is always expressed as a positive number.

ADDITION OF SIGNED NUMBERS

When two oppositely signed numbers having the same absolute value are added, the sum is zero.

$$(+10) + (-10) = 0$$

$$(-1.5) + (+1.5) = 0$$

$$(-.010) + (+.010) = 0$$

$$(+\frac{3}{4}) + (-\frac{3}{4}) = 0$$

If one of the two oppositely signed numbers is greater in absolute value, the sum is equal to the amount of that excess and carries the same sign as the number having the greater absolute value.

$$(+2) + (-1) = +1$$

$$(+8) + (-9) = -1$$

$$(-2.5) + (+2.0) = -.5$$

$$(-\frac{3}{4}) + (+\frac{1}{2}) = -\frac{1}{4}$$

TIP

To add signed numbers with the same sign, add the magnitudes of the numbers and keep the same sign. To add signed numbers with different signs, subtract the magnitudes of the numbers and use the sign of the number with the greater magnitude.

Exercise 9

Answers are on page 188.

1. $(+5) + (+8) =$
2. $(+6) + (-3) =$
3. $(+4) + (-12) =$
4. $(-7) + (+2) =$
5. $(-21) + (-17) =$
6. $(-9) + (-36) =$
7. $(+31) + (-14) =$
8. $(-16.3) + (-12.5) =$
9. $(-8\frac{1}{2}) + (+4\frac{1}{4}) =$
10. $(+66) + (-66) =$

SUBTRACTION OF SIGNED NUMBERS

Subtraction is the operation that finds the difference between two numbers, including the difference between signed numbers.

When subtracting signed numbers, it is helpful to refer to the number line.

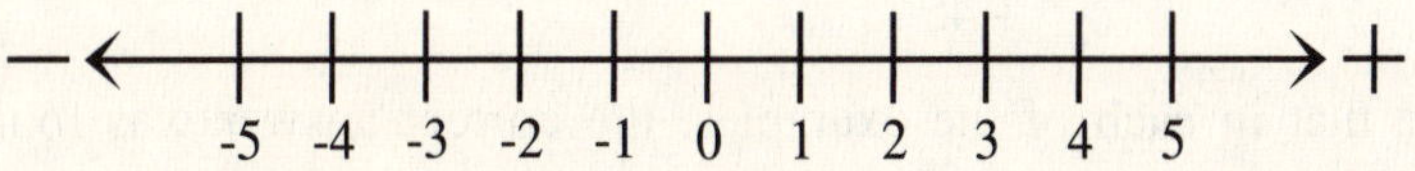

NOTE

Change the sign of the number being subtracted and follow the rules for addition.

For example, if we wish to subtract +2 from +5, we can use the number line to see that the difference is +3. We give the sign to the difference that represents the direction we are moving along the number line from the number being subtracted to the number from which you are subtracting. In this case, because we are subtracting +2 from +5, we count three units in a positive direction from +2 to +5 on the number line.

When subtracting signed numbers:

- The distance between the two numbers gives you the absolute value of the difference.
- The direction you have to move from the number being subtracted to get to the number from which you are subtracting gives you the sign of the difference.

Q Subtract –3 from +5.

Solution: Distance on the number line between –3 and +5 is 8 units. Direction is from negative to positive—a positive direction. Answer is +8.

Q Subtract –6 from –8.

Solution: Distance on number line between –6 and –8 is 2 units. Direction is from –6 to –8 — a negative direction. Answer is –2.

Q Subtract +1.30 from –2.70.

Solution: Distance between them on the number line is 4.0. Direction is from +1.30 to –2.70 — a negative direction. Answer is –4.0.

A quick way to subtract signed numbers accurately involves placing the numbers in columns, reversing the sign of the number being subtracted and then adding the two.

Q Subtract +26 from +15.

Solution:

$$\begin{array}{r} +15 \\ \underline{-\,+26} \end{array} = \begin{array}{r} +15 \\ \underline{-26} \\ -11 \end{array}$$

Q Subtract –35 from +10.

Solution:

$$\begin{array}{r} +10 \\ -\,\underline{-35} \end{array} = \begin{array}{r} +10 \\ \underline{+35} \\ +45 \end{array}$$

Notice that in each of the examples, the correct answer was found by reversing the sign of the number being subtracted and then adding.

Exercise 10

Answers are on page 188.

1. $(-6) - (-12) =$
2. $(+17) - (-8) =$
3. $(+45) - (+62) =$
4. $(-34) - (+21) =$
5. $(+4) - (-58) =$
6. $(+75) - (+27) =$
7. $(-12.6) - (-5.3) =$
8. $(-15\frac{1}{4}) - (+26\frac{1}{2}) =$
9. $(-35) - (+35) =$
10. $(+56.1) - (+56.7) =$

MULTIPLICATION OF SIGNED NUMBERS

Signed numbers are multiplied as any other numbers would be, with the following exceptions:

The product of two negative numbers is positive.

$(-3) \times (-6) = +18$

The product of two positive numbers is positive.

$(+3.05) \times (+6) = +18.30$

The product of a negative and positive number is negative.

$(+4\frac{1}{2}) \times (-3) = -13\frac{1}{2}$

$(+1) \times (-1) \times (+1) = -1$

CAUTION

Forgetting a sign will make your answer wrong. If there are an odd number of negative signs, the product is negative. An even number of negative signs gives you a positive product.

Exercise 11

Answers are on page 188.

1. $(+5) \times (+8) =$
2. $(+12) \times (-3) =$
3. $(-6) \times (-21) =$
4. $(-4) \times (-10) =$
5. $(+3.3) \times (-5.8) =$
6. $(-7.5) \times (+4.2) =$
7. $(-6\frac{1}{2}) \times (-7\frac{1}{4})$
8. $(+9) \times (-1) =$
9. $(0) \times (-5.7) =$
10. $(-12) \times (-12) =$

NOTE
If the signs are the same, the quotient is positive. If the signs are different, the quotient is negative.

DIVISION OF SIGNED NUMBERS

As with multiplication, the division of signed numbers requires you to observe three simple rules:

When dividing a positive number by a negative number, the result is negative.

$(+6) \div (-3) = -2$

When dividing a negative number by a positive number, the result is negative.

$(-6) \div (+3) = -2$

When dividing a negative number by a negative number or a positive number by a positive number, the result is positive.

$(-6) \div (-3) = +2$

$(+6) \div (+3) = +2$

Exercise 12

Answers are on page 188.

1. $(+3) \div (-1) =$
2. $(+36) \div (+12) =$
3. $(-45) \div (-9) =$
4. $(-75) \div (+3) =$
5. $(+5.6) \div (-.7) =$
6. $(-3.5) \div (-5) =$
7. $(+6\frac{1}{2}) \div (+3\frac{1}{4}) =$
8. $(-8.2) \div (-1) =$
9. $(+12\frac{1}{2}) \div (-12\frac{1}{2}) =$
10. $(0) \div (-19.6) =$

EQUATIONS

An equation is an equality. The values on either side of the equal sign in an equation must be equal. In order to learn the value of an unknown in an equation, do the same thing to both sides of the equation so as to leave the unknown on one side of the equal sign and its value on the other side.

Q $x - 2 = 8$

Add 2 to both sides of the equation:

$$x - 2 + 2 = 8 + 2$$

$$x = 10$$

Q $5x = 25$

Divide both sides of the equation by 5:

$$\frac{{}^{1}\not{5}x}{\not{5}_{1}} = \frac{25}{5}$$

$$x = 5$$

Q $y + 9 = 15$

Subtract 9 from both sides of the equation:

$$y + 9 - 9 = 15 - 9$$

$$y = 6$$

Q $a \div 4 = 48$

Multiply both sides of the equation by 4:

$${}^{1}\not{4}\left(\frac{a}{\not{4}_{1}}\right) = 48 \times 4$$

$$a = 192$$

Sometimes more than one step is required to solve an equation.

Q $6a \div 4 = 48$

First, multiply both sides of the equation by 4:

$$\frac{6a}{4} \times \frac{4}{1} = 48 \times 4$$

$$6a = 192$$

Then divide both sides of the equation by 6:

$$\frac{{}^{1}\not{6}a}{\not{6}_{1}} = \frac{192}{6}$$

$$a = 32$$

Exercise 13

Solve for x. Answers on page 188.

1. $x + 13 = 25$
2. $4x = 84$
3. $x - 5 = 28$
4. $x \div 9 = 4$
5. $3x + 2 = 14$
6. $\frac{x}{4} - 2 = 4$
7. $10x - 27 = 73$
8. $2x \div 4 = 13$
9. $8x + 9 = 81$
10. $2x \div 11 = 6$

GEOMETRY

CAUTION

Don't confuse the two formulas for calculating the circumference and the area of circles. A good way to keep them straight is to remember the square in πr^2. It should remind you that area must be in square units.

AREA OF PLANE FIGURES

Area is the space enclosed by a plane (flat) figure. A rectangle is a plane figure with four right angles. Opposite sides of a rectangle are of equal length and are parallel to each other. To find the area of a rectangle, multiply the length of the base of the rectangle by the length of its height. Area is always expressed in square units.

$A = bh$

$A = 9 \text{ ft.} \times 3 \text{ ft.}$

$A = 27 \text{ sq. ft.}$

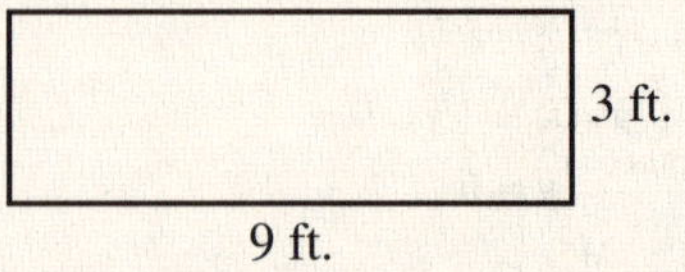

A square is a rectangle in which all four sides are the same length. The area of a square is found by squaring the length of one side, which is exactly the same as multiplying the square's length by its width.

$A = s^2$

$A = 4 \text{ in.} \times 4 \text{ in.}$

$A = 16 \text{ sq. in.}$

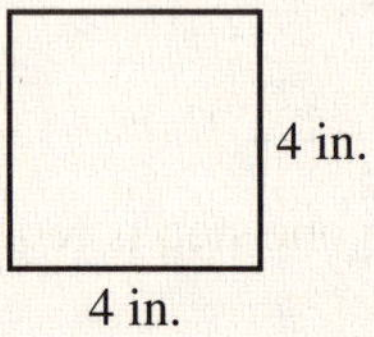

A triangle is a three–sided plane figure. The area of a triangle is found by multiplying the base by the altitude (height) and dividing by two.

$A = \frac{1}{2}bh$

$A = \frac{1}{2}(9 \text{ in.})(5 \text{ in.}) = \frac{45}{2}$

$A = 22\frac{1}{2} \text{ sq. in.}$

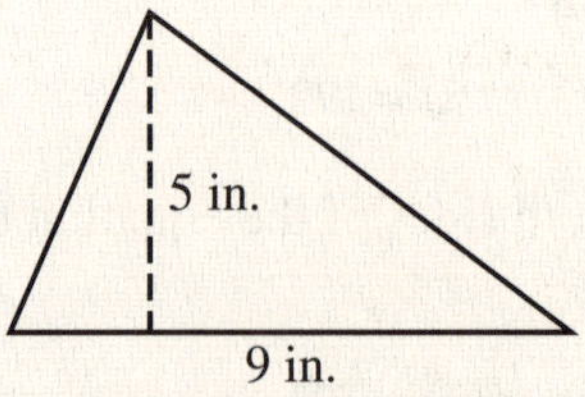

A circle is a perfectly round plane figure. The distance from the center of a circle to its rim is its radius. The distance from one edge to the other through the center is its diameter. The diameter is twice the length of the radius.

Pi(π) is a mathematical value equal to approximately 3.14 or $\frac{22}{7}$. Pi(π) is frequently used in calculations involving circles. The area of a circle is found by squaring the radius and multiplying it by π. You may leave the area in terms of pi unless you are told what value to assign π.

$A = \pi r^2$

$A = \pi (4 \text{ cm.})^2$

$A = 16\pi \text{ sq. cm.}$

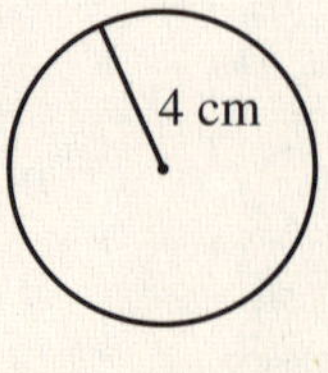

Exercise 14

Find the area of each figure. Answers are on page 189.

1.

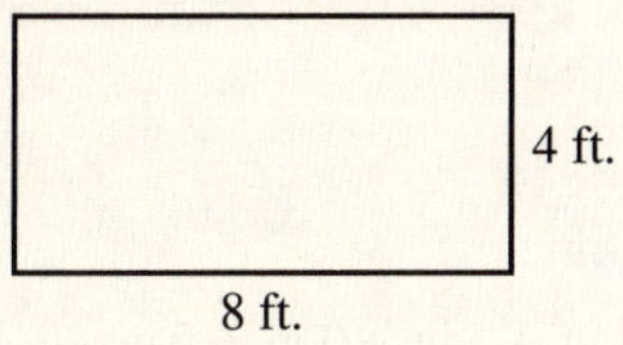

2.

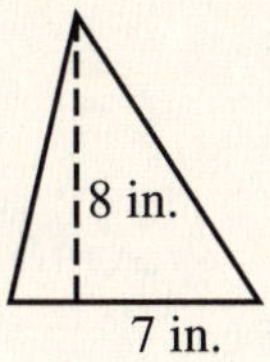

3.

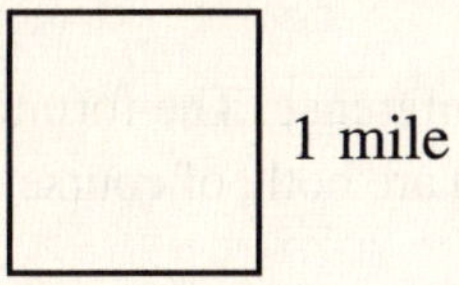

4.

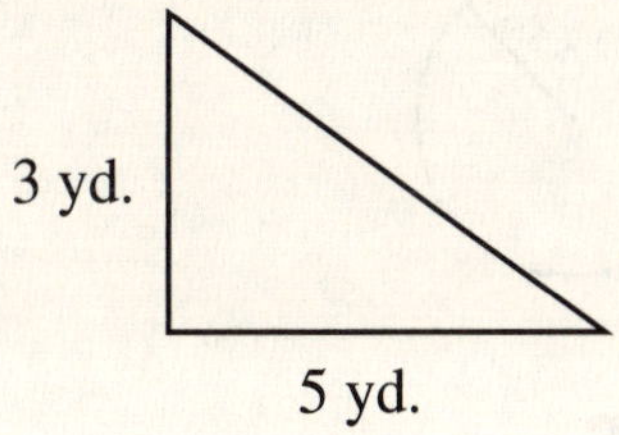

5.

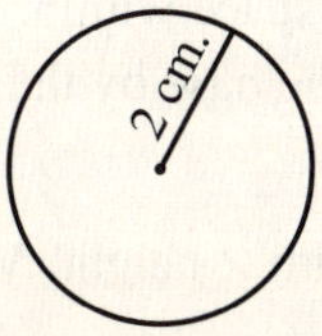

6.

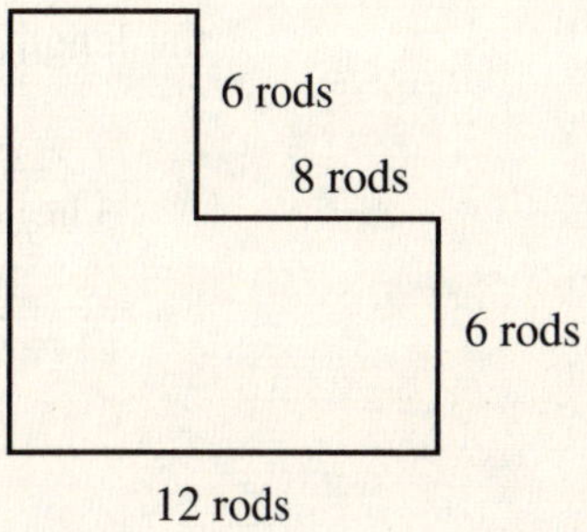

7.

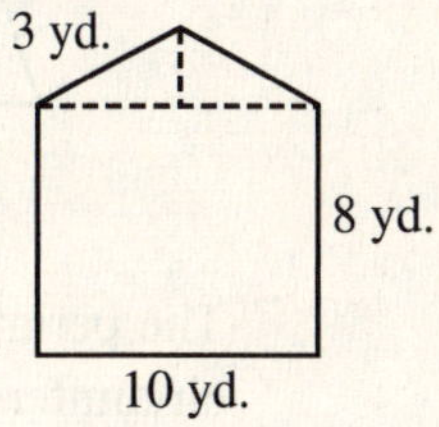

8.

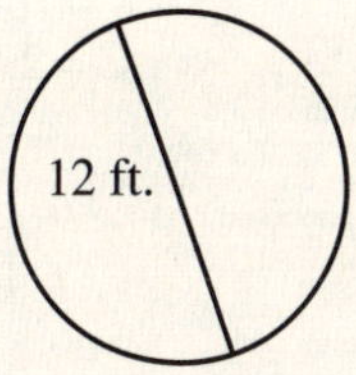

9.

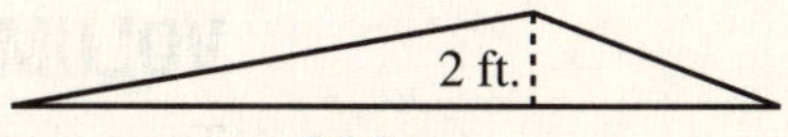

10.

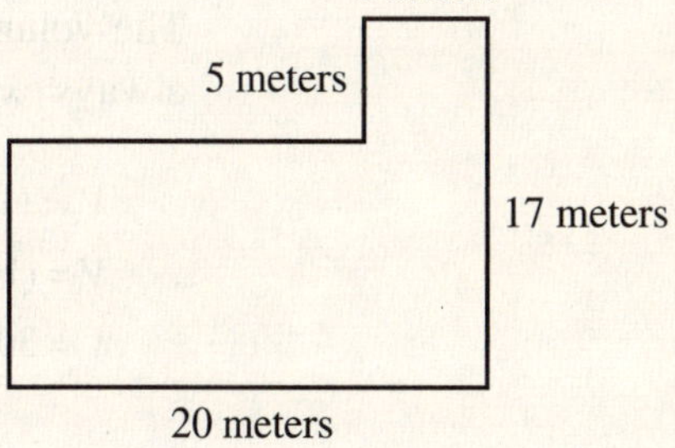

PERIMETER OF PLANE FIGURES

The *perimeter* of a plane figure is the distance around the outside. To find the perimeter of a polygon (a plane figure bounded by straight lines) just add the lengths of the sides.

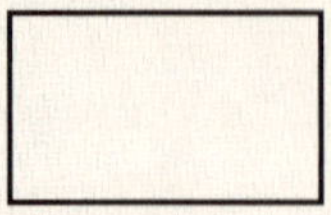

$P = 3$ in. + 5 in. + 3 in. + 5 in.
= 16 in.

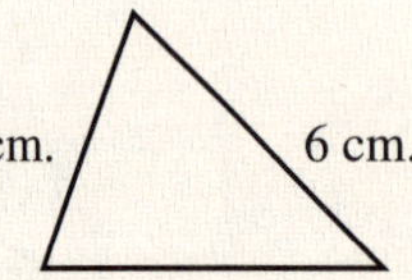

$P =$ 4 cm. + 6 cm. + 5 cm.
= 15 cm.

The perimeter of a circle is called the circumference. The formula for the circumference of a circle is πd or $2\pi r$, which are both, of course, the same thing.

$C = 2 \times 3 \times \pi = 6\pi$

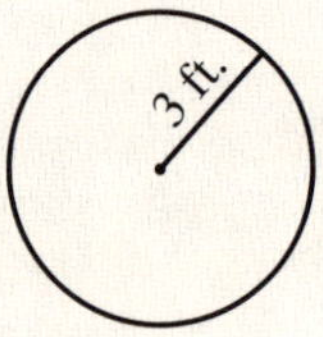

VOLUME OF SOLID FIGURES

The volume of a solid figure is the measure of the space within. To figure the volume of a solid figure, multiply the area of the base by the height or depth.

The volume of a rectangular solid is length × width × height. Volume is always expressed in cubic units.

$V = lwh$

$V =$ (10 in.) (6 in.) (5 in.)

$V =$ 300 cu. in.

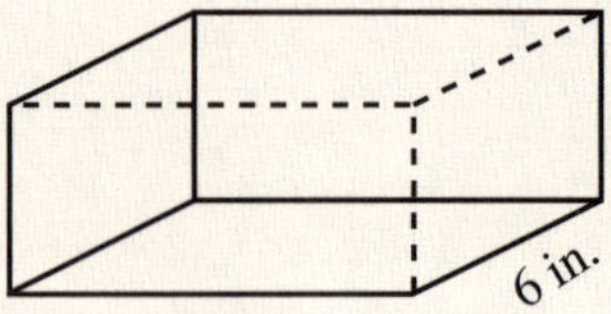

The volume of a cube is the cube of one side.

$V = s^3$

$V = (3 \text{ ft.})^3$

$V =$ 27 cu. ft.

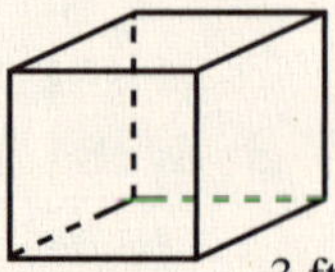

The volume of a cylinder is the area of the circular base (πr^2) times the height.

$V = \pi r^2 h$

$V = \pi(4 \text{ in.})^2 (5 \text{ in.})$

$V = \pi(16)(5) = 80\pi$ cu. in.

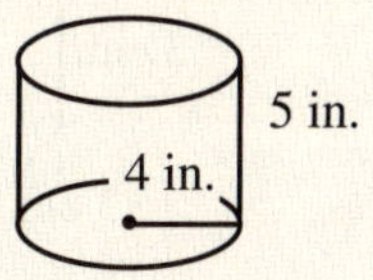

Exercise 15

Answers are on page 189.

1. Find the perimeter.

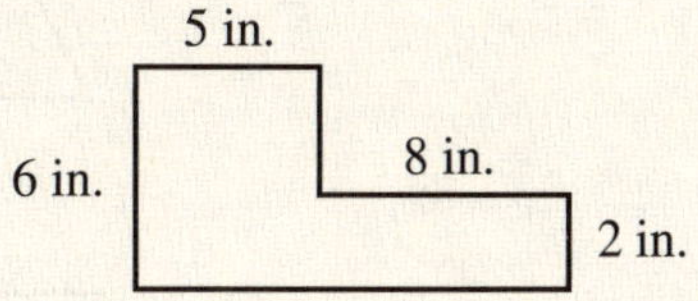

2. Find the volume.

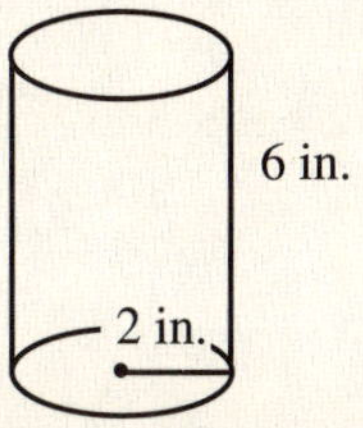

3. Find the circumference.

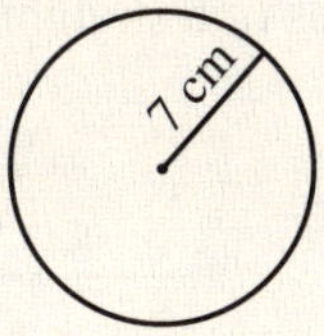

4. Find the volume.

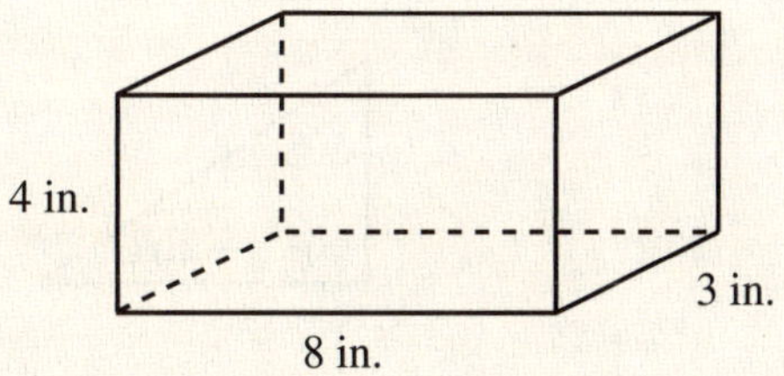

5. Find the volume.

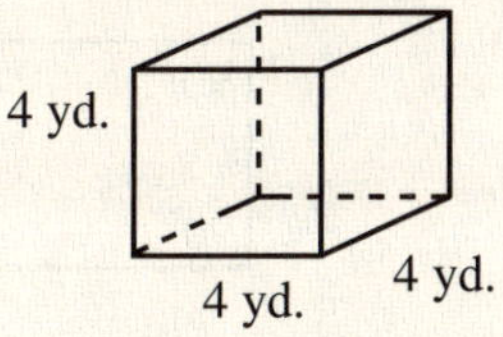

6. Find the perimeter.

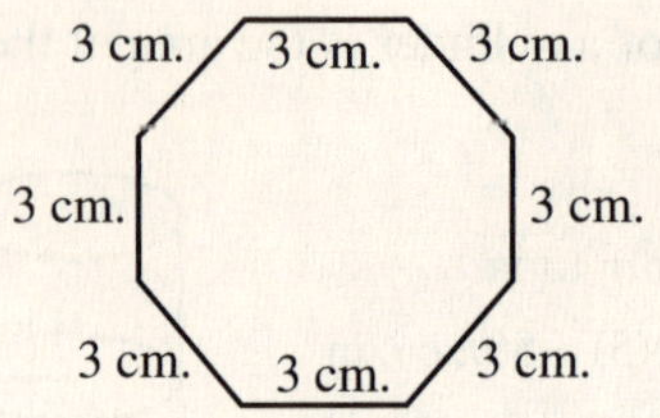

7. Find the perimeter.

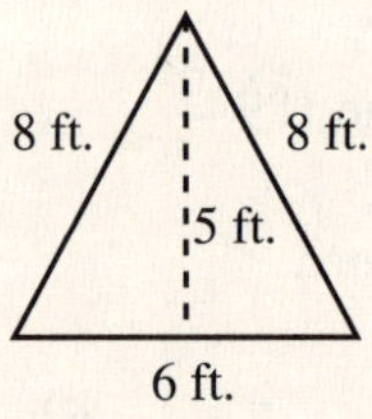

8. Find the perimeter.

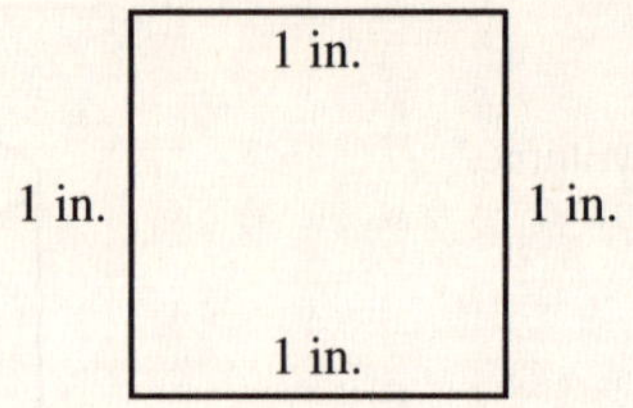

ANGLES

The sum of the angles of a straight line is 180°.

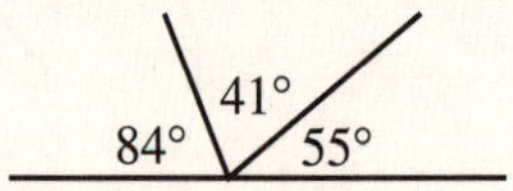

The sum of the angles of a triangle is 180°.

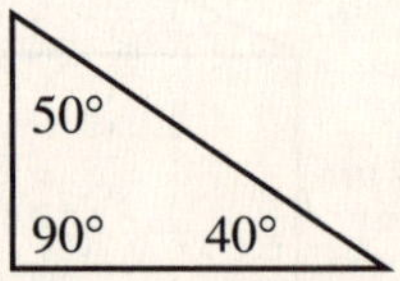

The sum of the angles of a rectangle is 360°.

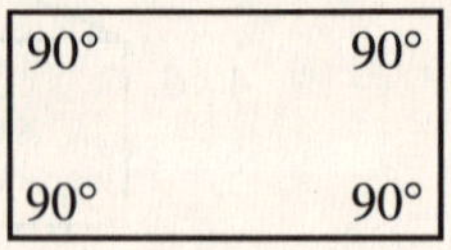

The sum of the angles of a circle is 360°.

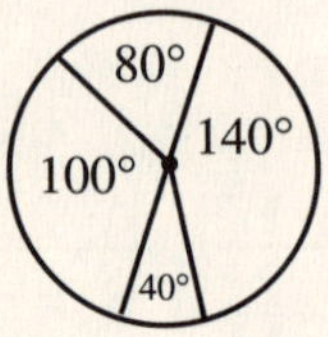

The sum of the angles of a polygon of n sides is $(n - 2)180°$.

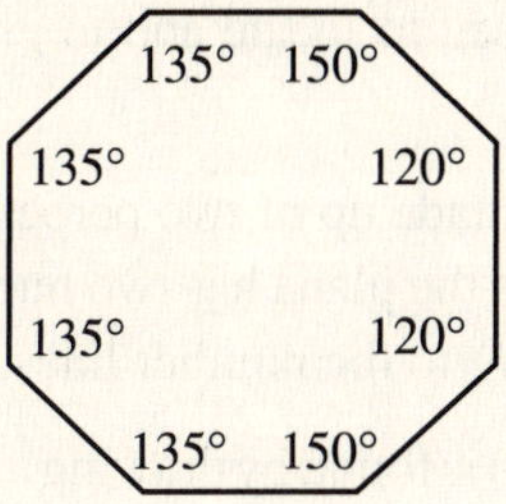

$(8 - 2)(180°) =$

$6 \times 180° = 1080°$

Exercise 16

What is the size of the unlabeled angle? Answers are on page 190.

1.

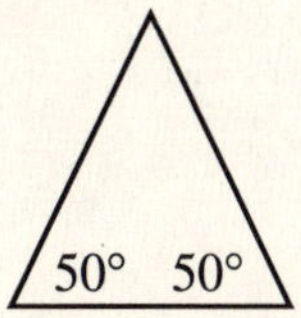

2.

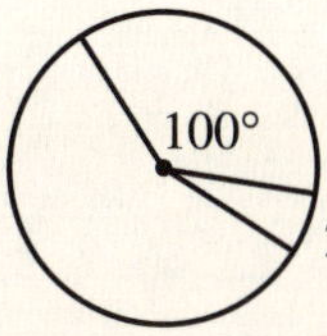

3

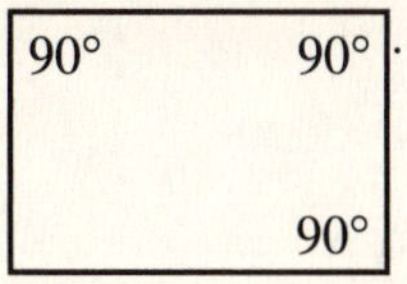

4.

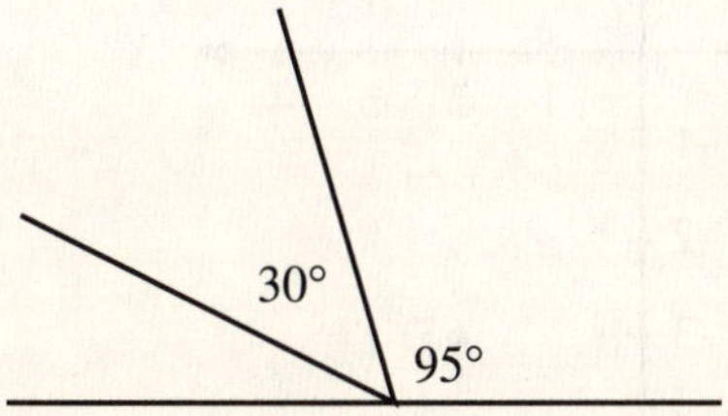

5.

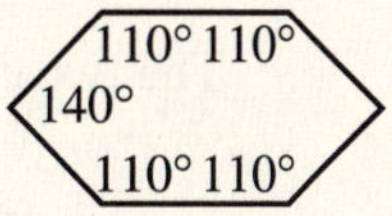

6.

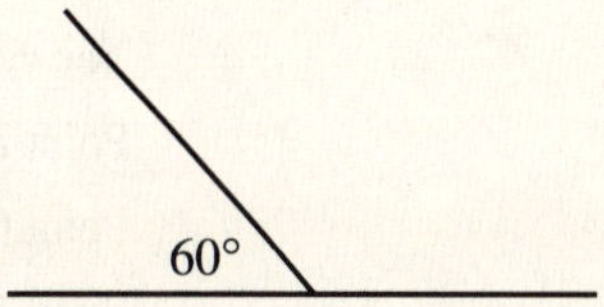

7.

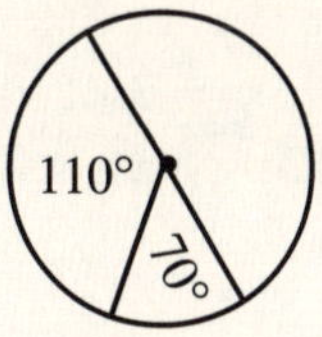

8.

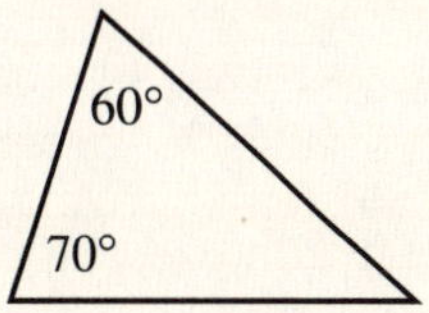

COORDINATE GEOMETRY

Coordinate geometry is used to locate and to graph points and lines on a plane.

The coordinate system is made up of two perpendicular number lines that intersect at 0. Any point on the plane has two numbers, or coordinates, that indicate its location relative to the number lines.

The *x*-coordinate (abscissa) is found by drawing a vertical line from the point to the horizontal number line (the *x*-axis). The number found on the *x*-axis is the abscissa.

The *y*-coordinate (ordinate) is found by drawing a horizontal line from the point to the vertical number line (the *y*-axis). The number found on the *y*-axis is the ordinate.

The two coordinates are always written in the order *(x, y)*.

The *x*-coordinate of point A is 3.

The *y*-coordinate of point A is 2.

The coordinates of point A are given by the ordered pair (3, 2).

Point B has coordinates (–1, 4).

Point C has coordinates (–4, –3).

Point D has coordinates (2, –3).

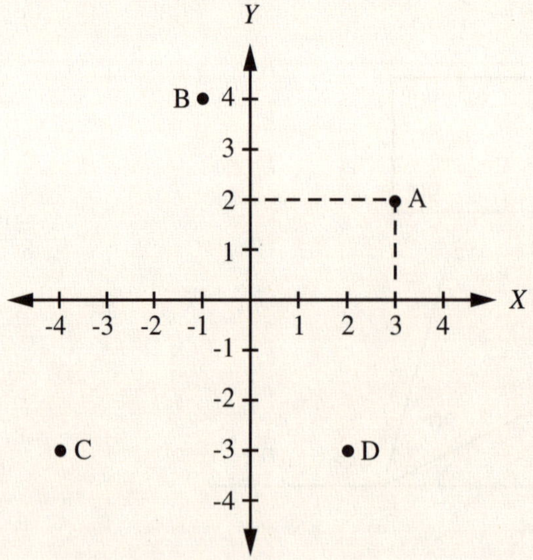

To graph a point whose coordinates are given, first locate the *x*-coordinate on the *x*-axis, then from that position move vertically the number of spaces indicated by the *y*-coordinate.

To graph (4, –2), locate 4 on the *x*-axis, then move –2 spaces vertically (2 spaces down) to find the given point.

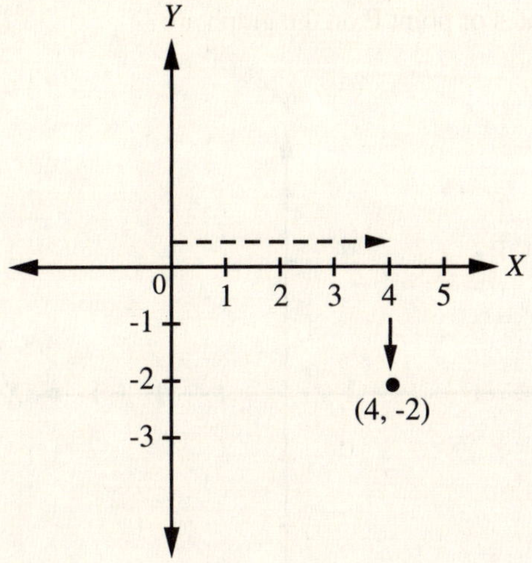

The point at which the *x*-axis and the *y*-axis meet has coordinates (0, 0) and is called the origin. Any point on the *y*-axis has 0 as its *x*-coordinate. Any point on the *x*-axis has 0 as its *y*-coordinate.

Exercise 17

Answers are on page 190.

1. In the graph below, the coordinates of point A are

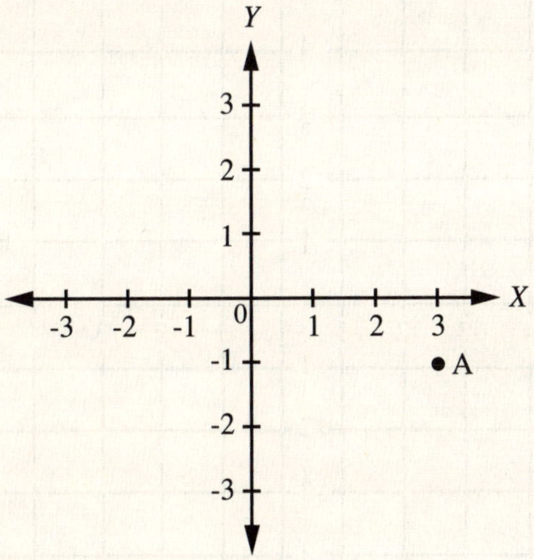

2. The coordinates of point P on the graph are

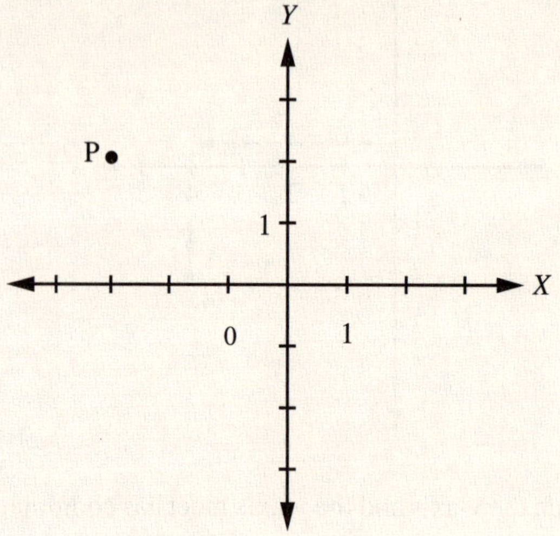

3. Which point is named by the ordered pair (5, 1)?

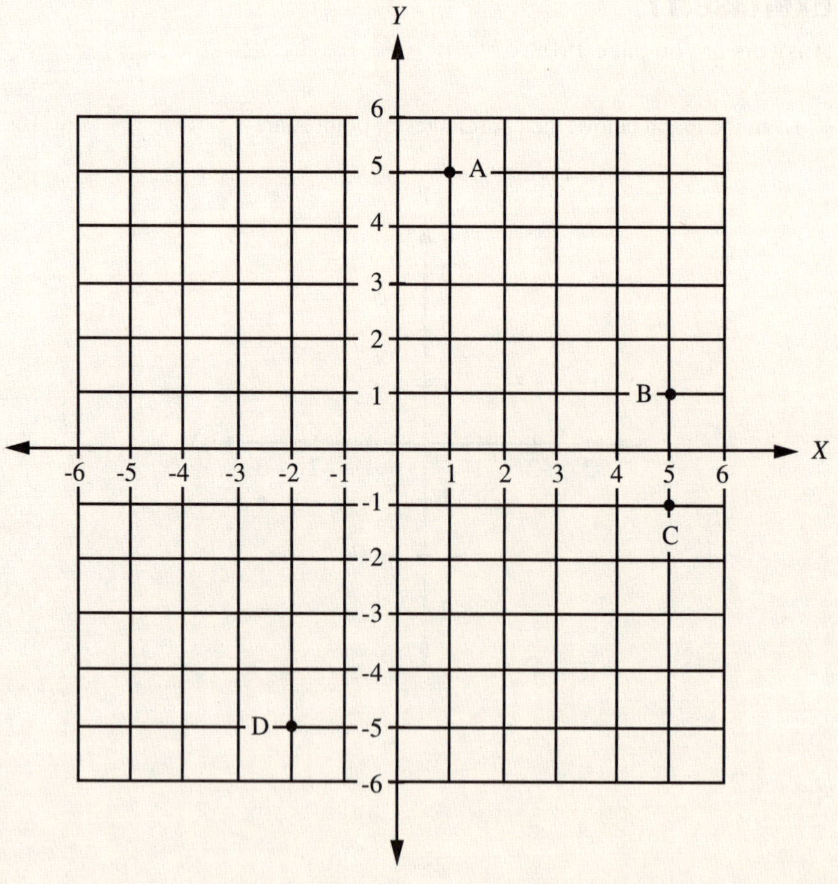

4. Which point might possibly have the coordinates (2, –3)?

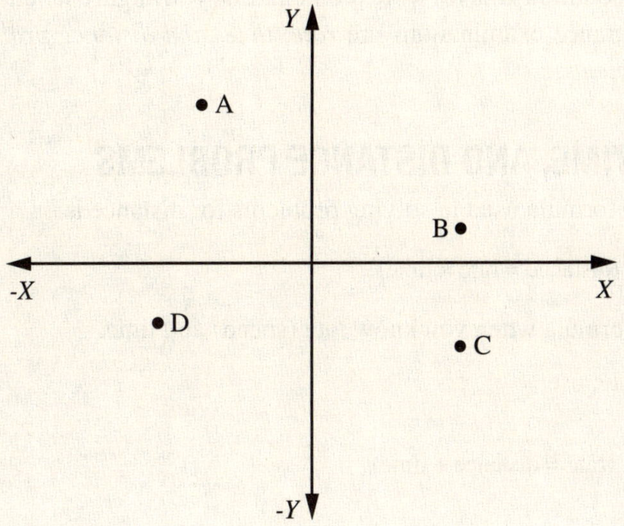

5. The point with the coordinates (3, 0) is

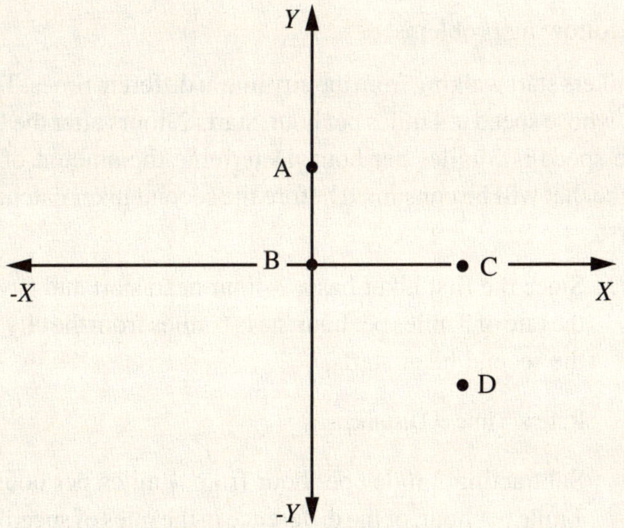

TIP
When solving word problems, remember to read the question carefully. The information given to you is important, but also examine the problem for information that is **not** given to you. The unknown information can be represented in the problem as *x*.

WORD PROBLEMS

Two very common kinds of word problems that you might encounter on high school entrance examinations are *rate, time, and distance problems* and *work problems*.

RATE, TIME, AND DISTANCE PROBLEMS

The basic formula used in solving problems for distance is:

$d = rt$ (distance = rate × time)

Use this formula when you know rate (speed) and time.

To find rate, use:

$r = \frac{d}{t}$ (rate = distance ÷ time)

To find time, use:

$t = \frac{d}{r}$ (time = distance ÷ rate)

Study the following problems:

Q Two hikers start walking from the city line at different times. The second hiker, whose speed is 4 miles per hour, starts 2 hours after the first hiker, whose speed is 3 miles per hour. Determine the amount of time and distance that will be consumed before the second hiker catches up with the first.

Solution 1: Since the first hiker has a 2–hour head start and is walking at the rate of 3 miles per hour, he is 6 miles from the city line when the second hiker starts.

Rate × Time = Distance

Subtracting 3 miles per hour from 4 miles per hour gives us 1 mile per hour, or the difference in the rates of speed of the two hikers. In other words, the second hiker gains one mile on the first hiker in every hour.

Because there is a 6–mile difference to cut down and it is cut down one mile every hour, it is clear that the second hiker will need 6 hours to overtake his companion.

In this time he will have traveled 4 × 6 = 24 miles. The first hiker will have been walking 8 hours, since he had a 2–hour head start, 8 × 3 = 24 miles.

or

Solution 2: One excellent way to solve distance (or mixture) problems is to organize all of the data in a chart. For distance problems, make columns for Rate, Time, and Distance and separate lines for each moving object. In the problem about the two hikers, the chart technique works like this:

STEP 1: Draw the chart.

	Rate ×	Time =	Distance
Hiker 1			
Hiker 2			

STEP 2: Since the problem states that Hiker 1 is traveling at 3 miles per hour and Hiker 2 is traveling at 4 miles per hour, enter these two figures in the Rate column.

	Rate ×	Time =	Distance
Hiker 1	3 mph		
Hiker 2	4 mph		

STEP 3: The problem does not tell us how long each hiker traveled, but it does say that Hiker 1 started 2 hours before Hiker 2. Therefore, if we use the unknown x to represent the number of hours Hiker 2 traveled, we can set Hiker 1's time as $x + 2$. Enter these two figures in the Time column.

	Rate ×	Time =	Distance
Hiker 1	3 mph	$x + 2$	
Hiker 2	4 mph	x	

STEP 4: Using the formula $D = R \times T$, we can easily find each hiker's distance by multiplying the figures for rate and time already in the chart.

For Hiker 1: $3(x + 2) = 3x + 6$

For Hiker 2: $4(x) = 4x$

	Rate ×	Time =	Distance
Hiker 1	3 mph	$x + 2$	$3x + 6$
Hiker 2	4 mph	x	$4x$

STEP 5: When the two hikers meet, each will have covered the same distance. Using this information, we can set up an equation:

Distance covered by Hiker 1		Distance covered by Hiker 2
$3x + 6$	$=$	$4x$

Solving this equation for x, we find that $x = 6$. This means that Hiker 1 has walked for 6 + 2 = 8 hours when Hiker 2 catches up to him.

STEP 6: Because Hiker 1 started 2 hours earlier than Hiker 2, he will have walked for 6 hours to catch up to Hiker 1.

STEP 7: Using this information, we can determine that Hiker 1 walked 8 hours at 3 miles per hour to cover 24 miles. Hiker 2 walked for 6 hours at 4 miles per hour to cover the same 24 miles.

Let's try another example: The same two hikers start walking toward each other along a road connecting two cities that are 60 miles apart. Their speeds are the same as in the preceding example, 3 and 4 miles per hour respectively. How much time will elapse before they meet?

Solution 1: In each hour of travel toward each other, the hikers will cut down a distance equal to the sum of their speeds, $3+4=7$ miles per hour. To meet they must cut down 60 miles, and at 7 miles per hour this would be:

$$\frac{D}{R} = T \frac{60}{7} = 8\frac{4}{7} \text{ hours.} \qquad \text{or}$$

Solution 2: In this problem we know that the distance traveled by Hiker 1 plus the distance traveled by Hiker 2 equals 60 miles and that the two hikers will have been traveling for the same length of time when they meet. Therefore, we set up an equation to represent this information and solve for x to find the time that will have elapsed before the two hikers meet:

$$3x + 4x = 60$$
$$7x = 60$$
$$x = 8\frac{4}{7}$$

The problem might also have asked: "How much distance must the slower hiker cover before the two hikers meet?" In such a case, we should have gone through the same steps plus one additional step:

The time consumed before meeting was $8\frac{4}{7}$ hours. To find the distance covered by the slower hiker, we merely multiply his rate by the time elapsed.

$$\text{R} \times \text{T} = \text{D} \qquad 3 \times 8\frac{4}{7} = 25\frac{5}{7}$$

Exercise 18

Answers begin on page 190.

1. A sailor on leave drove to Yosemite Park from his home at 60 miles per hour. On his trip home, his rate was 10 miles per hour less, and the trip took one hour longer. How far is his home from the park?

2. Two cars leave a restaurant at the same time and travel along a straight highway in opposite directions. At the end of three hours they are 300 miles apart. Find the rate of the slower car if one car travels at a rate 20 miles per hour faster than the other.

3. At 10:30 A.M., a passenger train and a freight train left from stations that were 405 miles apart and traveled toward each other. The rate of the passenger train was 45 miles per hour faster than that of the freight train. If they passed each other at 1:30 P.M., how fast was the passenger train traveling?

4. Susie left her home at 11 A.M. traveling along Route 1 at 30 miles per hour. At 1 P.M., her brother Richard left home and started after her on the same road at 45 miles per hour. At what time did Richard catch up to Susie?

5. How far can a man drive into the country if he drives out at 40 miles per hour, returns over the same road at 30 miles per hour, and spends 8 hours away from home including a one–hour stop for lunch?

6. At 10 A.M., two cars started traveling toward each other from towns 287 miles apart. They passed each other at 1:30 P.M. If the rate of the faster car exceeded the rate of the slower car by 6 miles per hour, find the rate in miles per hour of the faster car.

7. A driver covered 350 miles in 8 hours. Before noon he averaged 50 miles per hour, but after noon he averaged only 40 miles per hour. At what time did he leave?

8. At 3 P.M., a plane left Kennedy Airport for Los Angeles traveling at 600 mph. At 3:30 P.M., another plane left the same airport on the same route traveling at 650 mph. At what time did the second plane overtake the first?

9. A soldier with a 24-hour pass and no special plans left the base at 10 A.M. and walked out into the country at 4 miles per hour. He returned on the same road at 2 miles per hour. If he arrived back at the base at 4 P.M., how many miles into the country did he walk?

10. Two cars leave the gas station at the same time and proceed in the same direction along the same route. One car averages 36 miles per hour and the other 31 miles per hour. In how many hours will the faster car be 30 miles ahead of the slower car?

WORK PROBLEMS

Work problems generally involve two or more workers doing a job at different rates. The aim of work problems is to predict how long it will take to complete a job if the number of workers is increased or decreased. Work problems may also involve determining how fast pipes can fill or empty tanks. In solving pipe and tank problems, you must think of the pipes as workers.

In most work problems, a job is broken up into several parts, each representing a fractional portion of the entire job. For each part represented, the numerator should represent the time actually spent working, while the denominator should represent the total time needed for the worker to do the job alone. The sum of all the individual fractions must be 1 if the job is completed. The easiest way to understand this procedure is to carefully study the examples that follow. By following the step-by-step solutions, you will learn how to make your own fractions to solve the practice problems that follow and the problems you may find on your exam.

Q If A does a job in six days, and B does the same job in three days, how long will it take the two of them, working together, to do the job?

STEP 1: Write the fractions as follows.

$$\frac{\text{Time actually spent}}{\text{Time needed to do entire job alone}} \qquad \overset{\text{A}}{\frac{x}{6\text{ days}}} + \overset{\text{B}}{\frac{x}{3\text{ days}}} = 1$$

The variable x represents the amount of time each worker will work when both work together. 1 represents the completed job.

STEP 2: Multiply all the terms by the same number (in this case 6) in order to clear the fractions so as to work with whole numbers.

$$x + 2x = 6$$

STEP 3: Solve for x.

$$3x = 60$$
$$x = 2\text{ days}$$

Working together, A and B will get the job done in 2 days.

Let's try another example: A and B, working together, do a job in $4\frac{1}{2}$ days. B, working alone, is able to do the job in 10 days. How long would it take A to do the job working alone?

Solution:

STEP 1: Write the fractions as follows.

$$\frac{\text{Time actually spent}}{\text{Time needed to do entire job alone}} \qquad \overset{\text{A}}{\frac{4.5\text{ days}}{x}} + \overset{\text{B}}{\frac{4.5\text{ days}}{10\text{ days}}} = 1$$

STEP 2: Multiply all the terms by $10x$ to clear the fractions.

$$45 + 4.5x = 10x$$

STEP 3: Solve for x.

$$45 = 5.5x$$
$$x = 8.18 \text{ or } 8\frac{2}{11} \text{ days}$$

It would take A nearly $8\frac{1}{4}$ days to do the job alone.

Here is a third example: If A can do a job in 6 days that B can do in $5\frac{1}{2}$ days, and C can do in $2\frac{1}{5}$ days, how long would the job take if A, B, and C were working together?

STEP 1: This example is very similar to the first one. The number of workers is greater, but the procedure is the same. First write the fractions as follows.

$$\frac{\text{Time actually spent}}{\text{Time needed to do entire job alone}} \qquad \overset{\text{A}}{\frac{x}{6 \text{ days}}} + \overset{\text{B}}{\frac{x}{5.5 \text{ days}}} + \overset{\text{C}}{\frac{x}{2.2 \text{ days}}} = 1$$

Remember that 1 represents the completed job regardless of the number of days involved.

STEP 2: Multiply all terms by 33 to clear the fractions.

$$5.5x + 6x + 15x = 33$$

STEP 3: Solve for x.

$$26.5x = 33$$
$$x = 1.245 \text{ days}$$

A, B, and C all working together at their usual rates would get the job done in about $1\frac{1}{4}$ days.

Here is one last example: One pipe can fill a pool in 20 minutes, a second pipe can fill the pool in 30 minutes, and a third pipe can fill it in 10 minutes. How long would it take the three pipes together to fill the pool?

STEP 1: Treat the pipes as workers and write the fractions as follows.

$$\frac{\text{Time actually spent}}{\text{Time needed to do entire job alone}} \qquad \overset{\text{A}}{\frac{x}{20 \text{ mins.}}} + \overset{\text{B}}{\frac{x}{30 \text{ mins.}}} + \overset{\text{C}}{\frac{x}{10 \text{ mins.}}} = 1$$

STEP 2: Multiply all terms by 60 to clear the fractions.

$$3x + 2x + 6x = 60$$

STEP 3: Solve for x.

$$11x = 60$$
$$x = 5\frac{5}{11} \text{ minutes}$$

If the water flows from all three pipes at once, the pool will be filled in $5\frac{5}{11}$ minutes.

Exercise 19

Answers are on page 192.

1. John can complete a paper route in 20 minutes. Steve can complete the same route in 30 minutes. How long will it take them to complete the route if they work together?

2. Mr. Powell can mow his lawn twice as fast as his son Dick can. Together they do the job in 20 minutes. How many minutes would it take Mr. Powell to do the job alone?

3. Mr. White can paint his barn in 5 days. What part of the barn is still unpainted after he has worked for x days?

4. Mary can clean the house in 6 hours. Her younger sister Ruth can do the same job in 9 hours. In how many hours can they do the job if they work together?

5. A swimming pool can be filled by an inlet pipe in 3 hours. It can be drained by a drainpipe in 6 hours. By mistake, both pipes are opened at the same time. If the pool is empty, in how many hours will it be filled?

6. Mr. Jones can plow his field with his tractor in 4 hours. If he uses his manual plow, it takes three times as long to plow the same field. One day, after working with the tractor for two hours, he ran out of gas and had to finish with the manual plow. How long did it take to complete this job after the tractor ran out of gas?

7. Michael and Barry can complete a job in 2 hours when working together. If Michael requires 6 hours to do the job alone, how many hours does Barry need to do the job alone?

8. A girl can sweep the garage in 20 minutes, while her brother needs 30 minutes to do the same job. How many minutes will it take them to sweep the garage if they work together?

9. One printing press can print the school newspaper in 12 hours, while another press can print it in 18 hours. How long will the job take if both presses work simultaneously?

10. If John can do $\frac{1}{4}$ of a job in $\frac{3}{4}$ of a day, how many days will it take him to do the entire job?

ANSWERS AND EXPLANATIONS

EXERCISE 1

1. 0
2. 3
3. 0
4. 6
5. 0
6. 9
7. 5
8. 4
9. 2
10. 0
11. 0
12. 0
13. 1
14. 3
15. 5
16. 9
17. 12
18. 0
19. 1
20. 6

1. 180
2. .05
3. 1300
4. 36.2
5. .986
6. .0012
7. 45
8. .08328
9. 76,100
10. 6.886

EXERCISE 3

1. 44.809
2. 102.9531
3. 82.1
4. 18.01
5. 4.19
6. 34.23
7. 100.863
8. 17.19
9. .69
10. 837.92

EXERCISE 4

1. 20.272
2. 10.12
3. 60
4. 1.35
5. 1.51
6. 3
7. 36.03
8. 3.4
9. 2.43
10. 2.52

EXERCISE 5

1. $\frac{32}{20} = 1\frac{12}{20} = 1\frac{3}{5}$
2. $\frac{2}{8} = \frac{1}{4}$
3. $\frac{5}{6}$
4. $\frac{1}{5}$
5. $\frac{47}{24} = 1\frac{23}{24}$
6. $\frac{17}{12} = 1\frac{5}{12}$
7. $\frac{2}{6} = \frac{1}{3}$
8. $\frac{7}{24}$
9. $\frac{14}{12} = 1\frac{2}{12} = 1\frac{1}{6}$
10. $\frac{2}{9}$

EXERCISE 6

1. $\frac{2}{5}$
2. $2\frac{1}{3}$
3. 2
4. $\frac{15}{3} = 5$
5. $\frac{1}{3}$
6. $\frac{21}{16} = 1\frac{5}{16}$
7. $1\frac{13}{27}$
8. $\frac{7}{9}$
9. $\frac{4}{21}$
10. 1

EXERCISE 7

1. $.5 = 50\%$
2. $.875 = 87\frac{1}{2}\%$
3. $.833 = 83\frac{1}{3}\%$
4. $.75 = 75\%$
5. $.75 = 75\%$
6. $.666 = 66\frac{2}{3}\%$
7. $.60 = 60\%$
8. $.40 = 40\%$
9. $.25 = 25\%$
10. $.40 = 40\%$

EXERCISE 8

1. $32 \times .10 = 3.2$
2. $8 \div .25 = 32$
3. $\frac{12}{24} = \frac{1}{2} = .5 = 50\%$
4. $360 \times .20 = 72$
5. $\frac{5}{60} = \frac{1}{12} = .0833 = 8\frac{1}{3}\%$
6. $12 \div .08 = 150$
7. $36 \times .06 = 2.16$
8. $25 \div .05 = 500$
9. $\frac{70}{140} = \frac{1}{2} = .5 = 50\%$
10. $\frac{19}{100} = .19 = 19\%$

EXERCISE 9

1. +13
2. +3
3. –8
4. –5
5. –38
6. –45
7. +17
8. –28.8
9. $-4\frac{1}{4}$
10. 0

EXERCISE 10

1. +6
2. +25
3. –17
4. –55
5. +62
6. +48
7. –7.3
8. $-41\frac{3}{4}$
9. –70
10. –.6

EXERCISE 11

1. +40
2. –36
3. +126
4. +40
5. –19.14
6. –31.5
7. $+47\frac{1}{8}$
8. –9
9. 0
10. +144

EXERCISE 12

1. –3
2. +3
3. +5
4. –25
5. –8
6. +.7
7. +2
8. +8.2
9. –1
10. 0

EXERCISE 13

1. $x = 12$
2. $x = 21$
3. $x = 33$
4. $x = 36$
5. $x = 4$
6. $x = 24$
7. $x = 10$
8. $x = 26$
9. $x = 9$
10. $x = 33$

EXERCISE 14

1. $A = bh$

   $A = 8 \times 4 = 32$ sq. ft.

2. $A = \frac{1}{2}bh$

   $A = \frac{1}{2}(7 \times 8)$

   $A = \frac{1}{2}(56) = 28$ sq. in.

3. $A = s^2$

   $A = 1^2 = 1$ sq. mile

4. $A = \frac{1}{2}bh$

   $A = \frac{1}{2}(5 \times 3)$

   $A = \frac{1}{2}(15) = 7\frac{1}{2}$ sq. yds.

5. $A = \pi r^2$

   $A = \pi 2^2$

   $A = 4\pi$ sq. cm.

6. $A = bh$

   $A = 12 \times 6 + (12 - 8) \times 6$

   $A = 12 \times 6 + 4 \times 6$

   $A = 72 + 24 = 96$ sq. rds.

7. $A = bh$

   $A = 10 \times 8 = 80$ sq. yds.

   $A = \frac{1}{2}\text{bh}$

   $A = \frac{1}{2}(10 \times 3) = \frac{1}{2}(30)$

   $A = 15$ sq. yds.

   $80 + 15 = 95$ sq. yds.

8. $A = \pi \text{r}^2$

   $A = \pi 6^2$

   $A = 36\pi$ sq. ft.

9. $A = \frac{1}{2}bh$

   $A = \frac{1}{2}(26 \times 2) = \frac{1}{2}(52)$

   $A = 26$ sq. ft.

10. $A = bh$

    $A = 6 \times 5 + 20 \times (17 - 5)$

    $A = 6 \times 5 + 20 \times 12$

    $A = 30 + 240 = 270$ sq. meters

EXERCISE 15

1. $P = 6 + 5 + (6 - 2) + 8 + 2 + (8 + 5) = 38$ in.

2. $V = \pi r^2 h$

   $V = \pi \times 2^2 \times 6$

   $V = \pi \times 4 \times 6$

   $V = 24\pi$ cu. in.

3. $C = 2\pi r$

   $C = 2 \times \pi \times 7$

   $C = 14\pi$ cm.

4. $V = lwh$

   $V = 8 \times 3 \times 4$

   $V = 96$ cu. in.

5. $V = s^3$

   $V = 4^3 = 4 \times 4 \times 4$

   $V = 64$ cu. yd.

6. $P = 3 + 3 + 3 + 3 + 3 + 3 + 3 + 3$

   $P = 24$ cm.

7. $P = 8 + 8 + 6 = 22$ ft.

8. $P = 1 + 1 + 1 + 1 = 4$ in.

EXERCISE 16

1. 80°
2. 240°
3. 90°
4. 55°
5. 140°
6. 120°
7. 180°
8. 50°

EXERCISE 17

1. (3, –1) A vertical line through A meets the x-axis at 3; therefore, the x-coordinate is 3. A horizontal line through A meets the y-axis at –1; therefore, the y-coordinate is –1. The coordinates of point A are (3, –1).

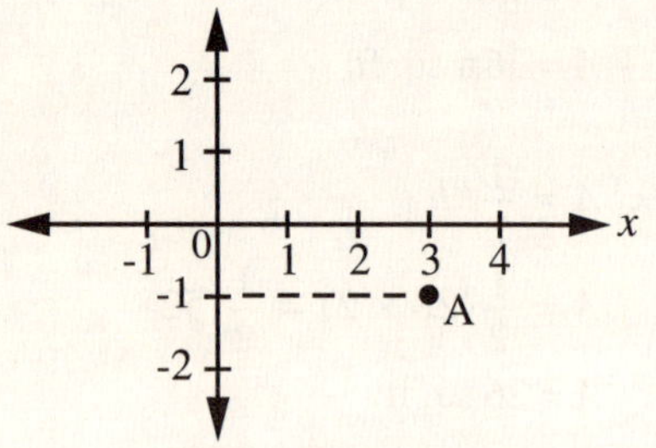

2. Point P has coordinates $x = -3$ and $y = 2$.

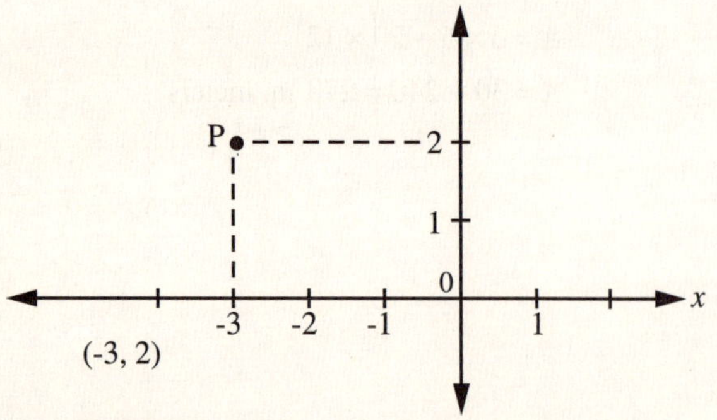

3. Because both coordinates are positive numbers, the point must be located in the upper-right quadrant of the graph. Location along the x-axis is always stated first, so the correct answer is point B.

4. Start by moving in a positive direction along the x-axis. Then you must move along the y-axis in a negative direction. The actual number of spaces you move is irrelevant, since point C is the only possible answer.

5. Again, make your moves in order. First move in the positive direction along the x-axis. Because the second coordinate is 0, make no move on the y-axis. Point C is your answer.

EXERCISE 18

To solve any type of motion problem, it is helpful to organize the information in a chart with columns for Rate, Time, and Distance. A separate line should be used for each moving object. Be very careful of units used. If the rate is given in *miles per hour*, the time must be in *hours* and the distance will be in *miles*.

1. 300 miles

	Rate ×	Time =	Distance
Going	60 mph	x	$60x$
Return	50 mph	$x + 1$	$50x + 50$

Let x = time of trip at 60 mph

The distances are, of course, equal.

$$60x = 50x + 50$$
$$10x = 50$$
$$x = 5$$

R × T = D; 60 mph × 5 hours = 300 miles

2. 40 mph

	Rate ×	Time =	Distance
Slow Car	x	3	$3x$
Fast Car	$x + 20$	3	$3x + 60$

Let x = rate of slower car

$3x + 60 + 3x$
←→
300 miles

$$3x + 3x + 60 = 300$$
$$6x = 240 \text{ mph}$$
$$x = 40 \text{ mph}$$

3. 90 mph

	Rate ×	Time =	Distance
Passenger	$x + 45$	3	$3x + 135$
Freight	x	3	$3x$

Let x = rate of freight train

$$3x + 135 + 3x = 405$$
$$6x = 270$$
$$x = 45$$
$$x + 45 = 45 + 45 = 90 \text{ mph}$$

4. 5 P.M.

	Rate ×	Time =	Distance
Susie	30	x	$30x$
Richard	45	$x - 2$	$45x - 90$

Let x = time Susie traveled

Richard left 2 hours later than Susie so he traveled for $x - 2$ hours. Since Richard caught up to Susie, the distances are equal.

$$30x = 45x - 90$$
$$90 = 15x$$
$$x = 6 \text{ hours}$$

Susie traveled for 6 hours. 11 A.M. + 6 hours = 5 P.M. when Richard caught up to her.

5. 120 miles

	Rate ×	Time =	Distance
Going	40	x	$40x$
Return	30	$7 - x$	$210 - 30x$

Let x = time for trip out

Total driving time = 8 – 1 = 7 hours

Therefore, time for return trip = $7 - x$ hours

$$40x = 210 - 30x$$
$$70x = 210$$
$$x = 3 \text{ hours}$$

R × T = D; 40 mph × 3 hours = 120 miles

6. 44 mph

	Rate ×	Time =	Distance
Slow Car	x	3.5	$3.5x$
Fast Car	$x + 6$	3.5	$3.5(x + 6)$

Let x = rate of slow car

The cars traveled from 10 A.M. to 1:30 P.M., which is 3.5 hours.

$$3.5x + 3.5\,(x + 6) = 287$$
$$3.5x + 3.5x + 21 = 287$$
$$7x + 21 = 287$$
$$7x = 266$$
$$x = 38 \text{ mph}$$
$$x + 6 = 44 \text{ mph}$$

7. 9 A.M.

	Rate ×	Time =	Distance
Before Noon	50	x	$50x$
After Noon	40	$8 - x$	$40(8 - x)$

Let x = hours traveled before noon

Note that the 8 hours must be divided into two parts.

$$50x + 40(8 - x) = 350$$
$$50x + 320 - 40x = 350$$
$$10x = 30$$
$$x = 3 \text{ hours}$$

If he traveled 3 hours before noon, he left at 9 A.M.

8. 9:30 P.M.

	Rate ×	Time =	Distance
3 p.m. Plane	600	x	$600x$
3:30 p.m. Plane	650	$x - \frac{1}{2}$	$650(x - \frac{1}{2})$

Let x = travel time of 3 P.M. plane.
The later plane traveled $\frac{1}{2}$ hour less.

$600x = 650(x - \frac{1}{2})$

$600x = 650x - 325$

$325 = 50x$

$x = 6\frac{1}{2}$ hours

The plane which left at 3 P.M. traveled for $6\frac{1}{2}$ hours. The time then was 9:30 P.M.

9. 8 miles

	Rate ×	Time =	Distance
Going	4	x	$4x$
Return	2	$6 - x$	$2(6 - x)$

Let x = time for walk out into country
The soldier was gone for 6 hours. Therefore, time of trip back = $6 - x$.

$4x = 2(6 - x)$

$4x = 12 - 2x$

$6x = 12$

$x = 2$ hours

R × T = D; 2 hours at 4 mph = 8 miles

10. 6 hours

	Rate ×	Time =	Distance
Faster Car	36	x	$36x$
Slower Car	31	x	$31x$

Let x = travel time

$36x - 31x = 30$

$5x = 30$

$x = 6$ hours

EXERCISE 19

1. 12 minutes

$$\frac{\text{Time actually spent}}{\text{Time needed to do entire job alone}} \qquad \overset{\text{John}}{\frac{x}{20}} + \overset{\text{Steve}}{\frac{x}{30}} = 1$$

Multiply all terms by 60 to clear the fractions.

$3x + 2x = 60$

$5x = 60$

$x = 12$

2. 30 minutes

It takes Mr. Powell x minutes to mow the lawn. Dick alone will take twice as long, or $2x$ minutes.

$$\frac{\text{Time actually spent}}{\text{Time needed to do entire job alone}} \qquad \overset{\text{Mr. Powell}}{\frac{20}{x}} + \overset{\text{Dick}}{\frac{20}{2x}} = 1$$

Multiply all terms by $2x$ to clear the fractions.

$40 + 20 = 2x$

$60 = 2x$

$x = 30$ minutes

3. $\frac{5-x}{5}$

In x days he has painted $\frac{x}{5}$ of the barn. To find what part is still unpainted, subtract the part completed from $1\left(\frac{5}{5}\right)$.

$$\frac{5}{5} - \frac{x}{5} = \frac{5-x}{5}$$

4. $3\frac{3}{5}$ hours

$$\frac{\text{Time actually spent}}{\text{Time needed to do entire job alone}} \qquad \overset{\text{Mary}}{\frac{x}{6}} + \overset{\text{Ruth}}{\frac{x}{9}} = 1$$

Multiply all terms by 18 to clear the fractions.

$$3x + 2x = 18$$
$$5x = 18$$
$$x = 3\frac{3}{5}$$

5. 6 hours

$$\frac{\text{Time actually spent}}{\text{Time needed to do entire job alone}} \qquad \overset{\text{Inlet}}{\frac{x}{3}} - \overset{\text{Drain}}{\frac{x}{6}} = 1$$

Multiply all terms by 6 to clear the fractions.

$$2x - x = 6$$
$$x = 6$$

Note that the two fractions are subtracted because the drainpipe does not help the inlet pipe but rather works against it.

6. 6 hours

$$\frac{\text{Time actually spent}}{\text{Time needed to do entire job alone}} \qquad \overset{\text{Tractor}}{\frac{2}{4}} + \overset{\text{Plow}}{\frac{x}{12}} = 1$$

You do not need to calculate the answer. Because half the job $\left(\frac{2}{4}\right)$ was completed by the tractor, the other half $\left(\frac{6}{12}\right)$ was done by the plow, and x, therefore, must equal 6.

7. 3 hours

$$\frac{\text{Time actually spent}}{\text{Time needed to do entire job alone}} \qquad \overset{\text{Michel}}{\frac{2}{6}} + \overset{\text{Barry}}{\frac{2}{x}} = 1$$

Multiple all the terms by $6x$ to clear the fractions.

$$2x + 12 = 6x$$
$$12 = 4x$$
$$x = 3$$

8. 12 minutes

$$\frac{\text{Time actually spent}}{\text{Time needed to do entire job alone}} \qquad \overset{\text{Girl}}{\frac{x}{20}} + \overset{\text{Brother}}{\frac{x}{30}} = 1$$

Multiply all the terms by 60 to clear the fractions.

$3x + 2x = 60$

$5x = 60$

$x = 12$

9. 7 hours 12 minutes

$$\frac{\text{Time actually spent}}{\text{Time needed to do entire job alone}} \qquad \overset{\text{Fast Press}}{\frac{x}{12}} + \overset{\text{Slower Press}}{\frac{x}{18}} = 1$$

Multiply all the terms by 36 to clear the fractions.

$3x + 2x = 36$

$5x = 36$

$x = 7.2$ hours = 7 hours 12 minutes

10. 3 days

If John completes $\frac{1}{4}$ of the job in $\frac{3}{4}$ day, it will take him 4 times as long to do the entire job.

$\frac{4}{1} \times \frac{3}{4} = 3$

MATHEMATICS EXERCISES

EXERCISE 1

Directions: In the following questions, work out each problem and mark the letter that corresponds to the correct answer. If the correct answer does not appear among the choices, mark (E) for "Not given." Answers are found at the end of this chapter.

1. 896×708

(A) 643,386

(B) 634,386

(C) 634,368

(D) 643,368

(E) Not given

2. $9\overline{)4266}$

(A) 447

(B) 477

(C) 474

(D) 475

(E) Not given

3. \$125.25 + .50 + 70.86 + 6.07

(A) \$201.68

(B) \$202.69

(C) \$200.68

(D) \$202.68

(E) Not given

4. $\begin{array}{r} \$1250.37 \\ -\ 48.98 \\ \hline \end{array}$

(A) $1,201.39

(B) $1,201.49

(C) $1,200.39

(D) $1,201.38

(E) Not given

5. $29\overline{)476.92}$

(A) 16.4445

(B) 17.4445

(C) 16.4555

(D) 17.4455

(E) Not given

6. $\begin{array}{r} 28 \\ 19 \\ 17 \\ +\,24 \\ \hline \end{array}$

(A) 87

(B) 88

(C) 90

(D) 89

(E) Not given

7. $3.7\overline{)2339.86}$

(A) 632.4

(B) 62.34

(C) 642.3

(D) 63.24

(E) Not given

8. $\begin{array}{r} 45{,}286 \\ \times\ \ 4\frac{1}{5} \\ \hline \end{array}$

(A) $190{,}021\frac{1}{5}$

(B) 190,234

(C) $190{,}201\frac{1}{5}$

(D) $190{,}202\frac{2}{5}$

(E) Not given

9. $\begin{array}{r} 8\frac{1}{6} \\ -\ 5\frac{2}{3} \\ \hline \end{array}$

(A) $3\frac{2}{3}$

(B) $2\frac{1}{3}$

(C) $3\frac{1}{6}$

(D) $2\frac{1}{2}$

(E) Not given

10. $\frac{1}{9} \times \frac{2}{3} \times \frac{7}{8} =$

(A) $\frac{6}{108}$

(B) $\frac{7}{108}$

(C) $\frac{14}{27}$

(D) $\frac{14}{108}$

(E) Not given

11. $4\frac{1}{3}\overline{)\frac{1}{4}}$

(A) $\frac{3}{52}$

(B) $\frac{5}{52}$

(C) $17\frac{1}{3}$

(D) $\frac{12}{52}$

(E) Not given

12. $\begin{array}{r} 78,523 \\ 21,457 \\ 3,256 \\ +\ 1,478 \\ \hline \end{array}$

(A) 104,715

(B) 105,714

(C) 104,814

(D) 105,814

(E) Not given

13. $\begin{array}{r} 12,689 \\ \times\quad 37 \\ \hline \end{array}$

(A) 569,493

(B) 468,493

(C) 469,493

(D) 568,493

(E) Not given

14. Find $6\frac{2}{3}\%$ of \$13.50.

(A) \$.89

(B) \$.91

(C) \$.88

(D) \$.95

(E) Not given

15. Rename $\frac{11}{16}$ as a decimal.

(A) .8675

(B) .6875

(C) .6785

(D) .6578

(E) Not given

EXERCISE 2

Directions: Work each problem on scratch paper or in the margins, then look at the answer choices. If your answer is among those choices, circle the letter before your answer. If your answer is not among the choices, circle (E) for "None of these." Answers are found at the end of this chapter.

1. $\begin{array}{r} 5239 \\ \times\ 706 \\ \hline \end{array}$

(A) 3,698,734

(B) 3,708,734

(C) 398,164

(D) 68,107

(E) None of these

2. $\begin{array}{r} 48,207 \\ \times\ \ 926 \\ \hline \end{array}$

(A) 44,639,682

(B) 45,739,682

(C) 45,638,682

(D) 46,739,682

(E) None of these

3. $4628 \div 7 =$

(A) 662 R1

(B) 661

(C) 661 R1

(D) 660 R6

(E) None of these

4. $419\overline{)5063}$

(A) 11 R408

(B) 12 R9

(C) 12 R37

(D) 14 R81

(E) None of these

5. \$59.60 ÷ \$0.40 =

(A) .149
(B) 1.49
(C) 14.9
(D) 149
(E) None of these

6. 3.41 + 5.6 + .873 =

(A) 4.843
(B) 9.883
(C) 15.264
(D) 17.743
(E) None of these

7. $\begin{array}{r} 58{,}769 \\ -\ 4{,}028 \\ \hline \end{array}$

(A) 54,641
(B) 44,741
(C) 54,741
(D) 53,741
(E) None of these

8. $.3 \times .08 =$

(A) .0024
(B) .024
(C) .240
(D) 2.40
(E) None of these

9. $.33\overline{)9.9}$

(A) .3
(B) 3
(C) 30
(D) 33
(E) None of these

10. 16% of 570 =

(A) 85.3
(B) 89.41
(C) 90.68
(D) 92
(E) None of these

11. 135 is what % of 900?

(A) 12%
(B) 15%
(C) 17.5%
(D) 19%
(E) None of these

Directions: Express all fractions in lowest terms.

12. $\frac{3}{4} + \frac{3}{8} =$

(A) $\frac{9}{8}$
(B) $\frac{8}{9}$
(C) $1\frac{1}{8}$
(D) $1\frac{3}{8}$
(E) None of these

13. $\begin{array}{r} 3\frac{1}{4} \\ 4\frac{1}{8} \\ +\ 4\frac{1}{2} \\ \hline \end{array}$

(A) $11\frac{5}{8}$
(B) $11\frac{3}{4}$
(C) $11\frac{7}{8}$
(D) 12
(E) None of these

14. $10\frac{2}{3}$
$-\ 9\frac{1}{2}$

(A) $1\frac{1}{3}$

(B) $1\frac{1}{2}$

(C) $1\frac{1}{6}$

(D) $\frac{13}{32}$

(E) None of these

15. $14\frac{7}{24}$
$-\ 5\frac{2}{3}$

(A) $8\frac{11}{12}$

(B) $8\frac{5}{6}$

(C) $9\frac{1}{3}$

(D) $9\frac{15}{24}$

(E) None of these

16. $\frac{8}{15} \times \frac{3}{4} =$

(A) $\frac{1}{5}$

(B) $\frac{2}{5}$

(C) $\frac{3}{5}$

(D) $\frac{3}{10}$

(E) None of these

17. $5\frac{1}{4} \times 2\frac{2}{7} =$

(A) 12

(B) $11\frac{3}{28}$

(C) $11\frac{4}{7}$

(D) $10\frac{3}{28}$

(E) None of these

18. $\frac{3}{4}\overline{\big)\frac{9}{16}}$

(A) $\frac{27}{64}$

(B) $\frac{3}{4}$

(C) $\frac{5}{8}$

(D) $\frac{7}{16}$

(E) None of these

19. $^-12 + {}^+4 =$

(A) $^+16$

(B) $^-8$

(C) $^+8$

(D) $^-16$

(E) None of these

20. $^-22 - {}^-18 =$

(A) $^+13$

(B) $^+6$

(C) $^-6$

(D) $^-30$

(E) None of these

21. $^{+}7 \times {}^{-}7 =$

(A) $^{+}49$

(B) 0

(C) $^{+}1$

(D) $^{-}14$

(E) None of these

22. $^{+}56 \div {}^{-}7 =$

(A) $^{-}6$

(B) $^{-}8$

(C) $^{+}8$

(D) $^{+}6$

(E) None of these

EXERCISE 3

Directions: Choose the correct answer to each problem and circle its letter. Answers are found at the end of this chapter.

✓= On Test X = Not on Test

1. Six girls sold the following number of boxes of cookies: 42, 35, 28, 30, 24, 27. What was the average number of boxes sold by each girl?

(A) 26

(B) 29

(C) 30

(D) 31

2. The cost of sending a telegram is 52 cents for the first ten words and $2\frac{1}{2}$ cents for each additional word. The cost of sending a 14 word telegram is

(A) 62 cents.

(B) 63 cents.

(C) 69 cents.

(D) 87 cents.

3. A stock clerk has on hand the following items:

500 pads worth four cents each

130 pencils worth three cents each

50 dozen rubber bands worth two cents per dozen

If, from this stock, he issues 125 pads, 45 pencils, and 48 rubber bands, the value of the remaining stock would be

(A) $6.43.

(B) $8.95.

(C) $17.63.

(D) $18.47.

4. As an employee at a clothing store, you are entitled to a 10% discount on all purchases. When the store has a sale, employees are also entitled to the 20% discount offered to all customers. What would you have to pay for a $60 jacket bought on a sale day?

(A) $6

(B) $10.80

(C) $36

(D) $43.20

5. How many square yards of linoleum are needed to cover a floor having an area of 270 square feet?

(A) 24

(B) 28

(C) 30

(D) 33

6. If a pie is divided into 40 parts, what percent is one part of the whole pie?

(A) .4

(B) 2.5

(C) 4.0

(D) 25

7. A recipe for 6 quarts of punch calls for $\frac{3}{4}$ cups of sugar. How much sugar is needed for 9 quarts of punch?

(A) $\frac{5}{8}$ of a cup

(B) $\frac{7}{8}$ of a cup

(C) $1\frac{1}{8}$ cups

(D) $2\frac{1}{4}$ cups

8. How many yards of ribbon will it take to make 45 badges if each badge uses 4 inches of ribbon?

(A) 5

(B) 9

(C) 11

(D) 15

9. Oil once sold at $42\frac{1}{2}$ cents a quart. The cost of 4 gallons of oil was

(A) $6.50.

(B) $6.60.

(C) $6.70.

(D) $6.80.

10. A clerk can add 40 columns of figures an hour by using an adding machine and 20 columns of figures an hour without using an adding machine. What is the total number of hours it will take the clerk to add 200 columns of figures if $\frac{3}{5}$ of the work is done by machine and the rest without the machine?

(A) 6 hours

(B) 7 hours

(C) 8 hours

(D) 9 hours

11. Two rectangular boards, each measuring 5 feet by 3 feet, are placed together to make one large board. How much shorter will the perimeter be if the two long sides are placed together than if the two short sides are placed together?

(A) 2 feet

(B) 4 feet

(C) 6 feet

(D) 8 feet

12. 1% of 8 =

(A) 8

(B) .8

(C) .08

(D) .008

13. When 81.3 is divided by 10 the quotient is

(A) 0.0813.

(B) 0.813.

(C) 8.13.

(D) 813.

14. +1 –1 +1 –1 +1. . . and so on, where the last number is +1 has a sum of

(A) 0.

(B) –1.

(C) +1.

(D) 2.

15. If a plane travels 1,000 miles in 5 hours 30 minutes, what is its average speed in miles per hour?

(A) $181\frac{9}{11}$

(B) 200

(C) 215

(D) $191\frac{1}{2}$

16. A jacket that normally sells for $35 can be purchased on sale for 2,975 pennies. What is the rate of discount represented by the sale price?

(A) 5%

(B) 10%

(C) 15%

(D) 20%

17. Perform the indicated operations and express your answer in inches: 12 feet, minus 7 inches, plus 2 feet 1 inch, minus 7 feet, minus 1 yard, plus 2 yards 1 foot 3 inches.
    (A) 130 inches
    (B) 128 inches
    (C) 129 inches
    (D) 131 inches

18. What is the value of x when $5x = 5 \times 4 \times 2 \times 0$?
    (A) 6
    (B) 8
    (C) 0
    (D) 1

19. A square has an area of 49 sq. in. The number of inches in its perimeter is
    (A) 7.
    (B) 28.
    (C) 14.
    (D) 98.

20. $(3 + 4)^3 =$
    (A) 21
    (B) 91
    (C) 343
    (D) 490

21. A roll of carpeting will cover 224 square feet of floor space. How many rolls will be needed to carpet a room 36' × 8' and another 24' × 9'?
    (A) 2.25
    (B) 4.50
    (C) 2.50
    (D) 4.25

22. A library contains 60 books on arts and crafts. If this is .05% of the total number of books on the shelves, how many books does the library own?
    (A) 120,000
    (B) 12,000
    (C) 1,200,000
    (D) 1,200

23. A court clerk estimates that the untried cases on the docket will occupy the court for 150 trial days. If new cases are accumulating at the rate of 1.6 trial days per day (Saturday and Sunday excluded) and the court sits 5 days a week, how many days' business will remain to be heard at the end of 60 trial days?
    (A) 168 trial days
    (B) 188 trial days
    (C) 185 trial days
    (D) 186 trial days

24. A house plan uses the scale $\frac{1}{4}$ inch = 1 foot, and in the drawing the living room is 7 inches long. If the scale is changed to 1 inch = 1 foot, what will the length of the living room be in the new drawing?
    (A) 18 in.
    (B) 28 in.
    (C) 30 in.
    (D) 36 in.

25. A store sold suits for \$65.00 each. The suits cost the store \$50.00 each. The percentage of increase of selling price over cost is
    (A) 40%.
    (B) $33\frac{1}{2}$%.
    (C) $33\frac{1}{3}$%.
    (D) 30%.

26. A man borrowed \$5,000 and agreed to pay $11\frac{1}{2}$% annual interest. If he repaid the loan in 6 months, how much interest would he pay?
    (A) \$2,875.00
    (B) \$5,750.00
    (C) \$287.50
    (D) \$575.00

27. After deducting a discount of 30%, the price of a coat was $35.00. The regular price of the coat was
(A) $116.67.
(B) $24.50.
(C) $50.00.
(D) $42.00.

28. Two cars start from the same point at the same time. One drives north at 20 miles an hour and the other drives south on the same straight road at 36 miles an hour. How many miles apart are they after 30 minutes?
(A) less than 10
(B) between 10 and 20
(C) between 20 and 30
(D) between 30 and 40

29. During his summer vacation, a boy earned $14.50 per day and saved 60% of his earnings. If he worked 45 days, how much did he save?
(A) $391.50
(B) $287.93
(C) $402.75
(D) $543.50

30. The number of cubic feet of soil needed for a flower box 3 feet long, 8 inches wide, and 1 foot deep is
(A) 24.
(B) 12.
(C) $4\frac{2}{3}$.
(D) 2.

31. The scale of a certain map is 4 inches = 32 miles. The number of inches that would represent 80 miles is
(A) 8.
(B) 12.
(C) 10.
(D) 16.

32. The daily almanac report for one day during the summer stated that the sun rose at 6:14 A.M. and set at 6:06 P.M. Find the number of hours and minutes in the time between the rising and setting of the sun on that day.
(A) 11 hr. 52 min.
(B) 12 hr. 8 min.
(C) 11 hr. 2 min.
(D) 12 hr. 48 min.

33. One piece of wire is 25 feet 8 inches long and another is 18 feet 10 inches long. What is the difference in length?
(A) 6 ft. 10 in.
(B) 6 ft. 11 in.
(C) 7 ft. 2 in.
(D) 7 ft. 4 in.

34. If a vehicle is to complete a 20-mile trip at an average rate of 30 miles per hour, it must complete the trip in
(A) 20 min.
(B) 30 min.
(C) 40 min.
(D) 50 min.

35. A snapshot measures $2\frac{1}{2}$ inches by $1\frac{7}{8}$ inches. It is to be enlarged so that the longer dimension will be 4 inches. The length of the enlarged shorter dimension will be
(A) $2\frac{1}{2}$ inches.
(B) 3 inches.
(C) $3\frac{3}{8}$ inches.
(D) $2\frac{5}{8}$ inches.

36. An adult's ski lift ticket costs twice as much as a child's. If a family of three children and two adults can ski for $49, what is the cost of an adult ticket?

(A) $7

(B) $10

(C) $12

(D) $14

37. A recipe calls for $1\frac{1}{2}$ cups of sugar. It is necessary to make eight times the recipe for a church supper. If 2 cups of sugar equal 1 pound, how many pounds of sugar will be needed to make the recipe for the supper?

(A) 4

(B) 6

(C) 8

(D) 10

38. In the fraction $\frac{1}{\Delta - 2}$, Δ can be replaced by all of the following except

(A) 0.

(B) +3.

(C) +2.

(D) –2.

39. If one pipe can fill a tank in $1\frac{1}{2}$ hours and another can fill the same tank in 45 minutes, how long will it take for the two pipes to fill the tank together?

(A) 1 hour

(B) $\frac{1}{2}$ hour

(C) $1\frac{1}{2}$ hours

(D) $\frac{1}{3}$ hour

40. Two cars are 550 miles apart, and traveling toward each other on the same road. If one travels at 50 miles per hour, the other at 60 miles per hour, and they both leave at 1:00 P.M., what time will they meet?

(A) 4:00 P.M.

(B) 4:30 P.M.

(C) 5:45 P.M.

(D) 6:00 P.M.

EXERCISE 4

Directions: Answer these questions. Answers are found at the end of this chapter.

1. Any number that is divisible by both 5 and 6 is also divisible by

(A) 11.

(B) 9.

(C) 7.

(D) 3.

2. 3,482,613 rounded to the nearest million is

(A) 2,000,000.

(B) 3,500,000.

(C) 3,000,000.

(D) 4,000,000.

3. The number that is *not* a factor of 120 is

(A) 5.

(B) 6.

(C) 7.

(D) 8.

4. What is the place value of 3 in 4.9236?

(A) hundredths

(B) thousandths

(C) ten thousandths

(D) hundred thousandths

5. Which symbol belongs in the circle?

.0983 ◯ .124

(A) <

(B) >

(C) =

(D) ≅

6. The greatest common factor of 24 and 12 is

(A) 2.

(B) 4.

(C) 6.

(D) 12.

7. 1000% is equal to

(A) .0001.

(B) .1.

(C) 10.

(D) 100.

8. In the simplest form, $\frac{12}{16}$ is

(A) $\frac{3}{4}$.

(B) $\frac{2}{3}$.

(C) $\frac{2}{6}$.

(D) $\frac{4}{8}$.

9. $\frac{9}{25}$ is equal to

(A) .036.

(B) .04.

(C) .36.

(D) .45.

10. What number belongs in the box? $^{-}5 + \square = 0$

(A) $^{-}5$

(B) 0

(C) $^{-}1$

(D) $^{+}5$

11. $\sqrt{81}$ is equal to

(A) 8.

(B) 9.

(C) 18.

(D) 40.5.

12. Solve for x: $\frac{x}{2} + 3 = 15$

(A) 18

(B) 20

(C) 22

(D) 24

13. If $y + 2 > 10$, then y must be

(A) smaller than 10.

(B) smaller than 8.

(C) greater than 8.

(D) equal to 0.

14. If $a + b = 200°$, and $c + d + e + f = 140°$, what is the number of degrees in angle g?

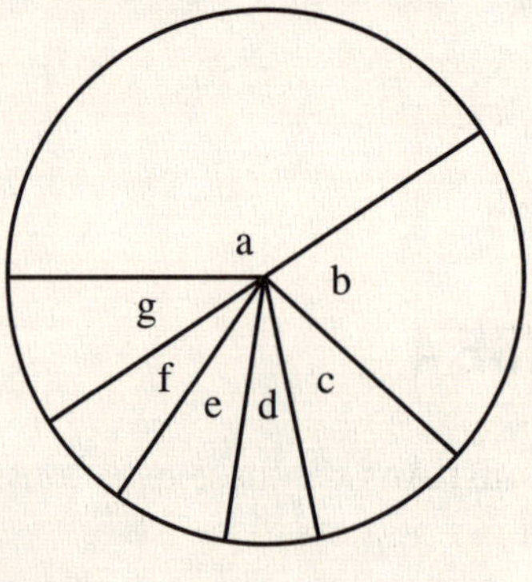

(A) 10°

(B) 20°

(C) 30°

(D) 45°

15. The area of the shaded portion of the rectangle below is

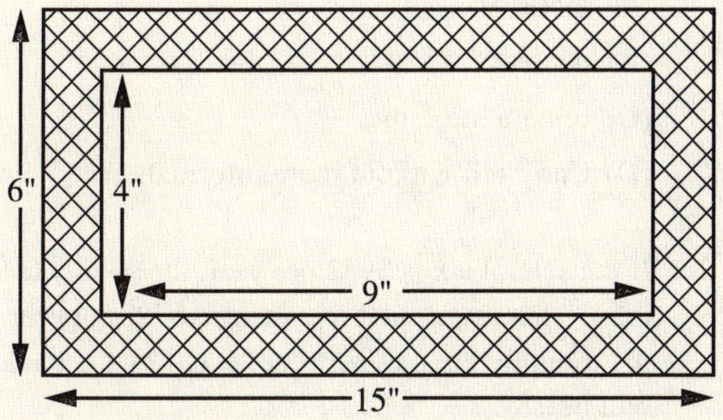

(A) 54 sq. in.
(B) 90 sq. in.
(C) 45 sq. in.
(D) 36 .sq. in.

16. Which point shown below corresponds to (8, 3)?

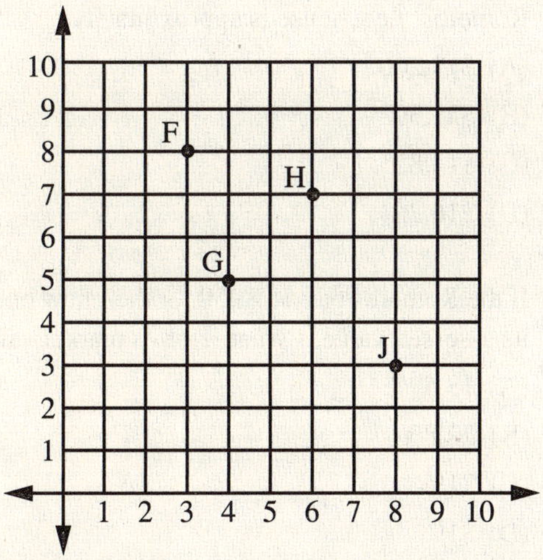

(A) Point F
(B) Point G
(C) Point H
(D) Point J

Questions 17–23 refer to the following information:

Mr. Shea, a shop teacher at the junior high school, owns a ski lodge in Vermont. The lodge is open to guests on weekends and during school vacations. Mr. Shea's regular rates, which include breakfast and dinner, are $25 per night for dormitory-style accommodations. He gives a 30% discount to all members of organized student groups from his community.

17. Sixteen members of Boy Scout Troop 60 and two of their leaders went on a ski weekend and stayed at Mr. Shea's lodge. The two-night cost of room and board for each boy was

(A) $25.
(B) $35.
(C) $50.
(D) $60.

18. The leaders shared a room instead of sleeping in the dormitory. The total bill for the two of them was $84 for the two nights. The surcharge *per person* for the semi-private room was

(A) 7%.
(B) 20%.
(C) 32%.
(D) 42%.

19. Lift tickets cost $20 per day for adults and $14 per day for juniors (persons under 13 years of age). Five of the boys were 12 years old, while the others were older. What was the total cost of lift tickets for a day of skiing?

(A) $220
(B) $290
(C) $330
(D) $390

20. Among the boys, $\frac{1}{4}$ considered themselves to be expert skiers. Of those who were less experienced, $\frac{3}{4}$ took ski lessons. Of those who took ski lessons, $\frac{1}{3}$ rented ski equipment. How many boys rented ski equipment?

(A) 9
(B) 6
(C) 4
(D) 3

21. The mountain on which the troop skied had 27 trails served by a T-bar, two J-bars, and three chair lifts. The proportion of trails to lifts was

(A) 5:1.
(B) 7:2.
(C) 9:3.
(D) 9:2.

22. One boy skied the length of a 4.6–mile trail in just under 14 minutes. His average speed was approximately
    (A) 15 mph.
    (B) 20 mph.
    (C) 25 mph.
    (D) 30 mph.

23. The bus chartered for the trip cost $250. The troop contributed $400 from its treasury to help defray expenses of the trip. Exclusive of lunches, lessons, and rentals the cost per person of the trip was
    (A) $64.11.
    (B) $71.13.
    (C) $75.28.
    (D) $83.07.

Questions 24–28 refer to the following information:

Clara's mother sells real estate. She is explaining monthly mortgage payments to Mr. and Mrs. Romero, who are about to purchase their first house. Clara's mother has told the Romeros that amortization is the amount that is repaid each month to reduce the amount of the loan. She has also explained that the bank that holds the mortgage will be in charge of paying real estate taxes on the property. The tax money will be collected in regular monthly installments as part of the Romero's mortgage payments. The rate of interest on the loan will be adjusted every six months according to fluctuations in the interest market, but the Romeros' payments will remain the same for a full year.

24. If the interest rates go up after the first six months, the monthly amortization of the Romeros' loan will
    (A) increase.
    (B) decrease.
    (C) remain the same.
    (D) Can't tell without more information.

25. If interest rates remain the same, the amount of monthly interest will
    (A) increase.
    (B) decrease.
    (C) remain the same.
    (D) Can't tell without more information.

26. If the school tax is $932 per year, the county tax is $424 per year, and the town tax is $783 per year, the monthly tax payments collected by the bank will be
    (A) $142.92.
    (B) $178.25.
    (C) $213.90.
    (D) $713.00.

27. If the tax rate is $.132 per $1000 of assessed value (not the true value), the assessed value of the Romeros' new house is approximately
    (A) $13,200.
    (B) $21,390.
    (C) $17,825.
    (D) $16,204.

28. If the Romeros pay $87,250 for their new house, its assessed value is what % of its market value?
    (A) 18.57%
    (B) 22.8%
    (C) 71%
    (D) 81%

Questions 29–32 refer to the following information:

On an icy day, the Bergs' car skidded into a telephone pole and suffered two smashed doors and a broken drive shaft. After four weeks in a body shop, the car was fully repaired. The Bergs' insurance company paid the body shop's bill, less the $200 deductible, which the Bergs paid.

29. For what portion of the year were the Bergs unable to use their car?

(A) $\frac{1}{4}$

(B) $\frac{1}{10}$

(C) $\frac{1}{12}$

(D) $\frac{1}{13}$

30. In the year before the accident, the Bergs' insurance premium was $1,100. The year following the accident, their premium rose to $1,500. The new premium was about what percent of the old premium?

(A) $26\frac{2}{3}\%$

(B) $36\frac{1}{3}\%$

(C) $136\frac{1}{3}\%$

(D) 140%

31. To match the blue paint of the car, the man in the body shop had to add $1\frac{1}{2}$ ounces of black paint to each pint of blue paint. He used three gallons of paint on the car. How much blue paint did he use?

(A) $2\frac{1}{4}$ pints

(B) $21\frac{3}{4}$ pints

(C) 24 pints

(D) $26\frac{1}{4}$ pints

32. Three men of about equal efficiency were assigned to work on the Bergs' car. One man worked on the car full–time. He was always assisted by one of the other men. If the full–time man had had to complete the job alone, the car would have been in the shop for

(A) 2 weeks.

(B) 4 weeks.

(C) 6 weeks.

(D) 8 weeks.

ANSWERS AND EXPLANATIONS TO MATHEMATICS EXERCISES

EXERCISE 1

1. **(C)**

$$\begin{array}{r} 896 \\ \times\ 708 \\ \hline 7168 \\ 62720 \\ \hline 634268 \end{array}$$

2. **(C)**

$$\begin{array}{r} 474 \\ 9\overline{)4266} \\ 36 \\ \hline 66 \\ 63 \\ \hline 36 \\ 36 \end{array}$$

3. **(D)** $202.68

4. **(A)** $1201.39

5. **(E)**

$$\begin{array}{r} 16.445551 = 16.4455 \\ 29\overline{)479.9200} \\ 29 \\ \hline 186 \\ 174 \\ \hline 129 \\ 116 \\ \hline 132 \\ 116 \\ \hline 160 \\ 145 \\ \hline 150 \\ 145 \\ \hline 50 \end{array}$$

6. **(B)** 88

7. **(A)**

$$\begin{array}{r} 63\,2.\,39 = 632.4 \\ 3.7\overline{)2339.8\;60} \\ 222 \\ \hline 119 \\ 111 \\ \hline 88 \\ 74 \\ \hline 146 \\ 111 \\ \hline 350 \\ 333 \\ \hline 17 \end{array}$$

8. **(C)** $\frac{1}{5} = .20$

$$\begin{array}{r} 45286 \\ \times\ 4.20 \\ \hline 9057\ 20 \\ 181144 \\ \hline 190201.20 = 190201\frac{1}{5} \end{array}$$

9. **(D)**

$$\begin{array}{r} 8\frac{1}{6} = 7\frac{7}{6} \\ -\ 5\frac{2}{3} = 5\frac{4}{6} \\ \hline 2\frac{3}{6} = 2\frac{1}{2} \end{array}$$

10. **(B)** $\frac{1}{9} \times \frac{\not{2}^{1}}{3} \times \frac{7}{\not{8}_4} = \frac{7}{108}$

11. **(A)** $\frac{1}{4} \div 4\frac{1}{3} = \frac{1}{4} \div \frac{13}{3} = \frac{1}{4} \times \frac{3}{13} = \frac{3}{52}$

12. **(E)** 104,714

13. **(C)**

$$\begin{array}{r} 12689 \\ \times\ 37 \\ \hline 88823 \\ 38067 \\ \hline 469493 \end{array}$$

14. **(E)** $\$13.50 \times 6\frac{2}{3}\% = \$13.50 \times .06\frac{2}{3}$

$= \frac{\$13.50}{1} \times \frac{.20}{3}$

$= \frac{\$2.7}{3} = \$.90$

15. **(B)** $\frac{11}{16} = $

$$\begin{array}{r} .6875 \\ 16\overline{)11.0000} \\ 9\ 6 \\ \hline 1\ 40 \\ 1\ 28 \\ \hline 120 \\ 112 \\ \hline 80 \\ 80 \\ \hline 0 \end{array}$$

EXERCISE 2

1. **(A)**
$$\begin{array}{r} 5239 \\ \times\,706 \\ \hline 31434 \\ 366730 \\ \hline 3698734 \end{array}$$

2. **(A)**
$$\begin{array}{r} 48207 \\ \times\,926 \\ \hline 289242 \\ 96414 \\ 433863 \\ \hline 44639682 \end{array}$$

3. **(C)**
$$\begin{array}{r} 661 \text{ R } 1 \\ 7\overline{)4628} \\ 42 \\ \hline 42 \\ 42 \\ \hline 8 \\ 7 \\ \hline 1 \end{array}$$

4. **(E)**
$$\begin{array}{r} 12 \text{ R } 35 \\ 419\overline{)5063} \\ 419 \\ \hline 873 \\ 838 \\ \hline 35 \end{array}$$

5. **(D)**
$$\begin{array}{r} 1\,49. \\ \$0.40\overline{)\$59.60} \\ 40 \\ \hline 196 \\ 160 \\ \hline 360 \\ 360 \\ \hline \end{array}$$

6. **(B)**
$$\begin{array}{r} 3.410 \\ 5.600 \\ +\ .873 \\ \hline 9.883 \end{array}$$

7. **(C)** 54,741

8. **(B)** .024 Add up the places to the right of the decimal point.

9. **(C)**
$$\begin{array}{r} 30. \\ .33\overline{)9.90} \end{array}$$

10. **(E)**
$$\begin{array}{r} 570 \\ \times\ .16 \\ \hline 34\,20 \\ 57\,0 \\ \hline 91.20 \end{array}$$

11. **(B)** 135 ÷ 900 = .15 = 15%

12. **(C)**
$$\begin{array}{r} \frac{3}{4} = \frac{6}{8} \\ +\frac{3}{8} = \frac{3}{8} \\ \hline \frac{9}{8} = 1\frac{1}{8} \end{array}$$

13. **(C)**
$$\begin{array}{r} 3\frac{1}{4} = 3\frac{2}{8} \\ 4\frac{1}{8} = 4\frac{1}{8} \\ +4\frac{1}{2} = 4\frac{4}{8} \\ \hline 11\frac{7}{8} \end{array}$$

14. **(C)**
$$\begin{array}{r} 10\frac{2}{3} = 10\frac{4}{6} \\ -9\frac{1}{2} = 9\frac{3}{6} \\ \hline 1\frac{1}{6} \end{array}$$

15. **(E)**
$$\begin{array}{r} 14\frac{7}{24} = 14\frac{7}{24} = 13\frac{31}{24} \\ -\ 5\frac{2}{3} = 5\frac{16}{24} = 5\frac{16}{24} \\ \hline 8\frac{15}{24} = 8\frac{5}{8} \end{array}$$

16. **(B)** $\frac{{}^{2}\not{8}}{\not{15}_{5}} \times \frac{{}^{1}\not{3}}{\not{4}_{1}} = \frac{2}{5}$

17. **(A)** $5\frac{1}{4} \times 2\frac{2}{7} = \frac{{}^{3}\not{21}}{\not{4}_{1}} \times \frac{{}^{4}\not{16}}{\not{7}_{1}} = \frac{12}{1} = 12$

18. **(B)** $\frac{9}{16} \div \frac{3}{4} = \frac{{}^{3}\not{9}}{\not{16}_{4}} \times \frac{{}^{1}\not{4}}{\not{3}_{1}} = \frac{3}{4}$

19. **(B)** When adding two numbers of unlike sign, subtract and assign the sign of the larger number.

20. **(E)** Minus negative = plus positive. The problem then reads: $^{-}22 + {}^{+}18 = {}^{+}4$. See answer 19.

21. **(E)** When multiplying two numbers of unlike sign, the product is always negative.

$^{+}7 \times {}^{-}7 = {}^{-}49$

22. **(B)** When you divide two numbers of unlike sign, the quotient is always negative.

EXERCISE 3

1. **(D)** To find the average, add all the numbers and divide the sum by the number of terms.

$42 + 35 + 28 + 30 + 24 + 27 = 186 \div 6 = 31$

2. **(A)** 14 words = 10 words + 4 words

10 words cost 52 cents

4 words @ 2.5 cents = $4 \times 2.5 = 10$ cents

52 cents + 10 cents = 62 cents

3. **(D)** 500 – 125 = 375 pads @ $.04 = $15.00

130 – 45 = 85 pencils @ $.03 = $2.55

50 dozen – 4 dozen = 46 dozen rubber bands @ $.02 = $.92

$15 + $2.55 + $.92 = $18.47

4. **(D)** $60 × .10 = $6 (employee discount)

$60 – $6 = $54

$54 × .20 = $10.80 (sale discount)

$54 – $10.80 = $43.20

5. **(C)** 9 square feet = 1 square yard

270 sq. ft. ÷ 9 = 30 sq. yds.

6. **(B)** The whole pie is 100%. Each part is $\frac{1}{40}$.

$100 \div 40 = 2.5\%$

7. **(C)** First find out how much sugar is needed for one quart of punch.

$\frac{3}{4}$ cups $\div 6 = \frac{3}{4} \div \frac{6}{1} = \frac{\cancel{3}^{1}}{4} \times \frac{1}{\cancel{6}_{2}} = \frac{1}{8}$

For 9 quarts of punch:

$9 \times \frac{1}{8} = \frac{9}{8} = 1\frac{1}{8}$

8. **(A)** 45 badges × 4 inches each = 180 inches needed. There are 36 inches in one yard. 180 inches ÷ 36 = 5 yards of ribbon needed.

9. **(D)** One gallon = four quarts

4 gals. = 16 qts.

16 qts. × $42\frac{1}{2}$ = 16 × $.425 = $6.80

10. **(B)** $\frac{3}{5}$ of 200 = 120 columns by machine @ 40 columns per hour = 3 hours

200 – 120 = 80 columns without machine @ 20 columns per hour = 4 hours

3 hours + 4 hours = 7 hours to complete the job.

11. **(B)** Perimeter = $2l + 2w$. If the two long sides are together the perimeter will be

$5 + 3 + 3 + 5 + 3 + 3 = 22$

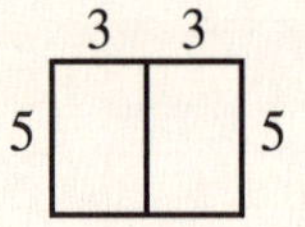

If the two short sides are together, the perimeter will be

$3 + 5 + 5 + 3 + 5 + 5 + = 26$

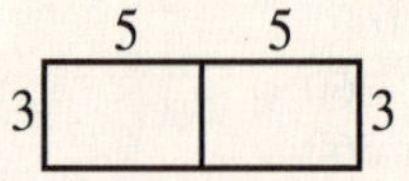

26 – 22 = 4 feet shorter

12. **(C)** To remove a % sign, divide the number by 100. Thus, $1\% = \frac{1}{100} = .01$. 1% of 8 is the same as 1% times 8 = .01 × 8 = .08

13. **(C)**

```
     8.13
10)81.30
   80
    13
    10
     30
     30
      0
```

14. **(C)** Each -1 cancels out the $+1$ before it. Because the final term is $+1$, which is not canceled out by a -1, the sum is $+1$.

15. **(A)** 5 hours 30 minutes = $5\frac{1}{2}$ hours

    $1000 \text{ mph} \div 5\frac{1}{2} \text{ hours} = 1000 \div \frac{11}{2} =$

    $1000 \times \frac{2}{11} = 181\frac{9}{11}$ mph

16. **(C)** 2,975 pennies = \$29.75

    \$35.00 – \$29.75 = \$5.25 amount of discount

    Rate of discount = $\frac{5.25}{35} \times 100 = .15 \times 100 = 15\%$

17. **(C)** First convert all the yards and feet into inches so that all addition and subtraction can be done using the same units.

12 feet =	144 inches
–7 inches =	–7 inches
+2 feet, 1 inch =	+25 inches
–7 feet =	–84 inches
–1 yard =	–36 inches
+2 yards, 1 foot, 3 inches =	<u>+87 inches</u>
	129 inches

18. **(C)** Any number multiplied by 0 equals 0. Since one multiplier on one side of the equals sign is 0, the product on that side of the sign must be 0. The value on the other side of the equals sign must also be 0.

    $5x = 5 \times 4 \times 2 \times 0$

    $5x = 40 \times 0$

    $5x = 0$

    $x = 0$

19. **(B)** Area of a square = s^2

    $49 = 7^2$

    one side = 7 inches

    $P = 4s$

    $P = 4'' \times 7'' = 28$ inches

20. **(C)** First perform the operation within the parentheses. To cube a number, multiply it by itself, two times.

    $(3 + 4)^3 = (7)^3 = 7 \times 7 \times 7 = 343$

21. **(A)**

First room: 36 ft. × 8 ft.	= 288 sq. ft.
Second room: 24 ft × 9 ft.	= <u>216</u> sq. ft.
Need:	504 sq. ft.

    504 ÷ 224 = 2.25 rolls needed

22. **(A)** .05% of the total (x) = 60

    $.0005x = 60$

    $x = 60 \div .0005 = 120{,}000$

23. **(D)** If the court does a day's work every day, it will dispense with 60 days' worth of new cases. The excess work is $.6 \times 60 = 36$ days of work. Add the 36 newly accumulated hours of excess work to the backlog of 150 days' work to learn that the court will be 186 trial days behind.

24. **(B)** $\frac{1}{4}$ in. = 1 ft., so 1 in. = 4 ft. and the living room is $7 \times 4 = 28$ ft. long. When the scale is changed to 1 in. = 1 ft., the 28-ft. living room will be 28 in. on the new drawing.

25. **(D)** To find percent of change, subtract the original figure from the new figure to determine amount of change; then divide the amount of change by the original figure to determine percent of change.

    \$65 – \$50 = \$15 ÷ 50 = .3 = 30%

26. **(C)** $11\frac{1}{2}$% of \$5,000 is \$575. Because he repaid the loan in one-half of a year, his interest payment is \$575 ÷ 2 = \$287.50.

27. **(C)** If 30% has been deducted, \$35 is 70% of the original price. To find out what a number is when a percent of it is given, rename the percent as a decimal and divide the given number by it.

    \$35 ÷ .70 = \$50

28. **(C)** One car went 20 mph for $\frac{1}{2}$ hour = 10 miles. The other went 36 mph for $\frac{1}{2}$ hour = 18 miles. Because they went in opposite directions, add the two distances to find the total number of miles apart: 10 + 18 = 28.

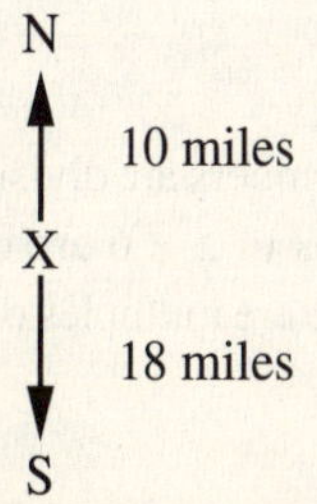

29. **(A)** The boy worked 45 days × \$14.50 per day, so he earned \$652.50. He saved 60% of \$652.50 = \$391.50.

30. **(D)** Rename 8 in. as $\frac{2}{3}$ ft. so that all measurements are in the same unit. Then multiply $l \times w \times h$.

$$3 \text{ ft.} \times \frac{2}{3} \text{ ft.} \times 1 \text{ ft.} = 2 \text{ cu. ft.}$$

31. **(C)** 4 in. = 32 miles, therefore 1 in. = 32 ÷ 4 = 8 miles. 80 miles would be represented by 10 in.

32. **(A)** You do not need to do complicated calculations to answer this question: 14 – 6 = 8. The sun was above the horizon for 8 minutes less than 12 hours, which is 11 hours 52 minutes (60 – 8 = 52).

33. **(A)** 25 ft. 8 in. = 24 ft. 20 in.
18 ft. 10 in. = 18 ft. 10 in.
6 ft. 10 in.

34. **(C)** No calculations are needed here. Note that a 20-mile trip at 60 mph (which is 1 mile per minute), would take 20 minutes. Because the vehicle is traveling half as fast (30 mph), the 20-mile trip should take twice as long, or 40 minutes.

35. **(B)** This is a proportion problem. Set up the proportion as follows:

$$\frac{2\frac{1}{2}}{4} = \frac{1\frac{7}{8}}{?}$$

Substitute x for ?:

$$\frac{2\frac{1}{2}}{4} = \frac{1\frac{7}{8}}{x}$$

Cross-multiply:

$$\frac{2\frac{1}{2}}{4} = \frac{1\frac{7}{8}}{x}$$

$$2\frac{1}{2}x = 4 \bullet 1\frac{7}{8}$$

Divide both sides by the coefficient of x and calculate:

$$\frac{5}{2}x = \frac{60}{8}$$

$$x = \frac{60}{8} \div \frac{5}{2}$$

$$x = \frac{60}{8} \times \frac{2}{5}$$

$$x = 3$$

36. **(D)** A child's ticket costs x dollars. Each adult ticket costs twice as much, or $2x$ dollars. $2(2x) = 2$ adult tickets; $3x = 3$ children tickets. Write a simple equation and solve for x.

$$2(2x) + 3x = \$49$$

$$4x + 3x = \$49$$

$$7x = 49$$

$$x = \$7$$

\$7 is the cost of a child's ticket; \$14 is the cost of an adult's ticket.

37. **(B)** $1\frac{1}{2}$ c. sugar × 8 = 12 c. sugar
12 c. ÷ 2 c. per lb. = 6 lb. of sugar

38. **(C)** By substituting +2 for the triangle, the denominator of the fraction becomes zero. A denominator of zero is undefined in mathematics.

39. **(B)** The first pipe can fill the tank in $1\frac{1}{2}$, or $\frac{3}{2}$, hours; that is, it can do $\frac{2}{3}$ of the job in 1 hour. The second pipe can fill the tank in 45 minutes, or $\frac{3}{4}$ of an hour, or it can do $\frac{4}{3}$ of the job in 1 hour. Together the pipes can complete $\frac{4}{3} + \frac{2}{3} = \frac{6}{3}$ of the job in one hour. $\frac{6}{3} = 2$, or twice the job in one hour. Therefore, together the two pipes could fill the tank in $\frac{1}{2}$ hour.

40. **(D)** The cars are traveling toward each other, so the distance between them is being reduced at 60 + 50 or 110 miles per hour. At a rate of 110 mph, 550 miles will be covered in 5 hours. If both cars left at 1:00 P.M., they should meet at 6:00 P.M.

EXERCISE 4

1. **(D)** Not many numbers are divisible by both 5 and 6. Only multiples of 5 × 6 are divisible by both. Multiples of 5 × 6 are multiples of 30, which are all divisible by 3.

2. **(C)** The seventh digit to the left of the decimal point is in the millionths place. Because 482 is less than 500, round down.

3. **(C)** 120 is not divisible by 7.

4. **(B)** The place values are: four ones, nine tenths, two hundredths, three thousandths, six ten thousandths.

5. **(A)** Look immediately to the right of the decimal point. 0 is less than 1.

6. **(D)** The greatest number by which both 12 and 24 can be divided is 12.

7. **(C)** To rename a percent as a decimal, move the decimal point two places to the left.

$$1000\% = 10.00$$

8. **(A)** To simplify $\frac{12}{16}$ to simplest form, divide both numerator and denominator by 4.

9. **(C)** The fraction bar in a fraction means divided by.

$$9 \div 25 = .36$$

10. **(D)** The positive and negative cancel each other out. Addition may be done in any order.

To check this problem, reverse the order of the addends.

$$5 - 5 = 0$$

11. **(B)** The square root of 81 is 9.

12. **(D)** $\frac{x}{2} + 3 = 15$

$$\frac{x}{2} = 15 - 3$$

$$\frac{x}{2} = 12$$

$$x = 12 \times 2$$

$$x = 24$$

13. **(C)** $y + 2 > 10$

$$y > 10 - 2$$

$$y > 8$$

y could be greater than 10; the only certainty is that it is greater than 8.

14. **(B)** The sum of the angles of a circle = 360° Angles *a* through *f* total 340°. Angle *g* must be 20°.

15. **(A)** The area of the entire rectangle is 6 in. × 15 in. = 90 sq. in. The area of the unshaded portion is 4 in. × 9 in. = 36 sq. in. 90 sq. in. – 36 sq. in. = 54 sq. in. in the shaded portion.

16. **(D)** In reading a graph, always read along the horizontal axis first.

17. **(B)** The charge for one night is $25; for two nights, $50. The Boy Scouts receive a 30% discount, so they pay 70%. 70% of $50 = $35.

18. **(B)** As part of the group, the leaders received the same 30% discount as the boys. If they had slept in the dormitory, they would have paid $35 each for the two nights. Their total bill (2 men, 2 nights) would have been $70. However, they paid extra for the privilege of the semiprivate room. To find percent of increase, subtract the original number from the new number and divide the difference by the original number.

$$\$84 - \$70 = \$14 \div \$70 = 20\%$$

19. **(C)** Of the 18 people, there are 13 adults and 5 juniors. The adult tickets cost $20 × 13 = $260. The junior tickets cost $14 × 5 = $70. The total cost of lift tickets for one day is $260 + $70 = $330.

20. **(D)** $\frac{1}{4}$ of 16 = 4 expert skiers. That leaves 16 – 4 = 12 less experienced skiers. $\frac{3}{4}$ of 12 = 9 that took ski lessons. $\frac{1}{3}$ of 9 = 3 that rented equipment.

21. **(D)** There were 27 trails and 6 lifts. Which simplifies to 9:2

22. **(B)** The formula for determining rate is $\frac{d}{t}$. The distance skied is 4.6 miles. The time, just under 14 minutes, is approximately .25 hour.

$$4.6 \div .25 = 18.4 \text{ mph.}$$

Because he skied the distance in slightly less than .25 hour, his average speed was very close to 20 mph.

23. **(A)** First add up the expenses:

16 boys paying $35 each for rooms =	$ 560
2 leaders' rooms =	$ 84
lift tickets for 2 days =	$ 660
bus =	$ 250
	$1554
Subtract the troop contribution	– 400
	$1154

Now divide by the 18 people:

$1154 ÷ 18 = $64.11 each

24. **(B)** If the interest rates go up, the amount of interest charged will go up. If the payments remain the same but a larger portion of those payments is interest, then a smaller portion of the payments will go toward amortization.

25. **(B)** Each month, part of the payment goes toward reducing the loan. Each month, the amount of the loan on which interest is being charged is slightly less. If the interest rates remain the same and the amount on which interest is being charged is lower, then the amount of interest which is being paid is lower, too.

26. **(B)** Add the three taxes to determine the total annual tax:

$$\$932 + \$424 + \$783 = \$2139$$

The tax is paid in 12 equal installments, so divide by 12:

$$\$2139 \div 12 = \$178.25$$

27. **(D)** Divide the total taxes by the tax rate to find the assessed valuation.

$$\$2139 \div \$.132 = \$16{,}204$$

28. **(A)** To find what percent one number is of another, create a fraction by putting the part over the whole and convert to a decimal by dividing.

$$\$16{,}205 \div \$87{,}250 = 18.57\%$$

29. **(D)** 4 weeks is $\frac{4}{52} = \frac{1}{13}$.

30. **(C)** Again find what percent one number is of another by creating a fraction. This time the part that you want to know about happens to be larger than the whole.

$$\$1500 \div \$1100 = 1.3636 = 136\frac{1}{3}\%$$

31. **(B)** 3 gallons = 24 pints. $1\frac{1}{2}$ ounces of black paint × 24 = 36 ounces of black paint. 36 ounces = $2\frac{1}{4}$ pints. 24 pints (in all) $-2\frac{1}{4}$ pints of black = $21\frac{3}{4}$ pints of blue.

32. **(D)** You do not have to calculate this problem. If you read carefully, you will see that 2 men worked full-time and the work took 4 weeks. If only one man, half the number, had worked, the job would have taken twice the time, or 8 weeks.

Summary: Hints for the Math Tests

- On the COOP exam, the section containing math problems is called Mathematics Concepts and Applications.
- If you are having special difficulties with any mathematic topic, talk with a teacher or refer back to any of your math textbooks.
- Use the exercises in this chapter to determine what you DON'T know well, and concentrate your study on those areas.
- When adding or subtracting decimals, it is important to keep the decimal points in line.
- The fastest way to find an equivalent fraction is to divide the denominator of the fraction you know by the denominator you want. Take the result and multiply it by the numerator.
- When solving a percentage problem, be sure to read the notation carefully, read the problem carefully, and use common sense.
- Remember the number line when subtracting signed numbers.
- Memorizing some simple rules will help you to move through the test more quickly and with less anxiety. An example of some of those rules is the following: The product of two negative numbers is positive; the product of two positive numbers is positive; the product of a negative number and a positive number is negative.
- Memorize the basic equations of geometry. These may not be given to you on the test. For example, to find the area of a rectangle, you must multiply the base times the height, $A=bh$.

Chapter 17

Series Reasoning

Series reasoning questions crop up on both the COOP and HSPT exams. On the COOP, these questions are called Sequences. On the HSPT, you find these questions in the Quantitative Skills section of the Mathematics test. Series reasoning questions—symbol series, number series, letter series, or mixed—are designed to test your ability to reason without words. These questions can be challenging, fun, and sometimes very frustrating.

In some ways, series questions are a lot like analogy questions—you remember, the questions that ask you to find the relationships between words. In series questions, you have to determine the relationship between a series of symbols, numbers, or letters, then choose the next item for the series.

This chapter gives you some in-depth instruction in working with series, by showing you how to complete number and letter series. These are the most common kinds of series questions that you'll encounter on both the COOP and the HSPT exams. The information and practice you get in this chapter will help you develop your own methods and strategies for solving these series questions. And you can use those same strategies to solve mixed series and even symbol series.

All series reasoning questions require the same concentration, the same logical thinking, and the same flexibility of approach. With all series reasoning questions you run the risk of working out a sequence and then finding that the answer you would choose to complete the sequence is not among the choices. Don't be discouraged! Just start over and try to determine what other relationship is reasonable.

ROAD MAP

- *Number Series*
- *Letter Series*
- *Mixed Series*
- *Symbol Series*
- *Series Question Tactics*
- *Series Reasoning Exercises*
- *Answers and Explanations*

NUMBER SERIES

Number series questions measure your ability to think with numbers and to see the relationship between elements of a series. Even though this type of task might be new and unfamiliar to you, the actual mathematics of number series questions is not complicated. The problems involve nothing more than simple arithmetic and a few of the concepts that were introduced in Chapter 16. What the questions do require of you is concentration; you must be able to see how the numbers in a series are related so that you can supply the next number in that series. You must be flexible enough in your thinking so that if the first pattern you consider for a series turns out to be invalid, you can try a different pattern.

There is a system with which to approach number series questions. Look hard at the series. The pattern might be obvious to you on inspection. A series such as 1, 2, 3, 1, 2, 3, 1. . . should not require any deep thought. Clearly, the sequence 1, 2, 3 is repeating itself over and over. The next number in the series must be 2. You might also instantly recognize the pattern of a simple series into which one number periodically intrudes. An example of such a series is 1, 2, 15, 3, 4, 15, 5. . . . The number 15 appears after each set of two numbers in a simple +1 series. The next number in this series is 6, which is followed by 15. Can you see why?

Here are five series questions, which you should be able to answer by inspection. Circle your answer choice.

1. 12, 10, 13, 10, 14. . .
   (A) 15
   (B) 14
   (C) 10
   (D) 9

2. 20, 40, 60, 20, 40. . .
   (A) 60
   (B) 20
   (C) 40
   (D) 80

3. 9, 2, 9, 4, 9. . .
   (A) 6
   (B) 9
   (C) 8
   (D) 4

4. 5, 8, 5, 8, 5. . .
   (A) 5
   (B) 8
   (C) 6
   (D) 9

5. 10, 9, 8, 7, 6. . .
   (A) 7
   (B) 4
   (C) 5
   (D) 6

Answers

1. **(C)** The series is a simple +1 series with the number 10 inserted after each step of the series.
2. **(A)** The sequence 20, 40, 60 repeats itself over and over again.
3. **(A)** This is a simple +2 series with the number 9 appearing before each member of the series.
4. **(B)** In this series the sequence 5, 8 repeats.
5. **(C)** You should be able to see that this is a descending series, each number is one less than the one before it. You can call this a –1 series.

Sometimes you might find that your ear is more adept than your eye. You might be able to "hear" a pattern or "feel" a rhythm more easily than you can "see" it. If you cannot immediately spot a pattern, try saying the series softly to yourself. First read the series through. If that does not help, try accenting the printed numbers and speaking the missing intervening numbers even more softly. Try grouping the numbers within the series into twos or threes. After grouping, try accenting the last number, or the first. If you read aloud 2, 4, 6, 8, 10, you will hear that the next number is 12. Likewise, if you see the series 31, 32, 33, 32, 33, 34, 34, and you group that series thus: 31, 32, 33/ 32, 33, 34/ 34. . . , you will feel the rhythm. The series consists of three-number mini-series. Each mini-series begins with a number one higher than the first number of the previous mini-series. The next number of the above series is 35, then 36, and then the next step will be 35, 36, 37.

You might be able to answer the next five series questions by inspection. If you cannot, try sounding them out.

1. 1, 2, 5, 6, 9, 10, 13
   (A) 14
   (B) 15
   (C) 16
   (D) 17

2. 2, 3, 4, 3, 4, 5, 4
   (A) 3
   (B) 4
   (C) 5
   (D) 6

3. 10, 10, 12, 14, 14, 16
   (A) 16
   (B) 18
   (C) 20
   (D) 22

4. 1, 2, 3, 2, 2, 3, 3, 2, 3
   (A) 1
   (B) 2
   (C) 3
   (D) 4

5. 10, 9, 8, 9, 8, 7, 8
   (A) 6
   (B) 7
   (C) 8
   (D) 9

Answers

1. **(A)** Read aloud (softly): 1, 2,   5, 6,   9, 10,   13
   whisper: 3, 4,   7, 8,   11, 12,

   The next number to read aloud is 14, to be followed by a whispered 15, 16, and then aloud again, 17.

2. **(C)** If you group the numbers into threes and read them aloud, accenting either the first or last number of each group, you should feel that each group of three begins and ends with a number one higher than the previous group. Read <u>2</u>, 3, 4/ <u>3</u>, 4, 5/ <u>4</u>, 5, 6; or 2, 3, <u>4</u>/ 3, 4, <u>5</u>/ 4, 5, <u>6</u>.
3. **(B)** Once more, group the numbers into threes. This time be certain to accent the third number in each group in order to sense the rhythm, and thereby the pattern, of the series: 10, 10, 12/ 14, 14, 16/ 18 . . .
4. **(D)** In this series, the rhythm emerges when you accent the first number in each group: <u>1</u>, 2, 3/ <u>2</u>, 2, 3/ <u>3</u>, 2, 3/ <u>4</u>, 2, 3.
5. **(B)** After you have seen a number of series of this type, you might be able to spot the pattern by inspection alone. If not, read aloud, group, and read again.

If you cannot hear the pattern of a series, the next step is to mark the degree and direction of change between the numbers. Most series progress by either + (plus) or – (minus) or a combination of both directions, so first try marking your changes in terms of + and –. If you cannot make sense of a series in terms of + and –, try × (times) and ÷ (divided by). You may mark the changes between numbers right on your exam paper, but be sure to mark the letter of the answer on your answer sheet when you figure it out. Only your answer sheet will be scored. The exam booklet will be collected, but it will not be scored.

Try this next set of practice questions. If you cannot "see" or "hear" the pattern, mark the differences between the numbers to establish the pattern. Then continue the pattern to determine the next number of the series.

1. 9, 10, 12, 15, 19, 24
   (A) 25
   (B) 29
   (C) 30
   (D) 31

2. 35, 34, 31, 30, 27, 26
   (A) 22
   (B) 23
   (C) 24
   (D) 25

3. 16, 21, 19, 24, 22, 27
   (A) 20
   (B) 25
   (C) 29
   (D) 32

4. 48, 44, 40, 36, 32, 28
   (A) 27
   (B) 26
   (C) 25
   (D) 24

5. 20, 30, 39, 47, 54, 60
   (A) 65
   (B) 66
   (C) 68
   (D) 70

Answers

1. **(C)** $9^{+1}\ 10^{+2}\ 12^{+3}\ 15^{+4}\ 19^{+5}\ 24^{+6}\ 30$
2. **(B)** $35^{-1}\ 34^{-3}\ 31^{-1}\ 30^{-3}\ 27^{-1}\ 26^{-3}\ 23$
3. **(B)** $16^{+5}\ 21^{-2}\ 19^{+5}\ 24^{-2}\ 22^{+5}\ 27^{-2}\ 25$
4. **(D)** $48^{-4}\ 44^{-4}\ 40^{-4}\ 36^{-4}\ 32^{-4}\ 28^{-4}\ 24$
5. **(A)** $20^{+10}\ 30^{+9}\ 39^{+8}\ 47^{+7}\ 54^{+6}\ 60^{+5}\ 65$

Arithmetical series such as those above might be interrupted by a particular number that appears periodically or by repetition of numbers according to a pattern. For example: 3, 6, 25, 9, 12, 25, 15, 18, 25. . . and 50, 50, 35, 40, 40, 35, 30, 30, 35. . . In these cases you must search a bit harder to spot both the arithmetic pattern and the pattern of repetition. When choosing your answer, you must be alert to the point at which the pattern was interrupted.

Do not repeat a number that has already been repeated, but do not forget to repeat before continuing the arithmetical pattern if repetition is called for at this point in the series.

1. 10, 13, 13, 16, 16, 19
   (A) 16
   (B) 19
   (C) 21
   (D) 22

2. 2, 4, 25, 8, 16, 25, 32
   (A) 25
   (B) 32
   (C) 48
   (D) 64

3. 80, 80, 75, 75, 70, 70
   (A) 60
   (B) 65
   (C) 70
   (D) 75

4. 35, 35, 32, 30, 30, 27
   (A) 25
   (B) 26
   (C) 27
   (D) 28

5. 76, 70, 12, 65, 61, 12
   (A) 12
   (B) 54
   (C) 55
   (D) 58

Answers

(r = repeat. ◯ = extraneous number repeated periodically.)

1. **(B)** 10^{+3} 13^{r} 13^{+3} 16^{r} 16^{+3} 19^{r} 19
2. **(D)** 2^{x2} 4^{x2} $\textcircled{25}$ 8^{x2} 16^{x2} $\textcircled{25}$ 32^{x2} 64
3. **(B)** 80^{r} 80^{-5} 75^{r} 75^{-5} 70^{r} 70^{-5} 65
4. **(A)** 35^{r} 35^{-3} 32^{-2} 30^{r} 30^{-3} 27^{-2} 25
5. **(D)** 76^{-6} 70^{-5} $\textcircled{12}$ 65^{-4} 61^{-3} $\textcircled{12}$ 58

LETTER SERIES

In letter series, each question consists of letters that are arranged according to a definite pattern. You must discover what that pattern is and then use that knowledge to determine which of the four alternatives offered is the missing letter or group of letters in the series. Series might be simple alphabetical progressions or intricate combinations that alternate between forward and backward steps.

Because each question is based on the twenty-six letters of the alphabet, it is a good idea to keep a copy of the alphabet in front of you as you work. Additionally, it is well worth your time to assign a number to each letter, jotting down the numbers from one to twenty-six directly under the letters to which they correspond. The seconds spent doing this might save you precious minutes as you work through the letter series.

There is more than one method of attack for letter series questions. You may solve these problems by inspection whenever possible. If that fails, try numerical analysis.

INSPECTION

The first line of attack should always be inspection, for this is the quickest and easiest approach. Look at the letters. Are they progressing in normal or reverse alphabetical order? Are the letters consecutive or do they skip one or more letters between terms? Are certain letters repeated? Here are some simple series that you should be able to solve by inspection only.

1. cadaeafaga
   (A) a
   (B) g
   (C) h
   (D) b

2. abccdeffghi
   (A) f
   (B) j
   (C) k
   (D) i

3. gij jlm mop
   (A) prq
   (B) prs
   (C) rst
   (D) qur

Answers

1. **(C)** The letters progress in consecutive alphabetical order, with the letter *a* inserted between each step. The next letter in this series must, therefore, be *h*.
2. **(D)** This is also a consecutive alphabetical progression, but here the third letter of each set is repeated. Thus we have: abcc deff ghii. Because only one *i* is given in the original series, the next letter must be the second *i* needed to complete the third set.
3. **(B)** This is a bit more difficult, but with the grouping already done for you, you should be able to solve it by inspection. The pattern is as follows: from the first letter skip one, then let the next letter in sequence follow immediately. Start each new three-letter sequence with the last letter of the previous sequence. The missing sequence begins with the *p* of the previous sequence, skips one letter to *r*, then continues immediately with *s*.

NUMERICAL ANALYSIS

If inspection does not make the answer apparent, switch to a numerical analysis of the series. Assign each letter in the series a numerical value according to its position in the alphabet. Write the direction and degree of difference between letters. Once you have done this, you will find yourself with a pattern of pluses and minuses similar to those you utilized in number series.

4. cdbefdghfij

   (A) h

   (B) k

   (C) f

   (D) l

5. abdgkp

   (A) q

   (B) u

   (C) w

   (D) v

6. mpt jmq gjn dgk

   (A) cfj

   (B) bei

   (C) kos

   (D) adh

Answers

A	B	C	D	E	F	G	H	I	J	K	L	M	N	O	P	Q	R	S	T	U	V	W	X	Y	Z
1	2	3	4	5	6	7	8	9	10	11	12	13	14	15	16	17	18	19	20	21	22	23	24	25	26

4. (A) c d b e f d g h f i j h

3 4 2 5 6 4 7 8 6 9 1 8

+1 −2 +3 +1 −2 +3 +1 −2 +3 +1 −2

Now it is obvious that the series progresses by the formula +1 −2 +3. According to this pattern, the next letter must be 10 −2, or 8, which corresponds to the letter *h*.

5. (D) a b d g k p v

1 2 4 7 11 16 22

+1 +2 +3 +4 +5 +6

The progression is obvious.

6. (D) m p t j m q g j n d g k a d h

13 16 20 10 13 17 7 10 14 4 7 11 1 4 8

+3 +4 −10 +3 +4 −10 +3 +4 −10 +3 +4 −10 +3 +4

Within each group of three, the pattern is +3, +4. Between groups of three, subtract ten.

MIXED SERIES

With mixed series you must once again ask yourself, "What's happening?" In what direction and in what manner are the numbers progressing? What about the letters? Are changes occurring in the relationships of numbers to letters? According to what pattern?

1. RA_1T_2 RA_3T_4 RA_1T_2 RA_4T_5 ____

   (A) RA_5T_6

   (B) RA_5T_4

   (C) RA_1T_2

   (D) R_1AT_2

2. $L^2M_2N^2O_3P^3Q_3R^2S_2T^2$ ____ $X^2Y_2Z^2$

   (A) $U_4V^4W_4$

   (B) $T_3\ U^3V_3$

   (C) $U^3V_3W^3$

   (D) $V^4W_3X^4$

Answers

1. **(C)** A good solid look at the groupings within the series shows that the unit RA_1T_2 intervenes between the other units of the series. With no further information on which to base any other features of the series, you must choose (C).
2. **(A)** The first thing that becomes clear in this mixed series is that the letters form a simple alphabetical progression. You can immediately narrow your choices to (A) and (C). On the basis of the information given, there is no way to know whether the numbers in the missing unit should be 3s or 4s, but we do have information about their position with relation to the letters. The pattern of the groups in which the numbers are 2s is superscript, subscript, superscript. In the only given group in which the numbers are not 2s, the pattern is subscript, superscript, subscript. Because, in addition, there is evidence of possible alternation of patterns, the proper choice is (A), in which the pattern of the numbers is subscript, superscript, subscript.

SYMBOL SERIES

In symbol series the figures might be unfamiliar and thus intimidating, but the task is the same. You must study the relationships of the individual members within a group and then determine what changes occur in that relationship as you move from one group to the next. While this activity is classified as nonverbal reasoning, you must verbalize to yourself exactly what is happening in the creation of the series.

1. 

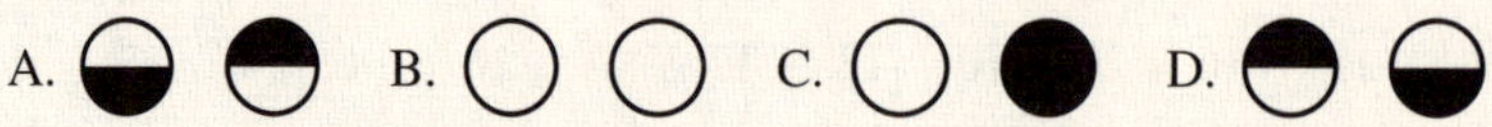

2. 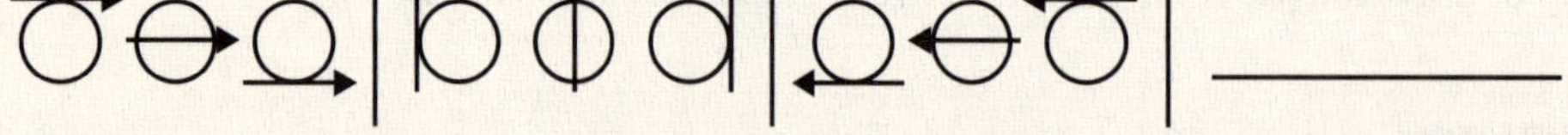

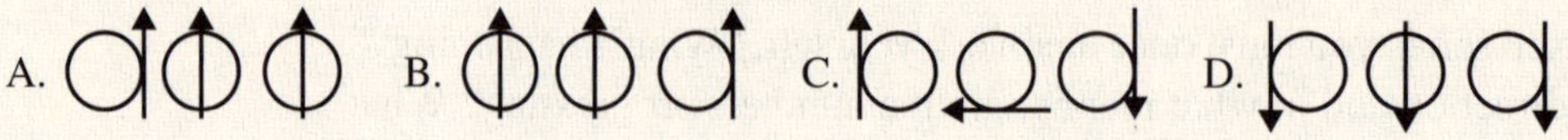

Answers

1. **(D)** If you look from the first group to the second, you will see that the second group is precisely the reverse of the first. Where the first is empty, upper half full, lower half full, the second is full, lower half full, upper half full. In the third group, the empty first circle of the first group is repeated, but the other two circles are reversed. Because the final group begins with a full circle (in both instances, the group with its first circle full follows a group with its first circle empty), the missing two circles should be the reverse of the second and third circles in the preceding group.
2. **(D)** In each group all of the arrows go in the same direction, and in each group the arrows go in a direction different from those in any other group. The arrows in the last group should point down. In all three groups, the middle arrow goes through the middle circle and the outer arrows go along the outer edges of the circles. This is clearest in the second group. Choice (D) fulfills all requirements best.

SERIES QUESTION TACTICS

1. Tackle first the questions that seem easiest for you. Questions generally tend to be arranged in order of difficulty, with the easiest questions first, but problems that might seem easy to some people might be more difficult to others, and vice versa. Answer quickly the questions that require little of your time and leave yourself extra time for the more difficult questions.

When you skip a question, put a mark before the question number in the test booklet and leave its answer space blank. When you return to a question that you have skipped, be sure to mark its answer in the correct space. The time you spend checking to make sure that question and answer number are alike is time well spent.

2. Follow the procedures outlined in this chapter. First, look for an obvious pattern. Second, sound out the series; if necessary, group the numbers and sound out again. Third, write the direction and amount of change between the numbers or letters.

If you do any figuring in the test booklet, be sure to mark the letter of the correct answer on your answer sheet. All answers must be marked on the answer sheet.

3. If none of the answers given fits the rule you have figured out, try again. Try to figure out a rule that makes one of the four answers a correct one.

4. Do not spend too much time on any one question. If a question seems impossible, skip it and come back to it later. A fresh look will sometimes help you find the answer. If you still cannot figure out the answer, guess. Remember that there is no penalty for a wrong answer.

5. Keep track of time. Because there is no penalty for a wrong answer, you will want to answer every question. Leave yourself time to go back to the questions you skipped to give them a second look. If you are not finished as the time limit approaches, mark random answers for the remaining questions.

SERIES REASONING EXERCISES

EXERCISE 1

Directions: Choose the number that should come next or that should fill the blank in the series.

1. 75, 75, 72, 72, 69, 69,

   (A) 63

   (B) 66

   (C) 68

   (D) 69

2. 12, 16, 21, 27, 31,

   (A) 33

   (B) 35

   (C) 36

   (D) 37

3. 22, 24, 12, 26, 28, 12,

   (A) 12

   (B) 30

   (C) 34

   (D) 36

4. 13, 22, 32, 43, ___ , 68

   (A) 53

   (B) 54

   (C) 55

   (D) 56

5. 4, 2, 1, $\frac{1}{2}$, $\frac{1}{4}$

   (A) 0

   (B) $\frac{1}{8}$

   (C) $\frac{3}{8}$

   (D) $\frac{1}{16}$

6. 100, 81, ____ , 49, 36

   (A) 60

   (B) 64

   (C) 65

   (D) 75

7. 32, 25, 86, 32, 25,

   (A) 5

   (B) 32

   (C) 68

   (D) 86

8. 51, 51, 30, 47, 47, 30, 43,

   (A) 30

   (B) 41

   (C) 43

   (D) 45

9. 3 3 9 | 15 15 21 | 27 27 ____

   (A) 1

   (B) 27

   (C) 30

   (D) 33

10. 95 90 86 | 83 78 74 | 51 ____ 42

    (A) 45

    (B) 46

    (C) 47

    (D) 50

11. 1 5 1 | 2 6 2 | 3 ____ 3

    (A) 0

    (B) 3

    (C) 4

    (D) 7

12. 50 52 48 | 35 37 33 | ____ 14 10

    (A) 9

    (B) 11

    (C) 12

    (D) 15

13. 39 40 80 | 10 11 22 | 17 18 ____
   (A) 9
   (B) 33
   (C) 36
   (D) 38

14. 36 12 4 | 63 21 7 | ____ 36 12
   (A) 72
   (B) 85
   (C) 97
   (D) 108

EXERCISE 2

Directions: Choose the letter or group of letters that should come next or that should fill the blank in the series.

1. n n o p p q r r s t
   (A) t
   (B) u
   (C) v
   (D) r

2. a j e b u q i y e p a
   (A) k
   (B) d
   (C) f
   (D) w

3. d e f d g h i g j k l j m n o
   (A) j
   (B) m
   (C) n
   (D) o

4. a c d a a c d b a c d c a c
   (A) a
   (B) b
   (C) c
   (D) d

5. a d h l b e i m c f j
   (A) l
   (B) m
   (C) n
   (D) o

6. z a z c z f z j z
   (A) g
   (B) o
   (C) z
   (D) s

7. hat | mat | rat | bat | ____
   (A) jat
   (B) qat
   (C) pat
   (D) uat

8. mnp | hik | bce | ____ | kln
   (A) uvx
   (B) gij
   (C) rqp
   (D) xyz

9. ZWT WTQ TQN ____ NKH
   (A) PNL
   (B) NLJ
   (C) MJG
   (D) QNK

10. ABC IRS GNO DHI ____
   (A) BDG
   (B) FKL
   (C) EJK
   (D) NYZ

EXERCISE 3

Directions: Choose the answer that will continue the pattern or sequence or that should fill the blank in the series.

1. $STPR_1$ STP_1R_2 $STPR_3$ ____ $STPR_5$
   (A) $STPR_4$
   (B) STP_4R_5
   (C) $ST_1P_2R_3$
   (D) STP_2R_3

2. $F^1G_2H^3I_4G_6H^7I_8J^9H_4I^5J_6K^7I^3J_4K^5L_6$ ____
   (A) $J^7K_8L^9M_{10}$
   (B) $M^5N_6O^7P_8$
   (C) $J^8K_9L^{10}M_{11}$
   (D) $K^1L_3M^5N_9$

3. $D_4F_6H_8E_5G_7I_9$ ____ $K_{11}M_{13}O_{15}P_{16}R_{18}T_{20}$
   (A) $J_{10}K_{11}L_{12}$
   (B) $J_{10}L_{12}N_{14}$
   (C) $J_{10}L_{11}N_{12}$
   (D) $J_{10}K_{12}L_{14}$

4. $R^2D^2R^2D_2R_2D_2R_2D^2D^2R^2$ ____
   (A) D_2R_2
   (B) R^2D_2
   (C) D^2R_2
   (D) D_2R^2

5. 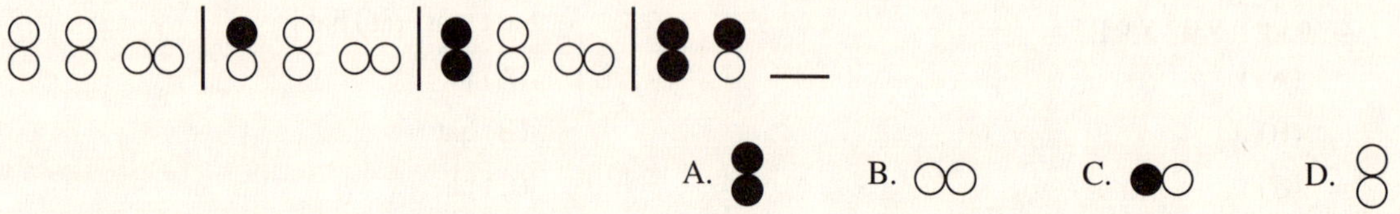

6. 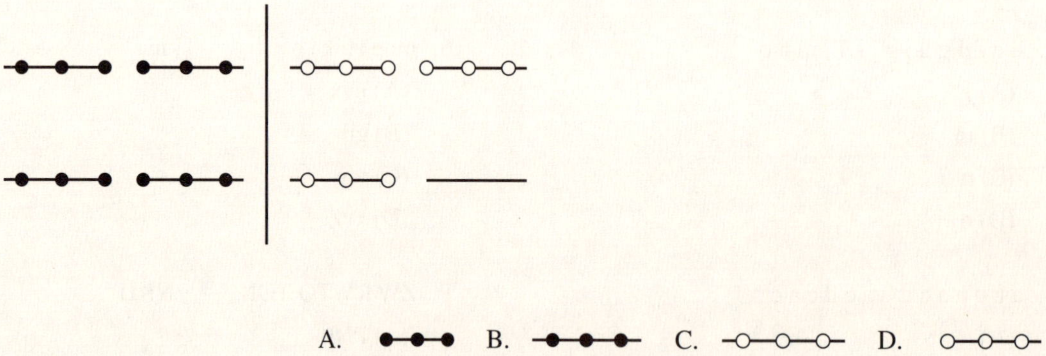

7. 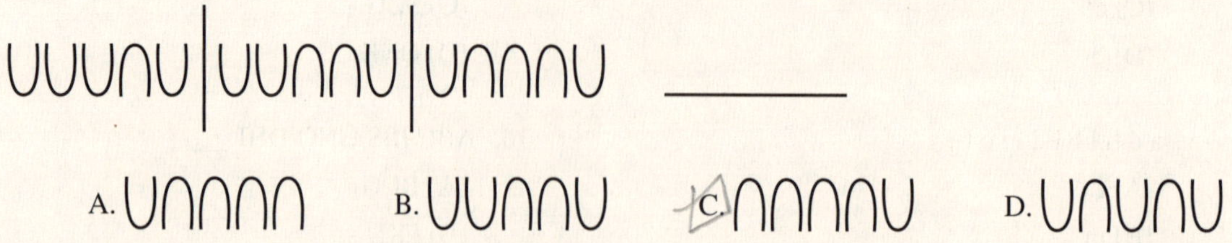

8.

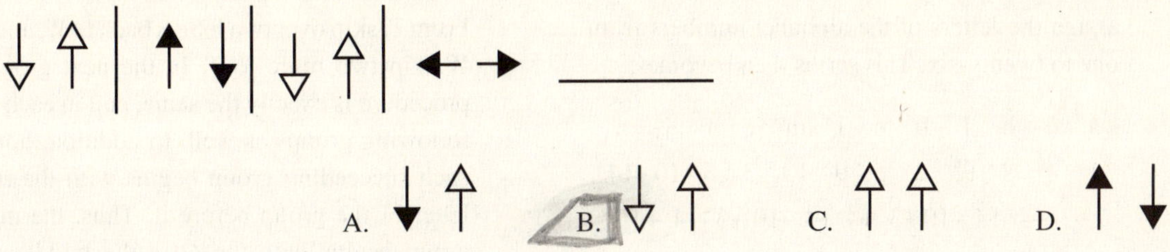

ANSWERS AND EXPLANATIONS

EXERCISE 1

1. **(B)** The pattern is: repeat the number, –3; repeat the number, –3; repeat the number, –3.
2. **(C)** The pattern is: +4, +5, +6; +4, +5, +6. The next number must be 31 + 5, which is 36.
3. **(B)** The basic pattern is a simple +2. The number 12 is inserted after each two terms of the series.
4. **(C)** The numbers are large, but the progression is simple. If you mark the differences between numbers, you will recognize: +9, +10, +11, +12, supply the +13 term, then continue with +14.
5. **(B)** This is a simple ÷ 2 series.
6. **(B)** This series consists of the squares of the whole numbers in descending order.
7. **(D)** This series follows no mathematical rule. You must solve it by inspection. The sequence 32, 25, 86 simply repeats.
8. **(C)** The basic pattern is: repeat the number, –4; repeat the number, –4. The number 30 appears each time after the repeat and before the –4.
9. **(D)** The entire series pattern is repeat, +6, +6; repeat, +6, +6. To answer the question, it is enough to recognize that the pattern within each segment of the series is: repeat, +6.
10. **(B)** Within each segment of the series, the pattern is: –5, –4. In the final segment, 51 – 5 = 46 – 4 = 42.
11. **(D)** You might see the pattern within each segment as +4, –4, or you might recognize by inspection or vocalization that each segment is simply a step up from the previous one.
12. **(C)** Within each segment, the pattern is +2, –4. Because there is no overall pattern for the series, you must establish the pattern in the first two segments, then apply it in reverse to determine the first term in the last segment. If the second term is two higher than the first, you can subtract 2 from the second term to determine the first.
13. **(C)** The pattern is +1, × 2.
14. **(D)** In the first two segments, you can establish that the pattern is ÷ 3. When you reach the third segment, multiply the second term by 3 to achieve the number that when divided by 3 equals 36.

EXERCISE 2

1. **(A)** This pattern alternates double and single letters in alphabetical order: nn o pp q rr s t. The next letter must be the second *t* needed to maintain the pattern.
2. **(A)** In this series, each set of two letters is a vowel followed by a consonant that contains the sound of the vowel with which it is paired: aj eb uq iy ep a. The only consonant offered that contains the sound of *a* is *k*.
3. **(B)** This series is an alphabetical progression of four-letter sequences where each fourth letter repeats the first letter of each sequence: defd ghig jklj mno. The missing letter is therefore the *m* needed to complete the fourth set.
4. **(D)** This pattern consists of the letters *acd* followed by consecutive letters of the alphabet. Thus: acda acdb acdc acd. The next letter must be *d* to complete the constant three-letter combination *acd*.

5. **(C)** The best way to visualize this pattern is to assign the letters of the alphabet numbers from one to twenty-six. This series then becomes:

a	d	h	l	b	e	i	m	c	f	j	n
1	4	8	12	2	5	9	13	3	6	10	14

+3 +4 +4 −10 +3 +4 +4 −10 +3 +4 +4

The last number must be 10 + 4, which is 14, corresponding to the letter n.

6. **(B)** Starting at the beginning of the alphabet, the space between letters increases by one with each new letter:

a c f j o

+2 +3 +4 +5

The letter *z* is a constant between each term. The next step in this series must be five letters after *j*, which is *o*.

7. **(C)** In this series, each set of three letters makes a word composed of a consonant plus *at*: hat, mat, rat, bat. The next segment, therefore, must consist of a consonant plus *at* that may be combined to form an English word.

8. **(A)** The easiest way to solve this series is to verify the numerical relationship within segments. In each instance, the sequence is +1, +2. The only option that satisfies this sequence is u + 1 = v + 2 = x.

9. **(D)** Look at the alphabet written out before you. From *Z*, skip over two letters back to *W*, and from *W* skip two more to *T*. In the next group, the procedure is exactly the same, and in each of the following groups as well. In addition, note that each succeeding group begins with the middle letter of the group before it. Thus, the missing group begins with the *Q* in the middle of the preceding group, continues with the skip of two back to *N*, and concludes with the further skip back to *K*.

10. **(C)** It is very important to have written the entire alphabet and to have assigned each letter its numerical equivalent in order to choose the answer to this question.

ABC	IRS	GNO	DHI	EJK
1 2 3	9 18 19	7 14 15	4 8 9	5 10 11
×2 +1	×2 +1	×2 +1	×2 +1	×2 +1

Obviously, you must figure out the relationship on groups other than the first one, then confirm that the relationship of the first three letters is not simple alphabetical succession. It is also clear that no group of three bears any external relationship to any other group of three letters. Only the relationship within a group of three will determine the correct answer. Only choice (C) satisfies the ×2, +1 formula.

EXERCISE 3

1. **(D)** Look at what you're given. In all groupings, the letters are the same. You might assume that the answer choice will contain those same letters. When there is only one subscript number, it is at the end. When there are two, they follow the last and the next to last letter. Your best guess, if you can find reasonable choices to fit, is that the number pattern appears to alternate: one number, two numbers, one number, two numbers. Choices (B) and (D) might fit into this pattern. Then look for the rationale for the numbers themselves. The numbers of the second group add to make the number of the third. Because the numbers of choice (D) add to make the number in the final group, this is the most logical choice.

2. **(A)** By inspection, you can find the pattern of the letters. Each succeeding group picks up with the second letter of the preceding group and proceeds in alphabetical order. This narrows your answer choice to (A) or (C). Now look at the numbers. Within each set of four, the numbers go in order, but there seems to be no rule by which numbers are assigned to succeeding groups. So you must look for a pattern of some sort. Note that even numbers always appear as subscripts and odd numbers are always superscripts. Now you know why (A) is the correct answer.

3. **(B)** Some series questions are easier than others. The numbers that follow the letters are the numbers assigned to the letters according to their position in the alphabet. Immediately, you may narrow to choices (A) and (B). Now look at the pattern of the letters. In each group there is a skip-one pattern. Because choice (A) gives letters in sequence, the correct answer must be (B).
4. **(C)** In the first four groupings, the 2s position themselves in all possible combinations around the *R* and the *D*. The fifth group reverses the positions of *R* and *D* and appears to begin anew the circuit of 2s around the letters. The final group, then, should continue the rotation of the 2s, following in the same manner as when the letters were in their original position. Thus, the second *D R* should have the 2s placed in the same manner as the second *R D*.
5. **(B)** As the pattern progresses, in each succeeding frame an additional circle is darkened. Thus in the first, none; in the second, one; in the third, two; and in the fourth, three. Because three circles have already been darkened in the fourth frame, the frame must be completed with undarkened circles, horizontal as in all frames.
6. **(D)** Because frames one and three are identical, you must assume that the pattern is of alternating identities and that frames two and four must also be identical.
7. **(C)** In the first three frames, the farthest-right figure is always a U shape. In the first frame, the next to the last figure is upended; in the second frame, an additional figure is upended, reading from right to left: in the third frame, three figures are upended. Logically, as the series progresses, the fourth frame should include the four left-hand figures upended, with only the farthest right maintaining its position as a U.
8. **(B)** The darkened figures seem to be following no particular pattern within themselves, but they do seem to be alternating frames with the undarkened figures. The positions of the undarkened arrows in the first and third frames are identical. There is no reason to expect their positions to change the next time they appear in the series. With the alternating dark, light pattern, the undarkened arrows are due to appear in the next frame, and choice (B) maintains their same position as in the two previous appearances.

Summary: Clues for Series Reasoning Questions

- On the COOP, these questions are called Sequences. On the HSPT, you find these questions in the Quantitative Skills section of the Mathematics test.
- In series questions, you have to determine the relationship between a series of symbols, numbers, or letters, then choose the next item for the series.
- First read the series through. If that does not help, try accenting the printed numbers and speaking the missing intervening numbers even more softly. Try grouping the numbers within the series into twos or threes. After grouping, try accenting the last number, or the first.
- It is a good idea to keep a copy of the alphabet in front of you as you work. Additionally, it is well worth your time to assign a number to each letter, jotting down the numbers from one to twenty-six directly under the letters to which they correspond.
- Study and practice the series reasoning question tactics in this chapter. Remember: answer the easy ones first; if you skip a question, make a mark on your answer sheet so you don't mark your answer sheet incorrectly; follow the system—look, sound, and group; don't spend too much time on any one question; and keep track of time.

Chapter 18

Comparisons

ROAD MAP

- *Geometric Comparisons*
- *Nongeometric Comparisons*
- *Comparison Exercises*
- *Answers and Explanations*

In this last section on quantitative and nonverbal skills, we'll look at comparison questions. The comparison questions in the Quantitative Skills section of the HSPT require a little bit of mathematical skill and a lot of patience and logical thinking. You can't rush through any of these questions! To get the maximum number of right answers, you have to study and count when you're answering geometric comparison questions. You begin by performing all of the operations of nongeometric comparison questions. Then you work through the answer choices one by one, eliminating each statement that proves to be false, based on the facts of the problem. When you find what you think is the correct choice, you still need to continue trying all of the other answers, as a check on your own reasoning. To give you a feel for these questions, let's work through a few together.

GEOMETRIC COMPARISONS

1. Examine (A), (B), and (C) and find the best answer.

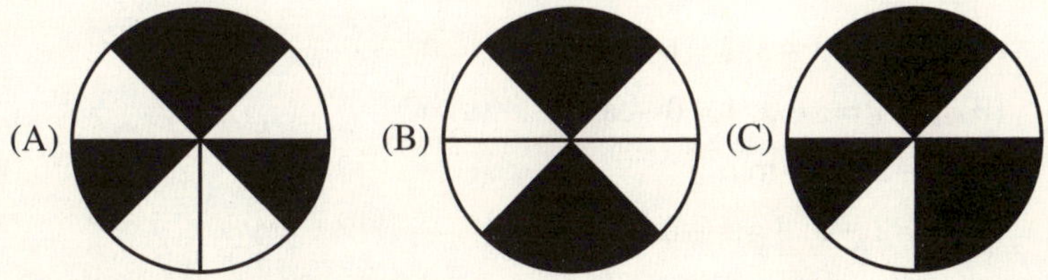

(A) (A) is more shaded than (B).

(B) (B) is more shaded than (A) and less shaded than (C).

(C) (A) and (B) are equally shaded and less shaded than (C).

(D) (A), (B) and (C) are equally shaded.

Begin by studying the three circles. Note that each circle is divided into eight segments. Now count the number of shaded segments in each circle, and write that number next to the letter of the circle. If you have counted accurately, you have written: (A) 4, (B) 4, (C) 5. Read the statements one by one, and mark true or false next to the letter of each statement. The statement in choice (A) is false because both (A) and (B) have four shaded segments. The statement in choice (B) must be marked false because it is not entirely true. (B) is indeed less shaded than (C), but it is not more shaded than (A).

CAUTION

Make sure you look at each figure carefully. Without careful examination, an optical illusion could give you the wrong first impression.

To be true, a statement must be 100% true. The statement in choice (C) is true. (A) and (B) arc equally shaded (4) and both are less shaded than (C) with its five shaded segments. Check out choice (D) just to be certain that you have not made an error. No problem here. The statement in choice (D) is clearly false.

2. The pie is divided into sixteen equal portions. Study the pie and find the best answer.

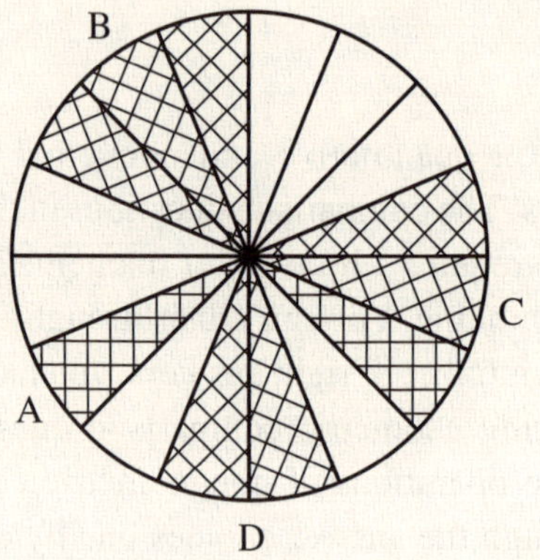

(A) A plus D equals B plus C.

(B) D minus A equals B minus C.

(C) C minus D equals A.

(D) B equals A plus C.

Begin by counting the pie wedges in each portion; write the number of wedges next to the letter—A (1), B (3), C (3), D (2). Now perform the very simple arithmetic for each statement.

(A) $1 + 2 = 3 + 3$; $3 = 6$—false

(B) $2 - 1 = 3 - 3$; $1 = 0$—false

(C) $3 - 2 = 1$—true

(D) $3 = 1 + 3$; $3 = 4$—false

NONGEOMETRIC COMPARISONS

1. Examine (A), (B), and (C) and find the best answer.

(A) $(5 \times 4) - 10$

(B) $(3 \times 6) + 4$

(C) $(8 \times 3) - 6$

(A) (B) is equal to (C) and greater than (A).

(B) (C) is greater than (A) but less than (B).

(C) (A) is greater than (C).

(D) (A) is less than (C) but more than (B).

Obviously, you must begin by performing the indicated operations.

(A) $20 - 10 = 10$

(B) $18 + 4 = 22$

(C) $24 - 6 = 18$

Now you can substitute these numbers for the letters in the four statements and choose the correct one.

(A) 22 is equal to 18 and greater than 10—false

(B) 18 is greater than 10 but less than 22—true

(C) 10 is greater than 18—false

(D) 10 is less than 18 but more than 22—false

2. Examine (A), (B), and (C) and find the best answer.

(A) 4^3

(B) 3^4

(C) $(3 \times 4)(4)$

(A) $A > B > C$

(B) $A = B > C$

(C) $C < B > A$

(D) $A = C < B$

First, perform the operations.

(A) $4^3 = 64$

(B) $3^4 = 81$

(C) $(3 \times 4)(4) = 12 \times 4 = 48$

Substitute the numbers in the statements.

(A) 64 is greater than 81, which is greater than 48—false

(B) 64 equals 81, which is greater than 48—false

(C) 48 is smaller than 81, which is greater than 64—true

(D) 64 is equal to 48, which is smaller than 81—false

COMPARISONS EXERCISES

Directions: Examine (A), (B), and (C) and find the best answer.

1.

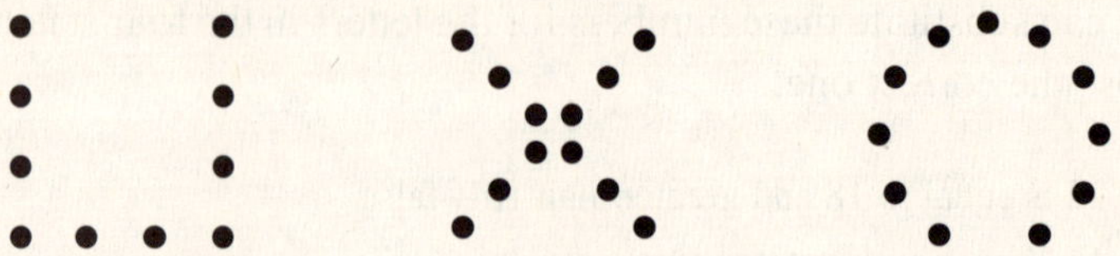

(A) (B) (C)

(A) **(B)** and **(C)** have the same number of dots.

(B) **(A)** has fewer dots than **(B)** but more dots than **(C)**.

(C) **(C)** has more dots than **(A)**.

(D) **(B)** has more dots than **(A)** and **(C)**, which have the same number of dots.

2. The distance from X to Y is one inch.

(A) (B) (C)

(A) Lines **(A)**, **(B)**, and **(C)** are of equal length.

(B) Line **(A)** is longer than lines **(B)** and **(C)**, which are of equal length.

(C) Line **(B)** is shorter than line **(A)** but longer than line **(C)**.

(D) Line **(A)** is shorter than line **(C)**.

3.

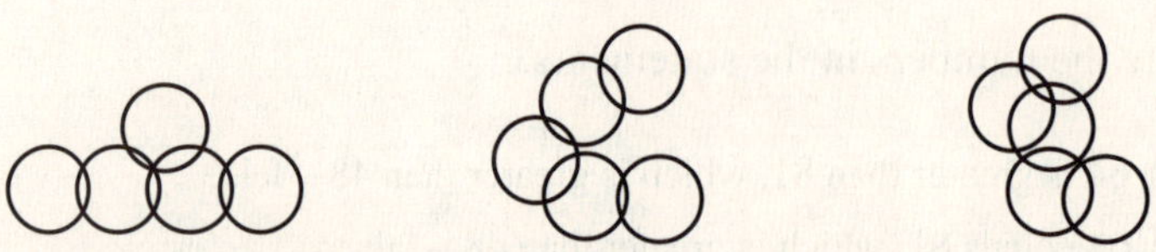

(A) (B) (C)

(A) **(C)** has more rings than **(A)**.

(B) **(A)** has the same number of rings as **(B)**.

(C) **(B)** and **(C)** have the same number of rings, which are more rings than **(A)**.

(D) **(B)** has fewer rings than either **(A)** or **(C)**.

4.

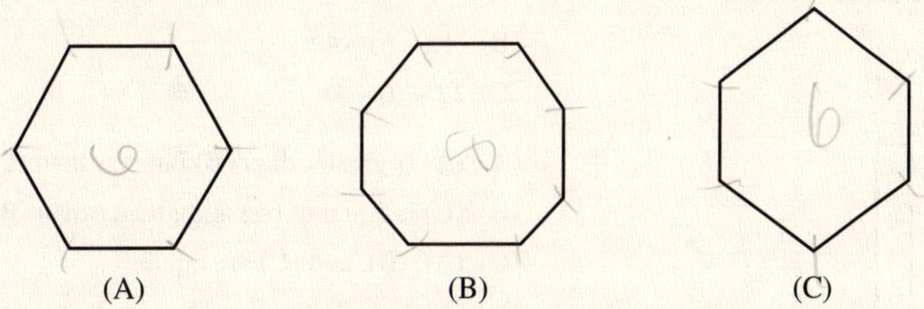

(A) (B) (C)

(A) **(C)** has more corners than **(A)**.

(B) **(B)** has the same number of corners as **(C)** and more corners than **(A)**.

(C) **(A)** has fewer corners than **(B)**.

(D) **(A)**, **(B)**, and **(C)** all have the same number of corners.

5.

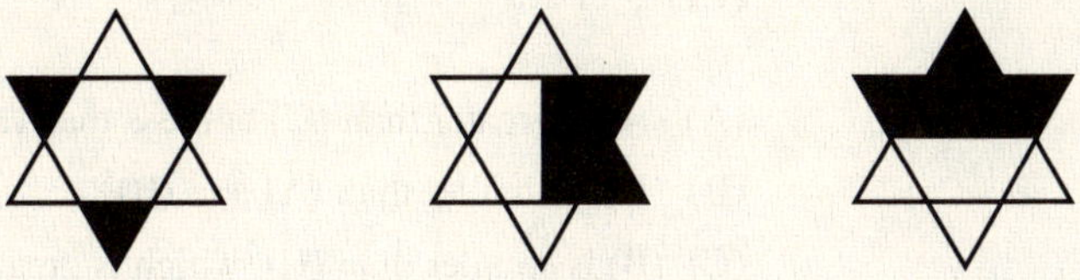

(A) (B) (C)

(A) **(C)** is more shaded than **(B)**, which is more shaded than **(A)**.

(B) **(C)** is more shaded than **(A)**, which is not less shaded than **(B)**.

(C) **(B)** and **(C)** are equally shaded.

(D) **(A)** and **(B)** are equally shaded.

6. Examine the rectangle and find the best answer.

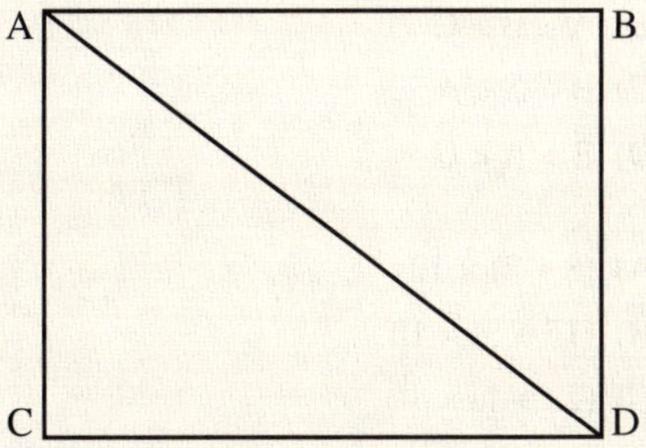

(A) AB is equal to CD, which is longer than AD

(B) BD is shorter than AC

(C) CD is longer than AD

(D) AC is equal to BD

7. Examine the graph and find the best answer.

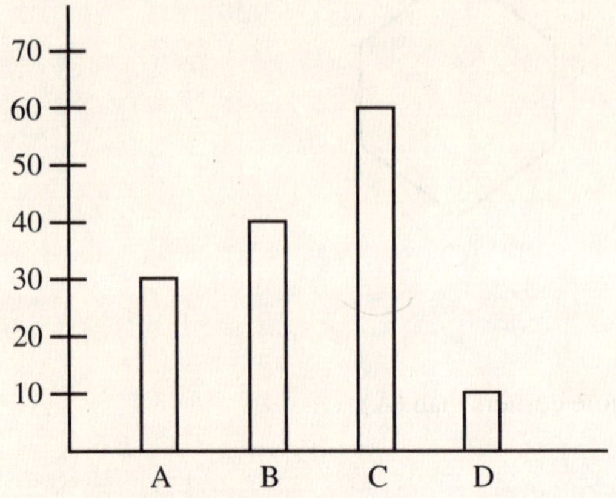

(A) C plus D minus A equals B.
(B) B plus D equals C.
(C) A plus B equals C.
(D) C minus D equals A plus B.

Directions: Examine (A), (B), and (C) and find the best answer.

8. (A) 30% of 30
(B) 25% of 40
(C) 20% of 50

(A) **(A)**, **(B)**, and **(C)** are equal.
(B) **(A)** and **(C)** are equal and are greater than **(B)**.
(C) **(A)** and **(B)** are equal and are less than **(C)**.
(D) **(B)** and **(C)** are equal and are greater than **(A)**.

9. (A) $(4 + 8) \times 10$
(B) $(8 + 10) \times 4$
(C) $(4 + 10) \times 8$

(A) **(A)** is greater than **(B)**, which is smaller than **(C)**.
(B) **(A)** and **(C)** are equal and are greater than **(B)**.
(C) **(C)** is greater than **(A)**, which is less than **(B)**.
(D) **(A)**, **(B)**, and **(C)** are equal.

10. (A) $(12 - 4) - 6$
(B) $(12 - 6) - 4$
(C) $12 - (6 - 4)$

(A) **(A)** is greater than **(B)** but less than **(C)**.
(B) **(C)** is equal to **(A)** and greater than **(B)**.
(C) **(A)**, **(B)**, and **(C)** are equal.
(D) **(A)** and **(B)** are equal but are less than **(C)**.

11. (A) $\frac{2}{3}$ of 27
(B) $\frac{2}{5}$ of 10
(C) $\frac{3}{7}$ of 28

(A) **(A)** is greater than **(C)** but less than **(B)**.
(B) **(C)** is smaller than **(A)** and **(B)**.
(C) **(B)** is smaller than **(C)**, which is greater than **(A)**.
(D) **(A)** is greater than **(C)**, which is greater than **(B)**.

12. (A) 8%
(B) .8
(C) .08%

(A) $A = B < C$
(B) $A < B > C$
(C) $B - C < A$
(D) $B > A < C$

13. (A) $(8 \div 2) \times 12$
(B) $(15 \div 3) \times 10$
(C) $(22 \div 1) \times 4$

(A) **(A)** is greater than **(B)**, which is less than **(C)**.
(B) **(C)** is greater than **(A)**, which is greater than **(B)**.
(C) **(A)** is equal to **(B)**, which is less than **(C)**.
(D) **(C)** is greater than **(A)**, which is less than **(B)**.

14. (A) $\sqrt{144}$
    (B) 3.5^2
    (C) $\frac{27}{2}$

    (A) A = B = C
    (B) A = B < C
    (C) B = C > A
    (D) A < B < C

15. (A) $7(x + 2y)$
    (B) $7x + 2y$
    (C) $7(x + 2y) + 2x$

    (A) **(C)** is greater than **(B)**, which is smaller than **(A)**.
    (B) **(B)** is smaller than **(C)**, which is smaller than **(A)**.
    (C) **(A)** is equal to **(B)**, which is smaller than **(C)**.
    (D) **(C)** is greater than **(A)**, which is smaller than **(B)**.

ANSWERS AND EXPLANATIONS

1. **(C)** (A) has 10 dots; (B) has 12 dots; (C) has 11 dots. 11 is greater than 10, so (C) has more dots than (A). Test the other statements, and you will find them all false.
2. **(D)** A straight line is the shortest distance between two points, so line (A) is the shortest line. The statement that declares that line (A) is shorter than either of the other two is the correct one.
3. **(B)** Each of the three figures has five rings, so any statement that speaks of more or fewer rings must be incorrect.
4. **(C)** (A) and (C) are hexagons with six sides and six corners; (B) is an octagon with eight sides and eight corners. Try this information out on the statements to find the true one.
5. **(A)** (C) is exactly half shaded; (B) is somewhat less than half shaded; (A) is very sparsely shaded. That is exactly the statement made in choice (A).
6. **(D)** In a rectangle, parallel sides are equal in length. Therefore, AB is equal to CD, and AC is equal to BD. AD is a hypotenuse. The hypotenuse is always the longest leg of a right triangle. AD cannot be shorter than any other line.
7. **(A)** Do the arithmetic. $60 + 10 = 30 + 40$. In other words, 70 equals 70, which is true. The other choices are all false. 40 plus 10 does not equal 60; 30 plus 40 does not equal 60; 60 minus 10 does not equal 30 plus 40.
8. **(D)** Do the arithmetic. 30% of 30 = 9; 25% of 40 = 10; 20% of 50 = 10. Therefore, (B) and (C) are equal and are both greater than (A).
9. **(A)** Do the arithmetic. $12 \times 10 = 120$; $18 \times 4 = 72$; $14 \times 8 = 112$. 120 is greater than 72, which is smaller than 112.
10. **(D)** Do the arithmetic. $8 - 6 = 2$; $6 - 4 = 2$; $12 - 2 = 10$. (A) and (B), both equaling 2, are equal but are far less than the 10 of (C).
11. **(D)** Do the arithmetic. $\frac{2}{3}$ of 27 = 18; $\frac{2}{5}$ of 10 = 4; $\frac{3}{7}$ of 28 = 12. 18 is greater than 12, which is greater than 10.
12. **(B)** Convert the percents to decimals so that the three numbers will be comparable. 8% = .08; .8 = .8; .08% = .0008. .08 is smaller than .8, which is greater than .0008.

13. **(D)** Do the arithmetic. $4 \times 12 = 48$; $5 \times 10 = 50$; $22 \times 4 = 88$. 88 is greater than 48, which is less than 50.

14. **(D)** Do the arithmetic. $\sqrt{144} = 12$; $3.5^2 = 12.25$; $27 \div 2 = 13.5$. 12 is smaller than 12.25, which is smaller than 13.5.

15. **(A)** You could substitute numerical values for x and y and arrive at the correct answer, but it is unnecessary to work with numbers. Simply perform the algebraic multiplications to make your comparisons. $7(x + 2y) = 7x + 14y$; $7x + 2y = 7x + 2y$; $7(x + 2y) + 2x = 7x + 14y + 2x = 9x + 14y$. $9x + 14y$ is greater than $7x + 2y$, which is smaller than $7x + 14y$.

Summary: Conquering Comparisons

- First perform all of the operations for nongeometric comparison questions.
- Next, work through all of the answer choices one by one and eliminate each statement that is false.
- Then, when you think you have found the correct answer, continue until you have tried each answer choice.

PART 4

Model Exams

PREVIEW

Chapter 19

First Model COOP Exam

ROAD MAP

- *Definitions for Memory Questions*
- *Test 1. Sequences*
- *Test 2. Analogies*
- *Test 3. Memory*
- *Test 4. Verbal Reasoning*
- *Test 5. Reading Comprehension*
- *Test 6. Mathematics Concepts and Applications*
- *Test 7. Language Expression*
- *Answers to First Model COOP Exam*
- *Answer Explanations for First Model COOP Exam*
- *Score Sheet*

Answer Sheet

Answers and explanations for all First Model COOP Exam questions follow the model exam.

TEST 1. SEQUENCES

1. Ⓐ Ⓑ Ⓒ Ⓓ	5. Ⓐ Ⓑ Ⓒ Ⓓ	9. Ⓐ Ⓑ Ⓒ Ⓓ	13. Ⓐ Ⓑ Ⓒ Ⓓ	17. Ⓐ Ⓑ Ⓒ Ⓓ
2. Ⓕ Ⓖ Ⓗ Ⓙ	6. Ⓕ Ⓖ Ⓗ Ⓙ	10. Ⓕ Ⓖ Ⓗ Ⓙ	14. Ⓕ Ⓖ Ⓗ Ⓙ	18. Ⓕ Ⓖ Ⓗ Ⓙ
3. Ⓐ Ⓑ Ⓒ Ⓓ	7. Ⓐ Ⓑ Ⓒ Ⓓ	11. Ⓐ Ⓑ Ⓒ Ⓓ	15. Ⓐ Ⓑ Ⓒ Ⓓ	19. Ⓐ Ⓑ Ⓒ Ⓓ
4. Ⓕ Ⓖ Ⓗ Ⓙ	8. Ⓕ Ⓖ Ⓗ Ⓙ	12. Ⓕ Ⓖ Ⓗ Ⓙ	16. Ⓕ Ⓖ Ⓗ Ⓙ	20. Ⓕ Ⓖ Ⓗ Ⓙ

TEST 2. ANALOGIES

1. Ⓐ Ⓑ Ⓒ Ⓓ	5. Ⓐ Ⓑ Ⓒ Ⓓ	9. Ⓐ Ⓑ Ⓒ Ⓓ	13. Ⓐ Ⓑ Ⓒ Ⓓ	17. Ⓐ Ⓑ Ⓒ Ⓓ
2. Ⓕ Ⓖ Ⓗ Ⓙ	6. Ⓕ Ⓖ Ⓗ Ⓙ	10. Ⓕ Ⓖ Ⓗ Ⓙ	14. Ⓕ Ⓖ Ⓗ Ⓙ	18. Ⓕ Ⓖ Ⓗ Ⓙ
3. Ⓐ Ⓑ Ⓒ Ⓓ	7. Ⓐ Ⓑ Ⓒ Ⓓ	11. Ⓐ Ⓑ Ⓒ Ⓓ	15. Ⓐ Ⓑ Ⓒ Ⓓ	19. Ⓐ Ⓑ Ⓒ Ⓓ
4. Ⓕ Ⓖ Ⓗ Ⓙ	8. Ⓕ Ⓖ Ⓗ Ⓙ	12. Ⓕ Ⓖ Ⓗ Ⓙ	16. Ⓕ Ⓖ Ⓗ Ⓙ	20. Ⓕ Ⓖ Ⓗ Ⓙ

TEST 3. MEMORY

1. Ⓐ Ⓑ Ⓒ Ⓓ	5. Ⓐ Ⓑ Ⓒ Ⓓ	9. Ⓐ Ⓑ Ⓒ Ⓓ	13. Ⓐ Ⓑ Ⓒ Ⓓ	17. Ⓐ Ⓑ Ⓒ Ⓓ
2. Ⓕ Ⓖ Ⓗ Ⓙ	6. Ⓕ Ⓖ Ⓗ Ⓙ	10. Ⓕ Ⓖ Ⓗ Ⓙ	14. Ⓕ Ⓖ Ⓗ Ⓙ	18. Ⓕ Ⓖ Ⓗ Ⓙ
3. Ⓐ Ⓑ Ⓒ Ⓓ	7. Ⓐ Ⓑ Ⓒ Ⓓ	11. Ⓐ Ⓑ Ⓒ Ⓓ	15. Ⓐ Ⓑ Ⓒ Ⓓ	19. Ⓐ Ⓑ Ⓒ Ⓓ
4. Ⓕ Ⓖ Ⓗ Ⓙ	8. Ⓕ Ⓖ Ⓗ Ⓙ	12. Ⓕ Ⓖ Ⓗ Ⓙ	16. Ⓕ Ⓖ Ⓗ Ⓙ	20. Ⓕ Ⓖ Ⓗ Ⓙ

TEST 4. VERBAL REASONING

1. Ⓐ Ⓑ Ⓒ Ⓓ	5. Ⓐ Ⓑ Ⓒ Ⓓ	9. Ⓐ Ⓑ Ⓒ Ⓓ	13. Ⓐ Ⓑ Ⓒ Ⓓ	17. Ⓐ Ⓑ Ⓒ Ⓓ
2. Ⓕ Ⓖ Ⓗ Ⓙ	6. Ⓕ Ⓖ Ⓗ Ⓙ	10. Ⓕ Ⓖ Ⓗ Ⓙ	14. Ⓕ Ⓖ Ⓗ Ⓙ	18. Ⓕ Ⓖ Ⓗ Ⓙ
3. Ⓐ Ⓑ Ⓒ Ⓓ	7. Ⓐ Ⓑ Ⓒ Ⓓ	11. Ⓐ Ⓑ Ⓒ Ⓓ	15. Ⓐ Ⓑ Ⓒ Ⓓ	19. Ⓐ Ⓑ Ⓒ Ⓓ
4. Ⓕ Ⓖ Ⓗ Ⓙ	8. Ⓕ Ⓖ Ⓗ Ⓙ	12. Ⓕ Ⓖ Ⓗ Ⓙ	16. Ⓕ Ⓖ Ⓗ Ⓙ	20. Ⓕ Ⓖ Ⓗ Ⓙ

TEAR HERE

TEST 5. READING COMPREHENSION

1. ⓐ ⓑ ⓒ ⓓ	9. ⓐ ⓑ ⓒ ⓓ	17. ⓐ ⓑ ⓒ ⓓ	25. ⓐ ⓑ ⓒ ⓓ	33. ⓐ ⓑ ⓒ ⓓ
2. ⓕ ⓖ ⓗ ⓙ	10. ⓕ ⓖ ⓗ ⓙ	18. ⓕ ⓖ ⓗ ⓙ	26. ⓕ ⓖ ⓗ ⓙ	34. ⓕ ⓖ ⓗ ⓙ
3. ⓐ ⓑ ⓒ ⓓ	11. ⓐ ⓑ ⓒ ⓓ	19. ⓐ ⓑ ⓒ ⓓ	27. ⓐ ⓑ ⓒ ⓓ	35. ⓐ ⓑ ⓒ ⓓ
4. ⓕ ⓖ ⓗ ⓙ	12. ⓕ ⓖ ⓗ ⓙ	20. ⓕ ⓖ ⓗ ⓙ	28. ⓕ ⓖ ⓗ ⓙ	36. ⓕ ⓖ ⓗ ⓙ
5. ⓐ ⓑ ⓒ ⓓ	13. ⓐ ⓑ ⓒ ⓓ	21. ⓐ ⓑ ⓒ ⓓ	29. ⓐ ⓑ ⓒ ⓓ	37. ⓐ ⓑ ⓒ ⓓ
6. ⓕ ⓖ ⓗ ⓙ	14. ⓕ ⓖ ⓗ ⓙ	22. ⓕ ⓖ ⓗ ⓙ	30. ⓕ ⓖ ⓗ ⓙ	38. ⓕ ⓖ ⓗ ⓙ
7. ⓐ ⓑ ⓒ ⓓ	15. ⓐ ⓑ ⓒ ⓓ	23. ⓐ ⓑ ⓒ ⓓ	31. ⓐ ⓑ ⓒ ⓓ	39. ⓐ ⓑ ⓒ ⓓ
8. ⓕ ⓖ ⓗ ⓙ	16. ⓕ ⓖ ⓗ ⓙ	24. ⓕ ⓖ ⓗ ⓙ	32. ⓕ ⓖ ⓗ ⓙ	40. ⓕ ⓖ ⓗ ⓙ

TEST 6. MATHEMATICS CONCEPTS AND APPLICATIONS

1. ⓐ ⓑ ⓒ ⓓ	9. ⓐ ⓑ ⓒ ⓓ	17. ⓐ ⓑ ⓒ ⓓ	25. ⓐ ⓑ ⓒ ⓓ	33. ⓐ ⓑ ⓒ ⓓ
2. ⓕ ⓖ ⓗ ⓙ	10. ⓕ ⓖ ⓗ ⓙ	18. ⓕ ⓖ ⓗ ⓙ	26. ⓕ ⓖ ⓗ ⓙ	34. ⓕ ⓖ ⓗ ⓙ
3. ⓐ ⓑ ⓒ ⓓ	11. ⓐ ⓑ ⓒ ⓓ	19. ⓐ ⓑ ⓒ ⓓ	27. ⓐ ⓑ ⓒ ⓓ	35. ⓐ ⓑ ⓒ ⓓ
4. ⓕ ⓖ ⓗ ⓙ	12. ⓕ ⓖ ⓗ ⓙ	20. ⓕ ⓖ ⓗ ⓙ	28. ⓕ ⓖ ⓗ ⓙ	36. ⓕ ⓖ ⓗ ⓙ
5. ⓐ ⓑ ⓒ ⓓ	13. ⓐ ⓑ ⓒ ⓓ	21. ⓐ ⓑ ⓒ ⓓ	29. ⓐ ⓑ ⓒ ⓓ	37. ⓐ ⓑ ⓒ ⓓ
6. ⓕ ⓖ ⓗ ⓙ	14. ⓕ ⓖ ⓗ ⓙ	22. ⓕ ⓖ ⓗ ⓙ	30. ⓕ ⓖ ⓗ ⓙ	38. ⓕ ⓖ ⓗ ⓙ
7. ⓐ ⓑ ⓒ ⓓ	15. ⓐ ⓑ ⓒ ⓓ	23. ⓐ ⓑ ⓒ ⓓ	31. ⓐ ⓑ ⓒ ⓓ	39. ⓐ ⓑ ⓒ ⓓ
8. ⓕ ⓖ ⓗ ⓙ	16. ⓕ ⓖ ⓗ ⓙ	24. ⓕ ⓖ ⓗ ⓙ	32. ⓕ ⓖ ⓗ ⓙ	40. ⓕ ⓖ ⓗ ⓙ

TEAR HERE

TEST 7. LANGUAGE EXPRESSION

1. ⓐ ⓑ ⓒ ⓓ	9. ⓐ ⓑ ⓒ ⓓ	17. ⓐ ⓑ ⓒ ⓓ	25. ⓐ ⓑ ⓒ ⓓ	33. ⓐ ⓑ ⓒ ⓓ
2. ⓕ ⓖ ⓗ ⓙ	10. ⓕ ⓖ ⓗ ⓙ	18. ⓕ ⓖ ⓗ ⓙ	26. ⓕ ⓖ ⓗ ⓙ	34. ⓕ ⓖ ⓗ ⓙ
3. ⓐ ⓑ ⓒ ⓓ	11. ⓐ ⓑ ⓒ ⓓ	19. ⓐ ⓑ ⓒ ⓓ	27. ⓐ ⓑ ⓒ ⓓ	35. ⓐ ⓑ ⓒ ⓓ
4. ⓕ ⓖ ⓗ ⓙ	12. ⓕ ⓖ ⓗ ⓙ	20. ⓕ ⓖ ⓗ ⓙ	28. ⓕ ⓖ ⓗ ⓙ	36. ⓕ ⓖ ⓗ ⓙ
5. ⓐ ⓑ ⓒ ⓓ	13. ⓐ ⓑ ⓒ ⓓ	21. ⓐ ⓑ ⓒ ⓓ	29. ⓐ ⓑ ⓒ ⓓ	37. ⓐ ⓑ ⓒ ⓓ
6. ⓕ ⓖ ⓗ ⓙ	14. ⓕ ⓖ ⓗ ⓙ	22. ⓕ ⓖ ⓗ ⓙ	30. ⓕ ⓖ ⓗ ⓙ	38. ⓕ ⓖ ⓗ ⓙ
7. ⓐ ⓑ ⓒ ⓓ	15. ⓐ ⓑ ⓒ ⓓ	23. ⓐ ⓑ ⓒ ⓓ	31. ⓐ ⓑ ⓒ ⓓ	39. ⓐ ⓑ ⓒ ⓓ
8. ⓕ ⓖ ⓗ ⓙ	16. ⓕ ⓖ ⓗ ⓙ	24. ⓕ ⓖ ⓗ ⓙ	32. ⓕ ⓖ ⓗ ⓙ	40. ⓕ ⓖ ⓗ ⓙ

TEAR HERE

First Model COOP Exam

DEFINITIONS FOR MEMORY QUESTIONS

Time—12 minutes

Directions: Read the nonsense words and their definitions aloud at least one time through the entire list. Commit them to memory.

1. A *procan* is a kind of dog.
2. *Tiher* means "to fly."
3. *Legod* is ice.
4. A *plifop* is a helicopter.
5. A *waftok* is a boot.
6. *Ragid* means "to snore."
7. *Minca* is candy.
8. A *toobo* is a hurricane.
9. A *glabara* is an elephant.
10. A *moskin* is a banana.
11. *Garcar* is the color red.
12. *Dystry* means "to read."
13. A *lopop* is a hole.
14. A *skosh* is a sardine.
15. A *calafa* is a palm tree.
16. A *freex* is a kind of musical instrument.
17. An *abartan* is a loud noise.
18. *Eteflo* is smoke.
19. A *nababa* is a rocking chair.
20. *Jepusu* is a sticky substance.

Use the full 12 minutes to memorize these words and their definitions. Do not go on until the signal is given.

TEST 1. SEQUENCES

Time—15 minutes

Directions: For questions 1 through 20, choose the part that would continue the pattern or sequence. Mark the letter of your answer on the answer sheet.

1. 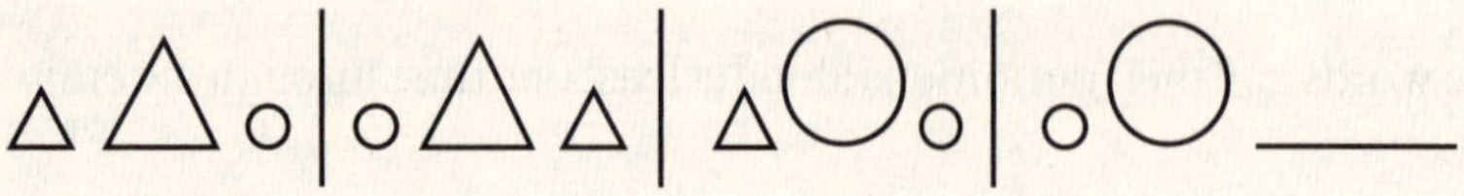

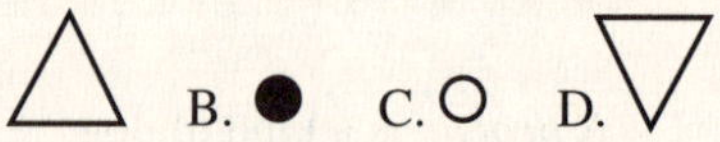

A. B. C. D.

2. 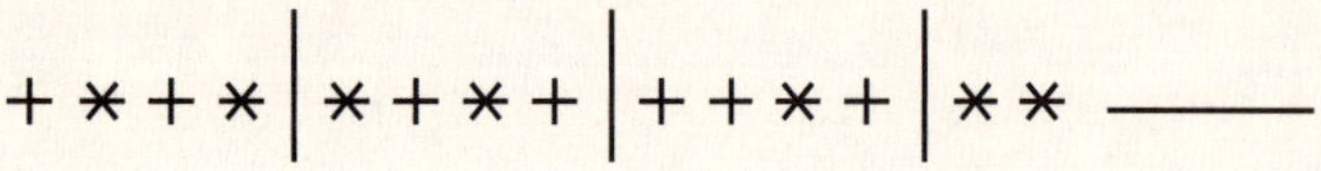

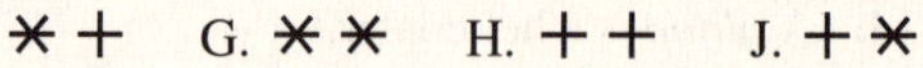

F. G. H. J.

3. 

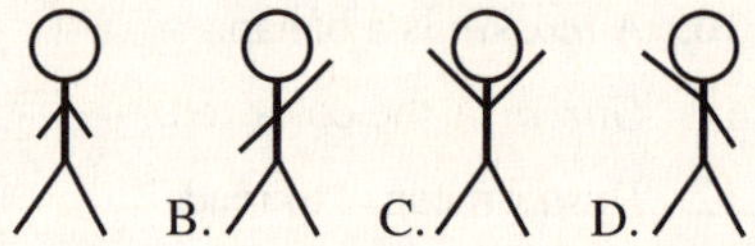

A. B. C. D.

4. 

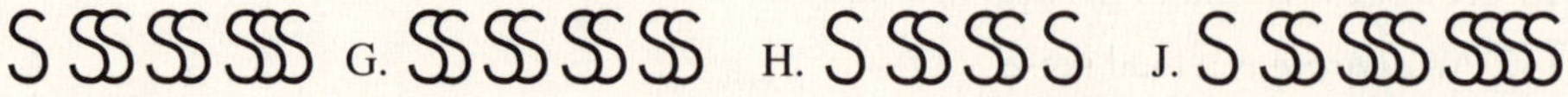

F. G. H. J.

5. 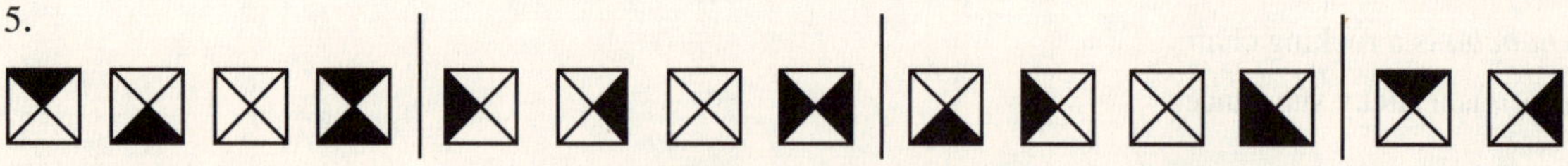

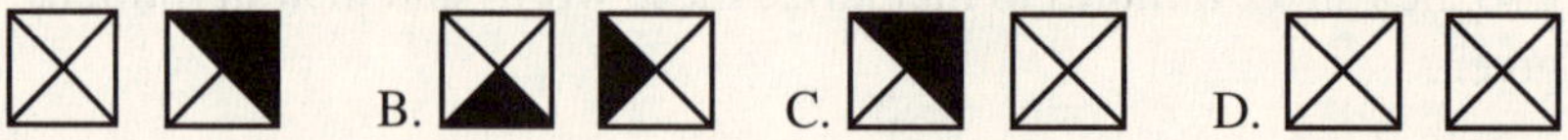

A. B. C. D.

6. 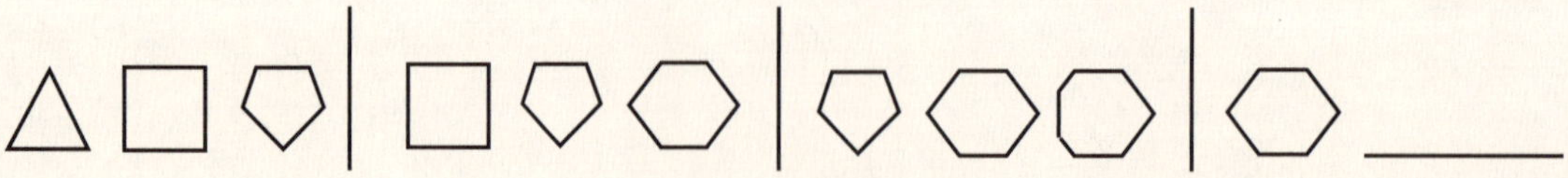

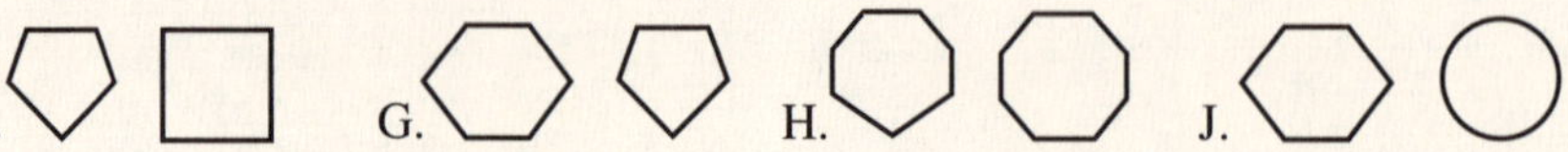

F. G. H. J.

7. 6 14 22 | 73 81 89 | 46 54 __ |
   (A) 58
   (B) 62
   (C) 64
   (D) 66

8. 36 31 31 | 12 7 7 | 81 __ 76 |
   (F) 81
   (G) 79
   (H) 76
   (J) 72

9. 33 40 34 | 51 58 52 | 65 __ 66 |
   (A) 70
   (B) 79
   (C) 71
   (D) 72

10. 96 24 6 | $\frac{1}{2}$ $\frac{1}{8}$ $\frac{1}{32}$ | __ 16 4 |
   (F) 32
   (G) 82
   (H) 58
   (J) 64

11. 8 16 9 | 25 50 43 | 19 38 __ |
   (A) 31
   (B) 27
   (C) 30
   (D) 25

12. 5 25 625 | 2 4 16 | 1 1 __ |
   (F) 0
   (G) 1
   (H) 2
   (J) 4

13. 21 15 26 | 15 15 20 | 10 __ 15 |
   (A) 15
   (B) 10
   (C) 20
   (D) 5

14. AB_5C_5 AB_5C_4 AB_4C_4 __ AB_3C_3
   (F) $A_5B_4C_3$
   (G) $A_4B_4C_3$
   (H) AB_3C_4
   (J) AB_4C_3

15. $F^1G^1H^1$ $F_2G^1H^1$ $F_2G_2H^1$ __ $F^3G_2H_2$
   (A) $F_2G_2H_2$
   (B) $F^1G_2H^3$
   (C) $F_2G_2H^3$
   (D) $F^2G_2H_2$

16. MKI_6 MK_5I_6 $M_4K_5I_6$ __ M_4KI
   (F) MK_5I_6
   (G) M_4K_5I
   (H) MK_5I
   (J) MKI_6

17. BCD FGH JKL MNP __
   (A) RST
   (B) QUR
   (C) QST
   (D) QRS

18. CADA EAFA GAHA __ KALA
   (F) HAKA
   (G) AIAJ
   (H) MANA
   (J) IAJA

19. PTL TLP LPT PTL __
   (A) LTP
   (B) TLP
   (C) LPT
   (D) TPL

20. ZYWV VUSR RQON __ JIGF
   (F) ONLK
   (G) NMLJ
   (H) MLKJ
   (J) NMKJ

STOP

IF YOU FINISH BEFORE TIME IS UP, CHECK OVER YOUR WORK ON TEST 1 ONLY. DO NOT GO BACK TO EITHER PREVIOUS TEST. DO NOT GO ON UNTIL THE SIGNAL IS GIVEN.

TEST 2. ANALOGIES

Time—7 minutes

Directions: For questions 1–20, choose the picture that should go in the empty box so that the bottom two pictures are related in the same way that the top two are related.

1.

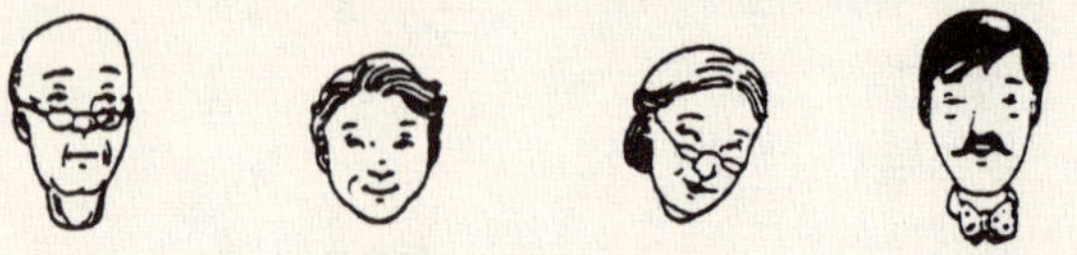

A. B. C. D.

2.

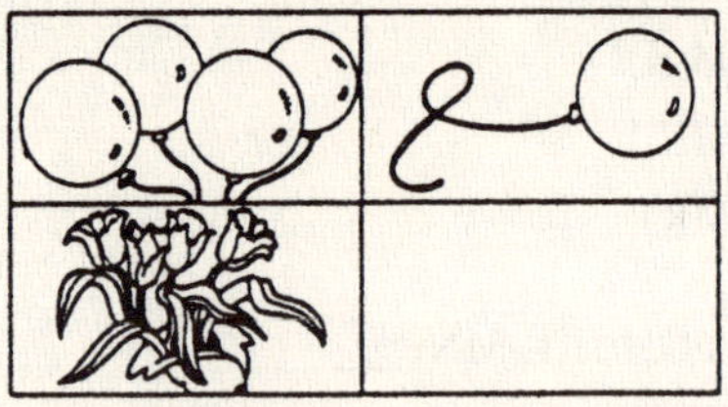

F. G. H. J.

3.

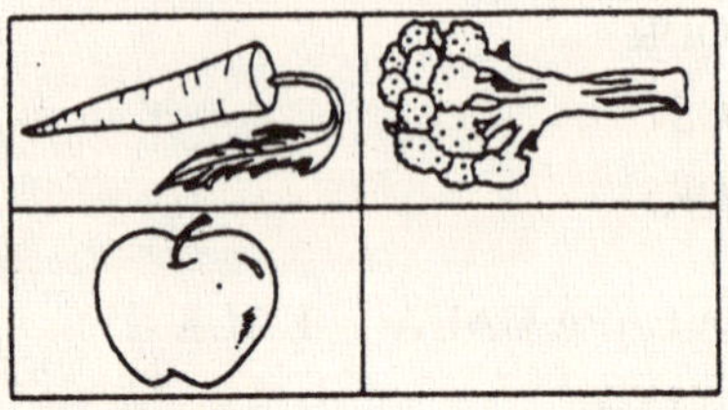

A. B. C. D.

4.

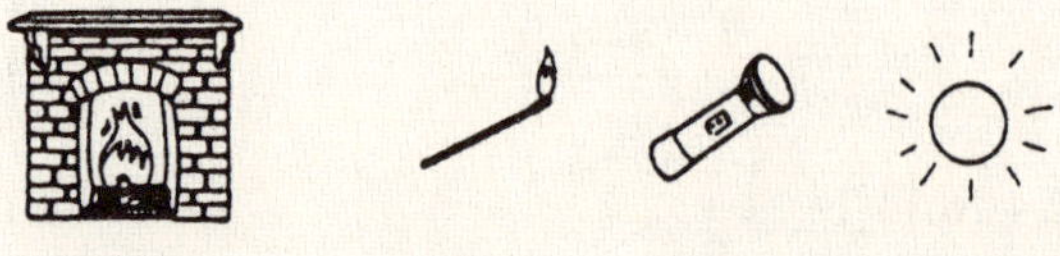

F. G. H. J.

5.

A. B C. D.

6

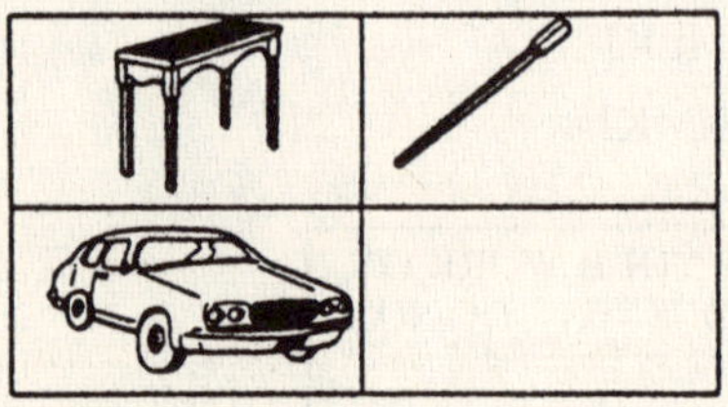

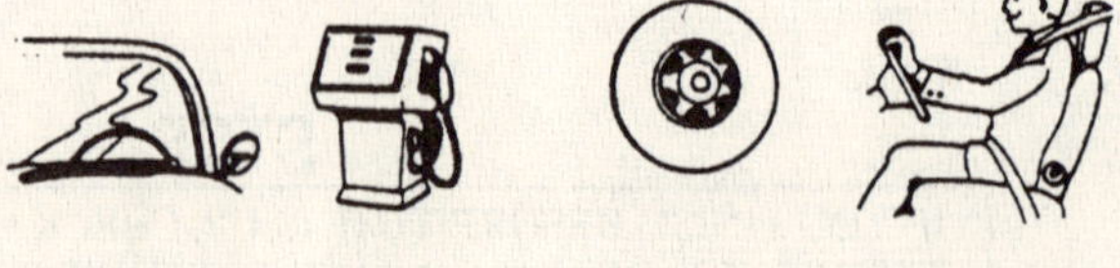

F. G. H. J.

7.

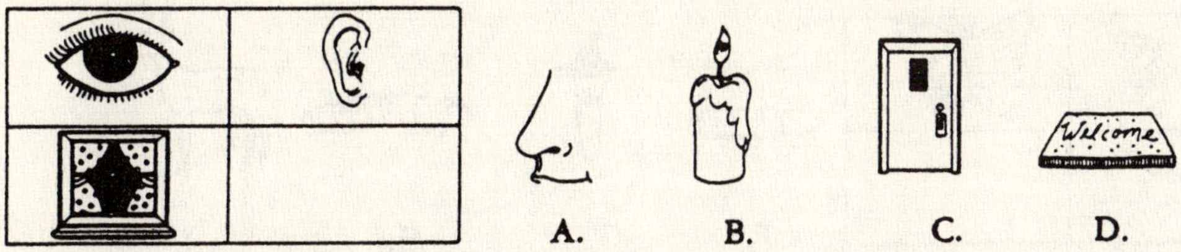

A. B. C. D.

8.

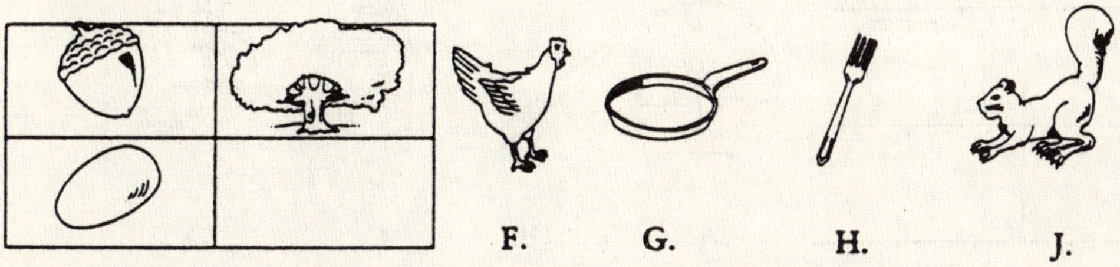

F. G. H. J.

9.

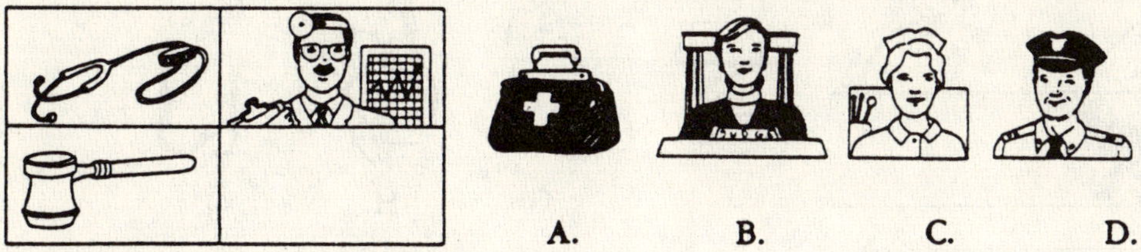

A. B. C. D.

10.

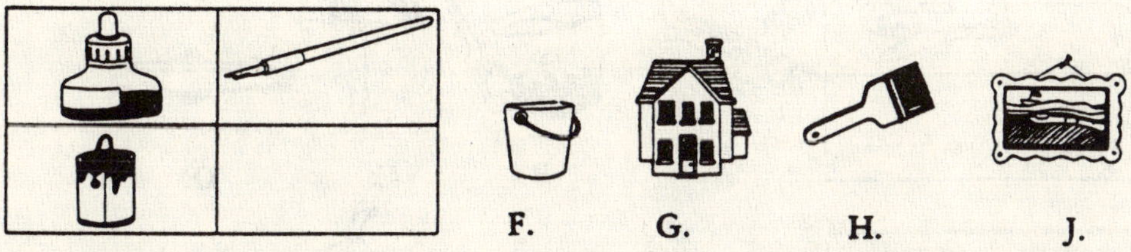

F. G. H. J.

11.

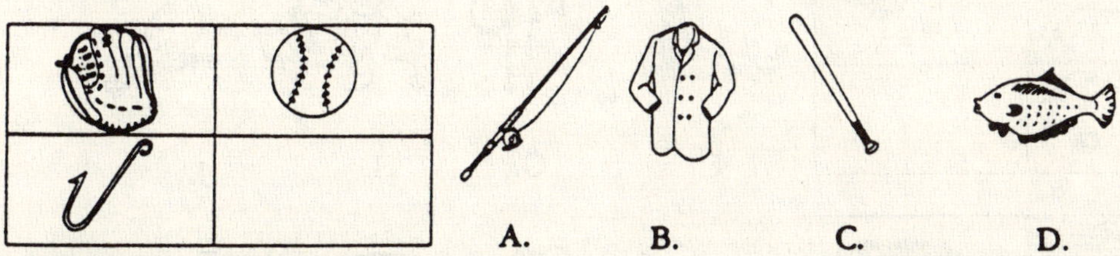

A. B. C. D.

12.

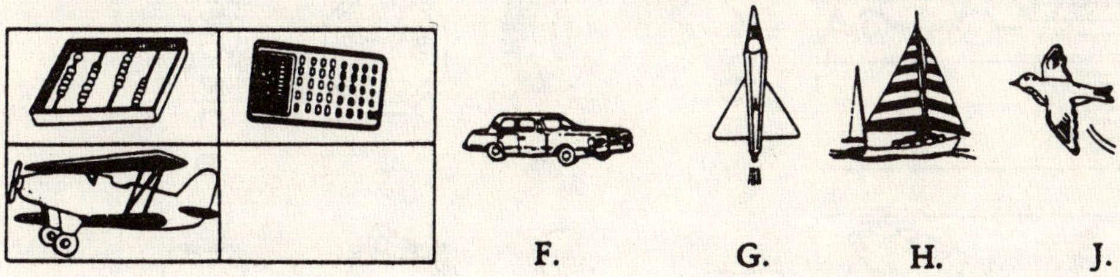

F. G. H. J.

13.

A. B. C. D.

GO ON TO THE NEXT PAGE

14.

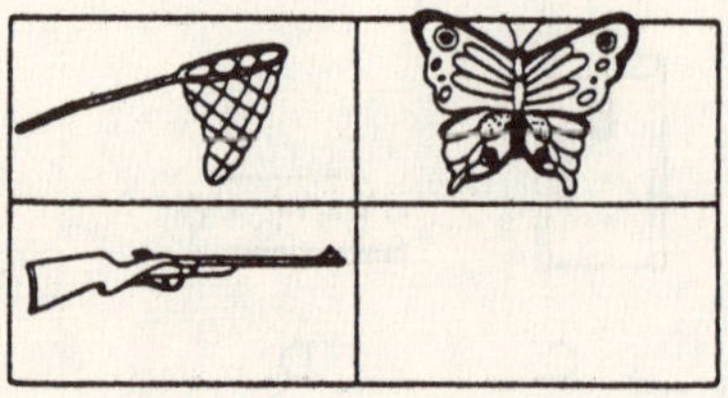

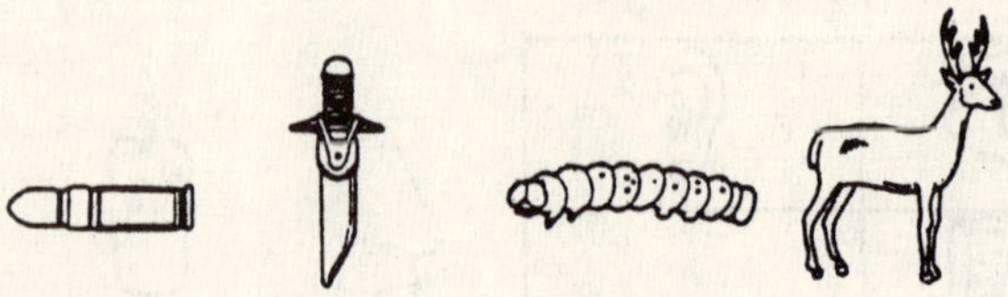

F. G. H. J.

15.

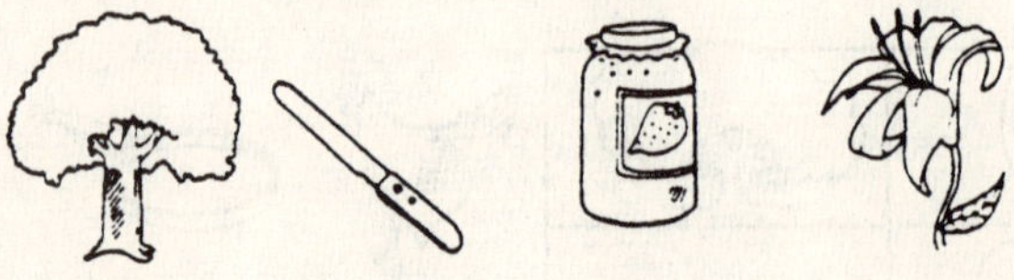

A. B. C. D.

16.

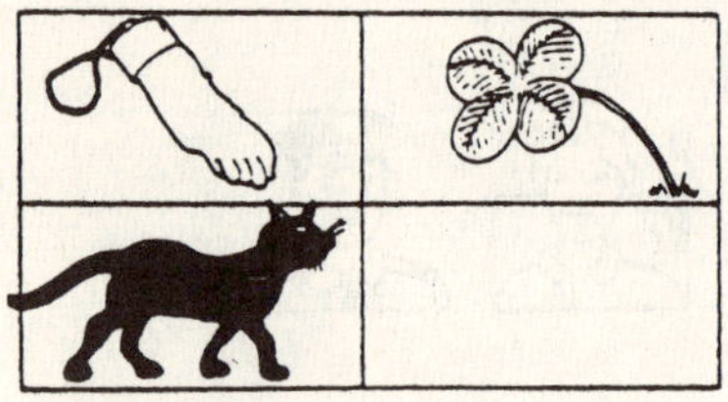

F. G. H. J.

17.

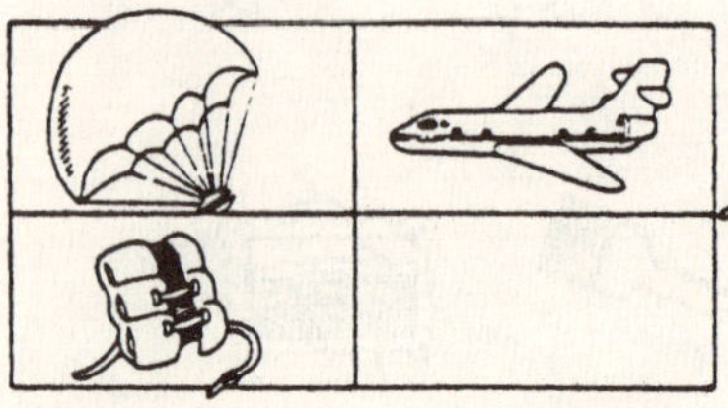

A. B. C. D.

18.

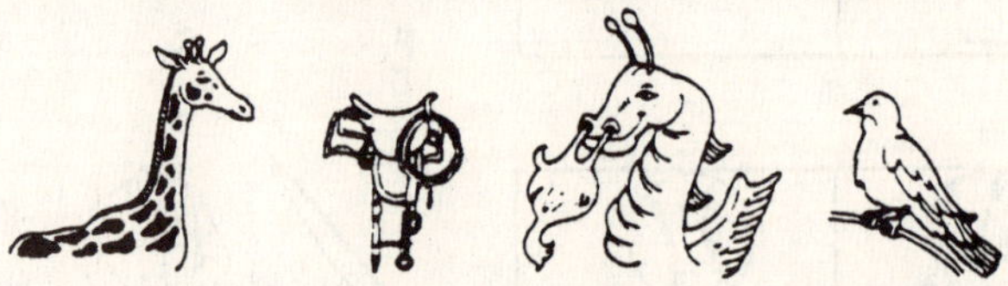

F. G. H. J.

19.

A. B. C. D.

20.

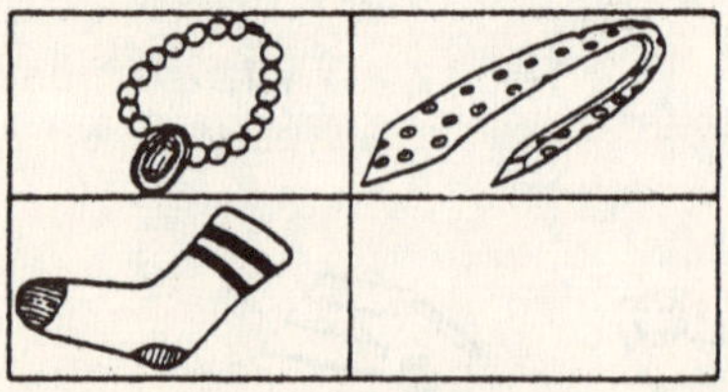

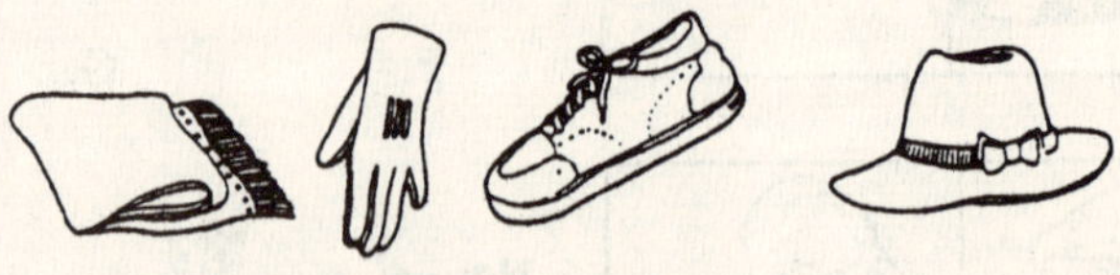

F. G. H. J.

STOP

IF YOU FINISH BEFORE TIME IS UP, CHECK OVER YOUR WORK ON TEST 2 ONLY. DO NOT GO BACK TO EITHER PREVIOUS TEST. DO NOT GO ON UNTIL THE SIGNAL IS GIVEN.

TEST 3. MEMORY

Time—5 minutes

Directions: Choose the word that means the same as the underlined word or phrase.

1. Which word is a boot?
   (A) skosh
   (B) waftok
   (C) eteflo
   (D) ragid
   (E) calafa

2. Which word means candy?
   (F) garcar
   (G) lopop
   (H) plifop
   (J) minca
   (K) nababa

3. Which word means a dog?
   (A) jepusu
   (B) dystry
   (C) tiher
   (D) moskin
   (E) procan

4. Which word means to read?
   (F) freex
   (G) tiher
   (H) dystry
   (J) abartan
   (K) legod

5. Which word means a palm tree?
   (A) calafa
   (B) abartan
   (C) ragid
   (D) toobo
   (E) plifop

6. Which word means to fly?
   (F) skosh
   (G) garcar
   (H) lopop
   (J) plifop
   (K) tiher

7. Which word means ice?
   (A) ragid
   (B) eteflo
   (C) legod
   (D) moskin
   (E) glabara

8. Which word means a sticky substance?
   (F) nababa
   (G) jepusu
   (H) dystry
   (J) glabara
   (K) freex

9. Which word means a loud noise?
   (A) tiher
   (B) toobo
   (C) nababa
   (D) abartan
   (E) waftok

10. Which word means banana?
    (F) moskin
    (G) procan
    (H) calafa
    (J) abartan
    (K) nababa

GO ON TO THE NEXT PAGE

11. Which word means the color red?
    (A) dystry
    (B) ragid
    (C) garcar
    (D) eteflo
    (E) freex

12. Which word means a helicopter?
    (F) toobo
    (G) nababa
    (H) waftok
    (J) plifop
    (K) tiher

13. Which word means a rocking chair?
    (A) glabara
    (B) nababa
    (C) abartan
    (D) procan
    (E) dystry

14. Which word means a sardine?
    (F) moskin
    (G) waftok
    (H) minca
    (J) tiher
    (K) skosh

15. Which word means to snore?
    (A) ragid
    (B) freex
    (C) jepusu
    (D) moskin
    (E) calafa

16. Which word means a hurricane?
    (F) lopop
    (G) toobo
    (H) minca
    (J) skosh
    (K) tiher

17. Which word means smoke?
    (A) freex
    (B) nababa
    (C) waftok
    (D) eteflo
    (E) procan

18. Which word means a hole?
    (F) lopop
    (G) dystry
    (H) garcar
    (J) legod
    (K) eteflo

19. Which word means a musical instrument?
    (A) plifop
    (B) calafa
    (C) freex
    (D) abartan
    (E) tiher

20. Which word means an elephant?
    (F) nababa
    (G) ragid
    (H) abartan
    (J) calafa
    (K) glabara

STOP

IF YOU FINISH BEFORE TIME IS UP, CHECK OVER YOUR WORK ON TEST 3 ONLY. DO NOT GO BACK TO EITHER PREVIOUS TEST. DO NOT GO ON UNTIL THE SIGNAL IS GIVEN.

TEST 4. VERBAL REASONING

Time—15 minutes

Directions: For questions 1–6, find the word that names a necessary part of the underlined word.

1. burning
   (A) flame
   (B) smoke
   (C) ash
   (D) heat

2. verbalize
   (F) verb
   (G) word
   (H) hearing
   (J) sound

3. legislation
   (A) laws
   (B) lawyers
   (C) senate
   (D) debate

4. terrarium
   (F) darkness
   (G) animals
   (H) water
   (J) earth

5. violin
   (A) bow
   (B) notes
   (C) strings
   (D) melody

6. chronometer
   (F) watch
   (G) standard
   (H) time
   (J) ticking

Directions: In questions 7–12, the words in the top row are related in some way. The words in the bottom row are related in the same way. For each item, find the word that completes the bottom row of words.

7. vest jacket coat
   sandal shoe
   (A) slipper
   (B) boot
   (C) ski
   (D) moccasin

8. gold mercury iron
   water air
   (F) oxygen
   (G) helium
   (H) steel
   (J) atmosphere

9. color odor sound
   feel see
   (A) hear
   (B) soft
   (C) sound
   (D) tell

10. forsythia tulip crocus
    holly poinsettia
    (F) lilac
    (G) mistletoe
    (H) wreath
    (J) tree

GO ON TO THE NEXT PAGE

11. bird dog spider
man horse
(A) crab
(B) fly
(C) eel
(D) unicorn

12. baseball football basketball
skiing shotput
(F) hockey
(G) soccer
(H) tennis
(J) marathon

Directions: For questions 13–17, find the statement that is true according to the given information.

13. Jeffrey is a law student. On Monday evenings he plays the violin in an orchestra. On Tuesdays and Thursdays he goes square dancing. On Friday afternoon Jeffrey fiddles for a children's folk dancing group.
(A) Jeffrey plays the violin at least twice a week.
(B) Jeffrey likes music better than the law.
(C) Jeffrey dances three times a week.
(D) Musicians are good dancers.

14. Debbie took the written Foreign Service Officer examination in December. Today Debbie received an appointment date for her Oral Assessment. Debbie is very happy.
(F) Debbie failed the written exam.
(G) Debbie is now a Foreign Service officer.
(H) Everyone who takes the Foreign Service Officer exam must take an oral exam as well.
(J) Debbie is still under consideration for appointment as a Foreign Service officer.

15. Bill and Dan were exploring an abandoned house. The windows swung loose, the floorboards creaked, and dust and cobwebs filled the air. Suddenly, the two boys ran from the house.
(A) The house was haunted.
(B) Something frightened the boys.
(C) There were bats flying about.
(D) Someone told the boys to get out.

16. Mr. and Mrs. Chen drive a blue Chevrolet station wagon that they keep in their driveway. Their son Warren has a red Toyota that he puts in the garage each night.
(F) Blue cars are less susceptible to ravages of weather than are red cars.
(G) The Chens have a one-car garage.
(H) Warren has a new car.
(J) Warren's car is garaged regularly.

17. Mark was distracted by his dog while jumping on the trampoline; he slipped and broke his right arm. That same afternoon the dog chased the cat up a tree. Another time Mark was walking his dog, the dog pulled Mark too fast; Mark fell and broke his right arm.
(A) Mark's dog is dangerous and must be destroyed.
(B) Mark should let his sister walk the dog.
(C) Mark is left-handed.
(D) Mark is accident-prone.

Directions: For questions 18–20, find the correct answer.

18. Here are some words translated from an artificial language.

    chekiruala means eating

    duangfrit means hidden

    duangruala means eaten

    Which word means *hiding*?

    (F) chekifrit

    (G) rualafrit

    (H) chekiduang

    (J) fritcheki

19. Here are some words translated from an artificial language.

    jokiohakaflis means creek

    luraohakaflis means river

    jokiohakasloo means pond

    Which word means *lake*?

    (A) slooohakalura

    (B) jokilurasloo

    (C) ohakasloolura

    (D) luraohakasloo

20. Here are some words translated from an artificial language.

    frushuwamba means dissolve

    uwambakuta means solution

    hamauwamba means resolve

    Which word means *resolution*?

    (F) kutafrush

    (G) hamauwambakuta

    (H) uwambakutahama

    (J) frushkutauwamba

STOP

IF YOU FINISH BEFORE TIME IS UP, CHECK OVER YOUR WORK ON TEST 4 ONLY. DO NOT GO BACK TO ANY PREVIOUS TEST. DO NOT GO ON UNTIL THE SIGNAL IS GIVEN.

TEST 5. READING COMPREHENSION

Time—40 minutes

Directions: For questions 1–40, read each passage and the questions following that passage. Find the answers.

Passage for questions 1–4

Yesterday morning I saw for the first time an animal that is rarely encountered face to face. It was a wolverine. Though relatively small, rarely weighing more than 40 pounds, he is, above all animals, the one most hated by the Indians and trappers. He is a fine tree climber and a relentless destroyer. Deer, reindeer, and even moose succumb to his attacks. We sat on a rock and watched him come, a bobbing rascal in blackish-brown. Since the male wolverine occupies a very large hunting area and fights to the death any male that intrudes on his domain, wolverines are always scarce, and in order to avoid extinction need all the protection that man can give. As a trapper, Henry wanted me to shoot him, but I refused, for this is the most fascinating and little-known of all our wonderful predators. His hunchback gait was awkward and ungainly, lopsided yet tireless.

1. Wolverines are very scarce because
   (A) they suffer in the survival of the fittest.
   (B) they are afraid of all humankind.
   (C) the males kill each other.
   (D) trappers take their toll of them.

2. Henry is
   (F) the author.
   (G) the author's dog.
   (H) the author's companion.
   (J) a hunchback.

3. The author of this selection is most probably a(n)
   (A) conscious naturalist.
   (B) experienced hunter.
   (C) inexperienced trapper.
   (D) young Indian.

4. Why do you suppose that the wolverine is so hated by Indians and trappers?
   (F) The wolverine climbs trees better than man.
   (G) Hunchback wolverines are incredibly ugly.
   (H) Wolverines are scarce and demand man's protection.
   (J) Wolverines are successful in destroying the same game that the Indians and trappers seek.

Passage for questions 5–8

The history of modern pollution problems shows that most have resulted from negligence and ignorance. We have an appalling tendency to interfere with nature before all of the possible consequences of our actions have been studied in depth. We produce and distribute radioactive substances, synthetic chemicals, and many other potent compounds before fully comprehending their effects on living organisms. Our education is dangerously incomplete.

It will be argued that the purpose of science is to move into unknown territory, to explore, and to discover. It can be said that similar risks have been taken before and that these risks are necessary to technological progress.

These arguments overlook an important element. In the past, risks taken in the name of scientific progress were restricted to a small place and a brief period of time. The effects of the processes we now strive to master are neither localized nor brief. Air pollution covers vast urban areas. Ocean pollutants have been discovered in nearly every part of the world. Synthetic chemicals spread over huge stretches of forest and farmland may remain in the soil for decades. Radioactive pollutants will be found in the biosphere for generations. The size and persistence of these problems have grown with the expanding power of modern science.

One might also argue that the hazards of modem pollutants are small compared to the dangers associated with other human activity. No estimate of the actual harm done by smog, fallout, or chemical residues can obscure the reality that the risks are being taken before being fully understood.

The importance of these issues lies in the failure of science to predict and control human intervention into natural processes. The true measure of the danger is represented by the hazards we will encounter if we enter the new age of technology without first evaluating our responsibility to the environment.

5. According to the author, the major cause of pollution problems is
   (A) designing synthetic chemicals to kill living organisms.
   (B) a lack of understanding of the history of technology.
   (C) scientists who are too willing to move into unknown territory.
   (D) changing our environment before understanding the effects of these changes.

6. The author believes that the risks taken by modern science are greater than those taken by earlier scientific efforts because
   (F) the effects may be felt by more people for a longer period of time.
   (G) science is progressing faster than ever before.
   (H) technology has produced more dangerous chemicals.
   (J) the materials used are more dangerous to scientists.

7. The author apparently believes that the problem of finding solutions to pollution depends on
   (A) the removal of present hazards to the environment.
   (B) the removal of all potential pollutants from their present uses.
   (C) overcoming technical difficulties.
   (D) the willingness of scientists to understand possible dangers before using new products in the environment.

8. The author seems to feel that the attitude of scientists toward pollution has been
   (F) concerned.
   (G) confused.
   (H) ignorant.
   (J) nonchalant.

Passage for questions 9–12

The kangaroo is found nowhere in the world but in Australasia. Ages ago, when that part of our earth was cut off from the Asian mainland, this fantastic animal from nature's long-ago was also isolated. There are about two dozen species distributed through Australia, southward to Tasmania and northward to New Guinea and neighboring islands. Some are no bigger than rabbits; some can climb trees. They are known by a variety of picturesque names: wallabies, wallaroos, potoroos, boongaries, and paddymelons. But the kangaroo—the one that is Australia's national symbol—is the great grey kangaroo of the plains, admiringly known throughout the island continent as the Old Man, and also as Boomer, Forester, and Man of the Woods. His smaller mate, in Australian talk, is called a flyer. Their baby is known as Joey.

A full-grown kangaroo stands taller than a man and commonly weighs 200 pounds. Even when he sits in his favorite position, reposing on his haunches and tilting back on the propping support of his "third leg"—his tail—his head is five feet or more above the ground. His huge hind legs, with steel-spring power, can send him sailing over a ten-foot fence with ease, or in a fight can beat off a dozen dogs. A twitch of his tail can break a man's leg like a matchstick.

Kangaroos provide an endless supply of tall tales to which wide-eyed visitors are treated in the land Down Under. The beauty of the tall tales about the kangaroos is that they can be almost as tall as you please and still be close to fact.

9. The amazing jumping power of the kangaroo is chiefly due to
   (A) the power of his hind legs.
   (B) the support of his tail.
   (C) his size.
   (D) his weight.

GO ON TO THE NEXT PAGE

10. Australasia is
    (F) another name for Australia.
    (G) an area that includes Australia and part of the continent of Asia.
    (H) Australia and some surrounding islands to the north and south of it.
    (J) all of the land in the Southern Hemisphere.

11. Which statement is true according to the passage?
    (A) The name "Old Man" shows the people's dislike of kangaroos.
    (B) Visitors to Australia hear very little about kangaroos.
    (C) A kangaroo's tail is a powerful weapon.
    (D) The most widely known species of kangaroo is no larger than a rabbit.

12. The author believes that the stories told about kangaroos are generally
    (F) harmful.
    (G) true.
    (H) suspicious.
    (J) beautiful.

Passage for questions 13–17

For generations, historians and boat lovers have been trying to learn more about the brave ship that brought the Pilgrims to America. The task is a difficult one because *Mayflower* was such a common name for ships back in early seventeenth-century England that there were at least twenty of them when the Pilgrims left for the New World.

An exact duplicate of the *Mayflower* has been built in England and given to the people of the United States as a symbol of goodwill and common ancestry linking Britons and Americans. The Pilgrims' *Mayflower* apparently was built originally as a fishing vessel. It seems to have been 90 feet long by 22 feet wide, displacing 180 tons of water. The duplicate measures 90 feet by 26 feet, displaces 183 tons of water, and has a crew of 21, as did the original vessel. The new *Mayflower* has no motor but travels faster than the old boat.

What happened to the historic boat? So far as can be told, the *Mayflower* went back to less colorful jobs and, not too many years later, was scrapped. What happened to the beams, masts, and planking is questionable. In the English city of Abingdon, there is a Congregational church that contains two heavy wooden pillars. Some say these pillars are masts from the *Mayflower*. A barn in the English town of Jordans seemed to be built on old ship timbers. Marine experts said these timbers were impregnated with salt and, if put together, would form a vessel 90 feet by 22 feet. The man who owned the farm when the peculiar barn was built was a relative of the man who appraised the *Mayflower* when it was scrapped.

So the original *Mayflower* may still be doing service ashore while her duplicate sails the seas.

13. A long search was made for the Pilgrims' boat because it
    (A) contained valuable materials.
    (B) might still do sea service.
    (C) has historical importance.
    (D) would link Great Britain and America.

14. It has been difficult to discover what happened to the original *Mayflower* because
    (F) many ships bore the same name.
    (G) it was such a small vessel.
    (H) the search was begun too late.
    (J) it has become impregnated with salt.

15. The British recently had a duplicate of the *Mayflower* built because
    (A) the original could not be located.
    (B) they wanted to make a gesture of friendship.
    (C) parts of the original could be used.
    (D) historians recommended such a step.

16. Compared with the original *Mayflower*, the modern duplicate
    (F) is longer.
    (G) is identical.
    (H) carries a larger crew.
    (J) is somewhat wider.

17. When the author says that the original boat might still be doing service ashore, he means that
    (A) it might be whole and intact somewhere.
    (B) present-day buildings might include parts of it.
    (C) it might be in a boat lover's private collection.
    (D) it might be in the service of pirates.

Passage for questions 18–21

A third of our lives is spent in the mysterious state of sleep. Throughout his history, man has attempted to understand this remarkable experience. Many centuries ago, for example, sleep was regarded as a type of anemia of the brain. Alemaeon, a Greek scientist, believed that blood retreated into the veins, and the partially starved brain went to sleep. Plato supported the idea that the soul left the body during sleep, wandered through the world, and woke up the body when it returned.

Recently, more scientific explanations of sleep have been proposed. According to one theory, the brain is put to sleep by a chemical agent that accumulates in the body when it is awake. Another theory is that weary branches of certain nerve cells break connections with neighboring cells. The flow of impulses required for staying awake is then disrupted. These more recent theories have to be subjected to laboratory research.

Why do we sleep? Why do we dream? Modern sleep research is said to have begun in the 1950s, when Eugene Aserinsky, a graduate student at the University of Chicago, and Nathaniel Kleitman, his professor, observed periods of rapid eye movements (REMs) in sleeping subjects. When awakened during these REM periods, subjects almost always remembered dreaming. On the other hand, when awakened during non-REM phases of sleep, the subjects rarely could recall their dreams.

Guided by REMs, it became possible for investigators to "spot" dreaming from outside and then awaken the sleeper to collect dream stories. They could also alter the dreamers' experiences with noises, drugs, or other stimuli before or during sleep.

Since the mid-1950s researchers have been drawn into sleep laboratories. There, bedrooms adjoin other rooms that contain recorders known as electroencephalograph (EEG) machines.

The EEG amplifies signals from sensors on the face, head, and other parts of the body, which together yield tracings of respiration, pulse, muscle tension, and changes of electrical potential in the brain that are sometimes called brain waves. These recordings supply clues to the changes of the sleeping person's activities.

18. Sleep has been the subject of awe for many centuries because
    (F) it is a form of anemia.
    (G) no one knows the destination of the wandering soul.
    (H) it is mysterious and remarkable.
    (J) dream interpretation is important.

19. According to this article,
    (A) sleep is caused by REMs.
    (B) we are awake for two-thirds of our lives.
    (C) modern sleep research began at the turn of the century.
    (D) dreams are caused by REMs.

20. Electroencephalograph recordings made during sleep provide clues about
    (F) broken nerve cells.
    (G) the content of dreams.
    (H) the meaning of dreams.
    (J) physical changes during sleep.

21. All of the following were mentioned as possible causes of sleep EXCEPT
    (A) exhausted nerve endings.
    (B) a buildup of certain body chemicals.
    (C) recurrent periods of rapid eye movement.
    (D) the absence of the conscious spirit.

Passage for questions 22–25

What is a cord of wood? Some people say the cord is the most elastic unit of measure ever devised by the mind of man. A "standard" cord is a pile of stacked wood $4 \times 4 \times 8$ feet; that's 128 cubic feet. How much of this is wood? That depends on what kind of wood, the size and

GO ON TO THE NEXT PAGE

straightness of the sticks, and who does the piling. Small crooked sticks, cut from hardwood limbs and piled by one of those cordwood artists who know how to make air spaces, may contain less than 30 cubic feet of solid wood per cord. Smooth, round wood such as birch or spruce, in sizes 8 inches and better, will average 100 cubic feet or more per cord. That's with the bark on. Peeled wood will make 10 to 12 percent more cubic volume in the same sized stack.

The heating value of wood varies enormously with the kind of tree. Black locust, white oak, hickory, black birch, and ironwood are the best. A cord of any of these woods, when seasoned, is worth approximately a ton of coal. Beech, yellow birch, sugar maple, ash, and red oak are next. White birch, cherry, soft maple, sycamore, and elm are comparatively poor fuel woods, with basswood, butternut, poplar, and the softwoods at the bottom of the scale.

22. The title that best expresses the main idea of this selection is
    (F) "Fuels."
    (G) "The Value of a Cord of Wood."
    (H) "Kinds of Trees."
    (J) "Standard Measures."

23. A standard cord of wood
    (A) always contains 128 cubic feet of wood.
    (B) will average 100 cubic feet of smooth wood.
    (C) contains less than 30 cubic feet of solid wood.
    (D) is stacked wood in a pile $4 \times 4 \times 8$ feet.

24. Removal of the bark from wood before stacking
    (F) increases the cubic volume of wood in a cord.
    (G) makes the stacking easier.
    (H) allows more air spaces in a cord of wood.
    (J) prevents seasoning of wood.

25. The cord is considered to be an elastic unit of measure because
    (A) if one jumps on a stack of wood, it is bouncy.
    (B) the amount of heat to be derived from a cord of wood varies with the kind of tree from which the wood comes.
    (C) the amount of wood in a cord varies with the wood itself and the method of stacking.
    (D) cord is string and can be stretched.

Passage for questions 26–29

As recently as the 1840s, most people believed that the earth, and man with it, was created a mere 6,000 to 7,000 years ago. For centuries, beautifully worked flints were regarded as the work of elves, a notion once far more plausible than the idea that man roamed the world's wildernesses in small bands long before the days of Greece and Rome. Even when these stones were accepted as man-made tools, they were attributed to the Romans or early Britons.

Today we think in wider terms. The earliest dated works of man have been found on the floor of Olduvai Gorge, a miniature Grand Canyon in East Africa, and include carefully made stone tools about 2,000,000 years old. Furthermore, fossil evidence suggests that members of the family of man used tools millions of years before that.

Opposition to these ideas began to fade during the late eighteenth and early nineteenth centuries. Excavators, mainly enthusiastic amateurs, pointed to material associated with the tools—fossil remains of men and extinct animals. Most geologists still thought in biblical terms, maintaining that such associations were accidental, that the Flood had mixed the bones of ancient animals and the tools and remains of recent man. But their last-ditch defenses crumbled with the finding of bones and tools together in unflooded and undisturbed deposits, including a number of important sites on the banks of the Somme River. British investigators came to check the French deposits, were convinced, and announced their conclusions in 1859, the year that saw publication of Darwin's *On the Origin of Species.* This date marks the beginning of modern research into human evolution.

26. All of the following types of archeological information were mentioned EXCEPT
    (F) carbon dating.
    (G) fossils.
    (H) flints.
    (J) extinct animals.

27. According to the article, man has lived on Earth for
    (A) about 7,000 years.
    (B) between 7,000 and 100,000 years.
    (C) about 2,000,000 years.
    (D) far more than 2,000,000 years.

28. The scientific turning point in theories about the age of man's existence was the
    (F) publication of *On the Origin of Species.*
    (G) discovery in France of the remains of extinct animals and men together.
    (H) new theological research of the Bible.
    (J) new theories about the Flood and its effects on mankind.

29. In the early nineteenth century
    (A) small bands of Romans roamed the earth.
    (B) geologists dated man's existence back 2,000,000 years.
    (C) the stones were accepted as ancient tools.
    (D) most people believed that man's existence was 6,000–7,000 years old.

Passage for questions 30–34

Eight of the city's twelve workers in Venetian glass recently finished one of the most unusual murals ever made for a New York skyscraper. It is an abstract, the creation of Hans Hofman, a 77-year-old German-born painter.

The mural covers 1,200 square feet of the outer wall of the elevator shaft in the William Kaufman Building at 711 Third Avenue. More than a half-million tiles in close to 500 shades of color have gone into it. Blue, red, and yellow are the chief colors. Each tile was made in Venice and is somewhat less than postage-stamp size. Each is beaten into a special everlasting concrete with a kind of flat wooden hand tool used for nothing else.

Mr. Hofman did the original color sketch about one-sixth the final size. This was photographed, and from the negative an enlargement was hand-colored by the artist, cut into sections, and sent in that form to the Vincent Foscato plant in Long Island City, which specializes in Venetian glass tile, or mosaic. There the Venetian specialists, whose trade has been handed down, father to son, through centuries, set each mosaic into place on the cartoon section, with painstaking fidelity to Mr. Hofman's color rendering. Although Mr. Foscato's plant keeps 1,400 shades of the glass mosaic, it had to have twelve additional shades specially made in Venice to match the sketch coloring for perfect blending. When all the sections had been filled and approved, they were carried by truck to the building lobby, the walls were covered with the special cement, and the workmen carefully beat each bit into place.

30. The best title for this selection would be
    (F) "Picture by German Artist to Hang in New York."
    (G) "New Mosaic Designed by Vincent Foscato."
    (H) "Unusual Photograph Decorates New York Building."
    (J) "Venetian Glass Mural Installed in Skyscraper."

31. The mosaic work was done by
    (A) Hans Hofman.
    (B) the 1,400 workers in the Foscato plant.
    (C) a dozen men skilled in photography.
    (D) two thirds of the New York workers in Venetian glass mosaics.

32. The original design was
    (F) painted on the wall of the Kaufman building.
    (G) a fraction of the size of the finished mural.
    (H) imported from Venice.
    (J) larger than the finished mural.

GO ON TO THE NEXT PAGE

33. In the making of the mural,
   (A) the shades of tile that the Foscato plant had in stock were not adequate.
   (B) 1,412 shades were needed
   (C) half a million colors were used.
   (D) over 500 shades of color were used.

34. Mr. Hofman
   (F) used only the most unusual shades of red, blue, and green.
   (G) had no further connection with the work after making the original sketch.
   (H) died shortly before the mural was completed.
   (J) colored the enlarged reproduction of the original.

Passage for questions 35–40

The dark and the sea are full of dangers to the fishermen of Norway. A whale might come and destroy the floating chain of corks that edges the nets, break it, and carry it off. Or a storm might come suddenly, unexpectedly, out of the night. The sea seems to turn somersaults. It opens and closes immense caverns with terrible clashes, chasing boats and fishermen who must flee from their nets and the expected catch. Then the fishermen might lift their nets as empty as they set them. At other times, the herring might come in such masses that the lines break from the weight when lifted, and the fishermen must return home empty handed, without line, nets, or herring.

But often the nets are full of herring that shine and glisten like silver. Once in awhile, a couple of fishermen will venture in their boats along the net lines to see whether the herring are coming, and when the corks begin to bob and jerk as if something were hitting the nets to which they are attached, then they know that the herring are there. The nets are being filled, and all the fishermen sit in quiet excitement. They dare only to whisper to each other, afraid to disturb, and quite overcome by the overwhelming generosity of the sea. Eyes shine in happy anticipation; hands are folded in thanks. Then muscles strain with power. It is as though the strength of the body doubled. They can work day and night without a thought of weariness. They need neither food nor rest; the thought of success keeps their vigor up almost endlessly. They will take food and rest when it is all over.

35. The best title for this passage is
   (A) "Hard Work in Norway."
   (B) "The Perils and Rewards of Fishing."
   (C) "Risky Business."
   (D) "The Generosity of the Sea."

36. The difficulties faced by the Norwegian fishermen include
   (F) the eating of the herring by whales.
   (G) it is difficult to be very calm.
   (H) interference by rough seas.
   (J) the jerking of the corks.

37. At the first indication that herring are entering the nets, the fishermen
   (A) try not to frighten the fish away.
   (B) strain every muscle to haul in the catch.
   (C) collect the nets quickly.
   (D) row quickly along the edge of the nets.

38. When the article says that the sea opens and closes immense caverns, it is referring to
   (F) caves along the shoreline.
   (G) deep holes in the ocean floor.
   (H) dangerous large boulders that get rolled around.
   (J) hollow pockets beneath very high waves.

39. The fishermen are described as
    - (A) strong, angry, and excitable.
    - (B) skillful, religious, and impatient.
    - (C) patient, brave, and grateful.
    - (D) surly, hardworking, and cautious.

40. Of the following, the one that is not mentioned as posing a problem to the fishermen is
    - (F) destruction of the nets.
    - (G) theft of the nets by other fishermen.
    - (H) too large a catch.
    - (J) whales.

STOP

IF YOU FINISH TEST 5 BEFORE TIME IS UP, CHECK OVER YOUR WORK ON THIS TEST ONLY. DO NOT RETURN TO ANY PREVIOUS TEST. DO NOT GO ON TO THE NEXT TEST UNTIL THE SIGNAL IS GIVEN.

TEST 6. MATHEMATICS CONCEPTS AND APPLICATIONS

Time—35 minutes

Directions: For questions 1–40, read each problem and find the answer.

1. Two hundred million, one hundred seventy-three thousand, and sixty-three =
   (A) 200,173,630
   (B) 2,173,063
   (C) 20,173,063
   (D) 200,173,063

2. Seventeen million sixty thousand thirty-four =
   (F) 1,760,034
   (G) 17,634
   (H) 17,060,034
   (J) 17,600,034

3. .5% is equal to
   (A) .5
   (B) .005
   (C) .05
   (D) $\frac{1}{2}$

4. A group of 6 people raised $690 for charity. One of the people raised 35% of the total. What was the amount raised by the other 5 people?
   (F) $241.50
   (G) $448.50
   (H) $449.50
   (J) $445.50

5. If a pie is divided into 40 parts, what percent is one part of the whole pie?
   (A) 40
   (B) 25
   (C) 4.0
   (D) 2.5

6. A millimeter is what part of a meter?
   (F) $\frac{1}{10}$
   (G) $\frac{1}{100}$
   (H) $\frac{1}{1,000}$
   (J) $\frac{1}{10,000}$

7. Find the area of a rectangle with a length of 176 feet and a width of 79 feet.
   (A) 13,904 sq. ft.
   (B) 13,854 sq. ft.
   (C) 13,304 sq. ft.
   (D) 13,804 sq. ft.

8. Mr. Lawson makes a weekly salary of $250 plus 7% commission on his sales. What will his income be for a week in which he made sales totaling $1,250?
   (F) $337.50
   (G) $87.50
   (H) $267.50
   (J) $327.50

9. Complete the following statement: $7(3 \times \_\_) + 4 = 2104$
   (A) 10 + 2
   (B) 10
   (C) 10^2
   (D) 10^3

10. Find the area of a triangle whose dimensions are: $b = 14$ inches, $h = 20$ inches.
    (F) 208 sq. inches
    (G) 280 sq. inches
    (H) 140 sq. inches
    (J) 288 sq. inches

11. What is the difference between $(4 \times 10^3) + 6$ and $(2 \times 10^3) + (3 \times 10) + 8$?
    (A) 168
    (B) 55,968
    (C) 3,765
    (D) 1,968

12. The set of common factors for 30 and 24 is
    (F) {1,2,3,6}
    (G) {1,2,3,4,6}
    (H) {1,2,4,6}
    (J) {1,2,4,6,12}

13. If the scale on a blueprint is $\frac{1}{4}$ inch = 1 foot, give the blueprint dimensions of a room that is actually 29 feet long and 23 feet wide.
    (A) $7\frac{1}{2}" \times 5\frac{1}{4}"$
    (B) $6\frac{3}{4}" \times 6"$
    (C) $7\frac{1}{4}" \times 5\frac{1}{2}"$
    (D) $7\frac{1}{4}" \times 5\frac{3}{4}"$

14. A scalene triangle has
    (F) two equal sides.
    (G) two equal sides and one right angle.
    (H) no equal sides.
    (J) three equal sides.

15. On a recent trip, the Smiths drove at an average speed of 55 miles per hour. If the trip took $5\frac{1}{2}$ hours, how many miles did they drive?
    (A) 320.75
    (B) 312.50
    (C) 320.5
    (D) 302.5

16. $\frac{17}{30}$ is greater than
    (F) $\frac{7}{8}$
    (G) $\frac{9}{20}$
    (H) $\frac{9}{11}$
    (J) $\frac{22}{25}$

17. 1 centimeter equals what part of a meter?
    (A) $\frac{1}{10}$
    (B) $\frac{1}{100}$
    (C) $\frac{1}{1,000}$
    (D) $\frac{1}{10,000}$

18. A baseball team won 18 games, which was 40% of its season. How many games did the team lose?
    (F) 25
    (G) 45
    (H) 32
    (J) 27

19. If $-2 < q < -1$, which of the following is true?
    (A) $q = \frac{1}{2}$
    (B) $q > -1$
    (C) $q > -8$
    (D) $q > -2$

20. Which pair of values for x and □ will make the following statement true?

    $2x \square 8$

    (F) (6. <)
    (G) (4, >)
    (H) (0, <)
    (J) (–3, >)

GO ON TO THE NEXT PAGE

21. $(6 \times 2) + (7 \times 3) =$

(A) $(6 \times 7) + (2 \times 3)$

(B) $(7 - 6) + (3 - 2)$

(C) $(7 \times 3) + (6 \times 2)$

(D) $(7 \times 3) \times (6 \times 2)$

22. Which of the following will substitute for x and make the statement below true?

$56 - (7 - x) = 53$

(F) 4

(G) 3

(H) 2

(J) 1

23. An angle that is greater than 90° and less than 180° is a(n)

(A) acute angle

(B) right angle

(C) reflex angle

(D) obtuse angle

24.

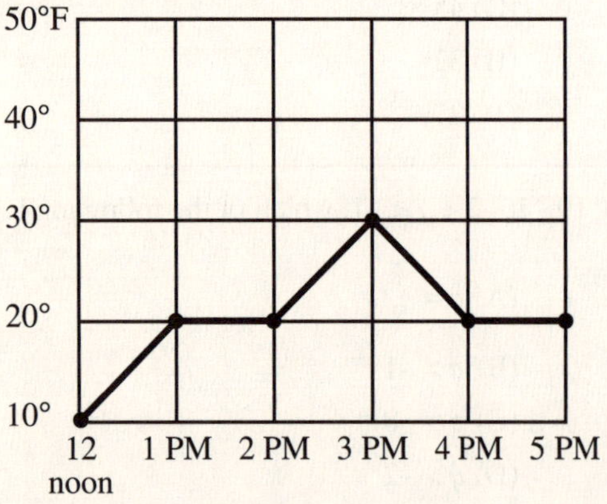

What was the average temperature on the afternoon shown on the above graph?

(F) 20°

(G) 24°

(H) 25°

(J) 30°

25. Mr. Jones has agreed to borrow $3,500 for one year at 10% interest. What is the total amount he will pay back to the bank?

(A) $3,675

(B) $350

(C) $3,700

(D) $3,850

26. Which of the following statements is true?

(F) $7 \times 11 > 78$

(G) $6 + 4 < 10.5$

(H) $8 - 3 = 7 + 4$

(J) $16 \div 2 > 9$

27. If one angle of a triangle measures 115°, then the sum of the other two angles is

(A) 245°

(B) 75°

(C) 195°

(D) 65°

28. At 20 miles per hour, how long does it take to travel one mile?

(F) 1 min.

(G) 2 min.

(H) 3 min.

(J) 4 min.

29. Find the circumference of a circle whose radius is 21 feet.

(A) 153 feet

(B) 65.94 feet

(C) 132 feet

(D) 1,769.4 feet

30. If $x > -4$, and $y < 2$, then $\{xy\}$ includes

(F) –4, 0, 1, 2

(G) –2, –1, 1, 2

(H) 1, 2, 3, 4

(J) –3, –2, –1, 0, 1

31. 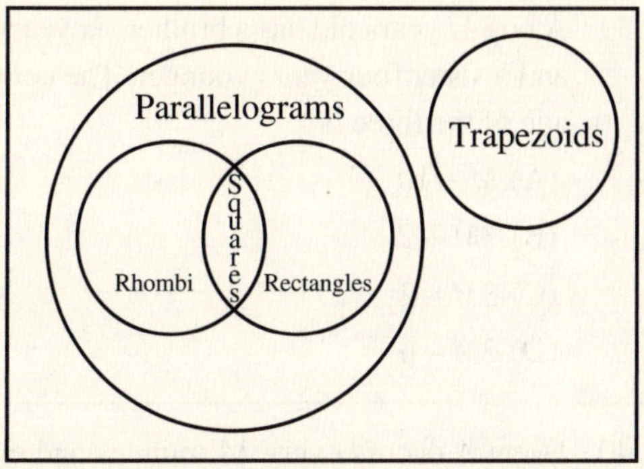

From the diagram above we know that

(A) all trapezoids are parallelograms.

(B) some rhombi are parallelograms.

(C) some rectangles are rhombi.

(D) all parallelograms are rectangles.

32. How many 2-inch tiles would have to be put around the outside edge of a 4-foot × 12-foot rectangle to completely frame the rectangle?

(F) 32

(G) 36

(H) 192

(J) 196

33. A certain highway intersection has had A accidents over a ten-year period, resulting in B deaths. What is the yearly average death rate for the intersection?

(A) A + B – 10

(B) $\frac{B}{10}$

(C) $10 - \frac{A}{B}$

(D) $\frac{AB}{12}$

34. Which point is named by the ordered pair (–4, 4)?

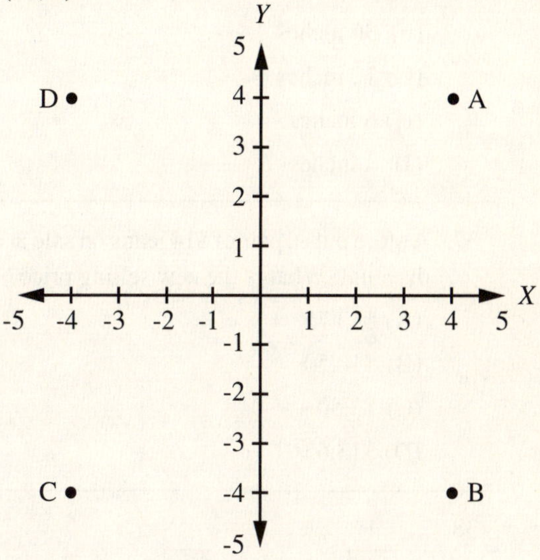

(F) A

(G) B

(H) C

(J) D

35. What are the coordinates of point P on the graph?

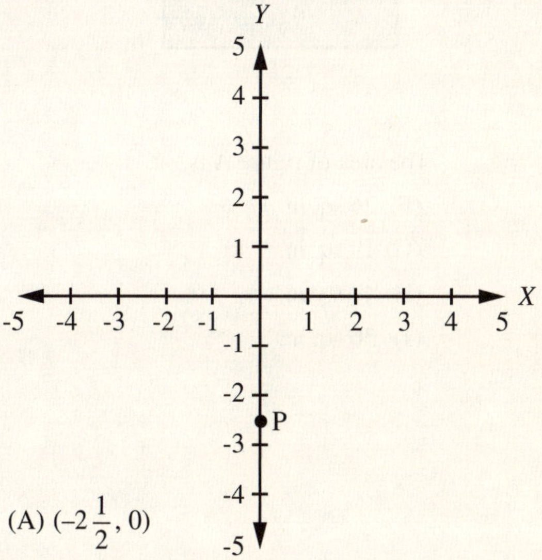

(A) $(-2\frac{1}{2}, 0)$

(B) $(0, -3\frac{1}{2})$

(C) $(0, -2\frac{1}{2})$

(D) $(-1, -2\frac{1}{2})$

GO ON TO THE NEXT PAGE

36. On a blueprint, 2 inches represent 24 feet. How long must a line be to represent 72 feet?
    (F) 36 inches
    (G) 12 inches
    (H) 6 inches
    (J) 4 inches

37. A store puts a pair of $14 jeans on sale at a 25% discount. What is the new selling price?
    (A) $13.75
    (B) $10.50
    (C) $3.50
    (D) $13.65

38.

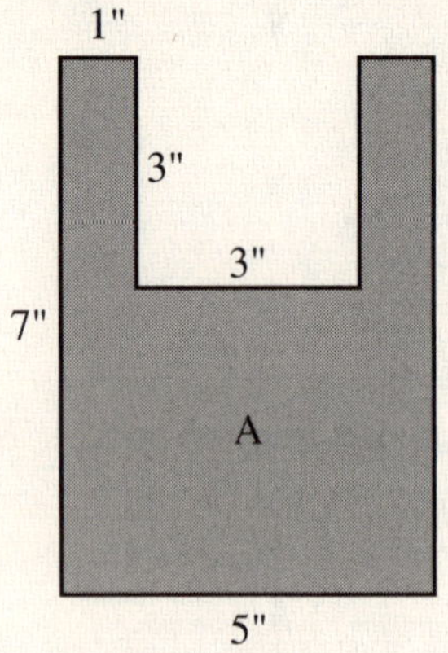

The area of figure A is
    (F) 26 sq. in.
    (G) 19 sq. in.
    (H) 44 sq. in.
    (J) 30 sq. in.

39. A boy *M* years old has a brother six years older and a sister four years younger. The combined age of the three is
    (A) $M + 10$
    (B) $3M + 2$
    (C) $3M - 2$
    (D) $2M - 6$

40. Event *A* occurs every 14 minutes and event *B* every 12 minutes. If they both occur at 1:00 p.m., when will be the next time that both occur together?
    (F) 2:12 p.m.
    (G) 1:48 p.m.
    (H) 2:24 p.m.
    (J) 3:48 p.m.

STOP

IF YOU FINISH THIS TEST BEFORE TIME IS UP, CHECK OVER YOUR WORK ON TEST 6 ONLY. DO NOT RETURN TO ANY PREVIOUS TEST. DO NOT GO ON TO THE NEXT TEST UNTIL THE SIGNAL IS GIVEN.

TEST 7. LANGUAGE EXPRESSION

Time—30 minutes

Directions: For questions 1–6, choose the word or phrase that best completes the sentence.

1. We had just finished shoveling the driveway _____ the plow came through again.
   (A) if
   (B) until
   (C) when
   (D) than
   (E) and

2. Fiction, _____ it is written regional dialect, must be grammatical.
   (F) unless
   (G) although
   (H) because
   (J) besides
   (K) when

3. _____ the railroad's spokesman announced that all trains were on or close to schedule, our train arrived 20 minutes late.
   (A) Because
   (B) In spite of
   (C) When
   (D) Before
   (E) Although

4. For me, watching the performers on the high wire is the _____ part of the circus.
   (F) scary
   (G) scariest
   (H) scaring
   (J) scared
   (K) scaringest

5. Once the pitcher ______ the pitch, the runner at first sprinted for second base.
   (A) has thrown
   (B) throwed
   (C) had thrown
   (D) was throwing
   (E) would throw

6. The review of that actor's performance was the ______ I have ever read.
   (F) most unkind
   (G) unkindliest
   (H) most unkindest
   (J) more unkindly
   (K) most not kind

Directions: For questions 7–12, choose the sentence that is correctly written.

7. (A) Don't worry John we all make mistakes.
   (B) Please don't worry. John, we all make mistakes.
   (C) While John doesn't worry and we all make mistakes.
   (D) Don't worry John; we all make mistakes.
   (E) Not to worry; John, we all make mistakes.

GO ON TO THE NEXT PAGE

8. (F) Returning from a frustrating day at the office, when the telephone rang in the middle of dinner.
   (G) When the telephone rang in the middle of dinner, returned from a frustrating day at the office.
   (H) We had just returned from a frustrating day at the office when the telephone rang in the middle of dinner.
   (J) We were just returning from a frustrating day at the office and the telephone rang and it was the middle of dinner.
   (K) In the middle of dinner, the telephone rang having just returned from a frustrating day at the office.

9. (A) Flinging himself at the heavy metal fire door, he pounded on it furiously.
   (B) Flinging himself at the heavy metal fire door and pounding on it furiously.
   (C) The heavy metal fire door was pounded furiously while flinging himself.
   (D) Flinging the heavy metal door and pounding furiously by himself.
   (E) Pounding furiously at the heavy metal door while flinging by himself.

10. (F) Recovering from jet lag and having traveled over 6,000 miles.
    (G) Traveling over 6,000 miles and having recovered from jet lag.
    (H) Recovering from jet lag and traveling over 6,000 miles we were.
    (J) We were recovering from jet lag after having traveled over 6,000 miles.
    (K) We traveled over 6,000 miles we recovered from jet lag.

11. (A) The world growing smaller and devising faster means of communication.
    (B) The world seems to grow smaller as faster means of communication are devised.
    (C) A smaller growing world and a faster means of communication being devised.
    (D) Faster means of communication devised and a world growing smaller.
    (E) Faster means of communication devising a smaller-growing world.

12. (F) When the flurry of angry words ended and it was evident that cool heads had not prevailed.
    (G) When the flurry of angry words had ended and it was evident that cool heads had not prevailed.
    (H) The flurry of angry words ended it was evident that cool heads had not prevailed.
    (J) Cool heads not prevailing the flurry of angry words evidently ending.
    (K) When the flurry of angry words had ended, it was evident that cool heads had not prevailed.

Directions: For questions 13–17, choose the sentence that uses verbs correctly.

13. (A) Even before the wind had stopped, the rain was slowed down.
    (B) After he had finished the test. He hurries off to catch the last train home.
    (C) He receives a gift when he brings home a good report card.
    (D) While we were rowing on the lake, a sudden squall almost capsizes the boat.
    (E) The people began to realize how much work she has done.

14. (F) If my trip is a success, I was back on Thursday.
    (G) I can't recall any time that George will break his word.
    (H) The door opens, and in walk Bob and Mary.
    (J) I will not understand why mother objected to my staying home today.
    (K) The defendant's testimony today was different from what it will be yesterday.

15. (A) When I tell her I'm sorry. I partly meant it.
(B) Everywhere I have gone, I will have been finding pollution in the air.
(C) He will be here when the letter carrier arrived.
(D) They gave the poor man some food when he knocked at the door.
(E) The boy runs away from home and became a marine.

16. (F) He will not be informed that he was required to work on weekends.
(G) Not only did I eat too much, but I will also drink to excess.
(H) After he stole the purse, he runs like a thief.
(J) When she graduates from high school, she will be eighteen years old.
(K) We eagerly awaited the pay envelopes that will be brought by the messenger.

17. (A) After he rescued the kitten, he rushes down the ladder to find its owner.
(B) Kelly rowed around the island and soon come in sight of the mainland.
(C) The captain welcomes us aboard, and the crew enjoyed showing us around the ship.
(D) Residents of the barrier island should listen to the weather forecast so that they anticipate a hurricane.
(E) Explanations of the correct answers follow each exercise so that you will learn from your errors.

Directions: For questions 18–21, choose the underlined word that is the simple subject of the sentence.

18. The noise (F) of thunder (G) is frightening (H) to adults (J) as well as to children (K).

19. When the police (A) arrived at the scene (B) of the accident (C), the ambulance (D) was already there (E).

20. Proper (F) idiomatic (G) form (H) requires the construction (J) "better than (K)."

21. Venetian (A) blinds (B) probably (C) did not originate (D) in Venice (E).

Directions: For questions 22–25, choose the underlined word or group of words that is the simple predicate (verb) of the sentence.

22. If it is addressed (F) correctly (G), the letter will be delivered (H) with the mailroom's (J) first morning run (K).

23. I feel (A) certain (B) that management will give (C) the promotion to the employee who shows (D) the greatest promise (E).

24. When you hear (F) the fire alarm (G) ringing (H), leave (J) the building without delay (K).

25. Since the baby now has gotten (A) a few teeth. I shall begin (B) to serve (C) her the same meals (D) that I prepare (E) for the rest of the family.

GO ON TO THE NEXT PAGE

Directions: For questions 26–28, choose the sentence that best combines the two underlined sentences into one.

26. Ecuador is South America's second smallest nation. It is no larger than the state of Colorado.
    (F) The second smallest nation in South America is no larger than the state of Colorado and it is Ecuador.
    (G) Ecuador, South America's second smallest nation, is no larger than the state of Colorado.
    (H) It is no larger than the state of Colorado and Ecuador is South America's second smallest nation.
    (J) The second smallest nation is Ecuador which is no larger than the state of Colorado and it is in South America.
    (K) The state of Colorado is the same size as the second smallest nation in South America and Ecuador is no larger.

27. Pollution may lead to the formation of low clouds. These clouds are extremely dangerous to our environment.
    (A) Low clouds are extremely dangerous to our environment and may be formed by pollution.
    (B) Dangerous pollution is caused by low clouds in our environment.
    (C) The formation of low clouds that are extremely dangerous to our environment may lead to pollution.
    (D) Dangerous low clouds in formation lead to extreme pollution of our environment.
    (E) The low clouds that tend to be formed by pollution are extremely dangerous to our environment.

28. The lands of the Northwest Territory had been claimed by several states. Virginia, Connecticut, Massachusetts, and New York all had claims in the territory before 1785.
    (F) Claims could be made in 1785 by several states in the Northwest Territory like Virginia, Connecticut, Massachusetts, and New York.
    (G) Claims in the Northwest Territory could be made of land before 1785 by the several states of Virginia, Connecticut, Massachusetts, and New York.
    (H) Before 1785, claims of land in the Northwest Territory were made by several states, namely Virginia, Connecticut, Massachusetts, and New York.
    (J) The several states of Virginia, Connecticut, Massachusetts, and New York claimed all the lands of the Northwest Territory before 1785.
    (K) Virginia, Connecticut, Massachusetts, and New York were all states before 1785 and they all had claims in the Northwest Territory.

Directions: For questions 29–31, choose the topic sentence that best fits the paragraph.

29. ________________________________.

    First, your ability to secure a position might depend on your English. Your prospective employer will notice how well you write the answers to the questions on your application blank. And when you are interviewed, he will notice how well you speak.
    (A) As you move up the success ladder, what you write and what you say will determine in part your rate of climb.
    (B) If you wish to enter business, there are three good reasons why you should study English.
    (C) You will need to write reports accurately and interestingly.

(D) You will need to talk effectively with your fellow workers, with your superiors, and perhaps with the public.

(E) New immigrants to the United States should not delay in beginning to learn the English language.

30. ______________________________.

On the one hand, we call history a science since the historian has a method for gathering evidence and evaluating it. On the other hand, it is less accurate in its ability to predict than a science should be. History can be literature because it involves the views and interpretations of the historian.

(F) History is sometimes compared to literature.

(G) The great history that has stirred people's minds has also been the theme of great literature.

(H) Is history a science?

(J) Historical fiction is a skillful blending of fact and fiction with no requirement for scientific accuracy.

(K) The question of whether history is a science or literature is difficult to answer.

31. ______________________________.

There are important areas in our lives in which opinions play a major role. Every time we look into the future, we depend on opinions. Every time we attempt to judge facts, we depend on opinions. And every time we attempt to advance into the "not yet known area," we depend on opinions.

(A) Opinions should not be taken lightly.

(B) Newspaper editorials are based upon opinion rather than upon facts.

(C) In some ways they actually go beyond facts.

(D) Scientific inquiry leaves no room for opinions.

(E) Highly opinionated persons can sometimes be quite overbearing.

Directions: For questions 32–34, choose the pair of sentences that best develops the topic sentence.

32. One of the most difficult problems in America today is that of homelessness.

(F) Homeless people tend to be dirty, lazy, and shiftless. They are an eyesore for honest, hardworking citizens.

(G) Homelessness was a problem during the Depression. The Salvation Army operated soup kitchens to feed the homeless.

(H) While the bulk of the homeless are single men, many are families with small children. Among the causes of homelessness are fires, poverty, and just plain hard luck.

(J) Some people are homeless by choice. Nomads like to wander from place to place without having to care for a stable residence.

(K) Home ownership is considered to be the American dream. Unfortunately, when money is in short supply, the banks provide very few mortgages.

GO ON TO THE NEXT PAGE

33. Many young people today are choosing to become vegetarians.
    (A) A vegetarian diet can be healthful, but it must be carefully planned. Complete proteins can be created by combining rice and beans in proper proportion.
    (B) Some religions frown upon vegetarianism. These religions require the eating of meat at certain ritual occasions.
    (C) If I were to tell my mother that I wanted to become a vegetarian, she would be very angry. My mother likes everyone at the table to eat the same food.
    (D) New vegetarians can be very annoying. Converts to new ideas or new ways often talk of nothing else.
    (E) Most restaurants now offer at least one vegetarian entree on their menus. In many cities, one can even find vegetarian restaurants.

34. One of the most important safety features on your car is the condition of the tires.
    (F) The first tires were made of solid rubber and were very uncomfortable to ride on. Later tires had an inflatable inner tube that gave a softer ride.
    (G) Studded tires give good traction on icy roads. Some states prohibit tire studs because they destroy the road surface.
    (H) Today's steel-belted radial tires give long service. If you use radials, you should put them on all four wheels.
    (J) When white-walled tires were first introduced, the white stripe was a sign of prestige and the wider the white wall, the costlier the tire. Nowadays, the cost of tires is determined by the quality of the rubber and the configuration of the tread.
    (K) Once the brakes are applied, it is the front tires that determine how quickly the car will stop and whether or not it will skid. Deep, matched treads on the two front tires will ensure a quick, smooth stop.

Directions: For questions 35–37, choose the sentence that does not belong in the paragraph.

35. (1) Human forms of cultural behavior are found among the Japanese monkey. (2) Members of the Japan Monkey Center have found among local monkey groups a wide variety of customs based on social learning. (3) The males of certain groups, for instance, take turns looking after the infants while the mothers are eating. (4) The scientists have also been able to observe the process by which behavioral innovations, such as swimming and sweet potato washing, developed and spread from individual to individual in the monkey group. (5) Japanese scientists found that female tigers swam more than male monkeys.
    (A) Statement 1
    (B) Statement 2
    (C) Statement 3
    (D) Statement 4
    (E) Statement 5

36. (1) The shaman deals mostly with illnesses that stem from a disturbance of the spirit. (2) He may also practice herbal therapy, but most often these cases are left to medicine men of lower standing. (3) Shamans wield great political power in many of the societies in which they are active. (4) Through divination or consultation with spirits, the shaman makes a diagnosis. (5) Usually the illness is diagnosed as a spirit loss or sorcery.
    (F) Statement 1
    (G) Statement 2
    (H) Statement 3
    (J) Statement 4
    (K) Statement 5

37. (1) Tecumseh found the torture and burning of a prisoner so revolting that without any voice in tribal matters as of yet, he protested. (2) In the spring of 1783, Tecumseh took part in his first battle against the whites, and at the age of fifteen, outshone even the ablest warriors of the

Shawnee. (3) He killed four men in the fight and helped Chikiska kill another. (4) The most any other Shawnee killed in the battle was two. (5) One white was taken prisoner.

(A) Statement 1

(B) Statement 2

(C) Statement 3

(D) Statement 4

(E) Statement 5

Directions: For questions 38–40, read the paragraph and choose the sentence that best fills the blank.

38. A handy all-round wrench that is generally included in every toolbox is the adjustable open-end wrench. This wrench is not intended to take the place of the regular solid open-end wrench. ____________. Its usefulness is achieved by being capable of fitting odd-sized nuts.

(F) As the jaw opening increases, the length of the wrench increases.

(G) Adjustable wrenches are available in varying sizes ranging from 4 to 24 inches in length.

(H) This flexibility is achieved although one jaw of the adjustable open-end wrench is fixed because the other jaw is moved along a slide by a thumbscrew adjustment.

(J) In addition, it is not built for use on extremely hard-to-turn items.

(K) There are times when, for engineering reasons, a definite force must be applied to a nut or bolt head.

39. Matter may change either by a physical change or by a chemical change. ____________. Changing water into ice or steam and dissolving sugar in water are examples of physical change. In a chemical change, molecules of new matter are formed that are different from the original matter.

(A) The burning of coal or the rusting of iron are examples of chemical change.

(B) There are four types of chemical reactions: synthesis, decomposition, single displacement, and double displacement.

(C) The form, size, or shape of matter is altered in a physical change, but the molecules remain unchanged.

(D) The molecules that enter the reaction are called *reactants.*

(E) When charcoal burns, carbon combines with oxygen to produce carbon dioxide.

40. Along the shores of the Indian Ocean is found a pretty little shellfish that is noted for furnishing what may have been the first money ever used. ____________. Millions of people around the ocean were using these cowries for money long before furs or cattle or other kinds of money were used anywhere, as far as is known. Cowries have been found in Assyria, many miles inland.

(F) Now, after thousands of years, there are still some tribes in Africa, India, and the South Seas that use cowries.

(G) In China they were used with several other kinds of shells.

(H) Its shell, called a cowrie, is white or light yellow and is about one inch long.

(J) Tortoise shells had the highest value, so it might be said that the tortoise shells were the dollar bills while the cowries were the coins.

(K) Cowries were used for money either separately or on strings.

STOP

IF YOU FINISH BEFORE TIME IS UP, CHECK OVER YOUR WORK ON TEST 7 ONLY. DO NOT RETURN TO ANY PREVIOUS TEST.

ANSWERS TO FIRST MODEL COOP EXAM

Answer Key

Test 1. SEQUENCES

1. C	5. A	9. D	13. A	17. D
2. J	6. H	10. J	14. J	18. J
3. B	7. B	11. A	15. A	19. B
4. G	8. H	12. G	16. G	20. J

Test 2. ANALOGIES

1. B	5. C	9. B	13. C	17. D
2. F	6. H	10. H	14. J	18. H
3. D	7. C	11. D	15. A	19. A
4. F	8. F	12. G	16. J	20. H

Test 3. MEMORY

1. B	5. A	9. D	13. B	17. D
2. J	6. K	10. F	14. K	18. F
3. E	7. C	11. C	15. A	19. C
4. H	8. G	12. J	16. G	20. K

Test 4. VERBAL REASONING

1. D	5. C	9. A	13. A	17. D
2. G	6. H	10. G	14. J	18. F
3. A	7. B	11. A	15. B	19. D
4. J	8. H	12. J	16. J	20. G

Test 5. READING COMPREHENSION

1. C	9. A	17. B	25. C	33. A
2. H	10. H	18. H	26. F	34. J
3. A	11. C	19. B	27. D	35. B
4. J	12. J	20. J	28. G	36. H
5. D	13. C	21. C	29. D	37. A
6. F	14. F	22. G	30. J	38. J
7. D	15. B	23. D	31. D	39. C
8. J	16. J	24. F	32. G	40. G

Test 6. MATHEMATICS CONCEPTS AND APPLICATIONS

1. D	9. C	17. B	25. D	33. B
2. H	10. H	18. J	26. G	34. J
3. B	11. D	19. D	27. D	35. C
4. G	12. F	20. H	28. H	36. H
5. D	13. D	21. C	29. C	37. B
6. H	14. H	22. F	30. J	38. F
7. A	15. D	23. D	31. C	39. B
8. F	16. G	24. F	32. J	40. H

Test 7. LANGUAGE EXPRESSION

1. C	9. A	17. E	25. B	33. A
2. F	10. J	18. F	26. G	34. K
3. E	11. B	19. D	27. E	35. E
4. G	12. K	20. H	28. H	36. G
5. C	13. C	21. B	29. B	37. A
6. F	14. H	22. H	30. K	38. J
7. D	15. D	23. A	31. A	39. C
8. H	16. J	24. J	32. H	40. H

FIRST MODEL COOP EXAM

Answers and Explanations

TEST 1. SEQUENCES

1. **(C)** In the first three segments, the pattern is small figure, large figure, small figure. The fourth segment begins: small figure, large figure... The final figure should be small. Because none of the figures are filled in, there is no reason for the final figure to be filled in.
2. **(J)** The pattern in the second segment is exactly the opposite of that in the first. The first two figures in the fourth segment give every indication that the fourth segment will be the exact opposite of the third. Choice (J) carries this out.
3. **(B)** The position of the arms governs. In the first segment, down, up/down, up; in the second, down, down/up (a reversal), up; in the third, down, up, up/down; in the fourth, down, up... If a reversal is offered, it would be most reasonable. Choice (B) offers this completion.
4. **(G)** In each succeeding segment, the number of double S's (SS) increases by one. The fourth segment should have four double S's.
5. **(A)** The third figure is always blank. This information narrows your choice to (A) or (D). In addition, the fourth figure is always a combination of the first two. This confirms (A) as the correct answer.
6. **(H)** The basis of the sequence is the number of sides of the figures. In the first segment, the number of sides is 3, 4, 5; in the second, 4, 5, 6; in the third, 5, 6, 7; the fourth must be 6, 7, 8.
7. **(B)** This is a +8 series. Within each segment, each number is 8 more than the number before it. 54 + 8 = 62.
8. **(H)** This time the pattern is –5 and repeat. Thus, from the first number in the last segment, 81, we subtract 5 to get 76, then repeat the 76.
9. **(D)** Within each segment the pattern is +7, –6.65 + 7 = 72; 72 – 6 = 66.
10. **(J)** The pattern is ÷4. In the first segment, 96 ÷ 4 = 24, and 24 ÷ 4 = 6; in the second segment, $\frac{1}{2} \div 4 = \frac{1}{8}$, and $\frac{1}{8} \div 4 = \frac{1}{32}$. Having established that the second number is the first divided by 4, multiply the second number of the fourth segment by 4 to find the first number.
11. **(A)** The pattern is ×2, –7; 38 – 7 = 31.
12. **(G)** Within each segment the series consists of repeated squares. 5 squared is 25; 25 squared is 625. 2 squared is 4; 4 squared is 16. 1 squared is 1; 1 squared is 1.
13. **(A)** Each segment consists of a +5 series with 15 in the middle. 21 + 5 = 26, 15 intervenes. 15 + 5 = 20, with 15 intervening to confuse you. 10 + 5 = 15. The 15 needed to fill the blank is the 15 that appears in each segment.
14. **(J)** The numbers and letters remain in the same relationship to one another throughout, that is, there is no number between A and B, and the numbers are always subscripts. The letters remain static. The pattern of the numbers appears to be 5 5, 5 4, 4 4, 4 3, 3 3. Isolating the numbers in this way, you can see the manner in which the numbers step down.
15. **(A)** The letters are static; each letter always has a number attached; odd numbers are superscripts, even numbers subscripts. The numbers are slowly increasing, with the changes occurring from left to right. The numbers in isolation read 111, 211, 221, 222, 322. Remember the superscript/subscript rule in choosing the answer.
16. **(G)** Because the letters are static and the numbers are all subscripts, concentrate at once on the pattern of the numbers: 6, 56, 456, 45, 4.
17. **(D)** The series consists of the consonants in alphabetical order.

18. **(J)** This series consists of the letters of the alphabet in alphabetical order, beginning with the letter *C*. The letter *A* appears after each letter in the series.
19. **(B)** This series consists of the three letters *P–T–L* in constant rotation. In each succeeding grouping of letters the first letter of the group before moves to the end of the group, and the other two letters move to the left, so the letter that was second in the previous group becomes the first letter of the next. After *PTL*, the *P* must move to the rear, and the next group must begin with *T* followed by *LP*.
20. **(J)** This series can be solved mathematically. Starting at the end of the alphabet, –1, –2, –1, repeat the last letter of the first group, then continue: –1, –2, –1, and so on.

TEST 2. ANALOGIES

1. **(B)** Mother is to daughter as father is to son. The analogy is one of parallel relationships.
2. **(F)** The analogy is that of the whole to one of its parts.
3. **(D)** Vegetable is to vegetable as fruit is to fruit. This is a part-to-part relationship. Carrot and lettuce are both part of the vegetable group. Apple and pear are both part of the fruit group.
4. **(F)** This is a relationship of new to old. A lamp is a modern version of the candle. A stove is a modern version of a fireplace.
5. **(C)** This is a relationship of degree. The mansion is a large, elegant version of the cabin. The stretch limousine is larger and more elegant than the pickup truck, though still a car.
6. **(H)** This is a functional relationship. The table leg holds up the table. The tire holds up the car. This could not be a simple part-to-whole relationship because too many car parts are offered as choices.
7. **(C)** This is a part-to-part relationship. Both eye and ear are parts of the head. Both window and door are parts of the house.
8. **(F)** This is a sequential relationship. From an acorn grows an oak tree; from an egg comes a chicken.
9. **(B)** This is a relationship between people and the tools they use. A stethoscope is used by a doctor; a gavel is used by a judge.
10. **(H)** The relationship is functional. Again, it is easiest read in reverse. A pen is used to apply ink; a brush is used to apply paint.
11. **(D)** Another functional relationship. This time read forward. The baseball glove catches the ball. The hook catches the fish.
12. **(G)** Sequential relationship. The abacus preceded the calculator as a mathematical aid. The biplane preceded the jet.
13. **(C)** Part-to-part relationship. Both collie and dachshund are part of the group of dogs. Both eagle and duck are part of the group of birds.
14. **(J)** This relationship is between a hunting implement and the animal hunted with it. The butterfly net is used to hunt the butterfly. The rifle is used to hunt the deer.
15. **(A)** This is a part-to-whole relationship. A slice of bread is part of a loaf; a leaf is part of a tree.
16. **(J)** Call this one what you will—association or part-to-part relationship. The rabbit's foot and four leaf clover are considered good luck. The black cat and the number 13 are considered bad luck.
17. **(D)** A parachute is a safety device on planes; a life preserver is a safety device on boats.
18. **(H)** This is a relationship between real animals and mythical ones. A unicorn is a type of mythical horse; a dragon is a type of mythical reptile.
19. **(A)** Cars travel on roads and trains travel on tracks.
20. **(H)** A necklace and a necktie are both worn around the neck. Socks and shoes are worn on your feet.

TEST 3. MEMORY

Most people find that the best way to learn nonsense words and their definitions is to form some sort of association in their minds, based on the form of the word or its meaning. By way of explanation, we offer possible associations by which you might have learned these words and definitions. These explanations are only suggestions as to how you might have learned; they are NOT the only useful associations.

1. **(B)** boot = waftok = water tog
2. **(J)** candy = minca = mint cavity
3. **(E)** dog = procan = canine
4. **(H)** to read = dystry = story
5. **(A)** palm tree = calafa = California leaf
6. **(K)** to fly = tiher = height, higher, or kite
7. **(C)** ice = legod = gelid
8. **(G)** sticky substance = jepusu = jelly
9. **(D)** loud noise = abartan = a bang
10. **(F)** banana = moskin = more skin
11. **(C)** red = garcar = garish carmine
12. **(J)** helicopter = plifop = flip flop
13. **(B)** rocking chair = nababa = "baba" (suggests a repetitive feeling of rocking)
14. **(K)** sardine = skosh = s + fish
15. **(A)** to snore = ragid = grate or drag
16. **(G)** hurricane = toobo = too (much) blow
17. **(D)** smoke = eteflo = steam float
18. **(F)** hole = lopop = plop
19. **(C)** a musical instrument = freex = flute or reed or xylophone
20. **(K)** elephant = glabara = large

TEST 4. VERBAL REASONING

1. **(D)** Flame and smoke often accompany burning, and ash often follows it. However, there can be no burning without heat; heat is the necessary component.
2. **(G)** To verbalize is to put into words; therefore, the essential ingredient of *verbalization* is *words.*
3. **(A)** Legislation is the enactment of laws. Laws may be enacted by any legislative body—city council, congress, or student organization. Debate is common but not required.
4. **(J)** A terrarium is an enclosure for growing and observing plants or plants and tiny animals indoors. A terrarium never has standing water, though water may be added for the benefit of the living things. Because there are always plants in a terrarium, there is always earth.
5. **(C)** The bow is an adjunct of a violin. Notes and melody are products. Strings are absolutely necessary to a violin.
6. **(H)** A chronometer is a device for measuring time. There must be time to measure. The chronometer may be a watch, a sundial, or even an hourglass.
7. **(B)** The relationship is progressive: from light covering, to heavier or warmer covering, to heaviest or most protective.
8. **(H)** The items above the line are all elements; those below the line all compounds. Oxygen and helium are both elements. Atmosphere is a more general term than a simple compound.
9. **(A)** Color, odor, and sound are all properties of matter. Feeling, seeing, and hearing are all sensory means for being affected by the properties of matter.
10. **(G)** Above the line are spring flowers. Below the line are winter flowers, particularly flowers associated with Christmas.
11. **(A)** Count the feet. Above the line: 2, 4, 8. Below the line: 2, 4, and the crab has 8. A fly has 6 legs; an eel, none at all and a unicorn, 4.
12. **(J)** Above the line are team sports. Below the line are individual sports.
13. **(A)** Jeffrey definitely plays the violin at least twice a week, on Monday and Friday. Although we know that Jeffrey enjoys both music and dancing, we have no way of knowing if he prefers either of these activities to the study of law. From this paragraph, you cannot tell how often Jeffrey dances.
14. **(J)** Chances are that Debbie did not fail the written exam because she is about to go for an Oral Assessment. Surely the person who failed the first step would not be called for the second. Likewise, we can assume that only people who pass the written exam take the oral exam. Otherwise, both exams could be scheduled in advance. If Debbie were already a Foreign Service officer, she would not need to go for an Oral Assessment. You might assume from this paragraph that Debbie is happy because she passed the exam and is still under consideration for appointment as a Foreign Service officer.

15. **(B)** The only certainty is that something frightened the boys, and they got out in a hurry.
16. **(J)** All of the choices could be true, but the only fact of which you may be certain is that Warren's car is garaged regularly.
17. **(D)** Clearly Mark is accident-prone and breaks his right arm easily. His dog is not dangerous; we do not even know if Mark has a sister; he may be learning to use his left hand out of necessity, but we do not know if he is left-or right-handed.
18. **(F)** In this language, the suffix comes before the stem of the word.

    cheki means *ing*

    ruala means *eat*

    duang means *en*

    frit means *hide* or *hid*
19. **(D)** Because the three given English words contain neither common prefixes, suffixes, nor stems, you must determine another basis on which to make your translation. All three words contain the central element *obaka.* Chances are that this element refers to water and that it must appear in the middle of the word *lake* as well. The two words that refer to moving water end in *flis.* Since a pond and lake are both still, *lake* will probably end with *sloo,* as does pond. Creek and pond are basically small versions of river and lake. *Creek* and *pond* both begin with *joki,* which probably means small. So *lura* probably means large. Choice (D) allows you to form a word based on all these assumptions. Large water still means lake.
20. **(G)** Pull apart each word, then reassemble the pieces to suit.

    frush means *dis*

    uwamba means *solve* or *solute* as a combination form

    kuta means *tion*

    bama means *re*

    If you are alert, all you need do is isolate the prefix meaning *re* and put it in front of the given word for *solution.*

TEST 5. READING COMPREHENSION

1. **(C)** ". . . the male wolverine occupies a very large hunting area and fights to the death any male. . . "
2. **(H)** Because Henry wanted the author to shoot the wolverine, Henry obviously was the author's companion.
3. **(A)** The attitude of the author is clearly that of a naturalist.
4. **(J)** In effect, wolverines are the Indians' and trappers' competition. Because the wolverines are successful, they are the hated competition.
5. **(D)** Both the first and last paragraphs make the point that we have been too quick to put into use chemicals and other technological developments before fully understanding their long-range effects.
6. **(F)** The third paragraph discusses this aspect of the problem.
7. **(D)** The author devotes his whole selection to the need for scientists to evaluate the impact of new products on the environment.
8. **(J)** Because the scientists have simply ignored the question of pollution, it might best be said that their attitude has been nonchalant.
9. **(A)** The kangaroo's hind legs are described as having "steel-spring power."
10. **(H)** The first paragraph tells us that kangaroos are found only in Australasia and that this part of the earth was cut off from the Asian mainland. Specifically, kangaroos are found in Australia, Tasmania to the south, and New Guinea to the north.
11. **(C)** The last sentence of the second paragraph makes this very clear. The name "Old Man" is an affectionate one.
12. **(J)** The author obviously enjoys tall tales about kangaroos. The author tells us that the tall tales may be close to fact, but not that they are true, so (J) is the *best* answer.
13. **(C)** Clues may be found in the first sentence, which states that historians are trying to learn more about the *Mayflower* and in the first sentence of the third paragraph, which describes the boat as historic.

14. **(F)** If you have this wrong, reread the first paragraph.
15. **(B)** The first sentence of the second paragraph answers this question.
16. **(J)** The original *Mayflower* was 22 feet wide; the duplicate is 26 feet wide.
17. **(B)** The author describes two buildings in England that may contain parts of the *Mayflower.*
18. **(H)** The first two sentences make it clear that sleep is mysterious and therefore the subject of awe.
19. **(B)** The answer to this question is found in the first sentence. Just subtract. The 1950s, when modern sleep research began is midcentury, not the turn of the century. Neither sleep nor dreams are caused by REMs.
20. **(J)** Respiration, pulse rate, muscle tension, and electrical changes in the brain are physical factors.
21. **(C)** REMs occur during sleep, but nowhere is it suggested that they cause sleep.
22. **(G)** The selection speaks of the value of a cord of wood in terms of how much wood there is in a cord and how much heat is produced by the wood.
23. **(D)** Read carefully. The third sentence is the definition.
24. **(F)** The last sentence of the first paragraph makes the statement.
25. **(C)** The elasticity of the measure is based on the fact that even though dimensions are standard, the actual amount of wood in a cord varies greatly.
26. **(F)** Carbon dating, the most recently developed method for determining the age of archeological finds and the most scientific, is not mentioned in this article.
27. **(D)** The second paragraph suggests that man used tools millions of years before 2,000,000 years ago.
28. **(G)** This is stated toward the end of the last paragraph. The Somme River is in France, and it is there that the British investigators went to check the French deposits.
29. **(D)** The 1840s are in the early to mid-nineteenth century.
30. **(J)** The selection is about the mural and how it was installed.
31. **(D)** Eight of the city's twelve workers in Venetian glass constitute two-thirds of such artisans.
32. **(G)** The original sketch was one-sixth the final size.
33. **(A)** The plant keeps 1,400 shades of glass in stock, but had to send to Venice for 12 additional ones. All 1,400 shades in stock were not necessarily used for this one mural.
34. **(J)** The procedure followed from original sketch to completion of the mural is outlined at the beginning of the third paragraph.
35. **(B)** The first paragraph speaks of the perils of fishing; the second about its rewards.
36. **(H)** The middle of the first paragraph discusses the problems created by rough seas. None of the other choices is mentioned as a difficulty.
37. **(A)** In the middle of the second paragraph, we learn that when fishermen note that herring are entering the nets they sit in quiet excitement so as not to frighten the fish away. They row along the net earlier in order to find out if the net is filling and haul in the nets later, when they are full.
38. **(J)** This phrase represents a powerful metaphor. Picture huge waves rising over empty space and crashing down upon fishermen and boats.
39. **(C)** All the other choices include at least one trait that is not ascribed to these fishermen.
40. **(G)** One might add honesty to the traits of the fishermen. Theft is not mentioned as a problem. If you had forgotten about the whales, reread the first sentence.

TEST 6. MATHEMATICS CONCEPTS AND APPLICATIONS

1. **(D)** Remember, the hundredths place will not be mentioned if its value is zero.
2. **(H)** Notice that the 6 is in the ten-thousands place.
3. **(B)** 1% = .01; one-half of 1 percent is written .005.

4. **(G)** One person raised 35% of \$690. \$690 ×.35 = \$241.50

The remainder raised by the others was \$690 – 241.50 = \$448.50

5. **(D)** The whole pie is 100%. Each part is $\frac{1}{40}$; 100 ÷ 40 = 2.5%.

6. **(H)** There are 1,000 millimeters in a meter.

7. **(A)** Area = length × width

= 176 ft. × 79 ft.

= 13,904 sq ft.

8. **(F)** His total income is equal to 7% of his sales plus \$250. 7% of his sales is \$1250 ×.07 = \$87.50 + \$250 = \$337.50

9. **(C)** Substitute *n* for the blank space.

$$7(3 \times n) + 4 = 2104$$
$$7(3n) + 4 = 2104$$
$$21n + 4 = 2104$$
$$21n = 2100$$
$$n = 100, \text{ or } 10^2$$

10. **(H)** The area of a triangle is found by using $A = \frac{1}{2}bh$.

$$A = \frac{1}{2} \times 14 \times 20$$
$$= 140 \text{ sq. in.}$$

11. **(D)**

$$(4 \times 10^3) + 6 = 4{,}006$$
$$-(2 \times 10^3) + (3 \times 10) + 8 = 2{,}038$$

The difference is 1,968.

12. **(F)** The set of factors for 24 is:

{1,2,3,4,6,8,12,24}

The set of factors for 30 is:

{1,2,3,5,6,10,15,30}

The set of common factors is: {1,2,3,6}

13. **(D)** For the length, 29 feet would be represented by 29 units of $\frac{1}{4}$ inch, resulting in $\frac{29}{4}$, or $7\frac{1}{4}$, inches. For the width, 23 feet would be represented by 23 units of $\frac{1}{4}$ inch, resulting in $\frac{23}{4}$, or $5\frac{3}{4}$, inches.

14. **(H)** A scalene triangle has no equal sides.

15. **(D)** Distance = rate × time

$= 55 \text{ mph} \times 5\frac{1}{2}$ hours

= 302.5 miles

16. **(G)** Note that $\frac{17}{30}$ is only slightly larger than $\frac{15}{30}$ or $\frac{1}{2}$. Answers F, H, and J are much closer in value to 1 than to $\frac{1}{2}$.

17. **(B)** 100 centimeters = 1 meter. Each centimeter is $\frac{1}{100}$ of a meter.

18. **(J)** If 18 games constituted 40% of the season, the season was 18 ÷ .40, or 45 games long. If the team won 18 games, it lost 45 – 18, or 27 games.

19. **(D)** The inequality should be conceptualized as "*q* is between –2 and –1." Because *q* must be closer to 0 than –2, it is *larger* than –2.

20. **(H)** If $x = 0$, then $2x < 8$ because $2(0) < 8$. None of the other pairs results in a true statement.

21. **(C)** The order in which numbers are added does not affect the sum; changing the signs does.

22. **(F)** We want the amount in the parentheses to be equal to 3. The value of *x* that will make the amount in parentheses equal to 3 is 4.

23. **(D)** Review your geometry if you got this wrong.

24. **(F)** The temperature over the 6 hours graphed was 10° + 20° + 20° + 30° + 20° + 20°= 120° ÷ 6 = 20°.

25. **(D)** He will pay back \$3,500 plus 10% interest. Ten percent of \$3,500 is \$350. \$3,500 + \$350 = \$3,850.

26. **(G)** Six plus four is ten, and ten is less than 10.5($10\frac{1}{2}$).

27. **(D)** The sum of the angles of a triangle is 180°. Therefore, 180° – 115° = 65°.

28. **(H)** Because distance = rate × time, time = distance ÷ rate. Therefore, time = $\frac{1}{20}$ of an hour = 3 minutes. Or, because 60 mph is 1 mile per minute, 20 mph is 1 mile every 3 minutes.

29. **(C)** Diameter = 2 • radius

$$\pi = \frac{22}{7}$$

Circumference = π • diameter

$$C = \pi \cdot 21 \cdot 2$$
$$C = \pi \cdot 42 = \frac{22}{7} \cdot 42 = 132 \text{ feet}$$

30. **(J)** The set {x,y} includes all those numbers larger than –4 and smaller than 2. Considering only whole numbers, this set includes –3, –2, –1, 0, and 1.

31. **(C)** Careful study of the Venn diagram shows overlap of the circles enclosing rectangles and rhombi, so some rectangles are rhombi as those same rhombi are rectangles. The other statements should read as follows: No trapezoids are parallelograms; all rhombi are parallelograms; and some parallelograms are rectangles, or all rectangles are parallelograms.

32. **(J)** There are 72 tiles along each length and 24 tiles along each width. 2 × 96 = 192 tiles along the perimeter. But 4 more are needed for the corners of the frame.

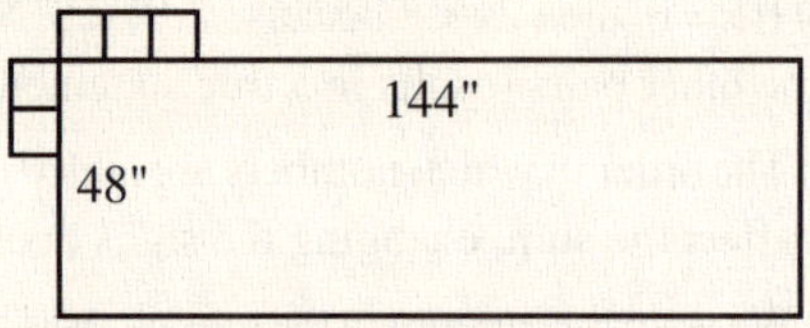

Hence, 196 tiles are needed.

33. **(B)** The number of accidents is irrelevant to the question. B deaths occurred in 10 years, so each year an average of one-tenth of B deaths occurred.

34. **(J)** First read to the left along the negative x-axis, then read up on the y-axis.

35. **(C)** Because point P has not moved along the y-axis, the x-coordinate is 0. Moving down on the y-axis, point P is located at $-2\frac{1}{2}$.

36. **(H)** If 2 inches equals 24 feet, 1 inch equals 12 feet. A line representing 72 feet, therefore, must be 6 inches long (72 ÷ 12 = 6).

37. **(B)** Reduce the $14.00 price by 25%.

    25% of $14.00 = $14 × .25 = $3.50

    $14.00 – $3.50 = $10.50 (new price)

    Therefore, (B) is the correct answer. Answer (A) indicates a reduction of only twenty-five cents. Answer (C) represents a reduction *to* 25% of the original price, or a 75% decrease in price.

38. **(F)** The area is most easily found by multiplying the length of the figure by its width, and then subtracting the area of the small 3" × 3" square.

    (7" × 5") – (3" × 3") = area

    35 sq. in – 9 sq. in. = 25 sq. in.

    Shapes such as this are often used for irregular pieces of carpeting or covering.

39. **(B)** The boy's age is M years. His older brother is $M + 6$ years old, and his younger sister is $M - 4$ years old. Adding the three ages together:

    $M + (M + 6) + (M - 4) = 3M + 2$

40. **(H)** This problem requires two steps. First, find the smallest number divisible by both 14 and 12 (the least common multiple, or LCM). Secondly, add the number to 1:00 and rename it as time of day. The LCM of 14 and 12 is 84. Both events will occur simultaneously 84 minutes past 1:00, or 2:24 p.m.

TEST 7. LANGUAGE EXPRESSION

1. **(C)** The sentence describes two activities, our shoveling and the plow's coming, in terms of their relationship in time. Of the two choices that refer to time, only *when* makes sense.

2. **(F)** The word that is required introduces an exception. *Unless* does this best.

3. **(E)** Try each choice in the sentence. *Because* and *before* are both illogical. *In spite of* is ungrammatical. *Although* highlights the contrast between statement and fact.

4. **(G)** There are far more than two circus acts, so in comparing the thrill value of various acts, we are seeking the superlative form of *scary*. *Most scary* (not offered) and *scariest* are equally correct. *Scaringest* is not a word.

5. **(C)** All of the action occurred in the past, so the blank must be filled by the past perfect, *had thrown.*

6. **(F)** Shakespeare used the form *most unkindest* in his play, *Julius Caesar*. However, in modern usage this construction is considered redundant. The superlative of *unkind* is *most unkind*. Likewise, the superlative of *unkindly* is *most unkindly*, making choice (G) incorrect.

7. **(D)** The two independent clauses are best connected by a semicolon. Choice (A) is a run-on

sentence; (B) is a comma splice; (C) is not a complete sentence. In (E), the first phrase is a colloquialism; it is not an independent clause.

8. **(H)** The independent clause is followed by a modifying dependent clause. Choices (F) and (G) are not complete sentences; (J) is a run-on. In (K) it appears that the telephone just returned from a frustrating day at the office.
9. **(A)** The second clause contains both subject, *he*, and verb, *pounded*. The subordinate clause with which the sentence begins modifies the main clause. Choices (B), (D), and (E) are not complete sentences; (C) is a complete sentence but makes no sense.
10. **(J)** A proper sentence contains subject and verb in reasonable proximity to each other so that the meaning is clear. Choice (H) contains both subject and verb, but the verb is so divided as to create a nonsense sentence; (F) and (J) have no subjects; (K) consists of two independent clauses with no connection.
11. **(B)** This is the only complete sentence offered.
12. **(K)** This well-written sentence begins with a subordinate clause that modifies the main clause that follows it. Choices (F), (G), and (J) are not complete sentences; (H) is a run-on.
13. **(C)** Both verbs are correctly in the present tense. Both choices (B) and (D) require the second verb to be in the past tense; in (A), the correct verb form should be *had slowed*; and choice (E) requires the past perfect tense, *had done*.
14. **(H)** The sentence is somewhat awkward, but it is correct. Both verbs are in the present tense because the action is simultaneous and is stated as if happening right now. The other choices all mix tenses in ridiculous order—one cannot, for instance, recall a future event.
15. **(D)** In this sentence, all activity occurred in the past. The other choices mix tenses in illogical order.
16. **(J)** The introductory clause speaks of a future event, so the second verb is correctly written in the future tense. The other choices combine tenses in illogical order.
17. **(E)** The explanations are there right now, in the present. Now that you know that they are there, you may turn to them and, in the immediate future, you will learn from your errors. Choices (A) and (C) offer illogical order of tenses. In (B), the correct past tense of the verb, *to come* is *came*. Choice (D) requires the auxiliary *can*. They should listen to the weather forecast so that they *can anticipate* a hurricane.
18. **(F)** The noise is frightening.
19. **(D)** *Police* is the subject of the introductory subordinate clause, but *ambulance* is the subject of the sentence.
20. **(H)** *Form* is the subject modified by the two adjectives that precede it.
21. **(B)** *Venetian* is an adjective modifying the subject, *blinds*.
22. **(H)** The *letter* is the subject of the sentence, and the letter *will be delivered*. *Run* is used here as a noun. *Is addressed* is the verb in the introductory prepositional clause, but it is not the predicate verb of the sentence
23. **(A)** The subject of the sentence is *I*, and I *feel*.
24. **(J)** *Hear* is the verb of the introductory subordinate clause, *leave* is the verb of the independent clause, hence the predicate verb of the sentence. The subject of the independent clause is understood to be *you*, even though unstated.
25. **(B)** Do not be misled by verbs in subordinate clauses or phrases. The subject is *I*, and I *shall begin*.
26. **(G)** The incorrect choices are all run-on sentences. Choice (G) then becomes the correct answer by default, but it also is by far the best combination because it focuses directly on the topic of the two sentences, *Ecuador*.
27. **(E)** All four choices are complete sentences, but only choice (E) accurately conveys the message of the two sentences. All the other choices distort the meaning.
28. **(H)** This is a comprehensive restatement of two rather long sentences. Choice (F) is awkward and inaccurate in that it places the states in the Northwest Territory and confines their claims to 1785 instead of before 1785; (G) is garbled; (J) makes an unwarranted absolutist statement about "all the lands"; and choice (K) makes an accurate statement but loses the meaning of the original two sentences.

29. **(B)** Consider that this answer is practically a "gift." Because the second sentence begins with the word *first*, it is obvious that the sentence that is about to offer *three good reasons* will be the topic sentence. If choice (B) were not offered, choice (A) might well have served as a topic sentence, but (B) is clearly better. The sense of choice (E) makes it a tempting choice, but the paragraph addresses *you,* while choice (E) is a third-person generalization. Choices (C) and (D) are quite obviously development sentences.
30. **(K)** Because the first development sentence begins with *On the one hand*, you should look for a topic sentence that offers an alternative. As in question 29, this question offers you a good second choice. If choice (K) were not offered, you would choose (H) because it raises the question of history's being a science, and the first development sentence speaks of history as a science. Still, the choice that raises the possibility of alternatives is the better of the two. The other choices prematurely introduce the subject of literature.
31. **(A)** The first development sentence is practically a restatement of the topic sentence. If opinions play a major role in important areas in our lives, obviously they should not be taken lightly. Choice (B) is clearly a development sentence; (C) could not possibly serve as a topic sentence because its subject is "they", which has no reference; (D) contradicts the paragraph; (E) might be a development sentence or might even belong in the next paragraph.
32. **(H)** The first sentence tells us that homelessness presents a difficult problem. Develop the paragraph by describing the extent and causes of the problem. Choice (F) is a statement of opinion that does not really address the problem. Choice (G) digresses into a narrow aspect of homelessness—hunger; it might appear later in the paragraph or in another paragraph of the same article. Choice (J) is totally irrelevant, and (K) addresses an entirely different topic, that of home ownership.
33. **(A)** Any one of the choices could possibly develop the paragraph, but the *best* development discusses the vegetarian diet itself.
34. **(K)** Note that the topic sentence speaks of the *condition* of the tires. Only choice (K) follows that theme.
35. **(E)** The paragraph is about Japanese monkeys and their human behaviors. Tigers have no place in this paragraph.
36. **(G)** The paragraph deals with shamans with respect to their diagnosis and treatment of illness. The political power of shamans is an interesting topic, but it is a topic for another paragraph.
37. **(A)** The paragraph is a description of Tecumseh's first battle and his role in it. Tecumseh's attitude toward the treatment of prisoners could follow development of the paragraph after sentence 5 or could appear in a new paragraph. The placement of Statement 1 at the beginning of this paragraph is clearly incorrect.
38. **(J)** The second sentence tells of one use for which the open-end wrench is not intended. Choice (J) tells of additional unintended use. Choices (F) and (G) address the length of the wrench rather than the opening of its jaws. Choice (H) logically follows the last sentence of the paragraph, and choice (K) is totally irrelevant.
39. **(C)** The paragraph will discuss two ways in which matter may change. The third sentence gives examples of physical change, and the fourth sentence describes a chemical change. It is reasonable to expect the missing sentence to describe a physical change. Choice (A) would logically follow the description of a chemical change. All other choices might best find their places in another paragraph.
40. **(H)** In a paragraph about the use of cowries as money, an explanation of exactly what a cowrie is should be offered as early as possible.

SCORE SHEET

CTB/McGraw-Hill will score your exam and will send your scaled scores and your percentile scores directly to the schools you indicated. Scaled scores are scores converted by a special formula to make comparable your performance on tests of unequal lengths and unequal importance. Percentile scores compare your performance on each test and the whole exam with the performance of other students who took the same exam at the same time. Your scores will *not* be reported either as raw scores—that is, number correct—nor as percents. Right now, however, you will find it very useful to convert your own scores on the model exam into simple percentages. In this way you can compare your own performance on each test of the exam with your performance on each other test. You can then focus your study where it will do you the most good.

Subject	**No. Correct**	÷	**No. of Questions**		× **100**	=	____**%**
Sequences	_____	÷	20 =	_____	× 100	=	_____%
Analogies	_____	÷	20 =	_____	× 100	=	_____%
Memory	_____	÷	20 =	_____	× 100	=	_____%
Verbal Reasoning	_____	÷	20 =	_____	× 100	=	_____%
Reading Comprehension	_____	÷	40 =	_____	× 100	=	_____%
Mathematics Concepts and Applications	_____	÷	40 =	_____	× 100	=	_____%
Language Expression	_____	÷	40 =	_____	× 100	=	_____%
TOTAL EXAM	_____	÷	200 =	_____	× 100	=	_____%

Chapter 20

Second Model COOP Exam

ROAD MAP

- *Definitions for Memory Questions*
- *Test 1. Sequences*
- *Test 2. Analogies*
- *Test 3. Memory*
- *Test 4. Verbal Reasoning*
- *Test 5. Reading Comprehension*
- *Test 6. Mathematics Concepts and Applications*
- *Test 7. Language Expression*
- *Answers to Second Model COOP Exam*
- *Answer Explanations for Second Model COOP Exam*
- *Score Sheet*

ANSWER SHEET

Answers and explanations for all Second Model COOP Exam questions follow the model exam.

TEST 1. SEQUENCES

1. Ⓐ Ⓑ Ⓒ Ⓓ	5. Ⓐ Ⓑ Ⓒ Ⓓ	9. Ⓐ Ⓑ Ⓒ Ⓓ	13. Ⓐ Ⓑ Ⓒ Ⓓ	17. Ⓐ Ⓑ Ⓒ Ⓓ
2. Ⓕ Ⓖ Ⓗ Ⓙ	6. Ⓕ Ⓖ Ⓗ Ⓙ	10. Ⓕ Ⓖ Ⓗ Ⓙ	14. Ⓕ Ⓖ Ⓗ Ⓙ	18. Ⓕ Ⓖ Ⓗ Ⓙ
3. Ⓐ Ⓑ Ⓒ Ⓓ	7. Ⓐ Ⓑ Ⓒ Ⓓ	11. Ⓐ Ⓑ Ⓒ Ⓓ	15. Ⓐ Ⓑ Ⓒ Ⓓ	19. Ⓐ Ⓑ Ⓒ Ⓓ
4. Ⓕ Ⓖ Ⓗ Ⓙ	8. Ⓕ Ⓖ Ⓗ Ⓙ	12. Ⓕ Ⓖ Ⓗ Ⓙ	16. Ⓕ Ⓖ Ⓗ Ⓙ	20. Ⓕ Ⓖ Ⓗ Ⓙ

TEST 2. ANALOGIES

1. Ⓐ Ⓑ Ⓒ Ⓓ	5. Ⓐ Ⓑ Ⓒ Ⓓ	9. Ⓐ Ⓑ Ⓒ Ⓓ	13. Ⓐ Ⓑ Ⓒ Ⓓ	17. Ⓐ Ⓑ Ⓒ Ⓓ
2. Ⓕ Ⓖ Ⓗ Ⓙ	6. Ⓕ Ⓖ Ⓗ Ⓙ	10. Ⓕ Ⓖ Ⓗ Ⓙ	14. Ⓕ Ⓖ Ⓗ Ⓙ	18. Ⓕ Ⓖ Ⓗ Ⓙ
3. Ⓐ Ⓑ Ⓒ Ⓓ	7. Ⓐ Ⓑ Ⓒ Ⓓ	11. Ⓐ Ⓑ Ⓒ Ⓓ	15. Ⓐ Ⓑ Ⓒ Ⓓ	19. Ⓐ Ⓑ Ⓒ Ⓓ
4. Ⓕ Ⓖ Ⓗ Ⓙ	8. Ⓕ Ⓖ Ⓗ Ⓙ	12. Ⓕ Ⓖ Ⓗ Ⓙ	16. Ⓕ Ⓖ Ⓗ Ⓙ	20. Ⓕ Ⓖ Ⓗ Ⓙ

TEST 3. MEMORY

1. Ⓐ Ⓑ Ⓒ Ⓓ Ⓔ	5. Ⓐ Ⓑ Ⓒ Ⓓ Ⓔ	9. Ⓐ Ⓑ Ⓒ Ⓓ Ⓔ	13. Ⓐ Ⓑ Ⓒ Ⓓ Ⓔ	17. Ⓐ Ⓑ Ⓒ Ⓓ Ⓔ
2. Ⓕ Ⓖ Ⓗ Ⓙ Ⓚ	6. Ⓕ Ⓖ Ⓗ Ⓙ Ⓚ	10. Ⓕ Ⓖ Ⓗ Ⓙ Ⓚ	14. Ⓕ Ⓖ Ⓗ Ⓙ Ⓚ	18. Ⓕ Ⓖ Ⓗ Ⓙ Ⓚ
3. Ⓐ Ⓑ Ⓒ Ⓓ Ⓔ	7. Ⓐ Ⓑ Ⓒ Ⓓ Ⓔ	11. Ⓐ Ⓑ Ⓒ Ⓓ Ⓔ	15. Ⓐ Ⓑ Ⓒ Ⓓ Ⓔ	19. Ⓐ Ⓑ Ⓒ Ⓓ Ⓔ
4. Ⓕ Ⓖ Ⓗ Ⓙ Ⓚ	8. Ⓕ Ⓖ Ⓗ Ⓙ Ⓚ	12. Ⓕ Ⓖ Ⓗ Ⓙ Ⓚ	16. Ⓕ Ⓖ Ⓗ Ⓙ Ⓚ	20. Ⓕ Ⓖ Ⓗ Ⓙ Ⓚ

TEST 4. VERBAL REASONING

1. Ⓐ Ⓑ Ⓒ Ⓓ	5. Ⓐ Ⓑ Ⓒ Ⓓ	9. Ⓐ Ⓑ Ⓒ Ⓓ	13. Ⓐ Ⓑ Ⓒ Ⓓ	17. Ⓐ Ⓑ Ⓒ Ⓓ
2. Ⓕ Ⓖ Ⓗ Ⓙ	6. Ⓕ Ⓖ Ⓗ Ⓙ	10. Ⓕ Ⓖ Ⓗ Ⓙ	14. Ⓕ Ⓖ Ⓗ Ⓙ	18. Ⓕ Ⓖ Ⓗ Ⓙ
3. Ⓐ Ⓑ Ⓒ Ⓓ	7. Ⓐ Ⓑ Ⓒ Ⓓ	11. Ⓐ Ⓑ Ⓒ Ⓓ	15. Ⓐ Ⓑ Ⓒ Ⓓ	19. Ⓐ Ⓑ Ⓒ Ⓓ
4. Ⓕ Ⓖ Ⓗ Ⓙ	8. Ⓕ Ⓖ Ⓗ Ⓙ	12. Ⓕ Ⓖ Ⓗ Ⓙ	16. Ⓕ Ⓖ Ⓗ Ⓙ	20. Ⓕ Ⓖ Ⓗ Ⓙ

TEAR HERE

TEST 5. READING COMPREHENSION

1. Ⓐ Ⓑ Ⓒ Ⓓ	9. Ⓕ Ⓖ Ⓗ Ⓙ	17. Ⓐ Ⓑ Ⓒ Ⓓ	25. Ⓕ Ⓖ Ⓗ Ⓙ	33. Ⓐ Ⓑ Ⓒ Ⓓ
2. Ⓕ Ⓖ Ⓗ Ⓙ	10. Ⓐ Ⓑ Ⓒ Ⓓ	18. Ⓕ Ⓖ Ⓗ Ⓙ	26. Ⓐ Ⓑ Ⓒ Ⓓ	34. Ⓕ Ⓖ Ⓗ Ⓙ
3. Ⓐ Ⓑ Ⓒ Ⓓ	11. Ⓕ Ⓖ Ⓗ Ⓙ	19. Ⓐ Ⓑ Ⓒ Ⓓ	27. Ⓕ Ⓖ Ⓗ Ⓙ	35. Ⓐ Ⓑ Ⓒ Ⓓ
4. Ⓕ Ⓖ Ⓗ Ⓙ	12. Ⓐ Ⓑ Ⓒ Ⓓ	20. Ⓕ Ⓖ Ⓗ Ⓙ	28. Ⓐ Ⓑ Ⓒ Ⓓ	36. Ⓕ Ⓖ Ⓗ Ⓙ
5. Ⓐ Ⓑ Ⓒ Ⓓ	13. Ⓕ Ⓖ Ⓗ Ⓙ	21. Ⓐ Ⓑ Ⓒ Ⓓ	29. Ⓕ Ⓖ Ⓗ Ⓙ	37. Ⓐ Ⓑ Ⓒ Ⓓ
6. Ⓕ Ⓖ Ⓗ Ⓙ	14. Ⓐ Ⓑ Ⓒ Ⓓ	22. Ⓕ Ⓖ Ⓗ Ⓙ	30. Ⓐ Ⓑ Ⓒ Ⓓ	38. Ⓕ Ⓖ Ⓗ Ⓙ
7. Ⓐ Ⓑ Ⓒ Ⓓ	15. Ⓕ Ⓖ Ⓗ Ⓙ	23. Ⓐ Ⓑ Ⓒ Ⓓ	31. Ⓕ Ⓖ Ⓗ Ⓙ	39. Ⓐ Ⓑ Ⓒ Ⓓ
8. Ⓕ Ⓖ Ⓗ Ⓙ	16. Ⓐ Ⓑ Ⓒ Ⓓ	24. Ⓕ Ⓖ Ⓗ Ⓙ	32. Ⓐ Ⓑ Ⓒ Ⓓ	40. Ⓕ Ⓖ Ⓗ Ⓙ

TEST 6. MATHEMATICS CONCEPTS AND APPLICATIONS

1. Ⓐ Ⓑ Ⓒ Ⓓ	9. Ⓕ Ⓖ Ⓗ Ⓙ	17. Ⓐ Ⓑ Ⓒ Ⓓ	25. Ⓕ Ⓖ Ⓗ Ⓙ	33. Ⓐ Ⓑ Ⓒ Ⓓ
2. Ⓕ Ⓖ Ⓗ Ⓙ	10. Ⓐ Ⓑ Ⓒ Ⓓ	18. Ⓕ Ⓖ Ⓗ Ⓙ	26. Ⓐ Ⓑ Ⓒ Ⓓ	34. Ⓕ Ⓖ Ⓗ Ⓙ
3. Ⓐ Ⓑ Ⓒ Ⓓ	11. Ⓕ Ⓖ Ⓗ Ⓙ	19. Ⓐ Ⓑ Ⓒ Ⓓ	27. Ⓕ Ⓖ Ⓗ Ⓙ	35. Ⓐ Ⓑ Ⓒ Ⓓ
4. Ⓕ Ⓖ Ⓗ Ⓙ	12. Ⓐ Ⓑ Ⓒ Ⓓ	20. Ⓕ Ⓖ Ⓗ Ⓙ	28. Ⓐ Ⓑ Ⓒ Ⓓ	36. Ⓕ Ⓖ Ⓗ Ⓙ
5. Ⓐ Ⓑ Ⓒ Ⓓ	13. Ⓕ Ⓖ Ⓗ Ⓙ	21. Ⓐ Ⓑ Ⓒ Ⓓ	29. Ⓕ Ⓖ Ⓗ Ⓙ	37. Ⓐ Ⓑ Ⓒ Ⓓ
6. Ⓕ Ⓖ Ⓗ Ⓙ	14. Ⓐ Ⓑ Ⓒ Ⓓ	22. Ⓕ Ⓖ Ⓗ Ⓙ	30. Ⓐ Ⓑ Ⓒ Ⓓ	38. Ⓕ Ⓖ Ⓗ Ⓙ
7. Ⓐ Ⓑ Ⓒ Ⓓ	15. Ⓕ Ⓖ Ⓗ Ⓙ	23. Ⓐ Ⓑ Ⓒ Ⓓ	31. Ⓕ Ⓖ Ⓗ Ⓙ	39. Ⓐ Ⓑ Ⓒ Ⓓ
8. Ⓕ Ⓖ Ⓗ Ⓙ	16. Ⓐ Ⓑ Ⓒ Ⓓ	24. Ⓕ Ⓖ Ⓗ Ⓙ	32. Ⓐ Ⓑ Ⓒ Ⓓ	40. Ⓕ Ⓖ Ⓗ Ⓙ

TEAR HERE

TEST 7. LANGUAGE EXPRESSION

1. Ⓐ Ⓑ Ⓒ Ⓓ Ⓔ	9. Ⓐ Ⓑ Ⓒ Ⓓ Ⓔ	17. Ⓐ Ⓑ Ⓒ Ⓓ Ⓔ	25. Ⓐ Ⓑ Ⓒ Ⓓ Ⓔ	33. Ⓐ Ⓑ Ⓒ Ⓓ Ⓔ
2. Ⓕ Ⓖ Ⓗ Ⓙ Ⓚ	10. Ⓕ Ⓖ Ⓗ Ⓙ Ⓚ	18. Ⓕ Ⓖ Ⓗ Ⓙ Ⓚ	26. Ⓕ Ⓖ Ⓗ Ⓙ Ⓚ	34. Ⓕ Ⓖ Ⓗ Ⓙ Ⓚ
3. Ⓐ Ⓑ Ⓒ Ⓓ Ⓔ	11. Ⓐ Ⓑ Ⓒ Ⓓ Ⓔ	19. Ⓐ Ⓑ Ⓒ Ⓓ Ⓔ	27. Ⓐ Ⓑ Ⓒ Ⓓ Ⓔ	35. Ⓐ Ⓑ Ⓒ Ⓓ Ⓔ
4. Ⓕ Ⓖ Ⓗ Ⓙ Ⓚ	12. Ⓕ Ⓖ Ⓗ Ⓙ Ⓚ	20. Ⓕ Ⓖ Ⓗ Ⓙ Ⓚ	28. Ⓕ Ⓖ Ⓗ Ⓙ Ⓚ	36. Ⓕ Ⓖ Ⓗ Ⓙ Ⓚ
5. Ⓐ Ⓑ Ⓒ Ⓓ Ⓔ	13. Ⓐ Ⓑ Ⓒ Ⓓ Ⓔ	21. Ⓐ Ⓑ Ⓒ Ⓓ Ⓔ	29. Ⓐ Ⓑ Ⓒ Ⓓ Ⓔ	37. Ⓐ Ⓑ Ⓒ Ⓓ Ⓔ
6. Ⓕ Ⓖ Ⓗ Ⓙ Ⓚ	14. Ⓕ Ⓖ Ⓗ Ⓙ Ⓚ	22. Ⓕ Ⓖ Ⓗ Ⓙ Ⓚ	30. Ⓕ Ⓖ Ⓗ Ⓙ Ⓚ	38. Ⓕ Ⓖ Ⓗ Ⓙ Ⓚ
7. Ⓐ Ⓑ Ⓒ Ⓓ Ⓔ	15. Ⓐ Ⓑ Ⓒ Ⓓ Ⓔ	23. Ⓐ Ⓑ Ⓒ Ⓓ Ⓔ	31. Ⓐ Ⓑ Ⓒ Ⓓ Ⓔ	39. Ⓐ Ⓑ Ⓒ Ⓓ Ⓔ
8. Ⓕ Ⓖ Ⓗ Ⓙ Ⓚ	16. Ⓐ Ⓑ Ⓒ Ⓓ Ⓚ	24. Ⓕ Ⓖ Ⓗ Ⓙ Ⓚ	32. Ⓐ Ⓑ Ⓒ Ⓓ Ⓚ	40. Ⓕ Ⓖ Ⓗ Ⓙ Ⓚ

TEAR HERE

Second Model COOP Exam

DEFINITIONS FOR MEMORY QUESTIONS

Time—12 minutes

Directions: Read the nonsense words and their definitions aloud at least one time through the entire list. Commit them to memory.

1. A *potho* is a furnace.
2. A *birbal* is an oriole.
3. A *tred* is an apple.
4. *Oblomo* means "to explode."
5. *Gnay* means "stop."
6. A *hortex* is an exam.
7. *Chohor* means "to laugh."
8. A *clolo* is a button.
9. A *grindle* is a child's toy.
10. A *lululoy* is a yellow vegetable.
11. A *blothink* is a psychiatrist.
12. A *rockflo* is a futon.
13. A *mostonica* is a cemetery.
14. *Chimichi* means "to sing."
15. A *hiwama* is a flood.
16. A *ganclan* is a member of a chain gang.
17. *Obalack* is the color white.
18. *Milikan* is illness.
19. *Plidl* means "to slip and fall."
20. *Shirocol* means "frozen."

Use the full 12 minutes to memorize these words and their definitions. Do not go on until the signal is given.

TEST 1. SEQUENCES

Time—15 minutes

Directions: For questions 1–20, choose the part that would continue the pattern or sequence. Mark the letter of your answer on the answer sheet.

1.
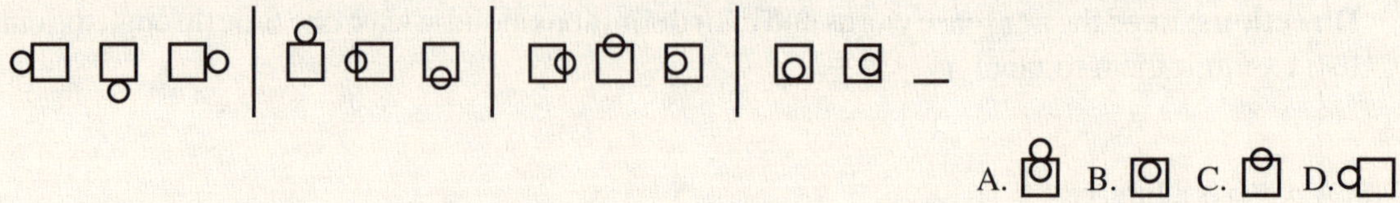

2.
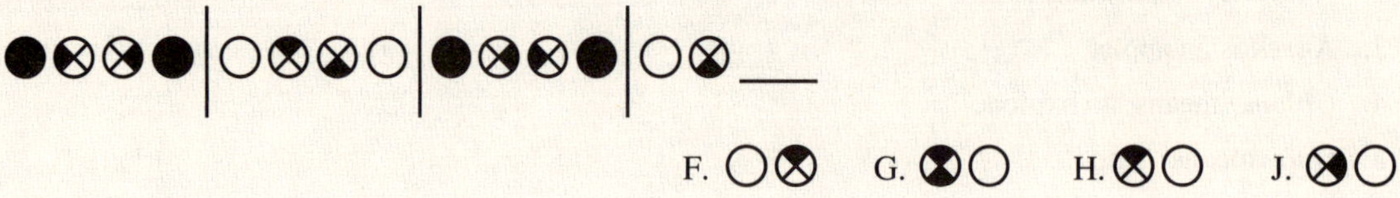

3.
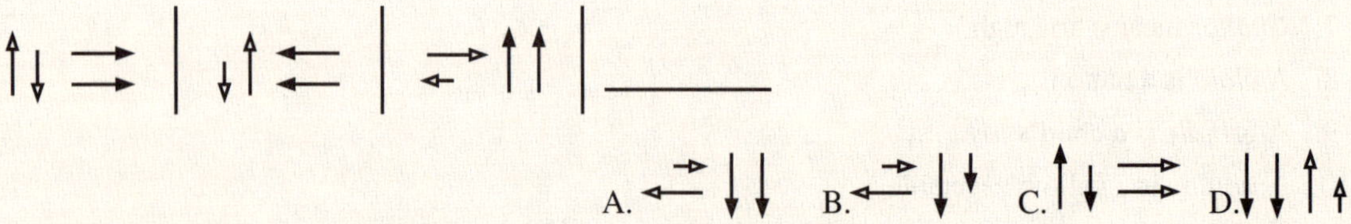

4.
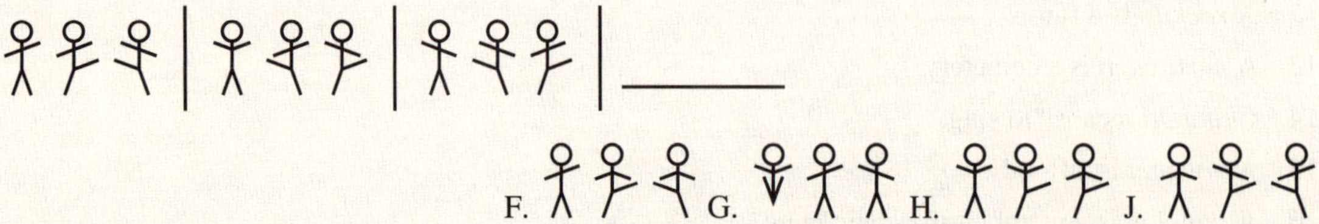

5.
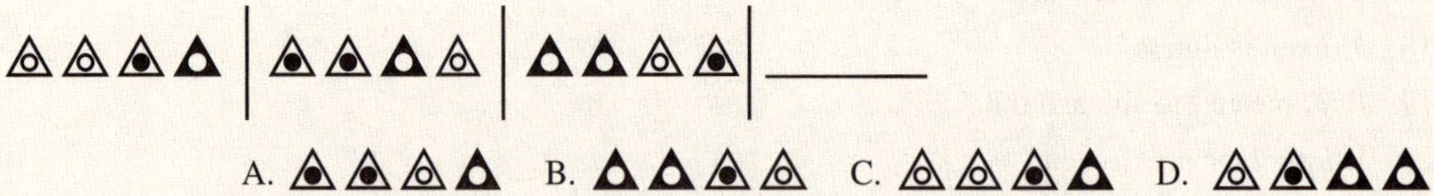

6.
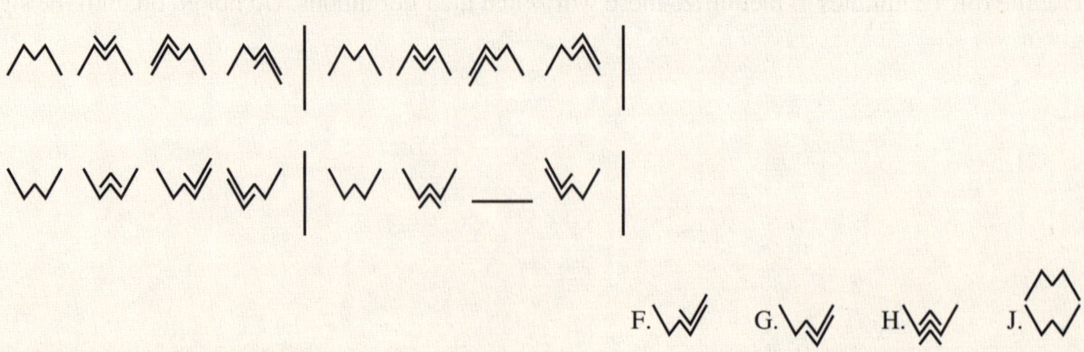

7. 44 39 35 | 87 82 78 | 61 56 _____
   (A) 53
   (B) 52
   (C) 50
   (D) 48

8. 3 6 3 | 12 24 12 | 9 _____ 9
   (F) 18
   (G) 3
   (H) 6
   (J) 27

9. 5 10 8 | 7 14 8 | 3 6 _____
   (A) 9
   (B) 7
   (C) 5
   (D) 8

10. 75 25 8.3 | 90 30 10 | _____ 7 2.3
   (F) 23
   (G) 21
   (H) 30
   (J) 15

11. 23 41 41 | 7 25 25 | 41 _____ 59
   (A) 23
   (B) 25
   (C) 59
   (D) 41

12. 2 4 6 | 3 6 9 | 4 8 _____
   (F) 16
   (G) 10
   (H) 12
   (J) 32

13. 100 80 90 | 60 40 50 | 80 _____ 70
   (A) 60
   (B) 90
   (C) 50
   (D) 100

14. $R_1S_2T^3$ $R^3S_1T_2$ $R_2S^3T_1$ _____ $R^3S_1T_2$
   (F) $R^1S_2T_3$
   (G) $R^3S_2T_1$
   (H) $R_3S_1T^2$
   (J) $R_1S_2T^3$

15. $P^6D^4Q^2$ $P^6D^4Q_2$ $P^6D_4Q_2$ _____ $P_6D_4Q^2$
   (A) $P^6D^4Q^2$
   (B) $P_6D_4Q_2$
   (C) $P_6D^4Q_2$
   (D) $P^6D_4Q^2$

16. $L^5M^5N_4$ $L^5M_4N_4$ $L_4M_4N_4$ _____ $L_4M^3N^3$
   (F) $L_4M_4N^3$
   (G) $L^5M_4N^3$
   (H) $L^5M^5N^5$
   (J) $L_4M^5N_3$

17. ABC FED GHI LRJ _____
   (A) ONM
   (B) NOP
   (C) MNO
   (D) MON

18. ABDB ACEB ADFB _____ AFHB
   (F) ADGB
   (G) AEGB
   (H) AFGB
   (J) ACGB

GO ON TO THE NEXT PAGE

19. ABC EFG JKL PQR _____
    (A) XYZ
    (B) UVW
    (C) TUV
    (D) WXY

20. ZYWX VUST RQOP _____ JIGH
    (F) MNKL
    (G) LKMN
    (H) NMKL
    (J) NMLK

STOP

IF YOU FINISH BEFORE TIME IS UP, CHECK OVER YOUR WORK ON THIS TEST ONLY. DO NOT GO ON TO THE NEXT TEST UNTIL THE SIGNAL IS GIVEN.

TEST 2. ANALOGIES

Time—7 minutes

Directions: For questions 1–20, choose the picture that should go in the empty box so that the bottom two pictures are related in the same way that the top two are related.

1. 

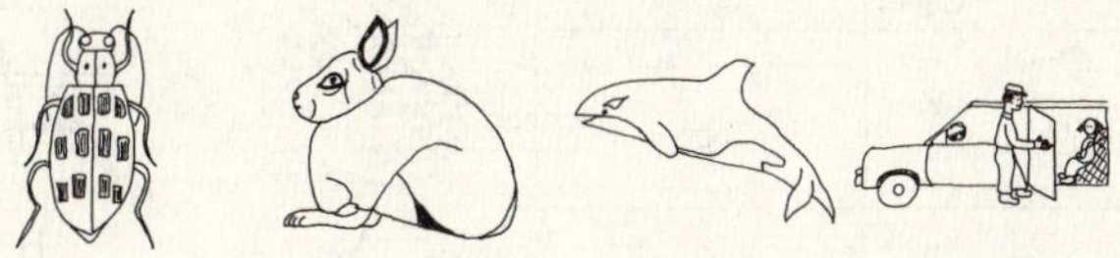

A. B. C. D.

2. 

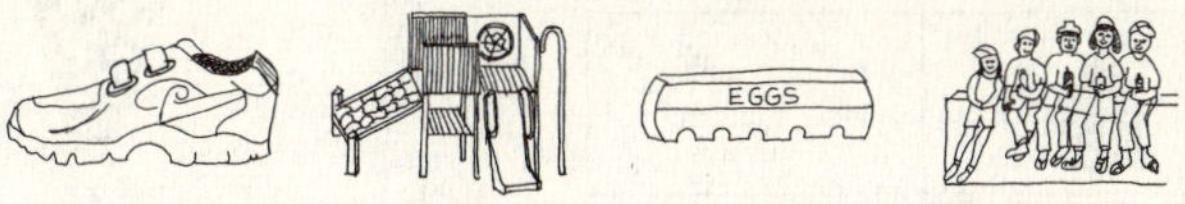

F. G. H. J.

3. 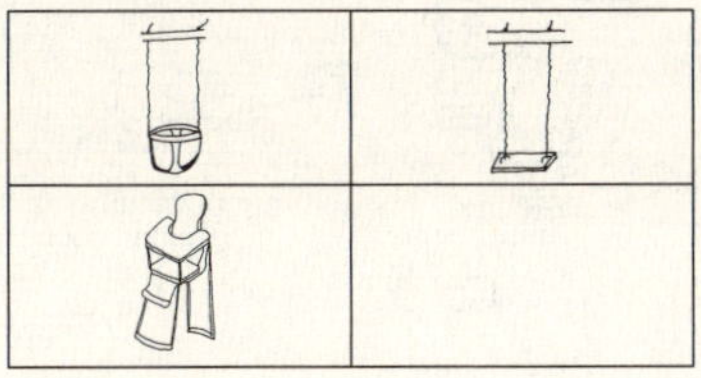

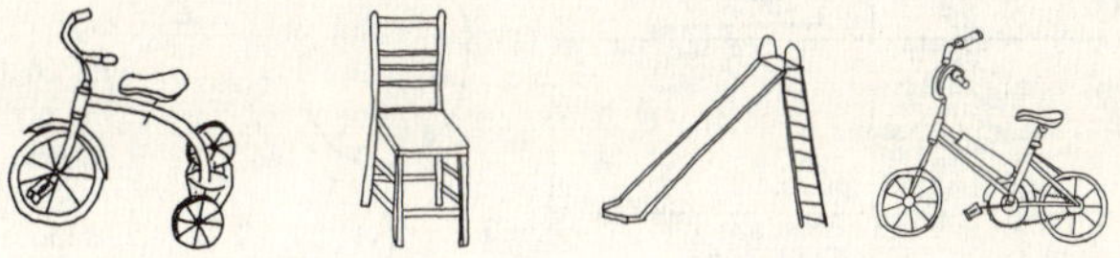

A. B. C. D.

4. 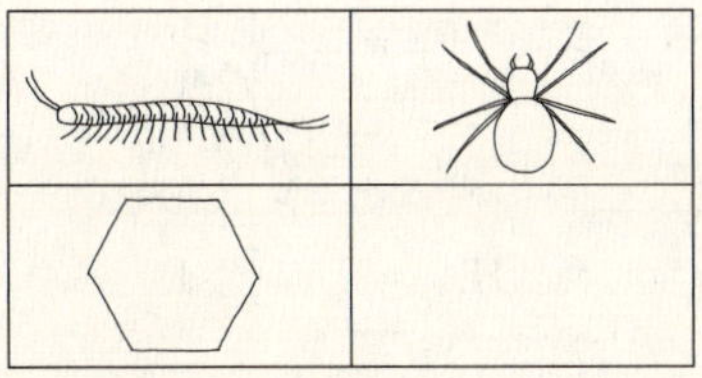

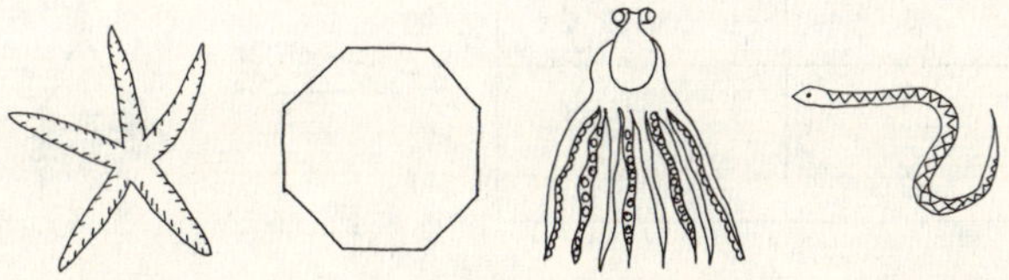

F. G. H. J.

5. 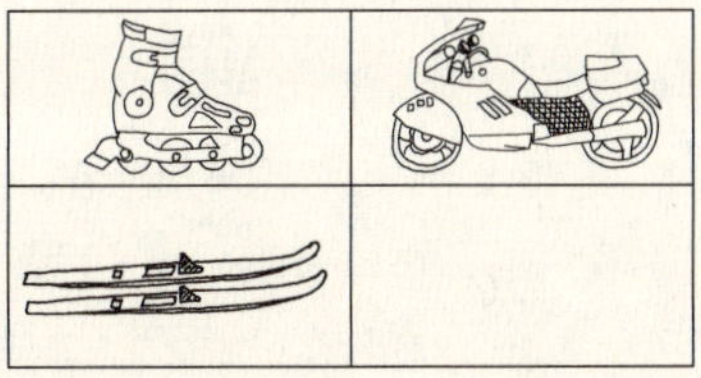

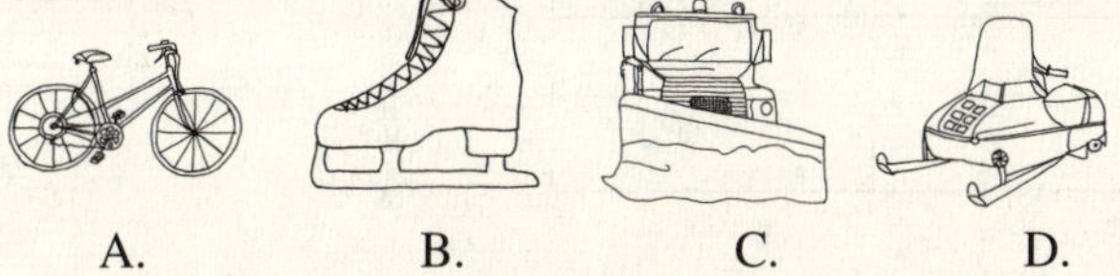

A. B. C. D.

GO ON TO THE NEXT PAGE

6. 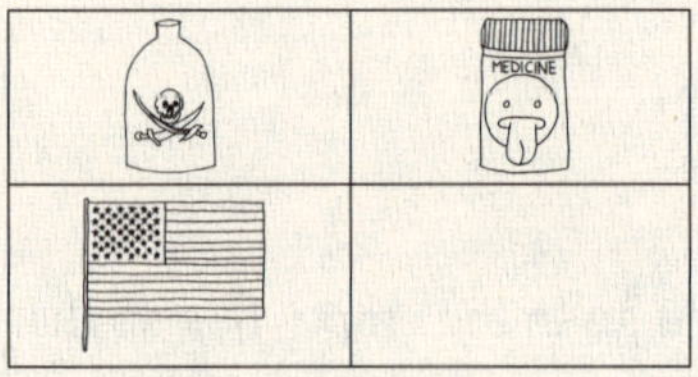

F.

G.

H.

J.

7. 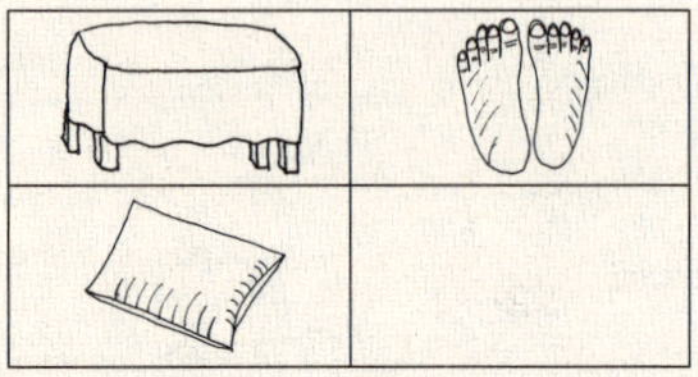

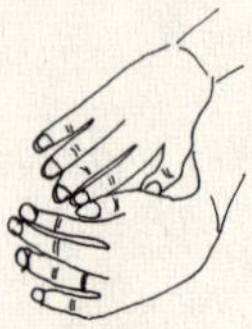
A.

B.

C.

D.

8. 

F.

G.

H.

J.

9. 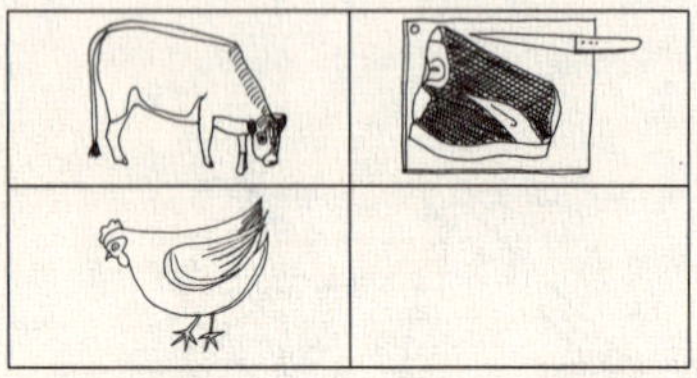

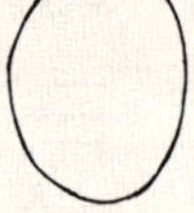
A.

B.

C.

D.

10. 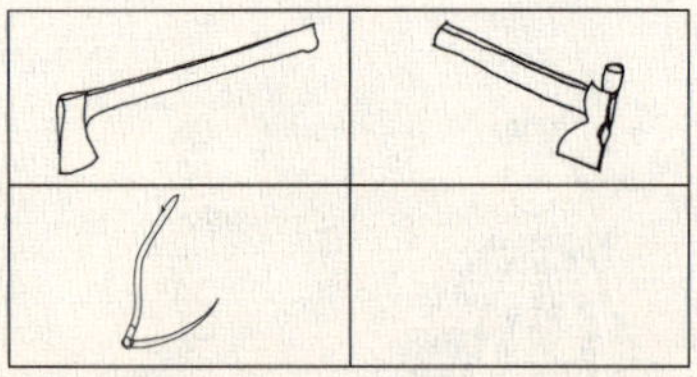

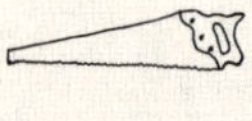
F.

G.

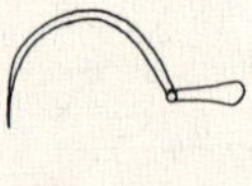
H.

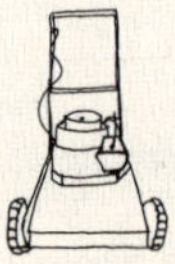
J.

11. 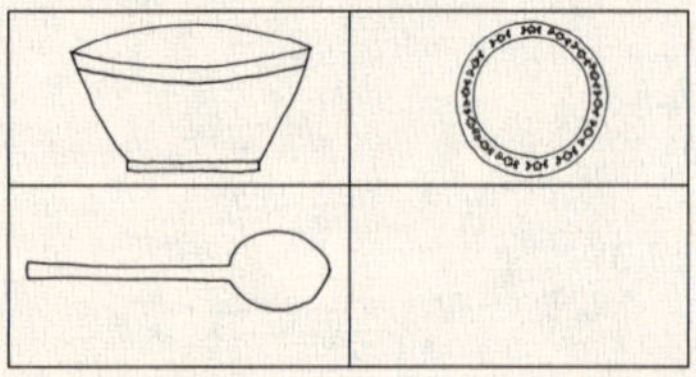

A.

B.

C.

D.

12. 

F. G. H. J.

13. 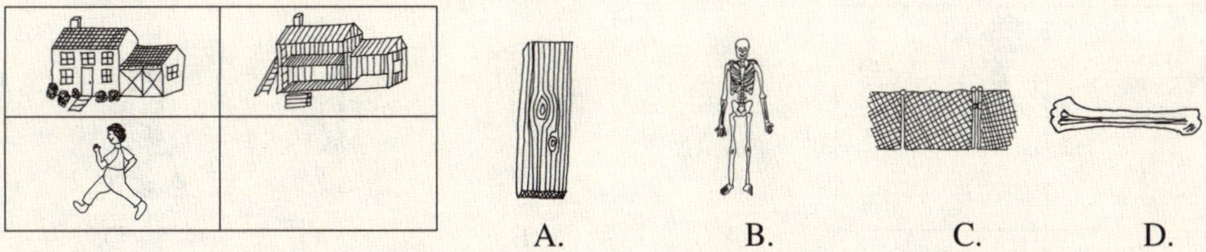

A. B. C. D.

14. 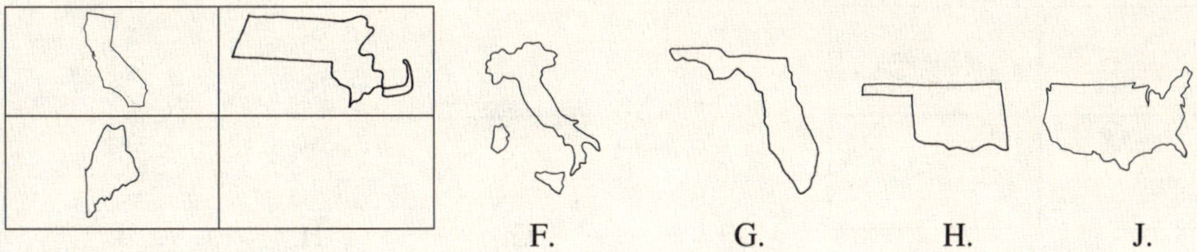

F. G. H. J.

15. 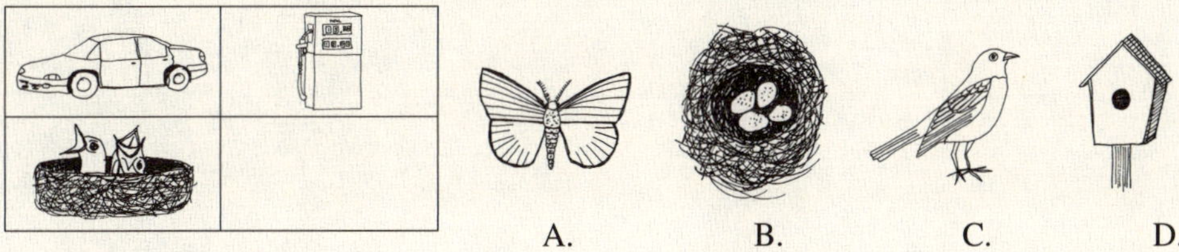

A. B. C. D.

16. 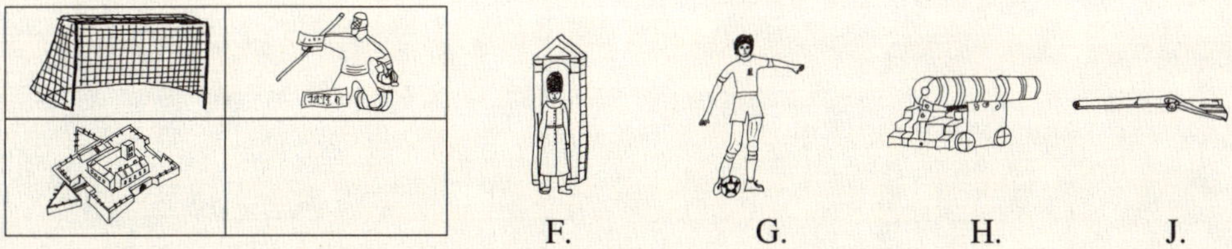

F. G. H. J.

17. 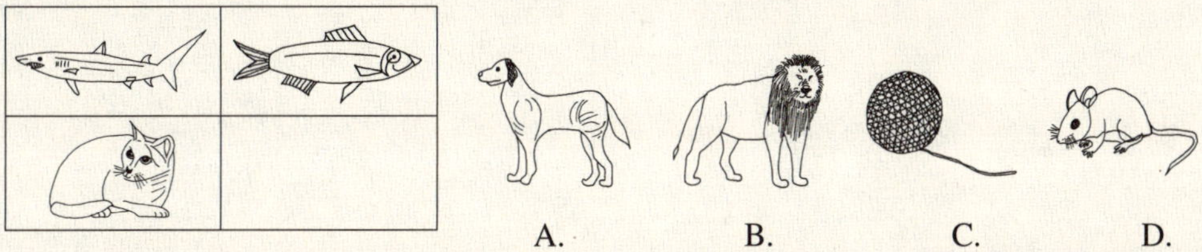

A. B. C. D.

GO ON TO THE NEXT PAGE

18.

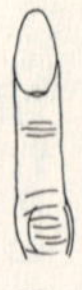

F.

G.

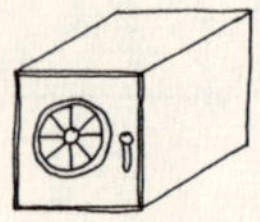

H.

J.

19.

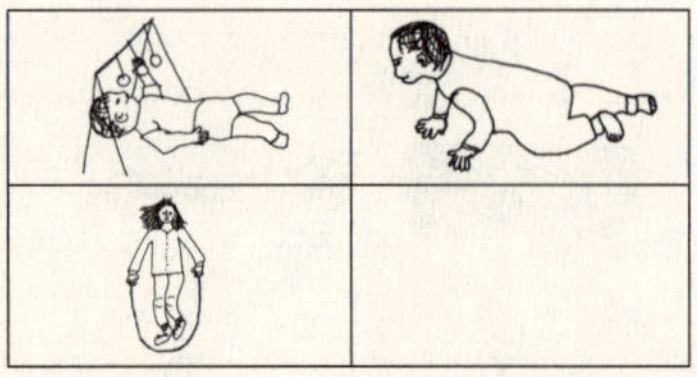

A.

B.

C.

D.

20.

F.

G.

H.

J.

STOP

IF YOU FINISH BEFORE TIME IS UP, CHECK OVER YOUR WORK ON TEST 2 ONLY. DO NOT RETURN TO TEST 1. DO NOT GO ON TO TEST 3 UNTIL THE SIGNAL IS GIVEN.

TEST 3. MEMORY

Time—5 minutes

Directions: Choose the word that means the same as the underlined word or phrase.

1. Which word means exam?
   (A) hortex
   (B) obalack
   (C) tred
   (D) hiwama
   (E) mostonica

2. Which word means psychiatrist?
   (F) potho
   (G) shirocol
   (H) chohor
   (J) chimichi
   (K) blothink

3. Which word means to explode?
   (A) ganclan
   (B) lululoy
   (C) oblomo
   (D) blothink
   (E) clolo

4. Which word means apple?
   (F) gnay
   (G) tred
   (H) plidl
   (J) grindle
   (K) chohor

5. Which word means member of a chain gang?
   (A) milikan
   (B) birbal
   (C) rockflo
   (D) ganclan
   (E) hortex

6. Which word means white?
   (F) obalack
   (G) chohor
   (H) oblomo
   (J) grindle
   (K) milikan

7. Which word means button?
   (A) mostonica
   (B) oblomo
   (C) clolo
   (D) ganclan
   (E) shirocol

8. Which word means stop?
   (F) hiwama
   (G) gnay
   (H) tred
   (J) blothink
   (K) birbal

9. Which word means furnace?
   (A) chimichi
   (B) obalack
   (C) lululoy
   (D) blothink
   (E) potho

10. Which word means futon?
    (F) plidl
    (G) mostonica
    (H) rockflo
    (J) chohor
    (K) oblomo

GO ON TO THE NEXT PAGE

11. Which word means <u>oriole</u>?
    (A) birbal
    (B) obalack
    (C) clolo
    (D) chohor
    (E) chimichi

12. Which word means <u>illness</u>?
    (F) grindle
    (G) mostonica
    (H) shirocol
    (J) milikan
    (K) potho

13. Which word means <u>a child's toy</u>?
    (A) lululoy
    (B) grindle
    (C) ganclan
    (D) tred
    (E) potho

14. Which word means <u>to sing</u>?
    (F) blothink
    (G) obalack
    (H) chimichi
    (J) chohor
    (K) milikan

15. Which word means <u>to slip and fall</u>?
    (A) rockflo
    (B) shirocol
    (C) hortex
    (D) plidl
    (E) clolo

16. Which word means <u>a yellow vegetable</u>?
    (F) oblomo
    (G) lululoy
    (H) milikan
    (J) ganclan
    (K) grindle

17. Which word means <u>frozen</u>?
    (A) obalack
    (B) potho
    (C) milikan
    (D) hiwama
    (E) shirocol

18. Which word means <u>to laugh</u>?
    (F) chohor
    (G) blothink
    (H) hiwama
    (J) ganclan
    (K) rockflo

19. Which word means <u>cemetery</u>?
    (A) hortex
    (B) mostonica
    (C) milikan
    (D) obalack
    (E) clolo

20. Which word means <u>flood</u>?
    (F) bloflo
    (G) chohor
    (H) birbal
    (J) hiwama
    (K) potho

STOP

IF YOU FINISH BEFORE TIME IS UP, CHECK OVER YOUR WORK ON TEST 3 ONLY. DO NOT GO BACK TO EITHER PREVIOUS TEST. DO NOT GO ON UNTIL THE SIGNAL IS GIVEN.

TEST 4. VERBAL REASONING

Times—15 minutes

Directions: For questions 1–6, find the word that names a necessary part of the underlined word.

1. <u>cartoon</u>
   (A) humor
   (B) animation
   (C) drawing
   (D) message

2. <u>heroine</u>
   (F) hero
   (G) woman
   (H) crisis
   (J) victim

3. <u>pump</u>
   (A) water
   (B) air
   (C) handle
   (D) pressure

4. <u>lantern</u>
   (F) light
   (G) glass
   (H) handle
   (J) fuel

5. <u>data</u>
   (A) numbers
   (B) information
   (C) charts
   (D) words

6. <u>biography</u>
   (F) facts
   (G) book
   (H) life
   (J) fame

Directions: In questions 7–12, the words in the top row are related in some way. The words in the bottom row are related in the same way. For each item, find the word that completes the bottom row of words.

7. red yellow blue
   orange green
   (A) turquoise
   (B) aqua
   (C) violet
   (D) gray

8. wind water sun
   coal gas
   (F) uranium
   (G) fission
   (H) wood
   (J) oil

GO ON TO THE NEXT PAGE

9. flamingo egret heron / finch chickadee

(A) sparrow

(B) woodpecker

(C) robin

(D) crane

10. saturated wet damp / doctor master

(F) nurse

(G) bachelor

(H) mistress

(J) hospital

11. apple tomato watermelon / plum mango

(A) pear

(B) cherry

(C) strawberry

(D) papaya

12. toe foot ankle / finger hand

(F) leg

(G) nail

(H) arm

(J) wrist

Directions: For questions 13–17, find the statement that is true according to the given information.

13. Bob walked into the convenience store and requested a package of cigarettes. The clerk asked Bob some questions. Bob left the store without cigarettes.

(A) Bob is too young to purchase cigarettes in this state.

(B) The store does not carry the brand that Bob prefers.

(C) Bob did not have enough money with him.

(D) The clerk did not sell cigarettes to Bob.

14. Tara purchased an airplane ticket for a vacation trip to Bermuda. The airplane crashed at take-off. Tara's name was not among the list of injured passengers.

(F) Tara missed the flight and was not on the airplane.

(G) Tara survived the crash.

(H) Tara was not injured.

(J) Tara never got to Bermuda.

15. A lavishly staged new play based on a very successful movie recently opened at a Broadway theater. A popular, but temperamental, aging actress was cast in the leading role. After three weeks, the play closed.

(A) The star walked out on the show.

(B) The movie was not suited to be performed as a stage play.

(C) The play was not a box office success.

(D) The play had only been scheduled for a three-week run.

16. Before Bernie left Tucson for a two-week vacation trip, he brought his dog, Michelle, to the home of his son Jack. Jack was unexpectedly called out of town on a business trip so he took Michelle to a kennel. Jack's business kept him away from Tucson for three days.

(F) Michelle spent some time at a kennel.

(G) The kennel is in Tucson.

(H) Jack took Michelle out of the kennel after three days.

(J) Michelle eagerly awaited Bernie's return.

17. When the weather in Canada gets very cold, the Canada geese fly south in search of a warmer climate and more plentiful food supply. In each flock, one goose is the leader, and other geese follow in a V-formation. It is January now, and there is a Canada goose in my backyard in Maine.

(A) The goose was injured and unable to continue its flight.

(B) The goose is not where it should be at this time.

(C) This goose finds Maine to be warm enough for it.

(D) This is an independent goose that refused to follow the leader.

Directions: For questions 18–20, find the correct answer.

18. Here are some words translated from an artificial language.

adabamikula means north pole

bomanitinkipu means south wind

adabagotono means north star

Which word means <u>east wind</u>?

(F) adabatinkipu

(G) manitutinkipu

(H) mikulamanitu

(J) manitugotono

19. Here are some words translated from an artificial language.

pataracolufax means biography

pataragantropo means biology

lognosocolufax means cartography

Which word means <u>geophysics</u>?

(A) damaniposiflo

(B) lognosodamani

(C) damanigantropo

(D) pataraposiflo

20. Here are some words translated from an artificial language.

elemehotuto means red fruit

zigarunaftama means green vegetable

zigarubiganinaftama means green leafy vegetable

Which word means <u>red flower</u>?

(F) hotutotoribuz

(G) biganieleme

(H) zigaruhotuto

(J) toribuzhotuto

STOP

IF YOU FINISH BEFORE TIME IS UP, CHECK OVER YOUR WORK ON TEST 4 ONLY. DO NOT GO BACK TO ANY PREVIOUS TEST. DO NOT GO ON UNTIL THE SIGNAL IS GIVEN.

TEST 5. READING COMPREHENSION

Time—40 minutes

Directions: For questions 1–40, read each passage and the questions following that passage. Find the answers.

Passage for questions 1–4

Using new tools and techniques, scientists, almost unnoticed, are remaking the world of plants. They have already remodeled 65 sorts of flowers, fruits, vegetables, and trees giving us, among other things, tobacco that resists disease, cantaloupes that are immune to the blight, and lettuce with crisper leaves. The chief new tool they are using is colchicine, a poisonous drug which has astounding effects upon growth and upon heredity. It creates new varieties with astonishing frequency, whereas such mutations occur rarely in nature. Colchicine has thrown new light on the fascinating jobs of the plant hunters. The Department of Agriculture sends agents all over the world to find plants native to other lands that can be grown here and that are superior to those already here. Scientists have crossed these foreign plants with those at home, thereby adding to our farm crops many desirable characteristics. The colchicine technique has enormously facilitated their work because hybrids so often can be made fertile and because it takes so few generations of plants now to build a new variety with the qualities desired.

1. The title that best expresses the ideas of the paragraph is
   (A) "Plant Growth and Heredity"
   (B) "New Plants for Old"
   (C) "Remodeling Plant Life"
   (D) "A More Abundant World"

2. Mutation in plant life results in
   (F) diseased plants
   (G) hybrids
   (H) new varieties
   (J) fertility

3. Colchicine speeds the improvement of plant species because it
   (A) makes possible the use of foreign plants
   (B) makes use of natural mutations
   (C) creates new varieties very quickly
   (D) can be used with 65 different vegetables, fruits, and flowers

4. According to the passage, colchicine is a
   (F) poisonous drug
   (G) blight
   (H) kind of plant hunter
   (J) hybrid plant

Passage for questions 5–8

The peopling of the Northwest Territory by companies from the eastern states, such as the Ohio Company under the leadership of Reverend Manasseh Cutler of Ipswich, Massachusetts, furnishes us with many interesting historical tales.

The first towns to be established were Marietta, Zanesville, Chillocothe, and Cincinnati. After the Ohio Company came the Connecticut Company, which secured all the territory bordering Lake Erie save a small portion known as fire lands and another portion known as Congress lands. The land taken up by the Connecticut people was called the Western Reserve and was settled almost entirely by New England people. The remainder of the state of Ohio was settled by Virginians and Pennsylvanians. Because the British controlled Lakes Ontario and Erie, the Massachusetts and Connecticut people made their journey into the Western Reserve through the southern part of the state. General Moses Cleaveland, the agent for the Connecticut Land Company, led a body of surveyors to the tract, proceeding by way of Lake Ontario. He quieted the Indian claims to the eastern portion of the reserve by giving them five hundred pounds, two heads of cattle, and one hundred gallons of whiskey. Landing at the mouth of the Conneaut River, General Moses Cleaveland and his party of fifty, including two women, celebrated Independence Day, 1796, with a feast of pork and beans with bread. A little later, a village was established at the mouth of the Cuyahoga River and was given the name of Cleaveland in honor of the agent of the company. It is related that the name was afterward shortened to Cleveland by one of the early editors because he could not get so many letters into the heading of his newspaper.

5. Reverend Manasseh Cutler
   (A) led the Ohio Company
   (B) owned the Western Reserve
   (C) led the Connecticut Land Company
   (D) settled the Congress lands

6. The title that best expresses the main idea of this selection is
   (F) "Control of the Great Lake Region"
   (G) "The Accomplishments of Reverend Manasseh Cutler"
   (H) "The Naming of Cleveland, Ohio"
   (J) "The Settling of the Northwest Territory"

7. In the last sentence of the selection, the word *related* is used to mean
   (A) associated with
   (B) rumored
   (C) reported
   (D) thought

8. The selection suggests that General Cleaveland at first found the Indians to be
   (F) extremely noisy people
   (G) hostile to his party of strangers
   (H) starving
   (J) eager to work with him

Passage for questions 9–12

From Gettysburg to the Battle of the Bulge, carrier pigeons have winged their way through skies fair and foul to deliver the vital messages of battle. Today, in spite of electronics and atomic weapons, these feathered heroes are still an important communication link in any army.

No one could be surer of this than the men at Fort Monmouth, New Jersey, the sole Army pigeon breeding and training center in this country. On the roosts at Fort Monmouth perch many genuine battle heroes, among them veteran G. I. Joe.

In 1943, 1,000 British troops moved speedily ahead of the Allied advance in Italy to take the small town of Colvi Vecchia. Since communications could not be established in time to relay the victory to headquarters, the troops were due for a previously planned Allied bombing raid. Then one of the men released carrier pigeon G. I. Joe. With a warning message on his back, he flew 20 miles in 20 minutes, arriving just as the bombers were warming up their engines. For saving the day for the British, the Lord Mayor of London later awarded G. I. Joe the Dickin Medal, England's highest award to an animal.

Even when regular message channels are set up, equipment can break or be overloaded or radio silence must be observed. Then the carrier pigeon comes into his own. Ninety-nine times out of a hundred, he completes his mission. In Korea, Homer the homing pigeon was flying from the front to a rear command post when he developed wing trouble. Undaunted, Homer made a forced landing, hopped the last two miles, and delivered his message. For initiative and loyalty, Homer was promoted to Pfc.—Pigeon First Class!

9. The writer of this selection evidently believes that carrier pigeons
   (A) have no usefulness in modern warfare
   (B) should be forced to fly only in emergencies
   (C) are remarkably reliable as message carriers
   (D) should receive regular promotions

GO ON TO THE NEXT PAGE

10. G. I. Joe was rewarded for
    (F) preventing unnecessary loss of life
    (G) guiding a bomber's flight
    (H) returning in spite of an injured wing
    (J) bringing the news of an allied victory

11. G. I. Joe's reward was a
    (A) promotion
    (B) reception given by the Lord Mayor
    (C) chance to retire to Fort Monmouth
    (D) medal

12. The word *vital* in the first paragraph means
    (F) extremely important
    (G) life saving
    (H) lively
    (J) deadly

Passage for questions 13–17

"There are many things from which I might have derived good, by which I have not profited, I dare say, Christmas among the rest. But I am sure I have always thought of Christmastime, when it has come round—apart from the veneration due to its sacred origin, if anything belonging to it *can* be apart from that—as a good time; a kind, forgiving, charitable, pleasant time; the only time I know of, in the long calendar of the year, when men and women seem by one consent to open their shut-up hearts freely and to think of people below them as if they really were fellow travelers to the grave, and not another race of creatures bound on other journeys. And therefore, Uncle, though it has never put a scrap of gold or silver in my pocket, I believe that it *has* done me good, and *will* do me good; and I say, God bless it!"

The clerk in the tank involuntarily applauded.

"Let me hear another sound from *you*," said Scrooge, "and you'll keep your Christmas by losing your situation! You're quite a powerful speaker, sir," he added, turning to his nephew. "I wonder you don't go into Parliament."

—From *A Christmas Carol*
by Charles Dickens

13. The word *veneration* probably means
    (A) worship
    (B) disapproval
    (C) agreement
    (D) love

14. The first speaker
    (F) is a very religious person
    (G) enjoys and celebrates Christmas
    (H) is defending Christmas
    (J) has been fired by Scrooge

15. The first speaker believes that Christmas
    (A) is a pleasant nuisance
    (B) brings out the best in people
    (C) has been separated from its religious origin
    (D) could be a profitable time of year

16. The phrase *by one consent* is synonymous with
    (F) affirmation
    (G) contractually
    (H) partially
    (J) unanimously

17. Scrooge probably is angry with
    (A) the speaker and the clerk
    (B) only the speaker
    (C) only the clerk
    (D) people who celebrate Christmas

Passage for questions 18–22

The police department of New York City has one branch that many do not know about even though it was established almost a century ago. This is the harbor precinct's 14-boat fleet of police launches, which patrol 578 miles of waters around the city, paying particular attention to the areas containing 500 piers and some 90 boat clubs.

The boats are equipped for various jobs. One boat is an ice breaker; another is equipped to render aid in the event of an airplane crash at La Guardia Airport. All of the boats are equipped with lifeline guns, heavy grappling irons to raise sunken automobiles, and lasso-sticks to rescue animals in the water. They have power pumps to bail out sinking craft, first-aid kits, extra life preservers, signal flags, and searchlights.

The force consists of 183 officers who have all had previous experience with boats. Some of the officers are Navy and Coast Guard veterans. Many members of the harbor police force have oceangoing Master's or Harbor Captain's licenses. All are highly trained in the care and handling of engines and in navigation. All are skilled in giving first aid, and each officer is a qualified radio operator and a trained marksman with a revolver.

The work of the police includes many tasks. One duty of this force is to check the operation of the fleet of 43 junk boats that ply their trade in the harbor, buying scrap, rope, and other items for resale ashore. These boats could just as easily be used to smuggle narcotics, gems, aliens, or spies into the country, so they are watched closely by the city's harbor police force. The officers also arrest those who break navigation laws or who endanger the safety of bathers by approaching too near the shore in speed boats. And during the last summer alone, police launches towed 450 disabled boats and gave some kind of help to thousands of others.

18. The harbor police were
    (F) introduced by order of the mayor
    (G) first used in the twentieth century
    (H) in use before the Civil War
    (J) introduced by Naval and Coast Guard veterans

19. The boats used
    (A) are uniform in design
    (B) can all serve as ice breakers
    (C) work at Kennedy Airport
    (D) vary in function

20. The harbor police
    (F) prevent the resale of scrap material
    (G) regulate the admission of spies
    (H) ensure the legal operation of junk boats
    (J) regulate disabled boats

21. The services of the harbor police include
    (A) towing, life saving, and salvage
    (B) customs collection, towing, and the sending of radio messages
    (C) first aid, the rescue of animals, and fire patrol
    (D) ice breaking, the collection of junk, and the transportation of aliens

22. Police boats
    (F) have no responsibility for bathers
    (G) assist boats of all kinds
    (H) warn offenders but do not make arrests
    (J) cannot detain other boats

Passage for questions 23–26

America's national bird, the bald eagle, which has flown high since the Revolutionary War, may soon be grounded. The eagle population of the United States is decreasing at an alarming rate, so the National Audubon Society has launched a full-scale survey to find out how many bald eagles are left and what measures are necessary to protect them from extinction. The survey, a year-long project, focuses attention on the bird chosen to appear on the Great Seal of the United States.

When it gained its official status over 200 years ago, the bald eagle was undisputed king of America's skies. Many thousands of the great birds roamed the country, and both the sight of the bald eagle and its piercing scream were familiar to almost every American. Today, naturalists fear that there are fewer than a thousand of them still in the lower forty-eight.

Nature is partly to blame. Severe hurricanes have destroyed many eggs, fledglings, and aeries, the eagles' mammoth nests. But man is the chief culprit. Despite legislation passed by Congress in 1940 to protect the emblematic birds, thousands of them have been gunned out of the skies by over-eager shooters who perhaps mistook them for large hawks.

The bald eagle was known as the bald-headed eagle when Congress began the search for a seal in 1776. The archaic meaning of bald—white or streaked with white—refers to his head, neck, and tail coloring

GO ON TO THE NEXT PAGE

rather than to any lack of plumage in our fine-feathered friend.

23. The Audubon Society is trying to
    (A) rid the country of the bald eagle
    (B) introduce the bald eagle into Alaska and Hawaii
    (C) prevent the extinction of the bald eagle in this country
    (D) have Congress pass a law forbidding the shooting of eagles

24. There are now
    (F) more eagles in this country than there were in 1776
    (G) fewer eagles here than there were over 200 years ago
    (H) many thousands of bald eagles
    (J) eagles whose scream is familiar to every American

25. Aeries are
    (A) fledglings
    (B) eggs
    (C) mating areas
    (D) nests

26. The eagle is called an *emblematic bird* because it is
    (F) bald
    (G) handsome and powerful
    (H) prized by hunters
    (J) a symbol of a nation

Passage for questions 27–30

You know, of course, that in China the Emperor is a Chinaman, and all the people around him are Chinamen, too. It happened a good many years ago, but that's just why it's worthwhile to hear the story, before it is forgotten. The Emperor's palace was the most splendid in the world; entirely and altogether made of porcelain, so costly, but so brittle, so difficult to handle that one had to be terribly careful. In the garden were to be seen the strangest flowers, and to the most splendid of them silver bells were tied, which tinkled so that nobody should pass by without noticing the flowers. Oh, the Emperor's garden had been laid out very smartly, and it extended so far that the gardener himself didn't know where the end was. If you went on and on, you came into the loveliest forest with high trees and deep lakes. The forest went right down to the sea, which was blue and deep; tall ships could sail right in under the branches of the trees; and in the trees lived a nightingale which sang so sweetly that even the poor fisherman, who had many other things to do, stopped still and listened when he had gone out at night to take up his nets and then heard the nightingale.

—From *The Nightingale*
by Hans Christian Andersen

27. The author wants to tell this story
    (A) before it is forgotten
    (B) because he is enchanted by China
    (C) because he is a writer and storyteller
    (D) in order to describe the garden

28. The Emperor's palace was made of
    (F) silver bells
    (G) high trees
    (H) porcelain
    (J) large stones and boulders

29. Silver bells were tied to flowers in the garden to
    (A) further enhance their beauty
    (B) draw attention to their beauty
    (C) accompany the singing of the nightingale
    (D) discourage flower picking

30. The Emperor's garden
    (F) was too large to care for
    (G) led into a lovely forest
    (H) housed a rare nightingale
    (J) was a source of pleasure for all in the kingdom

Passage for questions 31–35

On a population map of the world, deserts are shown as great blank spaces, but, in fact, these areas contribute many things to our lives.

When you go to the market to buy a box of dates, you are buying a bit of sunshine and dry air from the oases of the Sahara Desert or the Coachella Valley. Fresh peas or a lettuce salad for your winter dinner might be the product of an irrigation farmer in the Salt River Valley or the Imperial Valley. That fine broadcloth shirt you received for your birthday was made from silky, long-fibered cotton grown in Egypt. A half-wool, half-cotton sweater might contain Australian wool and Peruvian cotton, which are steppe and desert products.

These are only a few of the contributions these desert areas make to the quality of our lives. They have also made important cultural contributions.

Our number system is derived from the system used by the ancient civilizations of Arabia. The use of irrigation to make farming of dry areas possible was developed by the inhabitants of desert regions. The necessity of measuring water levels and noting land boundaries following flooding by the Nile River led to the development of mathematics and the practice of surveying and engineering. The desert people were also our early astronomers. They studied the locations of the stars in order to find their way across the limitless expanse of the desert at night.

31. The population of the world's deserts is
    (A) nomadic
    (B) scientific
    (C) vegetarian
    (D) sparse

32. The Imperial Valley produces
    (F) vegetables
    (G) winter dinners
    (H) shirts
    (J) irrigation

33. According to this passage, broadcloth is made of
    (A) wool
    (B) cotton
    (C) silk
    (D) half wool, half cotton

34. Culturally, desert civilizations have
    (F) far surpassed those of all other regions
    (G) made important contributions
    (H) not influenced western civilizations
    (J) been blank spaces

35. Surveying was developed because people needed to
    (A) study astronomy
    (B) find their way across the deserts
    (C) determine land boundaries after floods
    (D) irrigate their crops

Passage for questions 36–40

Residents of Montana laughingly refer to the small, windblown settlement of Ekalaka in the eastern Badlands as "Skeleton Flats," but as curious as it may sound, the name is appropriate.

So many fossils have been dug up in this otherwise unremarkable town that it has become a paradise for paleontologists, scientists who use fossils to study prehistoric life forms. In fact, dinosaur bones are so plentiful in this area that ranchers have been known to use them as doorstops!

Ekalaka's fame began to grow more than 50 years ago when Walter H. Peck, whose hobby was geology, found the bones of a Stegosaurus, a huge, plant-eating dinosaur. The entire community soon became infected with Peck's enthusiasm for his find, and everyone began digging for dinosaur bones. Led by the local science teacher, groups of people would go out looking for new finds each weekend, and they rarely returned empty-handed. It would seem there is no end to the fossil riches to be found in Ekalaka.

GO ON TO THE NEXT PAGE

Among the most prized finds were the remains of a Brontosaurus, an 80-foot-long monster that probably weighed 40 tons. The skeleton of a Triceratops was also found. The head of this prehistoric giant alone weighed more than 1,000 pounds. Careful searching also yielded small fossilized fishes, complete with stony scales, and the remains of a huge sea reptile.

The prize find was a Pachycephalosaurus, a dinosaur whose peculiar skull was several inches thick. When descriptions of it reached scientific circles in the East, there was great excitement because this particular prehistoric animal was then completely unknown to scientists.

36. In the first sentence, the writer places "Skeleton Flats" in quotation marks to show that this phrase is
    (F) a nickname given to the town by Montana residents, not the actual name of the town
    (G) spelled incorrectly
    (H) being spoken by someone other than the writer
    (J) a scientific term

37. This article is primarily about
    (A) paleontology
    (B) products in the state of Montana
    (C) fossil finds in Ekalaka
    (D) the Pachycephalosaurus

38. A paleontologist is
    (F) someone whose hobby is geology
    (G) a bone pit
    (H) a plant-eating dinosaur
    (J) someone who studies fossils

39. In the third paragraph, the writer is describing the
    (A) bones of a Stegosaurus
    (B) variety of fossils found in Ekalaka
    (C) town of Ekalaka
    (D) people of Ekalaka

40. Discovery of Pachycephalosaurus caused excitement because
    (F) its skull was several inches thick
    (G) it was the first evidence of this previously unknown creature
    (H) news of it quickly reached eastern scientific circles
    (J) it received a prize

STOP

IF YOU FINISH TEST 5 BEFORE TIME IS UP, CHECK OVER YOUR WORK ON THIS TEST ONLY. DO NOT RETURN TO ANY PREVIOUS TEST. DO NOT GO ON TO THE NEXT TEST UNTIL THE SIGNAL IS GIVEN.

TEST 6. MATHEMATICS CONCEPTS AND APPLICATIONS

Time—35 minutes

Directions: For questions 1–40, read each problem and find the answer.

1. Where $x = 1\frac{2}{3}$, the reciprocal of x equals

(A) $\frac{2}{3}$

(B) $\frac{5}{3}$

(C) $\frac{3}{5}$

(D) $\frac{1}{x}$

2. The product of $\frac{7}{16}$ and a number x is 1. The number is

(F) $1\frac{7}{16}$

(G) $\frac{16}{7}$

(H) $\frac{32}{14}$

(J) 1

3. $\dfrac{\frac{1}{x}+1}{1+\frac{1}{x}}$ is equivalent to

(A) 1

(B) $\frac{1}{x}$

(C) $\frac{1}{x}+2$

(D) 1 + x

4. $\dfrac{\frac{2}{3}+\frac{3}{8}}{\frac{1}{4}-\frac{3}{16}}$ equals

(F) $15\frac{2}{3}$

(G) $\frac{25}{16}$

(H) $\frac{13}{32}$

(J) $\frac{50}{3}$

5. In the formula $L = \frac{3}{4}bxh$, if $b = 2$, $x = 7$, and $h = \frac{1}{2}$, L equals

(A) $\frac{21}{2}$

(B) $\frac{21}{4}$

(C) $\frac{21}{8}$

(D) $\frac{7x}{4}$

6. Two angles of a triangle and 45° and 75°. What is the measure of the third angle?

(F) 60°

(G) 35°

(H) 180°

(J) 45°

7. 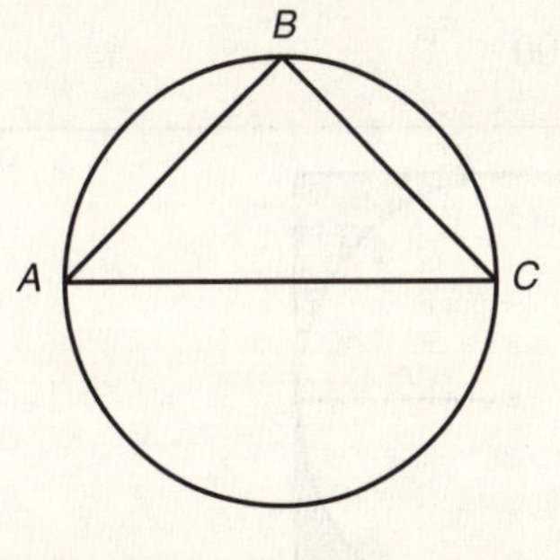

Isosceles ΔABC is inscribed in a circle that has a diameter of 10 centimeters. The area of the triangle is

(A) 78.5 sq. cm.

(B) 12.5 sq. cm.

(C) 25 sq. cm.

(D) 50 sq.

GO ON TO THE NEXT PAGE

8. The volume of a small warehouse measuring 75 feet long, 50 feet wide, and 30 feet high is

(F) 1,112,500 cubic feet

(G) 112,500 square feet

(H) 112,500 feet

(J) 112,500 cubic feet

9. A department store marks up its clothing 80% over cost. If it sells blue jeans for \$14, how much did the store pay for them?

(A) \$7.78

(B) \$17.50

(C) \$11.20

(D) \$1.12

10. The monthly finance charge on a charge account is $1\frac{1}{2}$% on the unpaid amount up to \$500, and 1% on the unpaid amount over \$500. What is the finance charge on an unpaid amount of \$750?

(F) \$22.50

(G) \$1.00

(H) \$10.00

(J) \$100.00

11.

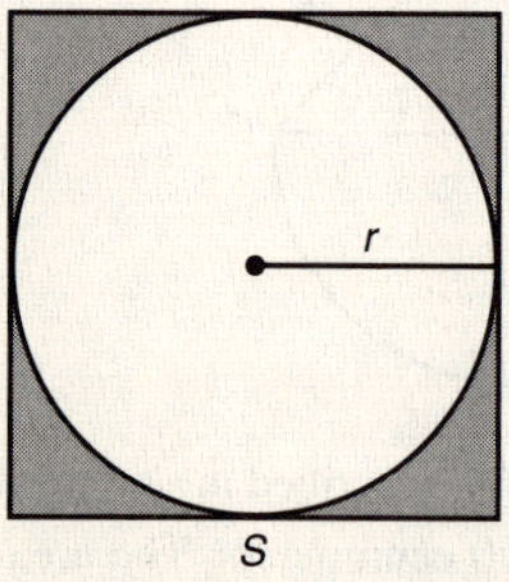

The square above has a side 4" long. The area of the shaded portion is

(A) $\frac{22}{7}$ sq. in.

(B) 16 sq. in.

(C) $3\frac{3}{7}$ sq. in.

(D) $4\frac{3}{7}$ sq. in.

12. The ratio of teachers to students in a certain school is 1:14. If there are fourteen teachers in the school, how many students are there?

(F) 14

(G) 196

(H) 206

(J) 176

13. Evaluate $\frac{100^4}{10^8}$

(A) 10^4

(B) 1000

(C) 1

(D) 10^{12}

14. If x is an odd whole number, which of the following also represents an odd number?

(F) $2x + 1$

(G) $x - 2$

(H) $4x - 3$

(J) all of the above

15. The sum of 4 hours 17 minutes, 3 hours 58 minutes, 45 minutes, and 7 hours 12 minutes is

(A) 15 hr. 32 min.

(B) 17 hr. 32 min.

(C) 16 hr. 12 min.

(D) 14 hr. 50 min.

16. If 8 lb. 12 oz. of fruit were to be divided among eight people how much would each receive?

(F) 1 lb. 1.5 oz.

(G) 10.5 oz.

(H) 2.0 lb.

(J) 13.5 oz.

17. In how much less time does a runner who finishes a marathon in 2 hours 12 minutes 38 seconds complete the race, than a runner who finishes in 3 hours 2 minutes 24 seconds?
(A) 48 min. 56 sec.
(B) 49 min. 46 sec.
(C) 1 hr. 51 min. 22 sec.
(D) 1 hr. 26 min. 12 sec.

18. The drawing of a wheel in a book is done at 1/16 scale. If the drawing is 1.8 inches in diameter, how big is the wheel?
(F) 32"
(G) 28.8"
(H) 24"
(J) .1125"

19. If a man runs M miles in T hours, his speed is
(A) M/T
(B) $M + T$
(C) $M - T$
(D) MT

20. How many square inches are there in R rooms, each having S square feet?
(F) RS
(G) $144RS$
(H) $9/RS$
(J) $S + R$

21. The ratio of the six inches to six feet is
(A) 1:6
(B) 12:1
(C) 1:12
(D) 24:1

22. Event A occurs every 4 years, event B every 11 years, and event C every 33 years. If they last occurred together in 1950, when will they next occur simultaneously?
(F) 3402
(G) 1983
(H) 2082
(J) 6804

23.
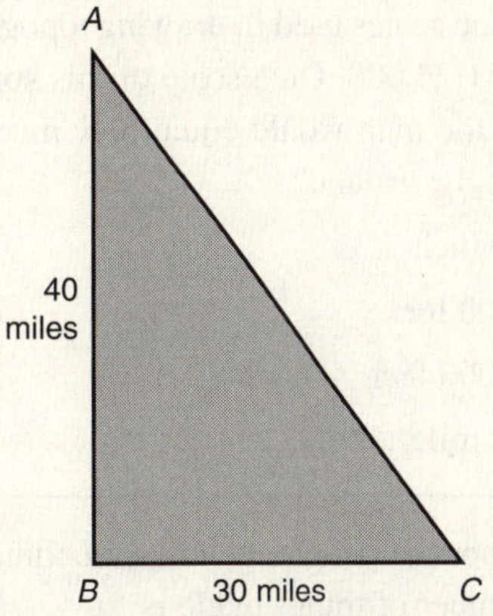

Two drivers begin at point C simultaneously. One drives from C to B to A. The other drives directly to A at 50 mph. How fast must the first person drive to get to A first?
(A) less than 50 mph
(B) less than 60 mph
(C) less than 70 mph
(D) more than 70 mph

24.
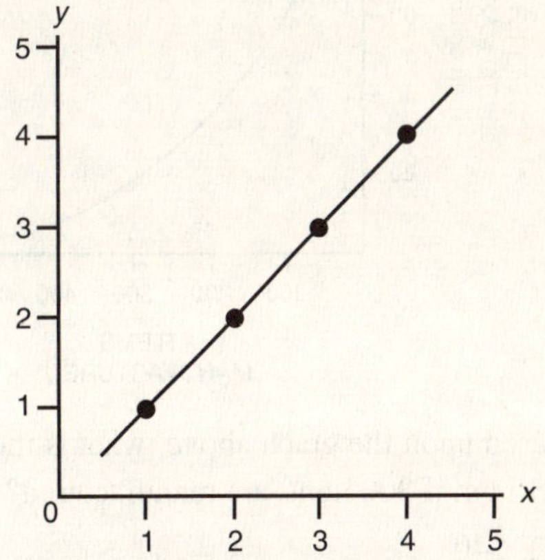

The graph above shows
(F) x increasing faster than y
(G) y increasing faster than x
(H) x increasing as fast as y
(J) no relationship between x and y

25. In the number 6,000,600,000, there are
(A) 6 billions and 6 hundred thousands
(B) 6 millions and 6 thousands
(C) 6 billions and 6 millions
(D) 6 millions and 60 thousands

GO ON TO THE NEXT PAGE

26. One of the scales used in drawing topographic maps is 1:24,000. On a scale of this sort, one inch on the map would equal how much distance on the ground?

(F) one inch

(G) 2,000 feet

(H) 24,000 feet

(J) one mile

27. If *A* number of people each make *L* things, the total number of things made is

(A) A/L

(B) $A + L$

(C) $A - L$

(D) AL

28.

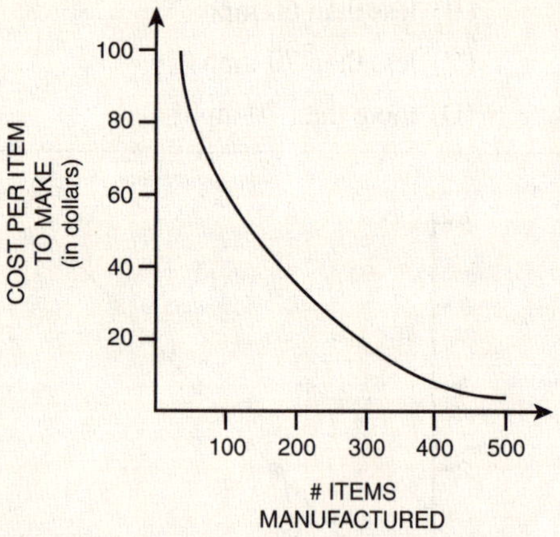

Based upon the graph above, what is the cost per item if 300 items are manufactured?

(F) $40

(G) $28

(H) $20

(J) >$20

29.

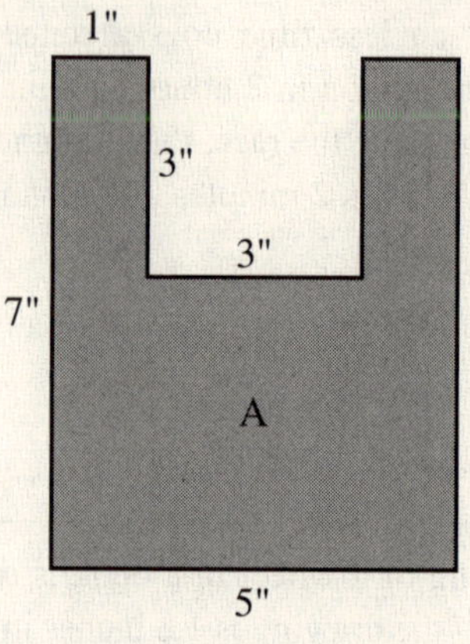

The perimeter of figure A is

(A) 19 in.

(B) 30 in.

(C) 23 sq. in.

(D) 19 sq. in.

30. Of 27 people in a certain group, fifteen are men and twelve are women. What is the ratio of men to women?

(F) 15:12

(G) 12:15

(H) 5:4

(J) 27:12

31.

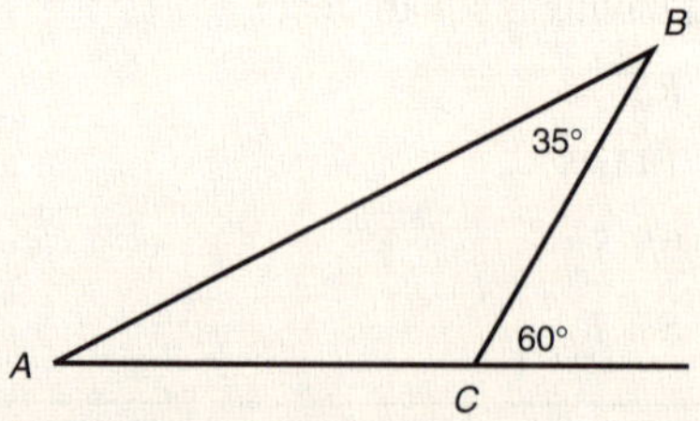

The measure of angle *A* is

(A) 15°

(B) 20°

(C) 25°

(D) 35°

32. The difference between 1,001,000 and 999,999 is

(F) 101,001

(G) 1,999

(H) 10,001

(J) 1,001

33. The surface area of a brick with the dimensions 6" × 3" × 2" is

(A) 36 sq. in.

(B) 72 sq. in.

(C) 128 sq. in.

(D) 72 cu. in.

34. Simplify:

–3 – [–2 + (5 – 6) –3]

(F) +3

(G) –1

(H) +1

(J) –3

35. Simplify:

$.6 + 1\frac{1}{2} + \frac{3}{4} =$

(A) 2.31

(B) 2.52

(C) 2.85

(D) $2\frac{13}{20}$

36. Simplify:

$-6 - [2 - (3a - b) + b] + a$

(F) $4 - 3a + 2b$

(G) $-6 + 3a + b$

(H) $-8 + 4a - 2b$

(J) $-8 + 3a - b$

37. Simplify:

–2 [–4 (2 – 1) + (3 + 2)]

(A) 18

(B) 2

(C) –18

(D) –2

38.

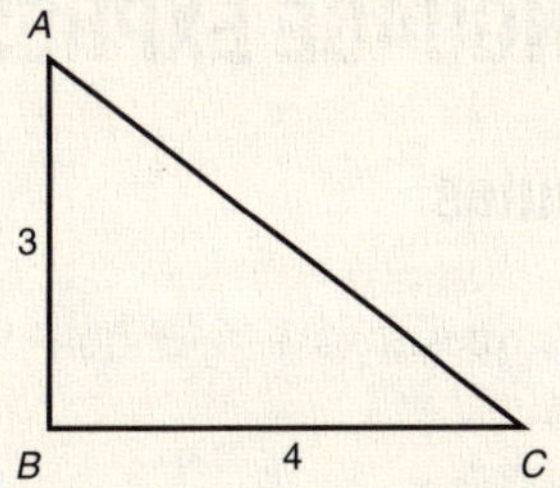

The length of $\overline{AC}$ in the triangle above is

(F) 4.5

(G) 3.5

(H) 5

(J) 4

39. 5:6 as 15:?

(A) 25

(B) 16

(C) 18

(D) 12

40. The ratio of surface area to volume of a cube having an edge of two inches is

(F) 2:3

(G) 1:3

(H) 6:1

(J) 3:1

STOP

IF YOU FINISH BEFORE TIME IS UP, CHECK OVER YOUR WORK ON TEST 6 ONLY. DO NOT GO BACK TO ANY PREVIOUS TEST. DO NOT GO ON UNTIL THE SIGNAL IS GIVEN.

TEST 7. LANGUAGE EXPRESSION

Time—30 minutes

Directions: For questions 1–6, choose the word that best completes the sentence.

1. The abandoned quarry was declared "off limits" to the boys; ______ they went there often.
   (A) meanwhile
   (B) therefore
   (C) moreover
   (D) besides
   (E) sometimes

2. A high school diploma by itself is not sufficient preparation for many occupations, ______ neither is a college degree.
   (F) also
   (G) because
   (H) but
   (J) thus
   (K) hence

3. My favorite running companion cannot join me this Saturday; ______ I shall enter the race myself.
   (A) moreover
   (B) furthermore
   (C) meanwhile
   (D) nevertheless
   (E) mainly

4. Children adjust to change ______ than do adults.
   (F) easier
   (G) more easier
   (H) more easy
   (J) more easily
   (K) most easily

5. The model ________ walk in that tight skirt.
   (A) can hardly
   (B) can't hardly
   (C) hardly can't
   (D) can hardly not
   (E) hardly cannot

6. As the student body _________ in size, we shall have to add more classrooms.
   (F) got bigger
   (G) will have grown
   (H) keeps getting bigger
   (J) grew more
   (K) has increased

Directions: For questions 7–12, choose the sentence that is correctly written.

7. (A) The truck with its huge load of crates, was beginning to roll down the hill.
   (B) The truck, with its huge load of crates; was beginning to roll down the hill.
   (C) The truck, with its huge load of crates, was beginning to roll down the hill.
   (D) The truck and its huge load of crates were beginning to roll down the hill.
   (E) The truck, and its huge load of crates, were beginning to roll down the hill.

8. (F) The storm was severe and blustery but it did not harm the passenger ship and no one was injured.
(G) The severe, blustery storm did no harm to the passenger ship and caused no injuries.
(H) The storm was severe and blustery and it did not harm the passenger ship; no one was injured.
(J) The severe and blustery storm it did not harm the passenger ship injuring no one.
(K) Because the severe, blustery storm did not harm the passenger ship it did not injure anyone.

9. (A) The student's statement relating to the missing papers being accurate.
(B) The student's statement, relating to the missing papers being accurate.
(C) The student's statement was relating to the missing papers being accurate.
(D) The student's statement, relating to the missing papers was accurate.
(E) The student's statement relating to the missing papers was accurate.

10. (F) Since you came late, we are not responsible for your having missed the first act.
(G) You came late since we are not responsible and you missed the first act.
(H) Since you came late; we are not responsible that you missed the first act.
(J) Coming late is not responsible for missing the first act.
(K) Since you came late and we are not responsible for your missing the first act.

11. (A) This is your last chance you won't have any other chances.
(B) This is your last chance; you won't have another.
(C) This being your last chance you will not have another chance.
(D) This is your last chance and no more chances.
(E) Since this is your last chance and you won't have any other chances.

12. (F) Impossible to ride a bicycle without moving the pedals.
(G) To ride a bicycle without moving the pedals being impossible.
(H) It is impossible to ride a bicycle without moving the pedals.
(J) It is impossible, for anyone to ride a bicycle, without moving the pedals.
(K) It is impossible and anyone cannot ride a bicycle without moving the pedals.

Directions: For questions 13–17, choose the sentence that uses verbs correctly.

13. (A) The study book would not of gotten to me in time to be of any use.
(B) After reading the book review, you will not have been an authority on the Aztecs.
(C) If you set your alarm for 6:30 A. M., you may be able to catch the 7:45 train.
(D) After my birthday next Wednesday, I had finally become old enough to drive.
(E) The boy walks his dog in the rain and was splashed by speeding cars.

14. (F) The green dragon breathed flames and smoke and will have started a forest fire.
(G) Whenever the wind blows, Martin's hay fever made his nose run.
(H) I will file my income tax early this year, therefore I received my refund very promptly.
(J) The cafeteria is closed today, so we will go to a restaurant for lunch.
(K) If the parents of the injured child will file a claim, they might have recovered the costs of his treatment.

GO ON TO THE NEXT PAGE

15. (A) Cinderella wished she could go to the ball, and her fairy godmother appears.
(B) Mary will put the clean plates away after the dishwasher washed them.
(C) A police officer is a public servant who has received a great deal of training.
(D) The old man smokes cigarettes for so many years.
(E) If the union thought the worker would be unfairly dismissed, it would have represented her at the hearing.

16. (F) When all the lights had been turned out, it will be very dark in the classroom.
(G) The pack of wild horses hears the thunder and stampeded through the canyon.
(H) The star of the show will be absent this evening, so we were treated to a performance by an understudy.
(J) St. Patrick's Day was cold and rainy, and many marchers will get wet.
(K) A power failure has disrupted service on the railroad, and all afternoon trains will be behind schedule.

17. (A) If the package finally arrives in today's mail, we will have been waiting three days for the shipment.
(B) Soon after he turned three years old, the little boy will tell everyone that he is three-and-a-half.
(C) The judge pronounced the sentence just one week after the jury will announce its verdict.
(D) After the snowstorm was over, everyone must shovel out.
(E) I find it very alarming when an airliner experiences mechanical difficulties and didn't tell anyone about it.

Directions: For questions 18–21, choose the underlined word that is the simple subject of the sentence.

18. Pliers (F) are made in many styles (G) and sizes (H) and are used to perform (J) many different operations (K).

19. When two different air masses (A) meet, they (B) do not readily mix but form a boundary (C) of separation (D) called a front (E).

20. When the king's (F) body (G) was exhumed recently, activation analysis (H) showed that his body (J) contained traces (K) of poisonous arsenic.

21. The simplest animals (A), called sponges (B), are marine animals (C) that feed on microscopic (D) organisms (E).

Directions: For questions 22–25, choose the underlined word or group of words that is the simple predicate (verb) of the sentence.

22. The resistance (F) offered (G) by the earth's atmosphere makes (H) meteors incandescent (J) in flight (K).

23. Conservation (A) of natural resources and control (B) of pollution (C) of air, water, and soil will preserve (D) existing (E) ecosystems.

24. For those questions answered (F) incorrectly, determine (G) why (H) your original answers are (J) incorrect (K).

25. I was surprised (A) to learn (B) that in some cultures (C) men help (D) with the housework (E).

Directions: For questions 26–28, choose the sentence that best combines the two underlined sentences into one.

26. Drivers between the ages of 16 to 18 have been involved in many accidents. Young people do not necessarily cause the accidents in which they are involved.
    - (F) Drivers who are 16 and 18 may or may not have caused the accidents they seem to be involved in.
    - (G) It is not necessary for 16-to-18 year old drivers to cause accidents in order to be involved in them.
    - (H) Drivers between the ages of 16 and 18 are involved in many accidents that they didn't cause.
    - (J) Between the ages of 16 and 18 young drivers are the cause of many accidents in which they are involved.
    - (K) Just because many 16-to-18 year old drivers are involved in accidents does not necessarily mean that these young people are the cause of the accidents.

27. Writing a good application letter is one of the first steps toward getting a job. Every teacher should help students learn to write such letters.
    - (A) Every teacher should help students to write good application letters for getting jobs.
    - (B) The first thing every teacher should do is teach students to get jobs by writing application letters.
    - (C) In preparing students to get jobs, every teacher should help the students to learn to write good application letters.
    - (D) Teachers should write good application letters so students will get jobs.
    - (E) If teachers help students learn to write good application letters, the students will get good jobs.

28. Companies that publish city directories make their profits in more than one way. They sell directories and they sell advertising.
    - (F) By selling advertising publishing companies sell directories and make profits.
    - (G) The advertising in city directories makes profits for the publishers who sell them.
    - (H) In more than one way publishing city directories makes a profit for companies that advertise and sell.
    - (J) Companies that publish city directories make their profits through the sales of the directories themselves and through the advertising in them.
    - (K) If a company that publishes city directories wants to make profits in more than one way, it will have to advertise directories and sell them.

GO ON TO THE NEXT PAGE

Directions: For questions 29–31, choose the topic sentence that best fit the paragraph.

29. ______________________________.

These people lose sight of an important fact. Many of the founding fathers of our country were comparatively young men. Today more than ever our country needs young, idealistic politicians.

(A) Young people don't like politics.

(B) Many people think that only older men and women who have had a great deal of experience should hold public office.

(C) The holding of public office should be restricted to highly idealistic people.

(D) Our Constitution prescribes certain minimum ages for certain elected federal officeholders.

(E) Young men and women should take part in politics at every level of government.

30. ______________________________.

Mass and weight are not the same. Mass is the amount of matter any object contains. Weight is the pull of gravity on that mass.

(F) Matter is anything that has mass and occupies space.

(G) The phenomenon of weightlessness in outer space is created by the weak pull of gravity.

(H) Matter is composed of basic substances known as *elements*.

(J) Atomic weight is the weight of one atom of an element expressed in atomic mass units.

(K) Two of the most commonly used measures of size and weight are the metric system and the English system.

31. ______________________________.

In some cases, it consists only of ordinances, with little or no attempt at enforcement. In other cases, good control is obtained through wise ordinances and an efficient inspecting force and laboratory. While inspection alone can do much toward controlling the quality and production of milk, there must also be frequent laboratory tests of the milk.

(A) The bacterial count of milk indicates the condition of the dairy and the methods of milk handling.

(B) When the milk-producing animals are free from disease, the milk that they provide registers a low bacterial count.

(C) Inefficient sterilization of equipment and utensils represented a source of milk contamination in dairies at the turn of the century.

(D) Not all public health sanitarians are equally trained nor equally conscientious.

(E) Most cities carrying on public health work exercise varying degrees of inspection and control over their milk supplies.

Directions: For questions 32–34, choose the pair of sentences that best develops the topic sentence.

32. A passage leads from the outer ear to a membrane called the eardrum.

(F) Earaches are caused by infection within the ear. Untreated chronic earaches may lead to eventual deafness.

(G) Sound waves striking the eardrum make it vibrate. On the other side of the eardrum lies a space called the middle ear.

(H) This tube ends near the throat opening of the nose, close to the tonsils. Doctors often remove both tonsils and adenoids in the same operation.

(J) The sounds we hear are created by the vibration of air waves. The frequency of the vibrations determines the pitch of the sound.

(K) Loss of any one of the senses is a frightening prospect. Loss of hearing often leads to profound depression because of its isolating effect.

33. Urban open-air markets originally came into existence spontaneously when groups of pushcart peddlers congregated in spots where business was good.

(A) There was confusion and disorder in these open-air markets because the peddlers paid no licensing fees. The strongest and toughest peddlers secured the best locations.

(B) One problem created by open-air markets is that of garbage in the streets. Another is obstruction of traffic.

(C) In some Asian countries, fixed stores represent a very small percent of all commerce. Nearly all buying and selling is done by merchants in the streets.

(D) Good business induced them to return to these spots daily, and unofficial open-air markets thus arose. These peddlers paid no fees, and cities received no revenue from them.

(E) The life of a pushcart peddler did not guarantee a steady income. In bad weather, the peddler simply packed up his wares and went home.

34. With well over a million different kinds of plants and animals living on earth, there is a need for a system of classification.

(F) The animal and plant kingdoms are the two principal kingdoms and contain virtually all life. Scientists have struggled to find the best method of grouping organisms for hundreds of years.

(G) Viruses are a type of life that scientists have difficulty in defining. They do not fit easily into any classification scheme because they do not have a true cell structure.

(H) The system currently in use is based principally upon relationships and similarities in structure. The scientific name consists of two terms identifying the genus and the species.

(J) The first letter of the genus is capitalized whereas the species is written in small letters. The scientific name for man is Homo sapien.

(K) Mammals are warm-blooded animals with hair or fur on their bodies. Mammals are divided into many orders based upon differences in body structure.

Directions: For questions 35–37, choose the sentence that does not belong in the paragraph.

35. (1) The island countries of the Caribbean area produce large quantities of oil, tropical fruits, and vegetables. (2) They are also rich in minerals. (3) The Caribbean Sea is to the American continent a central sea just as the Mediterranean is to the European continent. (4) This region is capable of supplying the United States with many goods formerly imported from Africa and Asia. (5) In exchange, the countries of this region need the manufactured goods that can be provided only by an industrial nation.

(A) Statement 1

(B) Statement 2

(C) Statement 3

(D) Statement 4

(E) Statement 5

36. (1) The dangers to which migratory birds are subjected during their journeys are but little less than those that would befall them if they remained in unsuitable zones. (2) During long oversea passages, fatigue and hunger weed out the weaklings. (3) Sudden storms and adverse winds strike migrating birds where no land is near, and they are often carried far from the goal they aimed at. (4) Predatory, birds accompany them, taking a toll en route, and predatory man waits for the tired wanderers with gun and net. (5) With the institution of bird banding, the study of bird migrations has become a fascinating science.

(F) Statement 1

(G) Statement 2

(H) Statement 3

(J) Statement 4

(K) Statement 5

GO ON TO THE NEXT PAGE

37. (1) A city of ants includes the queen, the workers, baby ants, and nurses that care for the baby ants. (2) Termites cause structural damage to houses by boring into foundation timbers while carpenter ants burrow tunnels into damp wood at any level of a building. (3) Ants begin their lives as small white eggs. (4) The eggs hatch into fat little white worms called larvae. (5) The larvae metamorphose to become pupae, and finally the pupae develop into baby ants.
(A) Statement 1
(B) Statement 2
(C) Statement 3
(D) Statement 4
(E) Statement 5

Directions: For questions 38–40, read the paragraph and choose the sentence that best fills the blank.

38. Many experiments on the effects of alcohol consumption show that alcohol decreases alertness and efficiency. It decreases self-consciousness and at the same time increases confidence and feelings of ease and relaxation. ______________________________. It destroys the fear of consequences.
(F) They become highway menaces.
(G) The alcohol content of one ounce of whiskey is equal to that in one can of beer and in one glass of wine.
(H) The legal drinking age has been set at 21 so as to save the lives of young drivers.
(J) It impairs attention and judgment.
(K) Alcohol may cause harm to a developing fetus, so women should not drink during pregnancy.

39. Arsonists are persons who set fires deliberately. They don't look like criminals, but they cost the nation millions of dollars in property loss and sometimes loss of life. ______________________________. Sometimes a shopkeeper sees no way out of losing his business and sets fire to it to collect the insurance. Some arsonists just like the excitement of seeing the fire burn and watching the firefighters at work.
(A) Arsonists set fires for many different reasons.
(B) Forest fires usually stem from carelessness or from natural causes rather than from the acts of arsonists.
(C) Another type of arsonist wants revenge and sets fire to the home or shop of someone he feels has treated him unfairly.
(D) Arsonists have even been known to help fight the fire.
(E) Arson is a difficult crime to detect because the fire itself tends to destroy the evidence.

40. Kindling temperature is the lowest temperature at which a substance catches fire and continues to burn. Different fuels have different kindling temperatures. ______________________________. Coal, because of its high kindling temperature, requires much heat before it will begin to burn. Matches are tipped with phosphorus or some other low kindling material to permit the small amount of heat produced by friction to ignite the match.
(F) Safety matches are so called because they can be ignited only by striking on a strip on the package in which they are sold.
(G) Paper catches fire easily because it has a low kindling temperature.
(H) The type of fire extinguisher to be used to put out a fire depends on the nature of the fire itself.
(J) The United States consumes so much energy that it is rapidly consuming its store of fossil fuels.
(K) Thin dry twigs are used as kindling wood for open fires.

STOP

IF YOU FINISH BEFORE TIME IS UP, CHECK OVER YOUR WORK ON TEST 7 ONLY. DO NOT RETURN TO ANY PREVIOUS TEST.

ANSWERS TO SECOND MODEL COOP EXAM

Answer Key

Test 1. SEQUENCES

1. B	5. C	9. D	13. A	17. C
2. H	6. G	10. G	14. J	18. G
3. A	7. B	11. C	15. B	19. D
4. J	8. F	12. H	16. F	20. H

Test 2. ANALOGIES

1. B	5. D	9. D	13. B	17. D
2. J	6. H	10. H	14. G	18. H
3. B	7. C	11. A	15. C	19. A
4. F	8. G	12. J	16. F	20. J

Test 3. MEMORY

1. A	5. D	9. E	13. B	17. E
2. K	6. F	10. H	14. H	18. F
3. C	7. C	11. A	15. D	19. B
4. G	8. G	12. J	16. G	20. J

Test 4. VERBAL REASONING

1. C	5. B	9. A	13. D	17. B
2. G	6. H	10. G	14. H	18. G
3. D	7. C	11. B	15. C	19. A
4. F	8. J	12. J	16. F	20. J

Test 5. READING COMPREHENSION

1. C	9. C	17. A	25. D	33. B
2. H	10. F	18. G	26. J	34. G
3. C	11. D	19. D	27. A	35. C
4. F	12. F	20. H	28. H	36. F
5. A	13. A	21. C	29. B	37. C
6. J	14. H	22. G	30. G	38. J
7. C	15. B	23. C	31. D	39. D
8. G	16. J	24. G	32. F	40. G

Test 6. MATHEMATICS CONCEPTS AND APPLICATIONS

1. C	9. A	17. B	25. A	33. B
2. G	10. H	18. G	26. G	34. F
3. A	11. C	19. A	27. D	35. C
4. J	12. G	20. G	28. H	36. H
5. B	13. C	21. C	29. B	37. D
6. F	14. J	22. H	30. H	38. H
7. C	15. C	23. D	31. C	39. C
8. J	16. F	24. H	32. J	40. J

Test 7. LANGUAGE EXPRESSION

1. B	9. E	17. A	25. A	33. D
2. H	10. F	18. F	26. K	34. H
3. D	11. B	19. B	27. C	35. C
4. J	12. H	20. H	28. J	36. K
5. A	13. C	21. A	29. B	37. B
6. K	14. J	22. H	30. F	38. J
7. C	15. C	23. D	31. E	39. A
8. G	16. K	24. G	32. G	40. G

SECOND MODEL COOP EXAM

Answers and Explanations

TEST 1. SEQUENCES

1. **(B)** The little circle is moving around the box in a counter-clockwise direction. In the first frame, the circle is on the outside of the box. After one complete circuit, the little circle straddles the perimeter of the box as it continues its counter-clockwise travel in the second frame. After the straddling circuit, the little circle moves into the box. The correct answer represents continuation of the circle in its counter-clockwise travel inside the box.
2. **(H)** Look at the first three frames and note that in each frame the first and last elements are identical. Eliminate choice (F). Look again at the first three frames and note that in each of the central elements only one segment is darkened. Eliminate choice (G). Now notice that within each frame, the single darkened elements are positioned opposite each other.
3. **(A)** In each of the first three frames, the two dark-headed arrows are of the same length and point in the same direction on the right. This pattern is carried out only in choice (A). Check to be certain of your choice by looking at the other two arrows. One is long, one short; both heads are clear; they point in opposite directions. This is consistent with the behavior of the left-hand arrows in the first three frames. All other choices break the pattern in more than one way.
4. **(J)** In the first three frames, the first figure stands on both legs. Eliminate choice (G). Looking again at the first figure, in each of the first three frames the arms are in a different position. Choice (J) offers the fourth position for this figure's arms. Confirm this by looking at the other two figures. The arm and leg positions are exactly reversed in the first and third frames. The arm and leg positions of the second and third figures in choice (J) are the reverse of those in the second frame.
5. **(C)** Of the four figures in each frame, the first two are always alike while the other two vary. There are only three different figures. The easiest way to derive a pattern is to assign a number to each figure. Thus, in the first frame, we have 1-1-2-3; in the second, 2-2-3-1; and in the third, 3-3-1-2. The progression shows that in each succeeding frame the figure in third position in the preceding frame is doubled. Thus, the fourth frame should consist of 1-1-2-3, as found in choice (C).
6. **(G)** Name the patterns. First frame: plain, vee, left up, right down. Second frame: plain, vee, left down, right up. Third frame: plain, vee, right up, left down. Fourth frame must follow the up-down, left-right reversal pattern established: plain, vee, right down, left up.
7. **(B)** In the first frame, $44 - 5 = 39$ and $39 - 4 = 35$. Try this pattern in the second frame, and you will see that the –5, –4 rule holds. In the third frame, $61 - 5 = 56$, so the answer is $56 - 4 = 52$.
8. **(F)** In each frame, the first and last numbers are the same, so you need only figure the relationship of the middle number to each of these. In both the first and second frames, the central number is 2 × the first, so choose $2 \times 9 = 18$ for your answer.
9. **(D)** In each frame, the second number is 2 × the first. However, the third number seems to follow no rule at all. Since the third number in each of the first two frames is 8, and 8 is offered as a choice, choose it and state to yourself the rule. "The third number is 8."
10. **(G)** The rule appears most clearly in the second frame: divide by 3, divide by 3. Applied to the first frame, it works. To choose the answer, you must choose the number that yields 7 when divided by 3. Multiply 7×3 to find 21.
11. **(C)** In each frame the second number is repeated, so you really might just guess that the middle number in the last frame will be the same as the last. To double check, you might note that the

second number in each frame is 18 more than the first.

12. **(H)** This problem looks simple, but you might have to look twice. In each frame, the first number becomes the addend for the progression. Thus, in the first frame 2 + 2 = 4; 4 + 2 = 6. In the second frame, 3 + 3 = 6; 6 + 3 = 9. And in the third, 4 + 4 = 8, and 8 + 4 = 12.
13. **(A)** In each frame, the first and second numbers set the limits, and the last number is half way between. So, in the last frame, 70 is halfway between 80 and the correct answer, 60.
14. **(J)** Look carefully and you will see that in every case *1* and *2* are subscripts and *3* is a superscript. The letters remain in the same order, and the numbers simply move in a clockwise direction around them.
15. **(B)** The numbers and the letters all remain in the same order, only the locations (that is subscript or superscript) of the numbers change. The logical progression between one superscript and two subscripts and two subscripts and one superscript is all subscripts.
16. **(F)** Again the letters remain the same and in the same order, but here the numbers both change and change their positions. Looking carefully, you will note that the odd numbers are superscripts while the even numbers are subscripts. Furthermore, the numbers themselves are decreasing in value one at a time. Concentrate on numbers alone: 5-5-4; 5-4-4; 4-4-4; fill in 4-4-3; then 4-3-3.
17. **(C)** This series is basically the alphabet, but every other set presents the letters in reverse order. As we reach the next set, we are back to alphabetical order again. If you quickly write the alphabet across the page in your test booklet, you will find alphabetic series much easier to figure out.
18. **(G)** Each set begins with *A* and ends with *B*. Then we find an alphabetic sequence beginning with *B* at the second position in each set and an alphabetic sequence beginning with *D* in the third position in each set.
19. **(D)** Within each grouping the letters move in direct alphabetical sequence. Between groups the space increases each time. Thus, moving from the first group to the second, we skip over one letter, *D*; from the second group to the third, over two letters, *H* and *I;* from the third group to the fourth, *M, N,* and *O*. Skip over four letters to choose the answer. The alphabet you have written in your test booklet will prove very helpful.
20. **(H)** This is a difficult question. You can see immediately that we are dealing with the alphabet in reverse and that no letters have been skipped. But what is the rule that governs? Assign a number to each letter in the first group, basing the number on natural sequence. Thus figure W-X-Y-Z would be 1-2-3-4; here they appear Z-Y-W-X or 4-3-1-2. Follow through with the remaining groupings and you will find that all adhere to the same 4-3-1-2 rule. Now it is easy to choose the answer.

TEST 2. ANALOGIES

1. **(B)** Large four-footed mammal is to small four-footed mammal as large car is to small car. Large is to small is not an adequate formulation of the relationship because the elephant is also larger than the bug. You must refine your relationship until you find only one answer.
2. **(J)** The mother has lots of children as the hen has lots of chickens.
3. **(B)** The analogy here is sequential. Progress is from high chair to chair as it is from baby swing to swing. If asked to locate another analogous relationship, you would choose that of the tricycle to the bicycle.
4. **(F)** The relationship here is that of more to fewer. The centipede has more legs than the spider. The hexagon has more sides than the starfish has arms. The octagon and the octopus both sport eight sides or arms (more than the hexagon, not fewer), and the snake has none at all.
5. **(D)** In-line skates are wheeled vehicles worn on the feet and propelled by the person wearing them; a motorcycle is a wheeled vehicle ridden by a person and propelled by a motor. Analogously, skis are runnered, worn on the feet, and propelled by the person wearing them; a snowmobile is a runnered vehicle ridden by a person and propelled by a motor.
6. **(H)** The skull and crossbones and the "Mister Yuk" face on containers are both symbols for

poisons. They say, "Danger. Don't eat or drink me." The American flag and the American eagle are both symbols for the United States. The hammer and sickle are the symbol for Russia. When faced with two possible choices to fit an analogy, you must refine the relationship. Here you must go beyond *symbol* to *symbol for the same thing*.

7. **(C)** A head goes on a pillow as feet go on a hassock. The relationship is one of purpose. The pillow goes on the bed, but that represents a reversal of the analogy.
8. **(G)** Pine cones are the seed carriers of the pine tree as acorns are the seed of the oak. Pine needles are part of the pine tree, but not the seed-carrying part.
9. **(D)** Steak is an edible part of the steer; a drumstick is an edible part of the chicken. The egg is an edible product of the chicken, but it is not part of the meat of the chicken that is eaten.
10. **(H)** The analogy is of large to small of objects with similar functions. Thus, an axe is a long-handled wood-chopping tool while the hatchet serves the same function but has a short handle. Similarly, the scythe is a long-handled grass-cutting tool while the sickle serves the same function but has a short handle.
11. **(A)** Sometimes it is easier to explain an analogy by reading down instead of across. Thus, one eats from a soup bowl with a soup spoon and from a plate with a fork. Actually, this analogy is easy enough to solve visually, without words at all.
12. **(J)** This analogy is based on association. The swimsuited woman is associated with the palm tree; think "hot." The igloo is associated with the parka-clad person; think "cold."
13. **(B)** To solve this analogy, think "outside is to inside." The human body bears the same relationship to its skeleton as the full, finished house bears to its framework.
14. **(G)** California is a coastal state of the far west; Massachusetts is its counterpart on the east coast. Maine is the northernmost state on the east coast, while Florida is southernmost. You could articulate this analogy as: "west is to east as north is to south." Actually, this analogy need not be so carefully refined. It would be adequate to say: "coastal state is to coastal state as coastal state is to coastal state." No other choice makes sense in the analogy. Oklahoma is totally inland.
15. **(C)** The car consumes gasoline; the source of that fuel is the gas pump. The baby birds consume worms, moths, and insects; the source of their fuel is the mother bird. Do not confuse the source of the fuel with the fuel itself.
16. **(F)** The hockey goal is guarded by the goalie; the fort is guarded by the sentry. The goalie and the sentry are both guardians of the gates; they have analogous functions.
17. **(D)** The analogy is that of the eater to the eaten. The shark eats the little fish; the cat eats the mouse.
18. **(H)** Milk, when not being drunk, is preserved in the refrigerator. A diamond ring, when not being worn, is preserved in a safe.
19. **(A)** The analogy is based on activities at different stages of development. The infant plays lying down and gets around by crawling. The child plays by jumping rope, for example, and gets around running. The child in the stroller is getting around passively. It does not fit into the analogy.
20. **(J)** The analogy is that of the rescuer to the rescued. The helicopter comes to the rescue of the people adrift in the lifeboat. The St. Bernard comes to the rescue of the hiker stranded in bad weather.

TEST 3. MEMORY

Most people find that the best way to learn nonsense words and their definitions is to form some sort association in their minds, basing their association on the form of the word or its meaning. By way of explanation, we offer possible associations by which you might have learned these words and definitions. These explanations are only suggestions as to how you might have learned: they are NOT the ONLY useful associations.

1. **(A)** exam = hortex = horror, terror, or exam itself from the *ex*
2. **(K)** psychiatrist = blothink = ink blot, think, or blow your mind
3. **(C)** to explode = oblomo = blow up
4. **(G)** apple = tred = tree red

5. **(D)** member of chain gang = ganclan = clang on the chain gang
6. **(F)** the color white = obalack = lack of black
7. **(C)** button = clolo = clothes lock
8. **(G)** stop = gnay = go—no
9. **(E)** furnace = potho = hot pot
10. **(H)** futon = rockflo = floor hard as a rock
11. **(A)** oriole = birbal = Baltimore bird
12. **(J)** illness = milikan = million aches
13. **(B)** child's toy = grindle = spindle or top
14. **(H)** to sing = chimichi = chime in
15. **(D)** to slip and fall = plidl = slide and plop
16. **(G)** yellow vegetable = lululoy = yellow, leafy
17. **(E)** frozen = shirocol = shivering cold or sheer as cold rock
18. **(F)** to laugh = chohor = chortle or chuckle
19. **(B)** cemetery = mostonica = moss on stones or mausoleum
20. **(J)** flood = hiwama = high water mark

TEST 4. VERBAL REASONING

1. **(C)** A cartoon always involves some sort of drawing. A cartoon usually involves animation, but animation may be lacking in a political cartoon. Humor and a message are common ingredients, but a cartoon may be simply decorative.
2. **(G)** The heroine must be a woman.
3. **(D)** What makes a pump work is pressure. If you were not certain of this answer, you could choose it by elimination. Because both water and air may be pumped, neither can be correct. As for handle, consider electric pumps.
4. **(F)** The necessary part of a lantern is light. The source of the light might be a bulb and the light can shine through mica or plastic as well as through glass.
5. **(B)** Information is absolutely necessary to the existence of data. Numbers, words, and charts all constitute information.
6. **(H)** A biography is the story of a life.
7. **(C)** Above the line are the primary colors of the spectrum, in order. Below the line are the mixed colors, also in order of appearance.
8. **(J)** Above the line are natural energy sources. Below the line are fossil fuels. Wood, uranium, and fission are all sources of power, but only oil is a fossil fuel.
9. **(A)** The birds above the line are all fish-eating wading birds. The birds below the line are seed eaters. A woodpecker eats insects; a robin eats worms; and a crane shares characteristics with the birds above the line not with those below.
10. **(G)** Above the line are degrees of wetness, from left to right most wet to least wet. Below the lines are academic degrees, from left to right the most highly educated doctorate, through the master's degree, to the bachelor's.
11. **(B)** Above the line are seed fruits; below the line the common factor is that all are stone fruits.
12. **(J)** The structures are connected in order.
13. **(D)** Because Bob went into the store alone and walked out empty-handed, we can safely conclude that the clerk did not sell cigarettes to Bob. No other assumption is supported by the facts as presented.
14. **(H)** If Tara's name was not on the injured list, Tara was not injured. She might have survived unscathed or have been killed. She might have missed the flight. As for choice (J), she might have changed her plans and taken a cruise to Bermuda instead. The possibility of an airline error in compiling the list of injured is not offered. Strictly on the basis of the situation described, you may correctly assume that Tara was not injured.
15. **(C)** Producers plan lavish stage productions to become long-running shows and always have contingency plans to replace actors as needed. There are many reasons why a show might not draw large audiences, but you can be certain that the reason for the premature closing was that the play was losing money; it was not a box office success.
16. **(F)** Michelle definitely spent some time at the kennel. We have no way of knowing where the kennel is nor at what point during Bernie's vacation Jack was called out of town. Bernie might have returned while Jack was out of town and might have taken Michelle home himself. And maybe Michelle was perfectly happy at the kennel or with Jack.

17. **(B)** We know that this is an out-of-place goose. Everything else is conjecture.

18. **(G)** *adaha* means *north*

    mikula means *pole*

    bomani means *south*

    tinkipu means *wind*

    gotono means *star*

    Therefore, *manitu* must mean *east* and manitutinkipu must mean east wind.

19. **(A)** If you study this question carefully, you do not need to actually translate at all. The word that you are trying to identify, geophysics, has no elements in common with any of the three words for which you are given translations. You can therefore eliminate any choice that contains any element that appears in any of the three initial words.

20. **(J)** In this language, the modifiers follow the noun.

    eleme means *fruit*

    naftama means *vegetable*

    hotuto means *red*

    zigaru means *green*

    bigani means *leafy*

    Therefore, *toribuz* must mean *flower*. Remember that in this language the modifier follows the noun. Choice (A) reverses this order. *Toribuzhotuto* means red flower.

TEST 5. READING COMPREHENSION

1. **(C)** Choosing the title for this paragraph takes more than one reading of the paragraph. This is not an easy question. After a couple of readings, however, you should be able to conclude that the all-inclusive subject of the paragraph is the remodeling of plants. An equally correct title, not offered here, might be "Uses and Effects of Colchicine."

2. **(H)** Buried in the middle of the paragraph is the sentence: "It creates new varieties with astonishing frequency, whereas such mutations occur but rarely in nature."

3. **(C)** This question becomes easy to answer after you have dealt with the previous question.

4. **(F)** The third sentence states that colchicine is a poisonous drug.

5. **(A)** The answer to this question of fact is in the first sentence.

6. **(J)** Do not be misled by the first sentence which introduces Reverend Manasseh Cutler, nor by the last portion of the selection which discusses the naming of Cleveland. The entire selection has to do with the settling of the Northwest Territory.

7. **(C)** In this context, the word *related* means reported or simply told.

8. **(G)** Read carefully. General Cleaveland *quieted the Indian claims;* he did not quiet the Indians. If the Indians were making claims, they were not eager to work with him. The selection suggests that General Cleaveland bought off the Indians with money, cattle, and whiskey.

9. **(C)** Clearly the writer of the selection is an admirer of carrier pigeons, praising their usefulness and reliability.

10. **(F)** G. I. Joe brought the news of an allied victory, but he was rewarded for the results of his bringing the news, for preventing unnecessary loss of life. If the British had not received news that their troops were already in the town of Colvi Vecchia, they would have sent out the raid and bombed their own soldiers. When two answers to a question seem right, you must choose the one that most specifically answers what is asked.

11. **(D)** The Lord Mayor of London gave G. I. Joe the Dickin Medal.

12. **(F)** In this sentence, *vital* means essential or extremely important. Often the messages do carry information of life-and-death significance, but important information does not necessarily immediately save lives.

13. **(A)** The context in which it is used should help you to choose this answer. "... Veneration due to its sacred origin..." implies something religious and related to worship.

14. **(H)** The speaker probably does celebrate and enjoy Christmas, but the primary reason for this speech is to defend the holiday to Uncle Scrooge by listing its advantages to mankind.

15. **(B)** This is the whole point of the first paragraph.
16. **(J)** Again, use of the word in context should lead you to its meaning. The paragraph speaks of goodwill among all men and women. This *one consent* therefore is <u>unanimous</u> good feeling.
17. **(A)** Read the last paragraph carefully. Scrooge is first reacting to the clerk who has just applauded the speech in defense of Christmas. Scrooge threatens the clerk with firing. He then turns and makes a sarcastic remark to his nephew. It can be assumed that he is angry with both characters.
18. **(G)** The harbor police force was established almost a century ago, that is, at the beginning of the twentieth century.
19. **(D)** The first sentence of the second paragraph says that the boats are equipped for various jobs. This means that they vary in function.
20. **(H)** By checking on the operation of the junk boats, the harbor police ensure that the activities of the junk boats are legal.
21. **(C)** Each of the other choices includes some activity that is not mentioned as an activity of the harbor police.
22. **(G)** The 450 disabled boats that were towed and the thousands that were assisted in other ways must surely have included a vast variety of different kinds of boats.
23. **(C)** This is the meaning of the second sentence of the first paragraph. You may be aware that the efforts of conservationists have paid off and that the population of bald eagles has been recovering over the last decade. Remember that your answers to reading comprehension questions must be based on information provided in the passage.
24. **(G)** Because the thrust of the selection is the threatened extinction of the bald eagle, you really do not need to search for the precise words that answer this question. However, you can find them in the second paragraph.
25. **(D)** This definition is given in the second sentence of the third paragraph: ". . . aeries, the eagles' mammoth nests."
26. **(J)** The bald eagle appears on the Great Seal of the United States, our national emblem. An emblem is a symbol. "Emblematic" is the adjective form of the noun, "emblem."
27. **(A)** Any one of the reasons might be accurate, but the author specifically tells you his reason in the second sentence.
28. **(H)** This is a fact question; see the third sentence.
29. **(B)** The old-fashioned language of this selection might require more than one reading, but this detail is found in the fourth sentence.
30. **(G)** The selection says that the garden extended so far that the gardener did not know where it ended, but it does not say that he was unable to care for it because of its size. In the sixth sentence we learn that the garden led into a lovely forest. The nightingale lived in the forest, not in the garden.
31. **(D)** Great blank spaces on a population map indicate a very sparse or scanty population. The fact that desert populations grow fruits and vegetables does not mean that they restrict their diets to these products.
32. **(F)** You may eat the vegetables at a winter dinner, but the farm only produces the vegetables; it does not cook the dinner.
33. **(B)** Broadcloth is made from silky cotton grown in Egypt.
34. **(G)** The third paragraph makes the statement that desert civilizations have made important cultural contributions, but it does not compare these contributions with those of any other civilizations. The last paragraph tells what these contributions are. It is obvious that these have had an impact on western civilizations.
35. **(C)** This need is explained in the middle of the last paragraph.
36. **(F)** The name of the town is *Ekalaka*, but they call it "Skeleton Flats."
37. **(C)** The answer to this main-idea question should be clear. The article is about the various fossil finds.
38. **(J)** This definition is in the second paragraph: ". . . paleontologists, scientists who use fossils to study prehistoric life forms." Walter Peck's hobby was geology, and in the course of pursuing his hobby, he made the first find.
39. **(D)** The third paragraph discusses the people of Ekalaka in terms of their enthusiasm for digging and fossil discovery. The various exciting finds are described in the fourth paragraph.
40. **(G)** The answer is nothing more than a restatement of the last sentence.

TEST 6. MATHEMATICS CONCEPTS AND APPLICATIONS

1. **(C)** The reciprocal of a fraction is the fraction "turned upside down," $1\frac{2}{3}$ is equivalent to $\frac{5}{3}$. The reciprocal of $\frac{5}{3}$ is $\frac{3}{5}$. The correct answer is (C). Choice (D) is a distractor. Because *x* has a precise value in the problem, we must choose an answer having a precise value.
2. **(G)** The product of any number and its reciprocal is 1. Therefore, $\frac{7}{16} \times \frac{16}{7} = 1$, and (G) is the correct choice. Even if you didn't know this rule, you could have examined the answers and eliminated both (F) because the product was greater than 1, and (J) because the product was less than 1. Answer (H) is equivalent to (G), but because it is *not* in lowest terms, it is a second choice.
3. **(A)** This problem looks much harder than it really is. The numerator of this complex fraction is the same as the denominator. When numerator and denominator are equivalent, the fraction is equal to 1.
4. **(J)** This is a complex fraction requiring all of your skills in working with fractions. To estimate the correct answer, note that the numerator is slightly larger than 1 ($\frac{2}{3} + \frac{3}{8} > 1$), and the denominator is equivalent to $\frac{4}{16} - \frac{3}{16}$, or $\frac{1}{16}$. Therefore, a number slightly larger than 1 divided by $\frac{1}{16}$ is slightly larger than 16. The closest answer is (J) $\frac{50}{3}$, which is equivalent to $16\frac{2}{3}$. To solve the problem by calculation, simplify the numerator and denominator, and then divide.
5. **(B)** This is a problem in which you must substitute the values given into the formula. After you do that, it is a simple problem.

$$L = \frac{3}{4} \times 2 \times 7 \times \frac{1}{2}$$

$$= \frac{3 \times 2 \times 7 \times 1}{4 \times 2} = \frac{42}{8} = \frac{21}{4}$$

Therefore, (B) is the correct answer. The other answers would have resulted if you had forgotten to multiply one of the numbers in the numerator. Answer (D) might have been chosen by someone who didn't know what to do but thought the most difficult-looking answer would be the best.

6. **(F)** The sum of the angles of a triangle is always 180°. The correct answer, therefore is (F) because 45° + 75° + 60° = 180°.
7. **(C)** Note that the base of the triangle is the same as the diameter of the circle. Because ΔABC is isosceles, its altitude is the same length as the radius of the circle. Use the formula for the area of a triangle, and substitute the correct values:

$$A = \frac{1}{2}ba$$

$$= \frac{1}{2} \times 10 \times 5$$

$$= 25 \text{ cm}^2$$

(A) is the area of the circle.

8. **(J)** These measurements describe a large rectangular room 30 feet high. Use the formula $V = l \times w \times h$ to find the volume:

$$V = 75 \text{ feet} \times 50 \text{ feet} \times 30 \text{ feet}$$

$$= 112{,}500 \text{ cubic feet}$$

Answers (G) and (H) use the wrong units. Volume is always measured in *cubic* units.

9. **(A)** A store markup of 100% would exactly double the price. An 80% markup almost doubles the price. The $14 jeans are priced at almost double their cost to the store. By estimation, the best answer is (A). To figure precisely, remember that an 80% markup is the equivalent of multiplying the cost by 180%, or 1.80.

cost × 1.80 = 14.00

cost = 14.00 ÷ 1.80

cost = $7.78

10. **(H)** The finance charge will be the sum of $1\frac{1}{2}$% of $500, plus 1% of $250. You can write this as follows:

(0.15 × 500) + (.01 × 250)

= 7.50 + 2.50 = $10.00

You can estimate the answer if you remember that percent means "hundredths of." One one-hundredth of $500 is $5.00; one one-hundredth of $250 is $2.50. The only answer near this sum is (H). Answers (G) and (J) would have resulted if you had misplaced a decimal point.

11. **(C)** The area of the shaded portion is equal to the area of the square, less the area of the circle. The length of the side of the square is equal to the diameter of the circle. Therefore, using $\frac{22}{7}$ for pi: $(4" \times 4") - (\pi 2^2) = 16$ sq. in. $- \frac{88}{7}$ sq. in. $= 3\frac{3}{7}$ sq. in. The correct answer is (C). If you answered (D), $4\frac{3}{7}$, check your skills in subtracting fractions from whole numbers.

12. **(G)** For each teacher, there are 14 students. Because there are 14 teachers, there must be 14×14, or 196, students.

13. **(C)** The long way to solve this problem is to multiply both the numerator and denominator out, and then divide. If you notice that 100^4 can also be written as 10^8, the answer is obviously (C).

$$100^4 = 10^2 \times 100^3 = 10^2 \times 10^2 \times 100^2 =$$

$$10^2 \times 10^2 \times 10^2 \times 100 = 10^2 \times 10^2 \times 10^2 \times 10^2 = 10^8$$

14. **(J)** In the whole number system, every other number is odd and every other number is even. If x is odd, $x + 1$ is even, $x + 2$ is odd, $x + 3$ is even, and so forth. Also, if x is odd, $x - 1$ is even, $x - 2$ is odd, and $x - 3$ is even. If an even or odd number is doubled, the outcome is even. Therefore, if x is odd, $2x + 1$ is odd, $x - 2$ is odd, and $4x - 3$ is odd.

15. **(C)** Arrange the periods of time in columns and add as you would add whole numbers.

4 hr.	17 min.
3 hr.	58 min.
	45 min.
+ 7 hr.	12 min.
14 hr.	132 min.

We know there are 60 minutes in each hour. Therefore, 132 minutes equals 2 hours 12 minutes. The correct answer for this addition is 16 hours 12 minutes, or answer (C). When working with units that measure time, volume, and length, it is usually best to represent the answer using as many larger units as possible. That's why 16 hours 12 minutes is preferable to 14 hours 132 minutes as an answer.

16. **(F)** You do not have to calculate this answer. If eight people share equally of 8 pounds and some ounces of fruit, each person would receive 1 pound and a few ounces. Only (F) is possible.

17. **(B)** This is a subtraction problem. You must find the difference between the lengths of time required to finish the race. As with other problems involving units of measurement, you must work carefully.

3 hr.	2 min.	24 sec.
−2 hr.	12 min.	38 sec.

Because 38 seconds is larger than 24 seconds and 12 minutes is larger than 2 minutes, borrow from the minutes column and the hour column and rewrite the problem as follows:

2 hr.	61 min.	84 sec.
−2 hr.	12 min.	38 sec.
0 hr.	49 min.	46 sec.

18. **(G)** If the drawing is at $\frac{1}{16}$ scale, it means that the drawing is $\frac{1}{16}$ the size of the actual wheel. Therefore. multiply the size of the drawing by 16.

$1.8 \times 16 = 28.8$ inches

19. **(A)** This problem asks you to find speed or rate. Speed or rate is found by dividing the distance traveled by the time required. The choice in which distance is divided by time is (A).

20. **(G)** R rooms each with S square feet contain a total of RS square feet. Because there are 144 square inches in each square foot, the rooms contain $144RS$ square inches.

21. **(C)**

Step 1. To find the correct ratio, write it as:

$$\frac{6 \text{ inches}}{6 \text{ feet}}$$

Step 2. Rewrite each quantity in inches.

$$\frac{6 \text{ inches}}{72 \text{ inches}}$$

Step 3. Simplify the ratio.

$$\frac{6}{72} = \frac{1}{12} = 1{:}12$$

22. **(H)** Here, three events occur periodically, so we must find the LCM of 4, 11, and 33, and add that number to 1950. That year will be the next common occurrence. The LCM of 4, 11, and 33 is 132. $1950 + 132 = 2082$.

23. **(D)** The is a two-step problem. First, find the length of the hypotenuse, so you know how far the other person is driving.

$$(AC)^2 = (AB)^2 + (BC)^2$$

$$= (40)^2 + (30)^2$$
$$= 1600 + 900$$
$$(AC) = \sqrt{2500} = 50 \text{ miles}$$

The person driving from C to A must drive 50 miles at 50 mph. He or she will get there in 1 hour. The other must drive 70 miles. To get there first, he or she must drive faster than 70 miles per hour.

24. **(H)** This graph contains a line that has points with coordinates (1,1), (2,2), (3,3) and (4,4). From one point to another, the value of the *x*-coordinate changes just as much as the value of the *y*-coordinate. This line is at a 45° angle from the *x*-axis and will be created whenever the *x*- and *y*-coordinates are equal.

25. **(A)** The first 6 is in the billions place; the second, in the hundred-thousands place. If you had trouble with this problem, review the sections on how to read numbers and determine place values in your math textbook.

26. **(G)** A scale of 1:24,000 means that 1 inch on the map equals 24,000 inches on the ground. 24,000 inches equals 2,000 feet.

27. **(D)** This is a *literal problem* requiring you to "think without numbers." Creating mental pictures might help you solve this type of problem. If each person in a group makes *L* number of things, the group's output will be the product of the number of people in the group and the number of things each makes. Answer (D) represents the product and is the correct choice.

28. **(H)** Find 300 on the horizontal axis. Draw a vertical line upward until you touch the line. Move horizontally from this point on the line to the vertical axis. Note that you touch the vertical axis at a point roughly equivalent to $20. We suggest you use a ruler to sketch your line.

29. **(B)** To find the perimeter we add up the dimensions of all of the sides. Note that there are some parts that have not been assigned measurements, so we have to infer that they are the same as those corresponding parts whose measurements have been designated. Beginning at the bottom and moving clockwise, the dimensions are:

   5" + 7" + 1" + 3" + 3" + 3" + 1" + 7"

   These equal 30 inches. If you chose (A), (C), or (D), you failed to add up all of the segments.

30. **(H)** The ratio of men to women is 15:12, but this ratio must be expressed in simplest form. Because 15 and 12 have 3 as a common factor, the ratio expressed correctly is 5:4. The ratio of women to men is 12:15 or 4:5.

31. **(C)** A straight line represents a "straight angle" of 180°. An angle of 60° is given, so m∠C must be 120° to complete the line. Knowing that all the angles in a triangle added together equal 180°,

$$m\angle A + m\angle B + m\angle C = 180^\circ$$
$$m\angle A + 35^\circ + 120^\circ = 180^\circ$$
$$m\angle A = 180^\circ - 155^\circ$$
$$m\angle A = 25^\circ$$

32. **(J)** This is a simple subtraction problem designed to test how carefully you can subtract. It is possible to calculate the correct answer without pencil and paper. 999,999 is only 1 less than a million, and 1,001,000 is 1,000 greater than a million. The difference, then, is 1,000 + 1, or 1,001. Or, you may figure the problem in the following way:

$$\begin{array}{r} 1{,}001{,}000 \\ -\ 999{,}999 \\ \hline 1{,}001 \end{array}$$

33. **(B)** The surface of a rectangular solid such as a brick is found by calculating the area of each face of the brick and finding the sum of the areas of the faces. The brick has 6 faces:

   Two faces 6" × 3"; total 36 sq. in.
   Two faces 6" × 2"; total 24 sq. in.
   Two faces 3" × 2"; total 12 sq. in.
   Total 72 sq. in.

   Area, even area of a solid figure, is expressed in square measure. Only volume is expressed in cubic measure.

34. **(F)**

   Step 1. $-3 - [-2 + (5 - 6) - 3]$
   Step 2. $-3 - [-2 + (-1) - 3]$
   Step 3. $-3 - [-2 - 1 - 3]$
   Step 4. $-3 - [-6]$
   Step 5. $-3 + 6 = +3$

35. **(C)** By far the easiest way to solve this problem is to rename the fractions as decimals: 6 + 1.5 + .75 = 2.85. If you were to rename as fractions, the correct answer would be $2\frac{17}{20}$.

36. **(H)** When simplifying, begin with the innermost grouping symbols first, and work your way outward.

Step 1. $-6 - [2 - (3a - b) + b] + a$

Step 2. $-6 - [2 - 3a + b + b] + a$

Step 3. $-6 - [2 - 3a + 2b] + a$

Step 4. $-6 - 2 + 3a - 2b + a$

Step 5. $-8 + 4a - 2b$

37. **(D)** Begin with the innermost parentheses and work your way outward. Note that a negative sign in front of a grouping symbol reverses the signs of all numbers within.

Step 1. $-2\,[-4(2 - 1) + (3 + 2)]$

Step 2. $-2\,[-4(1) + (5)]$

Step 3. $-2\,[-4 + 5]$

Step 4. $-2\,[+1] = -2$

38. **(H)** The Pythagorean Theorem is used to find the length of the sides of right triangles. The square of the length of the longest side (the hypotenuse) is equal to the sum of the squares of the other two sides. Once we know the square of the length of the longest side, it is easy to find the length.

$(AC)^2 = (AB)^2 + (BC)^2$

$(AC)^2 = 3^2 + 4^2$

$(AC)^2 = 25$

$AC = \sqrt{25} = 5$

39. **(C)** This proportion asks you to find the missing element. A proportion is a statement of equality between two ratios, so we know that 5 bears the same relationship to 15 as 6 does to the unknown number. Since 3×5 equals 15, we know 3×6 equals the unknown number. The number, thus, is 18. The completed proportion should read: 5:6 as 15:18. Proportions may also be written with a set of two colons replacing the word "as." In this case, the proportion would read: 5:6::15:18.

40. **(J)** Calculate the surface area of the cube. It has six faces, each 2" × 2". Its surface area, then, is 6 × 4 sq. in. or 24 sq. in. Its volume is found by multiplying its length × width × height, or 2" × 2" × 2" = 8 cu. in. The ratio of surface area to volume is 24:8, or 3:1.

TEST 7. LANGUAGE EXPRESSION

1. **(B)** *Nevertheless* or *but* might fill the blank well, but those choices are not offered. The sense of the sentence is that the boys did what was forbidden precisely because it was forbidden. *Therefore* fills the blank best.

2. **(H)** Only one word makes sense in this blank.

3. **(D)** Of all the choices offered, only one makes sense.

4. **(J)** The word in the blank tells how children adjust, so it must be an adverb. The adverbial form of *easy* is *easily*. Only two groups are being compared, so use *more*.

5. **(A)** *Hardly* is a negative word, so use of any form of *not* is inappropriate.

6. **(K)** The construction of the sentence allows for a verb expressing either continuing or past action. "Bigger in size" is a childish, redundant expression.

7. **(C)** The truck rolled down the hill. "With its huge load of crates" is additional information set apart within two commas. Choice (A) separates subject from predicate; the semicolon in (B) simply creates two sentence fragments; (D) and (E) introduce a plural verb for the singular subject.

8. **(G)** Choice (F) is a run-on sentence. The first clause of choice (H) is a run-on; in addition, it uses the conjunction *and* which makes no sense in context. Choice (J) inserts a redundant *it* and is awkward as well. In choice (K), the introductory subordinate clause must be separated from the independent clause by a comma.

9. **(E)** Choices (A) and (B) are sentence fragments; (C) makes no sense; (D) inserts an unnecessary comma separating subject from predicate.

10. **(F)** Choice (G) is both nonsensical and a run-on sentence. The semicolon in choice (H) is incorrectly used in place of a comma; (J) is nonsense; (K) is a sentence fragment.

11. **(B)** Choices (A) and (C) are run-on sentences; (D) connects an independent clause and a phrase with a coordinate conjunction; (E) is a sentence fragment.

12. **(H)** Choices (F) and (G) are sentence fragments; (J) incorrectly sets off a restrictive phrase with commas; (K) is a nonsensical run-on.

13. **(C)** What you do in the present allows for a future event. Choice (A) incorrectly uses *of* instead of the auxiliary *have*. All other wrong choices mix tenses in illogical order.
14. **(J)** As with question 13, the present sets the stage for the future. All other choices mix tenses illogically.
15. **(C)** The present situation was reached through a past activity. Choices (A) and (D) mix tenses in illogical order. Choice (B) cannot stand as is. Either "Mary *will put* the clean plates away after the dishwasher *has* washed them," or "Mary *put* the clean plates away after the dishwasher *had* washed them," would be acceptable. Choice (E) requires the construction *had thought*.
16. **(K)** One event leads to the next. All other choices order the tenses illogically.
17. **(A)** The verb construction is complex, but clear. If a condition is met in the near future, it will (in the future) confirm an ongoing past activity.
18. **(F)** The sentence is about pliers.
19. **(B)** The subject of the introductory clause is *air masses*, but the subject of the sentence itself is *they*. The remaining underlined nouns are all parts of the predicate; they tell us what *they form*.
20. **(H)** The *king's body* is the subject of the introductory clause, but the subject of the sentence is *analysis*.
21. **(A)** The fact that the simplest animals are called sponges is extra information. The subject of the sentence is *animals*.
22. **(H)** *Resistance* is the subject of the sentence, and the resistance *makes* the meteors incandescent in flight. The phrase, "offered by the earth's atmosphere," describes the resistance.
23. **(D)** Conservation and control *will preserve*.
24. **(G)** The subject of the sentence is not stated but must be understood to be *you*. The predicate of a sentence is never to be found in an introductory phrase or clause.
25. **(A)** The subject of the sentence is *I*, and I *was surprised*. The remainder of the sentence amplifies the predicate verb.
26. **(K)** Choice (F) loses sight of the range of ages involved and focuses only on 16- and 18-year old drivers; (G) makes no sense; both (H) and (J) make definite statements that these drivers are the cause of the accidents or not the cause, whereas the original statements only raise the possibility.
27. **(C)** Choice (A) suggests that the teachers should help the students write the letters rather than teaching them to write; (B) implies that letter-writing is the first activity in the classroom; in (D) the teachers write the letters; (E) offers an unwarranted guarantee that a good letter will procure a good job.
28. **(J)** All other choices miss the point of the two statements—that profits come from selling advertising and from selling directories.
29. **(B)** The first development sentence begins with "these people." The topic sentence must tell us who these people are. You can immediately eliminate choices (C), (D), and (E). Choice (B) then becomes clearly the best answer because it offers an opinion that contrasts with the bulk of the paragraph.
30. **(F)** Because the first development sentence tells of two dimensions that are not the same, and the remainder of the paragraph proceeds to define these two dimensions, it is reasonable to expect the topic sentence to lead into discussion of at least one of these dimensions.
31. **(E)** What consists only of ordinances with little or no attempt at enforcement? Only "the varying degrees of inspection and control" answers this question, so it must be the topic sentence.
32. **(G)** The topic sentence introduces the structure of the ear and specifically mentions the eardrum. Choice (G) tells of the function of the eardrum and then continues describing the structure of the ear. Choice (H) speaks of "this tube," but the reference is unclear. All other choices lead off on various tangents, all of them ear-related but none of them logically developing the topic sentence.
33. **(D)** The topic sentence promises a history of the development of open-air markets in urban locations. Choice (D) picks right up on the theme. Choices (A), (B), and (E) all focus in on the negative aspects of the open-air markets. Choice (C) digresses to the nature of open-air markets in other cultures.
34. **(H)** It is quite clear that a number of sentences must intervene between the topic sentence and choices (G), (J), and (K). The transition from the topic sentence to the first sentence of choice (F) is

smooth and logical, but the second sentence of choice (F) does not flow from the first. Choice (H) represents only the beginning of development of a complex paragraph, but it is a reasonable beginning.

35. **(C)** The paragraph concerns the economies of the Caribbean islands, their resources, produce, and trade. The Mediterranean Sea might make an interesting topic for comparison with the Caribbean, but it has no place in this paragraph.

36. **(K)** Bird-banding, while clearly related to a discussion of bird migration, belongs in another paragraph.

37. **(B)** The paragraph is about the structure of ant society and the life cycle of ants. It is not about the kinds of ants.

38. **(J)** The space should be filled with another sentence cataloging the effects of alcohol on the person who drinks it.

39. **(A)** The next two sentences tell some reasons for which an arsonist might set a fire. Choice (C) also gives a reason, but "another" must come later in the paragraph. (E) is incorrect because the paragraph is about *arsonists* not about *arson*.

40. **(G)** The second sentence, telling us that different fuels have different kindling temperatures, sets the stage. What follows should be a discussion of a number of fuels with respect to their kindling temperatures.

SCORE SHEET

CTB/McGraw-Hill will score your exam and will send your scaled scores and your percentile scores directly to the schools you indicated. Scaled scores are scores converted by a special formula to make comparable your performance on tests of unequal lengths and unequal importance. Percentile scores compare your performance on each test and the whole exam with the performance of other students who took the same exam at the same time. Your scores will *not* be reported either as raw scores—that is, number correct—nor as percents. Right now, however, you will find it very useful to convert your own scores on the model exam into simple percentages. In this way you can compare your own performance on each test of the exam with your performance on each other test. You can then focus your study where it will do you the most good.

Subject	**No. Correct**	÷	**No. of Questions**		× **100**	=	**____%**
Sequences	______	÷	20 =	______	× 100	=	______%
Analogies	______	÷	20 =	______	× 100	=	______%
Memory	______	÷	20 =	______	× 100	=	______%
Verbal Reasoning	______	÷	20 =	______	× 100	=	______%
Reading Comprehension	______	÷	40 =	______	× 100	=	______%
Mathematics Concepts and Applications	______	÷	40 =	______	× 100	=	______%
Language Expression	______	÷	40 =	______	× 100	=	______%
TOTAL EXAM	______	÷	200 =	______	× 100	=	______%

Now compare the percentage scores you just earned on the Second Model Coop Exam with the scores you achieved on the First Model Coop. If you have paid attention to the study chapters in this book and if you have concentrated especially on your areas of previous weakness, you should see a marked improvement in your performance. If you still see trouble spots, review the applicable study chapters again and, perhaps, consult a textbook or a teacher for further help and suggestions.

Subject	**First Model**	**Second Model**
Sequences	%	%
Analogies	%	%
Memory	%	%
Verbal Reasoning	%	%
Reading Comprehension	%	%
Mathematics Concepts and Applications	%	%
Language Expression	%	%
TOTAL EXAM	%	%

Chapter 21

First Model HSPT Exam

ROAD MAP

- *Verbal Skills*
- *Quantitative Skills*
- *Reading—Comprehension*
- *Reading—Vocabulary*
- *Mathematics—Concepts*
- *Mathematics—Problem-Solving*
- *Language*
- *Answers to First Model HSPT Exam*
- *Answer Explanations for First Model HSPT Exam*
- *Score Sheet*

Answer Sheet

Answers and explanations for all First Model HSPT Exam questions follow the model exam.

VERBAL SKILLS

1. Ⓐ Ⓑ Ⓒ Ⓓ	13. Ⓐ Ⓑ Ⓒ Ⓓ	25. Ⓐ Ⓑ Ⓒ Ⓓ	37. Ⓐ Ⓑ Ⓒ Ⓓ	49. Ⓐ Ⓑ Ⓒ
2. Ⓐ Ⓑ Ⓒ Ⓓ	14. Ⓐ Ⓑ Ⓒ Ⓓ	26. Ⓐ Ⓑ Ⓒ Ⓓ	38. Ⓐ Ⓑ Ⓒ	50. Ⓐ Ⓑ Ⓒ Ⓓ
3. Ⓐ Ⓑ Ⓒ Ⓓ	15. Ⓐ Ⓑ Ⓒ	27. Ⓐ Ⓑ Ⓒ Ⓓ	39. Ⓐ Ⓑ Ⓒ Ⓓ	51. Ⓐ Ⓑ Ⓒ Ⓓ
4. Ⓐ Ⓑ Ⓒ	16. Ⓐ Ⓑ Ⓒ Ⓓ	28. Ⓐ Ⓑ Ⓒ Ⓓ	40. Ⓐ Ⓑ Ⓒ Ⓓ	52. Ⓐ Ⓑ Ⓒ
5. Ⓐ Ⓑ Ⓒ Ⓓ	17. Ⓐ Ⓑ Ⓒ Ⓓ	29. Ⓐ Ⓑ Ⓒ Ⓓ	41. Ⓐ Ⓑ Ⓒ Ⓓ	53. Ⓐ Ⓑ Ⓒ Ⓓ
6. Ⓐ Ⓑ Ⓒ Ⓓ	18. Ⓐ Ⓑ Ⓒ Ⓓ	30. Ⓐ Ⓑ Ⓒ Ⓓ	42. Ⓐ Ⓑ Ⓒ Ⓓ	54. Ⓐ Ⓑ Ⓒ Ⓓ
7. Ⓐ Ⓑ Ⓒ Ⓓ	19. Ⓐ Ⓑ Ⓒ Ⓓ	31. Ⓐ Ⓑ Ⓒ Ⓓ	43. Ⓐ Ⓑ Ⓒ Ⓓ	55. Ⓐ Ⓑ Ⓒ
8. Ⓐ Ⓑ Ⓒ Ⓓ	20. Ⓐ Ⓑ Ⓒ Ⓓ	32. Ⓐ Ⓑ Ⓒ Ⓓ	44. Ⓐ Ⓑ Ⓒ Ⓓ	56. Ⓐ Ⓑ Ⓒ Ⓓ
9. Ⓐ Ⓑ Ⓒ Ⓓ	21. Ⓐ Ⓑ Ⓒ Ⓓ	33. Ⓐ Ⓑ Ⓒ	45. Ⓐ Ⓑ Ⓒ Ⓓ	57. Ⓐ Ⓑ Ⓒ Ⓓ
10. Ⓐ Ⓑ Ⓒ Ⓓ	22. Ⓐ Ⓑ Ⓒ	34. Ⓐ Ⓑ Ⓒ Ⓓ	46. Ⓐ Ⓑ Ⓒ Ⓓ	58. Ⓐ Ⓑ Ⓒ Ⓓ
11. Ⓐ Ⓑ Ⓒ Ⓓ	23. Ⓐ Ⓑ Ⓒ Ⓓ	35. Ⓐ Ⓑ Ⓒ Ⓓ	47. Ⓐ Ⓑ Ⓒ Ⓓ	59. Ⓐ Ⓑ Ⓒ Ⓓ
12. Ⓐ Ⓑ Ⓒ Ⓓ	24. Ⓐ Ⓑ Ⓒ	36. Ⓐ Ⓑ Ⓒ Ⓓ	48. Ⓐ Ⓑ Ⓒ Ⓓ	60. Ⓐ Ⓑ Ⓒ

TEAR HERE

QUANTITATIVE SKILLS

61. Ⓐ Ⓑ Ⓒ Ⓓ	72. Ⓐ Ⓑ Ⓒ Ⓓ	83. Ⓐ Ⓑ Ⓒ Ⓓ	94. Ⓐ Ⓑ Ⓒ Ⓓ	105. Ⓐ Ⓑ Ⓒ Ⓓ
62. Ⓐ Ⓑ Ⓒ Ⓓ	73. Ⓐ Ⓑ Ⓒ Ⓓ	84. Ⓐ Ⓑ Ⓒ Ⓓ	95. Ⓐ Ⓑ Ⓒ Ⓓ	106. Ⓐ Ⓑ Ⓒ Ⓓ
63. Ⓐ Ⓑ Ⓒ Ⓓ	74. Ⓐ Ⓑ Ⓒ Ⓓ	85. Ⓐ Ⓑ Ⓒ Ⓓ	96. Ⓐ Ⓑ Ⓒ Ⓓ	107. Ⓐ Ⓑ Ⓒ Ⓓ
64. Ⓐ Ⓑ Ⓒ Ⓓ	75. Ⓐ Ⓑ Ⓒ Ⓓ	86. Ⓐ Ⓑ Ⓒ Ⓓ	97. Ⓐ Ⓑ Ⓒ Ⓓ	108. Ⓐ Ⓑ Ⓒ Ⓓ
65. Ⓐ Ⓑ Ⓒ Ⓓ	76. Ⓐ Ⓑ Ⓒ Ⓓ	87. Ⓐ Ⓑ Ⓒ Ⓓ	98. Ⓐ Ⓑ Ⓒ Ⓓ	109. Ⓐ Ⓑ Ⓒ Ⓓ
66. Ⓐ Ⓑ Ⓒ Ⓓ	77. Ⓐ Ⓑ Ⓒ Ⓓ	88. Ⓐ Ⓑ Ⓒ Ⓓ	99. Ⓐ Ⓑ Ⓒ Ⓓ	110. Ⓐ Ⓑ Ⓒ Ⓓ
67. Ⓐ Ⓑ Ⓒ Ⓓ	78. Ⓐ Ⓑ Ⓒ Ⓓ	89. Ⓐ Ⓑ Ⓒ Ⓓ	100. Ⓐ Ⓑ Ⓒ Ⓓ	111. Ⓐ Ⓑ Ⓒ Ⓓ
68. Ⓐ Ⓑ Ⓒ Ⓓ	79. Ⓐ Ⓑ Ⓒ Ⓓ	90. Ⓐ Ⓑ Ⓒ Ⓓ	101. Ⓐ Ⓑ Ⓒ Ⓓ	112. Ⓐ Ⓑ Ⓒ Ⓓ
69. Ⓐ Ⓑ Ⓒ Ⓓ	80. Ⓐ Ⓑ Ⓒ Ⓓ	91. Ⓐ Ⓑ Ⓒ Ⓓ	102. Ⓐ Ⓑ Ⓒ Ⓓ	
70. Ⓐ Ⓑ Ⓒ Ⓓ	81. Ⓐ Ⓑ Ⓒ Ⓓ	92. Ⓐ Ⓑ Ⓒ Ⓓ	103. Ⓐ Ⓑ Ⓒ Ⓓ	
71. Ⓐ Ⓑ Ⓒ Ⓓ	82. Ⓐ Ⓑ Ⓒ Ⓓ	93. Ⓐ Ⓑ Ⓒ Ⓓ	104. Ⓐ Ⓑ Ⓒ Ⓓ	

READING—COMPREHENSION

113. Ⓐ Ⓑ Ⓒ Ⓓ	121. Ⓐ Ⓑ Ⓒ Ⓓ	129. Ⓐ Ⓑ Ⓒ Ⓓ	137. Ⓐ Ⓑ Ⓒ Ⓓ	145. Ⓐ Ⓑ Ⓒ Ⓓ
114. Ⓐ Ⓑ Ⓒ Ⓓ	122. Ⓐ Ⓑ Ⓒ Ⓓ	130. Ⓐ Ⓑ Ⓒ Ⓓ	138. Ⓐ Ⓑ Ⓒ Ⓓ	146. Ⓐ Ⓑ Ⓒ Ⓓ
115. Ⓐ Ⓑ Ⓒ Ⓓ	123. Ⓐ Ⓑ Ⓒ Ⓓ	131. Ⓐ Ⓑ Ⓒ Ⓓ	139. Ⓐ Ⓑ Ⓒ Ⓓ	147. Ⓐ Ⓑ Ⓒ Ⓓ
116. Ⓐ Ⓑ Ⓒ Ⓓ	124. Ⓐ Ⓑ Ⓒ Ⓓ	132. Ⓐ Ⓑ Ⓒ Ⓓ	140. Ⓐ Ⓑ Ⓒ Ⓓ	148. Ⓐ Ⓑ Ⓒ Ⓓ
117. Ⓐ Ⓑ Ⓒ Ⓓ	125. Ⓐ Ⓑ Ⓒ Ⓓ	133. Ⓐ Ⓑ Ⓒ Ⓓ	141. Ⓐ Ⓑ Ⓒ Ⓓ	149. Ⓐ Ⓑ Ⓒ Ⓓ
118. Ⓐ Ⓑ Ⓒ Ⓓ	126. Ⓐ Ⓑ Ⓒ Ⓓ	134. Ⓐ Ⓑ Ⓒ Ⓓ	142. Ⓐ Ⓑ Ⓒ Ⓓ	150. Ⓐ Ⓑ Ⓒ Ⓓ
119. Ⓐ Ⓑ Ⓒ Ⓓ	127. Ⓐ Ⓑ Ⓒ Ⓓ	135. Ⓐ Ⓑ Ⓒ Ⓓ	143. Ⓐ Ⓑ Ⓒ Ⓓ	151. Ⓐ Ⓑ Ⓒ Ⓓ
120. Ⓐ Ⓑ Ⓒ Ⓓ	128. Ⓐ Ⓑ Ⓒ Ⓓ	136. Ⓐ Ⓑ Ⓒ Ⓓ	144. Ⓐ Ⓑ Ⓒ Ⓓ	152. Ⓐ Ⓑ Ⓒ Ⓓ

TEAR HERE

TEAR HERE

READING—VOCABULARY

153. Ⓐ Ⓑ Ⓒ Ⓓ	158. Ⓐ Ⓑ Ⓒ Ⓓ	163. Ⓐ Ⓑ Ⓒ Ⓓ	168. Ⓐ Ⓑ Ⓒ Ⓓ	173. Ⓐ Ⓑ Ⓒ Ⓓ
154. Ⓐ Ⓑ Ⓒ Ⓓ	159. Ⓐ Ⓑ Ⓒ Ⓓ	164. Ⓐ Ⓑ Ⓒ Ⓓ	169. Ⓐ Ⓑ Ⓒ Ⓓ	174. Ⓐ Ⓑ Ⓒ Ⓓ
155. Ⓐ Ⓑ Ⓒ Ⓓ	160. Ⓐ Ⓑ Ⓒ Ⓓ	165. Ⓐ Ⓑ Ⓒ Ⓓ	170. Ⓐ Ⓑ Ⓒ Ⓓ	
156. Ⓐ Ⓑ Ⓒ Ⓓ	161. Ⓐ Ⓑ Ⓒ Ⓓ	166. Ⓐ Ⓑ Ⓒ Ⓓ	171. Ⓐ Ⓑ Ⓒ Ⓓ	
157. Ⓐ Ⓑ Ⓒ Ⓓ	162. Ⓐ Ⓑ Ⓒ Ⓓ	167. Ⓐ Ⓑ Ⓒ Ⓓ	172. Ⓐ Ⓑ Ⓒ Ⓓ	

MATHEMATICS—CONCEPTS

175. Ⓐ Ⓑ Ⓒ Ⓓ	180. Ⓐ Ⓑ Ⓒ Ⓓ	185. Ⓐ Ⓑ Ⓒ Ⓓ	190. Ⓐ Ⓑ Ⓒ Ⓓ	195. Ⓐ Ⓑ Ⓒ Ⓓ
176. Ⓐ Ⓑ Ⓒ Ⓓ	181. Ⓐ Ⓑ Ⓒ Ⓓ	186. Ⓐ Ⓑ Ⓒ Ⓓ	191. Ⓐ Ⓑ Ⓒ Ⓓ	196. Ⓐ Ⓑ Ⓒ Ⓓ
177. Ⓐ Ⓑ Ⓒ Ⓓ	182. Ⓐ Ⓑ Ⓒ Ⓓ	187. Ⓐ Ⓑ Ⓒ Ⓓ	192. Ⓐ Ⓑ Ⓒ Ⓓ	197. Ⓐ Ⓑ Ⓒ Ⓓ
178. Ⓐ Ⓑ Ⓒ Ⓓ	183. Ⓐ Ⓑ Ⓒ Ⓓ	188. Ⓐ Ⓑ Ⓒ Ⓓ	193. Ⓐ Ⓑ Ⓒ Ⓓ	198. Ⓐ Ⓑ Ⓒ Ⓓ
179. Ⓐ Ⓑ Ⓒ Ⓓ	184. Ⓐ Ⓑ Ⓒ Ⓓ	189. Ⓐ Ⓑ Ⓒ Ⓓ	194. Ⓐ Ⓑ Ⓒ Ⓓ	

MATHEMATICS—PROBLEM-SOLVING

199. Ⓐ Ⓑ Ⓒ Ⓓ	207. Ⓐ Ⓑ Ⓒ Ⓓ	215. Ⓐ Ⓑ Ⓒ Ⓓ	223. Ⓐ Ⓑ Ⓒ Ⓓ	231. Ⓐ Ⓑ Ⓒ Ⓓ
200. Ⓐ Ⓑ Ⓒ Ⓓ	208. Ⓐ Ⓑ Ⓒ Ⓓ	216. Ⓐ Ⓑ Ⓒ Ⓓ	224. Ⓐ Ⓑ Ⓒ Ⓓ	232. Ⓐ Ⓑ Ⓒ Ⓓ
201. Ⓐ Ⓑ Ⓒ Ⓓ	209. Ⓐ Ⓑ Ⓒ Ⓓ	217. Ⓐ Ⓑ Ⓒ Ⓓ	225. Ⓐ Ⓑ Ⓒ Ⓓ	233. Ⓐ Ⓑ Ⓒ Ⓓ
202. Ⓐ Ⓑ Ⓒ Ⓓ	210. Ⓐ Ⓑ Ⓒ Ⓓ	218. Ⓐ Ⓑ Ⓒ Ⓓ	226. Ⓐ Ⓑ Ⓒ Ⓓ	234. Ⓐ Ⓑ Ⓒ Ⓓ
203. Ⓐ Ⓑ Ⓒ Ⓓ	211. Ⓐ Ⓑ Ⓒ Ⓓ	219. Ⓐ Ⓑ Ⓒ Ⓓ	227. Ⓐ Ⓑ Ⓒ Ⓓ	235. Ⓐ Ⓑ Ⓒ Ⓓ
204. Ⓐ Ⓑ Ⓒ Ⓓ	212. Ⓐ Ⓑ Ⓒ Ⓓ	220. Ⓐ Ⓑ Ⓒ Ⓓ	228. Ⓐ Ⓑ Ⓒ Ⓓ	236. Ⓐ Ⓑ Ⓒ Ⓓ
205. Ⓐ Ⓑ Ⓒ Ⓓ	213. Ⓐ Ⓑ Ⓒ Ⓓ	221. Ⓐ Ⓑ Ⓒ Ⓓ	229. Ⓐ Ⓑ Ⓒ Ⓓ	237. Ⓐ Ⓑ Ⓒ Ⓓ
206. Ⓐ Ⓑ Ⓒ Ⓓ	214. Ⓐ Ⓑ Ⓒ Ⓓ	222. Ⓐ Ⓑ Ⓒ Ⓓ	230. Ⓐ Ⓑ Ⓒ Ⓓ	238. Ⓐ Ⓑ Ⓒ Ⓓ

LANGUAGE

239. Ⓐ Ⓑ Ⓒ Ⓓ	251. Ⓐ Ⓑ Ⓒ Ⓓ	263. Ⓐ Ⓑ Ⓒ Ⓓ	275. Ⓐ Ⓑ Ⓒ Ⓓ	287. Ⓐ Ⓑ Ⓒ Ⓓ
240. Ⓐ Ⓑ Ⓒ Ⓓ	252. Ⓐ Ⓑ Ⓒ Ⓓ	264. Ⓐ Ⓑ Ⓒ Ⓓ	276. Ⓐ Ⓑ Ⓒ Ⓓ	288. Ⓐ Ⓑ Ⓒ Ⓓ
241. Ⓐ Ⓑ Ⓒ Ⓓ	253. Ⓐ Ⓑ Ⓒ Ⓓ	265. Ⓐ Ⓑ Ⓒ Ⓓ	277. Ⓐ Ⓑ Ⓒ Ⓓ	289. Ⓐ Ⓑ Ⓒ Ⓓ
242. Ⓐ Ⓑ Ⓒ Ⓓ	254. Ⓐ Ⓑ Ⓒ Ⓓ	266. Ⓐ Ⓑ Ⓒ Ⓓ	278. Ⓐ Ⓑ Ⓒ Ⓓ	290. Ⓐ Ⓑ Ⓒ Ⓓ
243. Ⓐ Ⓑ Ⓒ Ⓓ	255. Ⓐ Ⓑ Ⓒ Ⓓ	267. Ⓐ Ⓑ Ⓒ Ⓓ	279. Ⓐ Ⓑ Ⓒ Ⓓ	291. Ⓐ Ⓑ Ⓒ Ⓓ
244. Ⓐ Ⓑ Ⓒ Ⓓ	256. Ⓐ Ⓑ Ⓒ Ⓓ	268. Ⓐ Ⓑ Ⓒ Ⓓ	280. Ⓐ Ⓑ Ⓒ Ⓓ	292. Ⓐ Ⓑ Ⓒ Ⓓ
245. Ⓐ Ⓑ Ⓒ Ⓓ	257. Ⓐ Ⓑ Ⓒ Ⓓ	269. Ⓐ Ⓑ Ⓒ Ⓓ	281. Ⓐ Ⓑ Ⓒ Ⓓ	293. Ⓐ Ⓑ Ⓒ Ⓓ
246. Ⓐ Ⓑ Ⓒ Ⓓ	258. Ⓐ Ⓑ Ⓒ Ⓓ	270. Ⓐ Ⓑ Ⓒ Ⓓ	282. Ⓐ Ⓑ Ⓒ Ⓓ	294. Ⓐ Ⓑ Ⓒ Ⓓ
247. Ⓐ Ⓑ Ⓒ Ⓓ	259. Ⓐ Ⓑ Ⓒ Ⓓ	271. Ⓐ Ⓑ Ⓒ Ⓓ	283. Ⓐ Ⓑ Ⓒ Ⓓ	295. Ⓐ Ⓑ Ⓒ Ⓓ
248. Ⓐ Ⓑ Ⓒ Ⓓ	260. Ⓐ Ⓑ Ⓒ Ⓓ	272. Ⓐ Ⓑ Ⓒ Ⓓ	284. Ⓐ Ⓑ Ⓒ Ⓓ	296. Ⓐ Ⓑ Ⓒ Ⓓ
249. Ⓐ Ⓑ Ⓒ Ⓓ	261. Ⓐ Ⓑ Ⓒ Ⓓ	273. Ⓐ Ⓑ Ⓒ Ⓓ	285. Ⓐ Ⓑ Ⓒ Ⓓ	297. Ⓐ Ⓑ Ⓒ Ⓓ
250. Ⓐ Ⓑ Ⓒ Ⓓ	262. Ⓐ Ⓑ Ⓒ Ⓓ	274. Ⓐ Ⓑ Ⓒ Ⓓ	286. Ⓐ Ⓑ Ⓒ Ⓓ	298. Ⓐ Ⓑ Ⓒ Ⓓ

TEAR HERE

FIRST Model HSPT Exam

VERBAL SKILLS

Time—16 minutes

Directions: Mark one answer—the answer you think is best—for each problem.

Example:

A. Travel most nearly means

A) stop.

B) move.

C) join.

D) interfere.

B. Mother is to daughter as father is to

A) uncle.

B) brother.

C) mother.

D) son.

Correct answer to example question A is (B), move. Correct answer to example question B is (D), son.

1. Which word does *not* belong with the others?
   (A) sundial
   (B) watch
   (C) time
   (D) clock

2. Which word does *not* belong with the others?
   (A) light
   (B) elated
   (C) gleeful
   (D) joyous

3. Red is to pink as black is to
   (A) beige.
   (B) white.
   (C) dark.
   (D) gray.

4. Ann reads faster than Sue. Karen reads faster than Ann. Karen reads more slowly than Sue. If the first two statements are true, the third is
   (A) true.
   (B) false.
   (C) uncertain.

5. Create most nearly means
   (A) destroy.
   (B) build.
   (C) discover.
   (D) invent.

6. Youth is to young as age is to
   (A) people.
   (B) parents.
   (C) grandmother.
   (D) old.

7. Which word does *not* belong with the others?
   (A) quality
   (B) honesty
   (C) sincerity
   (D) integrity

GO ON TO THE NEXT PAGE

8. Sand is to beach as black dirt is to
   (A) earth.
   (B) plants.
   (C) water.
   (D) farm.

9. Which word does *not* belong with the others?
   (A) day
   (B) time
   (C) month
   (D) hour

10. A salamander is a(n)
    (A) amphibian.
    (B) hammock.
    (C) spice.
    (D) fish.

11. Arrogant most nearly means
    (A) poised.
    (B) superior.
    (C) fragrant.
    (D) haughty.

12. Square is to circle as rectangle is to
    (A) round.
    (B) triangle.
    (C) oval.
    (D) cube.

13. One is to two as three is to
    (A) two.
    (B) five.
    (C) thirty.
    (D) six.

14. Which word does *not* belong with the others?
    (A) figure
    (B) number
    (C) add
    (D) letter

15. Paul is taller than Peter. Peter is shorter than John. Paul is taller than John. If the first two statements are true, the third is
    (A) true.
    (B) false.
    (C) uncertain.

16. A mellow peach is
    (A) ripe.
    (B) rotten.
    (C) yellow.
    (D) green.

17. Gossamer most nearly means
    (A) beautiful.
    (B) filmy.
    (C) eerie.
    (D) supernatural.

18. Coddle most nearly means
    (A) handle.
    (B) embrace.
    (C) pamper.
    (D) love.

19. Light is to lamp as heat is to
    (A) furnace.
    (B) light.
    (C) sun.
    (D) room.

20. Choir is to director as team is to
    (A) sport.
    (B) coach.
    (C) player.
    (D) athlete.

21. Diversify most nearly means
    (A) vary.
    (B) oppose.
    (C) change.
    (D) strengthen.

22. Harry is more intelligent than George. Sam is more intelligent than Ralph. Harry is more intelligent than Ralph. If the first two statements are true, the third is
    - (A) true.
    - (B) false.
    - (C) uncertain.

23. A superficial wound is
    - (A) serious.
    - (B) deep.
    - (C) facial.
    - (D) shallow.

24. A is north of B. B is north of C. C is south of A. If the first two statements are true, the third is
    - (A) true.
    - (B) false.
    - (C) uncertain.

25. A precocious child is
    - (A) precious.
    - (B) proper.
    - (C) tall.
    - (D) quick.

26. A sadistic remark is
    - (A) sad.
    - (B) silly.
    - (C) hurtful.
    - (D) sudden.

27. Which word does *not* belong with the others?
    - (A) college
    - (B) university
    - (C) school
    - (D) dormitory

28. Truncate most nearly means
    - (A) pack.
    - (B) cut.
    - (C) sound.
    - (D) transport.

29. A sallow face is
    - (A) ruddy.
    - (B) young.
    - (C) healthy.
    - (D) sickly.

30. An indigent person is
    - (A) delicate.
    - (B) intelligent.
    - (C) indignant.
    - (D) needy.

31. Table is to leg as automobile is to
    - (A) wheel.
    - (B) axle.
    - (C) door.
    - (D) fuel.

32. Which word does *not* belong with the others?
    - (A) dungeon
    - (B) residence
    - (C) dwelling
    - (D) domicile

33. All tumps are winged boscs. No blue boscs have wings. No tumps are blue. If the first two statements are true, the third is
    - (A) true.
    - (B) false.
    - (C) uncertain.

34. Which word does *not* belong with the others?
    - (A) prison
    - (B) jail
    - (C) reformatory
    - (D) punishment

35. Refuse means the *opposite* of
    - (A) reheat.
    - (B) accept.
    - (C) reveal.
    - (D) tidy.

GO ON TO THE NEXT PAGE

36. Ink is to pen as paint is to
    (A) canvas.
    (B) bucket.
    (C) wall.
    (D) brush.

37. Acquire means the *opposite* of
    (A) solo.
    (B) buy.
    (C) release.
    (D) collect.

38. River A is wider than River B. River B is narrower than River C. River A is wider than River C. If the first two statements are true, the third is
    (A) true.
    (B) false.
    (C) uncertain.

39. Scant means the *opposite* of
    (A) sparse.
    (B) scoundrel.
    (C) abundant.
    (D) straight.

40. Pinnacle means the *opposite* of
    (A) bridge.
    (B) base.
    (C) wall.
    (D) rummy.

41. Team is to captain as office is to
    (A) secretary.
    (B) accountant.
    (C) staff.
    (D) manager.

42. Which word does *not* belong with the others?
    (A) window
    (B) drape
    (C) shade
    (D) curtain

43. Corpulent means the *opposite* of
    (A) bulky.
    (B) singular.
    (C) company.
    (D) slender.

44. Naive means the *opposite* of
    (A) rural.
    (B) dull.
    (C) sophisticated.
    (D) funny.

45. Which word does *not* belong with the others?
    (A) fez
    (B) turban
    (C) glove
    (D) derby

46. Which word does *not* belong with the others?
    (A) gallery
    (B) audience
    (C) congregation
    (D) podium

47. Pledge most nearly means
    (A) promise.
    (B) beg.
    (C) join.
    (D) obey.

48. Depression is the *opposite* of
    (A) incline.
    (B) valley.
    (C) hill.
    (D) oppression.

49. Grapes cost more than apples but less than pineapples. Oranges cost more than apples but less than lemons. Apples cost the least of the fruits. If the first two statements are true, the third is
    (A) true.
    (B) false.
    (C) uncertain.

50. Which word does *not* belong with the others?
    (A) oak
    (B) elm
    (C) maple
    (D) fir

51. Diminish is the *opposite* of
    (A) trim.
    (B) augment.
    (C) decorate.
    (D) decrease.

52. Jay's batting average is better than Michael's. Michael's batting average is higher than Tom's. Jay's batting average is lower than Tom's. If the first two statements are true, the third is
    (A) true.
    (B) false.
    (C) uncertain.

53. Abandon is the *opposite* of
    (A) abdicate.
    (B) keep.
    (C) maintain.
    (D) encourage.

54. Which word does *not* belong with the others?
    (A) flexible
    (B) feasible
    (C) supple
    (D) malleable

55. A is northeast of B. C is southwest of D, but northwest of A. C is north of B. If the first two statements are true, the third is
    (A) true.
    (B) false.
    (C) uncertain.

56. Which word does *not* belong with the others?
    (A) leather
    (B) cotton
    (C) wool
    (D) fur

57. Which word does *not* belong with the others?
    (A) zipper
    (B) button
    (C) snap
    (D) seam

58. Dwindle most nearly means
    (A) shrink.
    (B) ooze.
    (C) leak.
    (D) spoil.

59. Which word does *not* belong with the others?
    (A) oxygen
    (B) water
    (C) helium
    (D) gold

60. Jon ran faster than Carl. Ron ran faster than George, but not as fast as Jon. Carl was the fastest runner. If the first two statements are true, the third is
    (A) true.
    (B) false.
    (C) uncertain.

STOP

END OF SECTION 1. IF YOU HAVE ANY TIME LEFT, GO OVER YOUR WORK IN THIS SECTION ONLY. DO NOT WORK IN ANY OTHER SECTION OF THE TEST.

QUANTITATIVE SKILLS

Time—30 minutes

Directions: Mark one answer—the answer you think is best—for each problem.

Example:

A. Look at this series: 1,3,5,7,9,.... What numeral should come next?

(A) 7

(B) 8

(C) 11

(D) 13

B. Examine (A), (B), and (C) and find the best answer.

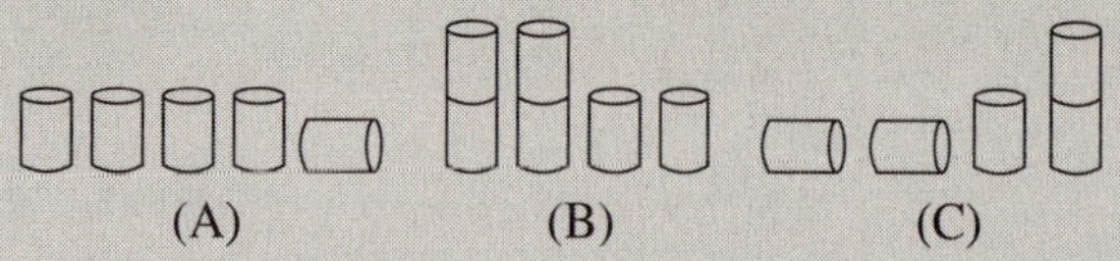

(A) **(B)** has more than **(A)** which has the same as **(C)**.

(B) **(A)**, **(B)**, and **(C)** are equal.

(C) **(A)** has less than **(C)** which is equal to **(B)**.

(D) **(B)** and **(C)** have the same.

C. What number added to 7 equals 6 times 3?

(A) 11

(B) 2

(C) 18

(D) 10

D. Examine (A), (B), and (C) and find the best answer.

(A) $(7 - 2) - 3$

(B) $(7 - 3) - 2$

(C) $7 - (3 - 2)$

(A) **(A)** is greater than **(C)**.

(B) **(A), (B)**, and **(C)** are equal.

(C) **(B)** is greater than **(C)**.

(D) **(A)** and **(B)** are equal.

The correct answer to example question A is (C), 11. The correct answer to example question B is (A). **(B)** has more than **(A)**, which has the same as **(C)**. The correct answer to example question C is (A), 11. The correct answer to example question D is (D). **(A)** and **(B)** are equal.

61. What number is 3 more than 20% of 40?
   (A) 11
   (B) 8
   (C) 5
   (D) 9

62. Look at this series: 32, 39, 46, 53,.... What number should come next?
   (A) 68
   (B) 61
   (C) 59
   (D) 60

63. Look at this series: 48, 39, 30, 21,.... What number should come next?
   (A) 17
   (B) 20
   (C) 29
   (D) 12

64. Examine (A), (B), and (C) and find the best answer.

(A) (B) (C)

   (A) **(A)** plus **(C)** is less than **(B)**.
   (B) **(C)** is equal to **(A)**.
   (C) **(A)** is greater than **(C)**.
   (D) **(C)** is less than **(B)** and greater than **(A)**.

65. Examine (A), (B), and (C) and find the best answer.

   (A) .625
   (B) $\frac{4}{7}$
   (C) $.297 \times 2.1$

   (A) **(B)** is less than **(A)** but greater than **(C)**.
   (B) **(A)** and **(C)** are equal and greater than **(B)**.
   (C) **(C)** is greater than **(A)** and **(B)**.
   (D) **(B)** is less than **(A)** and **(C)**.

66. What number is the cube of 5 divided by 5?
   (A) 15
   (B) 25
   (C) 75
   (D) 125

67. What number is $\frac{1}{2}$ of the average of 7, 18, 5, 39, 11?
   (A) 40
   (B) 5
   (C) 8
   (D) 20

68. Examine (A), (B), and (C) and find the best answer.

(A) (B) (C)

   (A) **(A)** is more shaded than **(B)**.
   (B) **(B)** and **(C)** are equally shaded.
   (C) **(C)** is less shaded than either **(A)** or **(B)**.
   (D) **(A)** and **(C)** are both less shaded than **(B)**.

69. Look at this series: 1, 4, 11, ____, 21, 24, 31,.... What number should fill the blank in the middle of the series?
   (A) 3
   (B) 14
   (C) 20
   (D) 22

70. Examine (A), (B), and (C) and find the best answer.

   (A) 10% of 80
   (B) 80% of 10
   (C) 10% of 80%

   (A) **(B)** is greater than **(A)** or **(C)**.
   (B) **(A)**, **(B)**, and **(C)** are equal.
   (C) **(A)** is equal to **(B)** and smaller than **(C)**.
   (D) **(A)** is greater than **(C)**.

GO ON TO THE NEXT PAGE

71. Look at this series: 1, 2, 4, 5, 10, 11,.... What number should come next?
   (A) 22
   (B) 12
   (C) 15
   (D) 21

72. Look at this series: 34, 40, 37, 36, 42, 39, 38,.... What three numbers should come next?
   (A) 44, 42, 41
   (B) 43, 40, 39
   (C) 44, 41, 40
   (D) 45, 42, 41

73. What number subtracted from 30 leaves 7 more than $\frac{3}{5}$ of 25?
   (A) 8
   (B) 15
   (C) 22
   (D) 23

74. What number is 5 more than $\frac{1}{3}$ of 18?
   (A) 6
   (B) 11
   (C) 1
   (D) 14

75. Examine (A), (B), and (C) and find the best answer.

   (A) $(8 \times 3) - 10$
   (B) $(5 \times 2) + 4$
   (C) $(4 \times 4) - 2$

   (A) **(C)** is greater than **(A)** and **(B)**.
   (B) **(A)** is greater than **(B)** and equal to **(C)**.
   (C) **(A)**, **(B)**, and **(C)** are equal.
   (D) **(B)** is greater than **(A)** and less than **(C)**.

76. Look at this series: 821, 812, 804, 797.... What number should come next?
   (A) 791
   (B) 788
   (C) 787
   (D) 790

77. Examine (A), (B), and (C) and find the best answer.

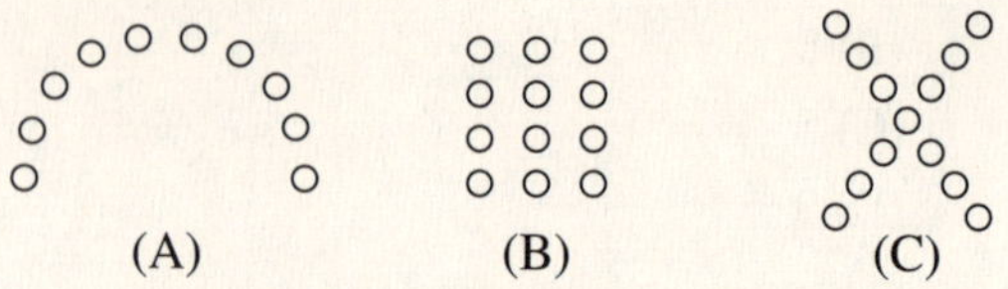

   (A) **(A)** has more circles than **(B)**.
   (B) **(B)** and **(C)** have the same number of circles.
   (C) **(B)** and **(C)** each have more circles than **(A)**.
   (D) **(A)** and **(C)** each have fewer circles than **(B)**.

78. Examine (A), (B), and (C) and find the best answer.

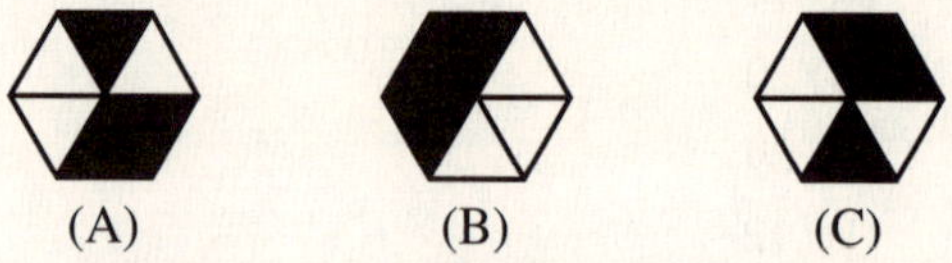

   (A) **(C)** is more shaded than **(B)**.
   (B) **(A)** and **(C)** are equally shaded and both are more shaded than **(B)**.
   (C) **(B)** is more shaded than **(A)** and less shaded than **(C)**.
   (D) **(A)**, **(B)**, and **(C)** are equally shaded.

79. Look at this series: 95, 99, ____, 107, 111. What number should fill the blank in the middle of the series?
   (A) 104
   (B) 98
   (C) 106
   (D) 103

80. What number divided by 4 is $\frac{1}{5}$ of 100?
   (A) 400
   (B) 20
   (C) 80
   (D) 200

81. Look at this series: 1, V, 6, X,.... What number should come next?
   (A) XV
   (B) 11
   (C) 10
   (D) IX

82. Examine (A), (B), and (C) and find the best answer.

(A) $\frac{1}{3}$ of 15

(B) $\frac{1}{4}$ of 16

(C) $\frac{1}{5}$ of 20

(A) **(A)** and **(B)** are each greater than **(C)**.

(B) **(A)**, **(B)**, and **(C)** are equal.

(C) **(C)** is greater than **(A)**.

(D) **(B)** and **(C)** are equal.

83. $\frac{1}{2}$ of what number is 7 times 3?

(A) 21

(B) 42

(C) 20

(D) 5

84. Examine (A), (B), and (C) and find the best answer.

(A) (B) (C)

(A) **(A)**, **(B)**, and **(C)** are equally shaded.

(B) **(B)** is less shaded than **(C)** and more shaded than **(A)**.

(C) **(A)** is more shaded than **(B)** or **(C)**.

(D) **(C)** is more shaded than **(A)**.

85. What number added to 6 is 3 times the product of 5 and 2?

(A) 16

(B) 4

(C) 30

(D) 24

86. Look at this series: 50, 48, 52, 50, 54, 52,.... What number should come next?

(A) 50

(B) 56

(C) 54

(D) 58

87. Examine (A), (B), and (C) and find the best answer.

(A) .4

(B) 4%

(C) $\frac{2}{5}$

(A) **(A)** is greater than **(C)**, which is greater than **(B)**.

(B) **(A)** is equal to **(C)** and greater than **(B)**.

(C) **(A)** is equal to **(B)** and greater than **(C)**.

(D) **(A)** is less than **(B)** and equal to **(C)**.

88. $\frac{3}{4}$ of what number is 6 times 4?

(A) 18

(B) 24

(C) 32

(D) 8

89. Look at this series: 12, 14, 28,___, 60,.... What number should fill the blank in this series?

(A) 19

(B) 16

(C) 40

(D) 30

90. Look at this series: 4, 5, 8, 11, 12, 15, 18, 19,.... What number should come next?

(A) 20

(B) 22

(C) 23

(D) 21

91. Examine the triangle and find the best answer.

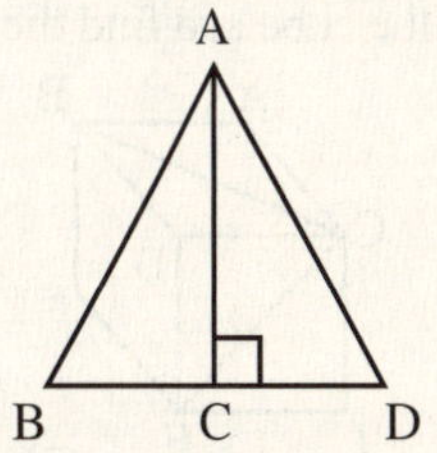

(A) AD is greater than CD.

(B) BA and AD are each less than BC.

(C) AB is equal to BC.

(D) AB is equal to AC plus BC.

GO ON TO THE NEXT PAGE

92. What number multiplied by 3 is 5 less than 29?

(A) 6

(B) 24

(C) 8

(D) 21

93. Look at this series: 23, 29, 32, 38, 41, __, 50,.... What number should fill the blank in this series?

(A) 42

(B) 47

(C) 44

(D) 51

94. Examine (A), (B), and (C) and find the best answer.

(A) $(10 \div 5) \times 10$

(B) $(5 \div 1) \times 4$

(C) $(20 \div 5) \times 5$

(A) **(A)** is equal to **(B)**, which is equal to **(C)**.

(B) **(A)** is equal to **(B)** and less than **(C)**.

(C) **(B)** is equal to **(C)** and less than **(A)**.

(D) **(C)** is greater than **(A)** and **(B)**.

95. Look at this series: 100, 101, 91, 92, 82,.... What two numbers should come next?

(A) 72, 74

(B) 72, 73

(C) 83, 73

(D) 84, 74

96. Examine the cube and find the best answer.

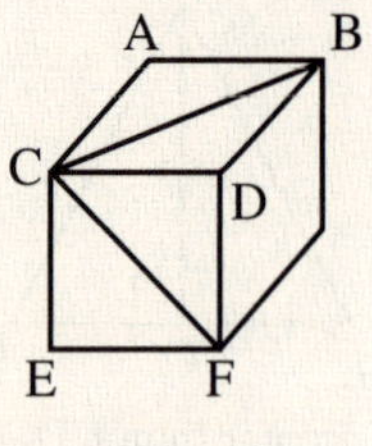

(A) CF is greater than CB.

(B) EF is less than AB.

(C) CB is equal to CE.

(D) CF is greater than AB.

97. What number divided by 2 leaves 4 more than 6?

(A) 5

(B) 10

(C) 20

(D) 4

98. Examine (A), (B), and (C) and find the best answer if both x and y are greater than zero.

(A) $5(x + y)$

(B) $5x + y$

(C) $5(x + y) + x$

(A) **(A)**, **(B)**, and **(C)** are equal.

(B) **(B)** is less than **(A)**, which is less than **(C)**.

(C) **(C)** is greater than **(A)** and less than **(B)**.

(D) **(A)** and **(B)** are equal.

99. Look at this series: 14, 28, 32, 64, 68, ... What number should come next?

(A) 136

(B) 138

(C) 72

(D) 76

100. What number subtracted from 7 leaves $\frac{1}{4}$ of 20?

(A) 13

(B) 5

(C) 12

(D) 2

101. Look at this series: A24, C28, E18, G22,.... What comes next?
   (A) H26
   (B) J14
   (C) H12
   (D) F20

102. Examine the graph and find the best answer.

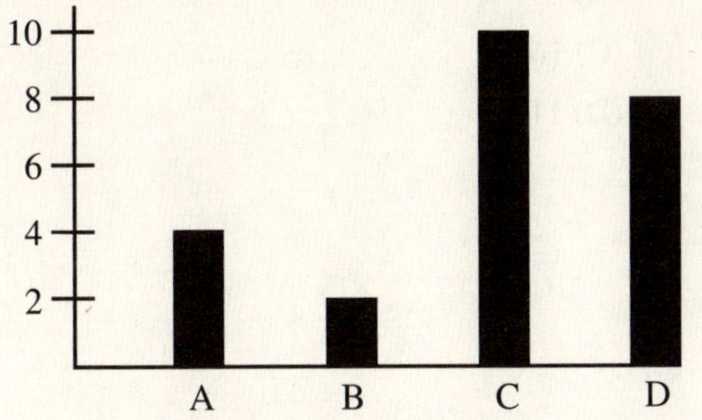

   (A) B plus C minus A equals D.
   (B) C minus A minus B equals D.
   (C) C plus D equals A plus B.
   (D) D minus B equals A plus C.

103. What number is 2 less than $\frac{3}{5}$ of 10?
   (A) 4
   (B) 8
   (C) 6
   (D) 2

104. Look at this series: 4, 16, 5, 25, 6,.... What number should come next?
   (A) 36
   (B) 30
   (C) 6
   (D) 20

105. Examine (A), (B), and (C) and find the best answer.

   (A) 5^2
   (B) 4^3
   (C) 2^4

   (A) A > B > C
   (B) B > A > C
   (C) A = B = C
   (D) B > A = C

106. Look at this series: 10, $7\frac{1}{2}$, 5, $2\frac{1}{2}$,.... What number should come next?
   (A) 1
   (B) $1\frac{1}{2}$
   (C) $\frac{1}{2}$
   (D) 0

107. What number is 8 times $\frac{1}{2}$ of 20?
   (A) 10
   (B) 80
   (C) 24
   (D) 28

108. Look at this series: 26, 30, 28, 27, 31, 29, 28,.... What three numbers should come next?
   (A) 32, 38, 24
   (B) 30, 28, 27
   (C) 32, 30, 29
   (D) 24, 26, 27

109. $\frac{1}{3}$ of what number added to 6 is 2 times 9?
   (A) 12
   (B) 36
   (C) 18
   (D) 3

GO ON TO THE NEXT PAGE

110. Examine the parallelogram and find the best answer.

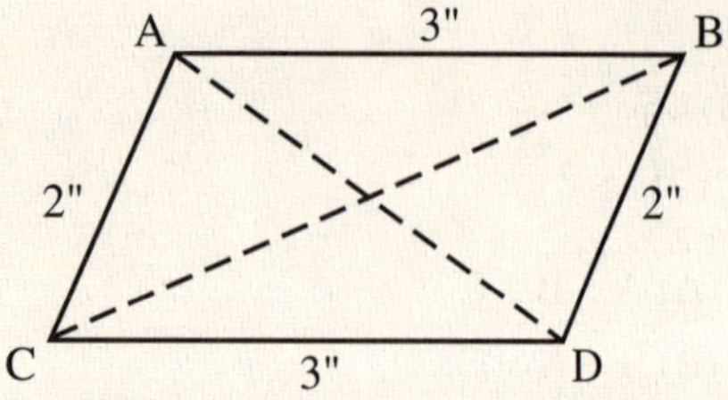

(A) The perimeter of the parallelogram is 10 inches.

(B) The area of the parallelogram is 5 square inches.

(C) The area of triangle ABD is greater than the area of triangle ACD.

(D) The perimeter of triangle BAC is equal to the perimeter of the parallelogram.

111. What number is 10 more than $\frac{4}{9}$ of 27?

(A) 37

(B) 12

(C) 2

(D) 22

112. What number is 7 less than 4 squared?

(A) 9

(B) 25

(C) 16

(D) 11

STOP

END OF SECTION 2. IF YOU HAVE ANY TIME LEFT, GO OVER YOUR WORK IN THIS SECTION ONLY. DO NOT WORK IN ANY OTHER SECTION OF THE TEST.

READING—COMPREHENSION

Time—25 minutes

Directions: Read each passage carefully. Then mark one answer—the answer you think is best—for each item.

Example:

The next test has short reading passages, each one followed by questions.

A. The reading passages on the next test will be

(A) all on one page.

(B) followed by questions.

(C) easy to read.

(D) very long.

The correct answer to example question A is (B), followed by questions.

Our planet Earth is divided into seven separate layers. The outer layer is called the crust and appears to be approximately twenty miles thick. Next in line are the four layers of the mantle. These layers <u>vary</u> in thickness from 250 to 1,000 miles. The <u>remaining</u> two layers are divided into the outer core and inner core. The thickness of the outer core has been determined to be slightly more than 1,200 miles, while that of the inner core is <u>slightly</u> less than 800 miles. Scientists calculate the location and depth of these layers by measuring and studying the speed and direction of earthquake waves. They have also determined that both temperature and pressure are much greater at the core than at the crust.

113. The thickest portion of the earth is the

(A) crust.

(B) outer core.

(C) mantle.

(D) inner core.

114. How many separate layers does the earth have?

(A) two

(B) twenty

(C) seven

(D) four

115. Which of the following is correct?

(A) No two sets of earthquake waves ever travel in the same direction.

(B) Earthquakes usually travel in the same direction.

(C) Earthquake waves travel at different speeds.

(D) Earthquake waves travel at the same speed but in different directions.

116. You would expect to find the kind of information in this passage in

(A) an encyclopedia.

(B) a science book.

(C) neither of these.

(D) both of these.

117. In going from the surface to the center of the earth, in which order would you pass through the layers?

(A) crust, outer core, mantle, inner core

(B) outer core, inner core, crust, mantle

(C) outer core, crust, inner core, mantle

(D) crust, mantle, outer core, inner core

GO ON TO THE NEXT PAGE

118. The word vary, as underlined and used in this passage, most nearly means
   (A) stabilize.
   (B) increase.
   (C) range.
   (D) arbitrate.

119. Which of the following is correct?
   (A) Scientists know the exact thickness of the crust.
   (B) Scientists believe they know the thickness of the crust.
   (C) The thickness of the crust cannot be determined.
   (D) Scientists cannot agree as to the thickness of the crust.

120. In comparing the core with the crust, you would find that at the core,
   (A) temperature and pressure are less.
   (B) pressure is greater, temperature is less.
   (C) temperature is greater, pressure is less.
   (D) temperature and pressure are greater.

121. The word slightly, as underlined and used in this passage, most nearly means
   (A) scarcely.
   (B) considerably.
   (C) a little.
   (D) at least.

122. The word remaining, as underlined and used in this passage, most nearly means
   (A) previous.
   (B) outer.
   (C) last.
   (D) prior.

The man is in utter darkness. Only the wavering beam of light from his flashlight pierces the blackness. The air, damp and cold, smells of dank, unseen, decaying material.

The man stumbles over stones, splashes into a hidden puddle. He bangs into a cold rocky wall. The flashlight cocks upward, and suddenly, the air is filled with the flutter of thousands of wings and the piping of tiny animal wails. He ducks, startled, then grins. He's found what he's looking for—bats!

For this man is a spelunker, another name for someone who explores caves for the fun of it. Spelunkers actually enjoy crawling on their stomachs in narrow, rocky tunnels far below the surface of the earth.

Spelunkers have discovered new caves. Some have formed clubs, sharing safety knowledge, developing new techniques, and teaching novices.

Spelunkers believe that earth's inner spaces are as exciting as the universe's outer spaces.

123. The first two paragraphs of this passage describe a cave's
   (A) rocks.
   (B) depth.
   (C) atmosphere.
   (D) streams.

124. The word wavering, as underlined and used in this passage, most nearly means
   (A) swaying.
   (B) steady.
   (C) strong.
   (D) shining.

125. The author of this passage is most likely a
   (A) spelunker.
   (B) cave scientist.
   (C) medical doctor.
   (D) magazine writer.

126. The cave the man was exploring was probably
   (A) large and dry.
   (B) deep underground.
   (C) near the surface.
   (D) dangerous.

127. According to this passage, what started the bats to suddenly fly about?
   (A) the spelunker
   (B) the damp and cold air
   (C) the flashlight
   (D) the sudden noise

128. The man ducked when the bats flew because he was

(A) angry.

(B) afraid.

(C) surprised.

(D) hurt.

129. The word utter, as underlined and used in this passage, most nearly means

(A) bovine.

(B) unspeakable.

(C) oppressive.

(D) great.

130. According to this passage, spelunkers ignore

(A) safety rules.

(B) light.

(C) discomfort.

(D) other spelunkers.

131. A good title for this passage would be

(A) "Batty About Bats."

(B) "Spelunkers—Underground Explorers."

(C) "Inner Space."

(D) "The Life of a Spelunker."

132. According to this passage, which word would most nearly describe spelunkers?

(A) experimental

(B) cautious

(C) antisocial

(D) adventurous

Litterbugs have a bad reputation, but the biggest litterbugs in history have, in fact, been very helpful to mankind.

For glaciers, in ancient times and today, are the greatest creators and distributors of litter. Of course, they don't drop tin cans, paper cups, and pop bottles; they dump rocks, boulders, sand, gravel, and mud all over the landscape, and it's this glacial debris that has helped create some of the world's most fertile farmland, such as that in America's Midwest.

Geologists describe glacial ice as true rock, different only in that it melts more easily than other rock. Because glacial ice is moving rock, it scrapes, bangs, and tears at the terrain over which it moves, breaking off chunks of all sizes. When the ice melts, the debris drops, and, if it is rich in minerals, creates fertile soil when it erodes.

It's too bad human litterbugs aren't as useful!

133. The richness of the soil in America's Midwest can be attributed, in part, to

(A) heavy annual rainfalls.

(B) scientific analysis.

(C) human litterbugs.

(D) ancient glacial debris.

134. Although the author of this passage describes glaciers as litterbugs, his attitude toward glaciers is one of

(A) love.

(B) gratitude.

(C) admiration.

(D) fear.

135. Which of the following is correct?

(A) Glacial ice is full of pop bottles.

(B) Glaciers are harmful.

(C) Glaciers erode the terrain.

(D) Glacial ice may be full of fertile soil.

136. According to this passage, history's biggest litterbugs are

(A) glaciers.

(B) people.

(C) rocks.

(D) bulldozers.

GO ON TO THE NEXT PAGE

137. The words most fertile, as underlined and used in this passage, most nearly mean
   (A) most icy.
   (B) flattest.
   (C) most rocky.
   (D) best growing.

138. Good soil contains
   (A) rocks.
   (B) minerals.
   (C) vitamins.
   (D) melted ice.

139. A good title for this passage might be
   (A) "A Lovely Litterbug."
   (B) "The Destructive Forces of Glaciers."
   (C) "Glaciers—Then and Now."
   (D) "The History of Glaciers."

140. This passage implies that the litter human beings drop is
   (A) useless.
   (B) ugly.
   (C) uninteresting.
   (D) unimportant.

141. The word terrain, as underlined and used in this passage, most nearly means
   (A) rock.
   (B) terror.
   (C) view.
   (D) land.

142. It could be said, on the basis of this passage, that glaciers change the
   (A) earth's atmosphere.
   (B) pollution rate.
   (C) mineral content of rocks.
   (D) earth's geography.

The superstition of witchcraft, which most people laugh at today, is still a matter of mystery and speculation.

Hundreds of thousands of people in Europe who were accused of being witches were executed during the Middle Ages and even as late as the early eighteenth century. Their deaths probably resulted from hysterical fears. Yet the judges undoubtedly were sincere in their desire to eliminate what they thought was a real danger. Some modern psychologists have theorized that so-called witches actually *were* dangerous. In essence, they say that a person who believes in the powers of witchcraft can be affected emotionally or physically—he may even die—because of a "witch's spell."

When Europeans immigrated to America, they brought their beliefs with them. There were a number of witchcraft trials in Massachusetts during the 1600s; however, after the execution of twenty Salem "witches" in 1692, prosecution for witchcraft didn't survive long in the New World.

Most people in the civilized world no longer believe in witchcraft. Nonetheless, the subject is fascinating for many people. As an example, the TV show "Bewitched" was a very popular program for more than five years.

143. This passage was probably printed in
   (A) a history book.
   (B) a magazine.
   (C) a psychology book.
   (D) an encyclopedia.

144. According to this passage, the mystery of witchcraft is
   (A) a major problem for psychologists.
   (B) of very little interest today.
   (C) still unsolved.
   (D) a major problem for sincere judges.

145. One of today's reminders of ancient witchcraft beliefs is
   (A) Halloween.
   (B) April Fools' Day.
   (C) the use of brooms.
   (D) the death penalty for certain crimes.

146. Which group can we be sure has had members who believed in witchcraft?
   (A) judges
   (B) TV producers
   (C) psychologists
   (D) newspaper reporters

147. This passage calls witchcraft a "superstition." Which of these would also be a superstition?
   (A) "Many hands make light work."
   (B) "Breaking a mirror brings bad luck."
   (C) "Eating sweets causes pimples."
   (D) "Great oaks from little acorns grow."

148. According to some psychologists, persons who *do* believe in witchcraft
   (A) can be harmed by it.
   (B) tend to laugh at it today.
   (C) are crazy.
   (D) tend to be dangerous.

149. The phrase In essence, as underlined and used in this passage, most nearly means
   (A) probably.
   (B) basically.
   (C) briefly.
   (D) finally.

150. The word fascinating, as underlined and used in this passage, most nearly means
   (A) frightening.
   (B) enjoyable.
   (C) frustrating.
   (D) interesting.

151. This passage suggests that what you believe
   (A) can hurt you.
   (B) should be based on facts.
   (C) does not affect you.
   (D) changes as you grow older.

152. A good title for this passage might be
   (A) "Witchcraft—Fact or Fiction?"
   (B) "The End of Witchcraft."
   (C) "Witchcraft in the New World."
   (D) "The Powers of Witchcraft."

READING—VOCABULARY

Directions: Choose the word that means the same or about the same as the underlined word.

153. a new perspective
   (A) receptacle
   (B) sight
   (C) picture
   (D) view

154. impair his vision
   (A) test
   (B) weaken
   (C) improve
   (D) destroy

155. the smallest hovel
   (A) hut
   (B) shovel
   (C) house
   (D) palace

156. to loathe
   (A) hate
   (B) love
   (C) help
   (D) lose

GO ON TO THE NEXT PAGE

157. to reproach
(A) approach
(B) praise
(C) blame
(D) steal

158. to be elated
(A) happy
(B) akin
(C) moved
(D) upset

159. his brusque manner
(A) foreign
(B) subtle
(C) soft
(D) abrupt

160. depress the key
(A) put away
(B) insert
(C) turn
(D) push down

161. quench your thirst
(A) end
(B) increase
(C) continue
(D) decrease

162. a famous exploit
(A) crime
(B) deed
(C) reputation
(D) journey

163. a deft move
(A) skillful
(B) dangerous
(C) thoughtless
(D) final

164. an interesting chronicle
(A) fairy tale
(B) record
(C) time
(D) item

165. that amiable soul
(A) casual
(B) honest
(C) fine
(D) likable

166. her astute mind
(A) shrewd
(B) careful
(C) stupid
(D) astounding

167. to sever contact
(A) cut
(B) maintain
(C) seek
(D) establish

168. the eminent man
(A) wicked
(B) destitute
(C) ancient
(D) outstanding

169. to terminate a contract
(A) end
(B) enter
(C) make
(D) determine

170. to hinder someone
(A) assist
(B) follow
(C) impede
(D) slight

171. a spirit of <u>contention</u>

(A) debate

(B) content

(C) inquiry

(D) calm

172. to <u>concede</u> defeat

(A) suspect

(B) admit

(C) realize

(D) refuse

173. to <u>forego</u> his rights

(A) usurp

(B) insure

(C) insist on

(D) give up

174. your <u>canny</u> guess

(A) uncertain

(B) mistaken

(C) clever

(D) insincere

STOP

END OF SECTION 3. IF YOU HAVE ANY TIME LEFT, GO OVER YOUR WORK IN THIS SECTION ONLY. DO NOT WORK IN ANY OTHER SECTION OF THE TEST.

MATHEMATICS—CONCEPTS

Time—45 minutes

Directions: Mark one answer—the answer you think is best—for each problem. You may use scratch paper when working these problems.

Example:

A. The number fifty-three is also written

(A) 43

(B) 53

(C) 52

(D) 63

The correct answer to example question A is (B), 53.

175. Which of the following is *not* a quadrilateral?

(A) square

(B) trapezoid

(C) triangle

(D) rectangle

176. $\{1, 3, 8, 10\} \cap \{2, 3, 8\} =$

(A) $\{1, 2\}$

(B) $\{1, 2, 3, 8, 10\}$

(C) $\{3, 8\}$

(D) $\{\ \}$

177. To the nearest tenth, 63.594 is written

(A) 63.6

(B) 64

(C) 63.59

(D) 64.5

178. Simplify: $3(-2)^3 =$

(A) –216

(B) –18

(C) 1

(D) –24

179. As a fraction, .24 is

(A) $\frac{24}{1000}$

(B) $\frac{6}{25}$

(C) $\frac{1}{4}$

(D) $\frac{100}{24}$

180. The measure of angle A is

(A) 15°

(B) 20°

(C) 25°

(D) 35°

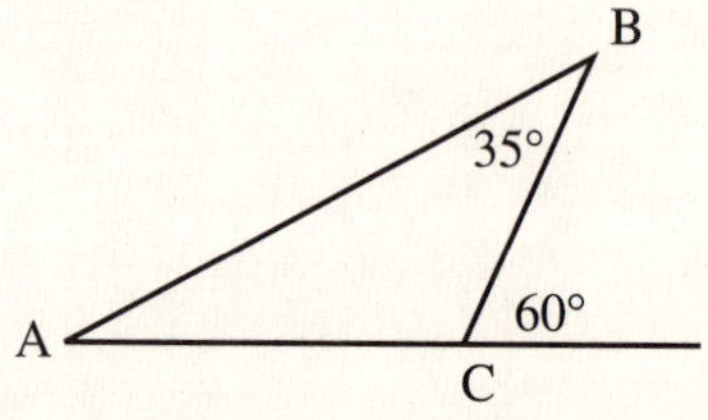

181. To multiply a number by 100, move the decimal point

(A) one place to the right.

(B) two places to the left.

(C) three places to the right.

(D) two places to the right.

182. Which of the following is a pair of reciprocals?

(A) (3, –3)

(B) $(3\frac{1}{3}, \frac{3}{10})$

(C) $(2^3, 3^2)$

(D) (0, 1)

183. The circumference of this circle is

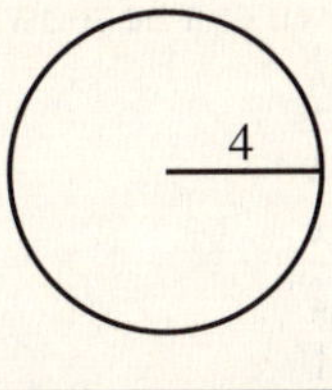

(A) 32π
(B) 16π
(C) 8π
(D) 4π

184. The ratio of 3 yards to 18 inches is
(A) 3 to 18
(B) 1 to 6
(C) 3 to 2
(D) 6 to 1

185. How many integers are between $\frac{33}{7}$ and 8.001?
(A) 3
(B) 6
(C) 5
(D) 4

186. Which of the following is true?
(A) $a \div (b + c) = \frac{a}{b} + \frac{a}{c}$
(B) $a(x + b) = ax + b$
(C) $a(x + b) = a(x) + a(b)$
(D) $a \div b = b(\frac{1}{a})$

187. The square root of 198 is between
(A) 19 and 20
(B) 98 and 100
(C) 90 and 100
(D) 14 and 15

188. In a base-five system of numeration, what are the next three counting numbers after $43_{(5)}$?
(A) $44_{(5)}$, $45_{(5)}$, $50_{(5)}$
(B) $44_{(5)}$, $45_{(5)}$, $46_{(5)}$
(C) $44_{(5)}$, $50_{(5)}$, $52_{(5)}$
(D) $44_{(5)}$, $100_{(5)}$, $101_{(5)}$

189. Which of these is a correctly written scientific notation?
(A) $.038 = 3.8 \times (\frac{1}{10})^2$
(B) $380 = 3.8 \times 10^3$
(C) $.38 = 3.8 \times (\frac{1}{10})^2$
(D) $3800 = 3.8 \times 10^2$

190. Which fraction shows the greatest value?
(A) $\frac{5}{9}$
(B) $\frac{2}{3}$
(C) $\frac{6}{7}$
(D) $\frac{7}{8}$

191. Which of the following is true?
(A) $8 \leq 6$
(B) $6 \geq 6$
(C) $.080 > .08$
(D) $15 < 8$

192. ΔABC is similar to ΔDBE. The length of $\overline{AB}$ is

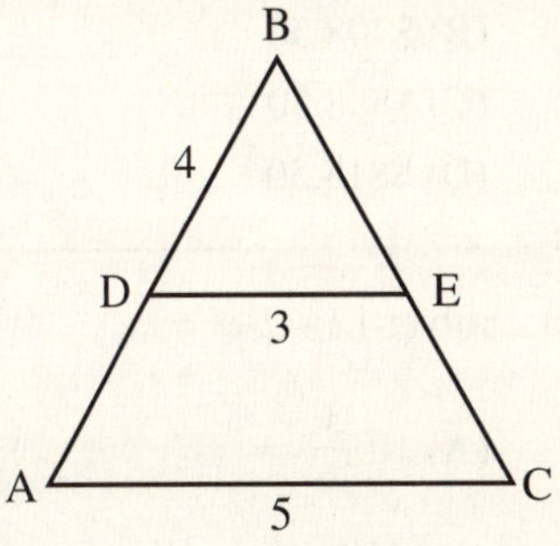

(A) $8\frac{1}{3}$
(B) $6\frac{1}{3}$
(C) $6\frac{2}{3}$
(D) $8\frac{2}{3}$

193. It is possible to have a right triangle that is also
(A) equilateral
(B) equiangular
(C) obtuse
(D) isosceles

GO ON TO THE NEXT PAGE

194. Which one of the following is *not* equal to $62\frac{1}{2}\%$?

(A) $\frac{10}{16}$

(B) $\frac{5}{8}$

(C) .625

(D) 62.5

195. The prime factorization of 12 is

(A) 2 • 2 • 3

(B) 4 + 8

(C) 6 • 2

(D) 4 • 3

196. The least common multiple of 2 and 6 is

(A) 6

(B) 12

(C) 3

(D) 2

197. If Bill can mow a lawn in x hours, what part of the lawn can he mow in 2 hours?

(A) $\frac{2}{x}$

(B) $\frac{x}{2}$

(C) $\frac{1}{2}$

(D) $\frac{1}{x}$

198. The associative property of addition states that

(A) $\frac{2}{3}+(\frac{1}{4}+\frac{1}{2})=\frac{2}{3}+(\frac{1}{2}+\frac{1}{4})$

(B) $(\frac{2}{3}+\frac{1}{2})+\frac{1}{4}=\frac{2}{3}+(\frac{1}{2}+\frac{1}{4})$

(C) $\frac{2}{3}(\frac{1}{4}+\frac{1}{2})=\frac{2}{3}(\frac{1}{4})+\frac{2}{3}(\frac{1}{2})$

(D) $\frac{2}{3}+\frac{1}{2}=\frac{2}{3}+\frac{1}{2}$

MATHEMATICS—PROBLEM-SOLVING

199. A movie theater sold 130 student tickets at $1.25 each and 340 adult tickets at $1.90 each. How much was collected?

(A) $798.50

(B) $708.50

(C) $808.50

(D) $818.50

200. Solve: $12-2\frac{3}{16}=$

(A) $10\frac{3}{16}$

(B) $9\frac{13}{16}$

(C) $10\frac{13}{16}$

(D) $9\frac{3}{16}$

201. Mr. Allen paid $54.24 for his telephone bills last year. How much did he pay, on the average, per month?

(A) $4.62 (C) $5.52

(B) $5.42 (D) $4.52

202. Bob has ten dollars less than four times the amount Tim has. If Bob has $88, how much does Tim have?

(A) $48

(B) $22

(C) $16

(D) $24.50

203. Solve: $6+(-12)+7+(-3)=$

(A) –2

(B) 2

(C) 28

(D) –8

204. The formula $F=\frac{9}{5}C+32$ converts temperature from Centigrade to Fahrenheit. What is the Fahrenheit temperature for 85° Centigrade?

(A) 153°

(B) 185°

(C) 175°

(D) 130°

205. If the 5% sales tax on a snowmobile was $42, what was the price of the snowmobile not including the tax?

(A) $840

(B) $210

(C) $820

(D) $640

206. Solve: $4\frac{1}{8} - 2\frac{2}{3} =$

(A) $2\frac{13}{24}$

(B) $2\frac{11}{24}$

(C) $1\frac{13}{24}$

(D) $1\frac{11}{24}$

207. If $-5 + 4x = 21$, $x =$

(A) 6.5

(B) 4

(C) 8.5

(D) 5.75

208. Solve: $3\frac{1}{3} \times 3\frac{3}{4} \times \frac{2}{5} =$

(A) $9\frac{1}{4}$

(B) 6

(C) 5

(D) $6\frac{2}{5}$

209. Mr. Symon paid $58.50 interest on a loan which had a 6% simple interest rate. How much did he borrow?

(A) $975

(B) $351

(C) $898

(D) $410

210. If a flagpole has a shadow 56 feet long when a 6-foot man's shadow is 14 feet long, what is the height of the flagpole?

(A) 24 feet

(B) 28 feet

(C) 20 feet

(D) 32 feet

211. If the perimeter of a rectangular region is 50 units, and the length of one side is 7 units, what is the area of the rectangular region?

(A) 291 square units

(B) 301 square units

(C) 126 square units

(D) 226 square units

212. If $4(3x - 2) = 16$, $x =$

(A) 1.5

(B) –2

(C) 2

(D) –1.5

213. If 18 is added to an integer, and the result is $\frac{5}{4}$ of the integer, what is the integer?

(A) 72

(B) 36

(C) 24

(D) –18

214. If $A = 6$ and $B = 3$, then $7A - 3B =$

(A) 7

(B) 5

(C) 36

(D) 33

215. Four years ago, Jim's father was 5 times as old as Jim. How old is Jim's father now if Jim is 12?

(A) 56

(B) 44

(C) 40

(D) 36

216. Solve: $2\frac{1}{2} + 7\frac{2}{3} + \frac{3}{4} =$

(A) $9\frac{1}{4}$

(B) $11\frac{1}{2}$

(C) $10\frac{11}{12}$

(D) $10\frac{1}{4}$

GO ON TO THE NEXT PAGE

217. If $N\%$ of 60 is 24, $N =$
(A) 40
(B) 25
(C) 125
(D) 150

218. If $10x - 3 = 2x + 4$, then x equals
(A) $\frac{9}{8}$
(B) $\frac{7}{8}$
(C) $\frac{8}{7}$
(D) $\frac{6}{7}$

219. The ratio of $\frac{3}{4}$ to $\frac{5}{2}$ is
(A) 10 to 3
(B) 15 to 8
(C) 3 to 10
(D) 8 to 15

220. What will a 9 ft. by 15 ft. rectangular rug cost at $5.00 a square yard?
(A) $75
(B) $60
(C) $675
(D) $225

221. Solve: $6.41\overline{)3.6537}$
(A) 67
(B) 57
(C) .57
(D) .67

222. What is the volume of this rectangular solid?
(A) 90 cu. in.
(B) 160 cu. in.
(C) 140 cu. in.
(D) 180 cu. in.

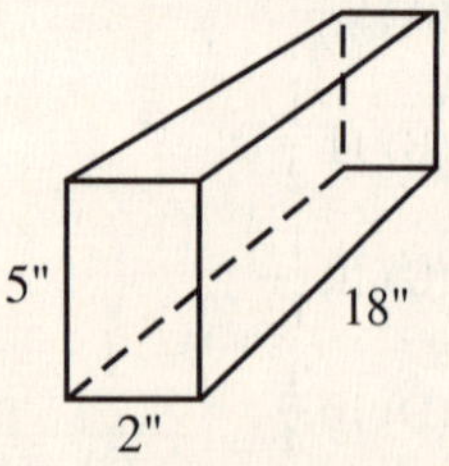

223. If $A = 3$, $B = 2$, and $C = 6$, then $\frac{3ABC}{2A} =$
(A) 18
(B) 24
(C) $4\frac{1}{2}$
(D) $4\frac{1}{6}$

224. Simplify: $\frac{5\frac{2}{3}}{2\frac{5}{6}}$
(A) $2\frac{1}{2}$
(B) $\frac{1}{2}$
(C) 2
(D) $1\frac{1}{3}$

225. If $\frac{5}{6}x = 30$, then $x =$
(A) 42
(B) 25
(C) 20
(D) 36

226. Solve: $65.14 \times .093$
(A) 6.05802
(B) 60.5802
(C) 605.602
(D) 6.05602

227. {26.80, 26.86, 26.92, 26.98, __} What number should come next in this set?
(A) 27.04
(B) 27.02
(C) 26.02
(D) 26.04

228. Solve: 72.528×109
(A) 1,377,032
(B) 7,805,452
(C) 1,378,032
(D) 7,905,552

229. The product of 11 and 12 is 3 more than N. What is N?

(A) 135

(B) 129

(C) 132

(D) 126

230. How many boards $1\frac{1}{3}$ feet long can be cut from a board $9\frac{1}{2}$ feet long?

(A) 9

(B) 6

(C) 7

(D) 8

231. Solve for x: $3x + 3 < 9 + x$

(A) $x = 6$

(B) $x > 3$

(C) $x < 3$

(D) $x > 6$

232. Solve: .602 + 4.2 + 5.03 =

(A) 11.47

(B) 9.802

(C) 9.832

(D) 10.441

233. Solve for x: $2.5x + 12.5 = 30$

(A) 7

(B) 9

(C) 17

(D) 70

234. Solve: $28\overline{)54,900}$

(A) 1,960 R20

(B) 1,858 R20

(C) 1,642 R12

(D) 1,868 R16

235. Solve: If $\sqrt{x+36} = 10$, then $x =$

(A) 8

(B) 64

(C) –16

(D) –4

236. Add in base 5: $143_{(5)}$
$+ 33_{(5)}$

(A) $131_{(5)}$

(B) $221_{(5)}$

(C) $231_{(5)}$

(D) $211_{(5)}$

237. Solve for x: $(\frac{2}{3} + \frac{1}{5}) - (\frac{1}{4} + \frac{1}{2}) = x$

(A) $\frac{13}{30}$

(B) $\frac{7}{60}$

(C) $\frac{51}{60}$

(D) $\frac{37}{60}$

238. If the tax rate is \$3.62 per \$100, how much tax must be paid on a home assessed at \$25,000?

(A) \$90.50

(B) \$80.50

(C) \$805

(D) \$905

STOP

END OF SECTION 4. IF YOU HAVE ANY TIME LEFT, GO OVER YOUR WORK IN THIS SECTION ONLY. DO NOT WORK IN ANY OTHER SECTION OF THE TEST.

LANGUAGE

Time—25 minutes

Examples:

Look for errors in capitalization, punctuation, usage, or spelling. Mark your answer sheet for the letter of the sentence that contains the error; if you find no error, mark (D) on your answer sheet.

A. (A) Sally was talking to her brother.
(B) Mother and i went to the store.
(C) We will get food for the picnic.
(D) No mistakes.

B. (A) Look up that word in the dictionary.
(B) Who discovered Florida?
(C) The potery was made by Indians.
(D) No mistakes.

The correct answer to example question A is (B), Mother and i went to the store. The correct answer to example question B is (C), The potery was made by Indians.

Directions: In questions 239–278, look for errors in capitalization, punctuation, or usage. If you find no mistake, mark (D) on your answer sheet.

239. (A) Jeff asked,"What color is the Easter bunny?"
(B) Steve won the annual polka contest.
(C) The letter was mailed on Memorial Day.
(D) No mistakes.

240. (A) Are you coming to my birthday party?
(B) The first snow fell on Sunday October 27.
(C) Jack's father drove us to the movies.
(D) No mistakes.

241. (A) We will be vacationing in sunny Italy.
(B) Dave will arrive at Kennedy international airport.
(C) We decided to have Charlie read the report.
(D) No mistakes.

242. (A) Jane's giving a report on <u>Born Free</u>.
(B) She fell down and broke her glasses.
(C) Ted said: "Did you see George's chess set?"
(D) No mistakes.

243. (A) Please wait for me after school.
(B) Mother, can I go to the movies?
(C) Bob and his brother will meet the train.
(D) No mistakes.

244. (A) The coach gave instructions to each of the girls on the team.
(B) Just forward the mail to Dan and me.
(C) Will all of us travel on one bus?
(D) No mistakes.

245. (A) Where in the world did you leave your gloves?
(B) The dog licked its chops after the meal.
(C) "Oh, that's terrible!" Sally cried.
(D) No mistakes.

246. (A) Detroit is the center of the automobile industry.
(B) Governor Jones was an officer in the Navy.
(C) Their making a terrible mistake.
(D) No mistakes.

247. (A) How is your cold?
(B) The rabbit got sick and died.
(C) Who's book is this?
(D) No mistakes.

248. (A) That is a pretty dress, isn't it, Sheila?
(B) How old is your pet, Alfie?
(C) Why are you so tired?
(D) No mistakes.

249. (A) How long has the train been gone?
(B) "Well," Jay said, let's get going."
(C) Jack's uncle is a fireman.
(D) No mistakes.

250. (A) Don told us where he'd bought his coat.
(B) What's your name, little girl?
(C) Yellowstone is run by the National Park Service.
(D) No mistakes.

251. (A) How are you, Jim?
(B) I'm fine, thank you.
(C) Did you notice that John left early?
(D) No mistakes.

252. (A) The teacher asked the child to bring the book home.
(B) Spring will begin at noon today.
(C) Let's share the candy with the whole group.
(D) No mistakes.

253. (A) Will, you're parents are very nice.
(B) Ted's family is buying a boat.
(C) My father is a textbook publisher.
(D) No mistakes.

254. (A) It was the most beautiful sight I've ever saw.
(B) Ed's aunt and uncle lived in the South for many years.
(C) Mattie is the older of the two.
(D) No mistakes.

255. (A) What is the matter with Sam's leg?
(B) The first show is at 2:30, isn't it'?
(C) How much is your plane ticket?
(D) No mistakes.

256. (A) The award was given jointly to Dierdre and I.
(B) John asked if he might go home early.
(C) Cats and dogs sometimes play well together.
(D) No mistakes.

257. (A) Have you seen Marie's new coat?
(B) Sue said, "I'm taking dancing lessons this year."
(C) People lay down when they are tired.
(D) No mistakes.

258. (A) Anne said. "we really should go now."
(B) You can always say Sam eats well—and often!
(C) I told them my study hall was second period.
(D) No mistakes.

259. (A) The boy threw his shoe in anger.
(B) I laid in bed all night without sleeping.
(C) Keep this as a secret between you and me.
(D) No mistakes.

260. (A) The Boy Scouts are meeting at Jim's tomorrow.
(B) Dr. Bell spoke at Northwestern University last night.
(C) Jack exclaimed, "Where is my present"?
(D) No mistakes.

GO ON TO THE NEXT PAGE

261. (A) She and I consider ourselves to be best friends.
(B) Do you know which of the spellings of too means also?
(C) There is a narrow path beside the railroad track.
(D) No mistakes,

262. (A) We would have called you if we'd known.
(B) May I open my eyes now?
(C) My brother-in-law lives in Butte, Montana.
(D) No mistakes.

263. (A) Actually, ice hockey is exciting to watch.
(B) Janet plays guitar almost as well as Tom.
(C) Does Dave like to talk to Debby Ann?
(D) No mistakes.

264. (A) Ken will graduate from Stanford this June.
(B) Jack is learning Kay to draw.
(C) Before we knew it, the class was over.
(D) No mistakes.

265. (A) When will you know what the assignment is?
(B) You should of seen the crowd at Paul's yesterday.
(C) Joe will be stationed at Fort Benning, Georgia.
(D) No mistakes.

266. (A) Dad's going fishing in Canada next week.
(B) Barb didn't know whether to laugh or to cry.
(C) Mom put to much baking powder in the cake.
(D) No mistakes,

267. (A) We have already sold too many tickets.
(B) If I knew the answer, I would be rich now.
(C) The artist works less hours than the carpenter.
(D) No mistakes.

268. (A) The tiny kitten sat licking it's wounds.
(B) If you wish, we will have chicken for dinner.
(C) It is so cloudy that we cannot see the Milky Way tonight.
(D) No mistakes.

269. (A) Everyone must sign their name on the register.
(B) I am all ready, but the taxi is not here yet.
(C) I do not believe that I have only two choices.
(D) No mistakes.

270. (A) If you don't know the answer, don't raise your hand.
(B) The baby is playing in its crib.
(C) Jeff is the taller of my three sons.
(D) No mistakes.

271. (A) Neither Lisa nor Liz has made the Honor Roll.
(B) I have much more free time than you.
(C) Everyone wants to have his own way.
(D) No mistakes.

272. (A) When he said that, everyone applauded.
(B) He was much more interesting than I thought he'd be.
(C) Helen asked Molly and I to come to her party.
(D) No mistakes.

273. (A) The sun set at 5:15 this afternoon.
(B) Mary set the table for dinner yesterday.
(C) Please set those books over there, Jim.
(D) No mistakes.

274. (A) The horse ran swiftly and won the race.
(B) I feel badly that I cannot attend your wedding.
(C) Most birds and some people fly south for the winter.
(D) No mistakes.

275. (A) This kind of movie may frighten small children.
(B) I'm glad to hear that you're planning to go to college.
(C) Myself has bought a new dress for the party.
(D) No mistakes.

276. (A) How many eggs did you use in this cake?
(B) I can't hardly wait for the school year to be over.
(C) Neither Shawn nor Sylvia has to work for her spending money.
(D) No mistakes.

277. (A) The childrens' boots got mixed up in the coatroom.
(B) Sheila is trying out for the marching band today.
(C) My sisters and I all went to camp last summer.
(D) No mistakes.

278. (A) I'll let you know if my parents can pick us up.
(B) Our whole class sent get-well cards to Hilda.
(C) Harry said he hadn't done nothing wrong.
(D) No mistakes.

Directions: For questions 279–288, look for mistakes in spelling only.

279. (A) Clarence Darrow was a distinguished trial lawyer.
(B) Apparantly Suzy couldn't find her umbrella.
(C) Alice will be married next Wednesday.
(D) No mistakes.

280. (A) Are you sure you can complete the assignment on time?
(B) The entire crew worked very efficently.
(C) Mary went to the library yesterday.
(D) No mistakes.

281. (A) It occured to me that I should write home.
(B) "What a dreadful comparison," Ida remarked.
(C) Bob's temperature was back to normal yesterday.
(D) No mistakes.

282. (A) Mary Lou is eligible for the committee.
(B) Discussion and argument are not the same thing.
(C) The chemist analized the solution in his laboratory.
(D) No mistakes.

283. (A) My brother's going out for athletics next year.
(B) "This is a small token of my esteem," he told his teacher.
(C) Mary dropped her handkerchief in the corridor.
(D) No mistakes.

284. (A) The general spoke of a possible winter offensive.
(B) Ted finally succeded in solving the puzzle.
(C) Thomas Alva Edison was a brilliant inventor.
(D) No mistakes.

285. (A) The schedule is posted on the bulletin board in the hall.
(B) Don discribed the play with sweeping gestures.
(C) Occasionally our class runs over into the next period.
(D) No mistakes.

GO ON TO THE NEXT PAGE

286. (A) Pete perfers to sit by the door.
(B) Joy has a very agreeable personality.
(C) We struggle with ourselves to overcome our faults.
(D) No mistakes.

287. (A) Did you hear the announcement about the picnic?
(B) While the initial cost is high, maintenance is low.
(C) Jan's coat is similar to mine.
(D) No mistakes.

288. (A) Al said it was not neccessary to read all of the plays.
(B) It's disappointing to have missed the picture.
(C) The original order was difficult to decipher.
(D) No mistakes.

Directions: For questions 289–298, look for errors in composition. Follow the directions for each question.

289. Choose the best word or words to join the thoughts together.

I left my books at school; ________ I won't be able to do my homework.

(A) therefore,
(B) nevertheless,
(C) however,
(D) None of these.

290. Choose the best word or words to join the thoughts together.

That area is experiencing great economic hardship; ________ its unemployment rate is very high.

(A) for example,
(B) in contrast,
(C) suprisingly,
(D) None of these.

291. Choose the group of words that best completes this sentence.

After a hard day at work, ____________

(A) sleep was something Mary did very well.
(B) Mary slept very well.
(C) Mary slept well afterwards.
(D) sleeping was what Mary did.

292. Which of these expresses the idea most clearly?
(A) Tom, every morning at breakfast, the paper he liked to read.
(B) At breakfast every morning it was the paper that Tom liked to read.
(C) At breakfast, reading the paper was what Tom liked to do every morning.
(D) Tom liked to read the paper every morning at breakfast.

293. Which of these expresses the idea most clearly?
(A) In order to hear her favorite musician perform, 50 miles it was that she drove.
(B) She drove 50 miles in order to hear her favorite musician perform.
(C) She drove, in order to hear her favorite musician perform, 50 miles.
(D) Her favorite musician performed, and she drove 50 miles in order to hear him perform.

294. Which of these best fits under the topic "History of the Automobile"?
(A) Cars require a great deal of attention and care in order to prevent problems from developing.
(B) The legal driving age varies from one state to another.
(C) The invention of the automobile cannot be credited to any one person.
(D) None of these.

295. Which of these expresses the idea most clearly?

(A) Kim liked the skateboard with the nylon wheels which his father had built.

(B) Kim liked the new skateboard his father had built with the nylon wheels.

(C) The skateboard with the nylon wheels which his father had built new Kim liked.

(D) His father had built a new skateboard which Kim liked with nylon wheels.

296. Which sentence does *not* belong in the paragraph?

(1) Everyone in the class was looking forward to the Halloween party. (2) Five students had difficulty with their math homework from the previous day. (3) Each student had prepared a snack to bring. (4) The costumes included four ghosts, five space creatures, and two pumpkins.

(A) sentence 1

(B) sentence 2

(C) sentence 3

(D) sentence 4

297. Which topic is best for a one-paragraph theme?

(A) How to Open Your Own Business

(B) Child Psychology

(C) The Geography of Asia and Africa

(D) None of these

298. Where should the sentence, "The government has set up laws restricting or forbidding the hunting of certain animals," be placed in the paragraph below?

(1) Many animal species are now becoming or have recently become extinct. (2) Both government and private efforts are being made to protect those species currently in danger. (3) It has also attempted to educate the public about the problem.

(A) between sentences 1 and 2

(B) between sentences 2 and 3

(C) after sentence 3

(D) The sentence does not fit in this paragraph.

STOP

END OF SECTION 5. IF YOU HAVE ANY TIME LEFT, GO OVER YOUR WORK IN THIS SECTION ONLY. DO NOT WORK IN ANY OTHER SECTION OF THE TEST.

ANSWERS TO FIRST MODEL HSPT EXAM

Answer Key

VERBAL SKILLS

1. C	13. D	25. D	37. C	49. A
2. A	14. C	26. C	38. C	50. D
3. D	15. C	27. D	39. C	51. B
4. B	16. A	28. B	40. B	52. B
5. D	17. B	29. D	41. D	53. B
6. D	18. C	30. D	42. A	54. B
7. A	19. A	31. A	43. D	55. A
8. D	20. B	32. A	44. C	56. B
9. B	21. A	33. A	45. C	57. D
10. A	22. C	34. D	46. D	58. A
11. D	23. D	35. B	47. A	59. B
12. C	24. A	36. D	48. C	60. B

QUANTITATIVE SKILLS

61. A	72. C	83. B	94. A	105. B
62. D	73. A	84. A	95. C	106. D
63. D	74. B	85. D	96. D	107. B
64. C	75. C	86. B	97. C	108. C
65. D	76. A	87. B	98. B	109. B
66. B	77. C	88. C	99. A	110. A
67. C	78. D	89. D	100. D	111. D
68. D	79. D	90. B	101. C	112. A
69. B	80. C	91. A	102. A	
70. D	81. B	92. C	103. A	
71. A	82. D	93. B	104. A	

READING—COMPREHENSION

113. B	121. C	129. D	137. D	145. A
114. C	122. C	130. C	138. B	146. A
115. C	123. C	131. B	139. A	147. B
116. D	124. A	132. D	140. A	148. A
117. D	125. D	133. D	141. D	149. B
118. C	126. B	134. B	142. D	150. D
119. B	127. C	135. D	143. B	151. A
120. D	128. C	136. A	144. C	152. A

READING—VOCABULARY

153. D	158. A	163. A	168. D	173. D
154. B	159. D	164. B	169. A	174. C
155. A	160. D	165. D	170. C	
156. A	161. A	166. A	171. A	
157. C	162. B	167. A	172. B	

MATHEMATICS—CONCEPTS

175. C	180. C	185. D	190. D	195. A
176. C	181. D	186. C	191. B	196. A
177. A	182. B	187. D	192. C	197. A
178. D	183. C	188. D	193. D	198. B
179. B	184. D	189. A	194. D	

MATHEMATICS—PROBLEM-SOLVING

199. C	207. A	215. B	223. A	231. C
200. B	208. C	216. C	224. C	232. C
201. D	209. A	217. A	225. D	233. A
202. D	210. A	218. B	226. A	234. A
203. A	211. C	219. C	227. A	235. B
204. B	212. C	220. A	228. D	236. C
205. A	213. A	221. C	229. B	237. B
206. D	214. D	222. D	230. C	238. D

LANGUAGE

239. C	251. D	263. D	275. C	287. D
240. B	252. A	264. B	276. B	288. A
241. B	253. A	265. B	277. A	289. A
242. C	254. A	266. C	278. C	290. A
243. B	255. D	267. C	279. B	291. B
244. D	256. A	268. A	280. B	292. D
245. D	257. C	269. A	281. A	293. B
246. C	258. A	270. C	282. C	294. C
247. C	259. B	271. D	283. D	295. A
248. D	260. C	272. C	284. B	296. B
249. B	261. D	273. D	285. B	297. D
250. D	262. D	274. B	286. A	298. B

FIRST MODEL HSPT EXAM

Answers and Explanations

VERBAL SKILLS

1. **(C)** *Time* is a general classification. The other choices are objects that tell time.
2. **(A)** *Elated, gleeful,* and *joyous* are synonyms.
3. **(D)** Cause-effect relationship. The effect of lightening red is pink; the effect of lightening black is gray.
4. **(B)** Because the first two statements are true and Karen reads faster than Ann, she must also read faster than Sue.
5. **(D)** *Create* means to bring into existence or to invent.
6. **(D)** Noun-adjective relationship.
7. **(A)** *Quality* is a general classification. The other choices are examples of good qualities.
8. **(D)** Part-whole relationship. Sand is part of the beach; black dirt is part of a farm.
9. **(B)** *Time* is a general classification. The other choices are measures of time.
10. **(A)** A *salamander* is an amphibian resembling a lizard.
11. **(D)** *Arrogant* means proud or haughty.
12. **(C)** Cause-effect relationship. Rounding the corners of a square produces a circle; rounding the corners of a rectangle produces an oval.
13. **(D)** Part-whole relationship. One is half of two; three is half of six.
14. **(C)** *Add* is a function. The others are general classifications of symbols.
15. **(C)** From the first two statements it is only certain that Peter is the shortest of the three boys. The relationship between Paul and John cannot be determined.
16. **(A)** A *mellow* fruit is one that is tender and sweet.
17. **(B)** Other synonyms for *gossamer* are insubstantial, delicate, *or* tenuous.
18. **(C)** *Coddle* means to treat with extreme care.
19. **(A)** Object-purpose relationship. The purpose of a lamp is to give light; the purpose of a furnace is to give heat.
20. **(B)** Object-purpose relationship. The purpose of a director is to lead a choir; the purpose of a coach is to lead a team.
21. **(A)** *Diversify* means to give variety to.
22. **(C)** The first two statements indicate no relationship between Harry and Ralph; therefore, the third statement is uncertain.
23. **(D)** A *superficial* wound is a surface wound.
24. **(A)** From the first two statements it is known that B is south of A. Because C is south of B, it must also be south of A.
25. **(D)** A *precocious* child is one who is advanced in development.
26. **(C)** A *sadistic* remark is intended to inflict pain.
27. **(D)** A *dormitory* is only one part of a school, university, or college.
28. **(B)** *Truncate* means to shorten or to cut off.

29. **(D)** A sallow complexion is of a sickly yellowish hue.
30. **(D)** An *indigent* person is impoverished.
31. **(A)** Part-whole relationship. A leg is a part of a table on which the table rests; a wheel is a part of a car on which the car rests.
32. **(A)** A *dungeon* is a place where people may be forced to stay. The other choices are places in which people choose to live.
33. **(A)** Because the first two statements are true, all tumps are a part of a larger set of boscs with wings. Blue boscs have no wings, therefore they cannot be tumps, nor can tumps be blue.
34. **(D)** *Punishment* is a general classification. The other choices describe specific types or places of punishment.
35. **(B)** *Refuse* means to decline; the opposite is *to accept*.
36. **(D)** Object-user relationship. Ink is used in a pen when applied; paint is used on a brush when applied.
37. **(C)** *Acquire* means to gain possession of; the opposite is *to release*.
38. **(C)** Though the first two statements are considered true, they do not provide any information as to the direct relationship between rivers A and C.
39. **(C)** *Scant* means meager; the opposite is *abundant*.
40. **(B)** *Pinnacle* means peak; the opposite is *base*.
41. **(D)** Part-whole relationship. The captain is the part of a team that guides the team; the manager is the part of an office that guides the office.
42. **(A)** A window may be covered by the other three choices.
43. **(D)** *Corpulent* means obese; the opposite is *slender*.
44. **(C)** *Naive* means artless; the opposite is *sophisticated*.
45. **(C)** A glove is a hand covering; all the other choices are head coverings.
46. **(D)** A podium is positioned at the front of an auditorium or theater. The other choices represent those who face the podium.
47. **(A)** To *pledge* is to promise.
48. **(C)** A *depression* is a low spot or a *hollow;* the opposite is a *hill*.
49. **(A)** Because the first two statements are true and all the fruits cost more than apples, apples must cost the least.
50. **(D)** A fir tree is an evergreen; all of the other trees are deciduous, losing their leaves.
51. **(B)** *Diminish* means to decrease; the opposite is *to augment*.
52. **(B)** Because the first two statements are true, Jay's batting average must be higher than Tom's.
53. **(B)** *Abandon* means to give up; the opposite is *to keep*.
54. **(B)** *Feasible* is an attribute of abstract things or ideas. The other choices are generally attributes applied to concrete objects.
55. **(A)** Because the first two statements are true and C is north of A, it must also be north of B.
56. **(B)** Cotton is a vegetable product; leather, wool, and fur are animal products.
57. **(D)** A *seam* is a type of closing. The other choices are things for opening and closing.
58. **(A)** *Dwindle* means to grow smaller.
59. **(B)** Oxygen, helium, and gold are elements; water is a compound of hydrogen and oxygen.
60. **(B)** Because the first two statements are true and the third statement is in direct opposition to the first, it cannot be true.

QUANTITATIVE SKILLS

61. **(A)** Start by finding 20% of 40: $.20 \times 40 = 8$. Then add 3: $8 + 3 = 11$.
62. **(D)** The pattern in this series is made by adding 7 to each number.
63. **(D)** The pattern in this series is made by subtracting 9 from each number.
64. **(C)** Determine the amount of money for (A), (B), and (C). Then test the alternatives given to see which is correct.
65. **(D)** (A) is .625; (B) is .571; (C) is .6237. Clearly (B) is less than both (A) and (C), which are not equal to each other.
66. **(B)** The cube of 5 is 125. 125 divided by 5 = 25.
67. **(C)** The sum of $7 + 18 + 5 + 39 + 11 = 80$. $80 \div 5 = 16$. $\frac{1}{2}$ of $16 = 8$.
68. **(D)** Determine how much of each box is shaded. Then test each alternative to see which is correct.
69. **(B)** The pattern in this series is +3, +7, +3, +7, and so on.
70. **(D)** Determine the amounts for (A), (B), and (C). Then test each alternative to see which is correct.
71. **(A)** The pattern in this series is +1, × 2, +1, × 2, and so on.
72. **(C)** The pattern in this series is +6, –3, –1, +6, –3, –1, and so on.
73. **(A)** Start this problem from the end and work forward:

    $\frac{3}{5} \times \frac{25}{1} = 15 \qquad 15 + 7 = 22$

    The number you're looking for is found by setting up an equation.

    $30 - ? = 22$

    $? = 30 - 22$

    $? = 8$

74. **(B)** Begin with $\frac{1}{3}$ of 18: $\frac{1}{3} \times \frac{18}{1} = 6$. Then, $6 + 5 = 11$.
75. **(C)** First determine the amounts of (A), (B), and (C). Then test each alternative to see which is true.
76. **(A)** The pattern in this series is –9, –8, –7, –6, and so on.
77. **(C)** Count the circles in (A), (B), and (C). Test each alternative to find the one that is true.
78. **(D)** Determine how much of each figure is shaded. Then test each alternative to find the one that is true.
79. **(D)** The pattern in this series is made by adding 4 to each number.
80. **(C)** Determine $\frac{1}{5}$ of 100: $\frac{1}{5} \times \frac{100}{1} = 20$. Multiply this result by 4 to find the answer:

    $20 \times 4 = 80$.

81. **(B)** The pattern in this series is +4, +1, +4, +1, and so on. Also, whenever 1 is added the result is expressed as an Arabic numeral; whenever 4 is added the result is expressed as a Roman numeral.
82. **(D)** Determine the amounts for (A), (B), and (C). Then test each alternative to find the one that is true.
83. **(B)** First find 7 times 3: $7 \times 3 = 21$. Double this result to find the answer: $2 \times 21 = 42$.
84. **(A)** Each box is shaded by $\frac{1}{2}$. Therefore, only (A) can be true.
85. **(D)** Figure this problem from the end and work forward:

    $5 \times 2 = 10$

    $3 \times 10 = 30$

    $6 + ? = 30$

    $? = 30 - 6 = 24$

86. **(B)** The pattern in this series is –2, + 4, –2, + 4, and so on.

87. **(B)** Change (A), (B), and (C) so that they are all the same form—either all fractions, decimals, or percents. Then test each alternative to see which is true.

88. **(C)** You can figure out this problem with algebra:

$$\frac{3}{4}\ ? = 6 \times 4$$

$$\frac{3}{4}\ ? = 24$$

$$? = \frac{24}{1} \times \frac{4}{3}$$

$$? = 32$$

89. **(D)** The pattern in this series is +2, × 2, +2, × 2, and so on.

90. **(B)** The pattern in this series is +1, +3, +3, +1, +3, +3, +1, and so on.

91. **(A)** The line drawn from point A to the base of triangle ABD divides this triangle into two right triangles, one of which is ΔACD. $\overline{AD}$ is the hypotenuse of this right triangle whose length must be greater than the length $\overline{CD}$, the base of ΔACD.

92. **(C)** Begin by subtracting 5 from 29. This number divided by 3 will provide the answer:

$$29 - 5 = 24$$

$$24 \div 3 = 8$$

93. **(B)** The pattern in this series is +6, +3, +6, +3, and so on.

94. **(A)** Determine the amounts for (A), (B), and (C). Then choose the best alternative. Be sure to do the operations in the parentheses first when figuring.

95. **(C)** The pattern in this series is +1, –10, +l, –10, and so on.

96. **(D)** Because the figure is a cube, all edges and sides are equal. When a diagonal line is drawn across one side, like $\overline{CF}$, it forms a hypotenuse of a right triangle whose length is longer than the length of either of its sides ($\overline{CE}$ and $\overline{EF}$). Because the sides of the cube are all equal, CF must also be longer than AB.

97. **(C)** This can be done with algebra. If *x* is the number you are looking for:

$$x \div 2 = 6 + 4$$

$$2(x \div 2) = (6 + 4)2$$

$$x = 20$$

98. **(B)** Perform the multiplications as indicated to arrive at these values:

(A) = $5x + 5y$

(B) = $5x + y$

(C) = $5x + 5y + x = 6x + 5y$

It can now be seen that (B) has the least value, (C) has the greatest value, and (A) has a value between these. Therefore, (B) is the correct answer.

99. **(A)** The pattern in this series is × 2, +4, × 2, +4, and so on.

100. **(D)** To begin, find $\frac{1}{4}$ of 20. This is the same as saying 20 ÷ 4, which equals 5. If *x* is the number you are looking for:

$$7 - x = 5$$

$$x = 2$$

101. **(C)** The pattern for the letters in this series is made by using every other letter starting with A. The pattern for the numbers is + 4, –10, + 4, –10, and so on.

102. **(A)** Determine the values for each bar in the graph by using the number scale to the left. Then choose the correct alternative.

103. **(A)** This can be set up as an algebraic equation. If x is the number you are looking for:

$$x = \frac{3}{5}(10) - 2$$
$$x = 6 - 2$$
$$x = 4$$

104. **(A)** The pattern in this series is made by taking numbers in sequential order (4, 5, 6, and so on) and following each number with its square.

105. **(B)** Determine the amounts for (A), (B), and (C). Then, decide which alternative is true.

(A) $5^2 = 25$

(B) $4^3 = 64$

(C) $2^4 = 16$

106. **(D)** The pattern in this series is made by subtracting $2\frac{1}{2}$ from each number.

107. **(B)** Begin by figuring $\frac{1}{2}$ of 20. This number multiplied by 8 will provide the answer:

$$\frac{1}{2} \times 20 = 10$$
$$8 \times 10 = 80$$

108. **(C)** The pattern in this series is +4, –2, –1, +4, –2, –1, and so on.

109. **(B)** This can be set up as an algebraic equation. If x is the number you are looking for:

$$6 + \frac{1}{3}x = 2 \times 9$$
$$6 + \frac{1}{3}x = 18$$
$$\frac{1}{3}x = 12$$
$$x = 36$$

110. **(A)** Test each of the alternatives to find the true one. To find the perimeter add the length of all four sides together:

$$2 + 3 + 2 + 3 = 10$$

111. **(D)** This can be set up as an algebraic equation. If x is the number you are looking for:

$$x = \frac{4}{9}(27) + 10$$
$$x = 12 + 10$$
$$x = 22$$

112. **(A)** First figure 4 squared. The number 7 less than 16 is 9:

$$4^2 = 4 \times 4 = 16$$
$$16 - 7 = 9$$

READING—COMPREHENSION

113. **(B)** See sentence 6.
114. **(C)** See sentence 1.
115. **(C)** This is an inferential question. Based on sentence 7, we know that both the speed and direction of earthquake waves vary. We do not know from this information if choice (A) is true, so we must assume that (C) is the best answer.
116. **(D)** Because of the nature of the information, it would be found in both sources mentioned.
117. **(D)** This answer is determined by the entire passage which describes the layers in order. The answer can be verified by eliminating choices (A), (B), and (C).
118. **(C)** *Vary* most closely means *range.*
119. **(B)** This is an inferential question. Though not specifically stated, the answer can be assumed based on sentence 2 and the phrase "appears to be."
120. **(D)** See the last sentence of the paragraph.
121. **(C)** In this passage, *slightly* most nearly means a *little.*
122. **(C)** *Remaining* most closely means *last.*
123. **(C)** This answer may be verified by eliminating choices (A), (B), and (D). Though rocks are mentioned, they are only a part of the entire description.
124. **(A)** In this case, *wavering* most nearly means *swaying.*
125. **(D)** This answer may be verified by eliminating choices (A), (B), and (C). A clue to the answer is the way the passage is written—without technical terms and in the third person.
126. **(B)** This is an inferential question. The answer may be verified by eliminating the other choices.
127. **(C)** This is the most specific, direct answer, though the other choices may have been indirectly related. The answer is found in paragraph 2.
128. **(C)** See paragraph 2, sentence 4.
129. **(D)** *Utter* most nearly means *great.*
130. **(C)** This is an inferential question. The answer may be verified by eliminating the other choices. See paragraphs 3 and 4.
131. **(B)** Though the author mentions bats, the passage covers the more general topic of spelunkers.
132. **(D)** The answer may be verified by eliminating the other choices.
133. **(D)** See paragraph 2, sentence 2.
134. **(B)** The answer may be verified by eliminating the other choices.
135. **(D)** See paragraph 3.
136. **(A)** See paragraph 1.
137. **(D)** In the passage, *most fertile* means *best growing.*
138. **(B)** See paragraph 3, sentence 3.
139. **(A)** This answer may be verified by eliminating the other three choices.
140. **(A)** See paragraph 4.
141. **(D)** In this passage, *terrain* most nearly means *land.*
142. **(D)** This answer may be verified by eliminating the other three choices.
143. **(B)** This answer may be verified by eliminating the other three choices. It covers several aspects of the topic—more than would be contained in just one type of book.
144. **(C)** See paragraph 1.

145. **(A)** This is a question based on your general knowledge.
146. **(A)** See paragraph 2.
147. **(B)** This answer is actually testing your vocabulary.
148. **(A)** See paragraph 3.
149. **(B)** As it is used in the passage, *in essence* most closely means *basically*.
150. **(D)** *Interesting* is the best answer; it could be substituted for *fascinating*.
151. **(A)** This is an inferential question. The answer is implied in paragraph 3.
152. **(A)** This answer may be verified by eliminating the other choices.

READING—VOCABULARY

153. **(D)** *Perspective* means "aspect," "attitude," or "view."
154. **(B)** To *impair* is to "spoil," "damage," or "weaken."
155. **(A)** A *hovel* is a "cottage," a "hut," or a "cabin."
156. **(A)** To *loathe* means to "detest," "abhor," or "hate" something or someone.
157. **(C)** To *reproach* is to "condemn," "chide," or "blame."
158. **(A)** To be *elate* is to be "jubilant," "exhilarated," or "happy."
159. **(D)** *Brusque* means to be "curt," or "blunt," or "abrupt."
160. **(D)** To *depress* something is to "squash," "flatten," or "push down."
161. **(A)** To *quench* is to "allay," "stifle," or "end."
162. **(B)** An *exploit* is an "escapade," "journey," or "venture."
163. **(A)** To be d*eft* means to be "dexterous," "expert," or "skillful."
164. **(B)** A *chronicle* is an "account," or a "history," or a "record" of something.
165. **(D)** To be an *amiable* person means to be " likeable."
166. **(A)** The meaning of the word *astute* is to be "keen" or "shrewd" or "clever."
167. **(A)** To *sever* something means to "divide," " split," or "cut" the object.
168. **(D)** *Eminent* means to be "distinguished," "important," or "outstanding."
169. **(A)** To *terminate* is to "end," "cancel," or "stop" something.
170. **(C)** To *hinder* means to "obstruct," "interfere," or "impede" something.
171. **(A)** To be in *contention* means to be in "strife," "discord," or "debate."
172. **(B)** To *concede* means to "admit," "allow," or "acknowledge."
173. **(D)** To *forego* means to "concede," "give up," or "relinquish."
174. **(C)** For something to be *canny* means to be "clever."

MATHEMATICS—CONCEPTS

175. **(C)** A quadrilateral is defined as a figure with four sides. A triangle has only three sides.
176. **(C)** The symbol ∩ stands for "intersection." The intersection of two or more sets is the set of elements common to both sets. In this case the common elements are 3 and 8.
177. **(A)** This problem requires you to "round off" the given number to the place one digit to the right of the decimal point.

178. **(D)** Always start with the operations in the parentheses first:

$(-2)^3 = (-2) \times (-2) \times (-2)$

$(-2)^3 = -8$

Then continue with the operations outside the parentheses:

$3 \times (-8) = -24$

Remember, a negative number times a positive number equals a negative number; a negative times a negative equals a positive.

179. **(B)** The digits 2 and 4 end in the hundredths place. This means $.24 = \frac{24}{100}$. When simplified to simplest form $\frac{24}{100} = \frac{6}{25}$.

180. **(C)** A straight line represents a "straight angle" of 180°. An angle of 60° is given, so m $\angle C$ must be 120° to complete the line. Knowing that all the angles in a triangle added together equal 180°,

$$m\angle A + m\angle B + m\angle C = 180^\circ$$
$$m\angle A + 35^\circ + 120^\circ = 180^\circ$$
$$m\angle A = 180^\circ - 155^\circ$$
$$m\angle A = 25^\circ.$$

181. **(D)** When multiplying by 10, 100, 1000, etc., move the decimal point one place to the right for each zero in the multiplier. In this example, 100 has two zeros, so the decimal point would be moved two places to the right.

182. **(B)** The reciprocal of a fraction is the fraction "reversed." To find the answer you would have to rename $3\frac{1}{3}$ as an improper fraction: $3\frac{1}{3} = \frac{10}{3}$; $\frac{10}{3}$ is the reciprocal of $\frac{3}{10}$.

183. **(C)** The formula for finding the circumference of a circle is π times the diameter. The diameter is 2 times the radius. In this case $2 \times 4 = 8$ is the diameter. Therefore,

$$C = d\pi$$
$$= 8\pi$$

184. **(D)** The components of this problem must be stated in the same units. Therefore, 3 yards = 108 inches. The ratio of 108 to 18 is simplified to 6 to 1.

185. **(D)** State $\frac{33}{7}$ as a decimal number.

$\frac{33}{7} = 4.714$

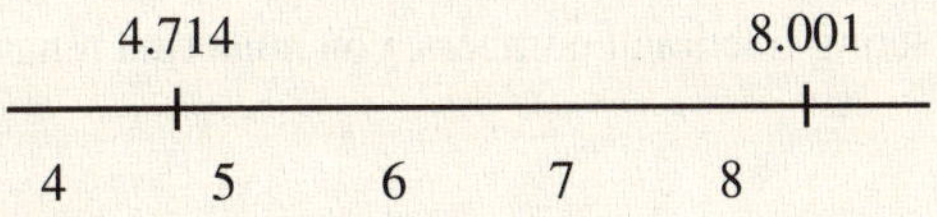

An integer is a whole number.

186. **(C)** The distributive property makes (C) true.

187. **(D)** $14^2 = 196$; $15^2 = 225$

188. **(D)** The base-five system uses only five symbols: 1, 2, 3, 4, and 0. Because of this, the other three alternatives are eliminated.

189. **(A)** When working with scientific notation, the exponent represents the number of places to move the decimal point in the multiplier. If the base of the exponent is 10, the decimal point moves to the right. If it is $\frac{1}{10}$, the decimal point moves to the left.

190. **(D)** This problem may be done without computation. The larger the denominator, the smaller the parts of the whole have been divided. The larger the numerator, the more parts are being considered. An alternative to this method is to find a common denominator and compare numerators. The largest numerator in this case shows the greatest value.

191. **(B)** The symbol means "greater than or equal to," and 6 is equal to 6.

192. **(C)** Figures are "similar" when their corresponding angles are equal and their corresponding sides are in proportion. To solve this problem, set up a ratio, assuming segment AB = $4 + n$.

$$\frac{3}{5} = \frac{4}{4 + n}$$

$$20 = 3(4 + n)$$

$$20 = 12 + 3n$$

$$8 = 3n$$

$$\frac{8}{3} = n$$

$$2\frac{2}{3} = n$$

Therefore, $4 + 2\frac{2}{3} = 6\frac{2}{3}$.

193. **(D)** By definition, an isosceles triangle is any triangle with two sides equal. Therefore, it is the only possible answer.

194. **(D)** For (D) to be equal, it would need the percent symbol after it.

195. **(A)** Prime factorization is factoring a number to the point where all factors are prime.

196. **(A)** The least common multiple is the least number divisible by both given numbers.

197. **(A)** This is done by ratios. The relationship between part of the lawn and the whole lawn is the same as the relationship between the time it takes to mow part of the lawn and the time it takes to mow the whole lawn.

198. **(B)** The associative property of addition means that you may group the numbers to be added in different ways and achieve the same sum.

MATHEMATICS—PROBLEM-SOLVING

199. **(C)** This involves multiplication and addition.

Student tickets	130 × $1.25 =	$162.50
Adult tickets	340 × $1.90 =	+ $646.00
Total	=	$808.50

200. **(B)** When subtracting fractional numbers, you must first rename the numbers with a common denominator.

$$12 - 2\frac{3}{16} =$$

$$\frac{192}{16} - \frac{35}{16} = \frac{157}{16}$$

$$= 9\frac{13}{16}$$

201. **(D)** There are 12 months in 1 year. If $54.24 is the total amount paid in a year, the average amount paid per month is $54.24 ÷ 12 = $4.52.

202. **(D)** First, add ten dollars to Bob's $88:

$88 + $10 = $98

Then, divide by 4:

$98 ÷ 4 = $24.50

203. **(A)** When expressed without the parentheses, this equation is 6 – 12 + 7 – 3. Solve by completing one part at a time:

$$6 - 12 + 7 - 3 =$$
$$-6 + 7 - 3 =$$
$$1 - 3 = -2$$

204. **(B)** Replace the *C* in the formula with 85 and solve:

$$F = \frac{9}{5}(85) + 32 =$$
$$153 + 32 = 185$$

205. **(A)** This can be set up as an algebraic equation. If *n* equals the price of the snowmobile, 5% of *n* equals \$42, or

$$.05n = \$42$$
$$n = \$42 \div .05$$
$$n = \$840$$

206. **(D)** Rename the number of the equation with a common denominator.

$$4\frac{1}{8} - 2\frac{2}{3} =$$
$$\frac{33}{8} - \frac{8}{3} =$$
$$\frac{99}{24} - \frac{64}{24} = \frac{35}{24}$$
$$= 1\frac{11}{24}$$

207. **(A)** Solve for *x:*

$$-5 + 4x = 21$$
$$4x = 21 + 5$$
$$4x = 26$$
$$x = \frac{26}{4}$$
$$x = 6.5$$

208. **(C)** Before multiplying, rename the mixed numbers as improper fractions:

$$3\frac{1}{3} \times 3\frac{3}{4} \times \frac{2}{5} =$$
$$\frac{10}{3} \times \frac{15}{4} \times \frac{2}{5} = \frac{300}{60} = 5$$

209. **(A)** This can be set up as an algebraic equation. If *n* is the amount Mr. Symon borrowed:

$$6\%(n) = 58.50$$
$$n = \frac{58.50}{6\%}$$
$$= \frac{58.50}{.06}$$
$$= 975$$

210. **(A)** This problem is done by ratios:

$$\frac{n}{6} = \frac{56}{14}$$

$$336 = 14n$$

$$\frac{336}{14} = n$$

$$24 = n$$

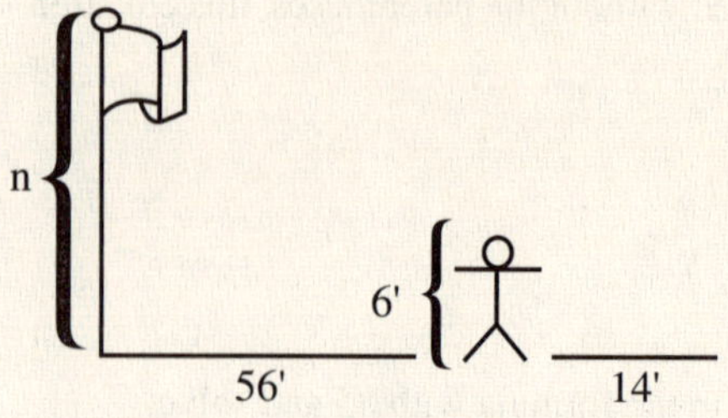

211. **(C)** By definition, the opposite sides of a rectangle are equal to each other. Because of this, if one side is 7 units, the opposite side is also 7 units. Consequently, 14 units account for two sides (7 + 7). The other two sides are each equal to (50 – 14) ÷ 2, or 18 units. Area is length times width—in this case:

$7 \times 18 = 126$ square units

212. **(C)** Solve for *x*:

$$4(3x - 2) = 16$$

$$12x - 8 = 16$$

$$12x = 24$$

$$x = \frac{24}{12}$$

$$x = 2$$

213. **(A)** Solve this as an algebraic equation with *n* as the unknown integer:

$$n + 18 = \frac{5}{4}n$$

$$18 = \frac{5}{4}n - n$$

$$18 = \frac{1}{4}n$$

$$72 = n$$

214. **(D)** Replace the letters with the given numbers and solve:

$$7A - 3B =$$

$$7(6) - 3(3) =$$

$$42 - 9 = 33$$

215. **(B)** Because Jim is now 12, four years ago he was 8. His father was then 5 times older, or 40. Now, 4 years later, Jim's father is 44.

216. **(C)** Convert the mixed numbers into improper fractions, then find the common denominator and add:

$$2\frac{1}{2} + 7\frac{2}{3} + \frac{3}{4} =$$

$$\frac{5}{2} + \frac{23}{3} + \frac{3}{4} =$$

$$\frac{30}{12} + \frac{92}{12} + \frac{9}{12} = \frac{131}{12}$$

$$= 10\frac{11}{12}$$

217. **(A)**

$$N\% \times 60 = 24$$
$$N\% = \frac{24}{60}$$
$$N\% = \frac{2}{5}$$
$$N\% = .4$$
$$N = 40$$

218. **(B)** Solve for *x:*

$$10x - 3 = 2x + 4$$
$$10x - 2x = 4 + 3$$
$$8x = 7$$
$$x = \frac{7}{8}$$

219. **(C)** To determine ratios, multiply the first numerator by the second denominator and the first denominator by the second numerator. Then reduce:

$\frac{3}{4}$ to $\frac{5}{2}$

6 to 20

3 to 10

220. **(A)** First convert the dimensions of the rug to yards. Multiply these to obtain the area. Multiply the area by $5.00 to determine the total cost.

A = 9 ft. × 15 ft. =

3 yd. × 5 yd. = 15 sq. yards

15 sq. yds. × $5.00 = $75

221. **(C)**

$$\begin{array}{r} .57 \\ 6.41\overline{)3.6537} \\ \underline{3.205} \\ 4487 \\ \underline{4487} \\ 0 \end{array}$$

222. **(D)** V = lwh

V = 18 × 2 × 5

V = 180 cu. in.

223. **(A)** Replace the letters in the problem with the given numbers.

$$\frac{3ABC}{2A} = \frac{3 \times 3 \times 2 \times 6}{2 \times 3}$$
$$= \frac{108}{6}$$
$$= 18$$

224. **(C)** Convert the mixed numbers into improper fractions. Then divide.

$$\frac{5\frac{2}{3}}{2\frac{5}{6}} = \frac{\frac{17}{3}}{\frac{17}{6}}$$

$$= \frac{17}{3} \div \frac{17}{6}$$

$$= \frac{17}{3} \times \frac{6}{17} = \frac{6}{3} = 2$$

225. **(D)**

$$\frac{5}{6}x = 30$$

$$x = \frac{30}{1} \bullet \frac{6}{5}$$

$$x = \frac{180}{5}$$

$$x = 36$$

226. **(A)** When solving this problem, remember that the number of decimal places to the right of the decimal point in the answer should equal the total number of places to the right of the decimal points in the two factors being multiplied.

$$\begin{array}{r} 65.14 \\ \times \quad .093 \\ \hline 19542 \\ 586260 \\ \hline 6.05802 \end{array}$$

227. **(A)** The pattern in this set is made by adding .06 to each number.

228. **(D)**

$$\begin{array}{r} 72528 \\ \times \quad 109 \\ \hline 652\ 752 \\ 000\ 00 \\ 7\ 252\ 8 \\ \hline 7{,}905{,}552 \end{array}$$

229. **(B)** Set this problem up as an algebraic equation.

$$11 \times 12 = N + 3$$

$$132 = N + 3$$

$$132 - 3 = N$$

$$129 = N$$

230. **(C)** Convert the mixed numbers into improper fractions. Then, divide the total length of the board by the length into which it will be cut.

$$9\frac{1}{2} \div 1\frac{1}{3} =$$

$$\frac{19}{2} \div \frac{4}{3} =$$

$$\frac{19}{2} \times \frac{3}{4} = \frac{57}{8}$$

$$= 7\frac{1}{8}$$

Though $\frac{1}{8}$ of a board is left, only 7 full-size boards can be made.

231. **(C)** $3x + 3 < 9 + x$

$$3x - x < 9 - 3$$

$$2x < 6$$

$$x < \frac{6}{2}$$

$$x < 3$$

232. **(C)** When adding decimal numbers, line up the decimal points.

$$\begin{array}{r} .602 \\ 4.2 \\ +\,5.03 \\ \hline 9.832 \end{array}$$

233. **(A)** $2.5x + 12.5 = 30$

$$2.5x = 30 - 12.5$$

$$2.5x = 17.5$$

$$x = \frac{17.5}{2.5}$$

$$x = 7$$

234. **(A)**

$$\begin{array}{r} 1960 \\ 28\overline{)54900} \\ \underline{28} \\ 269 \\ \underline{252} \\ 170 \\ \underline{168} \\ 20 \end{array}$$

235. **(B)** $\sqrt{x+36} = 10$

$$x + 36 = 10^2$$

$$x + 36 = 100$$

$$x = 100 - 36$$

$$x = 64$$

236. **(C)** $\begin{array}{r} 143_{(5)} \\ +\ 33_{(5)} \\ \hline 231_{(5)} \end{array}$

237. **(B)** Rename the fractions with a common denominator. Do the operations in parentheses first.

$$\left(\frac{2}{3}+\frac{1}{5}\right)-\left(\frac{1}{4}+\frac{1}{2}\right)=x$$

$$\left(\frac{10}{15}+\frac{3}{15}\right)-\left(\frac{1}{4}+\frac{2}{4}\right)=x$$

$$\frac{13}{15}-\frac{3}{4}=x$$

$$\frac{52}{60}-\frac{45}{60}=\frac{7}{60}$$

238. **(D)** First determine how many times 25,000 can be divided by 100:

25,000 ÷ 100 = 250

For *every* $100 in 25,000, $3.62 must be paid in taxes:

250 × 3.62 = $905.00

LANGUAGE

239. **(C)** *Day* should be capitalized.
240. **(B)** There should be a comma after *Sunday.*
241. **(B)** *International* and *Airport* should both be capitalized.
242. **(C)** There should be a comma after *said*, not a semicolon.
243. **(B)** *Can* refers to ability; *may* is used to request permission.
244. **(D)** No mistakes.
245. **(D)** No mistakes.
246. **(C)** The word *their* is incorrect in this context. The word should be *they're* (they are).
247. **(C)** The word *Who's* (who is) is incorrect in this context. The word should be *Whose.*
248. **(D)** No mistakes.
249. **(B)** There should be quotation marks before *let's* because it is a continuation of a direct quote.
250. **(D)** No mistakes.
251. **(D)** No mistakes.
252. **(A)** Because the action is from the teacher toward another place, the correct word is *take.*
253. **(A)** The word *you're* (you are) is incorrect in this context. The word should be *your.*
254. **(A)** The tense is incorrect. The last part of the sentence should read *I'd ever seen.*
255. **(D)** No mistakes.
256. **(A)** The object of the preposition *to* is Dierdre and *me.*
257. **(C)** The word *lay* is incorrect in this context. The word should be *lie.*
258. **(A)** The word *we* should be capitalized.
259. **(B)** The past tense of the verb *to lie* is *lay.*
260. **(C)** The question mark should be placed before the final quotation marks.
261. **(D)** No mistakes.

262. **(D)** No mistakes.
263. **(D)** No mistakes.
264. **(B)** The word *learning* is incorrect in this context. The word should be *teaching*.
265. **(B)** The word *of* is incorrect in this context. The word should be *have*.
266. **(C)** The preposition *to* is incorrect in this context. The word should be *too*, meaning excessive.
267. **(C)** The number of hours can be counted, therefore, *fewer*.
268. **(A)** The possessive of *it* is *its*. *It's* is the contraction for *it is*.
269. **(A)** *Everyone* is singular. The pronoun must be singular as well. Either *his* or *her* would be correct.
270. **(C)** There are three, so the comparative term must be *tallest*.
271. **(D)** No mistakes.
272. **(C)** The subjective *I* is incorrect in this context. The correct word is *me*, object of the verb *asked*.
273. **(D)** No mistakes.
274. **(B)** I feel *bad*. I would feel *badly* if something were wrong with my hands.
275. **(C)** The subject/verb of the sentence is *I have*.
276. **(B)** I *can hardly* wait. The double negative is incorrect.
277. **(A)** The apostrophe in *childrens* should be placed before the *s* since *children* is a plural word.
278. **(C)** The word *nothing* is incorrect in this context. The correct word is *anything*. The double negative is unacceptable.
279. **(B)** apparently
280. **(B)** efficiently
281. **(A)** occurred (see Spelling—Rule 9, page 103)
282. **(C)** analyzed
283. **(D)** No mistakes.
284. **(B)** succeeded
285. **(B)** described
286. **(A)** prefers
287. **(D)** No mistakes.
288. **(A)** necessary
289. **(A)** *Therefore* indicates the cause-and-effect relationship of the two clauses.
290. **(A)** The second clause provides an example.
291. **(B)** The subject (*Mary*) must follow the introductory phrase.
292. **(D)** No mistakes.
293. **(B)** The second clause offers the reason why she drove 50 miles.
294. **(C)** The invention of the automobile definitely belongs in a discussion of the history of the automobile.
295. **(A)** The clause with *nylon wheels* modifies *skateboard*.
296. **(B)** Sentences 1, 3, and 4 all concern preparation for the Halloween party.
297. **(D)** All of these topics are too broad for a one-paragraph theme.
298. **(B)** The given sentence should fall before sentence 3, because it refers to a singular noun and sentence two contains a plural noun. By placing the sentence between 2 and 3, the paragraph makes sense.

SCORE SHEET

Although your scores will not be reported as percentages, it might be helpful to convert your test scores to percentages so that you can see at a glance where your strengths and weaknesses lie. The numbers in parentheses represent the questions that test each skill area.

Subject	No. Correct	÷	No. of Questions	× 100 = __%
Verbal Analogies (3, 6, 8, 12, 13, 19, 20, 31, 36, 41)	_____	÷	10	= _____ × 100 = ___%
Synonyms (5, 10, 11, 16, 17, 18, 21, 23, 25, 26, 28, 29, 30, 47, 58)	_____	÷	15	= _____ × 100 = ___%
Logic (4, 15, 22, 24, 33, 38, 49, 52, 55, 60)	_____	÷	10	= _____ × 100 = ___%
Verbal Classification (1, 2, 7, 9, 14, 27, 32, 34, 42, 45, 46, 50, 54, 56, 57, 59)	_____	÷	16	= _____ × 100 = ___%
Antonyms (35, 37, 39, 40, 43, 44, 48, 51, 53)	_____	÷	9	= _____ × 100 = ___%
TOTAL VERBAL SKILLS	_____	÷	60	= _____ × 100 = ___%
Number Series (62, 63, 69, 71, 72, 76, 79, 81, 86, 89, 90, 93, 95, 99, 101, 104, 106, 108)	_____	÷	18	= _____ × 100 = ___%
Geometric Comparisons (64, 68, 77, 78, 84, 91, 96, 102, 110)	_____	÷	9	= _____ × 100 = ___%
Nongeometric Comparisons (65, 70, 75, 82, 87, 94, 98, 105)	_____	÷	8	= _____ × 100 = ___%
Number Manipulation (61, 66, 67, 73, 74, 80, 83, 85, 88, 92, 97, 100, 103, 107, 109, 111, 112)	_____	÷	17	= _____ × 100 = ___%
TOTAL QUANTITATIVE SKILLS	_____	÷	52	= _____ × 100 = ___%
Reading Comprehension (113–152)	_____	÷	40	= _____ × 100 = ___%
Reading—Vocabulary (153–174)	_____	÷	22	= _____ × 100 = ___%
TOTAL READING	_____	÷	62	= _____ × 100 = ___%
Mathematics—Concepts (175–198)	_____	÷	24	= _____ × 100 = ___%
Mathematics—Problem-Solving (199–238)	_____	÷	40	= _____ × 100 = ___%
TOTAL MATHEMATICS	_____	÷	64	= _____ × 100 = ___%
Punctuation and Capitalization (239–242, 248–251, 255, 258, 260, 277)	_____	÷	12	= _____ × 100 = ___%
Usage (243–247, 252–254, 256, 257, 259, 261–276, 278)	_____	÷	28	= _____ × 100 = ___%
Spelling (279–288)	_____	÷	10	= _____ × 100 = ___%
Composition (289–298)	_____	÷	10	= _____ × 100 = ___%
TOTAL LANGUAGE SKILLS	_____	÷	60	= _____ × 100 = ___%
TOTAL EXAM	_____	÷	298	= _____ × 100 = ___%

Chapter

22

Second Model HSPT Exam

ROAD MAP

- *Verbal Skills*
- *Quantitative Skills*
- *Reading—Comprehension*
- *Reading—Vocabulary*
- *Mathematics—Concepts*
- *Mathematics—Problem-Solving*
- *Language*
- *Answers to Second Model HSPT Exam*
- *Answer Explanations for Second Model HSPT Exam*
- *Score Sheet*

Answer Sheet

Answers and explanations for all Second Model HSPT Exam questions follow the model exam.

VERBAL SKILLS

1. Ⓐ Ⓑ Ⓒ Ⓓ	13. Ⓐ Ⓑ Ⓒ Ⓓ	25. Ⓐ Ⓑ Ⓒ Ⓓ	37. Ⓐ Ⓑ Ⓒ Ⓓ	49. Ⓐ Ⓑ Ⓒ Ⓓ
2. Ⓐ Ⓑ Ⓒ Ⓓ	14. Ⓐ Ⓑ Ⓒ Ⓓ	26. Ⓐ Ⓑ Ⓒ Ⓓ	38. Ⓐ Ⓑ Ⓒ Ⓓ	50. Ⓐ Ⓑ Ⓒ Ⓓ
3. Ⓐ Ⓑ Ⓒ	15. Ⓐ Ⓑ Ⓒ	27. Ⓐ Ⓑ Ⓒ	39. Ⓐ Ⓑ Ⓒ Ⓓ	51. Ⓐ Ⓑ Ⓒ
4. Ⓐ Ⓑ Ⓒ Ⓓ	16. Ⓐ Ⓑ Ⓒ Ⓓ	28. Ⓐ Ⓑ Ⓒ Ⓓ	40. Ⓐ Ⓑ Ⓒ Ⓓ	52. Ⓐ Ⓑ Ⓒ Ⓓ
5. Ⓐ Ⓑ Ⓒ Ⓓ	17. Ⓐ Ⓑ Ⓒ Ⓓ	29. Ⓐ Ⓑ Ⓒ Ⓓ	41. Ⓐ Ⓑ Ⓒ Ⓓ	53. Ⓐ Ⓑ Ⓒ Ⓓ
6. Ⓐ Ⓑ Ⓒ Ⓓ	18. Ⓐ Ⓑ Ⓒ Ⓓ	30. Ⓐ Ⓑ Ⓒ	42. Ⓐ Ⓑ Ⓒ Ⓓ	54. Ⓐ Ⓑ Ⓒ Ⓓ
7. Ⓐ Ⓑ Ⓒ Ⓓ	19. Ⓐ Ⓑ Ⓒ Ⓓ	31. Ⓐ Ⓑ Ⓒ Ⓓ	43. Ⓐ Ⓑ Ⓒ Ⓓ	55. Ⓐ Ⓑ Ⓒ Ⓓ
8. Ⓐ Ⓑ Ⓒ Ⓓ	20. Ⓐ Ⓑ Ⓒ	32. Ⓐ Ⓑ Ⓒ Ⓓ	44. Ⓐ Ⓑ Ⓒ	56. Ⓐ Ⓑ Ⓒ Ⓓ
9. Ⓐ Ⓑ Ⓒ Ⓓ	21. Ⓐ Ⓑ Ⓒ Ⓓ	33. Ⓐ Ⓑ Ⓒ Ⓓ	45. Ⓐ Ⓑ Ⓒ Ⓓ	57. Ⓐ Ⓑ Ⓒ Ⓓ
10. Ⓐ Ⓑ Ⓒ	22. Ⓐ Ⓑ Ⓒ Ⓓ	34. Ⓐ Ⓑ Ⓒ Ⓓ	46. Ⓐ Ⓑ Ⓒ Ⓓ	58. Ⓐ Ⓑ Ⓒ
11. Ⓐ Ⓑ Ⓒ Ⓓ	23. Ⓐ Ⓑ Ⓒ Ⓓ	35. Ⓐ Ⓑ Ⓒ Ⓓ	47. Ⓐ Ⓑ Ⓒ Ⓓ	59. Ⓐ Ⓑ Ⓒ Ⓓ
12. Ⓐ Ⓑ Ⓒ Ⓓ	24. Ⓐ Ⓑ Ⓒ Ⓓ	36. Ⓐ Ⓑ Ⓒ	48. Ⓐ Ⓑ Ⓒ Ⓓ	60. Ⓐ Ⓑ Ⓒ Ⓓ

TEAR HERE

QUANTITATIVE SKILLS

61. Ⓐ Ⓑ Ⓒ Ⓓ	72. Ⓐ Ⓑ Ⓒ Ⓓ	83. Ⓐ Ⓑ Ⓒ Ⓓ	94. Ⓐ Ⓑ Ⓒ Ⓓ	105. Ⓐ Ⓑ Ⓒ Ⓓ
62. Ⓐ Ⓑ Ⓒ Ⓓ	73. Ⓐ Ⓑ Ⓒ Ⓓ	84. Ⓐ Ⓑ Ⓒ Ⓓ	95. Ⓐ Ⓑ Ⓒ Ⓓ	106. Ⓐ Ⓑ Ⓒ Ⓓ
63. Ⓐ Ⓑ Ⓒ Ⓓ	74. Ⓐ Ⓑ Ⓒ Ⓓ	85. Ⓐ Ⓑ Ⓒ Ⓓ	96. Ⓐ Ⓑ Ⓒ Ⓓ	107. Ⓐ Ⓑ Ⓒ Ⓓ
64. Ⓐ Ⓑ Ⓒ Ⓓ	75. Ⓐ Ⓑ Ⓒ Ⓓ	86. Ⓐ Ⓑ Ⓒ Ⓓ	97. Ⓐ Ⓑ Ⓒ Ⓓ	108. Ⓐ Ⓑ Ⓒ Ⓓ
65. Ⓐ Ⓑ Ⓒ Ⓓ	76. Ⓐ Ⓑ Ⓒ Ⓓ	87. Ⓐ Ⓑ Ⓒ Ⓓ	98. Ⓐ Ⓑ Ⓒ Ⓓ	109. Ⓐ Ⓑ Ⓒ Ⓓ
66. Ⓐ Ⓑ Ⓒ Ⓓ	77. Ⓐ Ⓑ Ⓒ Ⓓ	88. Ⓐ Ⓑ Ⓒ Ⓓ	99. Ⓐ Ⓑ Ⓒ Ⓓ	110. Ⓐ Ⓑ Ⓒ Ⓓ
67. Ⓐ Ⓑ Ⓒ Ⓓ	78. Ⓐ Ⓑ Ⓒ Ⓓ	89. Ⓐ Ⓑ Ⓒ Ⓓ	100. Ⓐ Ⓑ Ⓒ Ⓓ	111. Ⓐ Ⓑ Ⓒ Ⓓ
68. Ⓐ Ⓑ Ⓒ Ⓓ	79. Ⓐ Ⓑ Ⓒ Ⓓ	90. Ⓐ Ⓑ Ⓒ Ⓓ	101. Ⓐ Ⓑ Ⓒ Ⓓ	112. Ⓐ Ⓑ Ⓒ Ⓓ
69. Ⓐ Ⓑ Ⓒ Ⓓ	80. Ⓐ Ⓑ Ⓒ Ⓓ	91. Ⓐ Ⓑ Ⓒ Ⓓ	102. Ⓐ Ⓑ Ⓒ Ⓓ	
70. Ⓐ Ⓑ Ⓒ Ⓓ	81. Ⓐ Ⓑ Ⓒ Ⓓ	92. Ⓐ Ⓑ Ⓒ Ⓓ	103. Ⓐ Ⓑ Ⓒ Ⓓ	
71. Ⓐ Ⓑ Ⓒ Ⓓ	82. Ⓐ Ⓑ Ⓒ Ⓓ	93. Ⓐ Ⓑ Ⓒ Ⓓ	104. Ⓐ Ⓑ Ⓒ Ⓓ	

READING—COMPREHENSION

113. Ⓐ Ⓑ Ⓒ Ⓓ	121. Ⓐ Ⓑ Ⓒ Ⓓ	129. Ⓐ Ⓑ Ⓒ Ⓓ	137. Ⓐ Ⓑ Ⓒ Ⓓ	145. Ⓐ Ⓑ Ⓒ Ⓓ
114. Ⓐ Ⓑ Ⓒ Ⓓ	122. Ⓐ Ⓑ Ⓒ Ⓓ	130. Ⓐ Ⓑ Ⓒ Ⓓ	138. Ⓐ Ⓑ Ⓒ Ⓓ	146. Ⓐ Ⓑ Ⓒ Ⓓ
115. Ⓐ Ⓑ Ⓒ Ⓓ	123. Ⓐ Ⓑ Ⓒ Ⓓ	131. Ⓐ Ⓑ Ⓒ Ⓓ	139. Ⓐ Ⓑ Ⓒ Ⓓ	147. Ⓐ Ⓑ Ⓒ Ⓓ
116. Ⓐ Ⓑ Ⓒ Ⓓ	124. Ⓐ Ⓑ Ⓒ Ⓓ	132. Ⓐ Ⓑ Ⓒ Ⓓ	140. Ⓐ Ⓑ Ⓒ Ⓓ	148. Ⓐ Ⓑ Ⓒ Ⓓ
117. Ⓐ Ⓑ Ⓒ Ⓓ	125. Ⓐ Ⓑ Ⓒ Ⓓ	133. Ⓐ Ⓑ Ⓒ Ⓓ	141. Ⓐ Ⓑ Ⓒ Ⓓ	149. Ⓐ Ⓑ Ⓒ Ⓓ
118. Ⓐ Ⓑ Ⓒ Ⓓ	126. Ⓐ Ⓑ Ⓒ Ⓓ	134. Ⓐ Ⓑ Ⓒ Ⓓ	142. Ⓐ Ⓑ Ⓒ Ⓓ	150. Ⓐ Ⓑ Ⓒ Ⓓ
119. Ⓐ Ⓑ Ⓒ Ⓓ	127. Ⓐ Ⓑ Ⓒ Ⓓ	135. Ⓐ Ⓑ Ⓒ Ⓓ	143. Ⓐ Ⓑ Ⓒ Ⓓ	151. Ⓐ Ⓑ Ⓒ Ⓓ
120. Ⓐ Ⓑ Ⓒ Ⓓ	128. Ⓐ Ⓑ Ⓒ Ⓓ	136. Ⓐ Ⓑ Ⓒ Ⓓ	144. Ⓐ Ⓑ Ⓒ Ⓓ	152. Ⓐ Ⓑ Ⓒ Ⓓ

TEAR HERE

TEAR HERE

READING—VOCABULARY

153. Ⓐ Ⓑ Ⓒ Ⓓ	158. Ⓐ Ⓑ Ⓒ Ⓓ	163. Ⓐ Ⓑ Ⓒ Ⓓ	168. Ⓐ Ⓑ Ⓒ Ⓓ	173. Ⓐ Ⓑ Ⓒ Ⓓ
154. Ⓐ Ⓑ Ⓒ Ⓓ	159. Ⓐ Ⓑ Ⓒ Ⓓ	164. Ⓐ Ⓑ Ⓒ Ⓓ	169. Ⓐ Ⓑ Ⓒ Ⓓ	174. Ⓐ Ⓑ Ⓒ Ⓓ
155. Ⓐ Ⓑ Ⓒ Ⓓ	160. Ⓐ Ⓑ Ⓒ Ⓓ	165. Ⓐ Ⓑ Ⓒ Ⓓ	170. Ⓐ Ⓑ Ⓒ Ⓓ	
156. Ⓐ Ⓑ Ⓒ Ⓓ	161. Ⓐ Ⓑ Ⓒ Ⓓ	166. Ⓐ Ⓑ Ⓒ Ⓓ	171. Ⓐ Ⓑ Ⓒ Ⓓ	
157. Ⓐ Ⓑ Ⓒ Ⓓ	162. Ⓐ Ⓑ Ⓒ Ⓓ	167. Ⓐ Ⓑ Ⓒ Ⓓ	172. Ⓐ Ⓑ Ⓒ Ⓓ	

MATHEMATICS—CONCEPTS

175. Ⓐ Ⓑ Ⓒ Ⓓ	180. Ⓐ Ⓑ Ⓒ Ⓓ	185. Ⓐ Ⓑ Ⓒ Ⓓ	190. Ⓐ Ⓑ Ⓒ Ⓓ	195. Ⓐ Ⓑ Ⓒ Ⓓ
176. Ⓐ Ⓑ Ⓒ Ⓓ	181. Ⓐ Ⓑ Ⓒ Ⓓ	186. Ⓐ Ⓑ Ⓒ Ⓓ	191. Ⓐ Ⓑ Ⓒ Ⓓ	196. Ⓐ Ⓑ Ⓒ Ⓓ
177. Ⓐ Ⓑ Ⓒ Ⓓ	182. Ⓐ Ⓑ Ⓒ Ⓓ	187. Ⓐ Ⓑ Ⓒ Ⓓ	192. Ⓐ Ⓑ Ⓒ Ⓓ	197. Ⓐ Ⓑ Ⓒ Ⓓ
178. Ⓐ Ⓑ Ⓒ Ⓓ	183. Ⓐ Ⓑ Ⓒ Ⓓ	188. Ⓐ Ⓑ Ⓒ Ⓓ	193. Ⓐ Ⓑ Ⓒ Ⓓ	198. Ⓐ Ⓑ Ⓒ Ⓓ
179. Ⓐ Ⓑ Ⓒ Ⓓ	184. Ⓐ Ⓑ Ⓒ Ⓓ	189. Ⓐ Ⓑ Ⓒ Ⓓ	194. Ⓐ Ⓑ Ⓒ Ⓓ	

MATHEMATICS—PROBLEM-SOLVING

199. Ⓐ Ⓑ Ⓒ Ⓓ	207. Ⓐ Ⓑ Ⓒ Ⓓ	215. Ⓐ Ⓑ Ⓒ Ⓓ	223. Ⓐ Ⓑ Ⓒ Ⓓ	231. Ⓐ Ⓑ Ⓒ Ⓓ
200. Ⓐ Ⓑ Ⓒ Ⓓ	208. Ⓐ Ⓑ Ⓒ Ⓓ	216. Ⓐ Ⓑ Ⓒ Ⓓ	224. Ⓐ Ⓑ Ⓒ Ⓓ	232. Ⓐ Ⓑ Ⓒ Ⓓ
201. Ⓐ Ⓑ Ⓒ Ⓓ	209. Ⓐ Ⓑ Ⓒ Ⓓ	217. Ⓐ Ⓑ Ⓒ Ⓓ	225. Ⓐ Ⓑ Ⓒ Ⓓ	233. Ⓐ Ⓑ Ⓒ Ⓓ
202. Ⓐ Ⓑ Ⓒ Ⓓ	210. Ⓐ Ⓑ Ⓒ Ⓓ	218. Ⓐ Ⓑ Ⓒ Ⓓ	226. Ⓐ Ⓑ Ⓒ Ⓓ	234. Ⓐ Ⓑ Ⓒ Ⓓ
203. Ⓐ Ⓑ Ⓒ Ⓓ	211. Ⓐ Ⓑ Ⓒ Ⓓ	219. Ⓐ Ⓑ Ⓒ Ⓓ	227. Ⓐ Ⓑ Ⓒ Ⓓ	235. Ⓐ Ⓑ Ⓒ Ⓓ
204. Ⓐ Ⓑ Ⓒ Ⓓ	212. Ⓐ Ⓑ Ⓒ Ⓓ	220. Ⓐ Ⓑ Ⓒ Ⓓ	228. Ⓐ Ⓑ Ⓒ Ⓓ	236. Ⓐ Ⓑ Ⓒ Ⓓ
205. Ⓐ Ⓑ Ⓒ Ⓓ	213. Ⓐ Ⓑ Ⓒ Ⓓ	221. Ⓐ Ⓑ Ⓒ Ⓓ	229. Ⓐ Ⓑ Ⓒ Ⓓ	237. Ⓐ Ⓑ Ⓒ Ⓓ
206. Ⓐ Ⓑ Ⓒ Ⓓ	214. Ⓐ Ⓑ Ⓒ Ⓓ	222. Ⓐ Ⓑ Ⓒ Ⓓ	230. Ⓐ Ⓑ Ⓒ Ⓓ	238. Ⓐ Ⓑ Ⓒ Ⓓ

LANGUAGE

239. Ⓐ Ⓑ Ⓒ Ⓓ	251. Ⓐ Ⓓ Ⓒ Ⓓ	263. Ⓐ Ⓑ Ⓒ Ⓓ	275. Ⓐ Ⓑ Ⓒ Ⓓ	287. Ⓐ Ⓑ Ⓒ Ⓓ
240. Ⓐ Ⓑ Ⓒ Ⓓ	252. Ⓐ Ⓑ Ⓒ Ⓓ	264. Ⓐ Ⓑ Ⓒ Ⓓ	276. Ⓐ Ⓑ Ⓒ Ⓓ	288. Ⓐ Ⓑ Ⓒ Ⓓ
241. Ⓐ Ⓑ Ⓒ Ⓓ	253. Ⓐ Ⓑ Ⓒ Ⓓ	265. Ⓐ Ⓑ Ⓒ Ⓓ	277. Ⓐ Ⓑ Ⓒ Ⓓ	289. Ⓐ Ⓑ Ⓒ Ⓓ
242. Ⓐ Ⓑ Ⓒ Ⓓ	254. Ⓐ Ⓑ Ⓒ Ⓓ	266. Ⓐ Ⓑ Ⓒ Ⓓ	278. Ⓐ Ⓑ Ⓒ Ⓓ	290. Ⓐ Ⓑ Ⓒ Ⓓ
243. Ⓐ Ⓑ Ⓒ Ⓓ	255. Ⓐ Ⓑ Ⓒ Ⓓ	267. Ⓐ Ⓑ Ⓒ Ⓓ	279. Ⓐ Ⓑ Ⓒ Ⓓ	291. Ⓐ Ⓑ Ⓒ Ⓓ
244. Ⓐ Ⓑ Ⓒ Ⓓ	256. Ⓐ Ⓑ Ⓒ Ⓓ	268. Ⓐ Ⓑ Ⓒ Ⓓ	280. Ⓐ Ⓑ Ⓒ Ⓓ	292. Ⓐ Ⓑ Ⓒ Ⓓ
245. Ⓐ Ⓑ Ⓒ Ⓓ	257. Ⓐ Ⓑ Ⓒ Ⓓ	269. Ⓐ Ⓑ Ⓒ Ⓓ	281. Ⓐ Ⓑ Ⓒ Ⓓ	293. Ⓐ Ⓑ Ⓒ Ⓓ
246. Ⓐ Ⓑ Ⓒ Ⓓ	258. Ⓐ Ⓑ Ⓒ Ⓓ	270. Ⓐ Ⓑ Ⓒ Ⓓ	282. Ⓐ Ⓑ Ⓒ Ⓓ	294. Ⓐ Ⓑ Ⓒ Ⓓ
247. Ⓐ Ⓑ Ⓒ Ⓓ	259. Ⓐ Ⓑ Ⓒ Ⓓ	271. Ⓐ Ⓑ Ⓒ Ⓓ	283. Ⓐ Ⓑ Ⓒ Ⓓ	295. Ⓐ Ⓑ Ⓒ Ⓓ
248. Ⓐ Ⓑ Ⓒ Ⓓ	260. Ⓐ Ⓑ Ⓒ Ⓓ	272. Ⓐ Ⓑ Ⓒ Ⓓ	284. Ⓐ Ⓑ Ⓒ Ⓓ	296. Ⓐ Ⓑ Ⓒ Ⓓ
249. Ⓐ Ⓑ Ⓒ Ⓓ	261. Ⓐ Ⓑ Ⓒ Ⓓ	273. Ⓐ Ⓑ Ⓒ Ⓓ	285. Ⓐ Ⓑ Ⓒ Ⓓ	297. Ⓐ Ⓑ Ⓒ Ⓓ
250. Ⓐ Ⓑ Ⓒ Ⓓ	262. Ⓐ Ⓑ Ⓒ Ⓓ	274. Ⓐ Ⓑ Ⓒ Ⓓ	286. Ⓐ Ⓑ Ⓒ Ⓓ	298. Ⓐ Ⓑ Ⓒ Ⓓ

TEAR HERE

Second Model HSPT Exam

VERBAL SKILLS

Time—16 minutes

Directions: Mark one answer—the answer you think is best—for each problem.

1. Which word does *not* belong with the others?
   (A) one
   (B) three
   (C) fourth
   (D) nine

2. Arouse is to pacify as agitate is to
   (A) smooth.
   (B) ruffle.
   (C) understand.
   (D) ignore.

3. Bagels are less expensive than muffins. Rolls are less expensive than bagels. Muffins are less expensive than rolls. If the first two statements are true, the third is
   (A) true.
   (B) false.
   (C) uncertain.

4. Query means the *opposite* of
   (A) argument.
   (B) answer.
   (C) square.
   (D) loner.

5. Impair most nearly means
   (A) direct.
   (B) improve.
   (C) stimulate.
   (D) weaken.

6. Which word does *not* belong with the others?
   (A) robbery
   (B) murder
   (C) death
   (D) burglary

7. If the wind is variable, it is
   (A) shifting.
   (B) mild.
   (C) chilling.
   (D) steady.

8. Egg is to beat as potato is to
   (A) yam.
   (B) bake.
   (C) eye.
   (D) mash.

9. If you obstruct the entrance to a building, you
   (A) block it.
   (B) enter it.
   (C) leave it.
   (D) cross it.

10. Barbara has five nickels more than Barry. Jane has 15¢ less than Barbara. Barry has more money than Jane. If the first two statements are true, the third is
    (A) true.
    (B) false.
    (C) uncertain.

GO ON TO THE NEXT PAGE

11. Which word does *not* belong with the others?
    (A) tuberculosis
    (B) measles
    (C) fever
    (D) flu

12. Cause means the *opposite* of
    (A) affect.
    (B) result.
    (C) question.
    (D) accident.

13. Skillful is to clumsy as deft is to
    (A) alert.
    (B) awkward.
    (C) dumb.
    (D) agile.

14. Which word does *not* belong with the others?
    (A) tent
    (B) igloo
    (C) cabin
    (D) cave

15. Pepper is the shaggiest dog in the obedience school class. Pretzel is a dachshund. Pepper and Pretzel are in the same obedience school class. If the first two statements are true, the third is
    (A) true.
    (B) false.
    (C) uncertain.

16. Pit is to peach as sun is to
    (A) planet.
    (B) moon.
    (C) orbit.
    (D) solar system.

17. Revenue most nearly means
    (A) taxes.
    (B) income.
    (C) expenses.
    (D) produce.

18. Which word does *not* belong with the others?
    (A) trapeze
    (B) wedge
    (C) lever
    (D) pulley

19. Which word does *not* belong with the others?
    (A) joy
    (B) sadness
    (C) tears
    (D) glee

20. Linda jumps rope faster than Mary but slower than Inez. Lori jumps faster than Inez but slower than Cleo. Mary is the slowest jumper in the group. If the first two statements are true, the third is
    (A) true.
    (B) false.
    (C) uncertain.

21. If a machine has manual controls, the machine is
    (A) self-acting.
    (B) simple.
    (C) hand-operated.
    (D) handmade.

22. Marshy most nearly means
    (A) swampy.
    (B) sandy.
    (C) wooded.
    (D) rocky.

23. Seal is to fish as bird is to
    (A) wing.
    (B) minnow.
    (C) worm.
    (D) snail.

24. Profit means the *opposite* of
    (A) ratio.
    (B) gross.
    (C) net.
    (D) loss.

25. Rest means the *opposite* of
   (A) sleep.
   (B) activity.
   (C) wake.
   (D) speak.

26. Which word does *not* belong with the others?
   (A) wind
   (B) gale
   (C) hurricane
   (D) zephyr

27. All people eaters are purple. No cyclops eat people. No cyclops are purple. If the first two statements are true, the third is
   (A) true.
   (B) false.
   (C) uncertain.

28. Stench most nearly means
   (A) puddle of slimy water.
   (B) pile of debris.
   (C) foul odor.
   (D) dead animal.

29. The judge who rules evidence to be immaterial means it is
   (A) unclear.
   (B) unimportant.
   (C) unpredictable.
   (D) not debatable.

30. Green books are heavier than red books but not as heavy as orange books. Orange books are lighter than blue books but not as light as yellow books. Yellow books are heavier than green books. If the first two statements are true, the third is
   (A) true.
   (B) false.
   (C) uncertain.

31. Shoe is to leather as highway is to
   (A) passage.
   (B) road.
   (C) trail.
   (D) asphalt.

32. Mend means the *opposite* of
   (A) give back.
   (B) change.
   (C) destroy.
   (D) clean.

33. Abstract means the *opposite* of
   (A) art.
   (B) absurd.
   (C) sculpture.
   (D) concrete.

34. A computer that does not function does not
   (A) operate.
   (B) finish.
   (C) stop.
   (D) overheat.

35. Which word does *not* belong with the others?
   (A) vitamin
   (B) protein
   (C) meat
   (D) calcium

36. All Ts are either green-eyed Ys or blue-tailed Gs. All blue-tailed Gs have brown eyes and red noses. Some Ts have red noses. If the first two statements are true, the third is
   (A) true.
   (B) false.
   (C) uncertain.

37. A sullen child is
   (A) grayish yellow.
   (B) soaking wet.
   (C) very dirty.
   (D) angrily silent.

GO ON TO THE NEXT PAGE

38. Which word does *not* belong with the others?
(A) stag
(B) monkey
(C) bull
(D) ram

39. Taste is to tongue as touch is to
(A) finger.
(B) eye.
(C) feeling.
(D) borrow.

40. Discord means the *opposite* of
(A) reward.
(B) record.
(C) harmony.
(D) music.

41. Which word does *not* belong with the others?
(A) aroma
(B) odor
(C) scent
(D) fumes

42. Which word does *not* belong with the others?
(A) ride
(B) creep
(C) hop
(D) run

43. Fatal most nearly means
(A) accidental.
(B) deadly.
(C) dangerous.
(D) beautiful.

44. Terry has won more races than Bill. Bill has won more races than Luis. Terry has won fewer races than Luis. If the first two statements are true, the third is
(A) true.
(B) false.
(C) uncertain.

45. Which word does *not* belong with the others?
(A) glass
(B) gauze
(C) brick
(D) lattice

46. If the packages were kept in a secure place, the place was
(A) distant.
(B) safe.
(C) convenient.
(D) secret.

47. Garish means the *opposite* of
(A) dull.
(B) damp.
(C) sweet.
(D) closed.

48. Horse is to foal as mother is to
(A) mare.
(B) son.
(C) stallion.
(D) father.

49. Which word does *not* belong with the others?
(A) gelatin
(B) tofu
(C) gum
(D) sourball

50. Counterfeit most nearly means
(A) mysterious.
(B) false.
(C) unreadable.
(D) priceless.

51. The thruway has more lanes than the parkway. The parkway has fewer lanes than the highway. The thruway has more lanes than the highway. If the first two statements are true, the third is
(A) true.
(B) false.
(C) uncertain.

52. Dog is to flea as horse is to
    (A) rider.
    (B) mane.
    (C) fly.
    (D) shoe.

53. The foghorn that sounded intermittently sounded
    (A) constantly.
    (B) annually.
    (C) using intermediaries.
    (D) at intervals.

54. Which word does *not* belong with the others?
    (A) Greek
    (B) Acrylic
    (C) Latin
    (D) Arabic

55. Diverse means the *opposite* of
    (A) definite.
    (B) understandable.
    (C) similar.
    (D) boring.

56. Finder is to reward as repenter is to
    (A) religion.
    (B) sin.
    (C) absolution.
    (D) contrition.

57. Which word does *not* belong with the others?
    (A) bend
    (B) explode
    (C) shatter
    (D) burst

58. The grocery store is south of the drugstore, which is between the gas station and the dry cleaner. The bookstore is north of the gas station. The grocery store is north of the dry cleaner. If the first two statements are true, the third is
    (A) true.
    (B) false.
    (C) uncertain.

59. Deception most nearly means
    (A) secrets.
    (B) fraud.
    (C) mistrust.
    (D) hatred.

60. Which word does *not* belong with the others?
    (A) cotton
    (B) linen
    (C) silk
    (D) nylon

STOP

END OF SECTION 1. IF YOU HAVE ANY TIME LEFT, GO OVER YOUR WORK IN THIS SECTION ONLY. DO NOT WORK IN ANY OTHER SECTION OF THE TEST.

QUANTITATIVE SKILLS

Time—30 minutes

Directions: Mark one answer—the answer you think is best—for each problem.

61. Look at this series: 23, 22, 20, 19, 16, 15, 11,…. What number should come next?
    (A) 9
    (B) 10
    (C) 7
    (D) 6

62. Examine (A), (B), (C), and (D) and find the best answer.

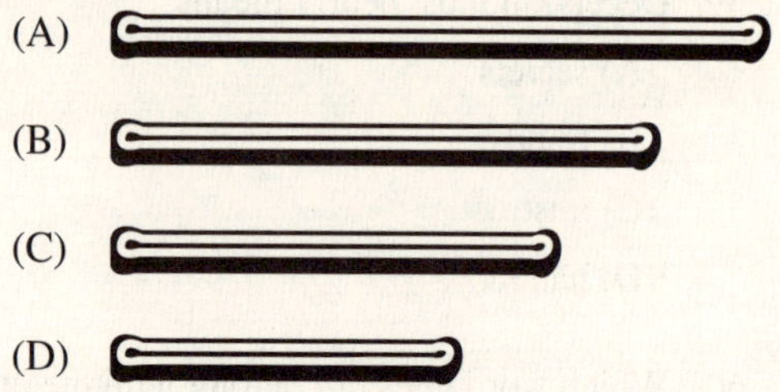

(A) **(A)** is longer than **(C)** but shorter than **(D)**.
(B) **(C)** is shorter than **(A)** minus **(D)**.
(C) **(B)** and **(D)** together are longer than **(A)**.
(D) **(C)** plus **(D)** are longer than **(A)** plus **(B)**.

63. Examine (A), (B), and (C) and find the best answer.
    (A) $3(2 + 3)$
    (B) $(2 + 3)^3$
    (C) $3(2) + 3$

(A) **(A)** plus **(C)** is greater than **(B)**.
(B) **(C)** is greater than **(A)**, which is smaller than **(B)**.
(C) **(A)** and **(B)** are equal.
(D) **(B)** is greater than **(A)** or **(C)**.

64. What number is 5 less than 60% of 40?
    (A) 24
    (B) 19
    (C) 29
    (D) 20

65. Look at this series: 50, 52, 48, 50, 46, 48, 44, …. What number should come next?
    (A) 46
    (B) 40
    (C) 50
    (D) 48

66. What number is 3 more than the cube of 4 divided by 4?
    (A) 61
    (B) 39
    (C) 67
    (D) 19

67. What number is 2 times the average of $6 + 12 + 4 + 41 + 7$?
    (A) 140
    (B) 14
    (C) 28
    (D) 30

68. Look at this series: 42, 40, 38, 35, 32, 28, 24, …. What two numbers should come next?
    (A) 20, 18
    (B) 18, 14
    (C) 19, 14
    (D) 20, 16

69. Look at this series: 27, 33, 25, __, 23, 29, 21, …. What number should fill the blank in the middle of the series?
    (A) 31
    (B) 24
    (C) 28
    (D) 30

70. Examine the triangle and find the best answer.

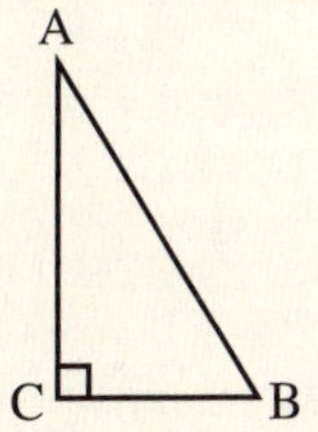

(A) AB is equal to AC
(B) m ∢ B is greater than m ∢ C.
(C) AB minus AC is equal to BC.
(D) m < A + m < B = m < C.

71. $\frac{2}{3}$ of what number is 6 times 4?
(A) 16
(B) 36
(C) 48
(D) 32

72. What number multiplied by 9 is 3 more than 42?
(A) 27
(B) 45
(C) 7
(D) 5

73. Examine (A), (B), and (C) and find the best answer.

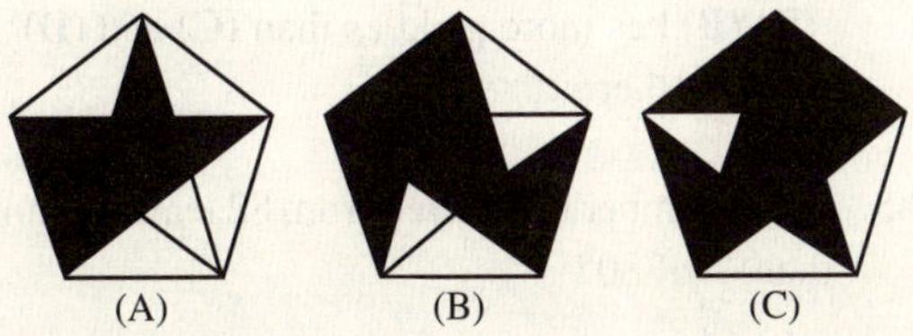

(A) **(B)** is less shaded than **(A)**.
(B) **(B)** and **(C)** are equally shaded.
(C) **(A)** and **(B)** are both less shaded than **(C)**.
(D) **(A)** and **(C)** are both more shaded than **(B)**.

74. Look at this series: 2, 11, 21, 32, 44, 57, …. What three numbers should come next?
(A) 71, 86, 102
(B) 68, 72, 94
(C) 70, 85, 101
(D) 72, 85, 105

75. Examine (A), (B), and (C) and find the best answer.
(A) .875
(B) $.33 \times 2.6$
(C) $\frac{7}{8}$

(A) **(A)**, **(B)**, and **(C)** are all equal.
(B) **(B)** is greater than **(C)**.
(C) **(B)** is less than **(A)**.
(D) **(A)** is greater than **(C)**.

76. The number that is 6 less than 69 is the product of 7 and what other number?
(A) 9
(B) 12
(C) 8
(D) 6

77. Examine (A), (B), and (C) and find the best answer.
(A) $\frac{1}{5}$ of 20
(B) $\frac{1}{4}$ of 24
(C) $\frac{1}{8}$ of 32

(A) **(B)** is equal to **(C)**.
(B) **(A)** is less than **(B)** and equal to **(C)**.
(C) **(A)** plus **(C)** equals **(B)**.
(D) **(B)** minus **(A)** equals **(C)**.

GO ON TO THE NEXT PAGE

78. Examine the pictograph and find the best answer.

Number of New Houses Built in XYZ Town Years A to D

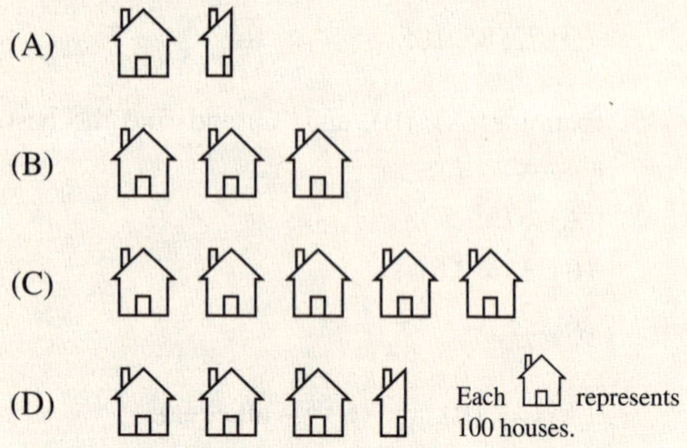

(A) One-half as many houses were built in year **(A)** as in year **(B)**.

(B) More houses were built in years **(A)** and **(B)** combined than in year **(C)**.

(C) Fewer houses were built in years **(A)** and **(D)** combined than in year **(C)**.

(D) An equal number of houses were built in years **(A)** and **(B)** combined as in year **(D)**.

79. Look at this series: 8, 16, 9, 18, 11, __ 15, 30, ... What number should fill the blank in this series?

(A) 12

(B) 22

(C) 19

(D) 7

80. Look at this series: 6, 7, 8, 10, 12, 15, 18, ... What number should come next?

(A) 20

(B) 21

(C) 22

(D) 23

81. The sum of 30% of a number and 50% of the same number is 96. What is the number?

(A) 60

(B) 120

(C) 136

(D) 150

82. By how much does the average of 12, 87, 72, and 41 exceed 25?

(A) 28

(B) 78

(C) 53

(D) 25

83. Look at this series: 24, 25, 23, 24, 21, 22, 18, ... What number should come next?

(A) 17

(B) 23

(C) 21

(D) 19

84. Examine (A), (B), (C), and (D) and find the best answer.

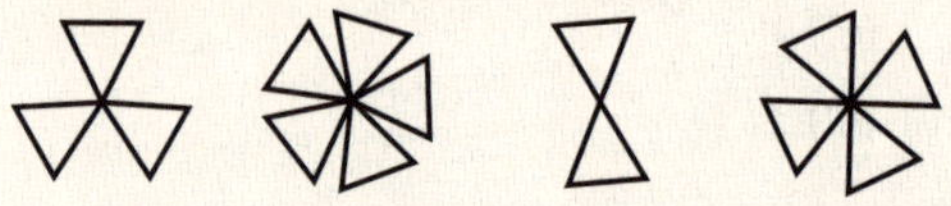

(A) (B) (C) (D)

(A) **(A)** has fewer paddles than **(B)** but more than **(D)**.

(B) **(A)** and **(D)** together are equal to **(B)** and **(C)** together.

(C) **(B)** has fewer paddles than **(A)** and **(C)** together.

(D) **(B)** has more paddles than **(C)** and **(D)** together.

85. What number subtracted from 82 leaves 3 more than $\frac{4}{5}$ of 80?

(A) 64

(B) 5

(C) 15

(D) 67

86. Look at this series: 5, 15, 24, 32, __, 45, 50, ... What number should fill the blank in this series?

(A) 39

(B) 40

(C) 37

(D) 55

87. Examine (A), (B), and (C) and find the best answer.

(A) 6^2

(B) 2^6

(C) $(2 \times 6)(6 \times 2)$

(A) **(A)** + **(B)** = **(C)**.

(B) **(C)** – **(B)** = **(A)**.

(C) **(A)** = **(B)** and both are smaller than **(C)**.

(D) **(C)** is greater than either **(A)** or **(B)**.

88. Examine (A), (B), and (C) and find the best answer.

(A) $(9 \times 5)+6$

(B) $(7 \times 8) - 5$

(C) $(15 \times 3) + (2 \times 3)$

(A) **(A)** is equal to **(B)**, which is equal to **(C)**.

(B) **(C)** is greater than **(B)** but equal to **(A)**.

(C) **(A)** is greater than **(B)**, which is less than **(C)**.

(D) **(C)** is greater than **(A)**.

89. What number added to 30 is 3 times the product of 8 and 4?

(A) 63

(B) 93

(C) 39

(D) 66

90. What number divided by 6 is $\frac{1}{8}$ of 96?

(A) 48

(B) 72

(C) 12

(D) 84

91. Look at this series: .125, .250, .375, .500, …. What number should come next?

(A) .620

(B) .625

(C) .728

(D) .875

92. Examine (A), (B), and (C) and find the best answer.

(A) **(C)** is more shaded than **(A)**.

(B) **(A)** and **(B)** are equally shaded and are more shaded than **(C)**.

(C) **(A)** is less shaded than **(B)** and more shaded than **(C)**.

(D) **(A)** and **(C)** are equally shaded.

93. What number is 15 more than $\frac{5}{9}$ of 99?

(A) 45

(B) 60

(C) 70

(D) 81

94. What number divided by $\frac{3}{4}$ yields a quotient that is equal to the divisor?

(A) $\frac{5}{8}$

(B) $\frac{7}{16}$

(C) $\frac{9}{16}$

(D) $\frac{3}{4}$

95. Examine (A), (B), and (C) and find the best answer.

(A) .8

(B) 80%

(C) $\frac{8}{10}\%$

(A) **(B)** is greater than **(A)** or **(C)**.

(B) **(A)** is greater than **(B)** plus **(C)**.

(C) **(A)**, **(B)**, and **(C)** are equal.

(D) **(C)** is smaller than both **(A)** and **(B)**.

GO ON TO THE NEXT PAGE

96. Examine the figure, and find the best answer.

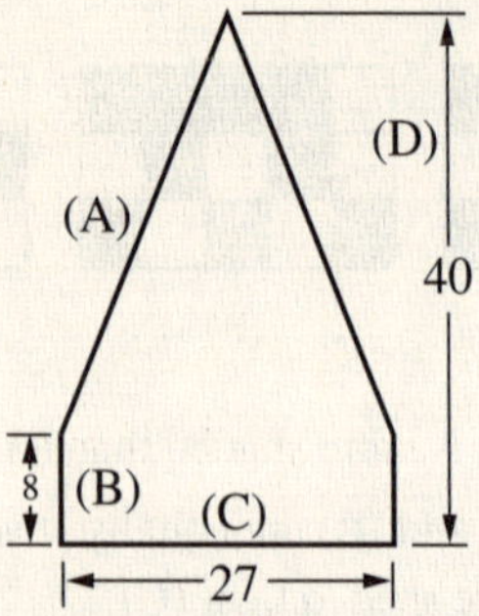

(A) Line **(A)** is shorter than line **(D)**, which is longer than line **(C)**.

(B) Line **(B)** is shorter than line **(A)**, which is longer than line **(D)**.

(C) Line **(C)** is longer than line **(D)**, which is longer than line **(B)**.

(D) Line **(B)** plus line **(C)** together equal the length of line **(D)**.

97. Look at this series: 81, 9, 64, 8, ______, 7, 36, ... What number should fill the blank in this series?

(A) 9

(B) 56

(C) 63

(D) 49

98. Look at this series: B25, E21, H17, K13, ... What comes next?

(A) M9

(B) N9

(C) N10

(D) O8

99. Look at this series: 1, 3, 3, 9, 9, 27, 27, ... What three numbers should come next?

(A) 81, 81, 729

(B) 27, 36, 36

(C) 27, 81, 81

(D) 81, 81, 243

100. If $\frac{3}{8}$ of a number is 9, then $83\frac{1}{3}\%$ of the number is

(A) 20

(B) 27

(C) 14

(D) 54

101. Examine the figure and choose the best answer.

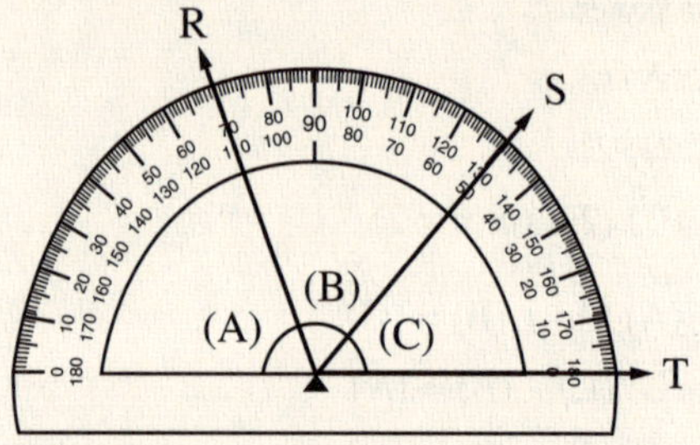

(A) Angle **(B)** plus angle **(C)** equals a right angle.

(B) Angle **(A)** is greater than angle **(C)**, which is smaller than angle **(B)**.

(C) Angle **(B)** minus angle **(C)** equals angle **(A)**.

(D) Angle **(A)** is equal to angle **(C)**.

102. Examine (A), (B), and (C) and choose the best answer.

(A) $\frac{1}{5}$ of 200

(B) 2^2 times 10

(C) $\frac{1}{2}$ of 8^2

(A) **(A)** is equal to **(B)** and greater than **(C)**.

(B) **(A)**, **(B)**, and **(C)** are all equal.

(C) **(B)** is greater than **(A)**, which is equal to **(C)**.

(D) **(A)** is greater than **(C)**, which is greater than **(B)**.

103. Look at this series: –19, –14, –12, –7, –5 .... What number should come next?

(A) 0

(B) 5

(C) –1

(D) 1

104. What number added to 60 is 3 times the product of 4 and 5?

(A) 10

(B) 0

(C) 15

(D) 5

105. Look at this series: .2, .1, .05, .025, …. What number should come next?

(A) .00625

(B) .0025

(C) .0125

(D) .055

106. What number is 12 less than $\frac{5}{8}$ of 96?

(A) 56

(B) 65

(C) 60

(D) 48

107. Examine (A), (B), and (C) and find the best answer.

(A) (B) (C)

(A) **(A)** is equal to **(C)**.

(B) **(B)** is greater than **(A)** and less than **(C)**.

(C) **(A)** is not greater than **(C)**, which is not greater than **(B)**.

(D) **(A)** plus **(B)** is not greater than **(C)**.

108. Look at this series: VI, IX, 12, 15, XVIII, …. What should come next?

(A) XXI

(B) 21

(C) XXII

(D) 22

109. Look at this series: $\frac{16}{2}, \frac{8}{2}, \frac{8}{4}, \frac{8}{8}, \frac{8}{16}$, … What number should come next?

(A) $\frac{16}{16}$

(B) $\frac{8}{32}$

(C) $\frac{16}{32}$

(D) $\frac{4}{8}$

110. Examine (A), (B), and (C) and find the best answer.

(A) 100% of 95

(B) 100% of 195%

(C) 95% of 100

(A) **(B)** is greater than **(A)**.

(B) **(C)** is greater than **(A)** plus **(B)**.

(C) **(A)** and **(C)** are equal and are greater than (B).

(D) **(A)** and **(C)** are equal and are smaller than **(B)**.

111. What number decreased by 40% of itself is 90?

(A) 150

(B) 36

(C) 60

(D) 145

112. Look at this series: 26, 18, 18, 12, 12, 8, 8, …. What two numbers should come next?

(A) 7, 7

(B) 8, 6

(C) 6, 4

(D) 6, 6

STOP

END OF SECTION 2. IF YOU HAVE ANY TIME LEFT, GO OVER YOUR WORK IN THIS SECTION ONLY. DO NOT WORK IN ANY OTHER SECTION OF THE TEST.

READING—COMPREHENSION

Time—25 minutes

Directions: Read each passage carefully. Then mark one answer—the answer you think is best—for each item.

Early in the 19th century, American youth was playing a game, somewhat like the English game of rounders, that contained all the elements of modern baseball. It was neither scientifically planned nor skillfully played, but it furnished considerable excitement for players and spectators alike. The playing field was a sixty-foot square with goals, or bases, at each of its four corners. A pitcher stationed himself at the center of the square, and a catcher and an indefinite number of fielders supported the pitcher and completed the team. None of these players, usually between 8 and 20 on a side, covered the bases. The batter was out on balls caught on the fly or the first bounce, and a base runner was out if he was hit by a thrown ball while off base. The bat was nothing more than a stout paddle with a two-inch-thick handle. The ball was apt to be an impromptu affair composed of a bullet, cork, or metal slug tightly wound with wool yarn and string. With its simple equipment and only a few rules, this game steadily increased in popularity during the first half of the century.

113. The title that best expresses the main idea of this selection is
(A) "Baseball Rules."
(B) "An English Game."
(C) "Baseball's Predecessor."
(D) "American Pastimes."

114. The rules of this game required
(A) 8 fielders.
(B) a pitcher, a catcher, and one fielder for each base.
(C) 20 fielders.
(D) no specific number of players.

115. The shape of the playing field was
(A) oblong.
(B) irregular.
(C) square.
(D) subject to no rules.

116. The game was
(A) scientifically planned.
(B) exciting for the players but boring to watch.
(C) boring for the players but exciting to watch.
(D) similar to an English game called "rounders."

117. The word impromptu, as underlined and used in this passage, most nearly means
(A) proven.
(B) unrehearsed.
(C) improvised.
(D) argued about.

118. This passage places the playing of this unnamed game roughly between the years of
(A) 1900 to 1950.
(B) 1800 to 1850.
(C) 1800 to 1830.
(D) 1900 to 1925.

119. This selection suggests that
(A) the game of baseball has grown more complicated over the years.
(B) the game described was very dangerous.
(C) baseball originated in the United States.
(D) the game described required skilled players.

120. According to the author, the popularity of this game was based largely upon
   (A) the excitement of watching skillful players.
   (B) the low cost of equipment.
   (C) the fact that none of the players covered the bases.
   (D) its being a new, strictly American game.

121. The word stout, as underlined and used in this passage, most nearly means
   (A) courageous.
   (B) fat.
   (C) that the bat was made from a stave of a beer barrel.
   (D) sturdy.

122. The writer of this selection
   (A) disdains this game because of its unprofessional aspects.
   (B) is nostalgic for days when games were simpler.
   (C) has prepared a factual report.
   (D) admires the ingenuity of American youth.

John J. Audubon, a bird watcher, once noticed that a pair of phoebes nested in the same place year after year, and he wondered if they might be the same birds. He put tiny silver bands on their legs, and the next spring the banded birds returned to the same nesting place.

This pair of phoebes were the first birds to be banded. Since that time, naturalists, with the aid of the federal government's Fish and Wildlife Department, band birds in an effort to study them. The bands, which are made of lightweight aluminum so as not to harm the birds, bear a message requesting finders to notify the department. Careful records of these notifications are kept and analyzed. In this way, naturalists have gained a great deal of knowledge about the nesting habits, migration patterns, and populations of a large variety of bird species. Most importantly, they are able to identify those species that are in danger of extinction.

123. Audubon banded phoebes because
   (A) he noticed that a pair of phoebes nested in the same place each year.
   (B) phoebes are in danger of extinction.
   (C) the federal government asked him to observe phoebes.
   (D) phoebes are easy to catch and band.

124. The message on bird bands is:
   (A) "Do not harm this bird."
   (B) "Kill this bird and send it to the Fish and Wildlife Department."
   (C) "Remove the band and send it to the Fish and Wildlife Department."
   (D) "Please notify the Fish and Wildlife Department as to where and when you saw this bird."

125. The word naturalists, as underlined and used in this passage refers to a(n)
   (A) employee of the Fish and Wildlife Department.
   (B) person who loves birds.
   (C) person who observes and studies nature.
   (D) person who develops theories about extinction of bird species.

126. The title below that best expresses the main idea of this passage is
   (A) "The Migration of Birds."
   (B) "One Method of Studying Birds."
   (C) "The Habits of Birds."
   (D) "The Work of John Audubon."

127. Audubon's purpose in banding the phoebes was to
   (A) satisfy his own curiosity.
   (B) start a government study of birds.
   (C) gain fame as the first birdbander.
   (D) chart the phoebes' migration patterns.

GO ON TO THE NEXT PAGE

128. Audubon proved his theory that
   (A) silver and aluminum are the best metals for birdbands.
   (B) the government should study birds.
   (C) phoebes are the most interesting bird to study.
   (D) at least some birds return to the same nesting place each spring.

129. The Fish and Wildlife Department is
   (A) a branch of the Audubon Society.
   (B) a group of naturalists.
   (C) an agency of the federal government.
   (D) a bird-banding organization.

130. The words migration patterns, as underlined and used in this passage, most nearly mean
   (A) random wanderings.
   (B) periodic movements.
   (C) food-gathering habits.
   (D) wintertime behavior.

131. The word extinction, as underlined and used in this passage, most nearly means
   (A) darkness.
   (B) resettlement.
   (C) inactivity.
   (D) disappearance.

132. The author's purpose in writing this selection was most probably to
   (A) convince readers to join in bird-banding efforts.
   (B) save birds from extinction.
   (C) encourage readers to cooperate with the Fish and Wildlife Department by reporting as requested.
   (D) praise John J. Audubon for his vision.

A vast stretch of land lies untouched by civilization in the back country of the Eastern portion of the African continent. With the occasional exception of a big-game hunter, foreigners never penetrate this area. Aside from the Wandorobo tribe, even the natives shun its confines because it harbors the deadly tsetse fly. The Wandorobo nomads depend on the forest for their lives, eating its roots and fruits, and making their homes wherever they find themselves at the end of the day.

One of the staples of their primitive diet, and their only sweet, is honey. They obtain it through an ancient, symbiotic relationship with a bird known as the Indicator. The scientific community finally confirmed the report, at first discredited, that this bird purposefully led the natives to trees containing the honeycombs of wild bees. Other species of honey guides are also known to take advantage of the foraging efforts of some animals in much the same way that the Indicator uses men.

This amazing bird settles in a tree near a Wandorobo encampment and chatters incessantly until the men answer it with whistles. It then begins its leading flight. Chattering, it hops from tree to tree, while the men continue their musical answering call. When the bird reaches the tree, its chatter becomes shriller and its followers examine the tree carefully. The Indicator usually perches just over the honeycomb, and the men hear the humming of the bees in the hollow trunk. Using torches, they smoke most of the bees out of the tree, but those that escape the nullifying effects of the smoke sting the men viciously. Undaunted, the Wandorobos free the nest, gather the honey, and leave a small offering for their bird guide.

133. The title that best expresses the topic of this selection is
   (A) "Life in the African Backwoods."
   (B) "The Wandorobo Tribe."
   (C) "Locating a Honeycomb."
   (D) "Men and Birds Work Together."

134. Most people avoid the back country of Eastern Africa because they
   (A) dislike honey.
   (B) fear the cannibalistic Wandorobo.
   (C) fear bee stings.
   (D) fear the tsetse fly.

135. The Wandoroo communicate with the Indicator bird by
   (A) whistling.
   (B) chattering.
   (C) playing musical instruments.
   (D) smoke signals.

136. The Indicator bird's name stems from the fact that it
(A) always flies in a northward line.
(B) points out locations of tsetse fly nests.
(C) leads men to honey trees.
(D) uses smoke to indicate the location of bees.

137. The reward of the Indicator bird is
(A) a symbiotic relationship.
(B) a musical concert.
(C) roots and fruits.
(D) some honey.

138. Smoke causes bees to
(A) fly away.
(B) sting viciously.
(C) hum.
(D) make honey.

139. Scientists at first discredited reports of the purposeful behavior of the Indicator bird because
(A) the Wandorobo are known to exaggerate in their stories.
(B) birds do not eat honey.
(C) honey guides take advantage of others of their own species only.
(D) the arrangement seemed so farfetched that they waited to confirm the reports scientifically.

140. The response of the Wandorobo toward bee stings is to
(A) ignore them.
(B) smoke the bees out.
(C) eat roots to nullify the effects of the stings.
(D) fear them.

141. The word incessantly, as underlined and used in the passage, most nearly means
(A) meaninglessly.
(B) continuously.
(C) raucously.
(D) softly.

142. According to the selection, one characteristic of the Wandorobo tribe is that its members
(A) avoid the country of the tsetse fly.
(B) have no permanent homes.
(C) lack physical courage.
(D) live entirely on a diet of honey.

"Sophistication by the reel" is the motto of Peretz Johannes, who selects juvenile films for Saturday viewing at the Museum of the City of New York. Sampling the intellectual climate of the young fans in this city for the past two years has convinced him that many people underestimate the taste level of young New Yorkers. Consequently, a year ago he began to show films ordinarily restricted to art movie distribution. The series proved enormously successful, and in September, when the program commenced for this season, youngsters from the five boroughs filled the theater.

As a student of history, Mr. Johannes has not confined himself to productions given awards in recent years, but has spent many hours among dusty reels ferreting out such prewar favorites as the silhouette films Lotte Reiniger made in Germany. One program included two films based on children's stories, "The Little Red Lighthouse" and "Mike Mulligan and His Steam Shovel." The movies are shown at 11 AM and 3 PM, with a short program of stories and a demonstration of toys presented during the intermission.

143. Mr. Johannes is a
(A) filmmaker.
(B) film critic.
(C) film selector.
(D) student of film.

144. Admission to the program described is
(A) limited to children in the neighborhood of the museum.
(B) for Manhattan only.
(C) available for all the city.
(D) for teenagers only.

GO ON TO THE NEXT PAGE

145. By his motto, "sophistication by the reel," Mr. Johannes means to imply that he
   (A) can convince students to remain in school through the lessons taught by his films.
   (B) introduces complex ideas and new perceptions by means of the movies.
   (C) considers all moviegoers to be immature.
   (D) feels that education on film is more effective than education in the classroom.

146. The words <u>ferreting out</u>, as underlined and used in the passage, most nearly mean
   (A) searching out.
   (B) dusting off.
   (C) editing.
   (D) protesting against.

147. The films are shown
   (A) year-round.
   (B) twice every day.
   (C) at the Museum of Modern Art.
   (D) on Saturday.

148. Mr. Johannes
   (A) followed an established policy in planning his programs.
   (B) has failed so far to secure a good audience.
   (C) limits his programs to the newest award-winning pictures.
   (D) evidently is a good judge of children's tastes.

149. Mr. Johannes found that children's taste in motion pictures
   (A) was more varied than had been thought.
   (B) ruled out pictures made before their own day.
   (C) was limited to cartoons.
   (D) was even poorer than adults had suspected.

150. Mr. Johannes would probably *not* choose to show
   (A) a film about a ballet dancer.
   (B) an X-rated film.
   (C) a film about the plight of migrant farmers.
   (D) a silent movie.

151. In the first sentence of the second paragraph, the reels are described as "dusty." The writer chose this word because
   (A) the cans in which the films were kept were very dirty.
   (B) the movies had not been shown in a long time.
   (C) many of the prewar films were about the plight of the farmers in the dust bowl of the Southwest.
   (D) the word *dusty* is a synonym for *stuffy*.

152. The silhouette films were probably popular with children because they
   (A) were made in Germany.
   (B) were not very colorful.
   (C) allowed for free run of the imagination to fill details.
   (D) had lively background music.

READING—VOCABULARY

Directions: Choose the word that means the same or about the same as the underlined word.

153. tedious work
 (A) technical
 (B) interesting
 (C) tiresome
 (D) confidential

154. to rescind an order
 (A) revise
 (B) cancel
 (C) misinterpret
 (D) confirm

155. diversity in the suggestions
 (A) similarity
 (B) value
 (C) triviality
 (D) variety

156. the problem of indigence
 (A) poverty
 (B) corruption
 (C) intolerance
 (D) laziness

157. a vindictive person
 (A) prejudiced
 (B) unpopular
 (C) petty
 (D) revengeful

158. unsatisfactory remuneration
 (A) payment
 (B) summary
 (C) explanation
 (D) estimate

159. a deficient program
 (A) excellent
 (B) inadequate
 (C) demanding
 (D) interrupted

160. a detrimental influence
 (A) favorable
 (B) lasting
 (C) harmful
 (D) restraining

161. accurate information
 (A) correct
 (B) good
 (C) ample
 (D) useful

162. to amplify one's remarks
 (A) soften
 (B) simplify
 (C) enlarge upon
 (D) repeat

163. to be legally competent
 (A) expert
 (B) ineligible
 (C) accused
 (D) able

164. infraction of the rules
 (A) violation
 (B) use
 (C) interpretation
 (D) part

165. a relevant magazine article
 (A) applicable
 (B) controversial
 (C) miscellaneous
 (D) recent

GO ON TO THE NEXT PAGE

166. an office manual
(A) laborer
(B) handbook
(C) typewriter
(D) handle

167. a computational device
(A) calculator
(B) adder
(C) mathematician
(D) machine

168. a conventional test
(A) agreeable
(B) public
(C) large-scale
(D) ordinary

169. the subject of controversy
(A) annoyance
(B) debate
(C) envy
(D) review

170. a diplomatic person
(A) well-dressed
(B) tactful
(C) domineering
(D) tricky

171. an irate student
(A) irresponsible
(B) untidy
(C) insubordinate
(D) angry

172. durable paint
(A) cheap
(B) long-lasting
(C) easily applied
(D) quick-drying

173. an extensive search
(A) complicated
(B) superficial
(C) thorough
(D) leisurely

174. the inception of the program
(A) beginning
(B) discussion
(C) rejection
(D) purpose

STOP

END OF SECTION 3. IF YOU HAVE ANY TIME LEFT, GO OVER YOUR WORK IN THIS SECTION ONLY. DO NOT WORK IN ANY OTHER SECTION OF THE TEST.

MATHEMATICS—CONCEPTS

Time—45 minutes

Directions: Mark one answer—the answer you think is best—for each problem. You may use scratch paper when working these problems.

175. Three hundred twenty-six million nine hundred thousand six hundred nineteen =
   (A) 3,269,619
   (B) 32,690,619
   (C) 326,960,019
   (D) 326,900,619

176. A number is changed if
   (A) 0 is added to it.
   (B) 1 is subtracted from it.
   (C) it is divided by 1.
   (D) it is multiplied by 1.

177. In the number 6,000,600,000, there are
   (A) 6 billions and 6 hundred thousands.
   (B) 6 millions and 6 thousands.
   (C) 6 billions and 6 millions.
   (D) 6 millions and 60 thousands.

178. Which is the longest time?
   (A) 1,440 minutes
   (B) 25 hours
   (C) $\frac{1}{2}$ day
   (D) 3,600 seconds

179. $5^3 \times 3^4 =$
   (A) $5 \times 3 \times 3 \times 4$
   (B) $5 \times 5 \times 5 \times 3 \times 3 \times 3$
   (C) $5 \times 5 \times 5 \times 3 \times 3 \times 3 \times 3$
   (D) $5 \times 5 \times 5 \times 5 \times 3 \times 3 \times 3$

180. $\frac{3 \times 8}{6 \times 5} =$
   (A) $\frac{2}{3}$
   (B) $\frac{1}{6}$
   (C) $\frac{3}{4}$
   (D) $\frac{4}{5}$

181. Which of the following has the same value as .5%?
   (A) .005%
   (B) $\frac{1}{2}$%
   (C) $\frac{1}{50}$%
   (D) $\frac{1}{500}$%

182. What is the total number of degrees found in angles A and C in the triangle below?

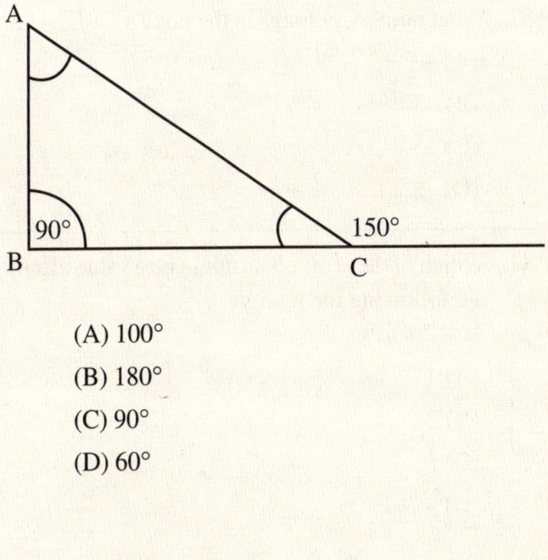

   (A) 100°
   (B) 180°
   (C) 90°
   (D) 60°

GO ON TO THE NEXT PAGE

183. If $x > 9$, then

(A) $x^2 > 80$

(B) $x^2 - 2 = 47$

(C) $x^2 < 65$

(D) $x^2 - 2 < 90$

184. Any number that is divisible by both 3 and 4 is also divisible by

(A) 8

(B) 9

(C) 12

(D) 16

185. Which symbol belongs in the circle?
.023 ○ .0086

(A) >

(B) <

(C) =

(D) ≅

186. The greatest common factor of 50 and 10 is

(A) 1

(B) 5

(C) 10

(D) 25

187. What number belongs in the box? +5 + □ = –3

(A) +3

(B) –3

(C) +8

(D) –8

188. Which of these numbers might be a value of x in the following inequality?
$3x + 2 > 12$

(A) 1

(B) 2

(C) 3

(D) 4

189. The area of the circle is

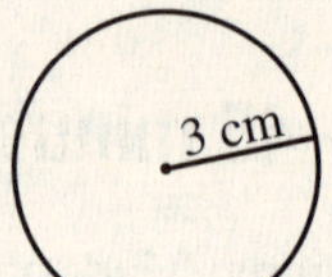

(A) 3 π cm.

(B) 6 π sq. cm.

(C) 9 π sq. cm.

(D) 36 π sq. cm.

190. If $x - 3 < 12$, x may be

(A) less than 15

(B) greater than 16

(C) equal to 15

(D) less than 18

191. The ratio of 3 quarts to 3 gallons is

(A) 3:1

(B) 1:4

(C) 6:3

(D) 4:1

192. Which pair of values for x and □ will make the following statement true? $2x$ □ 8

(A) (6, <)

(B) (4, >)

(C) (0, <)

(D) (–3, >)

193. How many sixths are there in $\frac{4}{5}$?

(A) $4\frac{4}{5}$

(B) $5\frac{1}{5}$

(C) 6

(D) $2\frac{2}{5}$

194. Set M = {1,2,3,4}; Set N = {2,5,6}. The intersection ∩ of the two sets is

(A) {2}

(B) {1,2,3,4,5,6}

(C) {3}

(D) {26}

195. If Mary is x years old now and her sister is 3 years younger, then 5 years from now her sister will be what age?

(A) $x + 5$ years

(B) $x + 3$ years

(C) $x + 2$ years

(D) 8 years

196. Write 493 in expanded form, using exponents.

(A) $(4 \times 10^2) + (9 \times 10) + 3$

(B) $(4 \times 10^3) + (9 \times 10^2) + (3 \times 10)$

(C) $(4 \times 10^1) + (9 \times 10) + 3$

(D) none of the above

197. Which of the following statements is true?

(A) $7 \times 11 > 78$

(B) $6 + 4 < 10.5$

(C) $8 - 3 = 7 + 4$

(D) $16 \div 2 > 9$

198.

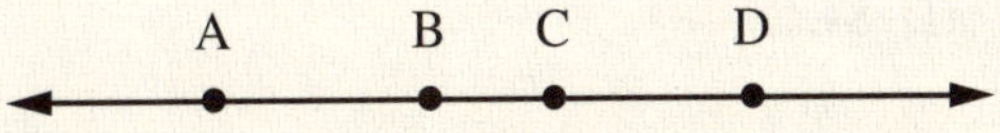

$\overline{AB} \cup \overline{BC}$

(A) $\overline{BD}$

(B) $\overline{BC}$

(C) $\overline{AD}$

(D) $\overline{AC}$

MATHEMATICS—PROBLEM-SOLVING

199. The ratio of teachers to students in a certain school is 1:14. If there are 14 teachers in the school, how many students are there?

(A) 14

(B) 196

(C) 206

(D) 176

200. On a blueprint, 2 inches represent 24 feet. How long must a line be to represent 72 feet?

(A) 36 inches

(B) 12 inches

(C) 6 inches

(D) 4 inches

201. A department store marks up its clothing 80% over cost. If it sells blue jeans for \$14, how much did the store pay for them?

(A) \$7.78

(B) \$17.50

(C) \$11.20

(D) \$1.12

202. The same store puts the same \$14 jeans on sale at a 25% discount. What is the new selling price?

(A) \$13.75

(B) \$10.50

(C) \$3.50

(D) \$13.65

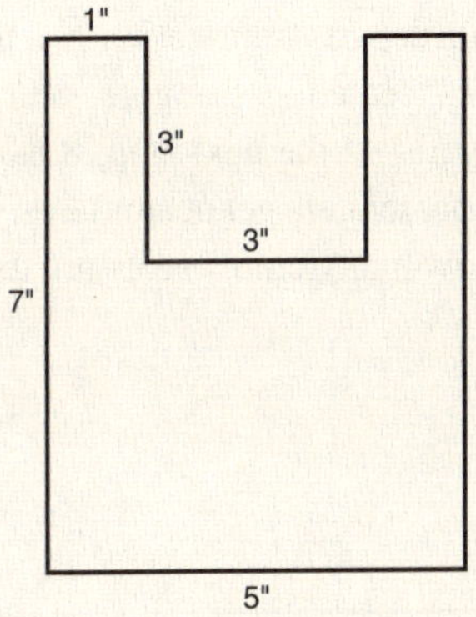

203. The perimeter of the figure above is

(A) 19 in.

(B) 30 in.

(C) 23 sq.in.

(D) 19 sq. in.

204. The area of the figure above is

(A) 26 sq. in.

(B) 19 sq. in.

(C) 44 sq. in.

(D) 30 sq. in.

GO ON TO THE NEXT PAGE

205. The charge for a particular long-distance call was \$1.56 for the first 3 minutes, and \$.22 for each additional minute. What was the total charge for a 16-minute call?

(A) \$5.80

(B) \$5.08

(C) \$2.86

(D) \$4.42

206. The winner of a race received $\frac{1}{3}$ of the total purse. The third-place finisher received $\frac{1}{3}$ of the winner's share. If the winner's share was \$2,700, what was the total purse?

(A) \$2,700

(B) \$8,100

(C) \$900

(D) \$1,800

207. As a train departs from station A, it has 12 empty seats, 14 seated passengers, and 4 standing passengers. At the next stop, 8 passengers get off, 13 passengers get on, and everyone takes a seat. How many empty seats are there?

(A) 1

(B) 2

(C) 3

(D) 4

208. In order to increase revenues, a municipality considers raising its sales tax from 5% to 8%. How much more will it cost to buy a \$250 television set if the 8% sales tax is approved?

(A) \$7.50

(B) \$10.00

(C) \$12.50

(D) \$15.50

209. Solve: $\dfrac{1\frac{3}{4}-\frac{1}{8}}{\frac{1}{8}}$

(A) 12

(B) 13

(C) 14

(D) 1

210. Solve: $2.01 \div 1.02 =$

(A) 1.97

(B) .507

(C) 3.03

(D) 2.0001

211. Solve: $-3 - [(2 - 1) - (3 + 4)] =$

(A) 3

(B) 12

(C) –6

(D) –9

212. 140% of 70 is

(A) 150

(B) 9.8

(C) 9,800

(D) 98

213.

$$\begin{array}{r} 5 \text{ gallons } 2 \text{ quarts } 1 \text{ pint} \\ -1 \text{ gallon } 3 \text{ quarts} \\ \hline \end{array}$$

(A) 4 gal. 9 qt. 1 pt.

(B) 2 gal. 2 qt. 1 pt.

(C) 3 gal. 3 qt. 1 pt.

(D) 2 gal. 6 qt. 2 pt.

214. Solve: $6 \div \frac{1}{3} + \frac{2}{3} \times 9 =$

(A) $\frac{2}{3}$

(B) 24

(C) 168

(D) 54

215. If $a = 9$, $b = 2$, and $c = 1$, the value of $\sqrt{a+3b+c}$ is

(A) 7

(B) 16

(C) 6

(D) 4

216. 7 is to 21 as $\frac{2}{3}$ is to

(A) 2

(B) 1

(C) $\frac{4}{3}$

(D) 3

217. The average of –10, 6, 0, –3, and 22 is

(A) 2

(B) –3

(C) –6

(D) 3

218. The number of telephones in Adelaide, Australia is 48,000. If this represents 12.8 telephones per 100 persons, the population of Adelaide to the nearest thousand is

(A) 128,000

(B) 375,000

(C) 378,000

(D) 556,000

219. A carpenter needs four boards, each 2 feet 9 inches long. If wood is sold only by the foot, how many feet must he buy?

(A) 9

(B) 10

(C) 11

(D) 12

220. What is the difference between $(4 \times 10^3) + 6$ and $(2 \times 10^3) + (3 \times 10) + 8$?

(A) 168

(B) 55,968

(C) 3,765

(D) 1,968

221. A square has an area of 49 sq. in. The number of inches in its perimeter is

(A) 7

(B) 28

(C) 14

(D) 98

222. $r = 35 - (3 + 6)(-n)$

$n = 2$

$r =$

(A) 53

(B) 17

(C) –53

(D) –17

223. $(3 + 4)^3 =$

(A) 21

(B) 91

(C) 343

(D) 490

224. Aluminum bronze consists of copper and aluminum, usually in the ratio of 10:1 by weight. If an object made of this alloy weighs 77 pounds, how many pounds of aluminum does it contain?

(A) 7.7

(B) 7.0

(C) 70.0

(D) 10

225. Mr. Lawson makes a weekly salary of $150 plus 7% commission on his sales. What will his income be for a week in which he makes sales totaling $945?

(A) $216.15

(B) $206.15

(C) $196.15

(D) $226.15

226. Solve for x: $x^2 + 5 = 41$

(A) ±6

(B) ±7

(C) ±8

(D) ±9

227. If 5 pints of water are needed to water each square foot of lawn, the minimum number of gallons of water needed for a lawn 8' by 12' is

(A) 60

(B) 56

(C) 80

(D) 30

228. Solve for x: $\frac{x}{2} + 36 = 37.25$

(A) 18.5

(B) 3.5

(C) 2.5

(D) 12.5

GO ON TO THE NEXT PAGE

229.

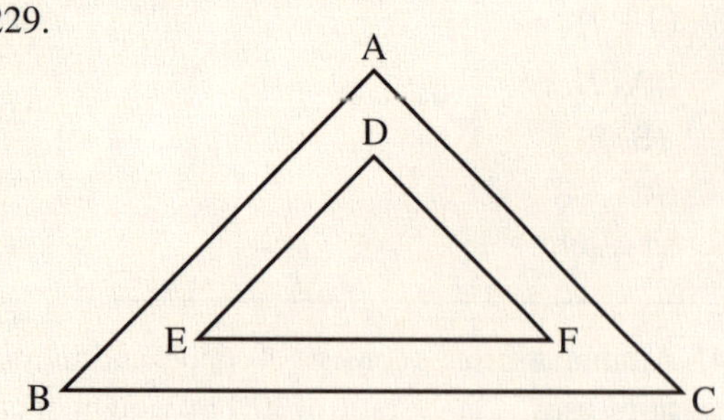

In the figure above, the sides of ΔABC are respectively parallel to the sides of ΔDEF. If the complement of $\angle A$ is 40°, then the complement of $\angle D$ is

(A) 20°

(B) 50°

(C) 60°

(D) 40°

230. Find the area of a rectangle with a length of 176 feet and a width of 79 feet.

(A) 13,904 sq. ft.

(B) 13,854 sq. ft.

(C) 13,304 sq. ft.

(D) 13,804 sq. ft.

231. Solve: $63 \div \frac{1}{9} = ?$

(A) 56

(B) 67

(C) 7

(D) 567

232. A house was valued at $83,000 and insured for 80% of that amount. Find the yearly premium if it is figured at $.45 per hundred dollars of value.

(A) $298.80

(B) $252.63

(C) $664.00

(D) $83.80

233. Solve: 72.61 ÷ .05 = ?

(A) 1.45220

(B) 145.220

(C) 1,452.20

(D) 14.522

234. Find the area of a triangle whose dimensions are $b = 12'$, $h = 14'$.

(A) 168 sq. ft.

(B) 84 sq. ft.

(C) 42 sq. ft.

(D) 24 sq. ft.

235. Increased by 150%, the number 72 becomes

(A) 188

(B) 108

(C) 180

(D) 170

236. If $14x - 2y = 32$ and $x + 2y = 13$, then $x = ?$

(A) 5

(B) 8

(C) 3

(D) 4

237. If $ab + 4 = 52$, and $a = 6$, $b = ?$

(A) 42

(B) 8

(C) 21

(D) 4

238. A group left on a trip at 8:50 AM and reached its destination at 3:30 PM. How long, in hours and minutes, did the trip take?

(A) 3 hours 10 minutes

(B) 4 hours 40 minutes

(C) 5 hours 10 minutes

(D) 6 hours 40 minutes

STOP

END OF SECTION 4. IF YOU HAVE ANY TIME LEFT, GO OVER YOUR WORK IN THIS SECTION ONLY. DO NOT WORK IN ANY OTHER SECTION OF THE TEST.

LANGUAGE

Time—25 minutes

Directions: This test is divided into three sections. Read the special instructions at the beginning of each section carefully as you come to them.

In questions 239–278, look for errors in capitalization, punctuation, or usage. Mark your answer sheet for the letter of the sentence that contains the error. If you find no error, mark (D) on your answer sheet.

239. (A) We had swum across the lake before the sun rose.
(B) Clearly visible on the desk were those letters he claimed to have mailed yesterday.
(C) John Kennedy effected many executive reforms during the tragically few years that he served as president of the United States.
(D) No mistakes.

240. (A) The loud noise of the cars and trucks aggravates those who live near the road.
(B) Joe seems slow on the track, but you will find few players quicker than he on the basketball court.
(C) Admirers of American ballet have made the claim that its stars can dance as well as or better than the best of the Russian artists.
(D) No mistakes.

241. (A) Rather than go with John, he decided to stay at home.
(B) Each of the nurses were scrupulously careful about personal cleanliness.
(C) His education had filled him with anger against those who he believed had hurt or humiliated him.
(D) No mistakes.

242. (A) After he had paid the fee and had seen the pictures he was quite satisfied.
(B) If I weren't dressed in this uniform, I wouldn't feel so conspicuous.
(C) I am depending on the medicine's being delivered without delay.
(D) No mistakes.

243. (A) Neither tears nor protests effected the least change in their parents' decision.
(B) Being able to trust his sources is indispensable for the investigative reporter.
(C) When you go to the library tomorrow, please take this book to the librarian who sits in the reference room.
(D) No mistakes.

244. (A) The government, announcing a bill of rights for its citizens, promised them equal rights under the law.
(B) Martin Luther King's birthday was recently designated a federal holiday.
(C) Remember that our Constitution is not self-executing; it must be interpreted and applied by the Supreme Court.
(D) No mistakes.

GO ON TO THE NEXT PAGE

245. (A) If you prepare systematically and diligently for the examination, one can be confident of passing it.
(B) Mary was so uninterested in the baseball game that she yawned unashamedly.
(C) If he had had the forethought to arrange an appointment, his reception might have been more friendly.
(D) No mistakes.

246. (A) Your telling the truth in the face of such dire consequences required great moral courage.
(B) No one among the students was more disgruntled than she when the assignments were handed out.
(C) A full hour before the party was to begin, the room was clean like it had never been before.
(D) No mistakes.

247. (A) For conscience's sake he gave himself up, though no suspicion had been directed toward him.
(B) Because they were unaware of his interest in the building, they did not understand why he felt so bad about it's being condemned.
(C) "I truly think," he said, "that we are entitled to have the day off in this snowstorm."
(D) No mistakes.

248. (A) Was it really she whom you saw last night?
(B) The distraught traveler asked Tom and I to give her directions to the nearest bus stop.
(C) Making friends is more rewarding than being antisocial.
(D) No mistakes.

249. (A) In his tales of adventure and romance, he predicted many scientific achievements of the 20th century.
(B) Today's *Times* has headlines about another woman who has just swum the English Channel.
(C) Some Third World countries have suggested that they be given the right to regularly censor what foreign journalists tell about their countries.
(D) No mistakes.

250. (A) Even if history does not repeat itself, knowledge of history can give current problems a familiar look.
(B) He proved to his own satisfaction that he was as clever as, if not more clever than, she.
(C) The citizens of Washington, like Los Angeles, prefer to commute by automobile.
(D) No mistakes.

251. (A) I have found one of those books that teaches how to build a model airplane.
(B) There are less derelicts in the downtown area since the crumbling building was razed.
(C) The ceremonies were opened by a colorful drum and bugle corps.
(D) No mistakes.

252. (A) Do not make a choice that changed the meaning of the original sentence.
(B) I would appreciate your treating me as if I were your sister.
(C) The contract should not have been awarded to the secretary's nephew.
(D) No mistakes.

253. (A) "To eat sparingly is advisable," said the doctor.
(B) "Which is the way to the science building?" asked the new student.
(C) She inquired, "Are you going to hand in your report before lunch?"
(D) No mistakes.

254. (A) A portion of the rental cost of the building, is based on the office space used by the agency.
(B) It is in everyone's interest for the poor to be assisted with heating costs.
(C) Do you understand the meaning of the expression, "full faith and credit"?
(D) No mistakes.

255. (A) You must explain that in the United States there is no government interference with the arts.
(B) The failure to pay back loans is a major cause of the failure of banks.
(C) The former Soviet Union was unsuccessful in curbing youth's "addiction" to hard rock and heavy metal.
(D) No mistakes.

256. (A) The convicted spy was hanged at sunrise.
(B) The lady looked well in her new boots.
(C) Neither the manager nor the employees want to work overtime.
(D) No mistakes.

257. (A) The town consists of three distinct sections, of which the western one is by far the larger.
(B) His speech is so precise as to seem affected.
(C) The door opens, and in walk John and Mary.
(D) No mistakes.

258. (A) His testimony today is different from that of yesterday.
(B) If you had studied the problem carefully, you would have found the solution more quickly.
(C) The flowers smelled so sweet that the whole house was perfumed.
(D) No mistakes.

259. (A) Never before have I seen anyone who has the skill John has when he repairs engines.
(B) There goes the last piece of cake and the last spoonful of ice cream.
(C) Every one of the campers but John and me is going on the hike.
(D) No mistakes.

260. (A) Chicago is larger than any other city in Illinois.
(B) The reason the new leader was so unsuccessful was that she had fewer responsibilities.
(C) Honor as well as profit are to be gained by these studies.
(D) No mistakes.

261. (A) That business is good appears to be true.
(B) The school secretary was pleased that the courses she had taken were relevant to her work.
(C) Strict accuracy is a necessary requisite in record keeping.
(D) No mistakes.

262. (A) The expression "Thanking you in advance" is unacceptable in modern practice.
(B) I like Burns's poem "To a Mountain Daisy."
(C) Venetian blinds—called that even though they probably did not originate in Venice, are no longer used in most homes.
(D) No mistakes.

263. (A) You see, you did mail the letter to yourself!
(B) Your introduction to your new classmates has been a pleasant experience, has it not.
(C) During the broadcast you are expected to stand, to salute, and to sing the fourth stanza of "America."
(D) No mistakes.

GO ON TO THE NEXT PAGE

264. (A) Participation in active sports produces both release from tension as well as physical well-being.
(B) One or the other of those clerks is responsible for these errors.
(C) None of the rocks which form the solid crust of our planet is more than two billion years old.
(D) No mistakes.

265. (A) We all prefer those other kinds of candy.
(B) The law prescribes when, where, and to whom the tax should be paid.
(C) Everything would have turned out right if she had only waited.
(D) No mistakes.

266. (A) Yesterday they laid their uniforms aside with the usual end-of-the-season regret.
(B) John told William that he was sure he had seen it.
(C) He determined to be guided by the opinion of whoever spoke first.
(D) No mistakes.

267. (A) Because a man understands a woman does not mean they are necessarily compatible.
(B) After much talk and haranguing, the workers received an increase in wages.
(C) If I am chosen, I will try and attend every meeting that is called.
(D) No mistakes.

268. (A) While driving through the mountain pass, the breathtaking scenes awed the travelers.
(B) I do not understand why mother should object to my playing the piano at the party.
(C) My experience in South Africa taught me that the climate there is quite different from ours.
(D) No mistakes.

269. (A) To learn to speak a foreign language fluently requires much practice.
(B) I could not help feel that her reasons for coming here were not honest.
(C) It would be interesting to compare the interior of one of the pyramids in Mexico with that of one of the pyramids in Egypt.
(D) No mistakes.

270. (A) "Complaints from the public," reports a government official, "are no longer considered to be a mere nuisance."
(B) Statistics tell us, "that heart disease kills more people than any other illness."
(C) According to a report released by the Department of Agriculture, the labor required to produce a bushel of wheat in 1830 was three hours.
(D) No mistakes.

271. (A) His written work has been done in so careless a manner that I refuse to read it.
(B) I never feel badly if after trying hard I fail to win a prize; the effort gives me satisfaction.
(C) Neither the United States nor, for that matter, any other country has seriously regretted having joined the United Nations.
(D) No mistakes.

272. (A) My landlord does not approve of my sending that letter to the local rent control agency.
(B) My artist friend and myself were the only guests in the gallery to truly appreciate the abstract paintings on display.
(C) The messenger will have gone to the airport before the package can be sent to the shipping room.
(D) No mistakes.

273. (A) Between you and me, I must say that I find this whole situation to be ridiculous.
(B) The dimensions of the envelope determine the quantity of material that can be enclosed.
(C) The reason why the train was so late today was because the previous train had been derailed.
(D) No mistakes.

274. (A) Due to the impending snowstorm, we will go directly home instead of stopping for ice cream.
(B) The eraser was lost after it had lain alongside the typewriter for weeks.
(C) Please distribute these newly arrived booklets among all the teachers in the building.
(D) No mistakes.

275. (A) The lecture was interrupted by the whirring, often much too loud, of the street-repair machinery right outside the window.
(B) Mandated school courses include mathematics, literature, history, and science; optional subjects include drama, marching band, and weaving,
(C) The pupil's account of his lateness is incredible, I will not give him a classroom pass.
(D) No mistakes.

276. (A) Winter came before the archaeologists could do anything more than mark out the burial site.
(B) A knock on the door having disrupted her concentration, she decided to wash her hair.
(C) Let's you and me settle the matter between ourselves.
(D) No mistakes.

277. (A) I recommend that you participate in all the discussions and heed the council of your elders.
(B) Upon graduation from the training course, my friend will be assigned to a permanent position.
(C) He finally realized that the extra practice had had a visible effect on his accuracy at the foul line.
(D) No mistakes.

278. (A) That unfortunate family faces the problem of adjusting itself to a new way of life.
(B) The secretary promptly notified the principal of the fire for which he was highly praised.
(C) All questions regarding procedure should be referred to a disinterested expert.
(D) No mistakes.

Directions: For questions 279–288, look for mistakes in spelling only.

279. (A) A novocaine shot promises only transient pain in place of agony from prolonged drilling.
(B) I will join the theater party next week if I am able to locate a responsible babysitter.
(C) That painting is so valuable that it is described as priceless.
(D) No mistakes.

280. (A) The circumference of a circle is the distance around its outer edge.
(B) Every accused is entitled to trial before an impartial jury.
(C) Now that the snow has been cleared from the streets, the mayor is able to rescind the no-parking order.
(D) No mistakes.

GO ON TO THE NEXT PAGE

281. (A) A timid person is likely to be terrified of weird noises in the night.
(B) Persons who are taking certain medicines should confine themselves to drinking caffeine-free coffee.
(C) Examinations such as this one are, unfortunately, a necessary evil.
(D) No mistakes.

282. (A) The eager young politician stood at the street comer handing out political pamphlets.
(B) If you do not watch your eating habits in a foreign country, you may return with an intestinal paresite.
(C) My childhood heroes were mainly cartoon characters.
(D) No mistakes.

283. (A) Begin to descend into the cave by way of the staircase just beyond the huge copper beech tree.
(B) Admissible evidence is evidence that has been collected in entirely legal ways.
(C) Since our army is so outnumbered, we might as well conceed defeat and limit our casualties.
(D) No mistakes.

284. (A) The scavengers desecrated many native graves.
(B) Be sure you enter your figures in a straight column.
(C) Even an exorbitant charge does not guarantee that the doctor will perform a thorough examination.
(D) No mistakes.

285. (A) The prologue to the play greatly enhanced its meaning.
(B) Retarded students may sometimes join their classmates for assembly programs and physical education classes.
(C) The error on the scoreboard was immediately noticable to all.
(D) No mistakes.

286. (A) The union and management agreed that the recommendation of the arbitrator would be binding.
(B) Parallel lines never meet.
(C) Drinking and driving often combine to conclude with a tragic accident.
(D) No mistakes.

287. (A) The hospital issued a daily bulletin regarding the movie star's medical condition.
(B) Please do not interrupt my telephone conversation.
(C) The newest soft contact lenses allow for extended wear.
(D) No mistakes.

288. (A) The manufacturer's reply was terse but cordial.
(B) Every student who was questioned gave a similar explanation.
(C) The writer has created a clever psuedonym for himself.
(D) No mistakes.

Directions: Questions 289–298 deal with the subject of composition. Follow the directions for each question.

289. Choose the best word or words to join the thoughts together.

The soldiers will not come home _____ the war is over.

(A) while
(B) since
(C) before
(D) None of these.

290. Choose the best word or words to join the thoughts together.

We enjoyed the movie _____ the long wait in line.

(A) during
(B) despite
(C) because of
(D) None of these.

291. Choose the group of words that best completes this sentence.

She avoided my look of surprise by _____

(A) staring at the ceiling steadily.
(B) staring up at the steady ceiling.
(C) staring up steadily at the ceiling.
(D) steadily staring at the ceiling.

292. Which of these expresses the idea most clearly?

(A) You can swim in tropical waters and see glass-bottomed boats, colorful fish, and coral reefs.
(B) You can see glass-bottomed fish swimming among coral reefs and colorful boats in tropical waters.
(C) In tropical waters you can see glass-bottomed boats, colorful fish, and coral reefs swimming.
(D) From glass-bottomed boats you can see colorful fish swimming in tropical waters among coral reefs.

293. Which of these expresses the idea most clearly?

(A) Backgammon is a complex game, and you must change strategies often to learn it well.
(B) Though backgammon is easy to learn, it is a complex game which requires frequent shifts of strategy when played well.
(C) To learn to play backgammon you must shift complex strategies easily.
(D) You must easily learn to shift strategies to play the complex game of backgammon well.

294. Choose the pair of sentences that best develops this topic sentence.

Computers came along at just the right moment.

(A) Cities were growing larger and spreading farther. People found they couldn't gather facts fast enough to make needed decisions.
(B) The computer is a mass of complex parts and flashing lights. However, it is still just a machine made by humans to serve humans.
(C) The most unusual use for computers lately has been in the supermarket. At the wave of a wand, the computer can read what a person has bought.
(D) The computer aids business by storing information. It is able to provide this information almost as soon as a problem comes up.

295. Which of the following sentences offers *least* support to the topic "The Need to Protect the Bald Eagle"?

(A) In flight the bald eagle is beautiful.
(B) Today, it enjoys the full protection of the law and seems to be slowly increasing.
(C) It is so plentiful that it is seen as a dangerous rival to the fishing industry.
(D) The game laws of Alaska are under local jurisdiction.

296. Which of these best fits under the topic, "The Squid—A Master of Disguise"?

(A) Because the squid is shy, it is often misunderstood.
(B) Little sacs of pigment enable the squid to change its color.
(C) In reality, they are adaptable, intelligent, and often beautiful.
(D) They propel themselves backward by squirting water out of a nozzle located near their heads.

GO ON TO THE NEXT PAGE

297. Which sentence does *not* belong in the paragraph?

(1) Intense religious zeal was the main reason for the Crusades, but it was not the only reason. (2) The Crusades weakened feudalism. (3) Businessmen saw good opportunities to set up new markets in the East. (4) Some knights hoped to win military glory and many just sought adventure.

(A) sentence 1

(B) sentence 2

(C) sentence 3

(D) sentence 4

298. Where should the sentence, "Man is learning," be placed in the paragraph below?

(1) His past experiences have taught him well. (2) He imports ladybugs to destroy aphids. (3) He irrigates, fertilizes, and rotates his crops.

(A) before sentence 1

(B) between sentences 1 and 2

(C) between sentences 2 and 3

(D) The sentence does not fit in this paragraph.

STOP

END OF SECTION 5. IF YOU HAVE ANY TIME LEFT, GO OVER YOUR WORK IN THIS SECTION ONLY. DO NOT WORK IN ANY OTHER SECTION OF THE TEST.

Answer Key

VERBAL SKILLS

1. C	13. B	25. B	37. D	49. D
2. A	14. D	26. A	38. B	50. B
3. B	15. C	27. C	39. A	51. A
4. B	16. D	28. C	40. C	52. C
5. D	17. B	29. B	41. D	53. D
6. C	18. A	30. B	42. A	54. B
7. A	19. C	31. D	43. B	55. C
8. D	20. A	32. C	44. B	56. C
9. A	21. C	33. D	45. C	57. A
10. B	22. A	34. A	46. B	58. C
11. C	23. C	35. C	47. A	59. B
12. B	24. D	36. A	48. B	60. D

QUANTITATIVE SKILLS

61. B	72. D	83. D	94. C	105. C
62. C	73. C	84. B	95. D	106. D
63. D	74. A	85. C	96. A	107. C
64. B	75. C	86. A	97. D	108. A
65. A	76. A	87. D	98. B	109. B
66. D	77. B	88. A	99. D	110. C
67. C	78. A	89. D	100. A	111. A
68. C	79. B	90. B	101. B	112. D
69. A	80. C	91. B	102. A	
70. D	81. B	92. D	103. A	
71. B	82. A	93. C	104. B	

READING—COMPREHENSION

113. C	121. D	129. C	137. D	145. B
114. D	122. C	130. B	138. A	146. A
115. C	123. A	131. D	139. D	147. D
116. D	124. D	132. C	140. A	148. D
117. C	125. C	133. D	141. B	149. A
118. B	126. B	134. D	142. B	150. B
119. A	127. A	135. A	143. C	151. B
120. B	128. D	136. C	144. C	152. C

READING—VOCABULARY

153. C	158. A	163. D	168. D	173. C
154. B	159. B	164. A	169. B	174. A
155. D	160. C	165. A	170. B	
156. A	161. A	166. B	171. D	
157. D	162. C	167. D	172. B	

MATHEMATICS—CONCEPTS

175. D	180. D	185. A	190. A	195. C
176. B	181. B	186. C	191. B	196. A
177. A	182. C	187. D	192. C	197. B
178. B	183. A	188. D	193. A	198. D
179. C	184. C	189. C	194. A	

MATHEMATICS—PROBLEM-SOLVING

199. B	207. C	215. D	223. C	231. D
200. C	208. A	216. A	224. B	232. A
201. A	209. B	217. D	225. A	233. C
202. B	210. A	218. B	226. A	234. B
203. B	211. A	219. C	227. A	235. C
204. A	212. D	220. D	228. C	236. C
205. D	213. C	221. B	229. D	237. B
206. B	214. B	222. A	230. A	238. D

LANGUAGE

239. C	251. B	263. B	275. C	287. B
240. A	252. A	264. A	276. D	288. C
241. B	253. D	265. D	277. A	289. C
242. A	254. A	266. B	278. B	290. B
243. D	255. D	267. C	279. B	291. D
244. D	256. B	268. A	280. A	292. D
245. A	257. A	269. D	281. D	293. B
246. C	258. D	270. B	282. B	294. A
247. B	259. B	271. B	283. C	295. C
248. B	260. C	272. B	284. D	296. B
249. C	261. C	273. C	285. C	297. B
250. C	262. C	274. A	286. A	298. A

Answers and Explanations

VERBAL SKILLS

1. **(C)** *Fourth* is an ordinal number. The other three are cardinal numbers.
2. **(A)** *Arouse* and *pacify* are antonyms, as are *agitate* and *smooth*. *Ruffle* is a synonym for *agitate*.
3. **(B)** From the least expensive to the most expensive: rolls—bagels—muffins. Muffins are more expensive than rolls, not less.
4. **(B)** Answer. A query is a question.
5. **(D)** To *impair* is to damage or to *weaken*.
6. **(C)** *Death* is the fact of dying. The other choices are crimes, one of which just happens to cause death.
7. **(A)** That which is *variable* is changeable, fluctuating, or *shifting*.
8. **(D)** The relationship is that of object to action. When one *beats* an *egg*, one performs a violent act upon the substance of the egg in preparation for eating. When one *mashes* a *potato*, one performs an analogous act upon the potato. Baking a potato prepares it for eating, but the act of baking is not analogous to the act of beating. If *mash* were not offered as a choice, *bake* might have served as the answer. You must always choose the best answer available.
9. **(A)** To *obstruct* is to clog or to *block*.
10. **(B)** Jane has 15¢ less than Barbara; Barry has 25¢ less than Barbara. Barry has less money than Jane, not more.
11. **(C)** *Fever* is a symptom. All the other choices are diseases.
12. **(B)** Result. The *result* is the end product of a *cause*. A synonym for *result* is "effect." Do not confuse "effect" with *affect*, which means "influence."
13. **(B)** The analogy is one of opposites or antonyms. *Clumsy* is the opposite of *skillful*; *awkward* is the opposite of *deft*. *Agile* is a synonym for *deft*.
14. **(D)** A cave is a naturally occurring shelter which might be used as a dwelling place. All the other choices are man-made.
15. **(C)** Pretzel, the dachshund, is clearly less shaggy than Pepper and so could be in the same dog obedience class, but there is no information to suggest that Pretzel even goes to obedience school.
16. **(D)** The relationship is that of part to whole, or, more specifically, that of the center to its surroundings. The *pit* is at the center of the *peach;* the *sun* is at the center of the *solar system*.
17. **(B)** *Revenue* means *income*. Taxes produce revenue, but they are not in themselves revenue.
18. **(A)** A *trapeze* is a short horizontal bar from which gymnasts and aerialists swing and upon which they perform. All the other choices are tools that make work easier.
19. **(C)** *Tears* may well come as a sign of emotion. All the other choices are emotions themselves.
20. **(A)** From fastest to slowest jumper we have: Cleo—Lori—Inez—Linda—Mary.
21. **(C)** *Manual*, as opposed to automatic or mechanical, means *hand-operated*.
22. **(A)** *Marshy* means "boggy" or *swampy*.
23. **(C)** The relationship is that of actor to object, or, if you like, eater to eaten. A *seal* eats *fish;* a *bird* eats *worms*.
24. **(D)** *Loss* is the opposite of *profit*.
25. **(B)** *Activity* is motion. *Rest* is freedom from activity.

26. **(A)** *Wind* is the general term for air in motion. All the other choices are descriptions of winds based upon wind speed.
27. **(C)** All people eaters are purple, but it does not necessarily follow that all things purple eat people. We cannot tell whether or not there are some cyclops that are purple even though they do not eat people.
28. **(C)** A *stench* is an offensive smell, or *foul odor.*
29. **(B)** The word *immaterial* means *unimportant.*
30. **(B)** From the heaviest to the lightest books we have: blue—orange—green—red—yellow. The yellow books are the lightest so they cannot be heavier than green.
31. **(D)** A *shoe* is made of *leather;* a *highway* is made of *asphalt.*
32. **(C)** Destroy. To mend is to repair.
33. **(D)** *Concrete* means "specific" or "particular." *Abstract* means "general" or "theoretical."
34. **(A)** To *function* is to *operate* or to "work."
35. **(C)** Meat is food. All the other choices are nutrients found in food.
36. **(A)** Because all Ts are either green-eyed Ys or blue-tailed Gs, it is reasonable to assume that some are blue-tailed Gs. Because all blue-tailed Gs have red noses, we can safely assume that some Ts, at least those which are blue-tailed Gs, have red noses.
37. **(D)** *Sullen* means "morose" or *angrily silent.* The word meaning "grayish yellow" is "sallow"; that meaning "soaking wet" is "sodden"; that meaning "very dirty" is "sordid."
38. **(B)** *Monkey* is the general term describing a whole class of primates, regardless of gender. All the other choices are specifically male animals.
39. **(A)** You *taste* with your *tongue* you *touch* with your *finger*. The sense of touch has to do with feeling, but the organ of touch to be found among the choices is *finger*, which is analogous to *tongue* in its relation to *taste.*
40. **(C)** Harmony. *Discord* means "deep disagreement." Music may be either harmonious or discordant.
41. **(D)** *Fumes* are gas, smoke, or vapor emanations. The other choices describe the smell of fumes.
42. **(A)** *Riding* is a passive act; an animal or machine does the transporting. All the other choices are active ways in which to move from one place to another.
43. **(B)** *Fatal* means "causing death" or *deadly.*
44. **(B)** Terry has won the most races of all.
45. **(C)** A *brick* is opaque. All the other choices are translucent.
46. **(B)** *Secure* means *safe*, as in "not exposed to danger."
47. **(A)** Dull. *Garish* means "gaudy" and "glaring."
48. **(B)** This is a sequential relationship. The sequence is from parent to child. *Horse* is the parent; *foal* the child. *Mother* is the parent; *son* the child. The gender of the parent and child is irrelevant to this analogy.
49. **(D)** A *sourball* is a very hard food. All the other choices are soft foods.
50. **(B)** That which is *counterfeit* is an "imitation made with intent to defraud" and, hence, *false.*
51. **(A)** In terms of most lanes to fewest lanes: thruway—highway—parkway.
52. **(C)** In this actor and object relationship, the actor serves as an irritant to the object. Thus, a *flea* irritates a *dog*; a *fly* irritates a *horse.* A rider might at times irritate a horse, but not with such consistency as a fly.
53. **(D)** The word *intermittently* means "recurring from time to time."
54. **(B)** *Acrylic* refers to a resin product—fiber, paint, or adhesive. The other choices refer to languages that are printed in different alphabets. If you had trouble with this, you were probably thinking of *Cyrillic*, the alphabet in which the Russian language is written.
55. **(C)** Similar. *Diverse* means "different."

56. **(C)** The *finder* seeks and receives a *reward;* the *repenter* seeks and receives *absolution* (from sin). *Contrition* is the feeling the repenter must have in order to repent. *Religion* may be associated with *repentance,* but without the same essential actor-to-object relationship.
57. **(A)** When an object *bends,* it changes shape or orientation but remains intact. All the other choices refer to breaking apart.
58. **(C)** We are told only relative positions with regard to north and south, but have no information as to proximity, or what is adjacent to what. We cannot tell from this information just where the grocery store is in relation to the dry cleaner.
59. **(B)** *Deception* means *fraud* or "subterfuge."
60. **(D)** *Nylon* is a synthetic fiber. All the other choices are natural fibers.

QUANTITATIVE SKILLS

61. **(B)** If you write the direction and amount of change between the numbers of the series, you see that the pattern of the series is –1, –2, –1, –3, –1, –4.... The next step is –1. 11 – 1 = 10.
62. **(C)** The relationships are clearly visible. Just read and examine carefully.
63. **(D)** First do the arithmetic. (A) is 15; (B) is 125; and (C) is 9. Obviously, (B) is greater than either (A) or (C).
64. **(B)** 60% of 40 = 24 – 5 = 19.
65. **(A)** The pattern is +2, –4, +2, –4, and so on. 44 + 2 = 46.
66. **(D)** The cube of 4 divided by 4 is the square of 4. 4^2 = 16. 16 + 3 = 19.
67. **(C)** 6 + 12 + 4 + 41 + 7 = 70 ÷ 5 = 14 × 2 = 28.
68. **(C)** The series so far is: –2, –2, –3, –3, –4, –4; next should come –5, –5. 24 – 5 = 19 – 5 = 14.
69. **(A)** The series on both sides of the blank reads +6, –8. 25 + 6 = 31. Then, to confirm, 31 – 8 = 23.
70. **(D)** Angle *C* is a right angle (90°). The three angles of a triangle must add up to 180°. Therefore, the sum of the other two angles is equal to 90°.
71. **(B)** 6 × 4 = 24. 24 is $\frac{2}{3}$ of 36.
72. **(D)** 42 + 3 = 45. 45 ÷ 9 = 5.
73. **(C)** Count up the shaded areas, taking note of the fact that some areas are larger than others. Then choose your answer by inspection and careful reading.
74. **(A)** The series reads: +9, +10, +11, +12, +13. Continue: 57 + 14 = 71 + 15 = 86 + 16 = 102.
75. **(C)** Make equivalent decimals of (A), (B), and (C). (B) = .858; (C) = .875, which makes it equal to (A). Now you can see that there is only one true statement.
76. **(A)** 69 – 6 = 63 ÷ 7 = 9.
77. **(B)** (A) is 4; (B) is 6; (C) is 4. Now just be careful.
78. **(A)** (A) is 150; (B) is 300; (C) is 500; and (D) is 350.
79. **(B)** Sometimes you must shift gears. Most series are based upon addition and subtraction, but not all. You cannot make sense of this series if you stick to the +8 with which you probably started out. The relationship between 9 and 18 and between 15 and 30 should make you think of multiplication. The series reads: × 2, –7, × 2, –7, × 2, –7.... 11 × 2 = 22. To confirm: 22 – 7 = 15.
80. **(C)** You should see that the pattern is developing: +1, +1, +2, +2, +3, +3, +4.... 18 + 4 = 22.
81. **(B)** Let *x* equal the number.

    30% + 50% = 80% = .80

    .80*x* = 96; *x* = 96 ÷ .80 = 120.
82. **(A)** 12 + 87 + 72 + 41 = 212 ÷ 4 = 53 - 25 = 28.

83. **(D)** The series +1, –2, +1, –3, +l, –4 now continues with +1. 18 + 1 = 19.

84. **(B)** Read, count, and reason carefully.

85. **(C)** $\frac{4}{5}$ of 80 = 64 + 3 = 67. 82 – 67 = 15.

86. **(A)** The series as we see it reads +10, +9, +8, __, +5. Fill in with 32 + 7 = 39 + 6 = 45.

87. **(D)** (A) is 36; (B) is 64; and (C) is 144. Plug in the numbers and find the answer.

88. **(A)** Work out the arithmetic and learn that (A), (B), and (C) all are equal to 51. Now there is only one true statement.

89. **(D)** $8 \times 4 = 32 \times 3 = 96 - 30 = 66$.

90. **(B)** $\frac{1}{8}$ of 96 = $12 \times 6 = 72$.

91. **(B)** The series may be interpreted as a repetition of +.125 or as increasing decimals of $\frac{1}{8}$, $\frac{2}{8}$, $\frac{3}{8}$, and so on.

92. **(D)** Count, then read carefully.

93. **(C)** $\frac{5}{9}$ of 99 = 55 + 15 = 70.

94. **(C)** The easiest way to find the solution is to try out each of the answers.

$$\frac{9}{16} \div \frac{3}{4} = \frac{9}{16} \times \frac{4}{3} = \frac{3}{4}; \frac{5}{8} \div \frac{3}{4} = \frac{5}{6}; \frac{7}{16} \div \frac{3}{4} = \frac{7}{12}; \frac{3}{4} \div \frac{3}{4} = 1.$$

95. **(D)** .8 and 80% are equal, but $\frac{8}{10}$% is only .008. Now it's easy.

96. **(A)** The order of the lengths of the lines, shortest to longest, is (B), (C), (A), (D).

97. **(D)** You should see quite readily that the series is based on squares followed by their positive number square roots in descending order. The missing number is the square of 7.

98. **(B)** The letters progress by +3. The numbers progress by –4. Three letters after *K* is *N*. 13 – 4 = 9.

99. **(D)** After you look beyond the first two numbers, you can see that the progression is $\times 3$, repeat the number, $\times 3$, repeat the number, $\times 3$, repeat the number. We pick up the series at $\times 3$. $27 \times 3 = 81$. Then repeat the number 81. Then, $81 \times 3 = 243$.

100. **(A)** If $\frac{3}{8}$ = 9, then $\frac{1}{8}$ = 3 and $\frac{8}{8}$ (the number) = 24. $83\frac{1}{3}$%, or $\frac{5}{6}$, of 24 = 20.

101. **(B)** The size of the angle is easily read on the arc of the protractor. (A) = 70°; (B) = 60°; and (C) = 50°. A right angle is 90°. Now, plug the angle sizes into the statements to find the answer.

102. **(A)** (A) is 40; (B) is 40; and (C) is 32. Use numbers in place of the letters and solve.

103. **(A)** Don't be thrown by the negative numbers. The series is: +5, +2, +5, +2. Next comes +5. –5 + 5 = 0.

104. **(B)** $4 \times 5 = 20 \times 3 = 60$. We need add nothing at all (0) to 60 to get 60.

105. **(C)** This is a simple ÷ 2 series; the decimals make it a bit confusing. .025 ÷ 2 = .0125.

106. **(D)** $\frac{5}{8}$ of 96 = 60 – 12 = 48.

107. **(C)** (A) is 21¢; (B) is 28¢; and (C) is 25¢. Replace letters with money amounts and answer the question.

108. **(A)** The progress of the series is +3. 18 + 3 = 21. However, in the small segment that we see, the series alternates two Roman numerals and two Arabic numbers. Having no reason to suppose that this alternation will change later in the series, we must assume that the next two entries will be Roman numerals. Hence, XXI is the correct form for the next number in the series.

109. **(B)** This is a ÷ 2 series which you might find somewhat hard to visualize in the fraction form. The correct answer, $\frac{8}{32}$, is $\frac{8}{16}$ ÷ 2. Rename the improper fractions as whole numbers to make this clear. $\frac{16}{2} = 8$; $\frac{8}{2} = 4$; $\frac{8}{4} = 2$; $\frac{8}{8} = 1$; $\frac{8}{16} = \frac{1}{2}$. Now $8 \div 2 = 4 \div 2 = 2 \div 2 = 1 \div 2 = \frac{1}{2}$, or $(\frac{8}{16})$, $\div 2 = \frac{1}{4}$, or $(\frac{8}{32})$.

110. **(C)** (A) is 95; (B) is 1.95; (C) is 95. Work with the numbers instead of the letters to find the answer.

111. **(A)** This is another instance in which it is easiest to try out the answers. 40% of 150 = 60. 150 – 60 = 90. Because the first choice works, there is no reason to continue. (B) and (C), being less than 90, could not

possibly be correct. If you wanted to be doubly sure (and if you had spare time) you could try 40% of 145 = 58. 145 – 58 = 87, which is not 90.

112. **(D)** The pattern being established is: –8, repeat the number, –6, repeat the number, –4, repeat the number. Logically, the next step is –2, repeat the number. 8 – 2 = 6; then repeat the 6.

READING—COMPREHENSION

113. **(C)** The selection is about a game that appears to be an early version of modern baseball.
114. **(D)** There were "usually between 8 and 20 players." The number of players was not fixed by rule. In fact, according to the last sentence, there were very few rules.
115. **(C)** One of the few rules defined the playing field as a 60-foot square.
116. **(D)** The first sentence tells us that the game was similar to the English game of rounders. The game probably derived its name from the fact that players ran around the bases. The second sentence assures us that the game was exciting for both players and spectators.
117. **(C)** The ball is described as a bullet, cork, or metal slug wound with yarn and string, obviously improvised to be put into service by that moment's group of players.
118. **(B)** The 19th century consists of the years in the 1800s. The game is placed in the early 19th century, from 1800 on. Its popularity increased throughout the first half of the century, so it clearly was played at least until 1850, and probably beyond.
119. **(A)** Compare your knowledge of the game of baseball as it is played today with the description of the game in the selection. You can readily see how much more complicated the game is today.
120. **(B)** The simple, improvised equipment made this a low-cost pastime. The players were not exceptionally skillful, and the game was only an American adaptation of an English game.
121. **(D)** The paddle with the thick handle was sturdy.
122. **(C)** The writer of the passage expresses no feeling whatsoever. This is nothing more than a clear, factual report.
123. **(A)** Phoebes might be easy to catch and band, but the reason that Audubon chose them was that it was a pair of phoebes which had piqued his curiosity.
124. **(D)** The selection says that the message on the band requests that the finder notify the Fish and Wildlife Department.
125. **(C)** Any one of the answer choices could be true, but as used in this passage, a naturalist is specifically a person who studies birds and nature in general.
126. **(B)** The selection describes birdbanding as one method of studying the nesting habits, migration patterns, and populations of birds.
127. **(A)** The clue to this answer is in the first sentence: "…he wondered if they might be the same birds."
128. **(D)** The second sentence tells us that Audubon's banded phoebes returned to the same nesting place. He could legitimately assume that at least some other birds behaved in the same way.
129. **(C)** See the second sentence of the second paragraph.
130. **(B)** *Migration* refers to group movements. *Patterns* implies some form of organization in the movements, that the movements might be periodic rather than random. Migration patterns tend to be seasonal and dictated by the need for food-gathering, but the question asks for a definition, not a reason.
131. **(D)** *Extinction* is the dying out and total disappearance of a species.
132. **(C)** In explaining the value of the Fish and Wildlife Department's endeavors in its studies of birds, the author is encouraging the public to cooperate in reporting sightings of banded birds.

133. **(D)** Although the selection does describe the Wandorobo tribe in some detail, the main topic of the selection is the manner in which birds and men work together in their quest for honey.

134. **(D)** People fear the tsetse fly because it carries the blood parasite that causes the often fatal African sleeping sickness.

135. **(A)** The Wandorobo whistle. The bird chatters.

136. **(C)** The Indicator bird indicates the location of honey trees. Men use the smoke to dislodge the bees.

137. **(D)** The small offering of honey left by the Wandorobo is the bird's reward. A symbiotic relationship is the association of two dissimilar organisms for their mutual benefit.

138. **(A)** Bees do not like smoke. Smoke causes them to fly away to escape from the smoky area. When the bees leave, the Wandorobo collect the honey. Those few bees that somehow avoid the effects of the smoke, perhaps by being outside the tree trunk at the time, sting viciously.

139. **(D)** Would you believe this account if scientists had not confirmed it? It does sound unbelievable. There is no support for the other choices in this passage.

140. **(A)** If the Wandorobo are undaunted by bee stings, they ignore the stings.

141. **(B)** The bird chatters without stopping until the men answer it with whistles and begin to follow.

142. **(B)** The last sentence of the first paragraph tells us that the Wandorobo are nomads who make their homes wherever they find themselves at the end of the day. The Wandorobo are the only tribe which travels in the forest infested with the tsetse fly. Their diet is roots and fruits. They are very courageous, even in the face of stinging bees.

143. **(C)** Mr. Johannes selects films for showing. He is a student of history.

144. **(C)** The last sentence of the first paragraph tells us that youngsters from all five boroughs of the City of New York attend the program.

145. **(B)** Mr. Johannes makes no far-reaching claims for long-term effects of his films. All he claims is that children are open to a broader range of concepts and visual presentations than those of their daily experience.

146. **(A)** To *ferret out* is to "dig" or to "search out." A ferret is a weasel-like animal that hunts out small rodents by flushing them out of their burrows.

147. **(D)** Read carefully. The film series begins in September. The films are shown at the Museum of the City of New York at 11 AM and 3 PM on Saturdays only.

148. **(D)** Because Mr. Johannes chooses a wide variety of films and regularly fills his theater, he is obviously a good judge of children's tastes.

149. **(A)** The answer is in the first paragraph.

150. **(B)** The audience consists of children.

151. **(B)** The word *dusty* is a metaphor for "long-unused" or "almost forgotten." The cans may well have been dust-laden from long disuse, but the reels were well preserved if he was able to show them. At any rate, (B) is certainly true while (A) only possibly might be true. Without (B) as a choice, (A) might have been correct. You must always choose the best answer.

152. **(C)** Silhouettes are one-color dark outline shapes against a light background. As such, the shapes present motion, form, and limited features, mainly profiles. Details can be filled by an active imagination. Choice (B), if anything, would argue against popularity.

READING—VOCABULARY

153. **(C)** *Tedious* means "monotonous," "boring," or *tiresome.*

154. **(B)** To *rescind* is to take back, to revoke, or to *cancel.*

155. **(D)** *Diversity* is difference, or *variety.*

156. **(A)** *Indigence* is destitution, or *poverty.* The word that means "laziness" is "indolence."
157. **(D)** *Vindictive* means "eager to get even" or *revengeful.*
158. **(A)** *Remuneration* is compensation, reward, or *payment.*
159. **(B)** *Deficient* means "lacking," "incomplete," or *inadequate.*
160. **(C)** *Detrimental* means "causing damage" or *harmful.*
161. **(A)** *Accurate* means "precise" or *correct.*
162. **(C)** To *amplify* is to make larger or stronger or to develop more fully, as with details and examples.
163. **(D)** To be *competent* is to be sufficient, permissible, authorized, or *able.*
164. **(A)** *Infraction* is breaking of the rules or *violation.*
165. **(A)** *Relevant* means "related to the matter at hand" or *applicable.*
166. **(B)** A *manual* is a book of instructions or a *handbook.*
167. **(D)** A *device* is a machine devised for a specific purpose. Be careful to define only the underscored word. A *calculator* is a "computational device."
168. **(D)** *Conventional* means "customary," "usual," or *ordinary.*
169. **(B)** *Controversy* is difference of opinion, argument, or *debate.*
170. **(B)** *Diplomatic* means *tactful* when dealing with people.
171. **(D)** *Irate* means *angry.*
172. **(B)** *Durable* means *long-lasting* even under conditions of hard use.
173. **(C)** *Extensive* means "comprehensive," "intensive," or *thorough.*
174. **(A)** The *inception* is the *beginning.*

MATHEMATICS—CONCEPTS

175. **(D)** The millions begin with the seventh digit to the left of the decimal place. Because you need 326 million, you can immediately eliminate choices (A) and (B). Read on: 900 thousand. You need look no further for the correct answer.
176. **(B)** You should know this answer instantly. If you do not, try out each option.
177. **(A)** The first 6 is in the billions place; the second, in the hundred-thousands place. If you had trouble with this problem, review the sections on how to read numbers and determine place values in your math textbook.
178. **(B)** You should recognize immediately that $\frac{1}{2}$ day is shorter than 25 hours and that 3600 seconds is far shorter than 1440 minutes. Narrowing down to the first two choices, you probably know that there are 1440 minutes in a day. If you do not know this, multiply 24 by 60 to see for yourself.
179. **(C)** You should know what the exponents mean. Count the 5s and 3s carefully.
180. **(D)** Multiply and simplify.

$$\frac{3\times 8}{6\times 5}=\frac{24}{30}=\frac{4}{5}$$

181. **(B)** $.5=\frac{1}{2}$. Therefore, .5% must equal $\frac{1}{2}$%.
182. **(C)** Because the sum of the angles of a triangle must always equal 180°, and because $m < B = 90°$, angles A and C together must equal 90°. Do not allow yourself to be diverted by extra information. $m < C$ of the triangle is equal to 30°, so $m < A$ = to 60°, but this knowledge is irrelevant to the question being asked. Do not waste time on unnecessary calculations.
183. **(A)** $9^2 = 81$. Because x is greater than 9, x^2 would have to be greater than 81. Obviously, then, x^2 is greater than 80.

184. **(C)** Many numbers are divisible by either 3 or 4, but not by both. All numbers that are divisible by both 3 and 4 are also divisible by their multiple, 12.

185. **(A)** Compare the digit in the hundredths place.

186. **(C)** The *greatest* common factor of 50 and 10 is 10 itself. 1 and 5 are also common factors, but they are smaller.

187. **(D)** For the sum to be smaller than the given number of an addition problem, the missing number must be negative.

188. **(D)** Begin as if you were solving an equation; subtract 2 from both sides. Now $3x > 10$. Quick inspection will show you that only 3×4 is greater than 10.

189. **(C)** The formula for determining the area of a circle is πr^2. $r = 3$; $r^2 = 3^2 = 9$.

190. **(A)** Because $x - 3 < 12$, x can be any number less than 15.

191. **(B)** Three gallons contain 12 quarts. The ratio is 3:12, or, in simplest form, 1:4.

192. **(C)** If $x = 0$, then $2x < 8$ because $2(0) < 8$. None of the other pairs results in a true statement.

193. **(A)** Simply divide $\frac{4}{5}$ by $\frac{1}{6}$ to find the answer. $\frac{4}{5} \div \frac{1}{6} = \frac{4}{5} \times \frac{6}{1} = \frac{24}{5} = 4\frac{4}{5}$.

194. **(A)** The intersection ($\cap$) of two sets has as its elements only those numbers which are in both original sets.

195. **(C)** Mary's age now = x.

Her sister's age now = $x - 3$.

In five years her sister's age will be $x - 3 + 5 = x + 2$.

196. **(A)** (B) is 4930; (C) is 133.

197. **(B)** $10 < 10.5$.

198. **(D)** The union of the two adjacent line segments creates one continuous line segment.

MATHEMATICS—PROBLEM-SOLVING

199. **(B)** For each teacher, there are 14 students. Because there are 14 teachers, there must be 14×14, or 196, students.

200. **(C)** If 2 inches equal 24 feet, 1 inch equals 12 feet. A line representing 72 feet, therefore, must be 6 inches long ($72 \div 12 = 6$).

201. **(A)** A store markup of 100% would exactly double the price. An 80% markup almost doubles the price. The $14 jeans are priced at almost double their cost to the store. By estimation, the best answer is (A). To figure precisely, remember that an 80% markup is the equivalent of multiplying the cost by 180%, or 1.80.

$$\text{cost} \times 1.80 = 14.00$$
$$\text{cost} = 14.00 \div 1.80$$
$$\text{cost} = \$7.78$$

202. **(B)** Reduce the $14.00 price by 25%.

25% of 14.00 = $14 × .25 = $3.50

$14.00 – 3.50 = $10.50 (new price)

Therefore, (B) is the correct answer. Answer (A) indicates a reduction of only 25 cents. Answer (C) represents a reduction *to* 25% of the original price, or a 75% decrease in price.

203. **(B)** To find the perimeter, we add up the dimensions of all of the sides. Note that there are some parts that have not been assigned measurements, so we have to infer that they are the same as those corresponding parts whose measurements have been designated. Beginning at the bottom and moving clockwise, the dimensions are:

$5" + 7" + 1" + 3" + 3" + 3" + 1" + 7"$

These equal 30 inches. The correct answer is (B). If you chose (A), (C) or (D), you failed to add up all of the segments.

204. **(A)** The area is most easily found by multiplying the length of the figure by its width, and then subtracting the area of the small 3" × 3" square.

$(7" \times 5") - (3" \times 3") = \text{area}$

35 sq. in. – 9 sq. in. = 26 sq. in.

Shapes such as this are often used for irregular pieces of carpeting or covering.

205. **(D)** A 16-minute call would cost $1.56 for the first 3 minutes, plus 22¢ for each of the 13 additional minutes. The total cost is found by $1.56 + 13(.22) = $4.42.

206. **(B)** You have to read only the first and third sentences of the problem. The information in the second sentence is not relevant to the problem. The winner received $\frac{1}{3}$ of the total, or $2,700. Thus, the total purse was $2,700 × 3 = $8,100.

207. **(C)** Number of seats = 12 + 14 = 26

Number of passengers at station A = 14 + 4 = 18

Number of passengers at next stop = 18 – 8 + 13 = 23

Number of empty seats = 26 – 23 = 3

208. **(A)** Raising the sales tax from 5% to 8% is a raise of 3%. 3% of $250 = .03 × $250 = $7.50.

209. **(B)** Simplify the numerator of the fraction, and then divide.

$$\frac{1\frac{3}{4}-\frac{1}{8}}{\frac{1}{8}} = \frac{1\frac{6}{8}-\frac{1}{8}}{\frac{1}{8}}$$

$$= \frac{1\frac{5}{8}}{\frac{1}{8}} = 1\frac{5}{8} \bullet \frac{8}{1}$$

$$= \frac{13}{8} \bullet \frac{8}{1} = 13$$

210. **(A)**

$$\begin{array}{r} 1.970 \\ 1.02\overline{)2.01000} \\ 1\,02 \\ \hline 99\,0 \\ 91\,8 \\ \hline 7\,20 \\ 7\,14 \\ \hline 60 \end{array}$$

211. **(A)** Begin working with the innermost parentheses and work your way out.

$-3 - [(2 - 1) - (3 + 4)]$

$= -3 - [(1) - (7)]$

$= -3 - [1 - 7]$

$= -3 - [-6]$

$= -3 + 6$

$= 3$

212. **(D)** This is a good problem to do in your head. Note that 10% of 70 is 7. 140%, then, is 14 × 7, or 98.

213. **(C)** Borrow a gallon and add it to 2 quarts. Rewrite the problem. Remember that you borrowed.

	4 gallons 6 quarts 1 pint
–	1 gallon 3 quarts 0 pints
	3 gallons 3 quarts 1 pint

214. **(B)** Bracket the multiplication and division first, and solve the problem.

$(6 \div \frac{1}{3}) + (\frac{2}{3} \times 9)$

$= 18 + 6$

$= 24$

215. **(D)** Substitute the values into the expression.

$\sqrt{9+3(2)+1}$

$= \sqrt{9+6+1}$

$= \sqrt{16}$

$= 4$

216. **(A)** 7 is one-third of 21, and $\frac{2}{3}$ is one-third of 2. As a proportion: $\frac{7}{21} = \frac{\frac{2}{3}}{x}$

217. **(D)** To find the average, find the sum of the addends and divide that sum by the number of addends.

$-10 + 6 + 0 + -3 + 22 = 15$

$15 \div 5 = 3$

218. **(B)** By knowing how many telephones are in Adelaide (48,000), and how many serve each group of 100 in the population (12.8), we can find how many groups of 100 are in the population.

48,000 telephones ÷ 12.8 telephones per 100 of population

= 3,750 groups of 100 in the population.

3,750 × 100 = 375,000 people.

219. **(C)** Four boards, each 2'9" long, total 11 feet. The carpenter must buy 11 feet of wood.

220. **(D)** $(4 \times 10^3) + 6 = 4{,}006$

$(2 \times 10^3) + (3 \times 10) + 8 = 2{,}038$

The difference is 1,968.

221. **(B)** Area of a square = s^2

$49 = 7^2$
one side = 7 inches
$P = 4s$
$P = 4 \times 7" = 28$ inches

222. **(A)** $r = 35 - (9)(-n)$
$r = 35 - (9)(-2)$
$r = 35 - (-18)$
$r = 35 + 18 = 53$

To subtract signed numbers, change the sign of the subtrahend and proceed as in algebraic addition.

223. **(C)** First perform the operation within the parentheses. To cube a number, multiply it by itself, two times.

$(3 + 4)^3 = (7)^3 = 7 \times 7 \times 7 = 343$

224. **(B)** Copper and aluminum in the ratio of 10:1 means 10 parts copper to 1 part aluminum.

Let x = weight of aluminum
Then $10x$ = weight of copper
$10x + x = 77$
$11x = 77$
$x = 7$

225. **(A)** His total income is equal to 7% of his sales plus \$150. 7% of his sales is \$945 × .07 = \$66.15:

\$66.15 + \$150 = \$216.15

226. **(A)** If
$x^2 + 5 = 41$
$x^2 = 41 - 5$
$x^2 = 36$
$x = \pm 6$

227. **(A)** The lawn is 8' × 12' = 96 sq. ft.
96 × 5 = 480 pints of water needed
8 pts. in 1 gal.; 480 ÷ 8 = 60 gallons needed

228. **(C)** $\frac{x}{2} + 36 = 37.25$
$\frac{x}{2} = 37.25 - 36$
$\frac{x}{2} = 1.25$
$x = 2.50$

229. **(D)** If the sides are parallel, the angles are congruent.

230. **(A)** Area = length × width

= 176 ft. × 79 ft.

= 13,904 sq. ft.

231. **(D)** $63 \div \frac{1}{9} = 63 \times \frac{9}{1} = 567$

This is a good answer to estimate. By dividing a number by $\frac{1}{9}$, you are, in effect, multiplying it by 9. Only one of the suggested answers is close.

232. **(A)** The amount the house was insured for is 80% of $83,000, or $66,400. The insurance is calculated at 45¢ per hundred, or $4.50 per thousand of value. Because there are 66.4 thousands of value, 66.4 × $4.50 per thousand equals the yearly premium of $298.80.

233. **(C)** The digits are all alike, so you do not need to calculate. Move the decimal point of the divisor two places to the right; do the same for the dividend.

234. **(B)** The formula for the area of a triangle is $A = \frac{1}{2}bh$. Plug in the numbers:

$$A = \frac{1}{2} \cdot 12 \cdot 14$$

$$A = 84 \text{ sq. ft.}$$

235. **(C)** This is a tricky question. It doesn't ask for 150% of 72, but rather to increase 72 by 150%. Because 150% of 72 = 108, we add 72 and 108 for the correct answer. Careful reading is an important factor in test success.

236. **(C)** Write down both equations and add them together.

$$\begin{array}{r} 14x - 2y = 32 \\ + \quad x + 2y = 13 \\ \hline 15x = 45 \\ x = 3 \end{array}$$

237. **(B)** If $a = 6$, $ab + 4 = 52$ becomes $6b + 4 = 52$.

$$\begin{aligned} \text{If } 6b + 4 &= 52 \\ 6b &= 52 - 4 \\ 6b &= 48 \\ b &= 8 \end{aligned}$$

238. **(D)** First convert to a 24–hour clock.

3:30 PM = 15:30

$$\begin{array}{r} 15{:}30 \\ -\ 8{:}50 \\ \hline 6{:}40 \end{array} = 6 \text{ hours } 40 \text{ minutes}$$

To subtract a greater number of minutes from a lesser number of minutes, "borrow" 60 minutes from the hour to enlarge the lesser number.

LANGUAGE

239. **(C)** *President of the United States* must be capitalized.

240. **(A)** To *aggravate* is to "make worse." The correct word should be *annoys*.

241. **(B)** Each of the nurses, one at a time, *was* careful. In (C), *who*, rather than *whom*, is correctly the subject of the clause "who had hurt or...."

242. **(A)** The long introductory phrase must be separated from the independent clause by a comma: After he had paid the fee and had seen the pictures, he was quite satisfied.

243. **(D)** No mistakes.

244. **(D)** No mistakes.

245. **(A)** Maintain the same voice throughout the sentence. "If *you* prepare, *you* can be confident." The statement, "If *one* prepares, *one* can be confident," would also be correct.

246. **(C)** "…the room was clean *as* it had never been before."

247. **(B)** The possessive form of *it* is *its*. *It's* is the contraction for *it is*.

248. **(B)** Tom and *me* are the objects of the verb *asked.*

249. **(C)** There is no reason for the word *countries* to begin with a capital letter.

250. **(C)** You cannot compare people with a city. "The citizens of Washington, like *those* of Los Angeles…."

251. **(B)** *Less* is a measure of bulk amount. *Fewer* gives the count of individuals.

252. **(A)** The choice that you have not yet made cannot have already changed the meaning of the sentence "Do not make a choice that *changes*…"

253. **(D)** No mistakes.

254. **(A)** The comma that separates subject from predicate does not belong there. The entire sentence at (C) is a question, so the question mark is correctly placed outside the quotation marks.

255. **(D)** No mistakes.

256. **(B)** It is unlikely that the new boots made the lady look healthy; they made her look *good*, that is, attractive.

257. **(A)** Three sections are being compared, so the superlative, *largest*, must be used. (C) might sound awkward, but both verbs are in the present tense, and the sentence is correct.

258. **(D)** No mistakes.

259. **(B)** The compound subject—piece of cake *and* spoonful of ice cream—requires a plural verb *go*.

260. **(C)** The subject of the sentence is the singular *honor*. The fact that profit is to be gained as well is additional information, not part of the subject. A singular subject requires a verb that agrees in number; therefore, the correct verb is *is*.

261. **(C)** A *requisite* is a *necessity*. "Necessary requisite" is redundant.

262. **(C)** Dashes used to set apart amplifying but extraneous information must be used in pairs. The comma after *Venice* should be replaced by a dash.

263. **(B)** This direct question should end with a question mark. In (C), a period *always* goes inside the quotation marks regardless of meaning.

264. **(A)** "Both" requires two objects connected by "and." Sports produce both release from tension *and* physical well-being.

265. **(D)** No mistakes.

266. **(B)** This sentence is ambiguous. To whom does the second *he* refer? Is John sure that John had seen it, or is John sure that William had seen it? In (A), *laid* is correctly used as the past tense of *lay*. In (C), *whoever* is the subject of the clause.

267. **(C)** Proper idiomatic form demands *try to attend.*

268. **(A)** The breathtaking scenes did not drive, but that is what the sentence implies. The *travelers* must be cast as the subject of the sentence. "While driving…, the travelers were awed by…."

269. **(D)** No mistakes.

270. **(B)** There is no direct quote here, so quotation marks are inappropriate, as is the comma following "us."

271. **(B)** Feeling *badly* refers to one's sense of touch. When referring to health or emotions, one feels *bad.*

272. **(B)** The correct subject of the sentence is "my artist friend and *I*." The reflexive *myself* is used only when something is reflecting back on me as, for instance, "I was beside myself with grief."

273. **(C)** The *reason why* is not *because*; The *reason why is that*…. Or the *reason that* is *because*…. In (A), *you and me* are correctly the objects of the preposition *between.*

274. **(A)** It is poor form to begin a sentence with "due to." The correct introduction to such an explanatory statement is "because of." In (B), the past participle of the verb *to lie* is *lain*.
275. **(C)** This error is called a "comma splice." The cure might be to create two sentences, with a period at the end of the first, or to join the two independent clauses with either a semicolon or a conjunction such as "so."
276. **(D)** No mistakes.
277. **(A)** The wrong word has been used. A "council" is a group; *counsel*, the required word, means "advice."
278. **(B)** Was the secretary highly praised for the fire? Was the principal highly praised for the fire? If the sentence means to say that the secretary was highly praised for promptly notifying the principal, then that is what the sentence should say.
279. **(B)** responsible
280. **(A)** circumference
281. **(D)** No mistakes.
282. **(B)** parasite
283. **(C)** concede
284. **(D)** No mistakes.
285. **(C)** noticeable (See Spelling—Rule 4, page 102)
286. **(A)** recommendation
287. **(B)** interrupt
288. **(C)** pseudonym
289. **(C)** The point is that the soldiers are busy fighting a war, but will return when the war is over. They will not return before the war is over because they are busy fighting it.
290. **(B)** Choice (A) represents an impossibility, and choice (C) is ridiculous. If the movie is very good, one might consider it to have been worth the wait.
291. **(D)** The ceiling is "up," so choices (B) and (C) can be eliminated as containing redundancies. "Steadily" describes the manner in which she stared and so should be placed next to the word it describes.
292. **(D)** "Glass-bottomed fish" and "coral reefs swimming" make no sense at all. Choice (A) is technically correct, but the whole purpose of glass-bottomed boats is to peer down to observe the fish swimming among the coral reefs.
293. **(B)** Choice (D) is totally garbled. (A) and (C) suggest that changing strategies is part of the learning process. The statement made by (B) is more reasonable.
294. **(A)** The growth of cities and the information explosion define the moment at which computers were needed.
295. **(C)** The threat that the bald eagle poses to the fishing industry counters the need to protect the bird.
296. **(B)** Changing one's color is a means for disguise.
297. **(B)** This sentence is an effect, not a reason.
298. **(A)** This sentence serves as a topic sentence and provides a subject. All the other sentences begin with pronouns referring to "man" and offer examples to bolster the topic sentence.

SCORE SHEET

Although your scores will not be reported as percentages, it may be helpful to convert your test scores to percentages so that you can see at a glance where your strengths and weaknesses lie. The numbers in parentheses represent the questions that test each skill area.

Subject	No. Correct	÷	No. of Questions	=		× 100 = __%
Verbal Analogies (2, 8, 13, 16, 23, 31, 39, 48, 52, 56)	____	÷	10	=	____	× 100 = ___%
Synonyms (5, 7, 9, 17, 21, 22, 28, 29, 34, 37, 43, 46, 50, 53, 59)	____	÷	15	=	____	× 100 = ___%
Logic (3, 10, 15, 20, 27, 30, 36, 44, 51, 58)	____	÷	10	=	____	× 100 = ___%
Verbal Classification (1, 6, 11, 14, 18, 19, 26, 35, 38, 41, 42, 45, 49, 54, 57, 60)	____	÷	16	=	____	× 100 = ___%
Antonyms (4, 12, 24, 25, 32, 33, 40, 47, 55)	____	÷	9	=	____	× 100 = ___%
TOTAL VERBAL SKILLS	____	÷	60	=	____	× 100 = ___%
Number Series (61, 65, 68, 69, 74, 79, 80, 83, 86, 91, 97, 98, 99, 103, 105, 108, 109, 112)	____	÷	18	=	____	× 100 = ___%
Geometric Comparisons (62, 70, 73, 78, 84, 92, 96, 101, 107)	____	÷	9	=	____	× 100 = ___%
Nongeometric Comparisons (63, 75, 77, 87, 88, 95, 102, 110)	____	÷	8	=	____	× 100 = ___%
Number Manipulation (64, 66, 67, 71, 72, 76, 81, 82, 85, 89, 90, 93, 94, 100, 104, 106, 111)	____	÷	17	=	____	× 100 = ___%
TOTAL QUANTITATIVE SKILLS	____	÷	52	=	____	× 100 = ___%
Reading Comprehension (113–152)	____	÷	40	=	____	× 100 = ___%
Reading Vocabulary (153–174)	____	÷	22	=	____	× 100 = ___%
TOTAL READING	____	÷	62	=	____	× 100 = ___%
Mathematics-Concepts (175–198)	____	÷	24	=	____	× 100 = ___%
Mathematics-Problem-Solving (199–238)	____	÷	40	=	____	× 100 = ___%
TOTAL MATHEMATICS	____	÷	64	=	____	× 100 = ___%
Punctuation and Capitalization (239, 242, 244, 247, 249, 253-255, 262, 263, 270, 275)	____	÷	12	=	____	× 100 = ___%
Usage (240, 241, 243, 245, 246, 248, 250–252, 256–261, 264–269, 271–274, 276–278)	____	÷	28	=	____	× 100 = ___%
Spelling (279–288)	____	÷	10	=	____	× 100 = ___%
Composition (289–298)	____	÷	10	=	____	× 100 = ___%
TOTAL LANGUAGE SKILLS	____	÷	60	=	____	× 100 = ___%
TOTAL EXAM	____	÷	298	=	____	× 100 = ___%

NOTES

NOTES

NOTES

NOTES

NOTES

NOTES

NOTES

NOTES

NOTES

NOTES

NOTES